Completely integrated with the text

Figure 3.14 ‖ There are no receptors at the place where the optic nerve leaves the eye. This enables the receptor's ganglion cell fibers to flow into the optic nerve. The absence of receptors in this area creates the blind spot.

DEMONSTRATION

Becoming Aware of the Blind Spot

Figure 3.15 ‖ [No caption]

Place the book on your desk. Close your right eye, and position yourself above the book so that Figure 3.15 is aligned with your left eye. Be sure the page is flat and, while looking at the cross, slowly move closer. As you move closer, be sure not to move your eye from the cross, but at the same time keep noticing the circle off to the side. At some point, around 3 to 9 inches from the book, the circle should disappear. When this happens the image of the circle is falling on your blind spot. ‖

Why aren't we usually aware of the blind spot? One reason is that the blind spot is located off to the side of our visual field, where objects are not in sharp focus. Because of this and because we don't know exactly where to look for it (as opposed to the demonstration, in which we are focusing our attention on the circle), the blind spot is hard to detect.

But the most important reason that we don't see the blind spot is that some mechanism in the brain "fills in" the place where the image disappears (Churchland & Ramachandran, 1996). The next demonstration illustrates an important property of this filling-in process.

DEMONSTRATION
Filling In the Blind Spot
Close your right eye and, with the cross in Figure 3.16 lined up with your left eye, move the "wheel" toward you. When the center of the wheel falls on your blind spot, notice how the spokes of the wheel fill in the hole (Ramachandran, 1992). ‖ V_L 3

spokes of the wheel in the second one.

Dark Adaptation of the Rods and Cones
A recent episode of the *Mythbusters* program on the Discovery Channel (2007) was devoted to investigating myths about pirates (Figure 3.17). One of the myths explored was that pirates wore eye patches to preserve night vision in one eye, so when they went from the bright light outside to the darkness belowdecks they could see with their previously patched eye. To determine whether this works, the mythbusters carried out some tasks in a dark room just after both of their eyes had been in the light and did some different tasks with an eye that had just previously been covered with a patch for 30 minutes. It isn't surprising that they completed the tasks much more rapidly when using the eye that had been patched. Anyone who has taken sensation and perception could have told the mythbusters that the eye patch would work because keeping an eye in the dark trig-

52   CHAPTER 3   Introduction to Vision

DEMONSTRATION

Filling In the Blind Spot

Close your right eye and, with the cross in Figure 3.16 lined up with your left eye, move the "wheel" toward you. When the center of the wheel falls on your blind spot, notice how the spokes of the wheel fill in the hole (Ramachandran, 1992). ‖ V_L 3

Throughout the text, a ***Virtual Lab*** icon directs students to specific animations and videos designed to help them visualize the material about which they are reading. The number beside each icon indicates the number of the relevant media element. At the end of each chapter, the titles of related ***Virtual Lab*** exercises are listed.

Accessible in three convenient ways!

Virtual Labs can be accessed via the **CD-ROM** that is packaged with each new text, through **CengageNOW™ for *Sensation and Perception*, Eighth Edition**, and through **WebTutor™** on WebCT® or Blackboard®.

Instructors: Contact your local Cengage Learning representative to help create the package that's just right for you and your students.

1.
2. CENGAGENOW
3. WebTUTOR

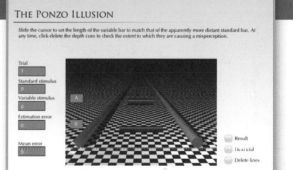

THE PONZO ILLUSION

Slide the cursor to set the length of the variable bar to match that of the apparently more distant standard bar. At any time, click-delete the depth cues to check the extent to which they are causing a misperception.

Trial

Standard stimulus

Variable stimulus

Estimation error

Mean error

Result
14 of trial
Delete lines

Accompanied by the *Virtual Lab Manual*

Virtual Lab Manual

The streamlined ***Virtual Lab Manual*** (available digitally on the CD-ROM and in a printed version) includes worksheets for the ***Virtual Lab*** experiments to encourage students to take a closer look at the labs and engage in analysis of the results.

Instructors—If you would like the printed version of the ***Virtual Lab Manual*** to be packaged with each new text, please use these ISBNs when placing your textbook order: ISBN-10: 0-495-76050-1 • ISBN-13: 978-0-495-76050-4.

Sensation and Perception

Eighth Edition

Sensation
and Perception

E. Bruce Goldstein

University of Pittsburgh
University of Arizona

WADSWORTH
CENGAGE Learning™

Australia • Brazil • Japan • Korea • Mexico • Singapore • Spain • United Kingdom • United States

DSWORTH
AGE Learning™

...n and Perception, Eighth Edition
... Goldstein

Senior Publisher: Linda Schreiber

Editors: Jon-David Hague, Jaime A. Perkins

Managing Development Editor: Jeremy Judson

Assistant Editor: Trina Tom

Editorial Assistant: Sarah Worrell

Media Editor: Lauren Keyes

Marketing Manager: Elisabeth Rhoden

Marketing Assistant: Molly Felz

Marketing Communications Manager: Talia Wise

Project Managers, Editorial Production: Mary Noel, Rita Jaramillo

Creative Director: Rob Hugel

Art Director: Vernon T. Boes

Print Buyer: Judy Inouye

Permissions Editors: Mandy Groszko, Tim Sisler

Production Service: Scratchgravel Publishing Services

Text Designer: Lisa Buckley

Art Editor: Lisa Torri

Photo Researcher: Laura Cordova

Copy Editor: Margaret C. Tropp

Cover Designer: Irene Morris

Cover Image: Color Blocks #40 by Nancy Crow photographed by J. Kevin Fitzsimons

Compositor: Newgen

For product information and technology assistance, contact us at
Cengage Learning Customer & Sales Support, 1-800-354-9706.

For permission to use material from this text or product, submit all requests online at **www.cengage.com/permissions**. Further permissions questions can be e-mailed to **permissionrequest@cengage.com**.

Library of Congress Control Number: 2008940684

ISBN-13: 978-0-495-60149-4
ISBN-10: 0-495-60149-7

Wadsworth
10 Davis Drive
Belmont, CA 94002-3098
USA

Cengage Learning is a leading provider of customized learning solutions with office locations around the globe, including Singapore, the United Kingdom, Australia, Mexico, Brazil, and Japan. Locate your local office at **www.cengage.com/global**.

Cengage Learning products are represented in Canada by Nelson Education, Ltd.

To learn more about Wadsworth, visit **www.cengage.com/wadsworth**.

Purchase any of our products at your local college store or at our preferred online store **www.ichapters.com**.

Printed in Canada
1 2 3 4 5 6 7 12 11 10 09

To my wife, Barbara, more than ever

and

To all of the students and teachers whose suggestions helped shape this edition

About the Author

E. Bruce Goldstein is Professor Emeritus of Psychology at the University of Pittsburgh and Adjunct Professor of Psychology at the University of Arizona. He has received the Chancellor's Distinguished Teaching Award from the University of Pittsburgh for his classroom teaching and textbook writing. He received his bachelor's degree in chemical engineering from Tufts University and his PhD in experimental psychology from Brown University; he was a postdoctoral fellow in the Biology Department at Harvard University before joining the faculty at the University of Pittsburgh. Bruce has published papers on a wide variety of topics, including retinal and cortical physiology, visual attention, and the perception of pictures. He is the author of *Cognitive Psychology: Connecting Mind, Research, and Everyday Experience,* 2nd Edition (Wadsworth, 2008), and the editor of the *Blackwell Handbook of Perception* (Blackwell, 2001) and the forthcoming two-volume *Sage Encyclopedia of Perception* (Sage, 2010).

Brief Contents

Contents

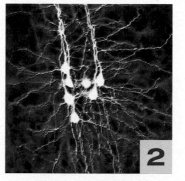

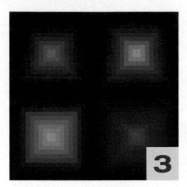

3 Introduction to Vision 43

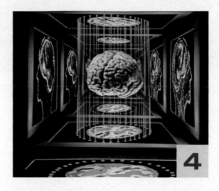

4 The Visual Cortex and Beyond 73

5 Perceiving Objects and Scenes 99

6 Visual Attention 133

Sound, the Auditory System, and Pitch Perception   259

11

Sound Localization and the Auditory Scene   291

12

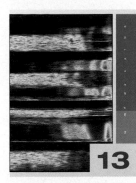

16 Perceptual Development 379

Virtual Lab Contents

Demonstrations

Preface

When I first began working on this book, Hubel and Wiesel were mapping orientation columns in the striate cortex and were five years away from receiving their Nobel Prize; Amoore's stereochemical theory, based largely on psychophysical evidence, was a prominent explanation for odor recognition; and one of the hottest new discoveries in perception was that the response properties of neurons could be influenced by experience. Today, specialized areas in the human brain have been mapped using brain imaging, olfactory receptors have been revealed using genetic methods, and the idea that the perceptual system is tuned to regularities in the environment is now supported by a wealth of both behavioral and physiological research.

But some things haven't changed. Teachers still stand in front of classrooms to teach students about perception, and students still read textbooks that reinforce what they are learning in the classroom. Another thing that hasn't changed is that teachers prefer texts that are easy for students to read, that present both classic studies and up-to-date research, and that present both the facts of perception and overarching themes and principles.

When I began teaching perception, I looked at the textbooks that were available and was disappointed, because none of them seemed to be written for students. They presented "the facts," but not in a way that seemed very interesting or inviting. I therefore wrote the first edition of *Sensation and Perception* with the idea of involving students in their study of perception by presenting the material as a story. The story is a fascinating one, because it is a narrative of one discovery following from another, and a scientific "whodunit" in which the goal is to uncover the hidden mechanisms responsible for our ability to perceive.

While my goal of writing this book has been to tell a story, this is, after all, a textbook designed for teaching. So in addition to presenting the story of perceptual research, this book also contains a number of features, all of which appeared in the seventh edition, that are designed to highlight specific material and to help students learn.

Features

- **Demonstrations** have been a popular feature of this book for many editions. They are integrated into the flow of the text and are easy enough to be carried out with little trouble, thereby maximizing the probability that students will do them. Some examples: Becoming Aware of the Blind Spot (Chapter 3); Non-Accidental Properties (Chapter 5—new); The Penumbra and Lightness Perception (Chapter 9); The Precedence Effect (Chapter 12); Perceiving Texture With a Pen (Chapter 14).

- **Methods** It is important not only to present the facts of perception, but also to make students aware of how these facts were obtained. Highlighted *Methods* sections, which are integrated into the ongoing discussion, emphasize the importance of methods, and the highlighting makes it easier to refer back to them when referenced later in the book. Examples: Measuring Dark Adaptation (Chapter 3); Dissociations in Neuropsychology (Chapter 4); Auditory Masking (Chapter 11).

- **Something to Consider** This end-of-chapter feature offers the opportunity to consider especially interesting new findings. Examples: The Mind–Body Problem (Chapter 2—new); How Do Neurons Become Specialized? (Chapter 4); Interactions Between Vision and Hearing (Chapter 12); Individual Differences in Tasting (Chapter 15).

- **Test Yourself** questions appear in the middle and at the end of each chapter. These questions are broad enough so students have to unpack the questions themselves, thereby making them more active participants in their studying.

- **Think About It** The *Think About It* section at the end of each chapter poses questions that require students to apply what they have learned and that take them beyond the material in the chapter.

- **If You Want to Know More** appears at the end of each chapter, and invites students to look into topics that were not fully covered in the chapter. A specific finding is described and key references are presented to provide a starting point for further investigation.

- **Virtual Lab** The *Virtual Lab* feature of this book enables students to view demonstrations and become participants in mini-experiments. The Virtual Lab has been completely revamped in this edition. More than 80 new items have been added to the 150 items carried over from the seventh edition. Most of these new items have been generously provided by researchers in vision, hearing, and perceptual development. Each item is indicated in the chapter by this numbered icon: VL. Students can access the Virtual Lab in a number of ways: the CD-ROM, Perception PsychologyNow, or WebTutor resource at **www.cengage.com/psychology/goldstein**.

- **Full-Color Illustrations** Perception, of all subjects, should be illustrated in color, and so I was especially pleased when the seventh edition became "full-color." What pleases me about the illustrations is not only how beautiful the color looks, but how well it serves pedagogy. The 535 figures in this edition (140 of them new) include photographs, which use color to illustrate both stimuli from experiments and perception in real-world contexts; graphs and diagrams; anatomical diagrams; and the results of brain-imaging experiments.

Supplement Package

Instructor's Manual With Test Bank

0-495-60151-9

Written by Stephen Wurst of SUNY at Oswego. For each chapter, this manual contains a detailed chapter outline, learning objectives, a chapter summary, key terms with page references, summary of labs on the Virtual Lab CD-ROM, and suggested websites, films, demonstrations, activities, and lecture topics. The test bank includes 40 multiple-choice questions (with correct answer, page reference, and question type) and 7 to 8 essay questions per chapter.

PowerLecture With JoinIn™ and ExamView®

0-495-60319-8

This one-stop lecture and class preparation tool contains ready-to-use Microsoft® PowerPoint® slides written by Terri Bonebright of De Pauw University, and allows you to assemble, edit, publish, and present custom lectures for your course. PowerLecture lets you bring together text-specific lecture outlines along with videos of your own materials, culminating in a powerful, personalized, media-enhanced presentation. The CD-ROM also includes JoinIn™, an interactive tool that lets you pose book-specific questions and display students' answers seamlessly within the Microsoft® PowerPoint® slides of your own lecture, in conjunction with the "clicker" hardware of your choice, as well as the ExamView® assessment and tutorial system, which guides you step by step through the process of creating tests.

CengageNOW™ for Goldstein's *Sensation and Perception*, Eighth Edition

0-495-80731-1

CengageNOW™ is an online teaching and learning resource that gives you more control in less time and delivers better outcomes—NOW. Flexible assignment and gradebook options provide you more control while saving you valuable time in planning and managing your course assignments. CengageNOW™ *Personalized Study* is a diagnostic tool consisting of chapter-specific pre- and post-tests and study plans that utilize multimedia resources to help students master the book's concepts. The study plans direct students to interactive *Virtual Labs* featuring animations, experiments, demonstrations, videos, and eBook pages from the text. Students can use the program on their own, or you can assign it and track their progress in your online gradebook.

Changes in This Edition

Here are some of the changes in this edition, which have been made both to make the book easier to read and to keep current with the latest research.

Taking Student Feedback Into Account

In past revisions I have made changes based on feedback that professors have provided based on their knowledge of the field and their experience in teaching from the book. In this edition, I have, for the first time, made use of extensive feedback provided by students based on their experience in using the book. I asked each of the 150 students in my class to write a paragraph in which they identified one thing in each chapter they felt could be made clearer. My students identified where and why they were having problems, and often suggested changes in wording or organization. When just one or two students commented on a particular section, I often used their comments to make improvements, but I paid the most attention when many students commented on the same material. I could write a "Top Ten" list of sections students thought should be revised, but instead I'll just say that student feedback resulted in numerous changes to every chapter in the book. Because of these changes, this is the most "student friendly" edition yet.

Improving Organization

The organization of material within every chapter has been evaluated with an eye toward improving clarity of presentation. A few examples:

- Chapters 2–4: These chapters set the stage for the rest of the book by introducing students to the basic principles of vision and physiology. Responding to feedback from users of the seventh edition, I now introduce basic physiological processes in Chapter 2.

This means that topics such as sensory coding, neural circuits, and receptive fields that were formerly in Chapters 3 and 4 are now introduced at the beginning of the book. Vision is introduced in Chapter 3, focusing on the retina, and higher-order visual processes are described in Chapter 4. This sequence of three chapters now flows more smoothly than in the seventh edition.

■ Chapter 5: Material on the physiology of object perception, which was formerly in the middle of the chapter, has been moved to the end, allowing for an uninterrupted discussion of behavioral approaches to understanding the perception of objects and scenes.

■ Chapter 14: Discussion of gate control theory is no longer at the end of the section on pain, but is now introduced early in the section. We first consider what motivated Melzack and Wall to propose the theory by describing how pain perception was explained in the early 1960s; then the theory is described, followed by a discussion of new research on cognitive influences on pain perception.

If you have used this book before, you will notice that the final chapter of the sixth edition, "Clinical Aspects of Vision and Hearing," is no longer in the book. This chapter, which was eliminated in the seventh edition to make room for other material, such as a new chapter on visual attention, described how vision and hearing can become impaired, what happens during eye and ear examinations, and some of the medical procedures that have been used to deal with these problems. Some of this material has been included in this edition, but for a fuller treatment, go to the book's website at **www.cengage.com/psychology/goldstein** for a reprint of that chapter.

Adding New Content

The updating of this edition is reflected in the inclusion of more than 100 new references, most to recent research. In addition, some earlier research has been added, and some descriptions from the seventh edition have been updated. Here are a few of these new additions.

Chapter 2: Introduction to the Physiology of Perception

■ Sparse coding
■ The mind–body problem

Chapter 4: The Visual Cortex and Beyond

■ Information flow in the lateral geniculate nucleus

Chapter 5: Perceiving Objects and Scenes

■ What is a scene?
■ Perceiving the gist of a scene
■ Perceiving objects in scenes (the effect of context on object perception)

■ Regularities in the environment
■ Will robot vision ever be as good as human vision?
■ Models of brain activity that can predict what a person is seeing

Chapter 6: Visual Attention

■ Perception without attention (updated)
■ Attention in autism

Chapter 7: Taking Action

■ Cortical response to the intention to take action
■ Neuropsychology of affordances
■ Mirror neurons and predicting another person's intentions
■ Behavioral and physiological responses during navigation by London taxi drivers
■ Neural prostheses: controlling movement with the mind

Chapter 8: Perceiving Motion

■ Aperture problem (updated)
■ Transcranial magnetic stimulation and biological motion

Chapter 9: Perceiving Color

■ Why two types of cones are necessary for color vision (clarified)
■ Information that opponent neurons add to the trichromatic receptor response
■ Memory color (updated)

Chapter 10: Perceiving Depth and Size

■ Relative disparity added to discussion of absolute disparity
■ Depth information across species
■ Is there a depth area in the brain?

Chapter 11: Sound, the Auditory System, and Pitch Perception

■ Ion flow and bending of inner hair cell cilia
■ Cochlear amplifier action of outer hair cells (updated)
■ Conductive hearing loss, sensorineural hearing loss, presybcusis, and noise-induced hearing loss
■ Potential for hearing loss from listening to MP3 players
■ "Pitch neurons" in the cortex that respond to fundamental frequency even if the fundamental is missing

Chapter 12: Sound Localization and the Auditory Scene

■ Cone of confusion
■ Jeffress "coincidence detector" circuit for localization
■ Broadly tuned ITD neurons and localization added to discussion of narrowly tuned neurons

- Architectural acoustics expanded, including acoustics in classrooms

Chapter 13: Speech Perception

- Transitional probabilities as providing information for speech segmentation
- Dual-stream model of speech perception
- Speech perception and action

Chapter 14: Cutaneous Senses

- The case of Ian Waterman, who lost his senses of touch and proprioception
- Gate control theory placed in historical perspective
- Brain activity in physically produced pain and pain induced by hypnosis

Chapter 15: The Chemical Senses

- Glomeruli as information-collecting units (updated)
- Higher-level olfactory processing, including the perceptual organization of smell
- Piriform cortex and perceptual learning
- How the orbitofrontal cortex response to pleasantness is affected by cognitive factors

Chapter 16: Perceptual Development

- Measurement of contrast sensitivity function (clarified)

Acknowledgments

It is a pleasure to acknowledge the following people who worked tirelessly to turn my manuscript into an actual book! Without these people, this book would not exist, and I am grateful to all of them.

- Jeremy Judson, my developmental editor, for keeping me on schedule, shepherding the book through the production process, and all those phone conversations.

- Anne Draus of Scratchgravel Production Services, for taking care of the amazing number of details involved in turning my manuscript into a book in her usual efficient and professional way.

- Peggy Tropp, for her expert and creative copy editing.

- Lauren Keyes for her attention to detail, for her technical expertise, and for being a pleasure to work with on the updating of the Virtual Labs.

- Armira Rezec, Saddleback College, for obtaining new items for the Virtual Lab, and for revising the Virtual Lab manual.

- Trina Tom, for her work on the ancillaries, especially the new Virtual Lab manual.

- Laura Cordova for her relentless quest for photo permissions.

- Lisa Torri, my art editor, for continuing the tradition of working on my book, which started many editions ago, and for all the care and creativity that went into making all of the illustrations happen.

- Mary Noel and Rita Jaramillo, senior content project managers, who coordinated all of the elements of the book during production and made sure everything happened when it was supposed to so the book would get to the printer on time.

- Vernon Boes, art guru, who directed the design for the book. Thanks, Vernon, for the therapeutic conversations, not to mention the great design and cover.

- Lisa Buckley for the elegant design and Irene Morris for the striking cover.

- Precision Graphics for the beautiful art renderings.

- Stephen Wurst, SUNY Oswego, for revising the Instructor's Manual and Test Bank, which he wrote for the previous edition.

In addition to the help I received from all of the above people on the editorial and production side, I also received a great deal of help from researchers and teachers. One of the things I have learned in my years of writing is that other people's advice is crucial. The field of perception is a broad one, and I rely heavily on the advice of experts in specific areas to alert me to emerging new research and to check my writing for accuracy. Equally important are all of the teachers of perception who rely on textbooks in their courses. They have read groups of chapters (and in a few cases, the whole book), with an eye to both accuracy of the material and pedagogy. I owe a great debt of thanks to this group of reviewers for their advice about how to present the material to their students. The following is a list of those who provided advice about content and teachability for this edition of the book.

Christopher Brown
Arizona State University

Carol Colby
University of Pittsburgh

John Culling
University of Cardiff

Stuart Derbyshire
University of Birmingham

Diana Deutsch
University of California, San Diego

Laura Edelman
Muhlenberg College

Jack Gallant
University of California, Berkeley

Mel Goodale
University of Western Ontario

Mark Hollins
University of North Carolina

Marcel Just
Carnegie-Mellon University

Kendrick Kay
University of California, Berkeley

Jeremy Loebach
Macalester College

David McAlpine
University College, London

Eriko Miyahara
California State University, Fullerton

Sam Musallam
University of Toronto

John Neuhoff
The College of Wooster

Crystal Oberle
Texas State University

Aude Oliva
Massachusetts Institute of Technology

Andrew Parker
University of Oxford

Mary Peterson
University of Arizona

David Pisoni
Indiana University

Jan Schnupp
University of Oxford

Bennett Schwartz
Florida International University

Alan Searleman
St. Lawrence University

Marc Sommer
University of Pittsburgh

Frank Tong
Vanderbilt University

Chris Urmson
Carnegie-Mellon University

Robert T. Weathersby
Eastern University

Shannon N. Whitten
University of Central Florida

Donald Wilson
New York University

Takashi Yamauchi
Texas A & M

Thomas Yin
University of Wisconsin

William Yost
Arizona State University

I also thank the following people who donated photographs and research records for illustrations that are new to this edition.

Moshe Bar
Harvard University

William Bosking
University of Texas

Mary Bravo
Rutgers University

Paul Breslin
Monell Chemical Senses Center

Beatriz Calvo-Merino
University College, London

Joseph Carroll
University of Wisconsin

Stuart Derbyshire
University of Birmingham

John Donahue
Brown University and Cyberkinetics, Inc.

Marc Ericson
Wright-Patterson Air Force Base

Li Fei-Fei
Princeton University

David Furness
Keele University

Gregory Hickok
University of California, Irvine

Andrew Hollingworth
University of Iowa

David Laing
University of New South Wales

Eleanor Maguire
University College, London

Pascal Mammassion
Université Paris Descartes

Edward Morrison
Auburn University

Claire Murphy
San Diego State University

Aude Oliva
Massachusetts Institute of Technology

Kevin Pelphrey
Yale University

Andrea Pierno
University of Padua

Maryam Shahbake
University of Western Sydney

Frank Tong
Vanderbilt University

Antonio Torralba
Massachusetts Institute of Technology

Chris Urmson
Tartan Racing, Carnegie-Mellon University

Brian Wandell
Stanford University

Donald Wilson
New York University

Finally, I thank all of the people and organizations who generously provided demonstrations and movies for the revised Virtual Lab CD-ROM.

ABC News
New York, New York

Edward Adelson
Massachusetts Institute of Technology

Michael Bach
University of Freiburg

Colin Blakemore
Cambridge University

Geoffrey Boynton
University of Washington

Diana Deutsch
University of California, San Diego

John Donahue
Brown University and Cyberkinetics, Inc.

Li Fei-Fei
Princeton University

Mary Hayhoe
University of Texas

Laurie Heller
Brown University

John Henderson
University of Edinburgh

George Hollich
Purdue University

Scott Johnson
University of California, Los Angeles

James Kalat
North Carolina State University

Stephen Neely
Boys Town Hospital, Omaha

Thomas Papathomas
Rutgers University

Phonak Corporation
Stafa, Switzerland

Andrea Pierno
University of Padua

Leila Reddy
Massachusetts Institute of Technology

Ronald Rensink
University of British Columbia

Sensimetrics Corporation
Malden, Massachusetts

Ladan Shams
University of California, Los Angeles

Nikolaus Troje
Queen's University

Chris Urmson
Tartan Racing, Carnegie-Mellon University

Peter Wenderoth
Macquarie University

Sensation and Perception

Chapter Contents

CHAPTER 1

Introduction to Perception

OPPOSITE PAGE Why are we able to perceive the forms, distances, colors, and lighting in this scene, even though it is a picture on a flat page? This is just one of the many questions about perception we will consider in this book.
Patrick Hyland Photography

VL The Virtual Lab icons direct you to specific animations and videos designed to help you visualize what you are reading about. The number beside each icon indicates the number of the clip you can access through your CD-ROM or your student website.

Some Questions We Will Consider:

▌ Why should you read this book? (p. 4)

▌ How are your perceptions determined by processes that you are unaware of? (p. 5)

▌ What is the difference between perceiving something and recognizing it? (p. 8)

▌ How can we measure perception? (p. 12)

Imagine that you have been given the following hypothetical science project.

Science project:
Design a device that can *locate, describe,* and *identify* all objects in the environment, including their distance from the device and their relationships to each other. In addition, make the device capable of traveling from one point to another, avoiding obstacles along the way.

Extra credit:
Make the device capable of having *conscious experience,* such as what people experience when they look out at a scene.

Warning:
This project, should you decide to accept it, is extremely difficult. It has not yet been solved by the best computer scientists, even though they have access to the world's most powerful computers.

Hint:
Humans and animals have solved the problems above in a particularly elegant way. They use (1) two spherical sensors called "eyes," which contain a light-sensitive chemical, to sense light; (2) two detectors on the sides of the head, which are fitted with tiny vibrating hairs to sense pressure changes in the air; (3) small pressure detectors of various shapes imbedded under the skin to sense stimuli on the skin; and (4) two types of chemical detectors to detect gases that are inhaled and solids and liquids that are ingested.

Additional note:
Designing the detectors is just the first step in designing the system. An information processing system is also needed. In the case of the human, this information processing system is a "computer" called the brain, with 100 billion active units and interconnections so complex that they have still not been completely deciphered. Although the detectors are an important part of the project, the design of the computer is crucial, because the information that is picked up by the detectors needs to be analyzed. Note that operation of the human system is still not completely understood and that the best scientific minds in the world have made little progress with the extra credit part of the problem. Focus on the main problem first, and leave conscious experience until later.

The "science project" above is what this book is about. Our goal is to understand the human model, starting with the detectors—the eyes, ears, skin receptors, and receptors in the nose and mouth—and then moving on to the computer—the brain. We want to understand how we sense things in the environment and interact with them. The paradox we face in searching for this understanding is that although we still don't understand perception, perceiving is something that occurs almost effortlessly. In most situations, we simply open our eyes and see what is around us, or listen and hear sounds, without expending any particular effort.

Because of the ease with which we perceive, many people see perception as something that "just happens," and don't see the feats achieved by our senses as complex or amazing. "After all," the skeptic might say, "for vision, a picture of the environment is focused on the back of my eye, and that picture provides all the information my brain needs to duplicate the environment in my consciousness." But the idea that perception is not complex is exactly what misled computer scientists in the 1950s and 1960s to propose that it would take only about a decade or so to create "perceiving machines" that could negotiate the environment with humanlike ease. That prediction, made half a century ago, has yet to come true, even though a computer defeated the world chess champion in 1997. From a computer's point of view, perceiving a scene is more difficult than playing world championship chess.

In this chapter we will begin by introducing some basic principles to help us understand the complexities of perception. We will first consider a few practical reasons for studying perception, then examine how perception occurs in a sequence of steps, and finally consider how to measure perception.

Why Read This Book?

The most obvious answer to the question "Why read this book?" is that it is required reading for a course you are taking. Thus, it is probably an important thing to do if you want to get a good grade. But beyond that, there are a number of other reasons for reading this book. For one thing, the material will provide you with information that may be helpful in other courses and perhaps even your future career. If you plan to go to graduate school to become a researcher or teacher in perception or a related area, this book will provide you with a solid background to build on. In fact, a number of the research studies you will read about were carried out by researchers who were introduced to the field of perception by earlier editions of this book.

The material in this book is also relevant to future studies in medicine or related fields, since much of our discussion is about how the body operates. A few medical applications that depend on knowledge of perception are devices to restore perception to people who have lost vision or hearing, and treatments for pain. Other applications include robotic vehicles that can find their way through unfamiliar environments, speech recognition systems that can understand what someone is saying, and highway signs that are visible to drivers under a variety of conditions.

But reasons to study perception extend beyond the possibility of useful applications. Because perception is something you experience constantly, knowing about how it works is interesting in its own right. To appreciate why, consider what you are experiencing right now. If you touch the page of this book, or look out at what's around you, you might get the feeling that you are perceiving exactly what is "out there" in the environment. After all, touching this page puts you in direct contact with it, and it seems likely that what you are seeing is what is actually there. But one of the things you will learn as you study perception is that everything you see, hear, taste, feel, or smell is created by the mechanisms of your senses. This means that what you are perceiving is determined not only by what is "out there," but also by the properties of your senses. This concept has fascinated philosophers, researchers, and students for hundreds of years, and is even more meaningful now because of recent advances in our understanding of the mechanisms responsible for our perceptions.

Another reason to study perception is that it can help you become more aware of the nature of your own perceptual experiences. Many of the everyday experiences that you take for granted—such as listening to someone talking, tasting food, or looking at a painting in a museum—can be appreciated at a deeper level by considering questions such as "Why does an unfamiliar language sound as if it is one continuous stream of sound, without breaks between words?" "Why do I lose my sense of taste when I have a cold?" and "How do artists create an impression of depth in a picture?" This book will not only answer these questions but will answer other questions that you may not have thought of, such as "Why don't I see colors at dusk?" and "How come the scene around me doesn't appear to move as I walk through it?" Thus, even if you aren't planning to become a physician or a robotic vehicle designer, you will come away from reading this book with a heightened appreciation of both the complexity and the beauty of the mechanisms responsible for your perceptual experiences, and perhaps even with an enhanced awareness of the world around you.

In one of those strange coincidences that occasionally happen, I received an e-mail from a student (not one of my own, but from another university) at exactly the same time that I was writing this section of the book. In her e-mail, "Jenny" made a number of comments about the book, but the one that struck me as being particularly relevant to the question "Why read this book?" is the following: "By reading your book, I got to know the fascinating processes that take place every second in my brain, that are doing things I don't even think about." Your reasons for reading this book may turn out to be totally different from Jenny's, but hopefully you will find out some things that will be useful, or fascinating, or both.

The Perceptual Process

One of the messages of this book is that perception does not just happen, but is the end result of complex "behind the scenes" processes, many of which are not available to your awareness. An everyday example of the idea of behind-the-scenes processes is provided by what's happening as you watch a play in the theater. While your attention is focused on the drama created by the characters in the play, another drama is occurring backstage. An actress is rushing to complete her costume change, an actor is pacing back and forth to calm his nerves just before he goes on, the stage manager is checking to be sure the next scene change is ready to go, and the lighting director is getting ready to make the next lighting change.

Just as the audience sees only a small part of what is happening during a play, your perception of the world around you is only a small part of what is happening as you perceive. One way to illustrate the behind-the-scenes processes involved in perception is by describing a sequence of steps, which we will call the *perceptual process*.

The perceptual process, shown in Figure 1.1, is a sequence of processes that work together to determine our experience of and reaction to stimuli in the environment. We will consider each step in the process individually, but first let's consider the boxes in Figure 1.1, which divide the process into four categories: *Stimulus, Electricity, Experience and Action,* and *Knowledge.*

Stimulus refers to what is out there in the environment, what we actually pay attention to, and what stimulates our receptors. *Electricity* refers to the electrical signals that are created by the receptors and transmitted to the brain. *Experience and Action* refers to our goal—to perceive, recognize, and react to the stimuli. *Knowledge* refers to knowledge we bring to the perceptual situation. This box is located above the other three boxes because it can have its effect at many different points in the process. We will consider each box in detail, beginning with the stimulus.

The Stimulus

The stimulus exists both "out there," in the environment, and within the person's body.

Environmental Stimuli and Attended Stimuli
These two aspects of the stimulus are in the environment. The environmental stimulus is all of the things in our environment that we can potentially perceive. Consider,

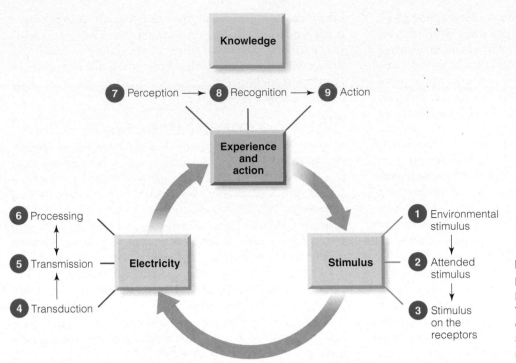

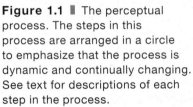

Figure 1.1 ▌ The perceptual process. The steps in this process are arranged in a circle to emphasize that the process is dynamic and continually changing. See text for descriptions of each step in the process.

for example, the potential stimuli that are presented to Ellen, who is taking a walk in the woods. As she walks along the trail she is confronted with a large number of stimuli (Figure 1.2a)—trees, the path on which she is walking, rustling noises made by a small animal scampering through the leaves. Because there is far too much happening for Ellen to take in everything at once, she scans the scene, looking from one place to another at things that catch her interest.

When Ellen's attention is captured by a particularly distinctive looking tree off to the right, she doesn't notice the interesting pattern on the tree trunk at first, but suddenly realizes that what she at first took to be a patch of moss is actually a moth (Figure 1.2b). When Ellen focuses on this moth, making it the center of her attention, it becomes the **attended stimulus**. The attended stimulus changes from moment to moment, as Ellen shifts her attention from place to place.

The Stimulus on the Receptors When Ellen focuses her attention on the moth, she looks directly at it,

1. Environmental stimulus   **2. Attended stimulus**   **3. Stimulus on the receptors**

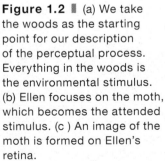

(a) The woods   (b) Moth on tree   (c) Image on Ellen's retina

Figure 1.2 ▌ (a) We take the woods as the starting point for our description of the perceptual process. Everything in the woods is the environmental stimulus. (b) Ellen focuses on the moth, which becomes the attended stimulus. (c) An image of the moth is formed on Ellen's retina.

and this creates an image of the moth and its immediate surroundings on the receptors of her retina, a 0.4-mm-thick network of light-sensitive receptors and other neurons that line the back of the eye (Figure 1.2c). (We will describe the retina and neurons in more detail in Chapters 2 and 3.) This step is important because the stimulus—the moth—is transformed into another form—an image on Ellen's retina.

Because the moth has been transformed into an image, we can describe this image as a *representation* of the moth. It's not the actual moth, but it stands for the moth. The next steps in the perceptual process carry this idea of representation a step further, when the image is transformed into electricity.

Electricity

One of the central principles of perception is that everything we perceive is based on electrical signals in our nervous system. These electrical signals are created in the receptors, which transform energy from the environment (such as the light on Ellen's retina) into electrical signals in the nervous system—a process called *transduction*.

Transduction Transduction is the transformation of one form of energy into another form of energy. For example, when you touch the "withdrawal" button on an ATM machine, the pressure exerted by your finger is transduced into electrical energy, which causes a device that uses mechanical energy to push your money out of the machine. Transduction occurs in the nervous system when energy in the environment—such as light energy, mechanical pressure, or chemical energy—is transformed into electrical energy. In our example, the pattern of light created on Ellen's

retina by the moth is transformed into electrical signals in thousands of her visual receptors (Figure 1.3a).

Transmission After the moth's image has been transformed into electrical signals in Ellen's receptors, these signals activate other neurons, which in turn activate more neurons (Figure 1.3b). Eventually these signals travel out of the eye and are transmitted to the brain. The transmission step is crucial because if signals don't reach the brain, there is no perception.

Processing As electrical signals are transmitted through Ellen's retina and then to the brain, they undergo **neural processing**, which involves interactions between neurons (Figure 1.3c). What do these interactions between neurons accomplish? To answer this question, we will compare how signals are transmitted in the nervous system to how signals are transmitted by your cell phone.

Let's first consider the phone. When a person says "hello" into a cell phone (right phone in Figure 1.4a), this voice signal is changed into electrical signals, which are sent out from the cell phone. This electrical signal, which represents the sound "hello," is relayed by a tower to the receiving cell phone (on the left), which transforms the signal into the sound "hello." An important property of cell phone transmission is that the signal that is *received* is the same as the signal that was *sent*.

The nervous system works in a similar way. The image of the moth is changed into electrical signals in the receptors, which eventually are sent out the back of the eye (Figure 1.4b). This signal, which represents the moth, is relayed through a series of neurons to the brain, which transforms this signal into a perception of the moth. Thus, with a cell

4. Transduction **5. Transmission** **6. Processing**

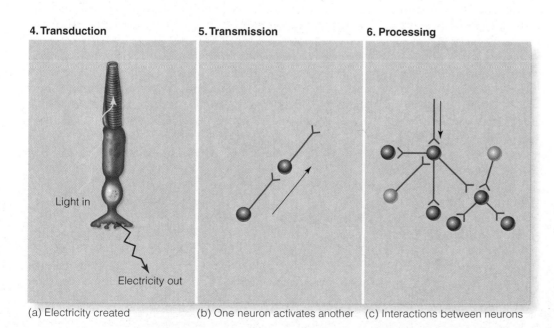

Light in

Electricity out

(a) Electricity created   (b) One neuron activates another   (c) Interactions between neurons

Figure 1.3 ▌ (a) *Transduction* occurs when the receptors create electrical energy in response to light. (b) *Transmission* occurs as one neuron activates the next one. (c) This electrical energy is *processed* through networks of neurons.

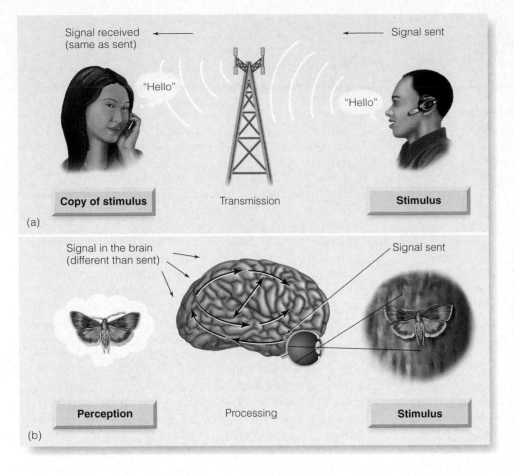

(a)

Signal received
(same as sent)

"Hello"

Copy of stimulus

Transmission

Signal sent

"Hello"

Stimulus

(b)

Signal in the brain
(different than sent)

Signal sent

Perception

Processing

Stimulus

Figure 1.4 ▌ Comparison of signal transmission by cell phones and the nervous system. (a) The sending cell phone on the right sends an electrical signal that stands for "hello." The signal that reaches the receiving cell phone on the left is the same as the signal sent. (b) The nervous system sends electrical signals that stand for the moth. The nervous system processes these electrical signals, so the signal responsible for perceiving the moth is different from the original signal sent from the eye.

phone, electrical signals that represent a stimulus ("hello") are transmitted to a receiver (another cell phone), and in the nervous system, electrical signals representing a stimulus (the moth) are also transmitted to a receiver (the brain).

There are, however, differences between information transmission in cell phones and in the nervous system. With cell phones, the signal received is the same as the signal sent. The goal for cell phones is to transmit an *exact copy* of the original signal. However, in the nervous system, the signal that reaches the brain is transformed so that, although it *represents* the original stimulus, it is usually very different from the original signal.

The transformation that occurs between the receptors and the brain is achieved by neural processing, which happens as the signals that originate in the receptors travel through a maze of interconnected pathways between the receptors and the brain and within the brain. In the nervous system, the original electrical representation of the stimulus that is created by the receptors is transformed by processing into a *new* representation of the stimulus in the brain. In Chapter 2 we will describe how this transformation occurs.

Experience and Action

We have now reached the third box of the perceptual process, where the "backstage activity" of transduction, trans-

mission, and processing is transformed into things we are aware of—perceiving, recognizing, and acting on objects in the environment.

Perception Perception is conscious sensory experience. It occurs when the electrical signals that represent the moth are transformed by Ellen's brain into her experience of seeing the moth (Figure 1.5a). In the past, some accounts of the perceptual process have stopped at this stage. After all, once Ellen *sees* the moth, hasn't she perceived it? The answer to this question is yes, she has *perceived* it, but other things have happened as well—she has recognized the form as a "moth" and not a "butterfly," and she has taken action based on her perception by walking closer to the tree to get a better look at the moth. These two additional steps—*recognition* and *action*—are behaviors that are important outcomes of the perceptual process.

Recognition Recognition is our ability to place an object in a category, such as "moth," that gives it meaning (Figure 1.5b). Although we might be tempted to group perception and recognition together, researchers have shown that they are separate processes. For example, consider the case of Dr. P., a patient described by neurologist Oliver Sacks (1985) in the title story of his book *The Man Who Mistook His Wife for a Hat.*

7. Perception　　　　**8. Recognition**　　　　**9. Action**

(a) Ellen perceives something on the tree.

(b) Ellen realizes it is a moth.

(c) Ellen walks toward the moth.

Figure 1.5 ▌ (a) Ellen has conscious perception of the moth. (b) She recognizes the moth. (c) She takes action by walking toward the tree to get a better view.

Dr. P., a well-known musician and music teacher, first noticed a problem when he began having trouble recognizing his students visually, although he could immediately identify them by the sound of their voices. But when Dr. P. began misperceiving common objects, for example addressing a parking meter as if it were a person or expecting a carved knob on a piece of furniture to engage him in conversation, it became clear that his problem was more serious than just a little forgetfulness. Was he blind, or perhaps crazy? It was clear from an eye examination that he could see well and, by many other criteria, it was obvious that he was not crazy.

Dr. P.'s problem was eventually diagnosed as **visual form agnosia**—an inability to recognize objects—that was caused by a brain tumor. He perceived the parts of objects but couldn't identify the whole object, so when Sacks showed him a glove, Dr. P. described it as "a continuous surface unfolded on itself. It appears to have five outpouchings, if this is the word." When Sacks asked him what it was, Dr. P. hypothesized that it was "a container of some sort. It could be a change purse, for example, for coins of five sizes." The normally easy process of object recognition had, for Dr. P., been derailed by his brain tumor. He could perceive the object and recognize parts of it, but couldn't perceptually assemble the parts in a way that would enable him to recognize the object as a whole. Cases such as this show that it is important to distinguish between perception and recognition.

Action Action includes motor activities such as moving the head or eyes and locomoting through the environment. In our example, Ellen looks directly at the moth and walks toward it (Figure 1.5c). Some researchers see action as an important outcome of the perceptual process because of its importance for survival. David Milner and Melvyn

Goodale (1995) propose that early in the evolution of animals the major goal of visual processing was not to create a conscious perception or "picture" of the environment, but to help the animal control navigation, catch prey, avoid obstacles, and detect predators—all crucial functions for the animal's survival.

The fact that perception often leads to action—whether it be an animal's increasing its vigilance when it hears a twig snap in the forest or a person's deciding to look more closely at something that looks interesting—means that perception is a continuously changing process. For example, the scene that Ellen is observing changes every time she shifts her attention to something else or moves to a new location, or when something in the scene moves.

The changes that occur as people perceive is the reason the steps of the perceptual process in Figure 1.1 are arranged in a circle. Although we can describe the perceptual process as a series of steps that "begin" with the environmental stimulus and "end" with perception, recognition, and action, the overall process is so dynamic and continually changing that it doesn't really have a beginning point or an ending point.

Knowledge

Our diagram of the perceptual process also includes a fourth box—Knowledge. **Knowledge** is any information that the perceiver brings to a situation. Knowledge is placed above the circle because it can affect a number of the steps in the perceptual process. Information that a person brings to a situation can be things learned years ago, such as when Ellen learned to tell the difference between a moth and a butterfly, or knowledge obtained from events that have just

Figure 1.6 ▌ See Perceiving a Picture in the Demonstration box below for instructions. (Adapted from Bugelski & Alampay, 1961.)

happened. The following demonstration provides an example of how perception can be influenced by knowledge that has just been acquired.

DEMONSTRATION

Perceiving a Picture

After looking at the drawing in Figure 1.6, close your eyes, turn the page, and open and shut your eyes rapidly to briefly expose the picture that is in the same location on the page as the picture above. Decide what the picture is; then read the explanation below it. Do this now, before reading further. ▌

Did you identify Figure 1.9 as a rat (or a mouse)? If you did, you were influenced by the clearly rat- or mouselike figure you observed initially. But people who first observe Figure 1.11 (page 14) instead of Figure 1.6 usually identify Figure 1.9 as a man. (Try this on someone else.) This demonstration, which is called the rat–man demonstration, shows how recently acquired knowledge ("that pattern is a rat") can influence perception.

An example of how knowledge acquired years ago can influence the perceptual process is the ability to categorize objects. Thus, Ellen can say "that is a moth" because of her knowledge of what moths look like. In addition, this knowledge can have perceptual consequences because it might help her distinguish the moth from the tree trunk. Someone with little knowledge of moths might just see a tree trunk, without becoming aware of the moth at all.

Another way to describe the effect of information that the perceiver brings to the situation is by distinguishing between bottom-up processing and top-down processing. Bottom-up processing (also called data-based processing) is processing that is based on incoming data. Incoming data always provide the starting point for perception because without incoming data, there is no perception. For Ellen, the incoming data are the patterns of light and dark on her retina created by light reflected from the moth and the tree (Figure 1.7a).

Top-down processing (also called knowledge-based processing) refers to processing that is based on knowledge (Figure 1.7b). For Ellen, this knowledge includes what she knows about moths. Knowledge isn't always involved in

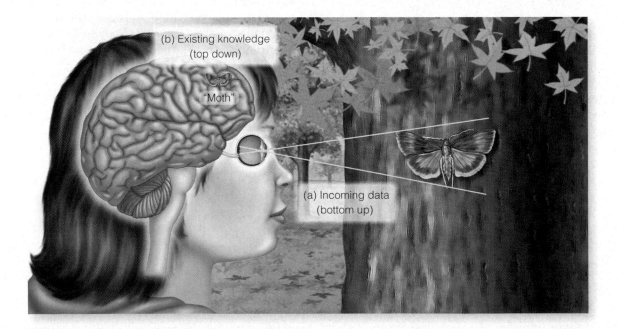

Figure 1.7 ▌ Perception is determined by an interaction between bottom-up processing, which starts with the image on the receptors, and top-down processing, which brings the observer's knowledge into play. In this example, (a) the image of the moth on Ellen's retina initiates bottom-up processing; and (b) her prior knowledge of moths contributes to top-down processing.

perception but, as we will see, it often is—sometimes without our even being aware of it.

Bottom-up processing is essential for perception because the perceptual process usually begins with stimulation of the receptors.[1] Thus, when a pharmacist reads what to you might look like an unreadable scribble on your doctor's prescription, she starts with the patterns that the doctor's handwriting creates on her retina. However, once these bottom-up data have triggered the sequence of steps of the perceptual process, top-down processing can come into play as well. The pharmacist sees the squiggles the doctor made on the prescription and then uses her knowledge of the names of drugs, and perhaps past experience with this particular doctor's writing, to help understand the squiggles. Thus, bottom-up and top-down processing often work together to create perception.

My students often ask whether top-down processing is always involved in perception. The answer to this question is that it is "very often" involved. There are some situations, typically involving very simple stimuli, in which top-down processing is probably not involved. For example, perceiving a single flash of easily visible light is probably not affected by a person's prior experience. However, as stimuli become more complex, the role of top-down processing increases. In fact, a person's past experience is usually involved in perception of real-world scenes, even though in most cases the person is unaware of this influence. One of the themes of this book is that our knowledge of how things usually appear in the environment can play an important role in determining what we perceive.

How to Approach the Study of Perception

The goal of perceptual research is to understand each of the steps in the perceptual process that lead to perception, recognition, and action. (For simplicity, we will use the term *perception* to stand for all of these outcomes in the discussion that follows.) To accomplish this goal, perception has been studied using two approaches: the *psychophysical approach* and the *physiological approach.*

The psychophysical approach to perception was introduced by Gustav Fechner, a physicist who, in his book *Elements of Psychophysics* (1860/1966), coined the term psychophysics to refer to the use of quantitative methods to measure relationships between stimuli (*physics*) and perception (*psycho*). These methods are still used today, but because a number of other, nonquantitative methods are also used, we will use the term *psychophysics* more broadly in this book

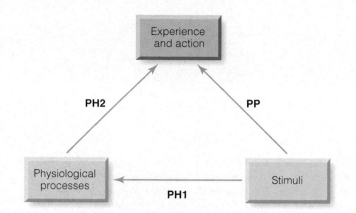

Figure 1.8 ▌ Psychophysical (PP) and physiological (PH) approaches to perception. The three boxes represent the three major components of the perceptual process (see Figure 1.1). The three relationships that are usually measured to study the perceptual process are the psychophysical (PP) relationship between stimuli and perception, the physiological (PH1) relationship between stimuli and physiological processes, and the physiological (PH2) relationship between physiological processes and perception.

to refer to any measurement of the relationship between stimuli and perception (PP in Figure 1.8). An example of research using the psychophysical approach would be measuring the stimulus–perception relationship (PP) by asking an observer to decide whether two very similar patches of color are the same or different (Figure 1.10a).

The **physiological approach to perception** involves measuring the relationship between stimuli and physiological processes (PH1 in Figure 1.8) and between physiological processes and perception (PH2 in Figure 1.8). These physiological processes are most often studied by measuring electrical responses in the nervous system, but can also involve studying anatomy or chemical processes.

An example of measuring the stimulus–physiology relationship (PH1) is measuring how different colored lights result in electrical activity generated in neurons in a cat's cortex (Figure 1.10b).[2] An example of measuring the physiology–perception relationship (PH2) would be a study in which a person's brain activity is measured as the person describes the color of an object he is seeing (Figure 1.10c).

You will see that although we can distinguish between the psychophysical approach and the physiological approach, these approaches are both working toward

---

[1] Occasionally perception can occur without stimulation of the receptors. For example, being hit on the head might cause you to "see stars," or closing your eyes and imagining something may cause an experience called "imagery," which shares many characteristics of perception (Kosslyn, 1994).

[2] Because a great deal of physiological research has been done on cats and monkeys, students often express concerns about how these animals are treated. All animal research in the United States follows strict guidelines for the care of animals established by organizations such as the American Psychological Association and the Society for Neuroscience. The central tenet of these guidelines is that every effort should be made to ensure that animals are not subjected to pain or distress. Research on animals has provided essential information for developing aids to help people with sensory disabilities such as blindness and deafness and for helping develop techniques to ease severe pain.

Figure 1.9 ▌ Did you see a "rat" or a "man"? Looking at the more ratlike picture in Figure 1.6 increased the chances that you would see this one as a rat. But if you had first seen the man version (Figure 1.11), you would have been more likely to perceive this figure as a man. (Adapted from Bugelski & Alampay, 1961.)

a common goal—to explain the mechanisms responsible for *perception*. Thus, when we measure how a neuron responds to different colors (relationship PH1) or the relationship between a person's brain activity and that person's perception of colors (relationship PH2), our goal is to explain the physiology behind how we *perceive* colors. Anytime we measure physiological responses, our goal is not simply to understand how neurons and the brain work; our goal is to understand how neurons and the brain *create perceptions*.

As we study perception using both psychophysical and physiological methods, we will also be concerned with how the knowledge, memories, and expectations that people bring to the situation influence their perceptions. These factors, which we have described as the starting place for top-down processing, are called cognitive influences on perception. Researchers study cognitive influences by measuring how knowledge and other factors, such as memories and expectations, affect each of the three relationships in Figure 1.8.

For example, consider the rat–man demonstration. If we were to measure the stimulus–perception relationship by showing just Figure 1.9 to a number of people, we would probably find that some people see a rat and some people see a man. But if we add some "knowledge" by first presenting the more ratlike picture in Figure 1.6, most people say "rat" when we present Figure 1.9. Thus, in this example, knowledge has affected the stimulus–perception relationship. As we describe research using the physiological approach, beginning in Chapter 2, we will see that knowledge can also affect physiological responding.

One of the things that becomes apparent when we step back and look at the psychophysical and physiological approaches is that each one provides information about different aspects of the perceptual process. Thus, to truly understand perception, we have to study it using both approaches, and later in this book we will see how some researchers have used both approaches in the same experiment. In the remainder of this chapter, we are going to describe some ways to measure perception at the psychophysical level. In Chapter 2 we will describe basic principles of the physiological approach.

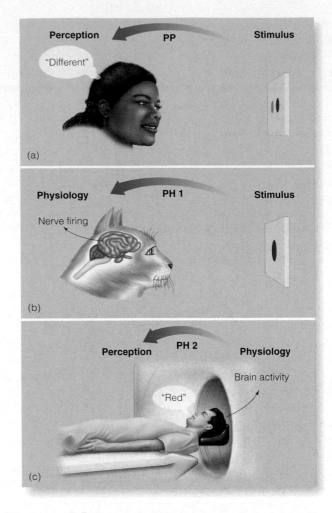

Figure 1.10 ▌ Experiments that measure the relationships indicated by the arrows in Figure 1.8. (a) The psychophysical relationship (PP) between stimulus and perception: Two colored patches are judged to be different. (b) The physiological relationship (PH1) between the stimulus and the physiological response: A light generates a neural response in the cat's cortex. (c) The physiological relationship (PH2) between the physiological response and perception: A person's brain activity is monitored as the person indicates what he is seeing.

Measuring Perception

We have seen that the psychophysical approach to perception focuses on the relationship between the *physical properties of stimuli* and the *perceptual responses to these stimuli*. There are a number of possible perceptual responses to a stimulus. Here are some examples taken from experiences that might occur while watching a college football game.

- *Describing:* Indicating characteristics of a stimulus. "All of the people in the student section are wearing red."
- *Recognizing:* Placing a stimulus in a specific category. "Number 12 is the other team's quarterback."

- *Detecting:* Becoming aware of a barely detectable aspect of a stimulus. "That lineman moved slightly just before the ball was snapped."

- *Perceiving magnitude:* Being aware of the size or intensity of a stimulus. "That lineman looks twice as big as our quarterback."

- *Searching:* Looking for a specific stimulus among a number of other stimuli. "I'm looking for Susan in the student section."

We will now describe some of the methods that perception researchers have used to measure each of these ways of responding to stimuli.

Description

When a researcher asks a person to describe what he or she is perceiving or to indicate when a particular perception occurs, the researcher is using the **phenomenological method**. This method is a first step in studying perception because it describes what we perceive. This description can be at a very basic level, such as when we notice that we can perceive some objects as being farther away than others, or that there is a perceptual quality we call "color," or that there are different qualities of taste, such as bitter, sweet, and sour. These are such common observations that we might take them for granted, but this is where the study of perception begins, because these are the basic properties that we are seeking to explain.

Recognition

When we categorize a stimulus by naming it, we are measuring *recognition*.

METHOD ▌ Recognition

Every so often we will introduce a new method by describing it in a "Method" section like this one. Students are sometimes tempted to skip these sections because they think the content is unimportant. However, you should resist this temptation because these methods are essential tools for the study of perception. These "Method" sections will help you understand the experiment that follows and will provide the background for understanding other experiments later in the book.

The procedure for measuring recognition is simple: A stimulus is presented, and the observer indicates what it is. Your response to the rat–man demonstration involved recognition because you were asked to name what you saw. This procedure is widely used in testing patients with brain damage, such as the musician Dr. P. with visual agnosia, described earlier. Often the stimuli in these experiments are pictures of objects rather than the actual object (thereby avoiding having to bring elephants and other large objects into the laboratory!).

Describing perceptions using the phenomenological method and determining a person's ability to recognize objects provides information about what a person is perceiving. Often, however, it is useful to establish a quantitative relationship between the stimulus and perception. One way this has been achieved is by methods designed to measure the amount of stimulus energy necessary for detecting a stimulus.

Detection

In Gustav Fechner's book *Elements of Psychophysics,* he described a number of quantitative methods for measuring the relationship between stimuli and perception. These methods—limits, adjustment, and constant stimuli—are called the classical psychophysical methods because they were the original methods used to measure the stimulus-perception relationship.

The Absolute Threshold The absolute threshold is the smallest amount of stimulus energy necessary to detect a stimulus. For example, the smallest amount of light energy that enables a person to just barely detect a flash of light would be the absolute threshold for seeing that light.

METHOD ▌ Determining the Absolute Threshold

There are three basic methods for determining the absolute threshold: the methods of *limits, adjustment,* and *constant stimuli.* In the method of limits, the experimenter presents stimuli in either ascending order (intensity is increased) or descending order (intensity is decreased), as shown in Figure 1.12, which indicates the results of an experiment that measures a person's threshold [VL] 1, 2 for hearing a tone.

On the first series of trials, the experimenter presents a tone with an intensity of 103, and the observer indicates by a "yes" response that he hears the tone. This response is indicated by a Y at an intensity of 103 on the table. The experimenter then presents another tone, at a lower intensity, and the observer responds to this tone. This procedure continues, with the observer making a judgment at each intensity, until he responds "no," that he did not hear the tone. This change from "yes" to "no," indicated by the dashed line, is the *crossover point,* and the threshold for this series is taken as the mean between 99 and 98, or 98.5. The next series of trials begins below the observer's threshold, so that he says "no" on the first trial (intensity 95), and continues until he says "yes" (when the intensity reaches 100). By repeating this procedure a number of times, starting above the threshold half the time and starting below the threshold half the time, the experimenter can determine the threshold by calculating the average of all of the crossover points.

Figure 1.11 ❚ Man version of the rat–man stimulus. (Adapted from Bugelski & Alampay, 1961.)

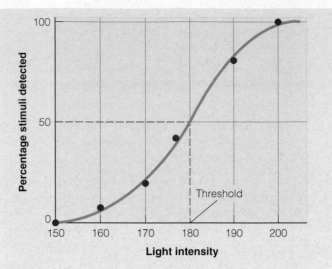

Figure 1.13 ❚ Results of a hypothetical experiment in which the threshold for seeing a light is measured by the method of constant stimuli. The threshold—the intensity at which the light is seen on half of its presentations—is 180 in this experiment.

In the **method of adjustment**, the observer or the experimenter adjusts the stimulus intensity continuously until the observer can just barely detect the stimulus. This method differs from the method of limits because the observer does not say "yes" or "no" as each tone intensity is presented. Instead, the observer simply adjusts the intensity until he or she can just barely hear the tone. For example, the observer might be told to turn a knob to decrease the intensity of a sound, until the sound can no longer be heard, and then to turn the knob back again so the sound is just barely audible. This just barely audible intensity is taken as the absolute threshold. This procedure can be repeated several times and the threshold [VL] **3, 4** determined by taking the average setting.

In the **method of constant stimuli**, the experimenter presents five to nine stimuli with different intensities in random order. The results of a hypothetical determi-

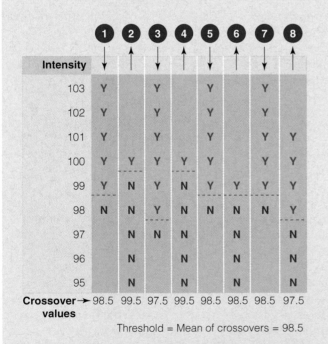

Intensity	1	2	3	4	5	6	7	8
103	Y		Y		Y		Y	
102	Y		Y		Y		Y	
101	Y		Y		Y		Y	Y
100	Y	Y	Y	Y	Y		Y	Y
99	Y	N	Y	N	Y	Y	Y	Y
98	N	N	Y	N	N	N	N	Y
97		N	N	N		N		N
96		N		N		N		N
95		N		N		N		N
Crossover values	98.5	99.5	97.5	99.5	98.5	98.5	98.5	97.5

Threshold = Mean of crossovers = 98.5

Figure 1.12 ❚ The results of an experiment to determine the threshold using the method of limits. The dashed lines indicate the crossover point for each sequence of stimuli. The threshold—the average of the crossover values—is 98.5 in this experiment.

nation of the threshold for seeing a light are shown in Figure 1.13. The data points in this graph were determined by presenting six light intensities 10 times each and determining the percentage of times that the observer perceived each intensity. The results indicate that the light with an intensity of 150 was never detected, the light with an intensity of 200 was always detected, and lights with intensities in between were sometimes detected and sometimes not detected. The threshold is usually defined as the intensity that results in detection on 50 percent of the trials. Applying this definition to the results in Figure 1.13 indicates that the threshold is [VL] **5** an intensity of 180.

The choice among the methods of limits, adjustment, and constant stimuli is usually determined by the accuracy needed and the amount of time available. The method of constant stimuli is the most accurate method because it involves many observations and stimuli are presented in random order, which minimizes how presentation on one trial can affect the observer's judgment of the stimulus presented on the next trial. The disadvantage of this method is that it is time-consuming. The method of adjustment is faster because observers can determine their threshold in just a few trials by adjusting the intensity themselves.

When Fechner published *Elements of Psychophysics,* he not only described his methods for measuring the absolute threshold but also described the work of Ernst Weber (1795–1878), a physiologist who, a few years before the publication of Fechner's book, measured another type of threshold, the difference threshold.

The Difference Threshold The difference threshold (called DL from the German *Differenze Limen,* which is translated as "difference threshold") is the smallest difference between two stimuli that a person can detect.

METHOD ▍ Determining the Difference Threshold

Fechner's methods can be used to determine the difference threshold, except that instead of being asked to indicate whether they detect a stimulus, participants are asked to indicate whether they detect a *difference* between two stimuli. For example, the procedure for measuring the difference threshold for sensing weight is as follows: Weights are presented to each hand, as shown in Figure 1.14; one is a standard weight, and the other is a comparison weight. The observer judges, based on weight alone (he doesn't see the weights), whether the weights are the same or different. Then the comparison weight is increased slightly, and the observer again judges "same" or "different." This continues (randomly varying the side on which the comparison is presented) until the observer says "different." The difference threshold is the difference between the standard and comparison weights when the observer first says "different." ▍VL▏ 6

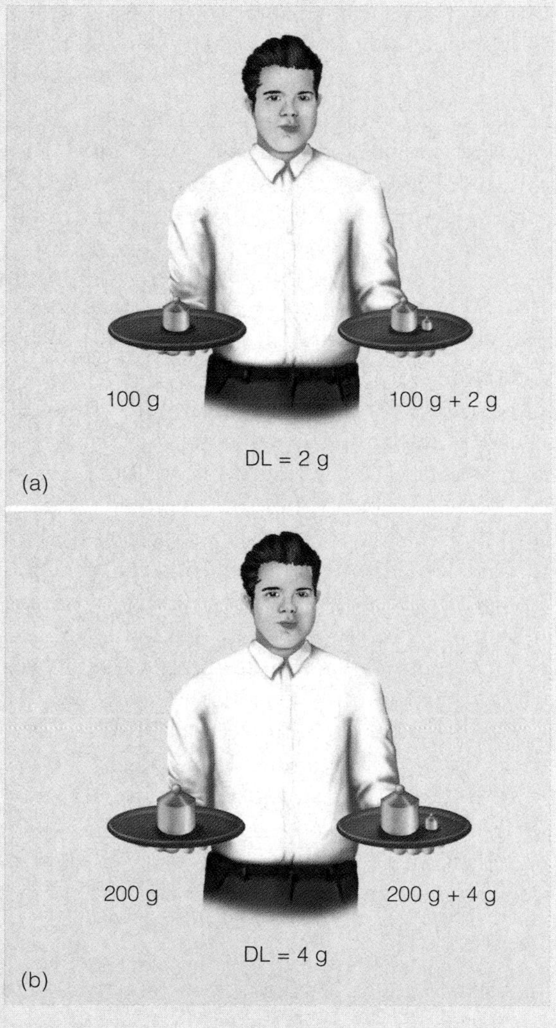

(a) 100 g | 100 g + 2 g
DL = 2 g

(b) 200 g | 200 g + 4 g
DL = 4 g

Figure 1.14 ▍ The difference threshold (DL). (a) The person can detect the difference between a 100-gram standard weight and a 102-gram weight but cannot detect a smaller difference, so the DL is 2 grams. (b) With a 200-gram standard weight, the comparison weight must be 204 grams before the person can detect a difference, so the DL is 4 grams. The Weber fraction, which is the ratio of DL to the weight of the standard, is constant.

Weber found that when the difference between the standard and comparison weights was small, his observers found it difficult to detect the difference in the weights, but they easily detected larger differences. That much is not surprising, but Weber went further. He found that the size of the DL depended on the size of the standard weight. For example, if the DL for a 100-gram weight was 2 grams (an observer could tell the difference between a 100- and a 102-gram weight, but could not detect smaller differences), then the DL for a 200-gram weight was 4 grams. Thus, as the magnitude of the stimulus increases, so does the size of the DL.

Research on a number of senses has shown that over a fairly large range of intensities, the ratio of the DL to the standard stimulus is constant. This relationship, which is based on Weber's research, was stated mathematically by Fechner as $DL/S = K$ and was called Weber's law. K is a constant called the **Weber fraction**, and S is the value of the standard stimulus. Applying this equation to our previous example of lifted weights, we find that for the 100-gram standard, $K = 2\,g/100\,g = 0.02$, and for the 200-gram standard, $K = 4\,g/200\,g = 0.02$. Thus, in this example, the Weber fraction (K) is constant. In fact, numerous modern investigators have found that Weber's law is true for most senses, as long as the stimulus intensity is not too close to the threshold (Engen, 1972; Gescheider, 1976). ▍VL▏ 7, 8

The Weber fraction remains relatively constant for a particular sense, but each type of sensory judgment has its own Weber fraction. For example, from Table 1.1 we can see that people can detect a 1 percent change in the intensity of an electric shock but that light intensity must be increased by 8 percent before they can detect a difference.

TABLE 1.1 ▍ **Weber Fractions for a Number of Different Sensory Dimensions**

Electric shock	0.01
Lifted weight	0.02
Sound intensity	0.04
Light intensity	0.08
Taste (salty)	0.08

Source: Teghtsoonian (1971).

Fechner's proposal of three psychophysical methods for measuring the threshold and his statement of Weber's law for the difference threshold were extremely important events in the history of scientific psychology because they demonstrated that mental activity could be measured quantitatively, which many people in the 1800s thought was impossible. But perhaps the most significant thing about these methods is that even though they were proposed in the 1800s, they are still used today. In addition to being used to determine thresholds in research laboratories, simplified versions of the classical psychophysical methods have been used to measure people's detail vision when determining prescriptions for glasses and measuring people's hearing when testing for possible hearing loss.

The classical psychophysical methods were developed to measure absolute and difference thresholds. But what about perceptions that occur above threshold? Most of our everyday experience consists of perceptions that are far above threshold, when we can easily see and hear what is happening around us. Measuring these above-threshold perceptions involves a technique called *magnitude estimation*.

Magnitude Estimation

If we double the intensity of a tone, does it sound twice as loud? If we double the intensity of a light, does it look twice as bright? Although a number of researchers, including Fechner, proposed equations that related perceived magnitude and stimulus intensity, it wasn't until 1957 that S. S. Stevens developed a technique called scaling, or **magnitude estimation**, that accurately measured this relationship (S. S. Stevens, 1957, 1961, 1962).

METHOD | Magnitude Estimation

The procedure for a magnitude estimation experiment is relatively simple: The experimenter first presents a "standard" stimulus to the observer (let's say a light of moderate intensity) and assigns it a value of, say, 10; he or she then presents lights of different intensities, and the observer is asked to assign a number to each of these lights that is proportional to the brightness of the standard stimulus. If the light appears twice as bright as the standard, it gets a rating of 20; half as bright, a 5; and so on. Thus, each light intensity has a brightness assigned to it by the observer. There are also magnitude estimation procedures in which no "standard" is used. But the basic principle is the same: The observer assigns numbers to stimuli that are proportional to perceived magnitude.

The results of a magnitude estimation experiment on brightness are plotted as the red curve in Figure 1.15. This graph plots the average magnitude estimates made by

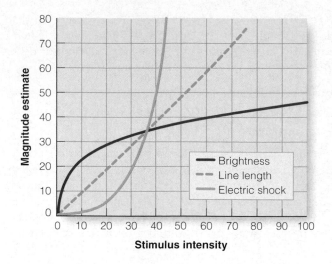

Figure 1.15 ▌ The relationship between perceived magnitude and stimulus intensity for electric shock, line length, and brightness. (Adapted from Stevens, 1962.)

a number of observers of the brightness of a light. This curve indicates that doubling the intensity does not necessarily double the perceived brightness. For example, when intensity is 20, perceived brightness is 28. If we double the intensity to 40, perceived brightness does not double, to 56, but instead increases only to 36. This result is called **response compression.** As intensity is increased, the magnitude increases, but not as rapidly as the intensity. To double the brightness, it is necessary to multiply the intensity by about 9.

Figure 1.15 also shows the results of magnitude estimation experiments for the sensation caused by an electric shock presented to the finger and for the perception of length of a line. The electric shock curve bends up, indicating that doubling the strength of a shock more than doubles the sensation of being shocked. Increasing the intensity from 20 to 40 increases perception of shock sensation from 6 to 49. This is called **response expansion.** As intensity is increased, perceptual magnitude increases more than intensity. The curve for estimating line length is straight, with a slope of close to 1.0, meaning that the magnitude of the response almost exactly matches increases in the stimulus (i.e., if the line length is doubled, an observer says it appears to be twice as long).

The beauty of the relationships derived from magnitude estimation is that the relationship between the intensity of a stimulus and our perception of its magnitude follows the same general equation for each sense. These functions, which are called **power functions**, are described by the equation $P = KS^n$. Perceived magnitude, P, equals a constant, K, times the stimulus intensity, S, raised to a power, n. This relationship is called **Stevens's power law.**

For example, if the exponent, n, is 2.0 and the constant, K, is 1.0, the perceived magnitude, P, for intensities 10 and 20 would be calculated as follows:

Intensity 10: $P = (1.0) \times (10)^2 = 100$

Intensity 20: $P = (1.0) \times (20)^2 = 400$

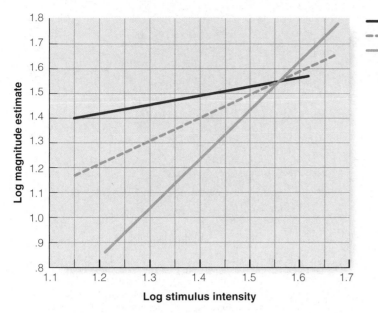

Figure 1.16 ▌ The three functions from Figure 1.15 plotted on log-log coordinates. Taking the logarithm of the magnitude estimates and the logarithm of the stimulus intensity turns the functions into straight lines. (Adapted from Stevens, 1962.)

In this example, doubling the intensity results in a fourfold increase in perceived magnitude, an example of response expansion.

One of the properties of power functions is that taking the logarithm of the terms on the left and right sides of the equation changes the function into a straight line. This is shown in Figure 1.16. Plotting the logarithm of the magnitude estimates in Figure 1.15 versus the logarithm of the stimulus intensities causes all three curves to become straight lines. The slopes of the straight lines indicate n, the exponent of the power function. Remembering our discussion of the three types of curves in Figure 1.15, we can see that the curve for brightness has a slope of less than 1.0 (response compression), the curve for estimating line length has a slope of about 1.0, and the curve for electric shock has a slope of greater than 1.0 (response expansion). Thus, the relationship between response magnitude and stimulus intensity is described by a power law for all senses, and the exponent of the power law indicates whether doubling the stimulus intensity causes more or less than a doubling of the response.

These exponents not only illustrate that all senses follow the same basic relationship, they also illustrate how the operation of each sense is adapted to how organisms function in their environment. Consider, for example, your experience of brightness. Imagine you are inside looking at a page in a book that is brightly illuminated by a lamp on your desk. Now imagine that you are looking out the window at a bright sidewalk that is brightly illuminated by sunlight. Your eye may be receiving thousands of times more light from the sidewalk than from the page of your book, but because the curve for brightness bends down (exponent 0.6), the sidewalk does not appear thousands of times brighter than the page. It does appear brighter, but not so much that you are blinded by the sunlit sidewalk.[3]

---
[3] Another mechanism that keeps you from being blinded by high-intensity lights is that your eye adjusts its sensitivity in response to different light levels.

The opposite situation occurs for electric shock, which has an exponent of 3.5, meaning that small increases in shock intensity cause large increases in pain. This rapid increase in pain even to small increases in shock intensity serves to warn us of impending danger, and we therefore tend to withdraw even from weak shocks.

Search

So far, we have been describing methods in which the observer is able to make a relatively leisurely perceptual judgment. When a person is asked to indicate whether he or she can see a light or tell the difference between two weights, the accuracy of the judgment is what is important, not the speed at which it is made. However, some perceptual research uses methods that require the observer to respond as quickly as possible. One example of such a method is **visual search**, in which the observer's task is to find one stimulus among many, as quickly as possible.

An everyday example of visual search would be searching for a friend's face in a crowd. If you've ever done this, you know that sometimes it is easy (if you know your friend is wearing a bright red hat, and no one else is), and sometimes it is difficult (if there are lots of people and your friend doesn't stand out). When we consider visual attention in Chapter 6, we will describe visual search experiments in which the observer's task is to find as rapidly as possible, a target stimulus that is hidden among a number of other stimuli. We will see that measuring reaction time—the time between presentation of the stimulus and the observer's response to the stimulus—has provided important information about mechanisms responsible for perception.

Other Methods of Measurement

Numerous other methods have been used to measure the stimulus–perception relationship. For example, in some experiments, observers are asked to decide whether two stimuli are the same or different, or to adjust the brightness or the colors of two lights so they appear the same, or to close their eyes and walk, as accurately as possible, to a distant target stimulus in a field. We will encounter methods such as these, and others as well, as we describe perceptual research in the chapters that follow.

Something to Consider: Threshold Measurement Can Be Influenced by How a Person Chooses to Respond

We've seen that we can use psychophysical methods to determine the absolute threshold. For example, by randomly presenting lights of different intensities, we can use the method of constant stimuli to determine the intensity to which a person reports "I see the light" 50 percent of the time. What determines this threshold intensity? Certainly, the physiological workings of the person's eye and visual system are important. But some researchers have pointed out that perhaps other characteristics of the person may also influence the determination of threshold intensity.

To illustrate this idea, let's consider a hypothetical experiment in which we use the method of constant stimuli to measure Julie's and Regina's thresholds for seeing a light. We pick five different light intensities, present them in random order, and ask Julie and Regina to say "yes" if they see the light and "no" if they don't see it. Julie thinks about these instructions and decides that she wants to be sure she doesn't miss any presentations of the light. She therefore decides to say "yes" if there is even the slightest possibility that she sees the light. However, Regina responds more conservatively because she wants to be totally sure that she sees the light before saying "yes." She is not willing to report that she sees the light unless it is clearly visible.

The results of this hypothetical experiment are shown in Figure 1.17. Julie gives many more "yes" responses than Regina and therefore ends up with a lower threshold. But given what we know about Julie and Regina, should we conclude that Julie's visual system is more sensitive to the lights than Regina's? It could be that their actual sensitivity to the lights is exactly same, but Julie's apparently lower threshold occurs because she is more willing than Regina to report that she sees a light. A way to describe this difference between these two people is that each has a different **response criterion**. Julie's response criterion is low (she says "yes" if there is the slightest chance a light is present), whereas Regina's response criterion is high (she says "yes" only when she is sure that she sees the light).

What are the implications of the fact that people may have different response criteria? If we are interested in how one person responds to different stimuli (for example, measuring how a particular person's threshold varies for

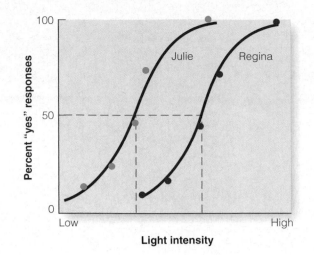

Figure 1.17 ▌ Data from experiments is which the threshold for seeing a light is determined for Julie (green points) and Regina (red points) by means of the method of constant stimuli. These data indicate that Julie's threshold is lower than Regina's. But is Julie really more sensitive to the light than Regina, or does she just appear to be more sensitive because she is a more liberal responder?

different colors of light), then we don't need to take response criterion into account because we are comparing responses within the same person. Response criterion is also not very important if we are testing many people and averaging their responses. However, if we wish to compare two people's responses, their differing response criteria could influence the results. Luckily, there is a way to take differing response criteria into account. This procedure is described in the Appendix, which discusses **signal detection theory**.

TEST YOURSELF 1.1

1. What are some of the reasons for studying perception?
2. Describe the process of perception as a series of steps, beginning with the environmental stimulus and culminating in the behavioral responses of perceiving, recognizing, and acting.
3. What is the role of higher-level or "cognitive" processes in perception? Be sure you understand the difference between bottom-up and top-down processing.
4. What does it mean to say that perception can be studied using different approaches?
5. Describe the different ways people respond perceptually to stimuli and how each of these types of perceptual response can be measured.
6. What does it mean to say that a person's threshold may be determined by more than the physiological workings of his or her sensory system?

THINK ABOUT IT

1. This chapter argues that although perception seems simple, it is actually extremely complex when we consider "behind the scenes" activities that are not obvious as a person is experiencing perception. Cite an example of a similar situation from your own experience, in which an "outcome" that might seem as though it was achieved easily actually involved a complicated process that most people are unaware of. (p. 5)

2. Describe a situation in which you initially thought you saw or heard something but then realized that your initial perception was in error. What was the role of bottom-up and top-down processing in this example of first having an incorrect perception and then realizing what was actually there? (p. 10)

IF YOU WANT TO KNOW MORE

1. *History.* The study of perception played an extremely important role in the development of scientific psychology in the first half of the 20th century. (p. 16)

   Boring, E. G. (1942). *Sensation and perception in the history of experimental psychology.* New York: Appleton-Century-Crofts.

2. *Disorders of recognition.* Dr. P.'s case, in which he had problems recognizing people, is just one example of many such cases of people with brain damage. In addition to reports in the research literature, there are a number of popular accounts of these cases written for the general public. (p. 13)

   Sacks, O. (1985). *The man who mistook his wife for a hat.* London: Duckworth.

   Kolb, B., & Whishaw, I. Q. (2003). *Fundamentals of human neuropsychology* (5th ed.). New York: Worth. (Especially see Chapters 13–17, which contain numerous descriptions of how brain damage affects sensory functioning.)

3. *Phenomenological method.* David Katz's book provides excellent examples of how the phenomenological method has been used to determine the experiences that occur under various stimulus conditions. He also describes how surfaces, color, and light combine to create many different perceptions. (p. 13)

   Katz, D. (1935). *The world of color* (2nd ed., R. B. MacLeod & C. W. Fox, Trans.). London: Kegan Paul, Trench, Truber.

4. *Top-down processing.* There are many examples of how people's knowledge can influence perception, ranging from early research, which focused on how people's motivation can influence perception, to more recent research, which has emphasized the effects of context and past learning on perception. (p. 10)

   Postman, L., Bruner, J. S., & McGinnis, E. (1948). Personal values as selective factors in perception. *Journal of Abnormal and Social Psychology, 43,* 142–154.

   Vernon, M. D. (1962). *The psychology of perception.* Baltimore: Penguin. (See Chapter 11, "The Relation of Perception to Motivation and Emotion.")

KEY TERMS

Absolute threshold (p. 13)
Action (p. 9)
Attended stimulus (p. 6)
Bottom-up processing (data-based processing) (p. 10)
Classical psychophysical methods (p. 13)
Cognitive influences on perception (p. 12)
Difference threshold (p. 15)
Environmental stimulus (p. 5)
Knowledge (p. 9)
Magnitude estimation (p. 16)
Method of adjustment (p. 14)

Method of constant stimuli (p. 14)
Method of limits (p. 13)
Neural processing (p. 7)
Perception (p. 8)
Perceptual process (p. 5)
Phenomenological method (p. 13)
Physiological approach to perception (p. 11)
Power function (p. 16)
Psychophysical approach to perception (p. 11)
Psychophysics (p. 11)
Rat-man demonstration (p. 10)
Reaction time (p. 17)

Recognition (p. 8)
Response compression (p. 16)
Response criterion (p. 18)
Response expansion (p. 16)
Signal detection theory (p. 18)
Stevens's power law (p. 16)
Top-down processing (knowledge-based processing) (p. 10)
Transduction (p. 7)
Visual form agnosia (p. 9)
Visual search (p. 17)
Weber fraction (p. 15)
Weber's law (p. 15)

MEDIA RESOURCES

The *Sensation and Perception* Book Companion Website

www.cengage.com/psychology/goldstein

See the companion website for flashcards, practice quiz questions, Internet links, updates, critical thinking exercises, discussion forums, games, and more!

CengageNOW

www.cengage.com/cengagenow

Go to this site for the link to CengageNOW, your one-stop shop. Take a pre-test for this chapter, and CengageNOW will generate a personalized study plan based on your test results. The study plan will identify the topics you need to review and direct you to online resources to help you master those topics. You can then take a post-test to help you determine the concepts you have mastered and what you will still need to work on.

Virtual Lab

VL

Your Virtual Lab is designed to help you get the most out of this course. The Virtual Lab icons direct you to specific media demonstrations and experiments designed to help you visualize what you are reading about. The number beside each icon indicates the number of the media element you can access through your CD-ROM, CengageNOW, or WebTutor resource.

The following lab exercises are related to material in this chapter:

1. *The Method of Limits* How a "typical" observer might respond using the method of limits procedure to measure absolute threshold.

2. *Measuring Illusions* An experiment that enables you to measure the size of the Müller-Lyer, horizontal–vertical, and simultaneous contrast illusions using the method of constant stimuli. The simultaneous contrast illusion is described in Chapter 3, and the Müller-Lyer illusion is described in Chapter 10.

3. *Measurement Fluctuation and Error* How our judgments of size can vary from trial to trial.

4. *Adjustment and PSE* Measuring the point of subjective equality for line length using the method of adjustment.

5. *Method of Constant Stimuli* Measuring the difference threshold for line length using the method of constant stimuli.

6. *Just Noticeable Difference* Measuring the just noticeable difference (roughly the same thing as difference threshold) for area, length, and saturation of color.

7. *Weber's Law and Weber Fraction* Plotting the graph that shows how Weber's fraction remains constant for different weights.

8. *DL vs. Weight* Plotting the graph that shows how the difference threshold changes for different weights.

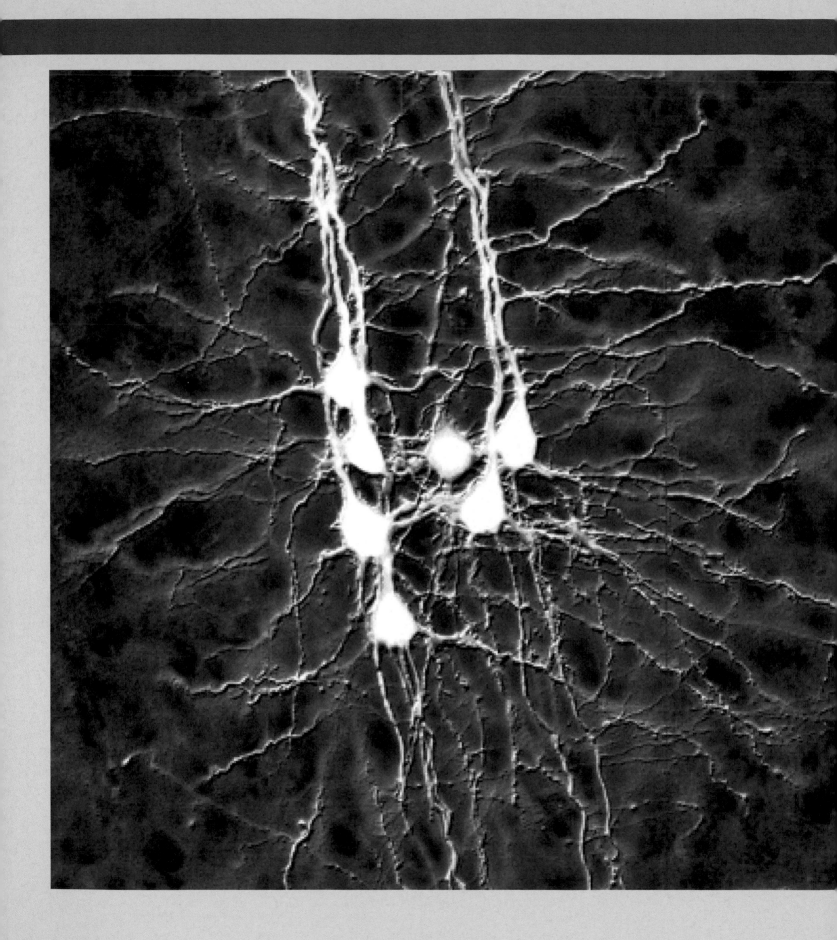

CHAPTER 2

Introduction to the Physiology of Perception

OPPOSITE PAGE Neurons, such as the ones shown here, form the communication and processing network of the nervous system. Understanding how neurons respond to perceptual stimuli is central to our understanding of the physiological basis of perception.
Copyright 2006 National Academy of Sciences, USA.

[VL] The Virtual Lab icons direct you to specific animations and videos designed to help you visualize what you are reading about. The number beside each icon indicates the number of the clip you can access through your CD-ROM or your student website.

Some Questions We Will Consider:

▌ How are physiological processes involved in perception? (p. 24)

▌ How can electrical signals in the nervous system represent objects in the environment? (p. 36)

In Chapter 1 we saw that electrical signals are the link between the environment and perception. The stimulus, first in the environment and then on the receptors, creates electrical signals in the nervous system, which through a miraculous and still not completely understood process become transformed into experiences like the colors of a sunset, the roughness of sandpaper, or smells from the kitchen. Much of the research you will read about in this book is concerned with understanding the connection between electrical signals in the nervous system and perception. The purpose of this chapter is to introduce you to the physiological approach to the study of perception and to provide the background you will need to understand the physiological material in the rest of the book.

The Brain: The Mind's Computer

Today we take it for granted that the brain is the seat of the mind: the structure responsible for mental functions such as memory, thoughts, language, and—of particular inter-

est to us—perceptions. But the idea that the brain controls mental functioning is a relatively modern idea.

Brief History of the Physiological Approach

Early thinking about the physiology of the mind focused on determining the anatomical structures involved in the operation of the mind.

Early Hypotheses About the Seat of the Mind In the fourth century B.C. the philosopher Aristotle (384–322 B.C.) stated that the heart was the seat of the mind and the soul (Figure 2.1a). The Greek physician Galen (ca. A.D. 130–200) saw human health, thoughts, and emotions as being determined by four different "spirits" flowing from the ventricles—cavities in the center of the brain (Figure 2.1b). This idea was accepted all the way through the Middle Ages and into the Renaissance in the 1500s and early 1600s. In the early 1630s the philosopher Rene Descartes, although still accepting the idea of flowing spirits, specified the pineal gland, which was thought to be located over the ventricles, as the seat of the soul (Figure 2.1c; Zimmer, 2004).

The Brain As the Seat of the Mind In 1664 Thomas Willis, a physician at the University of Oxford, published a book titled *The Anatomy of the Brain,* which was based on dissections of the brains of humans, dogs, sheep, and other animals. Willis concluded that the brain was responsible for mental functioning, that different functions

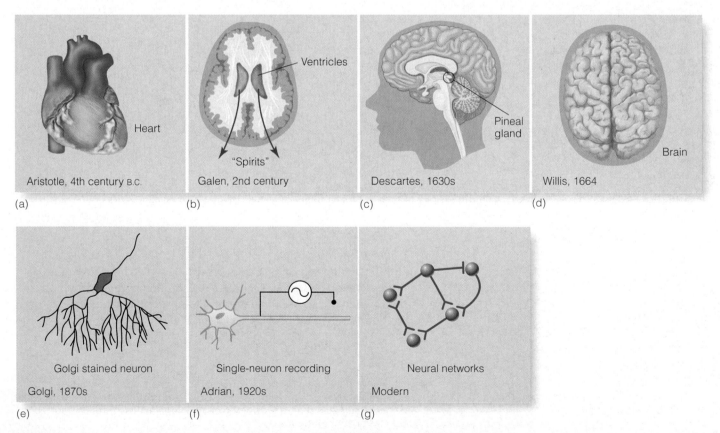

Figure 2.1 ▌ Some notable ideas and events regarding the physiological workings of the mind.

were located in different regions of the brain, and that disorders of the brain were disorders of chemistry (Figure 2.1d). Although these conclusions were correct, details of the mechanisms involved had to await the development of new technologies that would enable researchers to see the brain's microstructure and record its electrical signals.

Signals Traveling in Neurons One of the most important problems to be solved was determining the structure of the nervous system. In the 1800s, there were two opposing ideas about the nervous system. One idea, called **reticular theory**, held that the nervous system consisted of a large network of fused nerve cells. The other idea, **neuron theory**, stated that the nervous system consisted of distinct elements or cells.

An important development that led to the acceptance of neuron theory was the discovery of **staining**, a chemical technique that caused nerve cells to become colored so they stood out from surrounding tissue. Camillo Golgi (1873) developed a technique in which immersing a thin slice of brain tissue in a solution of silver nitrate created pictures like the one in Figure 2.2 in which individual cells were randomly stained (Figure 2.1e). What made this technique so useful was that only a few cells were stained, and the ones that were stained were stained completely, so it was possible to see the structure of the entire neuron. Golgi received the Nobel Prize for his research in 1906.

What about the signals in these neurons? By the late 1800s, researchers had shown that a wave of electricity is transmitted in groups of neurons, such as the optic nerve. To explain how these electrical signals result in different perceptions, Johannes Mueller in 1842 proposed the **doctrine of specific nerve energies**, which stated that our perceptions depend on "nerve energies" reaching the brain and that the specific quality we experience depends on which nerves are stimulated. Thus he proposed that activity in the optic nerve results in seeing, activity in the auditory nerve results in hearing, and so on. By the end of the 1800s, this idea had expanded to conclude that nerves from each of these senses reach different areas of the brain. This idea of separating different functions is still a central principle of nervous system functioning.

Recording From Neurons Details about how single neurons operate had to await the development of electronic amplifiers that were powerful enough to make visible the extremely small electrical signals generated by the neuron. In the 1920s Edgar Adrian (1928, 1932) was able to record electrical signals from single sensory neurons, an achievement for which he was awarded the Nobel Prize in 1932 (Figure 2.1f).

We can appreciate the importance of being able to record from single neurons by considering the following analogy: You walk into a large room in which hundreds of people are talking about a political speech they have just heard. There is a great deal of noise and commotion in the room as people react to the speech. However, based on just hearing this "crowd noise," all you can say about what is

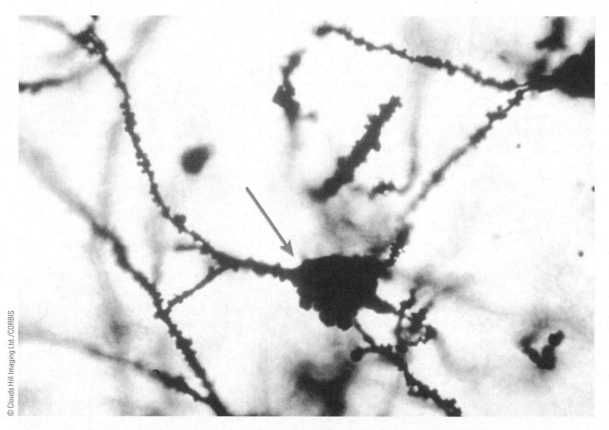

© Clouds Hill Imaging Ltd./CORBIS

Figure 2.2 ❙ A portion of the brain that has been treated with Golgi stain shows the shapes of a few neurons. The arrow points to a neuron's cell body. The thin lines are dendrites or axons (see Figure 2.4).

going on is that the speech seems to have generated a great deal of excitement. To get more specific information about the speech, you need to listen to what individual people are saying.

Just as listening to individual people provides valuable information about what is happening in a large crowd, recording from single neurons provides valuable information about what is happening in the nervous system. Recording from single neurons is like listening to individual voices. It is, of course, important to record from as many neurons as possible because just as individual people may have different opinions about the speech, different neurons may respond differently to a particular stimulus or situation.

The ability to record electrical signals from individual neurons ushered in the modern era of brain research, and in the 1950s and 1960s development of more sophisticated electronics and the availability of computers and the electron microscope made more detailed analysis of how neurons function possible. Most of the physiological research we will describe in this book had its beginning at this point, when it became possible to determine how individual neurons respond to stimuli in the environment and how neurons work together in neural networks (Figure 2.1g). We will now briefly describe the overall layout of the brain, to give you an overview of the entire system, and then zoom in to look in detail at some basic principles of neuron structure and operation.

Basic Structure of the Brain

In the first American textbook of psychology, Harvard psychologist William James (1890/1981) described the brain as the "most mysterious thing in the world" because of the amazing feats it achieves and the intricacies of how it achieves them. Although we are far from understanding all of the details of how the brain operates, we have learned a tremendous amount about how the brain determines our perceptions. Much of the research on the connection between the brain and perception has focused on activity in the **cerebral cortex**, the 2-mm-thick layer that covers the surface of the brain and contains the machinery for creating perception, as well as for other functions, such as language, memory, and thinking. A basic principle of cortical function is **modular organization**—specific functions are served by specific areas of the cortex.

One example of modular organization is how the senses are organized into **primary receiving areas**, the first areas in the cerebral cortex to receive the signals initiated by each sense's receptors (Figure 2.3). The primary receiving area for vision occupies most of the **occipital lobe**; the area for hearing is located in part of the **temporal lobe**; and the area for the skin senses—touch, temperature, and pain—is located in an area in the **parietal lobe**. The **frontal lobe** receives signals from all of the senses, and plays an important role in perceptions that involve the coordination of information received through two or more senses. As we study each sense in detail, we will see that other areas in addition to the primary receiving areas are also associated with each sense. For example,

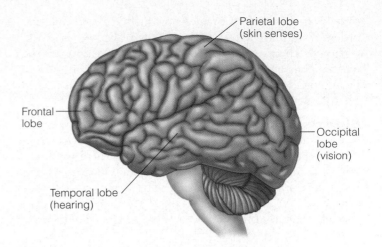

Figure 2.3 ▌ The human brain, showing the locations of the primary receiving areas for the senses in the temporal, occipital, and parietal lobes, and the frontal lobe, which is involved with integrating sensory functions.

there is an area in the temporal lobe concerned with the perception of form. We will consider the functioning of various areas of the brain in Chapters 3 and 4. In this chapter we will focus on describing the properties of neurons.

Neurons: Cells That Create and Transmit Electrical Signals

One purpose of neurons that are involved in perception is to respond to stimuli from the environment, and transduce these stimuli into electrical signals (see the *transduction* step of the perceptual process, page 7). Another purpose is to communicate with other neurons, so that these signals can travel long distances (see the *transmission* step of the perceptual process, page 7).

Structure of Neurons

The key components of neurons are shown in the neuron on the right in Figure 2.4. The **cell body** contains mechanisms to keep the cell alive; **dendrites** branch out from the cell body to receive electrical signals from other neurons; and the **axon**, or **nerve fiber**, is filled with fluid that conducts electrical signals. There are variations on this basic neuron structure: Some neurons have long axons; others have short axons or none at all. Especially important for perception are a type of neuron called **receptors**, which are specialized to respond to environmental stimuli such as pressure for touch, as in the neuron on the left in Figure 2.4. Figure 2.5 shows examples of receptors that are specialized for responding to (a) light (vision); (b) pressure changes in the air (hearing); (c) pressure on the skin (touch); (d) chemicals in the air (smell); and (e) chemicals in liquid form (taste). Although these receptors look different, they all have

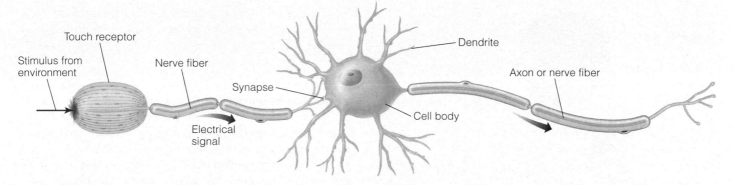

Figure 2.4 ▮ The neuron on the right consists of a cell body, dendrites, and an axon, or nerve fiber. The neuron on the left that receives stimuli from the environment has a receptor in place of the cell body.

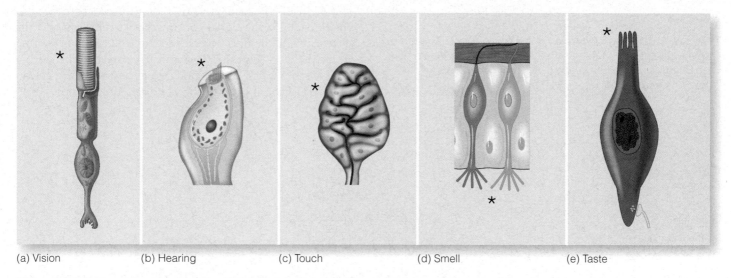

(a) Vision   (b) Hearing   (c) Touch   (d) Smell   (e) Taste

Figure 2.5 ▮ Receptors for (a) vision, (b) hearing, (c) touch, (d) smell, and (e) taste. Each of these receptors is specialized to transduce a specific type of environmental energy into electricity. Stars indicate the place on the receptor neuron where the stimulus acts to begin the process of transduction.

something in common: Part of each receptor, indicated by the star, reacts to environmental stimuli and triggers the generation of electrical signals, which eventually are transmitted to neurons with axons, like the one on the right in Figure 2.4. [VL] 1

Recording Electrical Signals in Neurons

We will be particularly concerned with recording the electrical signals from the axons of neurons. It is important to distinguish between single *neurons,* like the ones shown in Figure 2.4, and *nerves.* A **nerve**, such as the optic nerve, which carries signals out the back of the eye, consists of the axons (or nerve fibers) of many neurons (Figure 2.6), just as many individual wires make up a telephone cable. Thus, recording from an *optic nerve fiber* involves recording not from the optic nerve as a whole, but from one of the small fibers within the optic nerve.

METHOD ▮ Recording From a Neuron

Microelectrodes, small shafts of glass or metal with very fine tips, are used to record signals from single neurons. The key principle for understanding electrical signals in neurons is that we are always measuring the *difference in charge* between two electrodes. One of these electrodes, located where the electrical signals will occur, is the *recording electrode,* shown on the left in Figure 2.7a.[1] The other one, located some distance away so it is not affected by the electrical signals, is the *reference electrode.* The difference in charge between the recording and reference electrodes is displayed on an oscilloscope, which indicates the

---

[1] In practice, most recordings are achieved with the tip of the electrode positioned just outside the neuron because it is technically difficult to insert electrodes into the neuron, especially if it is small. However, if the electrode tip is close enough to the neuron, the electrode can pick up the signals generated by the neuron.

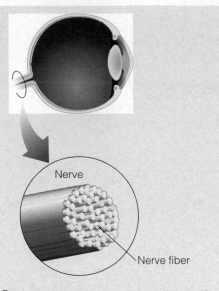

Figure 2.6 ▮ *Nerves* contain many *nerve fibers*. The optic nerve transmits signals out the back of the eye. Shown here schematically in cross section, the optic nerve actually contains about 1 million nerve fibers.

difference in charge by a small dot that creates a line as it moves across the screen, as shown on the right in Figure 2.7a.

$\boxed{V_L}$ **2**

When the nerve fiber is at rest, the oscilloscope records a difference in potential of −70 millivolts (where a millivolt is 1/1000 of a volt), as shown on the right in Figure 2.7a. This value, which stays the same as long as there are no signals in the neuron, is called the **resting potential**. In other words, the inside of the neuron is 70 mV negative compared to the outside, and remains that way as long as the neuron is at rest.

$\boxed{V_L}$ **3**

Figure 2.7b shows what happens when the neuron's receptor is stimulated so that a signal is transmitted down the axon. As the signal passes the recording electrode, the charge inside the axon rises to +40 millivolts compared to the outside. As the signal continues past the electrode, the charge inside the fiber reverses course and starts becoming negative again (Figure 2.7c), until it returns to the resting level (Figure 2.7d). This signal, which is called the **action potential**, lasts about 1 millisecond (1/1000 second).

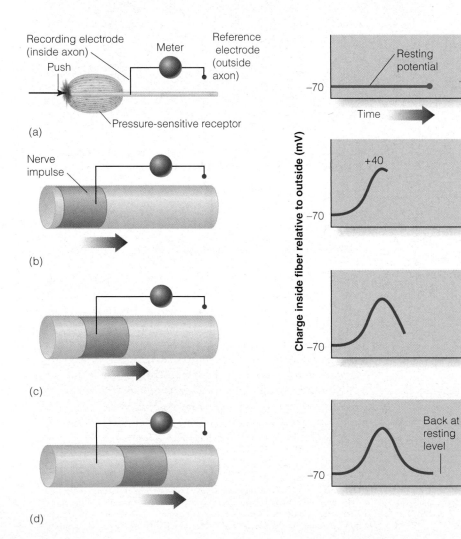

Figure 2.7 ▮ (a) When a nerve fiber is at rest, there is a difference in charge of −70 mV between the inside and the outside of the fiber. This difference is measured by the meter on the left; the difference in charge measured by the meter is displayed on the right. (b) As the nerve impulse, indicated by the red band, passes the electrode, the inside of the fiber near the electrode becomes more positive. This positivity is the rising phase of the action potential. (c) As the nerve impulse moves past the electrode, the charge inside the fiber becomes more negative. This is the falling phase of the action potential. (d) Eventually the neuron returns to its resting state.

Chemical Basis of Action Potentials

When most people think of electrical signals, they imagine signals conducted along electrical power lines or along the wires used for household appliances. We learn as young children that we should keep electrical wires away from liquid. But the electrical signals in neurons are created by and conducted through liquid.

The key to understanding the "wet" electrical signals transmitted by neurons is understanding the components of the neuron's liquid environment. Neurons are surrounded by a solution rich in ions, molecules that carry an electrical charge (Figure 2.8). Ions are created when molecules gain or lose electrons, as happens when compounds are dissolved in water. For example, adding table salt (sodium chloride, NaCl) to water creates positively charged sodium ions (Na^+) and negatively charged chlorine ions (Cl^-). The solution outside the axon of a neuron is rich in positively charged sodium (Na^+) ions, whereas the solution inside the axon is rich in positively charged potassium (K^+) ions.

Remember that the action potential is a rapid increase in positive charge until the inside of the neuron is +40 mV compared to the outside, followed by a rapid return to the baseline of −70 mV. These changes are caused by the flow of sodium and potassium ions across the cell membrane. Figure 2.9 shows the action potential from Figure 2.7, and also shows how the action potential is created by the flow of sodium and potassium ions. First sodium flows into the fiber, then potassium flows out, and this sequence of sodium-in, potassium-out continues as the action potential travels down the axon.

The records on the right in Figure 2.9 show how this flow of sodium and potassium is translated into a change of the charge inside the axon. The upward phase of the action potential—the change from −70 to +40 mV—occurs when positively charged sodium ions rush into the axon (Figure 2.9a). The downward phase of the potential—the change from +40 back to −70 mV—occurs when positively charged potassium ions rush out of the axon (Figure 2.9b). Once the action potential has passed the electrode, the charge inside the fiber returns to the resting potential of −70 mV (Figure 2.9c).

The changes in sodium and potassium flow that create the action potential are caused by changes in the fiber's permeability to sodium and potassium. Permeability is a property of the cell membrane that refers to the ease with which

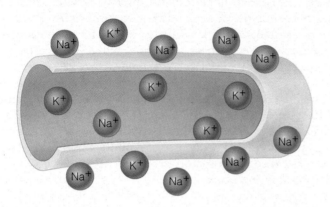

Figure 2.8 ▌ A nerve fiber, showing the high concentration of sodium outside the fiber and potassium inside the fiber. Other ions, such as negatively charged chlorine, are not shown.

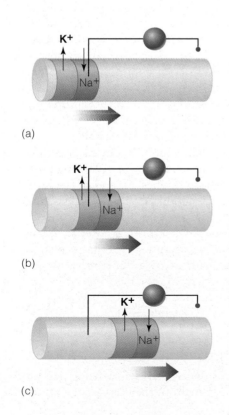

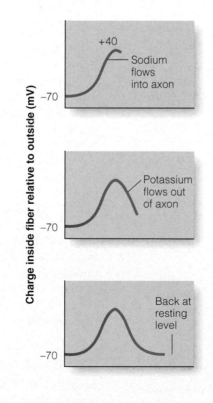

Figure 2.9 ▌ How the flow of sodium and potassium create the action potential. (a) As positively charged sodium (Na^+) flows into the axon, the inside of the neuron becomes more positive (rising phase of the action potential). (b) As positively charged potassium (K^+) flows out of the axon, the inside of the axon becomes more negative (falling phase of the action potential). (c) The fiber's charge returns to the resting level after the flow of Na^+ and K^+ has moved past the electrode.

a molecule can pass through the membrane. **Selective permeability** occurs when a membrane is highly permeable to one specific type of molecule, but not to others.

Before the action potential occurs, the membrane's permeability to sodium and potassium is low, so there is little flow of these molecules across the membrane. Stimulation of the receptor triggers a process that causes the membrane to become selectively permeable to sodium, so sodium flows into the axon. When the action potential reaches +40 mV, the membrane suddenly becomes selectively permeable to potassium, so potassium flows out of the axon. The action potential, therefore, is caused by changes in the axon's selective permeability to sodium and potassium.[2]

Basic Properties of Action Potentials

An important property of the action potential is that it is a **propagated response**—once the response is triggered, it travels all the way down the axon without decreasing in size. This means that if we were to move our recording electrode in Figure 2.7 or 2.9 to a position nearer the end of the axon, the response recorded as the action potential passed the electrode would still be an increase from −70 mV to +40 mV and then a decrease back to −70 mV. This is an extremely important property of the action potential because it enables neurons to transmit signals over long distances.

Another property is that the action potential remains the same size no matter how intense the stimulus is. We can demonstrate this by determining how the neuron fires to different stimulus intensities. Figure 2.10 shows what happens when we do this. Each action potential appears as a

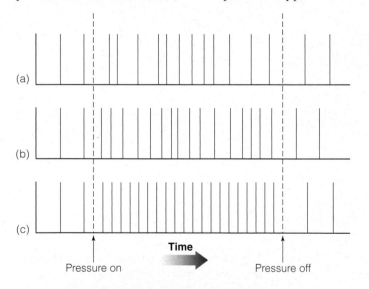

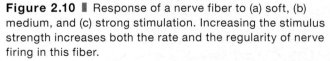

Figure 2.10 ▌ Response of a nerve fiber to (a) soft, (b) medium, and (c) strong stimulation. Increasing the stimulus strength increases both the rate and the regularity of nerve firing in this fiber.

---

[2] If this process were to continue, there would be a buildup of sodium inside the axon and potassium outside the axon. This buildup is prevented by a mechanism called the *sodium–potassium pump*, which is constantly transporting sodium out of the axon and potassium into the axon.

sharp spike in these records because we have compressed the time scale to display a number of action potentials.

The three records in Figure 2.10 represent the axon's response to three intensities of pushing on the skin. Figure 2.10a shows how the axon responds to gentle stimulation applied to the skin, and Figures 2.10b and 2.10c show how the response changes as the pressure is increased. Comparing these three records leads to an important conclusion: Changing the stimulus intensity does not affect the *size* of the action potentials but does affect the *rate* of firing. **VL 5**

Although increasing the stimulus intensity can increase the rate of firing, there is an upper limit to the number of nerve impulses per second that can be conducted down an axon. This limit occurs because of a property of the axon called the **refractory period**—the interval between the time one nerve impulse occurs and the next one can be generated in the axon. Because the refractory period for most neurons is about 1 ms, the upper limit of a neuron's firing rate is about 500 to 800 impulses per second.

Another important property of action potentials is illustrated by the beginning of each of the records in Figure 2.10. Notice that a few action potentials are occurring even before the pressure stimulus is applied. The action potentials that occur in the absence of stimuli from the environment is called **spontaneous activity**. This spontaneous activity establishes a baseline level of firing for the neuron. The presence of stimulation usually causes an increase in activity above this spontaneous level, but under some conditions it can cause firing to decrease below the spontaneous level.

What do these properties of the action potential mean in terms of their function for perceiving? The action potential's function is to communicate information. Increasing the stimulation of a receptor can cause a change in the rate of nerve firing, usually an increase in firing above the baseline level, but sometimes a decrease below the baseline level. These changes in nerve firing can therefore provide information about the intensity of a stimulus. But if this information remains within a single neuron, it serves no function. In order to be meaningful, this information must be transmitted to other neurons and eventually to the brain or other organs that can react to the information.

The idea that the action potential in one neuron must be transmitted to other neurons poses the following problem: Once an action potential reaches the end of the axon, how is the message that the action potential carries transmitted to other neurons? The problem is that there is a very small space between the neurons, known as a **synapse** (Figure 2.11). The discovery of the synapse raised the question of how the electrical signals generated by one neuron are transmitted across the space separating the neurons. As we will see, the answer lies in a remarkable chemical process that involves molecules called *neurotransmitters*. **VL 6**

Events at the Synapse

Early in the 1900s, it was discovered that when action potentials reach the end of a neuron, they trigger the release of chemicals called **neurotransmitters** that are stored in structures called *synaptic vesicles* in the sending neuron (Figure 2.11b). The neurotransmitter molecules flow into the synapse to small areas on the receiving neuron called **receptor sites** that are sensitive to specific neurotransmitters (Figure 2.11c). These receptor sites exist in a variety of shapes that match the shapes of particular neurotransmitter molecules. When a neurotransmitter makes contact with a receptor site matching its shape, it activates the receptor site and triggers a voltage change in the receiving neuron. A neurotransmitter is like a key that fits a specific lock. It has an effect on the receiving neuron only when its shape matches that of the receptor site.

Thus, when an electrical signal reaches the synapse, it triggers a chemical process that in turn triggers a change in voltage in the receiving neuron. The direction of this voltage change depends on the type of transmitter that is released

and the nature of the cell body of the receiving neuron. **Excitatory transmitters** cause the inside of the neuron to become more positive, a process called **depolarization**. Figure 2.12a shows this effect. In this example, the neuron becomes slightly more positive. Notice, however, that this response is much smaller than the positive action potential. To generate an action potential, enough excitatory neurotransmitter must be released to increase depolarization to the level indicated by the dashed line. Once depolarization reaches that level, an action potential is triggered. Because depolarization can trigger an action potential, it is called an **excitatory response**.

Inhibitory transmitters cause the inside of the neuron to become more negative, a process called **hyperpolarization**. Figure 2.12b shows this effect. Hyperpolarization is considered an **inhibitory response** because it can prevent the neuron from reaching the level of depolarization needed to generate action potentials.

We can summarize this description of the effects of excitatory and inhibitory transmitters as follows: The release of excitatory transmitters increases the chances that a neuron will generate action potentials and is associated with high rates of nerve firing. The release of inhibitory transmitters decreases the chances that a neuron will generate action potentials and is associated with lowering rates of nerve firing. Since a typical neuron receives both excitatory and inhibi-

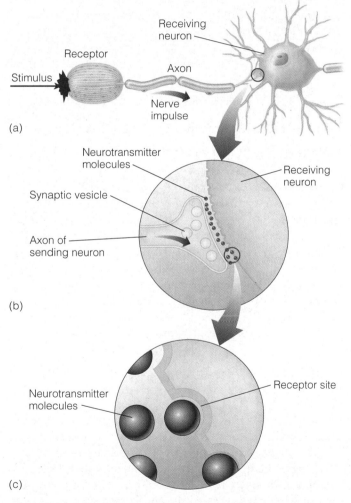

Figure 2.11 ▌ Synaptic transmission from one neuron to another. (a) A signal traveling down the axon of a neuron reaches the synapse at the end of the axon. (b) The nerve impulse causes the release of neurotransmitter molecules from the synaptic vesicles of the sending neuron. (c) The neurotransmitters fit into receptor sites and cause a voltage change in the receiving neuron.

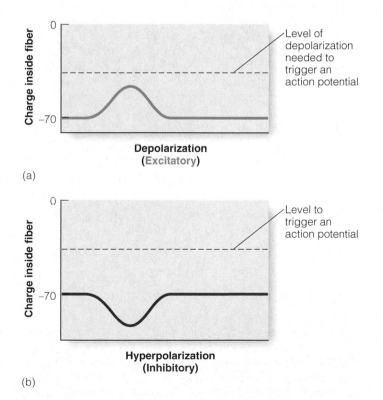

Figure 2.12 ▌ (a) Excitatory transmitters cause depolarization, an increased positive charge inside the neuron. (b) Inhibitory transmitters cause hyperpolarization, an increased negative charge inside the axon. The charge inside the axon must reach the dashed line to trigger an action potential.

tory transmitters, the response of the neuron is determined by the interplay of excitation and inhibition, as illustrated in Figure 2.13. In Figure 2.13a excitation (E) is much stronger than inhibition (I), so the neuron's firing rate is high. However, as inhibition becomes stronger and excitation becomes weaker, the neuron's firing decreases, until in Figure 2.13e inhibition has eliminated the neuron's spontaneous activity and has decreased firing to zero. <u>VL</u> 7

Why does inhibition exist? If one of the functions of a neuron is to transmit its information to other neurons, why would the action potentials in one neuron cause the release of inhibitory transmitter that decreases or eliminates nerve firing in the next neuron? The answer to this question is that the function of neurons is not only to transmit information but also to process it (see the *processing* step of the

perceptual process, page 7), and both excitation and inhibition are necessary for this processing.

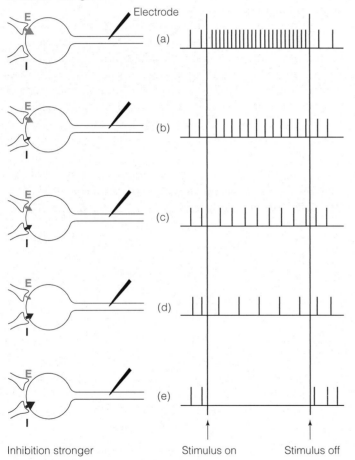

Excitation stronger

Electrode

(a)

(b)

(c)

(d)

(e)

Inhibition stronger

Stimulus on   Stimulus off

Figure 2.13 ▮ Effect of excitatory (E) and inhibitory (I) input on the firing rate of a neuron. The amount of excitatory and inhibitory input to the neuron is indicated by the size of the arrows at the synapse. The responses recorded by the electrode are indicated by the records on the right. The firing that occurs before the stimulus is presented is spontaneous activity. In (a) the neuron receives only excitatory transmitter, which causes the neuron to fire. In (b) to (e) the amount of excitatory transmitter decreases while the amount of inhibitory transmitter increases. As inhibition becomes stronger relative to excitation, firing rate decreases, until eventually the neuron stops firing.

Neural Processing: Excitation, Inhibition, and Interactions Between Neurons

In our description of perceptual processing in Chapter 1 we said that neural processing can transform the signals generated by the receptors (see page 7). The first step in understanding this process is to look at how excitation and inhibition work together in neural circuits. **Neural circuits** are groups of interconnected neurons. A neural circuit can consist of just a few neurons or many hundreds or thousands of neurons. To introduce the basic principles of neural circuits we will describe a few simple circuits. For our example we will use circuits that have receptors that respond to light.

Excitation, Inhibition, and Neural Responding

We will first describe a simple neural circuit and then increase the complexity of this circuit in two stages, noting how this increased complexity affects the circuit's response to the light. First, consider the circuit in Figure 2.14. This circuit shows seven receptors (indicated by blue ellipses), each of which synapses with another neuron (cell bodies, indicated by red circles). All seven of the synapses are excitatory (indicated by Y's). <u>VL</u> 8

We begin by illuminating receptor 4 with a spot of light and recording the response of neuron B. We then change this spot into a bar of light by adding light to illuminate receptors 3, 4, and 5 (3 through 5), then receptors 2 through 6,

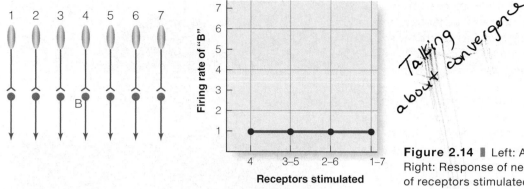

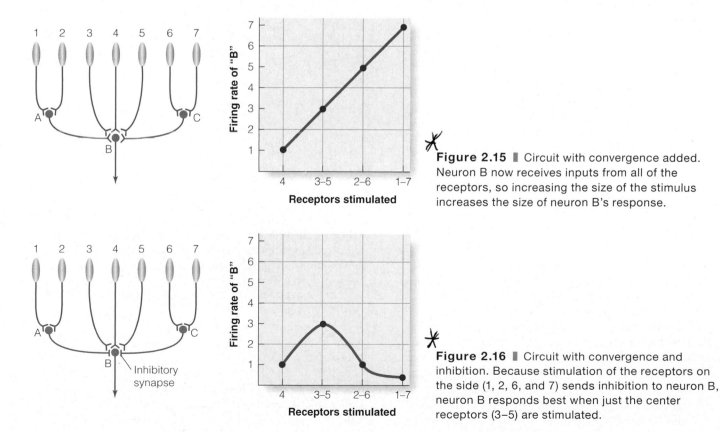

Figure 2.14 ▌ Left: A circuit with no convergence. Right: Response of neuron B as we increase the number of receptors stimulated.

and finally receptors 1 through 7. The response of neuron B, indicated on the graph in Figure 2.14, indicates that this neuron fires when we stimulate receptor 4 but that stimulating the other receptors has no effect on neuron B because it is only connected to receptor 4. Thus, the firing of neuron B simply indicates that its receptor has been stimulated and doesn't provide any further information about the light.

We now increase the complexity of the circuit by adding a property called **convergence**—the synapsing of more than one neuron onto a single neuron. In this circuit, shown in Figure 2.15, receptors 1 and 2 converge onto neuron A; 6 and 7 converge onto C; and 3, 4, and 5, and A and C converge onto B. As in the previous circuit, all of the synapses are excitatory; but, with the addition of convergence, cell B now collects information from all of the receptors. When we monitor the firing rate of neuron B, we find that each time we increase the length of the stimulus, neuron B's firing rate

increases, as shown in the graph in Figure 2.15. This occurs because stimulating more receptors increases the amount of excitatory transmitter released onto neuron B. Thus, in this circuit, neuron B's response provides information about the length of the stimulus.

We now increase the circuit's complexity further by adding two inhibitory synapses (indicated by T's) to create the circuit in Figure 2.16, in which neurons A and C inhibit neuron B. Now consider what happens as we increase the number of receptors stimulated. The spot of light stimulates receptor 4, which, through its excitatory connection, increases the firing rate of neuron B. Extending the illumination to include receptors 3 through 5 adds the output of two more excitatory synapses to B and increases its firing. So far, this circuit is behaving similarly to the circuit in Figure 2.15. However, when we extend the illumination further to also include receptors 2 and 6, something

Figure 2.15 ▌ Circuit with convergence added. Neuron B now receives inputs from all of the receptors, so increasing the size of the stimulus increases the size of neuron B's response.

Figure 2.16 ▌ Circuit with convergence and inhibition. Because stimulation of the receptors on the side (1, 2, 6, and 7) sends inhibition to neuron B, neuron B responds best when just the center receptors (3–5) are stimulated.

different happens: Receptors 2 and 6 stimulate neurons A and C, which, in turn, releases inhibitory transmitter onto neuron B, which decreases its firing rate. Increasing the size of the stimulus again to also illuminate receptors 1 and 7 increases the amount of inhibition and further decreases the response of neuron B.

In this circuit, neuron B fires weakly to small stimuli (a spot illuminating only receptor 4) or longer stimuli (a long bar illuminating receptors 1 through 7) and fires best to a stimulus of medium length (a shorter bar illuminating receptors 3 through 5). The combination of convergence and inhibition has therefore caused neuron B to respond best to a light stimulus of a specific size. The neurons that synapse with neuron B are therefore doing much more than simply transmitting electrical signals; they are acting as part of a neural circuit that enables the firing of neuron B to provide information about the stimulus falling on the receptors. The firing of a neuron like B might, for example, help signal the presence of a small spot of light, or a detail of a larger pattern.

So far our example has been theoretical. However, there is evidence that processing occurs in the nervous system, which involves convergence and inhibition, as shown in Figures 2.15 and 2.16. This evidence has been obtained by measuring a property of neurons called the neuron's *receptive field*.

Introduction to Receptive Fields

The receptive field of a neuron is the area on the receptors that influences the firing rate of the neuron. To describe receptive fields we will use the example of visual receptors, which line the back of the eye within the retina, and the optic nerve, which transmits signals out of the eye (Figure 2.6).

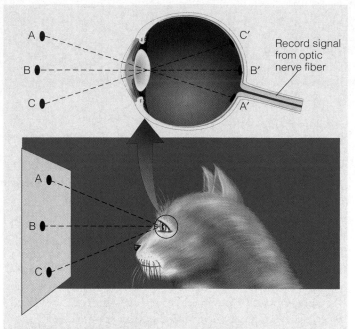

Figure 2.17 ▌ Recording electrical signals from a fiber in the optic nerve of an anesthetized cat. Each point on the screen corresponds to a point on the cat's retina.

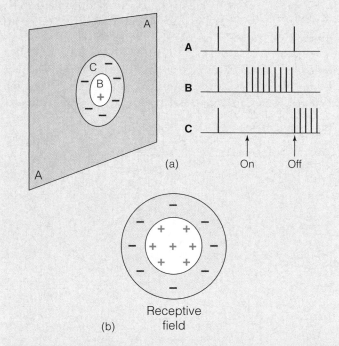

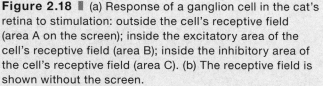

Figure 2.18 ▌ (a) Response of a ganglion cell in the cat's retina to stimulation: outside the cell's receptive field (area A on the screen); inside the excitatory area of the cell's receptive field (area B); inside the inhibitory area of the cell's receptive field (area C). (b) The receptive field is shown without the screen.

METHOD ▏ Determining a Neuron's Receptive Field

We will measure a receptive field of a neuron by stimulating a cat's retina with light and recording from a nerve fiber in the cat's optic nerve. Our goal is to determine the areas of the retina that, when stimulated, affect the firing of this neuron. The cat is anesthetized, and its eyes are focused on a screen like the one shown in Figure 2.17. Stimuli are presented on the screen, and since the cat's eye remains stationary, each of the stimuli on the screen is imaged on points on the cat's retina that correspond to points on the screen. Thus, a stimulus at point A on the screen creates an image on point A′ on the retina, B creates an image on B′, and C on C′.

The first step in determining the receptive field is to flash a small spot of light on the screen. Figure 2.18a shows that when light is flashed anywhere within area A on the screen, nothing happens (the signal shown is spontaneous activity). However, flashing spots of light in area B causes an increase in the neuron's firing (indicated by +), and flashing lights in area C causes a decrease in

---

firing (indicated by –). Since stimulating anywhere in area B causes an increase in the neuron's firing rate, this is called the excitatory area of the neuron's receptive field. Since stimulating in area C causes a decrease in firing rate, this is called the inhibitory area of the neuron's receptive field. Remembering that the definition of the receptive

The receptive field in Figure 2.18 is called a center-surround receptive field because the areas of the receptive field are arranged in a center region that responds one way and a surround region that responds in the opposite way. This particular receptive field is an excitatory-center-inhibitory-surround receptive field. There are also inhibitory-center-excitatory-surround receptive fields in which stimulating the center decreases firing and stimulating the surround increases firing.

The fact that the center and the surround of the receptive field respond in opposite ways causes an effect called center-surround antagonism. This effect is illustrated in Figure 2.19, which shows what happens as we increase the size of a spot of light presented to the neuron's receptive field. A small spot that is presented to the excitatory center of the receptive field causes a small increase in the rate of nerve firing (a), and increasing the light's size so that it covers the entire center of the receptive field increases the cell's response, as shown in (b). (We have used the term *cell* in place of *neuron* here. Because neurons are a type of cell, the word *cell* is often substituted for *neuron* in the research literature. In this book, we will often use these terms interchangeably.) **VL** **12, 13**

Center-surround antagonism comes into play when the spot of light becomes large enough so that it begins to cover the inhibitory area, as in (c) and (d). Stimulation of the inhibitory surround counteracts the center's excitatory response, causing a decrease in the neuron's firing rate. Thus, this neuron responds best to a spot of light that is the size of the excitatory center of the receptive field. Notice that this

sequence of increased firing when the spot size is increased and then decreased firing when the spot size is increased further is similar to what happened when we increased the number of receptors stimulated in the circuit of Figure 2.16. The neural circuit that created the receptive field in Figure 2.18 is a more complex version of our hypothetical circuit in Figure 2.16, but the basic principle of how excitation, inhibition, and convergence can determine how a neuron responds to stimuli is the same.

Center-surround receptive fields also occur in neurons in the skin. Figure 2.20 shows the receptive field of a neuron

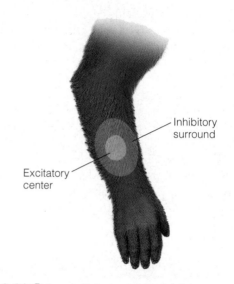

Figure 2.20 ▮ An excitatory-center-inhibitory-surround receptive field of a neuron in the monkey's thalamus. Note that just as in the visual system, the receptive field of the neuron is the area on the receptors (which are located just below the skin in this example) that, when stimulated, influence the responding of the neuron.

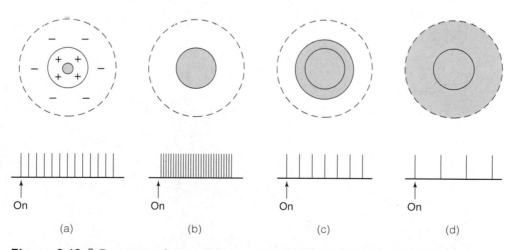

Figure 2.19 ▮ Response of an excitatory-center-inhibitory-surround receptive field as stimulus size is increased. Shading indicates the area stimulated with light. The response to the stimulus is indicated below each receptive field. The largest response occurs when the entire excitatory area is illuminated, as in (b). Increasing stimulus size further causes a decrease in firing due to center-surround antagonism. *(Adapted from Hubel and Wiesel, 1961.)*

receiving signals from receptors in a monkey's skin that increases its firing when the center area of a monkey's arm is touched, and decreases firing when the surrounding area is touched. Just as for the visual neuron, center-surround antagonism also occurs for this neuron. This means that this neuron responds best to a small stimulus presented to the center of the neuron's receptive field on the skin.

The Sensory Code: How the Environment Is Represented by the Firing of Neurons

We have seen that receptive fields enable us to specify a neuron's response. A neuron's receptive field indicates the location on the receptor surface (the retina or skin) that causes a neuron to respond *and* the size or shape of the stimulus that causes the best response.

But while acknowledging the importance of how receptive fields indicate the properties of neurons, let's not lose sight of the fact that we are interested in perception! We are interested not just in how neurons work, but in how the information in nerve impulses represents the things we perceive in the environment. The idea that nerve impulses can *represent* things in the environment is what is behind the following statement, written by a student in my class, Bernita Rabinowitz.

A human perceives a stimulus (a sound, a taste, etc.). This is explained by the electrical impulses sent to the brain. This is so incomprehensible, so amazing. How can one electrical impulse be perceived as the taste of a sour lemon, another impulse as a jumble of brilliant blues and greens and reds, and still another as bitter, cold wind? Can our whole complex range of sensations be explained by just the electrical impulses stimulating the brain? How can all of these varied and very concrete sensations—the ranges of perceptions of heat and cold, colors, sounds, fragrances and tastes—be merely and so abstractly explained by differing electrical impulses?

Bernita's question is an eloquent statement of the *problem of sensory coding:* How does the firing of neurons represent various characteristics of the environment? One answer that has been proposed to this question is called *specificity coding.*

Specificity Coding: Representation by the Firing of Single Neurons

Specificity coding is the representation of particular objects in the environment by the firing of neurons that are tuned to respond *specifically* to that object. To illustrate how this works, let's consider how specificity coding might signal the presence of the people's faces in Figure 2.21. According to

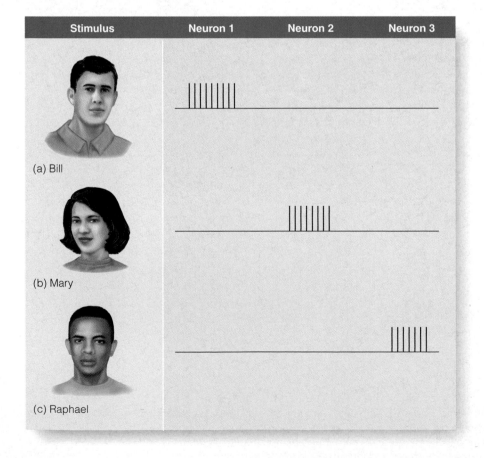

Figure 2.21 ▌ How faces could be coded by specificity coding. Each face causes one specialized neuron to respond.

specificity coding, Bill's face would be represented by the firing of a neuron that responds only to Bill's face (Figure 2.21a). Notice that neuron 1, which we could call a "Bill neuron," does not respond to Mary's face (Figure 2.21b) or Raphael's face (Figure 2.21c). In addition, other faces or types of objects would not affect this neuron. It fires only to Bill's face.

One of the requirements of specificity theory is that there are neurons that are specifically tuned to each object in the environment. This means that there would also have to be a neuron that fires only to Mary's face (Figure 2.21b) and another neuron that fires only to Raphael's face (right column of Figure 2.21c). The idea that there are single neurons that each respond only to a specific stimulus was proposed in the 1960s by Jerzy Konorski (1967) and Jerry Lettvin (see Barlow, 1995; Gross, 2002; Rose, 1996). Lettvin coined the term "grandmother cell" to describe this highly specific type of cell. A grandmother cell, according to Lettvin, is a neuron that responds only to a specific stimulus. This stimulus could be a specific image, such as a picture of your grandmother, or a concept, such as the idea of grandmothers in general (Gross, 2002). The neurons in Figure 2.21 would qualify as grandmother cells.

Is there any evidence for grandmother-type cells? Until recently, there was little evidence for neurons that respond to only one specific stimulus. However, recently, R. Quian Quiroga and coworkers (2005) recorded from neurons that respond to very specific stimuli. They recorded from eight patients with epilepsy who had electrodes implanted in their hippocampus or medial temporal lobe (MTL) to help localize precisely where their seizures originated, in preparation for surgery (Figure 2.22).

Patients saw a number of different views of specific individuals and objects plus pictures of other things, such as faces, buildings, and animals. Not surprisingly, a number of neurons responded to some of these stimuli. What was surprising, however, was that some neurons responded to a number of different views of just one person or building. For example, one neuron responded to all pictures of the actress Jennifer Aniston alone, but did not respond to faces of other famous people, nonfamous people, landmarks, animals, or other objects. Another neuron responded to pictures of actress Halle Berry. This neuron responded not only to photographs of Halle Berry, but to drawings of her, pictures of her dressed as Catwoman from *Batman,* and also to the words "Halle Berry" (Figure 2.22b). A third neuron responded to numerous views of the Sydney Opera House.

What is amazing about these neurons is that they respond to many different views of the stimulus, different modes of depiction, and even words signifying the stimulus. These neurons, therefore, are not responding to visual features of the pictures, but to *concepts*—"Jennifer Aniston," "Halle Berry," "Sydney Opera House"—that the stimuli represent.

It is important to note that these neurons were in the hippocampus and MTL—areas associated with the storage of memories. This function of these structures, plus the fact that the people who were tested had a history of past expe-

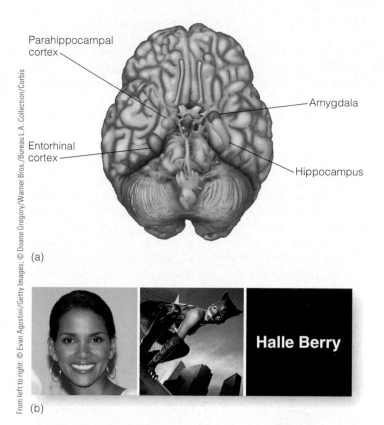

(a)

(b)

Figure 2.22 ▌ (a) Location of the hippocampus and some of the other structures that were studied by Quiroga and coworkers (2005). (b) Some of the stimuli that caused a neuron in the hippocampus to fire.

riences with these stimuli, may mean that familiar, well-remembered objects may be represented by the firing of just a few very specialized neurons.

But are these neurons grandmother cells? According to Quiroga and coworkers (2008), the answer is "no." They point out that it is unlikely that these neurons respond to only a single object or concept, for a number of reasons. First, if there were only one (or a few) neurons that responded to a particular person or concept, it would be extremely difficult to find it among the many hundreds of millions of neurons in the structures they were studying. One way to think about this is in terms of the proverbial difficulty of finding a needle in a haystack. Just as it would be extremely difficult to find a needle in a haystack, it would also be very difficult to find a neuron that responded *only* to Jennifer Aniston among the huge number of neurons in the hippocampus.

Quiroga and coworkers (2005, 2008) also point out that if they had had time to present more pictures, they might have found other stimuli that caused their neurons to fire; they estimate that cells in the areas they were studying probably respond to 50–150 different individuals or objects. The idea that neurons respond to a number of different stimuli is the basis of *distributed coding,* the idea that a particular object is represented not by the firing of a single neuron, but by the firing of *groups of neurons.*

Distributed Coding: Representation by the Firing of Groups of Neurons

Distributed coding is the representation of a particular object by the *pattern* of firing of groups of neurons. According to this idea, Bill's face might be represented by the pattern of firing of neurons 1, 2, and 3 shown in Figure 2.23a. Reading across the top row, we see that neuron 1 has a high firing rate, and neurons 2 and 3 have lower firing rates. Mary's face would be represented by a different pattern (Figure 2.23b), and Raphael's face by another pattern (Figure 2.23c). One of the advantages of distributed coding is that it doesn't require a specialized neuron for every object in the environment, as specificity coding does. Instead, distributed coding allows the representation of a large number of stimuli by the firing of just a few neurons. In our example, the firing of three neurons signals three faces, but these three neurons could help signal other faces as well. For example, these neurons can also signal Roger's face, with another pattern of firing (Figure 2.23d).

Sparse Coding: Distributed Coding With Just a Few Neurons

One question we can ask about distributed coding is, "If an object is represented by the pattern of firing in a group of neurons, how many neurons are there in this group?" Is a particular face indicated by the pattern of firing in thousands of neurons or in just a few? The idea that a particular object is represented by the firing of a relatively small number of neurons is called **sparse coding**.

One way to describe how sparse coding works in the nervous system is that it is somewhere between specificity coding, in which an object is represented by the firing of one type of very specialized neuron, and distributed coding, in which an object is represented by the pattern of firing of a large group of neurons. The neurons described by Quiroga and coworkers (2005, 2008) that probably respond to a small number of objects provide an example of sparse coding, and there is other evidence that the code for representing objects in the visual system, tones in the auditory system, and

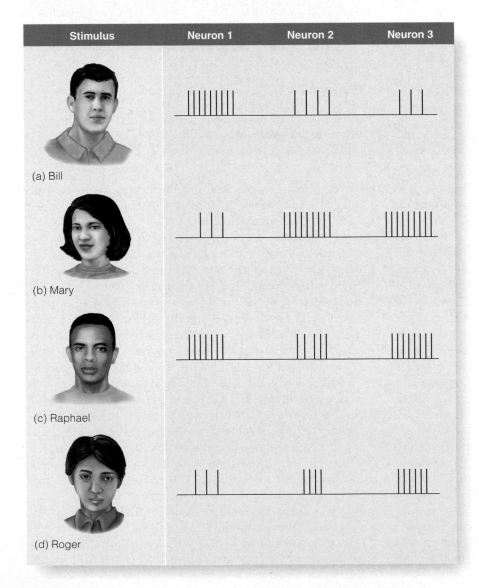

Figure 2.23 ▌ How faces could be coded by distributed coding. Each face causes all the neurons to fire, but the pattern of firing is different for each face. One advantage of this method of coding is that many faces could be represented by the firing of the three neurons.

odors in the olfactory system may, in fact, involve the pattern of activity across a relatively small number of neurons, as sparse coding suggests (Olshausen & Field, 2004).

Something to Consider: The Mind–Body Problem

One of the most famous problems in science is called the **mind–body problem**: How do physical processes such as nerve impulses or sodium and potassium molecules flowing across membranes (the body part of the problem) become transformed into the richness of perceptual experience (the mind part of the problem)?

The mind–body problem is what my student Bernita was asking about when she posed her question about how heat and cold, colors, sounds, fragrances and tastes can be explained by differing electrical impulses. One way to answer Bernita's question would be to explain how different perceptions might be represented by the firing of specialized neurons or by the pattern of firing of groups of neurons. Research that focuses on determining connections between stimuli in the environment and the firing of neurons is often referred to as research on the **neural correlate of consciousness (NCC)**, where consciousness can be roughly defined as our experiences.

Does determining the NCC qualify as a solution to the mind–body problem? Researchers often call finding the NCC the **easy problem of consciousness** because it has been possible to discover many connections between neural firing and experience (Figure 2.24a). But if NCC is the "easy" problem, what is the "hard" problem? We encounter the hard problem when we approach Bernita's question at a deeper level by asking not how physiological responses *correlate* with experience, but how physiological responses *cause* experience. To put it another way, how do physiological responses *become transformed* into experience? We can appreciate why this is called the **hard problem of consciousness** by stating it in molecular terms: How do sodium and potassium ions flowing across a membrane or the nerve impulses that result from this flow become the perception of a person's face or the experience of the color red (Figure 2.24b)?

Although researchers have been working to determine the physiological basis of perception for more than a century, the hard version of the mind–body problem is still unsolved. The first difficulty lies in figuring out how to go about studying the problem. Just looking for correlations may not be enough to determine how physiological processes *cause* experience. Because of the difficulty, most researchers have focused on determining the NCC. That doesn't mean the hard version of the mind–body problem will never be solved. Many researchers believe that doing research on the easy problem (which, after all, isn't really that easy) will eventually lead to a solution to the hard problem (see Baars, 2001; Block, in press; Crick & Koch, 2003).

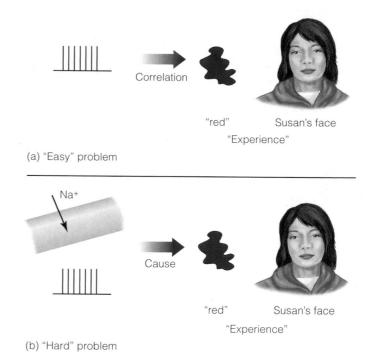

(a) "Easy" problem

(b) "Hard" problem

Figure 2.24 ▌ (a) Solving the "easy" problem of consciousness involves looking for *connections* between physiological responding and experiences such as perceiving "red" or "Susan's face." This is also called the search for the *neural correlate of consciousness*. (b) Solving the "hard" problem of consciousness involves determining how physiological processes such as ions flowing across the nerve membrane *cause* us to have experiences.

For now, there is quite a bit of work to be done on the easy problem. This approach to the physiology of perception is what the rest of this book is about.

TEST YOURSELF 2.2

1. Why is interaction between neurons necessary for neural processing? Be sure to understand how convergence and inhibition work together to achieve processing.
2. What is a neuron's receptive field, and how is it measured?
3. Describe a center-surround receptive field, and explain how center-surround antagonism affects firing as a stimulus spot is made bigger.
4. What is the sensory code? Describe specificity coding and distributed coding. Which type of coding is most likely to operate in sensory systems?
5. What is sparse coding? Can coding be both distributed and sparse?
6. What is the mind–body problem? What is the difference between the "easy" problem of consciousness and the "hard" problem of consciousness?

THINK ABOUT IT

1. Because the long axons of neurons look like electrical wires, and both neurons and electrical wires conduct electricity, it is tempting to equate the two. Compare the functioning of axons and electrical wires in terms of their structure and the nature of the electrical signals they conduct. (p. 29)

IF YOU WANT TO KNOW MORE

1. *Beyond "classic" receptive fields.* We defined a neuron's receptive field as "the area on the receptors that, when stimulated, influences the firing of the neuron."

But recent research has revealed that for some neurons, there are areas outside of the "classic" receptive field that cause no change in the firing of a neuron when stimulated alone, but can nonetheless influence the neuron's response to stimulation of an area inside the "classic" receptive field. (p. 34)

Vinje, B. V., & Gallant, J. L. (2002). Natural stimulation of the non-classical receptive field increases information transmission efficiency in V1. *Journal of Neuroscience, 22,* 2904–2915.

Zipser, K., Lamme, V. A. F., & Schiller, P. H. (1996). Contextual modulation in primary visual cortex. *Journal of Neuroscience, 16,* 7376–7389.

KEY TERMS

Action potential (p. 28)
Axon (p. 26)
Cell body (p. 26)
Center-surround antagonism (p. 35)
Center-surround receptive field (p. 35)
Cerebral cortex (p. 26)
Convergence (p. 33)
Dendrites (p. 26)
Depolarization (p. 31)
Distributed coding (p. 38)
Doctrine of specific nerve energies (p. 25)
Easy problem of consciousness (p. 39)
Excitatory area (p. 34)
Excitatory response (p. 31)
Excitatory transmitter (p. 31)
Excitatory-center-inhibitory-surround receptive field (p. 35)
Frontal lobe (p. 26)

Grandmother cell (p. 37)
Hard problem of consciousness (p. 39)
Hyperpolarization (p. 31)
Inhibitory area (p. 34)
Inhibitory response (p. 31)
Inhibitory transmitter (p. 31)
Inhibitory-center-excitatory-surround receptive field (p. 35)
Ions (p. 29)
Microelectrode (p. 27)
Mind–body problem (p. 39)
Modular organization (p. 26)
Nerve (p. 27)
Nerve fiber (p. 26)
Neural circuits (p. 32)
Neural correlate of consciousness (NCC) (p. 39)
Neuron theory (p. 25)
Neurotransmitter (p. 31)

Occipital lobe (p. 26)
Parietal lobe (p. 26)
Permeability (p. 29)
Pineal gland (p. 24)
Primary receiving areas (p. 26)
Propagated response (p. 30)
Receptive field (p. 34)
Receptor sites (p. 31)
Receptors (p. 26)
Refractory period (p. 30)
Resting potential (p. 28)
Reticular theory (p. 25)
Selective permeability (p. 30)
Sparse coding (p. 38)
Specificity coding (p. 36)
Spontaneous activity (p. 30)
Staining (p. 25)
Synapse (p. 30)
Temporal lobe (p. 26)
Ventricles (p. 24)

MEDIA RESOURCES

The *Sensation and Perception* Book Companion Website

www.cengage.com/psychology/goldstein

See the companion website for flashcards, practice quiz questions, Internet links, updates, critical thinking exercises, discussion forums, games, and more!

CengageNOW

www.cengage.com/cengagenow

Go to this site for the link to CengageNOW, your one-stop shop. Take a pre-test for this chapter, and CengageNOW will generate a personalized study plan based on your test results. The study plan will identify the topics you need to review and direct you to online resources to help you master those topics. You can then take a post-test to help you determine the concepts you have mastered and what you will still need to work on.

Virtual Lab

VL

Your Virtual Lab is designed to help you get the most out of this course. The Virtual Lab icons direct you to specific media demonstrations and experiments designed to help you visualize what you are reading about. The number beside each icon indicates the number of the media element you can access through your CD-ROM, CengageNOW, or WebTutor resource.

The following lab exercises are related to material in this chapter:

1. *Structure of a Neuron* Functions of different parts of a neuron.

2. *Oscilloscopes and Intracellular Recording* How nerve potentials are displayed on an oscilloscope.

3. *Resting Potential* Demonstrates the difference in charge between the inside and outside of the neuron when it is not conducting impulses.

4. *Phases of Action Potential* How sodium and potassium flow across the axon membrane during the action potential.

5. *Nerve Impulse Coding and Stimulus Strength* How neural activity changes as the intensity of a stimulus is varied.

6. *Synaptic Transmission* How electrical signals are transmitted from one neuron to another.

7. *Excitation and Inhibition* How excitation and inhibition interact to determine the firing rate of the postsynaptic neuron.

8. *Simple Neural Circuits* Presenting lights to receptors in three neural circuits illustrates how adding convergence and inhibition influences neural responding.

9. *Receptive Fields of Retinal Ganglion Cells* A classic 1972 film in which vision research pioneer Colin Blakemore describes the neurons in the retina and how center-surround receptive fields of ganglion cells are recorded from the cat's retina.

10. *Mapping Receptive Fields* Mapping the receptive field of a retinal ganglion cell.

11. *Receptive Field Mapping* Mapping the receptive fields of ganglion cells, LGN neurons, and cortical neurons.

12. *Stimulus Size and Receptive Fields* How the size of a stimulus relative to the receptive field affects the size of the neural response.

Chapter Contents

CHAPTER 3

Introduction to Vision

OPPOSITE PAGE This painting, *Arcturus II* by Victor Vasarely, consists of colored squares stacked one on top of the other. The diagonals we perceive radiating from the center of these patterns are not actually in the physical stimulus, but they are perceived because of interactions between excitation and inhibition in the visual system.
Hirshhorn Museum and Sculpture Garden, Smithsonian Institution, Gift of Joseph H. Hirshhorn, 1972. Photographer, Lee Stalsworth.

VL The Virtual Lab icons direct you to specific animations and videos designed to help you visualize what you are reading about. The number beside each icon indicates the number of the clip you can access through your CD-ROM or your student website.

Some Questions We Will Consider:

▌ How do chemicals in the eye called visual pigments affect our perception? (p. 47)

▌ How does the way neurons are "wired up" affect our perception? (p. 58)

▌ What do we mean when we say that perception is indirect? (p. 68)

Now that we know something about the psychophysical approach to perception (Chapter 1) and basic physiological principles (Chapter 2), we are ready to apply these approaches to the study of perception. In this chapter we describe what happens at the very beginning of the visual system, beginning when light enters the eye, and in Chapter 4 we will consider processes that occur in the visual areas of the brain. $\boxed{V_L}$ 1

Focusing Light Onto the Retina

Vision begins when visible light is reflected from objects into the eye.

Light: The Stimulus for Vision

Vision is based on visible light, which is a band of energy within the electromagnetic spectrum. The electromagnetic spectrum is a continuum of electromagnetic energy that is produced by electric charges and is radiated as waves (Figure 3.1). The energy in this spectrum can be described by its wavelength—the distance between the peaks of the electromagnetic waves. The wavelengths in the electromagnetic spectrum range from extremely short–wavelength gamma rays (wavelength = about 10^{-12} meters, or one ten-billionth of a meter) to long-wavelength radio waves (wavelength = about 10^{+4} meters, or 10,000 meters).

Visible light, the energy within the electromagnetic spectrum that humans can perceive, has wavelengths ranging from about 400 to 700 nanometers (nm), where 1 nanometer = 10^{-9} meters. For humans and some other animals, the wavelength of visible light is associated with the different colors of the spectrum. Although we will usually specify light in terms of its wavelength, light can also be described as consisting of small packets of energy called *photons*, with one photon being the smallest possible packet of light energy.

The Eye

The eye is where vision begins. Light reflected from objects in the environment enters the eye through the pupil and is focused by the cornea and lens to form sharp images of the objects on the retina, which contains the receptors for vision (Figure 3.2a). $\boxed{V_L}$ 2

There are two kinds of visual receptors, rods and cones, which contain light-sensitive chemicals called visual pigments that react to light and trigger electrical signals. These signals flow through the network of neurons that make up the retina (Figure 3.2b). The signals then emerge from the back of the eye in the optic nerve, which conducts signals toward the brain. The cornea and lens at the front of the eye and the receptors and neurons in the retina lining the back of the eye shape what we see by creating the transformations that occur at the beginning of the perceptual process.

Light Is Focused by the Eye

Once light is reflected from an object into the eye, it needs to be focused onto the retina. The cornea, the transparent covering of the front of the eye, accounts for about 80 percent of the eye's focusing power, but like the lenses in eyeglasses, it is fixed in place, so can't adjust its focus. The lens, which supplies the remaining 20 percent of the eye's focus-

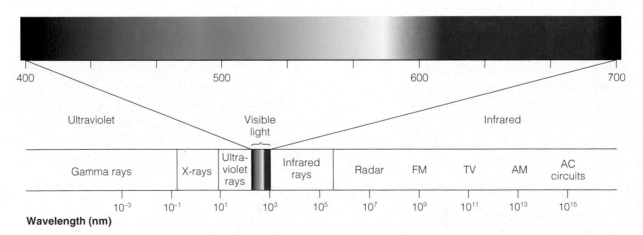

Figure 3.1 ▌ The electromagnetic spectrum, showing the wide range of energy in the environment and the small range within this spectrum, called visible light, that we can see. The wavelength is in nanometers (nm), where 1 nm = 10^{-9} meters.

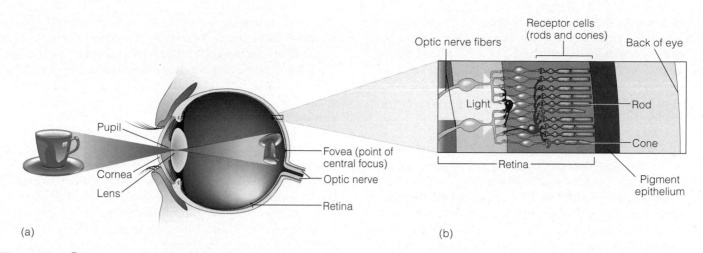

Figure 3.2 ▐ An image of the cup is focused on the retina, which lines the back of the eye. The close-up of the retina on the right shows the receptors and other neurons that make up the retina.

ing power, can change its shape to adjust the eye's focus for stimuli located at different distances.

We can understand how the lens adjusts its focus by first considering what happens when the eye is relaxed and a person views a small object that is far away. If the object is located more than about 20 feet away, the light rays that reach the eye are essentially parallel (Figure 3.3a), and these parallel rays are brought to a focus on the retina at point A. But if the object moves closer to the eye, the light rays reflected from this object enter the eye at more of an angle, which pushes the focus point back to point B (Figure 3.3b). However, the light is stopped by the back of the eye before it reaches point B, so the image on the retina is out of focus. If things remained in this state, the person would see the object as blurred.

A process called **accommodation** keeps this from happening. The ciliary muscles at the front of the eye tighten and increase the curvature of the lens so that it gets thicker (Figure 3.3c). This increased curvature bends the light rays passing through the lens to pull the focus point back to A to create a sharp image on the retina.

DEMONSTRATION

Becoming Aware of What Is in Focus

Accommodation occurs unconsciously, so you are usually unaware that the lens is constantly changing its focusing power so you can see clearly at different distances. This unconscious focusing process works so efficiently that most people assume that everything, near and far, is always in focus. You can demonstrate that this is not so by holding a pencil point up, at arm's length, and looking at an object that is at least 20 feet away. As you look at the faraway object, move the pencil point toward you without actually looking at it (stay focused on the far object). The pencil will probably appear blurred.

Then move the pencil closer, while still looking at the far object, and notice that the point becomes more blurred and

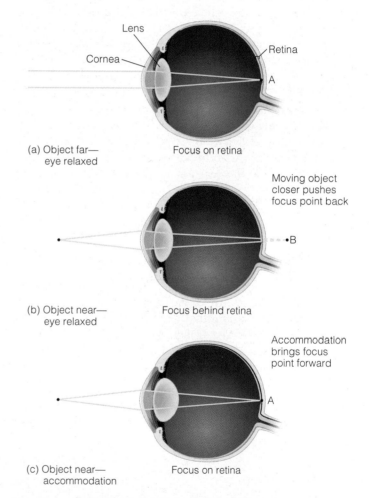

(a) Object far—   Focus on retina
eye relaxed

(b) Object near—   Focus behind retina
eye relaxed

(c) Object near—   Focus on retina
accommodation

Figure 3.3 ▐ Focusing of light rays by the eye. (a) Rays of light coming from a small light source that is more than 20 feet away are approximately parallel. The focus point for parallel light is at A on the retina. (b) Moving an object closer to the relaxed eye pushes the focus point back. Here the focus point is at B, but light is stopped by the back of the eye. (c) Accommodation of the eye (indicated by the fatter lens) increases the focusing power of the lens and brings the focus point for a near object back to A on the retina.

appears double. When the pencil is about 12 inches away, focus on the pencil point. You now see the point sharply, but the faraway object you were focusing on before has become blurred. Now, bring the pencil even closer until you can't see the point sharply no matter how hard you try. Notice the strain in your eyes as you try unsuccessfully to bring the point into focus. ▮

When you changed focus during this demonstration, you were changing your accommodation. Accommodation enables you to bring both near and far objects into focus, although objects at different distances are not in focus at the same time. But accommodation has its limits. When the pencil was too close, you couldn't see it clearly, even though you were straining to accommodate. The distance at which your lens can no longer adjust to bring close objects into focus is called the **near point**.

The distance of the near point increases as a person gets older, a condition called **presbyopia** (for "old eye"). The near point for most 20-year-olds is at about 10 cm, but it increases to 14 cm by age 30, 22 cm at 40, and 100 cm at 60 (Figure 3.4). This loss of ability to accommodate occurs because the lens hardens with age, and the ciliary muscles become weaker. These changes make it more difficult for the lens to change its shape for vision at close range.

Though this gradual decrease in accommodative ability poses little problem for most people before the age of 45, at around that age the ability to accommodate begins to decrease rapidly, and the near point moves beyond a comfortable reading distance. There are two solutions to this problem. One is to hold reading material farther away. If you've ever seen someone holding a book or newspaper at arm's length, the person is employing this solution. The other solution is to wear glasses that add to the eye's focusing power, so it can bring light to a focus on the retina.

Of course, many people who are far younger than 45 need to wear glasses to see clearly. Most of these people have **myopia**, or **nearsightedness**, an inability to see distant objects clearly. The reason for this difficulty, which affects more than 70 million Americans, is illustrated in Figure 3.5a: The myopic eye brings parallel rays of light into focus at a point in front of the retina so that the image reaching the retina is blurred. This problem can be caused by either of two factors: (1) **refractive myopia**, in which the cornea and/or the lens bends the light too much, or (2) **axial myopia**, in which the eyeball is too long. Either way, images of faraway objects are not focused sharply, so objects look blurred.

How can we deal with this problem? One way to create a focused image on the retina is to move the stimulus closer. This pushes the focus point farther back (see Figure 3.3b), and if we move the stimulus close enough, we can push the focus point onto the retina (Figure 3.5b). The distance at which the spot of light becomes focused on the retina is called the **far point**; when the spot of light is at the far point, a myope can see it clearly.

Although a person with myopia can see nearby objects clearly (which is why a myopic person is called nearsighted), objects beyond the far point are still out of focus. The solution to this problem is well known to anyone with myopia: corrective eyeglasses or contact lenses. These corrective lenses bend incoming light so that it is focused as if it were at the far point, as illustrated in Figure 3.5c. Notice that the lens placed in front of the eye causes the light to enter the eye at exactly the same angle as light coming from the far point in Figure 3.5b.

Although glasses or contact lenses are the major route to clear vision for people with myopia, surgical procedures in which lasers are used to change the shape of the cornea have been introduced that enable people to experience good vision without corrective lenses. More than 1 million Americans a year have laser-assisted in situ keratomileusis (LASIK) surgery. LASIK involves sculpting the cornea with a type of laser called an excimer laser, which does not heat tissue. A small flap, less than the thickness of a human hair, is cut into the surface of the cornea. The flap is folded out of the way, the cornea is sculpted by the laser so that it focuses light onto the retina, and the flap is then folded back into place. The result, if the procedure is successful, is good vision without the need for glasses.

A person with **hyperopia**, or **farsightedness**, can see distant objects clearly but has trouble seeing nearby objects.

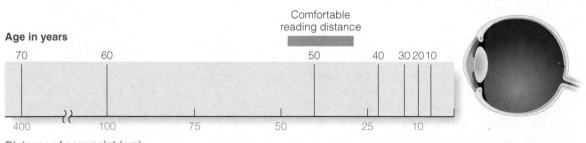

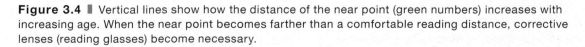

Figure 3.4 ▮ Vertical lines show how the distance of the near point (green numbers) increases with increasing age. When the near point becomes farther than a comfortable reading distance, corrective lenses (reading glasses) become necessary.

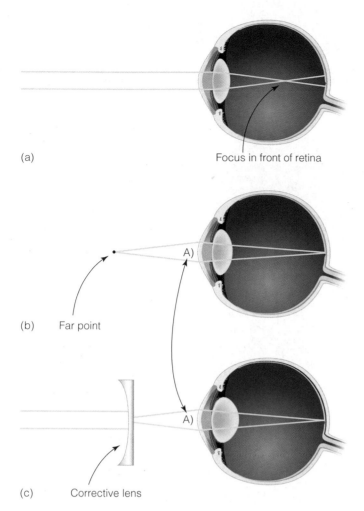

(a)

Focus in front of retina

(b) Far point

(c) Corrective lens

Figure 3.5 ▮ Focusing of light by the myopic (nearsighted) eye. (a) Parallel rays from a distant spot of light are brought to a focus in front of the retina, so distant objects appear blurred. (b) As the spot of light is moved closer to the eye, the focus point is pushed back until, at the far point, the rays are focused on the retina, and vision becomes clear. (c) A corrective lens, which bends light so that it enters the eye at the same angle as light coming from the far point, brings light to a focus on the retina. Angle A is the same in (b) and (c).

In the hyperopic eye, the focus point for parallel rays of light is located behind the retina, usually because the eyeball is too short. By accommodating to bring the focus point back to the retina, people with hyperopia are able to see distant objects clearly.

Nearby objects, however, are more difficult for a person with hyperopia to deal with because a great deal of accommodation is required to return the focus point to the retina. The constant need to accommodate when looking at nearby objects (as in reading or doing close-up work) results in eyestrain and, in older people, headaches. Headaches do not usually occur in young people because they can accommodate easily, but older people, who have more difficulty accommodating because of presbyopia, are more likely to

experience headaches and may therefore require a corrective lens that brings the focus point forward onto the retina.

Focusing the image clearly onto the retina is the initial step in the process of vision. But it is important to realize that although a sharp image on the retina is essential for clear vision, we do not see the image on the retina. Vision occurs not in the retina, but in the brain, and before the brain can create vision, the light on the retina must be transformed into electricity.

Transforming Light Into Electricity

The transformation of light into electricity is the process of transduction we introduced in Chapter 1 (p. 7).

The Visual Receptors and Transduction

Transduction is carried out by *receptors*, neurons specialized for receiving environmental energy and transforming this energy into electricity (see page 7). The receptors for vision are the *rods* and the *cones*. As we will see shortly, the rods and cones have different properties that affect our perception. However, they both function similarly during transduction, so to describe transduction we will focus on the rod receptor shown in Figure 3.6.

The key part of the rod for transduction is the **outer segment**, because it is here that the light acts to create electricity. Rod outer segments contain stacks of discs (Figure 3.6a). Each disc contains thousands of **visual pigment molecules**, one of which is highlighted in Figure 3.6b. Zooming in on an individual molecule, we can see that the molecule is a long strand of protein called **opsin**, which loops back and forth across the disc membrane seven times (Figure 3.6c). Our main concern is one particular place where a molecule called **retinal** is attached. Each visual pigment molecule contains only one of these tiny retinal molecules. The retinal is crucial for transduction, because it is the part of the visual pigment that is sensitive to light.

Transduction is triggered when the light-sensitive retinal absorbs one photon of light. (Remember that a photon is the smallest possible packet of light energy.) Figure 3.7 shows what happens. Before light is absorbed, the retinal is next to the opsin (Figure 3.7a). (Only a small part of the opsin, where the retinal is attached, is shown here). When a photon of light hits the retinal, it changes shape, so it is sticking out from the opsin. This change in shape is called **isomerization**, and it is this step that triggers the transformation of the light entering the eye into electricity in the receptors.

How Does Transduction Occur?

Saying that isomerization of the visual pigment results in transduction is just the first step in explaining how light is

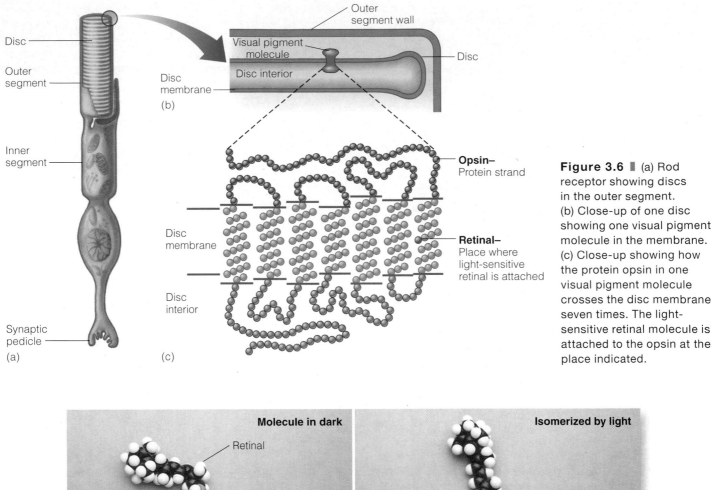

Figure 3.6 ▌ (a) Rod receptor showing discs in the outer segment. (b) Close-up of one disc showing one visual pigment molecule in the membrane. (c) Close-up showing how the protein opsin in one visual pigment molecule crosses the disc membrane seven times. The light-sensitive retinal molecule is attached to the opsin at the place indicated.

Disc

Outer segment

Inner segment

Synaptic pedicle

(a)

Outer segment wall

Visual pigment molecule

Disc interior

Disc membrane

(b)

Disc

Opsin– Protein strand

Retinal– Place where light-sensitive retinal is attached

Disc membrane

Disc interior

(c)

Molecule in dark

Retinal

Opsin

Isomerized by light

Bruce Goldstein

Figure 3.7 ▌ Model of a visual pigment molecule. The horizontal part of the model shows a tiny portion of the huge opsin molecule near where the retinal is attached. The smaller molecule on top of the opsin is the light-sensitive retinal. The model on the left shows the retinal molecule's shape before it absorbs light. The model on the right shows the retinal molecule's shape after it absorbs light. This change in shape is one of the steps that results in the generation of an electrical response in the receptor.

transformed into electricity. Because isomerization of the visual pigment molecule is a chemical process, one way to approach the problem of transduction would be to study the chemistry of visual pigments in a chemistry or physiology laboratory or to study physiological relationships PH1 and PH2 in Figure 3.8, which is our diagram of the perceptual process from Chapter 1 (Figure 1.8). But there is also another way to approach this problem. We can learn something about the physiological process of transduction by doing psychophysical experiments, in which we measure relationship PP to provide information about the underlying physiology.

How can measuring a psychophysical relationship tell us about physiology? We can appreciate how this is possible by considering what happens when a doctor listens to a person's heartbeat during a physical exam. As the doctor listens, he is using his perception of the heartbeat to draw conclusions about the physiological condition of the heart. For example, a clicking sound in the heartbeat can indicate that one or more of the heart's valves may not be operating properly.

Just as a doctor can draw conclusions about the physiology of the heart by listening to the sounds the heart is making, the psychologist Selig Hecht (Hecht, Shlaer, &

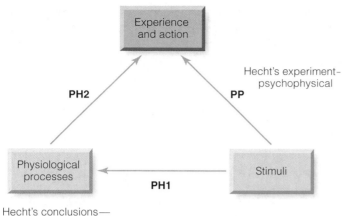

Figure 3.8 ▌ The three main components of the perceptual process (see Figures 1.1 and 1.10). Hecht was able to draw physiological (PH) conclusions based on the measurement of a psychophysical (PP) relationship.

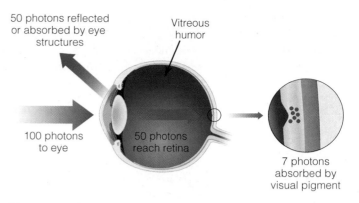

Figure 3.9 ▌ The observer in Hecht et al.'s (1942) experiment could see a spot of light containing 100 photons. Of these, 50 photons reached the retina, and 7 photons were absorbed by visual pigment molecules.

Pirenne, 1942) was able to draw conclusions about the physiology of transduction by determining a person's ability to see dim flashes of light.

Hecht's Psychophysical Experiment The starting point for Hecht's experiment was his knowledge that transduction is triggered by the isomerization of visual pigment molecules and that it takes just one photon of light to isomerize a visual pigment molecule. With these facts in hand, Hecht did a psychophysical experiment that enabled him to determine how many visual pigment molecules need to be isomerized for a person to see. He accomplished this by using the method of constant stimuli (see page 14) to determine a person's absolute threshold for seeing a brief flash of light. What was special about this experiment is that Hecht used a precisely calibrated light source, so he could determine the threshold in terms of the number of photons needed to see.

Hecht found that a person could detect a flash of light that contained 100 photons. To determine how many visual pigment molecules were isomerized by this flash, he considered what happened to those 100 photons before they reached the visual pigment. The first thing that happens is that about half the photons bounce off the cornea or are absorbed by the lens and by the vitreous humor, a jellylike substance that fills the inside of the eye (Figure 3.9). Thus, only 50 of the original 100 photons actually reach the retina at the back of the eye. But of these 50, only about 7 are absorbed by the light-sensitive retinal part of the visual pigment. The rest hit the larger opsin (which is not sensitive to light) or may slip between the visual receptors. This means that a person sees a flash of light when only 7 visual pigment molecules are isomerized (also see Sackett, 1972, who obtained a similar result).

But Hecht wasn't satisfied just to show that a person sees a light when 7 visual pigment molecules are activated.

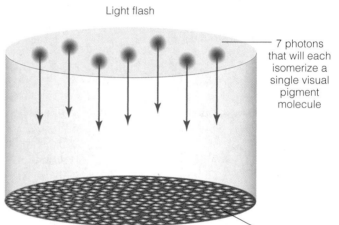

Figure 3.10 ▌ How Hecht reasoned about what happened at threshold, when observers were able to see a flash of light when 7 photons were absorbed by visual pigment molecules. The 7 photons that were absorbed are shown poised above 500 rod receptors. Hecht reasoned that because there were only 7 photons but 500 receptors, it is likely that each photon entered a separate receptor. Thus, only one visual pigment molecule was isomerized per rod. Because the observer perceived the light, each of 7 rods must have been activated.

He also wanted to determine how many visual pigment molecules must be isomerized to activate a single rod receptor. We can understand how he determined this by looking at Figure 3.10, which shows that the light flash Hecht's observers saw covered about 500 receptors. Because Hecht had determined that the observers saw the light when only 7 visual pigment molecules were isomerized, the figure shows the 7 photons that cause this isomerization approaching the 500 receptors.

With this picture of 7 photons approaching 500 receptors in mind, Hecht asked the following question: What is the likelihood that any two of these photons would enter the same receptor? The answer to this question is "very small." It is therefore unlikely that 2 of the 7 visual pigment molecules that each absorbed a photon Hecht's experiment would be in the same receptor. Hecht concluded that only 1 visual pigment molecule per receptor was isomerized when his observer's reported seeing the light; therefore, a rod receptor can be activated by the isomerization of only 1 visual pigment molecule. Hecht's conclusions can be summarized as follows:

1. A person can see a light if 7 rod receptors are activated simultaneously.

2. A rod receptor can be activated by the isomerization of just 1 visual pigment molecule.

The beauty of Hecht's experiment is that he used the psychophysical approach, measuring relationship PP in Figure 3.8, to draw conclusions about the physiological operation of the visual system. You will see, as you read this book, that this technique of discovering physiological mechanisms from psychophysical results has been used to study the physiological mechanisms responsible for perceptions ranging from color and motion in vision to the pitch of sounds for hearing to the ability to perceive textures with the sense of touch.

The Physiology of Transduction Hecht's demonstration that it takes only one photon to activate a rod receptor posed a challenge for physiological researchers, because they needed to explain how isomerization of just one of the millions of visual pigment molecules in a rod can activate the receptor. Hecht carried out his experiment in the 1940s when physiological and chemical tools were not available to solve this problem, so it wasn't until 30 years later that researchers in physiology and chemistry laboratories were able to discover the mechanism that explained Hecht's result.

Physiological and chemical research determined that isomerization of a single visual pigment molecule triggers thousands of chemical reactions, which in turn trigger thousands more (Figure 3.11). A biological chemical that in small amounts facilitates chemical reactions in this way is called an *enzyme*; therefore, the sequence of reactions triggered by the activated visual pigment molecule is called the **enzyme cascade**. Just as lighting one match to a fuse can trigger a fireworks display consisting of thousands of points of light, isomerizing one visual pigment molecule can cause a chemical effect that is large enough to activate the entire rod receptor. For more specific details as to how this is accomplished, see "If You Want to Know More #3" at the end of this chapter.

Pigments and Perception

Vision can occur only if the rod and cone visual pigments transform the light entering the eye into electricity. We will now see, however, that these pigments not only determine whether or not we see, but also shape specific aspects of our perceptions. We will show how the properties of visual pigments help determine how sensitive we are to light, by comparing perception determined by the rod receptors to perception determined by the cone receptors. To accomplish this, we need to consider how the rods and cones are distributed in the retina.

Distribution of the Rods and Cones

From the cross section of the retina in Figure 3.2b you can see that the rods and cones are interspersed in the retina. In the part of the retina shown in this picture, there are more rods than cones. The ratio of rods and cones depends, however, on location in the retina. Figure 3.12, which shows how the rods and cones are distributed in the retina, indicates that

1. There is one small area, the fovea, that contains only cones. When we look directly at an object, its image falls on the fovea.

2. The **peripheral retina**, which includes all of the retina outside of the fovea, contains both rods and cones. It is important to note that although the fovea is the place where there are *only* cones, there are many cones in the peripheral retina. The fovea is so small (about the size of this "o") that it contains only about 1 percent, or 50,000, of the 6 million cones in the retina (Tyler, 1997a, 1997b).

3. There are many more rods than cones in the peripheral retina because most of the retina's receptors are located there and because there are about 120 million rods and 6 million cones.

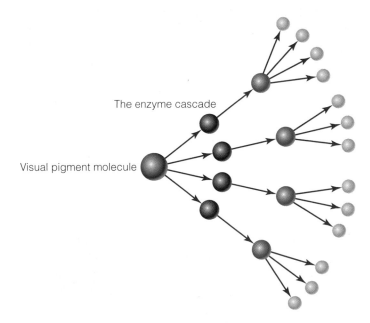

The enzyme cascade

Visual pigment molecule

Figure 3.11 ▌ This sequence symbolizes the enzyme cascade that occurs when a single visual pigment molecule is activated by absorption of a quantum of light. In the actual sequence of events, each visual pigment molecule activates hundreds more molecules, which, in turn, each activate about a thousand more molecules. Thus, isomerization of one visual pigment molecule activates about a million other molecules.

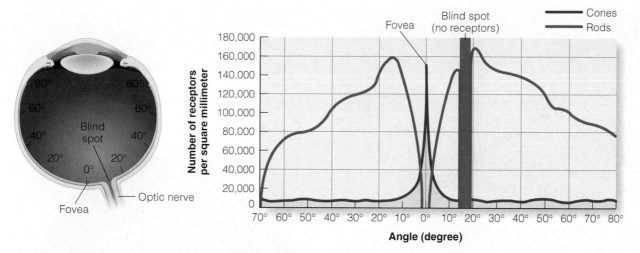

Figure 3.12 ▮ The distribution of rods and cones in the retina. The eye on the left indicates locations in degrees relative to the fovea. These locations are repeated along the bottom of the chart on the right. The vertical brown bar near 20 degrees indicates the place on the retina where there are no receptors because this is where the ganglion cells leave the eye to form the optic nerve. *(Adapted from Lindsay & Norman, 1977.)*

One way to appreciate the fact that the rods and cones are distributed differently in the retina is by considering what happens when functioning receptors are missing from one area of the retina. A condition called **macular degeneration,** which is most common in older people, destroys the cone-rich fovea and a small area that surrounds it. This creates a "blind spot" in central vision, so when a person looks at something he or she loses sight of it (Figure 3.13a).

Another condition, called **retinitis pigmentosa,** is a degeneration of the retina that is passed from one generation to the next (although not always affecting everyone in a family). This condition first attacks the peripheral rod recep-

tors and results in poor vision in the peripheral visual field (Figure 3.13b). Eventually, in severe cases, the foveal cone receptors are also attacked, resulting in complete blindness.

Before leaving the rod–cone distribution shown in Figure 3.12, note that there is one area in the retina, indicated by the vertical brown bar on the graph, where there are no receptors. Figure 3.14 shows a close-up of the place where this occurs, which is where the optic nerve leaves the eye. Because of the absence of receptors, this place is called the **blind spot.** Although you are not normally aware of the blind spot, you can become aware of it by doing the following demonstration.

(a)

(b)

Figure 3.13 ▮ (a) In a condition called macular degeneration, the fovea and surrounding area degenerate, so the person cannot see whatever he or she is looking at. (b) In retinitis pigmentosa, the peripheral retina initially degenerates and causes loss of vision in the periphery. The resulting condition is sometimes called "tunnel vision."

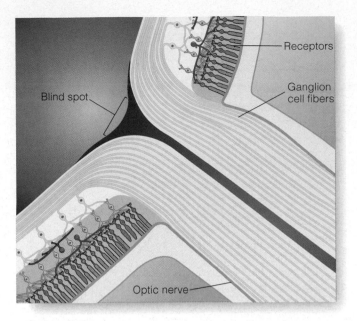

Figure 3.14 ❙ There are no receptors at the place where the optic nerve leaves the eye. This enables the receptor's ganglion cell fibers to flow into the optic nerve. The absence of receptors in this area creates the blind spot.

DEMONSTRATION

Becoming Aware of the Blind Spot

Place the book on your desk. Close your right eye, and position yourself above the book so that the cross in Figure 3.15 is aligned with your left eye. Be sure the page is flat and, while looking at the cross, slowly move closer. As you move closer, be sure not to move your eye from the cross, but at the same time keep noticing the circle off to the side. At some point, around 3 to 9 inches from the book, the circle should disappear. When this happens the image of the circle is falling on your blind spot. ❙

Figure 3.15 ❙

Why aren't we usually aware of the blind spot? One reason is that the blind spot is located off to the side of our visual field, where objects are not in sharp focus. Because of this and because we don't know exactly where to look for it (as opposed to the demonstration, in which we are focusing our attention on the circle), the blind spot is hard to detect.

But the most important reason that we don't see the blind spot is that some mechanism in the brain "fills in" the place where the image disappears (Churchland & Ramachandran, 1996). The next demonstration illustrates an important property of this filling-in process.

DEMONSTRATION

Filling in the Blind Spot

Close your right eye and, with the cross in Figure 3.16 lined up with your left eye, move the "wheel" toward you. When the center of the wheel falls on your blind spot, notice how the spokes of the wheel fill in the hole (Ramachandran, 1992). ❙ V_L 3

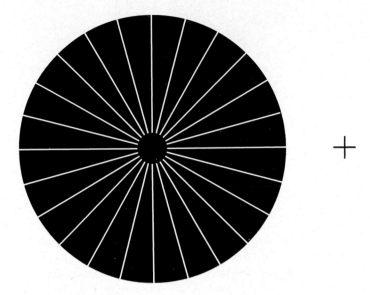

Figure 3.16 ❙ View the pattern as described in the text, and observe what happens when the center of the wheel falls on your blind spot. (From Ramachandran, 1992.)

These demonstrations show that the brain does not fill in the area served by the blind spot with "nothing"; rather, it creates a perception that matches the surrounding pattern—the white page in the first demonstration, and the spokes of the wheel in the second one.

Dark Adaptation of the Rods and Cones

A recent episode of the *Mythbusters* program on the Discovery Channel (2007) was devoted to investigating myths about pirates (Figure 3.17). One of the myths explored was that pirates wore eye patches to preserve night vision in one eye, so when they went from the bright light outside to the darkness belowdecks they could see with their previously patched eye. To determine whether this works, the mythbusters carried out some tasks in a dark room just after both of their eyes had been in the light and did some different tasks with an eye that had just previously been covered with a patch for 30 minutes. It isn't surprising that they completed the tasks much more rapidly when using the eye that had been patched. Anyone who has taken sensation and perception could have told the mythbusters that the eye patch would work because keeping an eye in the dark trig-

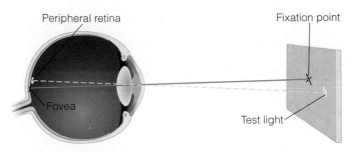

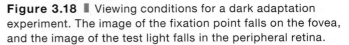

Figure 3.18 ▌ Viewing conditions for a dark adaptation experiment. The image of the fixation point falls on the fovea, and the image of the test light falls in the peripheral retina.

Figure 3.17 ▌ Why did pirates wear eye patches? Did they all have exactly the same eye injury? Were they trying to look scary? Or were they dark adapting the patched eye?

gers a process called **dark adaptation**, which causes the eye to increase its sensitivity in the dark. (Whether pirates actually used patches to dark adapt their eyes to help them see when going belowdecks remains a plausible, but unproven, hypothesis.) We are going to describe dark adaptation and show how it can be used to illustrate a difference between the rods and cones.

You may have noticed that when the lights are turned off it is difficult to see at first, but that eventually you begin seeing things that were previously not visible. However, as you experience your eye's increasing sensitivity in the dark, it is probably not obvious that your eyes increase their sensitivity in two distinct stages: an initial rapid stage and a later, slower stage. These two stages are revealed by measurement of the **dark adaptation curve**—a plot of how visual sensitivity changes in the dark, beginning with when the lights are extinguished.

We will now describe three ways of measuring the dark adaptation curve, to show that the initial rapid stage is due to adaptation of the cone receptors and the second, slower stage is due to adaptation of the rod receptors. We will first describe how to measure a two-stage dark adaptation curve that is caused by both the rods and the cones. We will then measure the dark adaptation of the cones alone and of the rods alone and show how the different adaptation rates of the rods and the cones can be explained by differences in their visual pigments.

In all of our dark adaptation experiments, we ask our observer to adjust the intensity of a small, flashing test light so that he or she can just barely see it. This is similar to the psychophysical *method of adjustment* that we described in Chapter 1 (see page 14). In the first experiment, our observer looks at a small fixation point while paying attention to a flashing test light that is off to the side (Figure 3.18). Because the observer is looking directly at the fixation point, its image falls on the fovea, and the image of the test light falls in the periphery. Thus, the test light stimulates both rods and cones. The dark adaptation curve is measured as follows.

The first step in measuring dark adaptation is to light adapt the observer by exposure to light. While the adapting light is on, the observer indicates his or her sensitivity by adjusting the intensity of a test light so it can just barely be seen. This is called the **light-adapted sensitivity**, because it is measured while the eyes are adapted to the light. Once the light-adapted sensitivity is determined, the adapting light is extinguished, so the observer is in the dark. The course of dark adaptation is usually measured by having the observer turn a knob to adjust the intensity of the test light so it can just barely be seen. Because the observer is becoming more sensitive to the light, he or she must continually decrease the light's intensity to keep it just barely visible. The result, shown as the red curve in Figure 3.19, is a dark adaptation curve.

The dark adaptation curve shows that as dark adaptation proceeds, the observer becomes more sensitive to the light. Note that higher sensitivity is at the bottom of this graph, so as the dark adaptation curve moves downward, the observer's sensitivity is increasing.

The dark adaptation curve indicates that the observer's sensitivity increases in two phases. It increases rapidly for the first 3 to 4 minutes after the light is extinguished and then levels off; it begins increasing again at about 7 to 10 minutes and continues to do so until about 20 or 30 minutes after the light was extinguished (red curve in Figure 3.19). The sensitivity at the end of dark adaptation, labeled **dark-adapted sensitivity**, is about 100,000 times greater than the light-adapted sensitivity measured before dark adaptation began.

Measuring Cone Adaptation To measure dark adaptation of the cones alone, we have to ensure that the image of the test light stimulates only cones. We achieve this by having the observer look directly at the test light so its image will fall on the all-cone fovea, and by making the test light small enough so that its entire image falls within the fovea. The dark adaptation curve determined by this procedure is indicated by the green line in Figure 3.19. This

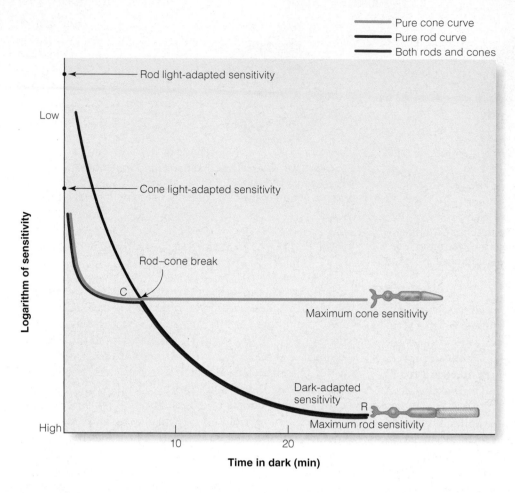

Legend:
- Pure cone curve
- Pure rod curve
- Both rods and cones

Rod light-adapted sensitivity

Low

Logarithm of sensitivity

Cone light-adapted sensitivity

Rod–cone break

C

Maximum cone sensitivity

Dark-adapted sensitivity

R

High

Maximum rod sensitivity

10   20

Time in dark (min)

Figure 3.19 ▌ Three dark adaptation curves. The red line is the two-stage dark adaptation curve, with an initial cone branch and a later rod branch. The green line is the cone adaptation curve. The purple curve is the rod adaptation curve. Note that the downward movement of these curves represents an *increase* in sensitivity. The curves actually begin at the points indicating "light-adapted sensitivity," but there is a slight delay between the time the lights are turned off and when measurement of the curves begin. *(Partial data from "Rhodopsin Measurement and Dark Adaptation in a Subject Deficient in Cone Vision," by W. A. H. Ruston, 1961, Journal of Psychology, 156, 193–205. Copyright © 1961 by Wiley–Blackwell. All rights reserved. Reproduced by permission.)*

curve, which reflects only the activity of the cones, matches the initial phase of our original dark adaptation curve but does not include the second phase. Does this mean that the second part of the curve is due to the rods? We can show that the answer to this question is "yes" by doing another experiment.

Measuring Rod Adaptation We know that the green curve of Figure 3.19 is due only to cone adaptation because our test light was focused on the all-cone fovea. Because the cones are more sensitive to light at the beginning of dark adaptation, they control our vision during the early stages of dark adaptation, so we don't see what is happening to the rods. In order to reveal how the sensitivity of the rods is changing at the very beginning of dark adaptation, we need to measure dark adaptation in a person who has no cones. Such people, who have no cones due to a rare genetic defect, are called **rod monochromats**. Their all-rod retinas provide a way for us to study rod dark adaptation without interference from the cones. (Students sometimes wonder why we can't simply present the test flash to the peripheral retina, which contains mostly rods. The answer is that there are a few cones in the periphery, which influence the beginning of the dark adaptation curve.)

Because the rod monochromat has no cones, the light-adapted sensitivity we measure just before we turn off the lights is determined by the rods. The sensitivity we deter-

mine, which is labeled "rod light-adapted sensitivity" in Figure 3.19, is much lower than the light-adapted sensitivity we measured in the original experiment. Once dark adaptation begins, the rods increase their sensitivity and reach their final dark-adapted level in about 25 minutes (purple curve in Figure 3.19) (Rushton, 1961).

Based on the results of our three dark adaptation experiments, we can summarize the process of dark adaptation in a normal observer as follows: As soon as the light is extinguished, the sensitivity of *both* the cones *and* the rods begins increasing. However, because our vision is controlled by the receptor system that is most sensitive, the cones, which are more sensitive at the beginning of dark adaptation, determine the early part of the dark adaptation curve.

But what is happening to the sensitivity of the rods during this early part of dark adaptation? The rods are increasing their sensitivity in the dark during the cone part of the dark adaptation curve. After about 3 to 5 minutes, the cones are finished adapting, so their curve levels off. Meanwhile, the rods' sensitivity continues to increase, until by about 7 minutes of dark adaptation the rods have caught up to the cones and then become more sensitive than the cones. Once the rods become more sensitive, they begin controlling the person's vision, and the course of rod dark adaptation becomes visible. The place where the rods begin to determine the dark adaptation curve is called the **rod–cone break**.

Why do the rods take about 20 to 30 minutes to reach their maximum sensitivity (point R on the curve), compared to only 3 to 4 minutes for the cones (point C)? The answer to this question involves a process called *visual pigment regeneration,* which occurs more rapidly in the cones than in the rods.

Visual Pigment Regeneration When light hits the light-sensitive retinal part of the visual pigment molecule, it is isomerized and triggers the transduction process (Figure 3.7). It then separates from the opsin part of the molecule. This separation causes the retina to become lighter in color, a process called **visual pigment bleaching.** This bleaching is shown in Figure 3.20, which shows a picture of a frog retina that was taken moments after it was illuminated with light (Figure 3.20a). The red color is the visual pigment. As the light remains on, more and more of the pigment's retinal is isomerized and breaks away from the opsin, so the retina's color changes (Figures 3.20b and c).

Does this mean that all of our pigment eventually becomes bleached if we stay in the light? This would be a bad situation because we need intact visual pigment molecules to see. Luckily, even in the light, as some molecules are absorbing light, isomerizing, and splitting apart, molecules that have been split apart are undergoing a process called **visual pigment regeneration** in which the retinal and opsin become rejoined.

As you look at the page of this book, some of your visual pigment molecules are isomerizing and bleaching, as shown in Figure 3.20, and others are regenerating. This means that under most normal light levels your eye always contains some bleached visual pigment and some intact visual pigment. If you were to turn out the lights, then bleached visual pigment would continue to regenerate, but there would

be no more isomerization, so eventually your retina would contain only intact (unbleached) visual pigment molecules.

As retinal combines with opsin in the dark, the pigment regains its darker red color. William Rushton (1961) devised a procedure to measure the regeneration of visual pigment in humans by measuring this darkening of the visual pigment that occurs during dark adaptation. Rushton's measurements showed that cone pigment takes 6 minutes to regenerate completely, whereas rod pigment takes more than 30 minutes. When he compared the course of pigment regeneration to the rate of psychophysical dark adaptation, he found that the rate of cone dark adaptation matched the rate of cone pigment regeneration and the rate of rod dark adaptation matched the rate of rod pigment regeneration.

Rushton's result demonstrated two important connections between perception and physiology:

1. Our sensitivity to light depends on the concentration of a chemical—the visual pigment.

2. The speed at which our sensitivity is adjusted in the dark depends on a chemical reaction—the regeneration of the visual pigment.

We can appreciate the fact that the increase in sensitivity we experience during dark adaptation is caused by visual pigment regeneration by considering what happens when the visual pigment can't regenerate because of a condition called **detached retina.** A major cause of detached retinas is traumatic injuries of the eye or head, as when a baseball player is hit in the eye by a line drive. When part of the retina becomes detached, it has become separated from a layer that it rests on, called the *pigment epithelium,* which contains enzymes that are necessary for pigment regeneration (see Figure 3.2b). The result is that once visual pigments

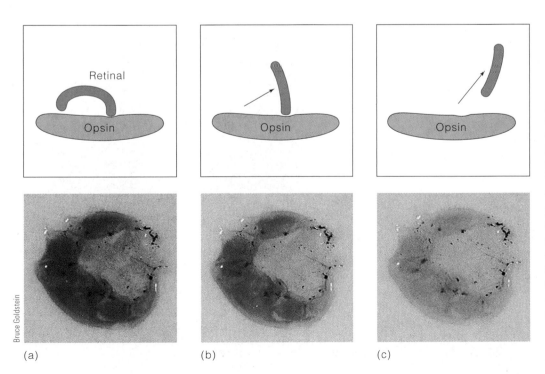

(a)   (b)   (c)

Bruce Goldstein

Figure 3.20 ▌ A frog retina was dissected from the eye in the dark and then exposed to light. (a) This picture was taken just after the light was turned on. The dark red color is caused by the high concentration of visual pigment in the receptors that are still in the unbleached state, as indicated by the closeness of the retinal and opsin in the diagram above the retina. Only a small part of the opsin molecule is shown. (b, c) As the pigment isomerizes, the retinal and opsin break apart, and the retina becomes *bleached,* as indicated by the lighter color.

are bleached, so the retinal and opsin are separated, they can no longer be recombined in the detached part of the retina, and the person becomes blind in the area of the visual field served by this area of the retina.

Spectral Sensitivity of the Rods and Cones

Another way to show that perception is determined by the properties of the visual pigments is to compare rod and cone spectral sensitivity—an observer's sensitivity to light at each wavelength across the visible spectrum.

Measuring Spectral Sensitivity In our dark adaptation experiments, we used a white test light, which contains all wavelengths in the visible spectrum. To determine spectral sensitivity, we use flashes of monochromatic light, light that contain only a single wavelength. We determine the threshold for seeing these monochromatic lights for wavelengths across the visible spectrum (see Figure 3.1). For example, we might first determine the threshold for seeing a 420-nm (nanometer) light, then a 440-nm light, and so on, using one of the psychophysical methods for measuring threshold described in Chapter 1. The result is the curve in Figure 3.21a, which shows that the threshold for seeing light is lowest in the middle of the spectrum; that is, less light is needed to see wavelengths in the middle of the spectrum than to see wavelengths at either the short- or long-wavelength ends of the spectrum.

The ability to see wavelengths across the spectrum is often plotted not in terms of threshold versus wavelength as in Figure 3.21a, but in terms of sensitivity versus wavelength. We can convert threshold to sensitivity with the following equation: sensitivity = 1/threshold. When we do this for the curve in Figure 3.21a, we obtain the curve in Figure 3.21b, which is called the spectral sensitivity curve.

We measure the cone spectral sensitivity curve by having people look directly at the test light, so that it stimulates only the cones in the fovea, and presenting test flashes of wavelengths across the spectrum. We measure the rod spectral sensitivity curve by measuring sensitivity after the eye is dark adapted (so the rods control vision because they are the most sensitive receptors) and presenting test flashes off to the side of the fixation point.

The cone and rod spectral sensitivity curves, shown in Figure 3.22, show that the rods are more sensitive to short-wavelength light than are the cones, with the rods being most sensitive to light of 500 nm and the cones being most sensitive to light of 560 nm. This difference in the sensitivity of the cones and the rods to different wavelengths means that as vision shifts from the cones to the rods during dark adaptation, we become relatively more sensitive to short-wavelength light—that is, light nearer the blue and green end of the spectrum.

You may have noticed an effect of this shift to short-wavelength sensitivity if you have observed how green foliage seems to stand out more near dusk. The shift from cone

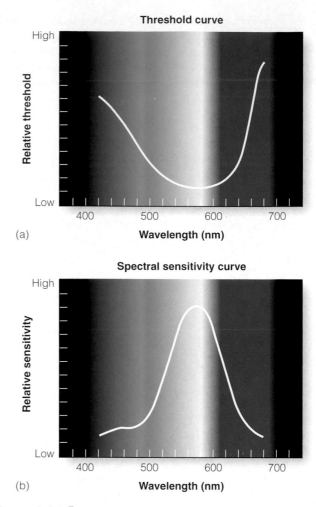

(a)

(b)

Figure 3.21 ▌ (a) The threshold for seeing a light versus wavelength. (b) Relative sensitivity versus wavelength—the *spectral sensitivity curve. (Adapted from Wald, 1964.)*

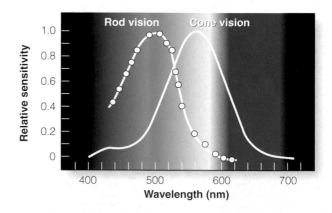

Figure 3.22 ▌ Spectral sensitivity curves for rod vision (left) and cone vision (right). The maximum sensitivities of these two curves have been set equal to 1.0. However, the relative sensitivities of the rods and the cones depend on the conditions of adaptation: The cones are more sensitive in the light, and the rods are more sensitive in the dark. The circles plotted on top of the rod curve are the absorption spectrum of the rod visual pigment. *(From Wald, 1964; Wald & Brown, 1958.)*

vision to rod vision that causes this enhanced perception of short wavelengths during dark adaptation is called the Purkinje (Pur-kin'-jee) shift, after Johann Purkinje, who described this effect in 1825. You can experience this shift in color sensitivity that occurs during dark adaptation by closing one of your eyes for about 5–10 minutes, so it dark adapts, and then switching back and forth between your eyes and noticing how the blue flower in Figure 3.23 is brighter compared to the red flower in your dark-adapted eye.

Rod and Cone Absorption Spectra The difference between the rod and cone spectral sensitivity curves is caused by differences in the absorption spectra of the rod and cone visual pigments. An **absorption spectrum** is a plot of the amount of light absorbed by a substance versus the wavelength of the light. The absorption spectra of the rod and cone pigments are shown in Figure 3.24. The rod pigment absorbs best at 500 nm, the blue-green area of the spectrum.

There are three absorption spectra for the cones because there are three different cone pigments, each contained in its own receptor. The short-wavelength pigment (S) absorbs light best at about 419 nm; the medium-wavelength pigment (M) absorbs light best at about 531 nm; and the long-wavelength pigment (L) absorbs light best at about 558 nm. $\boxed{VL}$ **4**

The absorption of the rod visual pigment closely matches the rod spectral sensitivity curve (Figure 3.22),

and the short-, medium-, and long-wavelength cone pigments that absorb best at 419, 531, and 558 nm, respectively, add together to result in a psychophysical spectral sensitivity curve that peaks at 560 nm. Because there are fewer short-wavelength receptors and therefore much less of the short-wavelength pigment, the spectral sensitivity curve is determined mainly by the medium- and long-wavelength pigments (Bowmaker & Dartnall, 1980; Stiles, 1953).

It is clear from the evidence we have presented that the rod and cone sensitivity in the dark (dark adaptation) and sensitivity to different wavelengths (spectral sensitivity) are determined by the properties of the rod and cone visual pigments. But, of course, perception is not determined just by what is happening in the receptors. Signals travel from the receptors through a network of neurons in the retina, and then leave the eye in the optic nerve. Next we consider how what happens in this network of neurons affects perception.

TEST YOURSELF 3.1

1. Describe the structure of the eye and how moving an object closer to the eye affects how light entering the eye is focused on the retina.
2. How does the eye adjust the focusing of light by accommodation? Describe the following conditions that can cause problems in focusing: presybopia, myopia, hyperopia. Be sure you understand the difference between the near point and the far point, and can describe the various solutions to focusing problems, including corrective lenses and surgery.
3. Describe the structure of a rod receptor. What is the structure of a visual pigment molecule, and where are visual pigments located in the receptor? What must happen in order for the visual pigment to be isomerized?
4. Describe the psychophysical experiment that showed that it takes 7 photons to see and 1 photon to excite a rod, and the physiological mechanism that explains how this is possible.

Figure 3.23 ▍ Flowers for demonstrating the Purkinje shift. See text for explanation.

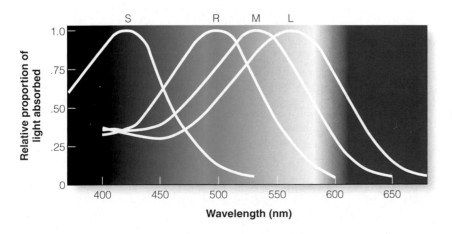

Figure 3.24 ▍ Absorption spectra of the rod pigment (R), and the short- (S), medium- (M), and long-wavelength (L) cone pigments. *(From Dartnall, Bowmaker, & Mollon, 1983.)*

5. Where on the retina does a researcher need to present a stimulus to test dark adaptation of the cones? How can adaptation of the rods be measured without any interference from the cones?

6. Describe how rod and cone sensitivity changes starting when the lights are turned off and how this change in sensitivity continues for 20–30 minutes in the dark.

7. What happens to visual pigment molecules when they (a) absorb light and (b) regenerate? What is the connection between visual pigment regeneration and dark adaptation?

8. What is spectral sensitivity? How is a cone spectral sensitivity curve determined? A rod spectral sensitivity curve?

9. What is an absorption spectrum? How do rod and cone pigment absorption spectra compare, and what is their relationship to rod and cone spectral sensitivity?

Neural Convergence and Perception

We've seen how perception can be shaped by properties of the visual pigments in the receptors. We now move past the receptors to show how perception is also shaped by neural circuits in the retina.

Figure 3.25a is a cross section of the retina that has been stained to reveal the retina's layered structure. Figure 3.25b shows the five types of neurons that make up these layers. Signals generated in the receptors (R) travel to the **bipolar cells** (B) and then to the **ganglion cells** (G). The receptors and bipolar cells do not have long axons, but the ganglion cells have axons like the neurons in Figure 2.4. These axons transmit signals out of the retina in the optic nerve (see Figure 3.14). $\boxed{V_L}$ **5, 6**

In addition to the receptors, bipolars, and ganglion cells, there are two other types of neurons, the **horizontal cells** and **amacrine cells**, which connect neurons across the retina. Signals can travel between receptors through the horizontal cells and between bipolar cells and between ganglion cells through the amacrine cells. We will return to the horizontal and amacrine cells later in the chapter. For now we will focus on the direct pathway from the receptors to the ganglion cells. We focus specifically on the property of **neural convergence** (or just *convergence* for short) that occurs when one neuron receives signals from many other neurons. We introduced convergence in Chapter 2 (page 33). Now let's see how it applies to the neurons in the retina.

In Figure 3.25b the ganglion cell on the right receives signals from three receptors (indicated by light color). A great deal of convergence occurs in the retina because there are 126 million receptors, but only 1 million ganglion cells. Thus, on the average, each ganglion cell receives signals from 126 receptors. We can show how convergence can affect perception by continuing our comparison of the rods and cones. An important difference between rods and cones is that the signals from the rods converge more than do the signals from the cones. We can appreciate this difference by noting that there are 120 million rods in the retina, but only 6 million cones. On the average, about 120 rods pool their signals to one ganglion cell, but only about 6 cones send signals to a single ganglion cell.

This difference between rod and cone convergence becomes even greater when we consider the foveal cones. (Remember that the fovea is the small area that contains only cones.) Many of the foveal cones have "private lines" to ganglion cells, so that each ganglion cell receives signals from only one cone, with no convergence. The greater convergence of the rods compared to the cones translates into two differences in perception: (1) the rods result in better sensitivity than the cones, and (2) the cones result in better detail vision than the rods.

Why Rods Result in Greater Sensitivity Than Cones

One reason rod vision is more sensitive than cone vision is that it takes less light to generate a response from an individual rod receptor than from an individual cone receptor (Barlow & Mollon, 1982; Baylor, 1992). But there is another reason as well: The rods have greater convergence than the cones.

We can understand why the amount of convergence is important for determining sensitivity by expanding our discussion of neurotransmitters from Chapter 2 (see page 31). We saw that the release of excitatory transmitter at the synapse increases the chances that the receiving neuron will fire. This means that if a neuron receives excitatory transmitter from a number of neurons it will be more likely to fire.

Keeping this basic principle in mind, we can see how the difference in rod and cone convergence translates into differences in the maximum sensitivities of the cones and the rods. In the two circuits in Figure 3.26, five rod receptors converge onto one ganglion cell and five cone receptors each send signals onto their own ganglion cells. We have left out the bipolar, horizontal, and amacrine cells in these circuits for simplicity, but our conclusions will not be affected by these omissions.

For the purposes of our discussion, we will assume that we can present small spots of light to individual rods and cones. We will also make the following additional assumptions:

1. One unit of light intensity causes the release of one unit of excitatory transmitter, which causes one unit of excitation in the ganglion cell.

2. The threshold for ganglion cell firing is 10 units of excitation. That is, the ganglion cell must receive 10 units of excitation to fire.

3. The ganglion cell must fire before perception of the light can occur.

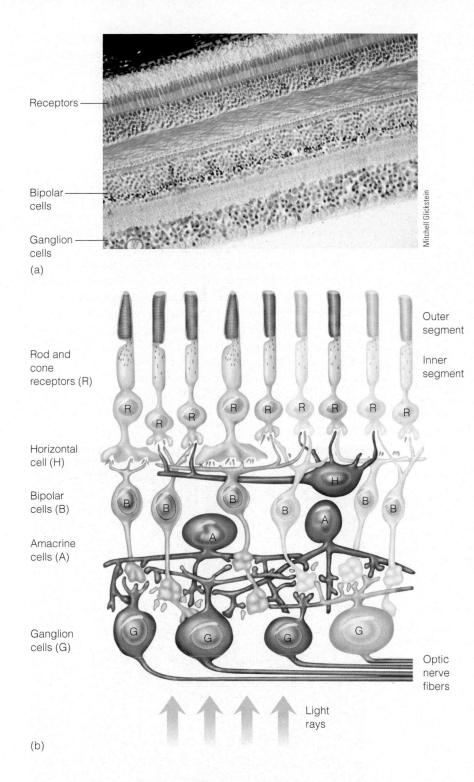

Receptors

Bipolar cells

Ganglion cells

Mitchell Glickstein

(a)

Outer segment

Inner segment

Rod and cone receptors (R)

Horizontal cell (H)

Bipolar cells (B)

Amacrine cells (A)

Ganglion cells (G)

Optic nerve fibers

Light rays

(b)

Figure 3.25 ▌ (a) Cross section of a monkey retina, which has been stained to show the various layers. Light is coming from the bottom. The red circles are cell bodies of the receptors, bipolar cells, and ganglion cells. (b) Cross section of the primate retina showing the five major cell types and their interconnections: receptors (R), bipolar cells (B), ganglion cells (G), horizontal cells (H), and amacrine cells (A). Signals from the three highlighted rods on the right reach the highlighted cell. This is an example of convergence. *(Based on "Organization of the Private Retina," by J. E. Dowling and B. B. Boycott,* Proceedings of the Royal Society of London, B, 1966, 166, pp. 80–111. *Used by Permission of the Royal Society of London and John Dowling.)*

When we present spots of light with an intensity of 1 to each receptor, the rod ganglion cell receives 5 units of excitation, 1 from each of the 5 rod receptors. Each of the cone ganglion cells receives 1 unit of excitation, 1 from each cone receptor. Thus, when intensity = 1, neither the rod nor the cone ganglion cells fire. If, however, we increase the intensity to 2, as shown in the figure, the rod ganglion cell receives 2 units of excitation from each of its 5 receptors, for a total of 10 units of excitation. This total reaches the threshold for the rods' ganglion cell, it fires, and we see the light. Meanwhile, at the same intensity, the cones' ganglion cells are still below threshold, each receiving only 2 units of excitation. For the cones' ganglion cells to fire, we must increase the intensity to 10.

The operation of these circuits demonstrates that one reason for the rods' high sensitivity compared to the cones' is the rods' greater convergence. Many rods summate their responses by feeding into the same ganglion cell, but only one or a few cones send their responses to a single ganglion cell. The fact that rod and cone sensitivity is determined

VL 7

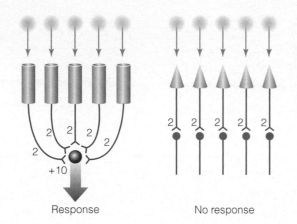

Figure 3.26 ▍ The wiring of the rods (left) and the cones (right). The dot and arrow above each receptor represents a "spot" of light that stimulates the receptor. The numbers represent the number of response units generated by the rods and the cones in response to a spot intensity of 2.

Response　　　　No response

not by individual receptors but by groups of receptors converging onto other neurons means that when we describe "rod vision" and "cone vision" we are actually referring to the way *groups* of rods and cones participate in determining our perceptions.

Why We Use Our Cones to See Details

While rod vision is more sensitive than cone vision because the rods have *more* convergence, the cones have better visual acuity—detail vision—because they have *less* convergence. One way to appreciate the high acuity of the cones is to think about the last time you were looking for one thing that was hidden among many other things. This could be searching for an eraser on the clutter of your desk or locating your friend's face in a crowd. To find what you are looking for, you usually need to move your eyes from one place to another. When you move your eyes to look at different things in this way, what you are doing is scanning with your cone-rich fovea (remember that when you look directly at something, its image falls on the fovea). This is necessary because your visual acuity is highest in the fovea; objects that are imaged on the peripheral retina are not seen as clearly.

DEMONSTRATION

Foveal Versus Peripheral Acuity

D I H C N R L A Z I F W N S M Q P Z K D **X**

You can demonstrate that foveal vision is superior to peripheral vision for seeing details by looking at the X on the right and, without moving your eyes, seeing how many letters you can identify to the left. If you do this without cheating (resist the urge to look to the left!), you will find that although you can read the letters right next to the X,

which are imaged on or near the fovea, you can read only a few of the letters that are off to the side, which are imaged on the peripheral retina. ▍

Visual acuity can be measured in a number of ways, one of which is to determine how far apart two dots have to be before a space can be seen between them. We make this measurement by presenting a pair of closely spaced dots and asking whether the person sees one or two dots. We can also measure acuity by determining how large the elements of a checkerboard or a pattern of alternating black and white bars must be for the pattern to be detected. Perhaps the most familiar way of measuring acuity involves the eye chart in an optometrist's or ophthalmologist's office.

In the demonstration above, we showed that acuity is better in the fovea than in the periphery. Because you were light adapted, the comparison in this demonstration was between the foveal cones, which are tightly packed, and the peripheral cones, which are more widely spaced. Comparing the foveal cones to the rods results in even greater differences in acuity. We can make this comparison by measuring how acuity changes during dark adaptation.

The picture of the bookcase in Figure 3.27 simulates the change in acuity that occurs during dark adaptation.

Bruce Goldstein

Figure 3.27 ▍ Simulation of the change from colorful sharp perception to colorless fuzzy perception that occurs during the shift from cone vision to rod vision during dark adaptation.

The books on the top shelf represent the details we see when viewing the books in the light, when our cones are controlling vision. The books on the middle shelf represent how we might perceive the details midway through the process of dark adaptation, when the rods are beginning to determine our vision, and the books on the bottom shelf represent the poor detail vision of the rods. (Also note that color has disappeared. We will describe why this occurs in Chapter 9.) The poor detail vision of the rods is why it is difficult to read in dim illumination.

We can understand how differences in rod and cone wiring explain the cones' greater acuity by returning to our rod and cone neural circuits. As we stimulate the receptors in the circuits in Figure 3.28 with two spots of light, each with

an intensity of 10, we will ask the following question: Under what conditions can we tell, by monitoring the output of the ganglion cells, that there are two separate spots of light? We begin by presenting the two spots next to each other, as in Figure 3.28a. When we do this, the rod ganglion cell fires, and the two adjacent cone ganglion cells fire. The firing of the single rod ganglion cell provides no hint that two separate spots were presented, and the firing of the two adjacent cone ganglion cells could have been caused by a single large spot. However, when we spread the two spots apart, as in Figure 3.28b, the output of the cones signals two separate spots, because there is a silent ganglion cell between the two that are firing, but the output of the rods' single ganglion cell still provides no information that would enable us to say that there are two spots. Thus, the rods' convergence decreases their ability to resolve details (Teller, 1990). $\boxed{V_L}$ 8

We have seen that the large amount of convergence that occurs in the rods results in high sensitivity, and the low amount of convergence of the cones results in high acuity. This is an example of how what we see depends both on what's out there in the environment and on the physiological workings of our visual system. When we are looking directly at something under high illumination, cone vision, aided by low neural convergence, enables us to see details, as in the top shelf of the bookcase in Figure 3.27. When we are looking at something under low illumination, rod vision, aided by high neural convergence, enables us to make out things that are dimly illuminated, but we see few details, as in the bottom shelf of the bookcase. In the next section we will consider how another physiological mechanism—the decrease in the rate of nerve firing caused by inhibition—can also influence what we perceive.

Lateral Inhibition and Perception

The neural circuit in Figure 3.29 may look familiar because it is the circuit from Chapter 2 that introduced the idea that neural processing is achieved by convergence and inhibition. We saw that the convergence and inhibition in this circuit caused neuron B to respond best to stimulation by a small

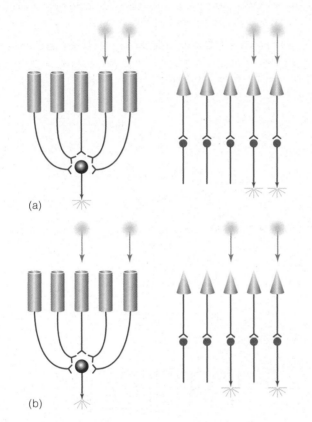

Figure 3.28 ▌ Neural circuits for the rods (left) and the cones (right). The receptors are being stimulated by two spots of light.

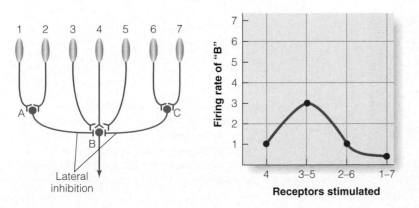

Figure 3.29 ▌ Circuit with convergence and inhibition from Figure 2.16. Lateral inhibition arrives at neuron B from A and from C.

spot of light on receptors 3, 4, and 5. We are now going to look at some perceptual effects of inhibition by focusing on **lateral inhibition**—inhibition that is transmitted across the retina. An example of lateral inhibition is the connections between neurons A and B and C and B in Figure 3.29. Notice that activation of neurons A or C results in the release of inhibitory transmitter onto neuron B.

To understand how lateral inhibition can cause perceptual effects, we will look at an experiment using a primitive animal called the *Limulus,* more familiarly known as the horseshoe crab (Figure 3.30).

What the Horseshoe Crab Teaches Us About Inhibition

In an experiment that is now considered a classic, Keffer Hartline, Henry Wagner, and Floyd Ratliff (1956) used the *Limulus* to demonstrate how lateral inhibition can affect the response of neurons in a circuit. They chose the *Limulus* because the structure of its eye makes it possible to stimulate individual receptors. The *Limulus* eye is made up of hundreds of tiny structures called **ommatidia,** and each ommatidium has a small lens on the eye's surface that is located directly over a single receptor. Each lens and receptor is roughly the diameter of a pencil point (very large compared to human receptors), so it is possible to illuminate and record from a single receptor without illuminating its neighboring receptors.

When Hartline and coworkers recorded from the nerve fiber of receptor A, as shown in Figure 3.31a, they found that illumination of that receptor caused a large response. But when they added illumination to the three nearby receptors at B, the response of receptor A decreased (Figure 3.31b). They also found that increasing the illumination of B decreased A's response even more (Figure 3.31c). Thus, illumination of the neighboring receptors inhibited the firing of receptor A. This decrease in the firing of receptor A is

caused by lateral inhibition that is transmitted across the *Limulus*'s eye by the fibers of the *lateral plexus,* shown in Figure 3.31.

VL 9

Just as the lateral plexus transmits signals laterally in the *Limulus,* the horizontal and amacrine cells (see Figure 3.25) transmit signals across the human retina. We will now see how lateral inhibition may influence how humans perceive light and dark.

Lateral Inhibition and Lightness Perception

We will now describe three perceptual phenomena that have been explained by lateral inhibition. Each of these phenomena involves the perception of lightness—the perception of shades ranging from white to gray to black.

The Hermann Grid: Seeing Spots at Intersections Notice the ghostlike gray images at the intersections of the white "corridors" in the display in Figure 3.32,

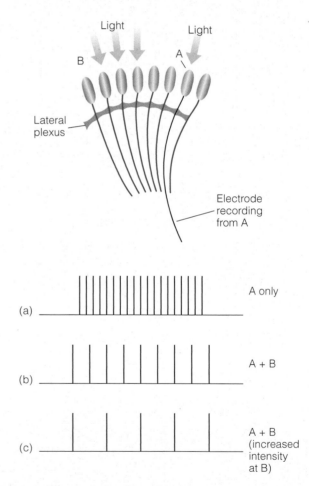

Figure 3.31 ❚ A demonstration of lateral inhibition in the *Limulus.* The records show the response recorded by the electrode in the nerve fiber of receptor A: (a) when only receptor A is stimulated; (b) when receptor A and the receptors at B are stimulated together; (c) when A and B are stimulated, with B at an increased intensity. *(Adapted from Ratliff, 1965.)*

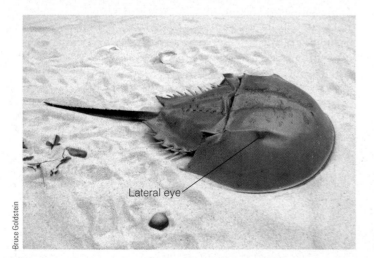

Figure 3.30 ❚ A *Limulus,* or horseshoe crab. Its large eyes are made up of hundreds of ommatidia, each containing a single receptor.

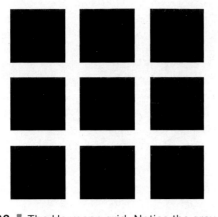

Figure 3.32 ▮ The Hermann grid. Notice the gray "ghost images" at the intersections of the white areas, which decrease or vanish when you look directly at an intersection.

which is called the **Hermann grid**. You can prove that this grayness is not physically present by noticing that it is reduced or vanishes when you look directly at an intersection or, better yet, when you cover two rows of black squares with white paper.

Figure 3.33 shows how the dark spots at the intersections can be explained by lateral inhibition. Figure 3.33a shows four squares of the grid and five receptors that are stimulated by different parts of the white corridors. Receptor A is stimulated by light at the intersection of the two white corridors, where the gray spot is perceived, and the surrounding receptors B, C, D, and E are located in the corridors. It is important to note that all five of these receptors receive the same stimulation, because they are all receiving illumination from the white areas.

Figure 3.33b shows a three-dimensional view of the grid and the receptors. This view shows each receptor sending signals to a bipolar cell. It also shows that each of the bipolar cells sends lateral inhibition, indicated by the arrows, to receptor A's bipolar cell. We are interested in determining the output of the bipolar cell that receives signals from receptor A. We are assuming, for the purposes of this example, that our perception of the lightness at A is determined by the response of its bipolar cell. (It would be more accurate to use ganglion cells because they are the neurons that send signals out of the retina, but to simplify things for the purposes of this example, we will focus on the bipolar cells.)

The size of the bipolar cell response depends on how much stimulation it receives from its receptor *and* on the amount that this response is decreased by the lateral inhibition it receives from its neighboring cells. Let's assume that light falling on A generates a response of 100 units in its bipolar cell. This would be the response of the bipolar cell if no inhibition were present. We determine the amount of inhibition by making the following assumption: The lateral inhibition sent by each receptor's bipolar cell is one-tenth of each receptor's response. Because receptors B, C, D, and E receive the same illumination as receptor A, their response is also 100. Taking one-tenth of this, we determine that each of these receptors is responsible for 10 units of lateral inhibition. To calculate the response of A's bipolar cell, we start with A's initial response of 100 and subtract the inhibition sent from the other four bipolar cells, as follows: $\boxed{V_L}$ **10, 11**
$100 - 10 - 10 - 10 - 10 = 60$ (Figure 3.33c).

Now that we have calculated the response of the bipolar cell stimulated by A, we repeat the same calculation for receptor D, which is in the corridor between two black areas (Figure 3.34). The calculation is the same as the one we just did, but with one important difference. Two of the surrounding receptors, F and H are illuminated dimly because they fall under black squares. If we assume their response is only 20, this means the effect of the inhibition associated with these receptors will be 2, and the output of the bipolar cell receiving signals from D will be $100 - 10 - 2 - 10 - 2 = 76$ (Figure 3.34c).

These outputs make a prediction about perception: Because the response associated with receptor A (at the intersection) is smaller than the response associated with receptor D (in the corridor between the black squares), the

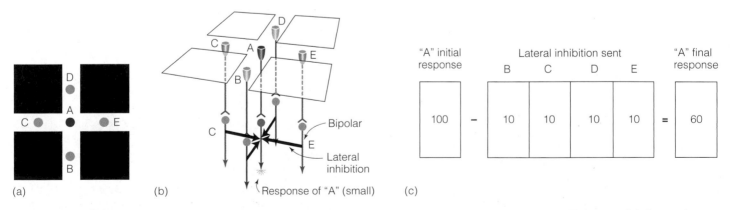

Figure 3.33 ▮ (a) Four squares of the Hermann grid, showing five of the receptors under the pattern. Receptor A is located at the intersection, and B, C, D, and E have a black square on either side. (b) Perspective view of the grid and five receptors, showing how the receptors connect to bipolar cells. Receptor A's bipolar cell receives lateral inhibition from the bipolar cells associated with receptors B, C, D, and E. (c) The calculation of the final response of receptor A's bipolar cell starts with A's initial response (100) and subtracts the inhibition associated with each of the other receptors.

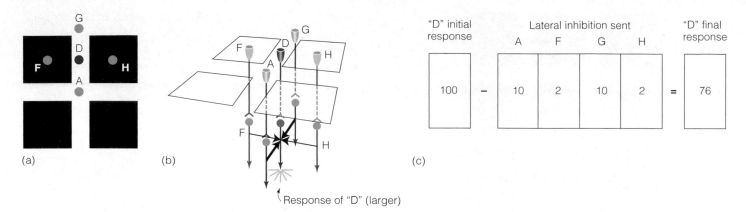

Response of "D" (larger)

Figure 3.34 ▌ (a) Four squares of the Hermann grid, as in Figure 3.33, but now focusing on receptor D, which is flanked by two black squares. Receptor D is surrounded by receptors A, F, G, and H. Notice that receptors F and H are located under the two black squares, so they receive less light than the other receptors. (b) Perspective view showing the inhibition received by the bipolar cells associated with receptor D. Notice that D receives less inhibition than A did in the previous example, because two of the bipolar cells that are sending lateral inhibition (F and H) are associated with receptors that are illuminated more dimly. (c) The calculation of the final response of receptor D indicates that it responds more than A in the previous example.

intersection should appear darker than the corridor. This is exactly what happens—we perceive grey images at the intersections. Lateral inhibition therefore explains the dark images at the intersection. (Although the fact that these images disappear when we look at the intersection directly must be explained by some other mechanism).

Mach Bands: Seeing Borders More Sharply Another perceptual effect that can be explained by lateral inhibition is **Mach bands**, illusory light and dark bands near a light–dark border. Mach bands were named after the Austrian physicist and philosopher Ernst Mach, who also lent his name to the "Mach number" that indicates speed compared to the speed of sound (Mach 2 = twice the speed of sound). You can see Mach bands in Figure 3.35 by looking just to the left of the light–dark border for a faint light band (at B) and just to the right of the border for a faint dark band (at C). (There are also bands at the other two borders in this figure.) ⏹ VL **12, 13, 14**

DEMONSTRATION

Creating Mach Bands in Shadows

Mach bands can be demonstrated using gray stripes, as in Figure 3.35, or by casting a shadow, as shown in Figure 3.36. When you do this, you will see a dark Mach band near the border of the shadow and a light Mach band on the other side of the border. The light Mach band is often harder to see than the dark band. ▌

The reason Mach bands are interesting is that, like the spots in the Hermann grid, they are an illusion—they are not actually present in the pattern of light. If we determine the intensity across the stripes in Figure 3.35a by measuring

the amount of light reflected from this pattern as we move along the line between A and D, we obtain the result shown in Figure 3.35b. The light intensity remains the same across the entire distance between A and B then drops to a lower level and remains the same between C and D.

Because the intensities remain constant across the light stripe on the left and the dark stripe on the right, the small bands we perceive on either side of the border must be illusions. Our perception of these illusory bands is represented graphically in Figure 3.35c, which indicates what we *perceive* across the two stripes. The upward bump at B represents the slight increase in lightness we see to the left of the border, and the downward bump at C represents slight *decrease* in lightness we see to the right of the border.

By using the circuit in Figure 3.37 and doing a calculation like the one we did for the Hermann grid, we can show that Mach bands can be explained by lateral inhibition. Each of the six receptors in this circuit sends signals to bipolar cells, and each bipolar cell sends lateral inhibition to its neighbors on both sides. Receptors A, B, and C fall on the light side of the border and so receive intense illumination; receptors D, E, and F fall on the darker side and receive dim illumination.

Let's assume that receptors A, B, and C generate responses of 100, whereas D, E, and F generate responses of 20, as shown in Figure 3.37. Without inhibition, A, B, and C send the same responses to their bipolar cells, and D, E, and F send the same responses to their bipolar cells. If perception were determined only by these responses, we would see a bright bar on the left with equal intensity across its width and a darker bar on the right with equal intensity across its width. But to determine what we perceive, we need to take lateral inhibition into account. We do this with the following calculation:

1. Start with the response received by each bipolar cell: 100 for A, B, and C, and 20 for D, E, and F.

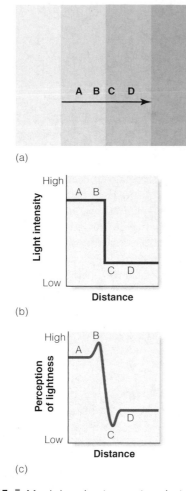

(a)

(b)

(c)

Figure 3.35 ▌ Mach bands at a contour between light and dark. (a) Just to the left of the contour, near B, a faint light band can be perceived, and just to the right at C, a faint dark band can be perceived. (b) The physical intensity distribution of the light, as measured with a light meter. (c) A plot showing the perceptual effect described in (a). The bump in the curve at B indicates the light Mach band, and the dip in the curve at C indicates the dark Mach band. The bumps that represent our perception of the bands are not present in the physical intensity distribution.

Figure 3.36 ▌ Shadow-casting technique for observing Mach bands. Illuminate a light-colored surface with your desk lamp and cast a shadow with a piece of paper.

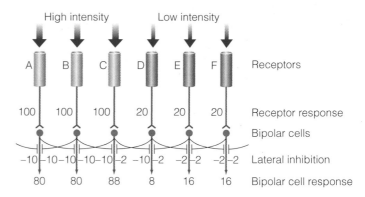

Figure 3.37 ▌ Circuit to explain the Mach band effect based on lateral inhibition. The circuit works like the one for the Hermann grid in Figure 3.34, with each bipolar cell sending inhibition to its neighbors. If we know the initial output of each receptor and the amount of lateral inhibition, we can calculate the final output of the receptors. (See text for a description of the calculation.)

2. Determine the amount of inhibition that each bipolar cell receives from its neighbor on each side. As with the Hermann grid, we will assume that each cell sends inhibition to the cells on either side, equal to one-tenth of that cell's initial output. Thus, cells A, B, and C will send $100 \times 0.1 = 10$ units of inhibition to their neighbors, and cells D, E, and F will send $20 \times 0.1 = 2$ units of inhibition to their neighbors.

3. Determine the final response of each cell by subtracting the amount of inhibition received, from the initial response. Remember that each cell receives inhibition from its neighbor on either side. (We assume here that cell A receives 10 units of inhibition from an unseen cell on its left and that F receives 2 units of inhibition

from an unseen cell on its right.) Here is the calculation for each cell:

Cell A: Final response $100 - 10 - 10 = 80$
Cell B: Final response $100 - 10 - 10 = 80$
Cell C: Final response $100 - 10 - 2 = 88$
Cell D: Final response $20 - 10 - 2 = 8$
Cell E: Final response $20 - 2 - 2 = 16$
Cell F: Final response $20 - 2 - 2 = 16$

The graph of these neural responses, shown in Figure 3.38, looks similar to the graph in Figure 3.35c, where there is an increase in brightness on the light side of the border at C and a decrease in brightness on the dark side at D.

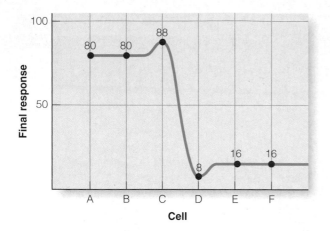

Figure 3.38 ❙ A plot showing the final receptor output calculated for the circuit in Figure 3.37. The bump at B and the dip at C correspond to the light and dark Mach bands, respectively.

The lateral inhibition in our circuit has therefore created a neural pattern that looks like the Mach bands we perceive. A circuit similar to this one, but of much greater complexity, is probably responsible for the Mach bands that we see.

Lateral Inhibition and Simultaneous Contrast Simultaneous contrast occurs when our perception of the brightness or color of one area is affected by the presence of an adjacent or surrounding area. V_L **15, 16, 17**

DEMONSTRATION

Simultaneous Contrast

When you look at the two small squares in Figure 3.39, the one on the left appears much darker than the one on the right. Now, punch two holes 2 inches apart in a card or a piece of paper, position the two holes over the squares so the

background is masked off, and compare your perception of the small squares. ❙

You may have been surprised to see that the small squares look the same when viewed through the holes. Your perception occurs because the two small squares are actually identical shades of gray. The illusion that they are different, which is created by the differences in the areas surrounding each square, is the simultaneous contrast effect.

An explanation for simultaneous contrast that is based on lateral inhibition is diagrammed in Figure 3.40, which shows an array of receptors that are stimulated by a pattern like the one in Figure 3.39. The receptors under the two small squares receive the same illumination. However the receptors under the light area surrounding the square on the left are intensely stimulated, so they send a large amount of inhibition to the receptors under the left square (indicated by the large arrows). The receptors under the dark area surrounding the square on the right are less intensely stimulated, so they send less inhibition to the receptors under the right square (small arrows). Because the cells under the left square receive

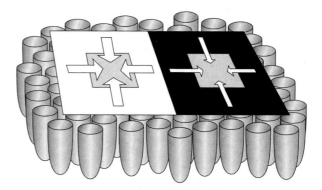

Figure 3.40 ❙ How lateral inhibition has been used to explain the simultaneous contrast effect. The size of the arrows indicate the amount of lateral inhibition. Because the square on the left receives more inhibition, it appears darker.

Figure 3.39 ❙ Simultaneous contrast. The two center squares reflect the same amount of light into your eyes but look different because of simultaneous contrast.

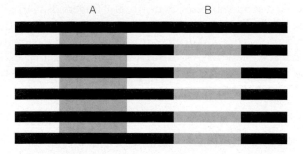

Figure 3.41 ▮ White's illusion. The rectangles at A and B appear different, even though they are printed from the same ink and reflect the same amount of light. *(From White, 1981.)*

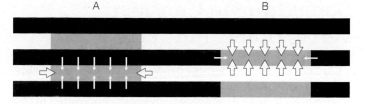

Figure 3.43 ▮ The arrows indicate the amount of lateral inhibition received by parts of rectangles A and B. Because the part of rectangle B is surrounded by more white, it receives more lateral inhibition. This would predict that B should appear darker than A (as in the simultaneous contrast display in Figure 3.39), but the opposite happens. This means that lateral inhibition cannot explain our perception of White's illusion.

more inhibition than the cells under the right square, their response is decreased more, they fire less than the cells under the right square, and the left square therefore looks darker.

The above explanation based on lateral inhibition makes sense and is still accepted by some researchers, although it is difficult for lateral inhibition to explain the following perception: If we start at the edge of the center square on the left and move toward the middle of the square, the lightness appears to be the same, all across the square. However, because lateral inhibition would affect the square more strongly near the edge, we would expect that the square would look lighter near the border and darker in the center. The fact that this does not occur suggests that lateral inhibition cannot be the whole story behind simultaneous contrast. In fact, psychologists have created other displays that result in perceptions that can't be explained by the spread of lateral inhibition.

A Display That Can't Be Explained by Lateral Inhibition

Look at the two rectangles in Figure 3.41, which is called **White's illusion** (White, 1981). Rectangle A, on the left, looks much darker than rectangle B, on the right. However, rectangles A and B reflect the same amount of light. This is hard to believe, because the two rectangles look so different, but you can prove this to yourself by using white paper to

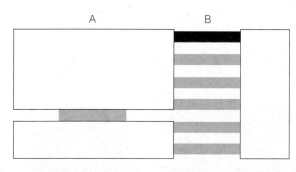

Figure 3.42 ▮ When you mask off part of the White's illusion display, as shown here, you can see that rectangles A and B are actually the same. (Try it!)

mask off part of the display and comparing parts of rectangles A and B, as in Figure 3.42. VL 18

What causes the rectangles on the left and right to look so different, even though they are reflecting the same amount of light? Figure 3.43 shows part of rectangle A, on the left, and part of rectangle B, on the right. The amount of lateral inhibition that affects each area is indicated by the arrows, with larger arrows indicating more inhibition, just as in Figure 3.40. It is clear that area B receives more lateral inhibition, because more of its border is surrounded by white. Because area B receives more lateral inhibition than area A, an explanation based on lateral inhibition would predict that area B should appear darker, like the left square in the simultaneous contrast display in Figure 3.40. But the opposite happens—rectangle B appears lighter! Clearly, White's illusion can't be explained by lateral inhibition.

What's happening here, according to Alan Gilchrist and coworkers (1999), is that our perception of lightness in influenced by a principle called **belongingness**, which states that an area's appearance is influenced by the part of the surroundings to which the area appears to belong. According to this idea, our perception of rectangle A would be affected by the light background, because it appears to be resting on it. Similarly, our perception of rectangle B would be affected by the dark bars, because it appears to be resting on them. According to this idea, the light area makes area A appear darker and the dark bars make area B appear lighter.

Whether or not this idea of belongingness turns out to the be correct explanation, there is no question that some mechanism other than lateral inhibition is involved in our perception of White's illusion and many other displays (see Adelson, 1993; Benary, 1924; Knill & Kersten, 1991; Williams, McCoy, & Purves, 1998). It isn't surprising that there are perceptions we can't explain based just on what is happening in the retina. There is still much more processing to be done before perception occurs, and this processing happens later in the visual system, in the visual receiving area of the cortex and beyond, as we will see VL 19–26 in Chapter 4.

Something to Consider: Perception Is Indirect

The experience of perception connects us with our environment. But perception does more than that. It gives us the feeling that we are in *direct contact* with the environment. As I look up from my writing, I can tell that there is a coffee cup sitting on the table directly in front of me. I know where the cup is, so I can easily reach for it, and as I pick it up I feel the smooth texture of the cup's ceramic finish. As I drink the coffee, I sense heat, and also the coffee's taste and smell. But as much as I feel that all of these experiences are due to my direct contact with the coffee cup and the liquid in it, I know that this feeling of directness is largely an illusion. Perception, as we will see throughout this text, is an indirect process.

We have already demonstrated the indirectness of perception by considering the mechanisms responsible for vision. I see the cup not because of any direct contact with it, but because the light that is reflected from the cup is focused onto my retina and then changed into electricity, which is then processed by mechanisms such as convergence, excitation, and inhibition.

"Well, vision may be indirect," you might say, "but how about the perceptions of heat and texture that occur from picking up the cup? Weren't your fingers in direct contact with the cup?" The answer to this question is, yes, it is true that my fingers were in direct physical contact with the cup, but my perception of the heat of the coffee and the texture of the cup's finish was due to the stimulation of temperature-sensitive and pressure-sensitive receptors in my fingers, which translated the temperature and pressure into electrical impulses, just as the light energy that causes vision is translated into electrical impulses.

Smell and taste are also indirect because these experiences occur when chemicals travel through the air to receptor sites in the nose and tongue. Stimulation of these receptor sites causes electrical signals that are processed by the nervous system to create the experiences of smell and taste. Hearing is the same. Air pressure changes transmitted through the air cause vibrations of receptors inside the ear, and these vibrations generate the electrical signals our auditory system uses to create the experience of sound.

The amazing thing about perception is that despite this indirectness, it seems so real. And it is real, in the sense that our perceptions usually provide us with accurate information about what's out there in the distance or what's up close under our noses or beneath our fingers. But in all of these cases, this information is created through the actions of receptors that change environmental stimulation into electrical signals and by the actions of convergence, excitation, and inhibition that transform electrical signals as they travel through the nervous system.

TEST YOURSELF 3.2

1. What is convergence, and how can the differences in the convergence of rods and cones explain (a) the rods' greater sensitivity in the dark and (b) the cones' better detail vision?
2. Describe the experiment that demonstrated the effect of lateral inhibition in the *Limulus*.
3. How can lateral inhibition explain the "spots" that are perceived at the intersections of the Hermann grid?
4. What are Mach bands, and how can lateral inhibition explain our perception of them? Be sure to understand the calculations used in conjunction with the circuit in Figure 3.37.
5. What is simultaneous contrast? How has it been explained by lateral inhibition? What are some problems with this explanation?
6. How does White's illusion demonstrate that there are some perceptual "lightness" effects that lateral inhibition cannot explain? What does this mean about the location of the mechanism that determines lightness perception?
7. What does it mean to say that all perception is indirect?

THINK ABOUT IT

1. In the demonstration "Becoming Aware of What Is in Focus" on page 45, you saw that we see things clearly only when we are looking directly at them so that their image falls on the cone-rich fovea. But consider the common observation that the things we aren't looking at do not appear "fuzzy," that the entire scene appears "sharp" or "in focus." How can this be, in light of the results of the demonstration? (p. 45)
2. Here's an exercise you can do to get more in touch with the process of dark adaptation: Find a dark place

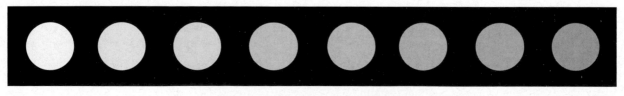

Figure 3.44 ▌ Dark adaptation test circles.

where you will make some observations as you adapt to the dark. A closet is a good place to do this because it is possible to regulate the intensity of light inside the closet by opening or closing the door. The idea is to create an environment in which there is dim light (no light at all, as in a darkroom with the safelight out, is too dark). Take this book into the closet, opened to this page. Close the closet door all the way so it is very dark, and then open the door slowly until you can just barely make out the white circle on the far left in the Figure 3.44, but can't see the others or can see them only as being very dim. As you sit in the dark, become aware that your sensitivity is increasing by noting how the circles to the right in the figure slowly become visible over a period of about 20 minutes. Also note that once a circle becomes visible, it gets easier to see as time passes. If you stare directly at the circles, they may fade, so move your eyes around every so often. Also, the circles will be easier to see if you look slightly above them. (p. 52)

3. Ralph, who is skeptical about the function of lateral inhibition, says, "OK, so lateral inhibition causes us to see Mach bands and the spots at the intersections of the Hermann grid. Even though these perceptual effects are interesting, they don't seem very important to me. If they didn't exist, we would see the world in just about the same way as we do with them." (a) How would you respond to Ralph if you wanted to make an argument for the importance of lateral inhibition? (b) What is the possibility that Ralph could be right? (p. 61)

4. Look for shadows, both inside and outside, and see if you can see Mach bands at the borders of the shadows. Remember that Mach bands are easier to see when the border of a shadow is slightly fuzzy. Mach bands are not actually present in the pattern of light and dark, so you need to be sure that the bands are not really in the light but are created by your nervous system. How can you accomplish this? (p. 64)

IF YOU WANT TO KNOW MORE

1. *Disorders of focusing.* Many people wear glasses to compensate for the fact that their optical system does not focus a sharp image on their retinas. The three most common problems are farsightedness, nearsightedness, and astigmatism. (p. 46)
   Goldstein, E. B. (2002). *Sensation and perception* (6th ed.). Belmont, CA: Wadsworth. (See Chapter 16, "Clinical Aspects of Vision and Hearing.")

2. *LASIK eye surgery.* For more information about LASIK, see the following U.S. Food and Drug Administration website (p. 46):
   http://www.fda.gov/cdrh/lasik

3. *Transduction.* The molecular basis of transduction, in which light is changed into electrical energy, is a process that involves sequences of chemical reactions. (p. 47)
   Burns, M., & Lamb, T. D. (2004). Visual transduction by rod and cone photoreceptors. In L. M. Chalupa & J. S. Werner (Eds.), *The visual neurosciences.* Cambridge, MA: MIT Press.

4. *A disorder of dark adaptation.* There is a rare clinical condition called Oguchi's disease, in which adaptation of the rods is slowed so that it takes 3 or 4 hours for the rods to reach their maximum sensitivity in the dark. What makes this condition particularly interesting is that the rate of rod visual pigment regeneration is normal, so there must be a problem somewhere between the visual pigments and the mechanism that determines sensitivity to light. (p. 54)
   Carr, R. E., & Ripps, H. (1967). Rhodopsin kinetics and rod adaptation in Oguchi's disease. *Investigative Ophthalmology, 6,* 426–436.

KEY TERMS

Absorption spectrum (p. 57)
Accommodation (p. 45)
Amacrine cells (p. 58)
Axial myopia (p. 46)
Belongingness (p. 67)
Bipolar cells (p. 58)
Blind spot (p. 51)
Cone (p. 44)
Cornea (p. 44)
Dark adaptation (p. 53)
Dark adaptation curve (p. 53)
Dark-adapted sensitivity (p. 53)
Detached retina (p. 55)
Electromagnetic spectrum (p. 44)
Enzyme cascade (p. 50)

Eye (p. 44)
Far point (p. 46)
Farsightedness (p. 46)
Fovea (p. 50)
Ganglion cells (p. 58)
Hermann grid (p. 63)
Horizontal cells (p. 58)
Hyperopia (p. 46)
Isomerization (p. 47)
Laser-assisted in situ keratomileusis (LASIK) (p. 46)
Lateral inhibition (p. 62)
Lens (p. 44)
Light-adapted sensitivity (p. 53)
Lightness (p. 62)

Limulus (p. 62)
Mach bands (p. 64)
Macular degeneration (p. 51)
Monochromatic light (p. 56)
Myopia (p. 46)
Near point (p. 46)
Nearsightedness (p. 46)
Neural convergence (p. 58)
Ommatidia (p. 62)
Opsin (p. 47)
Optic nerve (p. 44)
Outer segment (p. 47)
Peripheral retina (p. 50)
Presbyopia (p. 46)
Pupil (p. 44)

MEDIA RESOURCES
The *Sensation and Perception* Book Companion Website

www.cengage.com/psychology/goldstein

See the companion website for flashcards, practice quiz questions, Internet links, updates, critical thinking exercises, discussion forums, games, and more!

CengageNOW

www.cengage.com/cengagenow

Go to this site for the link to CengageNOW, your one-stop shop. Take a pre-test for this chapter, and CengageNOW will generate a personalized study plan based on your test results. The study plan will identify the topics you need to review and direct you to online resources to help you master those topics. You can then take a post-test to help you determine the concepts you have mastered and what you will still need to work on.

Virtual Lab

V_L

Your Virtual Lab is designed to help you get the most out of this course. The Virtual Lab icons direct you to specific media demonstrations and experiments designed to help you visualize what you are reading about. The number beside each icon indicates the number of the media element you can access through your CD-ROM, CengageNOW, or WebTutor resource.

The following lab exercises are related to material in this chapter:

1. *A Day Without Sight* A segment from *Good Morning America* in which Diane Sawyer talks with people who have lost their sight about the experience of being blind.

2. *The Human Eye* A drag-and-drop exercise to test your knowledge of parts of the eye.

3. *Filling In* A demonstration of how the visual system can fill in empty areas to complete a pattern.

4. *Types of Cones* Absorption spectra showing that each cone absorbs light in a different region of the spectrum.

5. *Cross Section of the Retina* A drag-and-drop exercise to test your knowledge of the neurons in the retina.

6. *Visual Path Within the Eyeball* How electrical signals that start in the rods and cones are transmitted through the retina and out the back of the eye in the optic nerve.

7. *Receptor Wiring and Sensitivity* When light is presented to the receptors, rod ganglion cells fire at lower light intensities than cone ganglion cells.

8. *Receptor Wiring and Acuity* When spots of light are presented to rod and cone receptors, detail information is present in the cone ganglion cells but not the rod ganglion cells.

9. *Lateral Inhibition* How lateral inhibition affects the firing of one neuron when adjacent neurons are stimulated.

10. *Lateral Inhibition in the Hermann Grid* How lateral inhibition can explain the firing of neurons that cause the "spots" in the Hermann grid.

11. *Receptive Fields of Retinal Ganglion Cells* A classic 1972 film in which vision research pioneer Colin Blakemore describes the neurons in the retina, and how center-surround receptive fields of ganglion cells are recorded from the cat's retina.

12. *Intensity and Brightness* Mapping the physical intensity across a display that produces Mach bands and comparing this intensity to perceived brightness across the display.

13. *Vasarely Illusion* A demonstration of how lateral inhibition can affect our perception of a picture. (Courtesy of Edward Adelson.)

14. *Pyramid Illusion* Another demonstration of the Vasarely illusion. (Courtesy of Michael Bach.)

15. *Simultaneous Contrast* How varying the intensity of the surround can influence perception of the brightness of squares in the center.

16. *Simultaneous Contrast: Dynamic* How perception of a gray dot changes as it moves across a background that is graded from white to black.

17. *Simultaneous Contrast 2* Animation illustrating simultaneous contrast. (Courtesy of Edward Adelson.)

18. *White's Illusion* An animation of White's illusion. (Courtesy of Edward Adelson.)

19. *Craik-Obrien-Cornsweet Effect* A perceptual effect caused by the fact that the visual system responds best to sharp changes of intensity. (Courtesy of Edward Adelson.)

20. *Criss-Cross Illusion* A contrast illusion based on the idea that the visual system takes illumination into account in determining the perception of lightness. (Courtesy of Edward Adelson.)

21. *Haze Illusion* An illustration of how lightness cues can affect an area's appearance. (Courtesy of Edward Adelson.)

22. *Knill and Kersten's Illusion* An illustration of how our perception of shading caused by curvature can affect lightness perception. (Courtesy of Edward Adelson.)

23. *Koffka Ring* A demonstration showing how the spatial configuration of a pattern can affect lightness perception. (Courtesy of Edward Adelson.)

24. *The Corrugated Plaid* A demonstration showing how the orientation of a surface can affect lightness perception. (Courtesy of Edward Adelson.)

25. *Snake Illusion* Another contrast demonstration that can't be explained by lateral inhibition. (Courtesy of Edward Adelson.)

26. *Hermann Grid, Curving* A version of the Hermann grid that can't be explained by lateral inhibition. (Courtesy of Michael Bach.)

Chapter Contents

CHAPTER 4

The Visual Cortex and Beyond

OPPOSITE PAGE Brain imaging technology has made it possible to visualize both the structure and functioning of different areas of the brain.
© Barry Blackman/Taxi/Getty Images.

VL The Virtual Lab icons direct you to specific animations and videos designed to help you visualize what you are reading about. The number beside each icon indicates the number of the clip you can access through your CD-ROM or your student website.

Some Questions We Will Consider:

▐ How can brain damage affect a person's perception? (p. 88)

▐ Are there separate brain areas that determine our perception of different qualities? (p. 91)

▐ How has the operation of our visual system been shaped by evolution and by our day-to-day experiences? (p. 94)

In Chapters 2 and 3 we described the steps of the perceptual process that occur in the retina. We can summarize this process as follows for vision: Light is reflected from an object into the eye. This light is focused to form an image of that object on the retina. Light, in a pattern that illuminates some receptors intensely and some dimly, is absorbed by the visual pigment molecules that pack the rod and cone outer segments. Chemical reactions in the outer segments transduce the light into electrical signals. As these electrical signals travel through the retina, they interact, excite, and inhibit, eventually reaching the ganglion cells, which because of this processing have center-surround receptive fields on the retina. After being processed by the retina these electrical signals are sent out the back of the eye in fibers of the optic nerve. It is here that we pick up our story.

Following the Signals From Retina to Cortex

In this chapter we follow the signals from the retina to the visual receiving area of the cortex, and then to other areas beyond the visual receiving area. Our quest, in following these signals to the visual cortex and beyond, is to determine the connection between these signals and what we perceive. One way researchers have approached this problem is by determining how neurons at various places in the visual system respond to stimuli presented to the retina. The first step in describing this research is to look at the overall layout of the visual system.

The Visual System

Figure 4.1a, which is an overview of the visual system, pictures the pathway that the neural signals follow once they leave the retina. Most of the signals from the retina travel out of the eye in the optic nerve to the **lateral geniculate nucleus (LGN)** in the thalamus. From here, signals travel to the **primary visual receiving** area in the occipital lobe of the cortex. The visual receiving area is also called the **striate cortex** because of the white stripes (striate = striped) that are created within this area of cortex by nerve fibers that

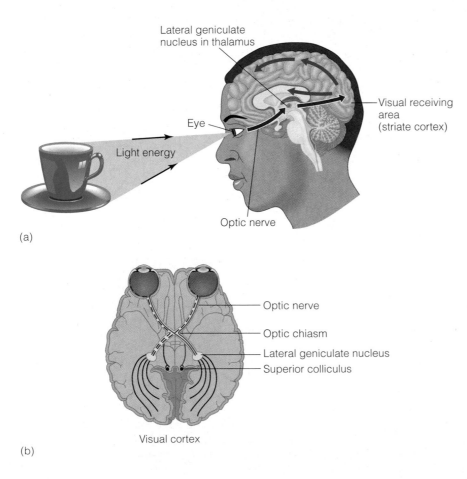

(a)

(b)

Figure 4.1 ▐ (a) Side view of the visual system, showing the three major sites along the primary visual pathway where processing takes place: the eye, the lateral geniculate nucleus, and the visual receiving area of the cortex. (b) Visual system seen from underneath the brain showing how some of the nerve fibers from the retina cross over to the opposite side of the brain at the optic chiasm.

run through it (Glickstein, 1988). From the striate cortex, signals are transmitted along two pathways, one to the temporal lobe and the other to the parietal lobe (blue arrows). Visual signals also reach areas in the frontal lobe of the brain.

VL 1

Figure 4.1b shows the visual system as seen from the underside of the brain. In addition to showing the pathway from eye to LGN to cortex, this view also indicates the location of the **superior colliculus**, an area involved in controlling eye movements and other visual behaviors that receives about 10 percent of the fibers from the optic nerve. This view also shows how signals from half of each retina cross over to the opposite side of the brain.

From the pictures of the visual system in Figure 4.1 it is clear that many areas of the brain are involved in vision. We begin considering these visual areas by following signals in the optic nerve to the first major area where visual signals are received—the lateral geniculate nucleus.

Processing in the Lateral Geniculate Nucleus

What happens to the information that arrives at the lateral geniculate nucleus? One way to answer this question is to record from neurons in the LGN to determine what their receptive fields look like.

Receptive Fields of LGN Neurons Recording from neurons in the LGN shows that LGN neurons have the same center-surround configuration as retinal ganglion cells (see Figure 2.18). Thus, neurons in the LGN, like neurons in the optic nerve, respond best to small spots of light on the retina. If we just consider the receptive fields of LGN neurons, we might be tempted to conclude that nothing is happening there. But further investigation reveals that a major function of the LGN is apparently not to create new receptive field properties, but to regulate neural information as it flows from the retina to the visual cortex (Casagrande & Norton, 1991; Humphrey & Saul, 1994).

Information Flow in the Lateral Geniculate Nucleus The LGN does not simply receive signals from the retina and then transmit them to the cortex. Figure 4.2a shows that it is much more complex than that. Ninety percent of the fibers in the optic nerve arrive at the LGN. (The other 10 percent travel to the superior colliculus.) But these signals are not the only ones that arrive at the LGN. The LGN also receives signals from the cortex, from the brain stem, from other neurons in the thalamus (T), and from other neurons in the LGN (L). Thus, the LGN receives information from many sources, including the cortex, and then sends its output to the cortex.

Figure 4.2b indicates the amount of flow between the retina, LGN, and cortex. Notice that (1) the LGN receives more input back from the cortex than it receives from the retina (Sherman & Koch, 1986; Wilson, Friedlander, & Sherman, 1984); and (2) the smallest signal of all is from

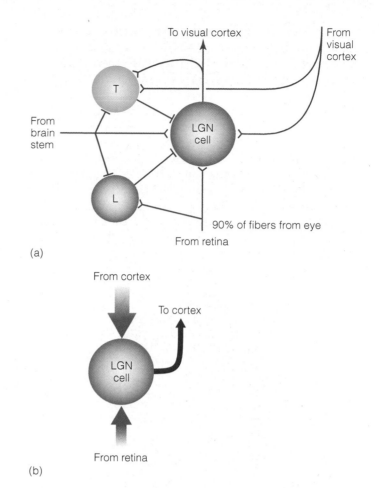

Figure 4.2 ▮ (a) Inputs and outputs of an LGN neuron. The neuron receives signals from the retina and also receives signals from the cortex, from elsewhere in the thalamus (T), from other LGN neurons (L), and from the brain stem. Excitatory synapses are indicated by Y's and inhibitory ones by T's. (b) Information flow into and out of the LGN. The sizes of the arrows indicate the sizes of the signals. *(Part a adapted from Kaplan, Mukherjee, & Shapley, 1993.)*

the LGN to the cortex. For every 10 nerve impulses the LGN receives from the retina, it sends only 4 to the cortex. This decrease in firing that occurs at the LGN is one reason for the suggestion that one of the purposes of the LGN is to regulate neural information as it flows from the retina to the cortex.

But the LGN not only regulates information flowing through it; it also organizes the information. Organizing information is important. It is the basis of finding a document in a filing system or locating a book in the library and, as we will see in this chapter, in the filing of information that is received by structures in the visual system. The LGN is a good place to begin discussing the idea of organization, because although this organization begins in the retina, it becomes more obvious in the LGN. We will see that the signals arriving at the LGN are sorted and organized based on the eye they came from, the receptors that generated them, and the type of environmental information that is represented in them.

Organization by Left and Right Eyes The lateral geniculate nucleus (LGN) is a bilateral structure, which means there is one LGN in the left hemisphere and one in the right hemisphere. Viewing one of these nuclei in cross section reveals six layers (Figure 4.3). Each layer receives signals from only one eye. Layers 2, 3, and 5 (red layers) receive signals from the **ipsilateral eye**, the eye on the same side of the body as the LGN. Layers 1, 4, and 6 (blue layers) receive signals from the **contralateral eye**, the eye on the opposite side of the body from the LGN. Thus, each eye sends half of its neurons to the LGN that is located in the left hemisphere of the brain and half to the LGN that is located in the right hemisphere. Because the signals from each eye are sorted into different layers, the information from the left and right eyes is kept separated in the LGN.

Organization as a Spatial Map To introduce the idea of spatial maps, we first consider Figure 4.4. When the man looks at the cup, points A, B, and C on the cup are imaged on points A, B, and C of the retina, and each place on the retina corresponds to a specific place on the lateral geniculate nucleus (LGN). This correspondence between points on the LGN and points on the retina creates a **retinotopic map** on the LGN—a map in which each point on the LGN corresponds to a point on the retina. We can determine what this map looks like by recording from neurons in the LGN.

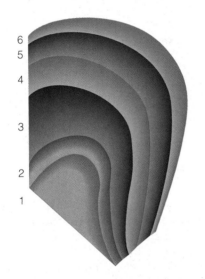

Figure 4.3 ▌ Cross section of the LGN showing layers. Red layers receive signals from the ipsilateral (same side of the body) eye. Blue layers receive signals from the contralateral (opposite side) eye.

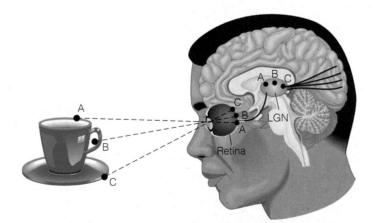

Figure 4.4 ▌ Points A, B, and C on the cup create images at A, B, and C on the retina and cause activation at points A, B, and C on the lateral geniculate nucleus (LGN). The correspondence between points on the LGN and retina indicates that there is a retinotopic map on the LGN.

METHOD ▌ Determining Retinotopic Maps by Recording From Neurons

The retinotopic map on the LGN has been determined by recording from neurons in the LGN with an electrode that penetrates the LGN obliquely (at a small angle to the surface), as shown in Figure 4.5. In this example, we are recording from the neurons at A, B, and C in layer 6 of the LGN.

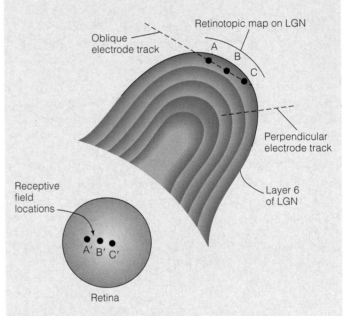

Figure 4.5 ▌ Retinotopic mapping of neurons in the LGN. The neurons at A, B, and C in layer 6 of the LGN have receptive fields located at positions A′, B′, and C′ on the retina. This mapping can be determined by recording from neurons encountered along an oblique electrode track. Also, neurons along a perpendicular electrode track all have their receptive fields at about the same place on the retina.

Recording from the neuron at A, we determine the location of the neuron's receptive field on the retina by stimulating different places on the retina with spots of light until the neuron responds. The location of the neuron's receptive field is indicated by A′ on the retina. When we repeat this procedure with an electrode at B and then at C, we find that B's receptive field is at B′ on the retina,

The correspondence between locations on the retina and locations on the LGN means that neurons entering the LGN are arranged so that fibers carrying signals from the same area of the retina end up in the same area of the LGN, each location on the LGN corresponds to a location on the retina, and neighboring locations on the LGN correspond to neighboring locations on the retina. Thus, the receptive fields of neurons that are near each other in the LGN, such as neurons A, B, and C, in layer 6 (Figure 4.5), are adjacent to each other at A', B', and C' on the retina.

Retinotopic maps occur not only in layer 6, but in each of the other layers as well, and the maps of each of the layers line up with one another. Thus, if we lower an electrode perpendicularly, as shown in Figure 4.5, all of the neurons we encounter along the electrode track will have receptive fields at the same location on the retina. This is an amazing feat of organization: One million ganglion cell fibers travel to each LGN, and on arriving there, each fiber goes to the correct LGN layer (remember that fibers from each eye go to different layers) and finds its way to a location next to other fibers that left from the same place on the retina. Meanwhile, all of the other fibers are doing the same thing in the other layers! The result is aligned, overlapping retinotopic maps in each of the LGN's six layers.

Receptive Fields of Neurons in the Striate Cortex

We are now ready to move from the LGN to the visual cortex. As we saw in Figure 4.1, a large area of the cortex is involved in vision. In fact, more than 80 percent of the cortex responds to visual stimuli (Felleman & Van Essen, 1991). The idea that most of the cortex responds when the retina is stimulated is the result of research that began in the late 1950s. In the early 1950s, we knew little about visual cortical function; a 63-page chapter on the physiology of vision that appeared in the 1951 *Handbook of Experimental Psychology* devoted less than a page to the visual cortex (Bartley, 1951). But by the end of that decade, David Hubel and Thorsten Wiesel (1959) had published a series of papers in which they described both receptive field properties and organization of neurons in the striate cortex. For this research and other research on the visual system, Hubel and Wiesel received the Nobel prize in physiology and medicine in 1982. We will see later in this chapter how other researchers pushed our knowledge of visual physiology to areas beyond the striate cortex, but first let's consider Hubel and Wiesel's research.

Using the procedure described in Chapter 2 (page 34) in which receptive fields are determined by flashing spots of light on the retina, Hubel and Wiesel found cells in the striate cortex with receptive fields that, like center-surround receptive fields of neurons in the retina and LGN, have excitatory and inhibitory areas. However, these areas are arranged side by side rather than in the center-surround configuration (Figure 4.6a). Cells with these side-by-side receptive fields are called **simple cortical cells**. VL 2

We can tell from the layout of the excitatory and inhibitory areas of the simple cell shown in Figure 4.6a that a cell with this receptive field would respond best to vertical bars. As shown in Figure 4.6b, a vertical bar that illuminates only the excitatory area causes high firing, but as the bar is tilted so the inhibitory area is illuminated, firing decreases.

The relationship between orientation and firing is indicated by a neuron's orientation tuning curve, which is determined by measuring the responses of a simple cortical cell to bars with different orientations. The tuning curve in Figure 4.6c shows that the cell responds with 25 nerve

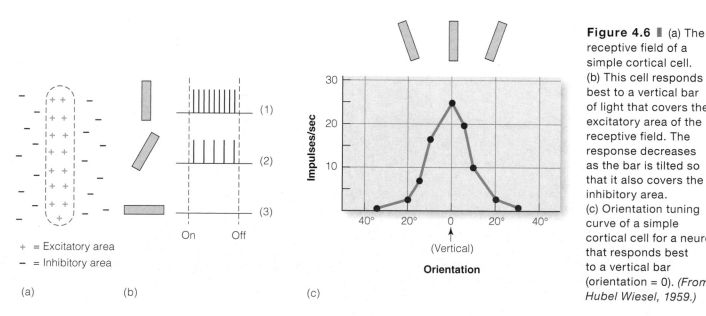

+ = Excitatory area
− = Inhibitory area

On Off

(a)   (b)   (c)

Figure 4.6 ▍ (a) The receptive field of a simple cortical cell. (b) This cell responds best to a vertical bar of light that covers the excitatory area of the receptive field. The response decreases as the bar is tilted so that it also covers the inhibitory area. (c) Orientation tuning curve of a simple cortical cell for a neuron that responds best to a vertical bar (orientation = 0). *(From Hubel Wiesel, 1959.)*

impulses per second to a vertically oriented bar and that the cell's response decreases as the bar is tilted away from the vertical, and begins stimulating inhibitory areas of the neuron's receptive field. Notice that a bar tilted 20 degrees from the vertical elicits only a small response. This particular simple cell responds best to a bar with a vertical orientation, but there are other simple cells that respond to other orientations, so there are neurons that respond to all of the orientations that exist in the environment. VL 3

Although Hubel and Wiesel were able to use small spots of light to map the receptive fields of simple cortical cells like the one in Figure 4.6, they found that many of the cells they encountered in the cortex refused to respond to small spots of light. In his Nobel lecture, Hubel describes how he and Wiesel were becoming increasingly frustrated in their attempts to get these cortical neurons to fire, when something startling happened: As they inserted a glass slide containing a spot stimulus into their slide projector, a cortical neuron "went off like a machine gun" (Hubel, 1982). The neuron, as it turned out, was responding not to the spot at the center of the slide that Hubel and Wiesel had planned to use as a stimulus, but to the image of the slide's edge moving downward on the screen as the slide dropped into the projector (Figure 4.7). Upon realizing this, Hubel and Wiesel changed their stimuli from small spots to moving lines and were then able to find cells that responded to oriented moving bars. As with simple cells, a particular neuron had a preferred orientation. VL 4

Hubel and Wiesel discovered that many cortical neurons respond best to moving barlike stimuli with specific orientations. **Complex cells**, like simple cells, respond best to bars of a particular orientation. However, unlike simple cells, which respond to small spots of light or to stationary stimuli, most complex cells respond only when a correctly oriented bar of light moves across the entire receptive field. Further, many complex cells respond best to a particular direction of movement (Figure 4.8a). Because these neurons

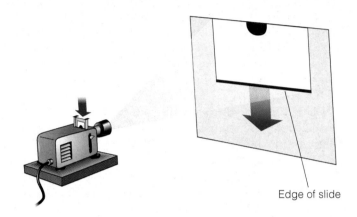

Edge of slide

Figure 4.7 ▌ When Hubel and Wiesel dropped a slide into their slide projector, the image of the edge of the slide moving down unexpectedly triggered activity in a cortical neuron.

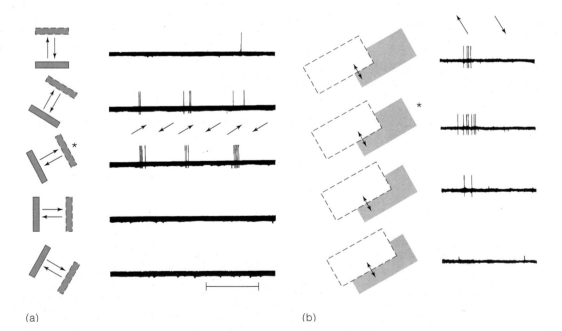

(a)　　　　　　　　　　　　　　(b)

Figure 4.8 ▌ (a) Response of a complex cell recorded from the visual cortex of the cat. The stimulus bar is moved back and forth across the receptive field. The cell fires best when the bar is positioned with a specific orientation and is moved in a specific direction (*). (From Hubel & Wiesel, 1959.) (b) Response of an end-stopped cell recorded from the visual cortex of the cat. The stimulus is indicated by the light area on the left. This cell responds best to a medium-sized corner that is moving up (*). *(From "Receptive fields and functional architecture in two non-striate visual areas (18 and 19) of the fat," by D. H. Hubel and T. N. Wiesel, 1965,* Journal of Neurophysiology, 28, *229–289.)*

don't respond to stationary flashes of light, their receptive fields are not indicated by pluses and minuses, but by indicating the area which, when stimulated, elicits a response in the neuron.

Another type of cell, called **end-stopped cells**, fire to moving lines of a specific length or to moving corners or angles. Figure 4.8b shows a light corner stimulus that is being moved up and down across the retina. The records to the right indicates that the neuron responds when the corner moves upward. The neuron's response increases as the corner-shaped stimulus gets longer, but then stops responding when the corner becomes too long (Hubel & Wiesel, 1965).

Hubel and Wiesel's finding that some neurons in the cortex respond only to oriented lines was an extremely important discovery because it indicates that neurons in the cortex do not simply respond to "light"; they respond to some patterns of light and not to others. This makes sense because the purpose of the visual system is to enable us to perceive objects in the environment, and many objects can be at least crudely represented by lines of various orientations. Thus, Hubel and Wiesel's discovery that neurons respond selectively to stationary and moving lines was an important step toward determining how neurons respond to more complex objects.

Because simple, complex, and end-stopped cells fire in response to specific features of the stimulus, such as orientation or direction of movement, they are sometimes called **feature detectors**. Table 4.1, which summarizes the properties of the five types of neurons we have described so far, illustrates an important fact about neurons in the visual system: As we travel farther from the retina, neurons fire to more complex stimuli. Retinal ganglion cells respond best

to spots of light, whereas cortical end-stopped cells respond best to bars of a certain length that are moving in a particular direction.

Do Feature Detectors Play a Role in Perception?

Neural processing endows neurons with properties that make them feature detectors, which respond best to a specific type of stimulus. But just showing that neurons *respond* to specific stimuli doesn't prove that they have anything to do with the *perception* of these stimuli. One way to establish a link between the firing of these neurons and perception is by using a psychophysical procedure called *selective adaptation*.

Selective Adaptation and Feature Detectors

When we view a stimulus with a specific property, neurons tuned to that property fire. The idea behind **selective adaptation** is that if the neurons fire for long enough, they become fatigued, or adapt. This adaptation causes two physiological effects: (1) the neuron's firing rate decreases, and (2) the neuron fires less when that stimulus is immediately presented again. According to this idea, presenting a vertical line causes neurons that respond to vertical lines to respond, but as these presentations continue, these neurons eventually begin to fire less to vertical lines. Adaptation is *selective* because only the neurons that respond to verticals or near-verticals adapt, and other neurons do not.

The basic assumption behind a *psychophysical* selective adaptation experiment is that if these adapted neurons have anything to do with perception, then adaptation of neurons that respond to verticals should result in the *perceptual effect* of becoming selectively less sensitive to verticals, but not to other orientations. Many selective adaptation experiments have used a stimulus called a *grating stimulus* and a behavioral measure called the *contrast threshold*.

Grating Stimuli and the Contrast Threshold Grating stimuli are alternating bars. Figure 4.9a shows gratings with black and white bars. This figure shows gratings with a number of different orientations. Figure 4.9b shows gratings with a number of different contrasts. High-contrast gratings are on the left, and lower-contrast gratings are on the right. A grating's **contrast threshold** is the difference in intensity at which the bars can just barely be seen. The difference between the bars in the grating on the far right of Figure 4.9b is close to the contrast threshold, because further decreases in the difference between the light and dark bars would make it difficult to see the bars. The following method describes the measurement of contrast thresholds in a selective adaptation experiment. $\boxed{V_L}$ 5

TABLE 4.1 ▌ **Properties of Neurons in the Optic Nerve, LGN, and Cortex**

TYPE OF CELL	CHARACTERISTICS OF RECEPTIVE FIELD
Optic nerve fiber (ganglion cell)	Center-surround receptive field. Responds best to small spots, but will also respond to other stimuli.
Lateral geniculate	Center-surround receptive fields very similar to the receptive field of a ganglion cell.
Simple cortical	Excitatory and inhibitory areas arranged side by side. Responds best to bars of a particular orientation.
Complex cortical	Responds best to movement of a correctly oriented bar across the receptive field. Many cells respond best to a particular direction of movement.
End-stopped cortical	Responds to corners, angles, or bars of a particular length moving in a particular direction.

(a)

(b)

Figure 4.9 ▌ (a) Grating stimuli showing gratings with different orientations. (b) A vertical grating. The contrast is high for the grating on the left, and becomes lower for the ones on the right.

METHOD ▌ Selective Adaptation to Orientation

Selective adaptation to orientation involves the following three steps:

1. Measure a person's *contrast threshold* to stimuli with a number of different orientations (Figure 4.10a).
2. Adapt the person to one orientation by having the person view a high contrast *adapting stimulus* for a minute or two. In this example, the adapting stimulus is a vertical grating (Figure 4.10b).
3. Remeasure the contrast threshold of all of the test stimuli presented in step 1 (Figure 4.10c). **VL** **6, 7**

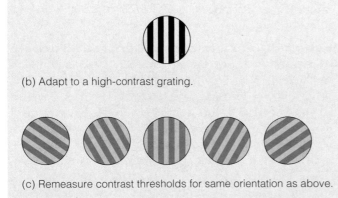

(a) Measure contrast threshold at a number of orientations.

(b) Adapt to a high-contrast grating.

(c) Remeasure contrast thresholds for same orientation as above.

Figure 4.10 ▌ Procedure for a selective adaptation experiment.

Figure 4.11a shows the results of a selective adaptation experiment in which the adapting stimulus was a vertically oriented grating. This graph indicates that adapting with the vertical grating caused a large increase in contrast threshold for the vertically oriented test grating. That is, the contrast of a vertical grating had to be increased for the person to see the bars. This is what we would expect if the vertical adapting stimulus selectively affects neurons that were tuned to respond best to verticals.

The important result of this experiment is that our psychophysical curve shows that adaptation selectively affects only some orientations, just as neurons selectively respond to only some orientations. In fact, comparing the psychophysically determined selective adaptation curve (4.11a) to the orientation tuning curve for a simple cortical neuron (4.11b) reveals that they are very similar. The psychophysical curve is slightly wider because the adapting grating affects not only neurons that respond best to verticals, but also more weakly affects some neurons that respond to nearby orientations. The near-match between the orientation selectivity of neurons and the perceptual effect of selective adaptation supports the idea that orientation detectors play a role in perception.

Selective Rearing and Feature Detectors

Further evidence that feature detectors are involved in perception is provided by selective rearing experiments. The idea behind **selective rearing** is that if an animal is reared in an environment that contains only certain types of stimuli, then neurons that respond to these stimuli will become more prevalent. This follows from a phenomenon called **neural plasticity** or **experience-dependent plasticity**—the idea that the response properties of neurons can be shaped by perceptual experience. According to this idea, rearing an animal in an environment that contains only vertical lines should result in the animal's visual system having neurons that respond predominantly to verticals.

This result may seem to contradict the results of the selective adaptation experiment just described, in which exposure to verticals *decreases* the response to verticals. However, the selective rearing effect occurs over a longer timescale and is strongest in young animals, whose visual systems are still developing. Thus, when a kitten is exposed only to verticals, some adaptation to vertical orientations may take place (causing the response to verticals to decrease), but as the animal develops, vertically responding neurons become the only neurons that respond at all.

One way to describe the results of selective rearing experiments is "Use it or lose it." This effect was demonstrated in a classic experiment by Colin Blakemore and Grahame Cooper (1970) in which they placed kittens in striped tubes like the one in Figure 4.12a, so that each kitten was exposed to only one orientation, either vertical or horizontal. The kittens were kept in the dark from birth to 2 weeks of age, at which time they were placed in the tube for 5 hours a day; the

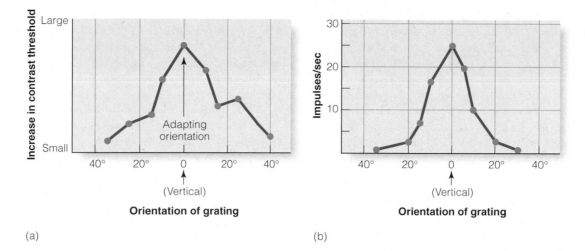

Figure 4.11 ▌ (a) Results of a psychophysical selective adaptation experiment. This graph shows that the participant's adaptation to the vertical grating causes a large decrease in her ability to detect the vertical grating when it is presented again, but has less effect on gratings that are tilted to either side of the vertical. (b) Orientation tuning curve of the simple cortical neuron from Figure 4.6.

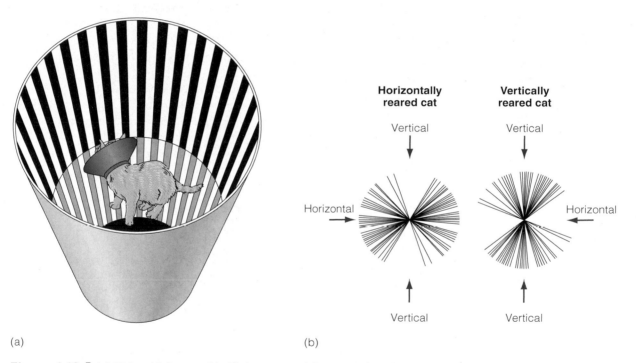

Figure 4.12 ▌ (a) Striped tube used in Blakemore and Cooper's (1970) selective rearing experiments. (b) Distribution of optimal orientations for 52 cells from a cat reared in an environment of horizontal stripes, on the left, and for 72 cells from a cat reared in an environment of vertical stripes, on the right. *(Reprinted by permission from Macmillan Publishers Ltd., Copyright 1970. From Blakemore, C., & Cooper, G. G. (1970). Development of the brain depends on the visual environment.* Nature, 228, 477–478.)

rest of the time they remained in the dark. Because the kittens sat on a Plexiglas platform, and the tube extended both above and below them, there were no visible corners or edges in their environment other than the stripes on the sides of the tube. The kittens wore cones around their head to prevent them from seeing vertical stripes as oblique or horizontal stripes by tilting their heads; however, according to Blake-

more and Cooper, "The kittens did not seem upset by the monotony of their surroundings and they sat for long periods inspecting the walls of the tube" (p. 477).

When the kittens' behavior was tested after 5 months of selective rearing, they seemed blind to the orientations that they hadn't seen in the tube. For example, a kitten that was reared in an environment of vertical stripes would pay

$\boxed{V_L}$ 8

attention to a vertical rod but ignored a horizontal rod. Following behavioral testing, Blakemore and Cooper recorded from cells in the visual cortex and determined the stimulus orientation that caused the largest response from each cell.

Figure 4.12b shows the results of this experiment. Each line indicates the orientation preferred by a single neuron in the cat's cortex. This cat, which was reared in a vertical environment, has many neurons that respond best to vertical or near-vertical stimuli, but none that respond to horizontal stimuli. The horizontally responding neurons were apparently lost because they hadn't been used. The opposite result occurred for the horizontally reared cats. The parallel between the orientation selectivity of neurons in the cat's cortex and the cat's behavioral response to the same orientation provides more evidence that feature detectors are involved in the perception of orientation. This connection between feature detectors and perception was one of the major discoveries of vision research in the 1960s and 1970s. Another advance was the description of how these neurons were organized in the brain.

Maps and Columns in the Striate Cortex

We've seen that retinotopic maps exist on the LGN. This organization, in which nearby points on a structure receive signals from nearby locations on the retina, also occurs in the striate cortex.

Maps in the Striate Cortex

Figure 4.13 shows the results of an experiment by Hubel and Wiesel (1965), when they recorded from a series of neurons along an oblique electrode track in the cat's visual cortex. As for the LGN experiment in Figure 4.5, record-

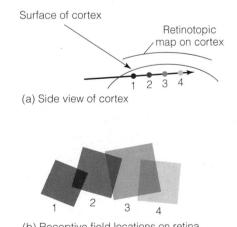

(a) Side view of cortex

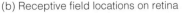

(b) Receptive field locations on retina

Figure 4.13 ❚ Retinotopic mapping of neurons in the cortex. When the electrode penetrates the cortex obliquely, the receptive fields of neurons recorded from the numbered positions along the track are displaced, as indicated by the numbered receptive fields; neurons near each other in the cortex have receptive fields near each other on the retina.

ings were made from neurons encountered as the electrode was inserted into the cortex, first neuron 1, then 2, and so on. Hubel and Wiesel found that the receptive field of each neuron was displaced slightly on the retina, as indicated by the squares in Figure 4.13b, but that receptive fields of neurons close to each other along the electrode track had receptive fields that were close to each other on the retina. Thus, nearby points on the cortex receive signals ⟨VL⟩ **9, 10** from nearby locations in the retina.

Retinotopic mapping indicates that information about objects near each other in the environment is processed by neurons near each other in the cortex. This makes sense in terms of efficiency of functioning. Adjacent areas in the environment can affect one another, as evidenced by the simultaneous contrast effect shown in Figure 3.39, so processing would be more efficient if areas that are adjacent in the environment were also adjacent in the visual system.

Another example of physiology serving functionality is that the area representing the cone-rich fovea is much larger than one would expect from the fovea's small size. Even though the fovea accounts for only 0.01 percent of the retina's area, signals from the fovea account for 8 to 10 percent of the retinotopic map on the cortex (Van Essen & Anderson, 1995). This apportioning the small fovea with a large area on the cortex is called the **cortical magnification factor** (Figure 4.14).

The cortical magnification factor in the human cortex has been determined using a technique called *brain imaging,* which makes it possible to create pictures of the brain's activity (Figure 4.15). We will describe the procedure of brain imaging and how this procedure has been used to measure the cortical magnification factor in humans.

METHOD ❚ Brain Imaging

Brain imaging refers to a number of techniques that result in images that show which areas of the brain are active. One of these techniques, **positron emission tomography (PET)**, was introduced in 1976 (Hoffman et al., 1976; Ter-Pogossian et al., 1975). In the PET proce-

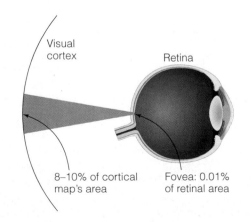

Visual cortex

Retina

8–10% of cortical map's area

Fovea: 0.01% of retinal area

Figure 4.14 ❚ The magnification factor in the visual system. The small area of the fovea is represented by a large area on the visual cortex.

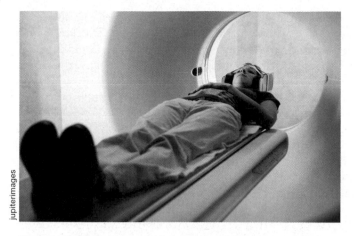

Figure 4.15 ▌ A person in a brain scanning apparatus.

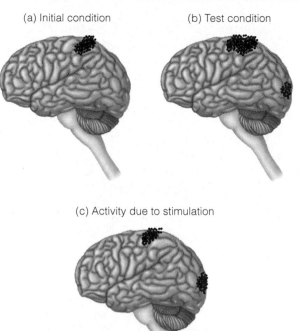
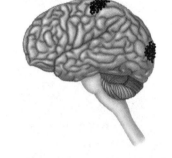

(a) Initial condition   (b) Test condition

(c) Activity due to stimulation

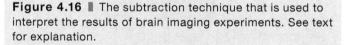

Figure 4.16 ▌ The subtraction technique that is used to interpret the results of brain imaging experiments. See text for explanation.

dure, a person is injected with a low dose of a radioactive tracer that is not harmful. The tracer enters the bloodstream and indicates the volume of blood flow. The basic principle behind the PET scan is that changes in the activity of the brain are accompanied by changes in blood flow, and monitoring the radioactivity of the injected tracer provides a measure of this blood flow.

PET enabled researchers to track changes in blood flow to determine which brain areas were being activated. To use this tool, researchers developed the sub-traction technique, in which brain activity is measured in two conditions: (1) an *initial condition,* before the stimulus of interest is presented; and (2) a *test condition,* in which the stimulus of interest is presented. For example, if we were interested in determining which areas of the brain are activated by manipulating an object with the hand, the initial condition would be when the person is holding the object in his or her hand (Figure 4.16a) and the test condition would be when the person is manipulating the object (Figure 4.16b). Subtracting the activity record in the initial condition from the activity in the test condition indicates the brain activation connected with manipulating the object (Figure 4.16c).

Another neuroimaging technique is functional magnetic resonance imaging (fMRI). Like PET, fMRI is based on the measurement of blood flow. Because hemoglobin, which carries oxygen in the blood, contains a ferrous molecule and therefore has magnetic properties, presenting a magnetic field to the brain causes the hemoglobin molecules to line up like tiny magnets.

fMRI indicates the presence of brain activity because the hemoglobin molecules in areas of high brain activity lose some of the oxygen they are transporting. This makes the hemoglobin more magnetic, so these molecules respond more strongly to the magnetic field. The fMRI apparatus determines the relative activity of various areas of the brain by detecting changes in the magnetic response of the hemoglobin that occurs when a person perceives a stimulus or engages in a specific be-

havior. The subtraction technique described above for PET is also used for the fMRI. Because fMRI doesn't require radioactive tracers and because it is more accurate, this technique has become the main method for localizing brain activity in humans.

Robert Dougherty and coworkers (2003) used brain imaging to determine the magnification factor in the human visual cortex. Figure 4.17a shows the stimulus display viewed by the observer, who was in an fMRI scanner. The observer looked directly at the center of the screen, so the dot at the center fell on the fovea. During the experiment stimulus light was presented in two places: (1) near the center (red area), which illuminated a small area near the fovea; and (2) farther from the center (blue area), which illuminated an area in the peripheral retina. The areas of the brain activated by these two stimuli are indicated in Figure 4.17b. This activation illustrates the magnification factor because stimulation of the small area near the fovea activated a greater area on the cortex (red) than stimulation of the larger area in the periphery (blue).

The large representation of the fovea in the cortex is also illustrated in Figure 4.18, which shows the space that would be allotted to words on a page (Wandell et al., 2007a, 2007b). Notice that the letter "a," which is near where the person is looking (red arrow), is represented by a much larger area in the cortex than letters that are far from where

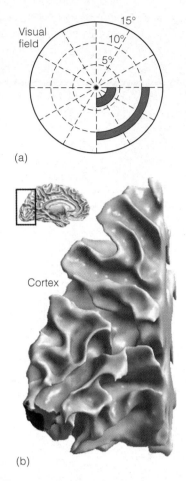

(a)

Cortex

(b)

Figure 4.17 ▌ (a) Red and blue areas show the extent of stimuli that were presented while a person was in an fMRI scanner. (b) Red and blue indicate areas of the brain activated by the stimulation in (a). *(From Dougherty et al., 2003.)*

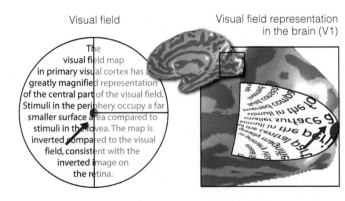

Figure 4.18 ▌ Demonstration of the magnification factor. A person looks at the red spot on the text on the left. The area of brain activated by each letter of the text is shown on the right. The arrows point to the letter *a* in the text on the left, and the area in the brain activated by the *a* on the right. *(From Wandell et al., 2007b.)*

the person is looking. The extra cortical space allotted to letters and words at which the person is looking provides the extra neural processing needed to accomplish tasks such as reading that require high visual acuity (Azzopardi & Cowey, 1993).

The connection between cortical area and acuity has been confirmed by Robert Duncan and Geoffrey Boynton (2003). They measured brain activation with the fMRI and visual acuity using a psychophysical task. The fMRI indicated that the magnification factor was not the same for all of their observers. Some people had more cortical space allotted to their foveas than other people, and those with more cortical space also had better acuity. Apparently, good acuity is associated not only with sharp focusing of images on the retina, and the small amount of convergence of the cones, but also with the relatively large amount of brain area devoted to the all-cone fovea.

Columns in the Striate Cortex

Determining the retinotopic map and the magnification factor has kept us near the surface of the cortex. We are now going to consider what is happening below the surface by looking at the results of experiments in which recording electrodes were inserted perpendicular to the surface of the cortex. Doing this has revealed that the cortex is organized into a number of different kinds of columns.

Location Columns Hubel and Wiesel (1965) recorded from neurons along a perpendicular electrode track as shown in Figure 4.19a, which shows a side view of the

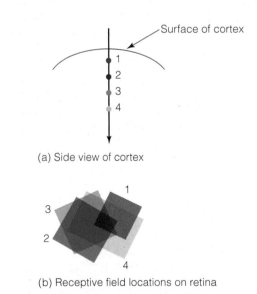

Figure 4.19 ▌ When an electrode penetrates the cortex perpendicularly, the receptive fields of the neurons encountered along this track overlap. The receptive field recorded at each numbered position along the electrode track is indicated by a correspondingly numbered square. *(This figure was published in* Neuron, 56, Wandell, B. A., Dumoulin, S. O., & Brewer, A. A., Visual field maps in human cortex, 366–383. Copyright Elsevier, 2007.)*

cortex. The receptive fields of neurons 1, 2, 3, and 4, indicated by the squares in Figure 4.19b, are all located at about the same place on the retina. Hubel and Wiesel concluded from this result that the cortex is organized into location columns that are perpendicular to the surface of the cortex so that all of the neurons within a location column have their receptive fields at the same location on the retina.

Orientation Columns As Hubel and Wiesel lowered their electrodes along the perpendicular track, they noted not only that the neurons along this track had receptive fields with the same location on the retina, but that these neurons all preferred stimuli with the same orientations. Thus, all cells encountered along the electrode track at A in Figure 4.20 fired the most to horizontal lines, whereas all those along electrode track B fired the most to lines oriented at about 45 degrees. Based on this result, Hubel and Wiesel concluded that the cortex is organized into orientation columns, with each column containing cells that respond best to a particular orientation. (Also see "If You Want to Know More #1," at the end of the chapter, for another technique for revealing orientation columns.)

Hubel and Wiesel also showed that adjacent columns have cells with slightly different preferred orientations. When they moved an electrode through the cortex obliquely, as was done for the LGN (Figure 4.5), so that the electrode cut across orientation columns, they found that the neurons' preferred orientations changed in an orderly fashion, so a column of cells that respond best to 90 degrees is right next to the column of cells that respond best to 85 degrees (Figure 4.21). Hubel and Wiesel also found that as they moved their electrode 1 millimeter across the cortex, their electrode passed through orientation columns that represented the entire range of orientations.

Ocular Dominance Columns Neurons in the cortex are also organized with respect to the eye to which they respond best. About 80 percent of the neurons in the cortex respond to stimulation of both the left and right eyes.

However, most neurons respond better to one eye than to the other. This preferential response to one eye is called ocular dominance, and neurons with the same ocular dominance are organized into ocular dominance columns in the cortex. This means that each neuron encountered along a perpendicular electrode track responds best to the same eye.

Ocular dominance columns can also be observed during oblique penetrations of the cortex. A given area of cortex usually contains cells that all respond best to one of the eyes, but when the electrode is moved about 0.25 to 0.50 mm across the cortex, the neurons respond best to the other eye. Thus, the cortex consists of a series of columns that alternate in ocular dominance in a left-right-left-right pattern.

Hypercolumns Hubel and Wiesel proposed that all three types of columns could be combined into one larger unit called a hypercolumn. Figure 4.22 is a schematic diagram called the *ice-cube model* (because it is shaped like an ice cube) that Hubel and Wiesel used to depict a hypercolumn. This diagram shows two side-by-side hypercolumns. Each hypercolumn contains a single location column (since it responds to stimuli presented to a particular place on the retina), left and right ocular dominance columns, and a complete set of orientation columns that cover all possible stimulus orientations from 0 to 180 degrees.

Hubel and Wiesel thought of a hypercolumn as a "processing module" that processes information about any stimulus that falls within the location on the retina served by the hypercolumn. They based this proposal on the fact that each hypercolumn contains a full set of orientation columns, so that when a stimulus of any orientation is presented to the area of retina served by the hypercolumn, neurons within the hypercolumn that respond to that orientation will be activated.

Research done since Hubel and Wiesel's proposal of the ice-cube model has shown that the actual organization of

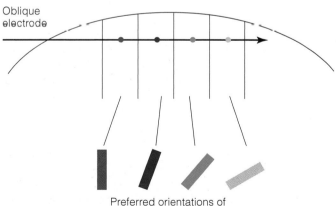

Oblique electrode

Preferred orientations of neurons in each column

Figure 4.21 ▌ If an electrode is inserted obliquely into the cortex, it crosses a sequence of orientation columns. The preferred orientation of neurons in each column, indicated by the bars, changes in an orderly way as the electrode crosses the columns. The distance the electrode is advanced is exaggerated in this picture.

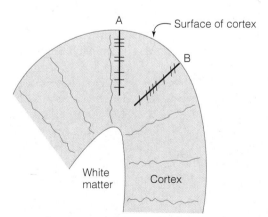

A

Surface of cortex

B

White matter

Cortex

Figure 4.20 ▌ All of the cortical neurons encountered along track A respond best to horizontal bars (indicated by the red lines cutting across the electrode track). All of the neurons along track B respond best to bars oriented at 45 degrees.

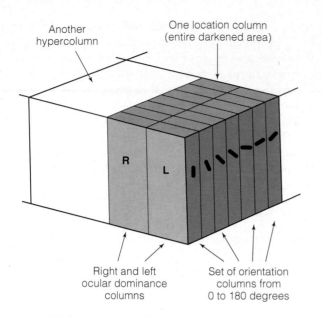

Another hypercolumn

One location column (entire darkened area)

R L

Right and left ocular dominance columns

Set of orientation columns from 0 to 180 degrees

Figure 4.22 ▌ Schematic diagram of a hypercolumn as pictured in Hubel and Wiesel's ice-cube model. The light area on the left is one hypercolumn, and the darkened area on the right is another hypercolumn. The darkened area is labeled to show that it consists of one location column, right and left ocular dominance columns, and a complete set of orientation columns.

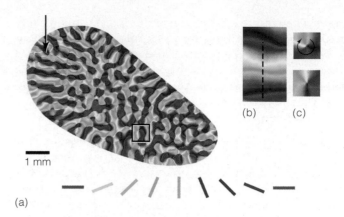

1 mm

(b) (c)

(a)

Figure 4.23 ▌ (a) Picture of the arrangement of columns that respond to different orientations, determined in the tree shrew cortex by a brain-scanning technique called *optical imaging*. Each color represents a different orientation. Colors correspond to the orientations indicated by the bars at the bottom; for example, an electrode inserted into a light blue area will record from neurons that prefer vertical orientations. (b) In some places, orientations are lined up, so moving across the cortex in a straight line encounters all of the orientations in order (dashed line); see the arrow on the left in Figure 4.23a. (c) In other places, orientations are arranged in a "pinwheel," so preferred orientation changes in an orderly way as we start with vertical (blue) and move across the brain in a small circle, indicated by the arrow; see the square in Figure 4.23a. *(Adapted from Bosking et al., 1997, Journal of Neuroscience, 17, 2112–2127, © 1997 by the Society of Neuroscience. All rights reserved. Reproduced by permission.)*

the three kinds of columns is far more complex than the picture in Figure 4.22. Figure 4.23a shows the results of an experiment that determined the layout of orientation columns using brain imaging. In some cases columns that prefer different orientations are lined up, as in Figure 4.23b (the arrow on the left of Figure 4.23a locates one of these areas), and in some cases orientations are arranged in a "pinwheel" as in Figure 4.23c, so all orientations are represented by traveling in a circle around a center point (see the small square in Figure 4.23a).

Both Hubel and Wiesel's ice-cube model and the more complex arrangement of orientations shown in Figure 4.23 indicate that an oriented stimulus activates neurons located in orientation columns in the cortex.

How Is an Object Represented in the Striate Cortex?

How is an object represented in the striate cortex? That is, how does the electrical activity in the cortex *stand for* the object in the environment? To begin, we will consider the situation in Figure 4.24, in which an observer is looking at a tree. Looking at the tree results in an image on the retina, which then results in a pattern of activation on the striate cortex that looks something like the tree because of the retinotopic map in the cortex. Notice, however, that the activation is distorted compared to the actual object. More space is allotted to the top of the tree, where the observer is looking, because the magnification factor allots more space on the cortex to the parts of the image that fall on the observer's fovea.

But the pattern of activation on the surface of the cortex doesn't tell the whole story. To appreciate how the tree is represented by activity that is occurring under the surface of the cortex, we will focus just on the trunk, which is essentially a long oriented bar. To determine which neurons in the cortex will be activated by a long oriented bar, let's return to the idea of a hypercolumn. Remember that a hypercolumn processes information from a specific area of the retina. This area is fairly small, however, so a long bar will stimulate a number of hypercolumns. Since our trunk is oriented vertically, it will activate neurons within the vertical (90-degree) orientation column within each hypercolumn, as shown in Figure 4.25.

Thus, a large stimulus, which stretches across the retina, will stimulate a number of different orientation columns, each in a location in the cortex that is separated from the other orientation columns. Therefore, our tree trunk has been translated into activity in a number of separated orientation columns, and this activity looks quite different from the shape of the stimulus, which is a single continuous bar.

Although it may be surprising that the tree is represented in a number of separate columns in the cortex, it simply confirms a basic property of our perceptual system: the cortical representation of a stimulus does not have to *resemble* the stimulus; it just has to contain information that *represents* the stimulus. The representation of the tree in the

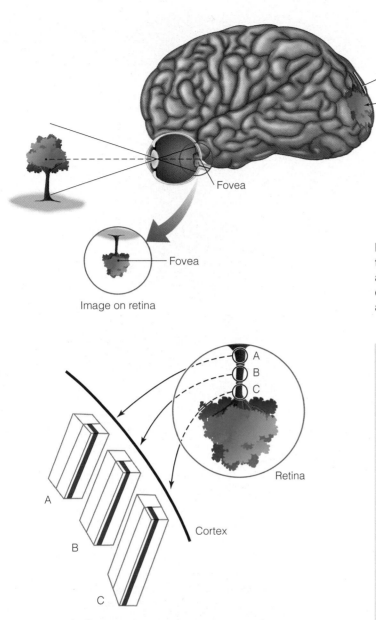

Figure 4.24 ▎ Looking at the tree creates an image on the observer's retina, and this image on the retina causes a pattern of activation on the visual cortex. This pattern is distorted because of the magnificaton factor (more space is allotted to the top of the tree, where the observer is looking.)

Figure 4.25 ▎ How the trunk of the tree pictured in Figure 4.24 would activate a number of different orientation columns in the cortex.

visual cortex is contained in the firings of neurons in separate cortical columns. Of course, this representation in the striate cortex is only the first step in representing the tree. As we will now see, signals from the striate cortex travel to a number of other places in the cortex for further processing.

TEST YOURSELF 4.1

1. Describe receptive fields of neurons in the LGN. What is the evidence that the LGN is involved in regulating information flow in the visual system?
2. Describe how the LGN is organized in layers, and describe retinotopic mapping in the LGN.

3. Describe the characteristics of simple, complex, and end-stopped cells in the cortex. Why have these cells been called feature detectors?
4. How has the psychophysical procedure of selective adaptation been used to demonstrate a link between feature detectors and the perception of orientation? Be sure you understand the rationale behind a selective adaptation experiment and also how we can draw conclusions about physiology from the results of this psychophysical procedure.
5. How has the procedure of selective rearing been used to demonstrate a link between feature detectors and perception? Be sure you understand the concept of neural plasticity.
6. How is the retina mapped onto the striate cortex? What is the cortical magnification factor, and what function does it serve?
7. How was neural recording used to determine the existence of location, orientation, and ocular dominance columns in the striate cortex?
8. Describe (a) the ice-cube model of organization and (b) the pinwheel arrangement of orientation columns.
9. How is a simple object, such as a tree, represented by electrical activity in the cortex?

Streams: Pathways for What, Where, and How

So far, as we have been looking at types of neurons in the cortex, and how the cortex is organized into maps and columns, we have been describing research primarily from the 1960s and 1970s. Most of the research during this time was concerned with the striate cortex or areas near the striate cortex. Although a few pioneers had looked at visual functioning outside the striate cortex (Gross, Bender, & Roche-Miranda, 1969), it wasn't until the 1980s that a large number of researchers began investigating how stimulation of the retina causes activity in areas far beyond the striate cortex.

One of the most influential ideas to come out of this research is that there are pathways, or "streams," that transmit information from the striate cortex to other areas in the brain. This idea was introduced in 1982, when Leslie Ungerleider and Mortimer Mishkin described experiments that distinguished two streams that served different functions.

Streams for Information About What and Where

Ungerleider and Mishkin (1982) used a technique called *ablation* (also called *lesioning*). Ablation refers to the destruction or removal of tissue in the nervous system.

METHOD | Brain Ablation

The goal of a brain ablation experiment is to determine the function of a particular area of the brain. This is accomplished by first determining an animal's capacity by testing it behaviorally. Most ablation experiments have used monkeys because of the similarity of their visual system to that of humans and because monkeys can be trained to determine perceptual capacities such as acuity, color vision, depth perception, and object perception.

Once the animal's perception has been measured, a particular area of the brain is ablated (removed or destroyed), either by surgery or by injecting a chemical at the area to be removed. Ideally, one particular area is removed and the rest of the brain remains intact. After ablation, the monkey is retrained to determine which perceptual capacities remain and which have been affected by the ablation.

Ungerleider and Mishkin presented monkeys with two tasks: (1) an object discrimination problem and (2) a landmark discrimination problem. In the object discrimination problem, a monkey was shown one object, such as a rectangular solid, and was then presented with a two-choice task like the one shown in Figure 4.26a, which included the "target" object (the rectangular solid) and another stimulus, such as the triangular shape. If the monkey pushed aside the target object, it received the food reward that was hidden in a well under the object. The landmark discrimination problem is shown in Figure 4.26b. Here, the monkey's task was to remove the food well cover that was closest to the tall cylinder.

In the ablation part of the experiment, part of temporal lobe was removed in some monkeys. After ablation,

(a) Object discrimination

(b) Landmark discrimination

Figure 4.26 ❚ The two types of discrimination tasks used by Ungerleider and Mishkin. (a) Object discrimination: Pick the correct shape. Lesioning the temporal lobe (shaded area) makes this task difficult. (b) Landmark discrimination: Pick the food well closer to the cylinder. Lesioning the parietal lobe makes this task difficult. *(From Mishkin, Ungerleider, & Macko, 1983.)*

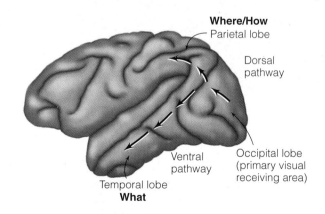

Where/How
Parietal lobe
Dorsal pathway
Occipital lobe (primary visual receiving area)
Ventral pathway
Temporal lobe
What

Figure 4.27 ❚ The monkey cortex, showing the *what*, or ventral, pathway from the occipital lobe to the temporal lobe, and the *where*, or dorsal, pathway from the occipital lobe to the parietal lobe. The *where* pathway is also called the *how* pathway. *(From Mishkin, Ungerleider, & Macko, 1983.)*

behavioral testing showed that the object discrimination problem was very difficult for these monkeys. This result indicates that the pathway that reaches the temporal lobes is responsible for determining an object's identity. Ungerleider and Mishkin therefore called the pathway leading from the striate cortex to the temporal lobe the *what* pathway (Figure 4.27).

Other monkeys, which had their parietal lobes removed, had difficulty solving the landmark discrimination problem. This result indicates that the pathway that leads to the parietal lobe is responsible for determining an object's location. Ungerleider and Mishkin therefore called the pathway leading from the striate cortex to the parietal lobe the *where* pathway.

The *what* and *where* pathways are also called the **ventral pathway** (what) and the **dorsal pathway** (where), because the lower part of the brain, where the temporal lobe is located, is the ventral part of the brain, and the upper part of the brain, where the parietal lobe is located, is the dorsal part of the brain. The term *dorsal* refers to the back or the upper surface of an organism; thus, the dorsal fin of a shark or dolphin is the fin on the back that sticks out of the water. Figure 4.28 shows that for upright, walking animals such as humans, the dorsal part of the brain is the top of the brain. (Picture a person with a dorsal fin sticking out of the top of his or her head!) *Ventral* is the opposite of dorsal, hence it refers to the lower part of the brain.

The discovery of two pathways in the cortex—one for identifying objects (what) and one for locating objects (where)—led some researchers to look back at the retina and LGN. Using both recordings from neurons and ablation, they found that properties of the ventral and dorsal streams are established by two different types of ganglion cells in the retina, which transmit signals to different layers of the LGN. Thus, the cortical ventral and dorsal streams can actually be traced back to the retina and LGN. (For more about research on the origins of processing streams in the retina and LGN, see "If You Want to Know More #2" VL 11 at the end of the chapter.)

Although there is good evidence that the ventral and dorsal pathways serve different functions, it is important to note that (1) the pathways are not totally separated, but have connections between them; and (2) signals flow not only "up" the pathway toward the parietal and temporal lobes, but "back" as well (Merigan & Maunsell, 1993; Ungerleider & Haxby, 1994). It makes sense that there would be communication between the pathways because in our everyday behavior we need to both identify and locate objects, and we routinely coordinate these two activities every time we identify something (for example, a pencil) and take action with regard to it (picking up the pencil and writing with it). Thus, there are two distinct pathways, but some information is shared between them. The "backward" flow of information, called *feedback*, provides information from higher centers that can influence the signals flowing into the system. This feedback is one of the mechanisms behind top-down processing, introduced in Chapter 1 (page 10).

Streams for Information About What and How

Although the idea of ventral and dorsal streams has been generally accepted, David Milner and Melvyn Goodale (1995; see also Goodale & Humphrey, 1998, 2001) have suggested that rather than being called the *what* and *where* streams, the ventral and dorsal streams should be called the *what* and *how* streams. The ventral stream, they argue, is for perceiving objects, an idea that fits with the idea of *what*. However, they propose that the dorsal stream is for taking action, such as picking up an object. Taking this action would involve knowing the location of the object, consistent with the idea of *where*, but it also involves a physical interaction with the object. Thus, reaching to pick up a pencil involves information about the pencil's location *plus* movement of the hand toward the pencil. According to this idea, the dorsal stream provides information about *how* to direct action with regard to a stimulus.

Evidence supporting the idea that the dorsal stream is involved in how to direct action is provided by the discovery of neurons in the parietal cortex that respond (1) when a monkey looks at an object and (2) when it reaches toward the object (Sakata et al., 1992; also see Taira et al., 1990). But the most dramatic evidence supporting the idea of a dorsal "action," or *how*, stream comes from **neuropsychology**—the study of the behavioral effects of brain damage in humans.

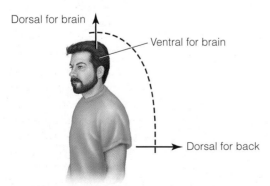

Figure 4.28 ▌ *Dorsal* refers to the back surface of an organism. In upright standing animals such as humans, dorsal refers to the back of the body *and* to the top of the head, as indicated by the arrows and the curved dashed line. Ventral is the opposite of dorsal.

METHOD ▌ **Dissociations in Neuropsychology**

One of the basic principles of neuropsychology is that we can understand the effects of brain damage by studying **dissociations**—situations in which one function is absent while another function is present. There are two kinds of dissociations: **single dissociations**, which can be studied in a single person, and **double dissociations**, which require two or more people.

To illustrate a single dissociation, lets consider a woman, Alice, who has suffered damage to her temporal lobe. She has difficulty naming objects but has no

TABLE 4.2 ▌ A Double Dissociation

	NAMING OBJECTS	DETERMINING OBJECTS' LOCATIONS
(a) ALICE: Temporal lobe damage (ventral stream)	NO	YES
(b) BERT: Parietal lobe damage (dorsal stream)	YES	NO

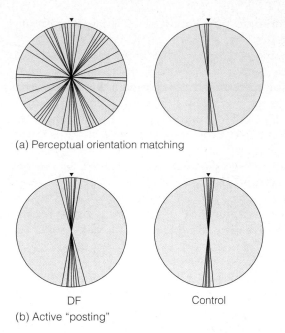

(a) Perceptual orientation matching

DF   Control

(b) Active "posting"

Figure 4.29 ▌ Performance of D.F. and a person without brain damage on two tasks: (a) judging the orientation of a slot; and (b) placing a card through the slot. See text for details. *(From Milner & Goodale, 1995.)*

trouble indicating where they are located (Table 4.2a). Alice demonstrates a single dissociation—one function is present (locating objects) and another is absent (naming objects). From a single dissociation such as this, in which one function is lost while another function remains, we can conclude that two functions (in this example, locating and naming objects) involve different mechanisms, although they may not operate totally independently of one another.

We can illustrate a double dissociation by finding another person who has one function present and another absent, but in a way opposite to Alice. For example, Bert, who has parietal lobe damage, can identify objects but can't tell exactly where they are located (Table 4.2b). The cases of Alice and Bert, taken together, represent a double dissociation. Establishing a double dissociation enables us to conclude that two functions are served by different mechanisms *and* that these mechanisms operate independently of one another.

The Behavior of Patient D.F. The method of determining dissociations was used by Milner and Goodale (1995) to study D.F., a 34-year-old woman who suffered damage to her ventral pathway from carbon monoxide poisoning caused by a gas leak in her home. One result of the brain damage was that D.F. was not able to match the orientation of a card held in her hand to different orientations of a slot. This is shown in the left circle in Figure 4.29a. Each line in the circle indicates the orientation to which D.F. adjusted the card. Perfect matching performance would be indicated by a vertical line for each trial, but D.F.'s responses are widely scattered. The right circle shows the accurate performance of the normal controls.

Because D.F. had trouble orienting a card to match the orientation of the slot, it would seem reasonable that she would also have trouble *placing* the card through the slot because to do this she would have to turn the card so that it was lined up with the slot. But when D.F. was asked to "mail" the card through the slot, she could do it! Even though D.F. could not turn the card to match the slot's orientation, once she started moving the card toward the slot,

she was able to rotate it to match the orientation of the slot (Figure 4.29b). Thus, D.F. performed poorly in the static orientation-matching task but did well as soon as *action* was involved (Murphy, Racicot, & Goodale, 1996). Milner and Goodale interpreted D.F.'s behavior as showing that there is one mechanism for judging orientation and another for coordinating vision and action.

These results for D.F. demonstrate a single dissociation, which indicates that judging orientation and coordinating vision and action involve different mechanisms. To show that these two functions are not only served by different mechanisms but are also *independent* of one another, we have to demonstrate a double dissociation. As we saw in the example of Alice and Bert, this involves finding a person whose symptoms are the opposite of D.F.'s, and such people do, in fact, exist. These people can judge visual orientation, but they can't accomplish the task that combines vision and action. As we would expect, whereas D.F.'s ventral stream is damaged, these other people have damage to their dorsal streams.

Based on these results, Milner and Goodale suggested that the ventral pathway should still be called the *what* pathway, as Ungerleider and Mishkin suggested, but that a better description of the dorsal pathway would be the *how* pathway, or the **action pathway**, because it determines *how* a person carries out an *action*. As sometimes occurs in science, not everyone uses the same terms. Thus, some researchers call the dorsal stream the *where* pathway and some call it the *how* or action pathway.

The Behavior of People Without Brain Damage In our normal daily behavior we aren't aware of two visual processing streams, one for *what* and the other for *how*, because they work together seamlessly as we perceive objects and take actions toward them. Cases like that of D.F., in which one stream is damaged, reveal the existence of these two streams. But what about people without damaged brains? Psychophysical experiments that measure how people perceive and react to visual illusions have demonstrated the dissociation between perception and action that was evident for D.F.

Figure 4.30a shows a stimulus called the **rod and frame illusion**, which was used in one of these experiments. In this illusion, the two small lines inside the tilted squares appear slightly tilted in opposite directions, even though they are parallel vertical lines.

Richard Dyde and David Milner (2002) presented their observers with two tasks: a matching task and a grasping task. In the *matching task,* observers adjusted the matching

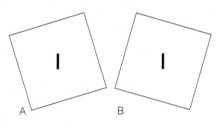

(a) Rod and frame illusion

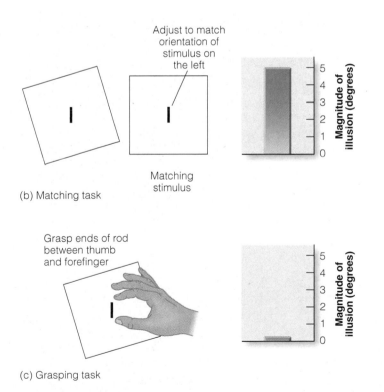

Adjust to match orientation of stimulus on the left

Matching stimulus

(b) Matching task

Grasp ends of rod between thumb and forefinger

(c) Grasping task

Figure 4.30 ▌ (a) Rod and frame illusion. Both small lines are oriented vertically. (b) Matching task and results. (c) Grasping task and results. See text for details.

stimulus, a rod located in an upright square (on the right) until it appeared to match the orientation of the vertical rod in the tilted square (on the left) (Figure 4.30b). This provided a measure of how much the tilted square made the vertical rod on the left appear tilted. The results, shown on the right, indicate that observers had to adjust the matching stimulus to 5 degrees from vertical in order to make it match their perception of the rod in the tilted square.

In the *grasping task,* observers grasped a rod in the tilted square between their thumb and forefinger (Figure 4.30c). The positioning of the thumb and forefinger was measured using a special position-sensing device attached to the observers' fingers. The result, shown on the right, indicates that observers positioned their fingers appropriately for the rod's orientation. Thus the tilted square did not affect the accuracy of grasping.

The rationale behind this experiment is that because these two tasks involve different processing streams (matching task = ventral, or *what,* stream; grasping task = dorsal, or *how,* stream), they may be affected differently by the presence of the surrounding frames. In other words, conditions that created a *perceptual visual illusion* (matching task) had no effect on the person's ability to *take action* with regard to the stimulus (grasping task). These results support the idea that perception and action are served by different mechanisms. Thus, an idea that originated with observations of patients with brain damage is supported by the performance of observers without brain damage.

Modularity: Structures for Faces, Places, and Bodies

We have seen how the study of the visual system has progressed from Hubel and Wiesel's discovery of neurons in the striate cortex that respond to oriented bars, to discovery of the ventral and dorsal streams. We now return to where we left off with Hubel and Wiesel to consider more research on the types of stimuli to which individual neurons respond.

As researchers moved outside the striate cortex, they found neurons that responded best to more complex stimuli. For example, Keiji Tanaka and his coworkers (Ito et al., 1995; Kobatake & Tanaka, 1994; Tanaka, 1993; Tanaka et al., 1991) recorded from cells in the temporal cortex that responded best to complex stimuli, such as the disc with a thin bar shown in Figure 4.31a. This cell, which responds best to a circular disc with a thin bar, responds poorly to the bar alone (Figure 4.31b) or the disc alone (Figure 4.31c). The cell does respond to the square shape with the bar (Figure 4.31d), but not as well to the circle and bar.

In addition to discovering neurons that respond to complex stimuli, researchers also found evidence that neurons that respond to similar stimuli are often grouped together in one area of the brain. A structure that is specialized to process information about a particular type of stimulus is

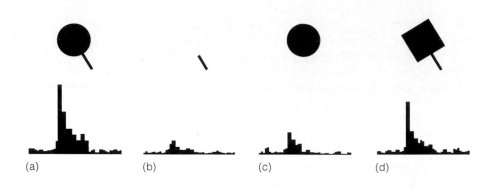

Figure 4.31 ▍ How a neuron in a monkey's temporal lobe responds to a few stimuli. This neuron responds best to a circular disc with a thin bar. *(Adapted from Tanaka et al., 1991.)*

(a) (b) (c) (d)

called a module. There is a great deal of evidence that there are specific areas in the temporal lobe that respond best to particular types of stimuli.

Face Neurons in the Monkey's IT Cortex

Edmund Rolls and Martin Tovee (1995) measured the response of neurons in the monkey's inferotemporal (IT) cortex (Figure 4.32a). When they presented pictures of faces and pictures of nonface stimuli (mostly landscapes and food), they found many neurons that responded best to faces. Figure 4.33 shows the results for a neuron that responded briskly to faces but hardly at all to other types of stimuli.

You may wonder how there could be neurons that respond best to complex stimuli such as faces. We have seen how neural processing that involves the mechanisms of convergence, excitation, and inhibition can create neurons that respond best to small spots of light (Figure 2.16). The same mechanisms are presumably involved in creating neurons that respond to more complex stimuli. Of course, the neural circuits involved in creating a "face-detecting" neuron must be extremely complex. However, the potential for this complexity is there. Each neuron in the cortex receives inputs from an average of 1,000 other neurons, so the number of potential connections between neurons in the cortex

is astronomical. When we consider the vast complexity of the neural interconnections that must be involved in creating a neuron that responds best to faces, it is easy to agree with William James's (1890/1981) description of the brain as "the most mysterious thing in the world."

Areas for Faces, Places, and Bodies in the Human Brain

Brain imaging (see Method, page 82) has been used to identify areas of the human brain that contain neurons that respond best to faces, and also to pictures of scenes and human bodies. In one of these experiments, Nancy Kanwisher and coworkers (1997) first used fMRI to determine brain activity in response to pictures of faces and other objects,

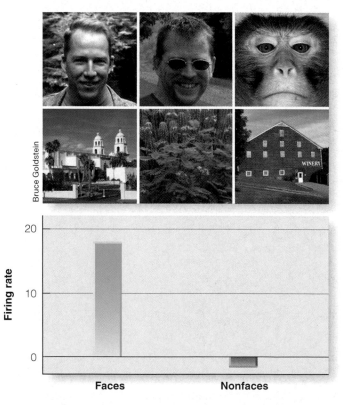

Figure 4.33 ▍ Size of response of a neuron in the monkey's IT cortex that responds to face stimuli but not to nonface stimuli. *(Based on data from Rolls & Tovee, 1995.)*

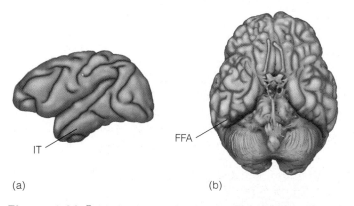

Figure 4.32 ▍ (a) Monkey brain showing the location of the inferotemporal (IT) cortex. (b) Human brain showing the location of the fusiform face area (FFA), which is located just under the temporal lobe.

such as scrambled faces, household objects, houses, and hands. When they subtracted the response to the other objects from the response to the faces, Kanwisher and coworkers found that activity remained in an area they called the fusiform face area (FFA), which is located in the fusiform gyrus on the underside of the brain directly below the IT cortex (Figure 4.32b). They interpreted this result to mean that the FFA is specialized to respond to faces.

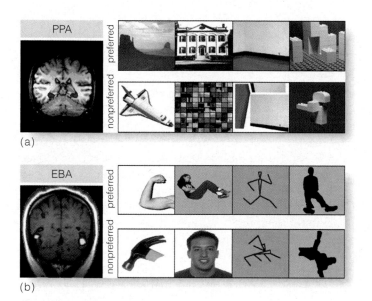

(a)

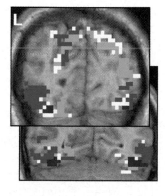

(b)

Figure 4.34 ▌ (a) The parahippocampal place area is activated by places (top row) but not by other stimuli (bottom row). (b) The extrastriate body area is activated by bodies (top), but not by other stimuli (bottom). *(From Kanwisher, N., The ventral visual object pathway in humans: Evidence from fMRI. In* The Visual Neurosciences, *2003, pp. 1179–1189. Edited by Chalupa, L., & Werner, J., MIT Press.)*

Additional evidence of an area specialized for the perception of faces is that damage to the temporal lobe causes prosopagnosia—difficulty recognizing the faces of familiar people. Even very familiar faces are affected, so people with prosopagnosia may not be able to recognize close friends or family members—or even their own reflection in the mirror—although they can easily identify people as soon as they hear them speak (Burton et al., 1991; Hecaen & Angelerques, 1962; Parkin, 1996).

In addition to the FFA, which contains neurons that are activated by faces, two other specialized areas in the temporal cortex have been identified. The **parahippocampal place area (PPA)** is activated by pictures depicting indoor and outdoor scenes like those shown in Figure 4.34a (Aguirre et al., 1998; R. Epstein et al., 1999; R. Epstein & Kanwisher, 1998). Apparently what is important for this area is information about spatial layout, because activation occurs both to empty rooms and to rooms that are completely furnished (Kanwisher, 2003). The other specialized area, the **extrastriate body area (EBA)**, is activated by pictures of bodies and parts of bodies (but not by faces), as shown in Figure 4.34b (Downing et al., 2001).

We have come a long way from Hubel and Wiesel's simple and complex cells in the striate cortex that respond best to oriented lines. The existence of neurons that are specialized to respond to faces, places, and bodies brings us closer to being able to explain how perception is based on the firing of neurons. It is likely that our perception of faces, landmarks, and people's bodies depends on specifically tuned neurons in areas such as the FFA, PPA, and EBA.

But it is also important to recognize that even though stimuli like faces and buildings activate specific areas of the brain, these stimuli also activate other areas of the brain as well. This is illustrated in Figure 4.35, which shows the re-

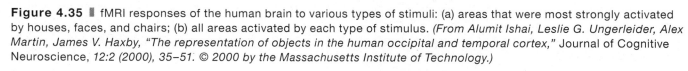

(a) Segregation by category

(b) Response magnitude

Houses   Faces   Chairs

Maximal Respose to:
- Houses
- Chairs
- Faces
- No difference

Percent Activation

−1 0 +1 +2

Figure 4.35 ▌ fMRI responses of the human brain to various types of stimuli: (a) areas that were most strongly activated by houses, faces, and chairs; (b) all areas activated by each type of stimulus. *(From Alumit Ishai, Leslie G. Ungerleider, Alex Martin, James V. Haxby, "The representation of objects in the human occipital and temporal cortex,"* Journal of Cognitive Neuroscience, *12:2 (2000), 35–51. © 2000 by the Massachusetts Institute of Technology.)*

sults of an fMRI experiment on humans. Figure 4.35a shows that pictures of houses, faces, and chairs cause maximum activation in three separate areas in the IT cortex. However, each type of stimulus also causes substantial activity within the other areas, as shown in the three panels limited to just these areas (Figue 4.35b; Ishai et al., 2000; Ishai et al., 1999). Thus, the idea of specialized modules is correct, but shouldn't be carried too far. Objects may cause a focus of activity in a particular area, but they are represented in the cortex by activity that is distributed over a wide area (J. D. Cohen & Tong, 2001; Riesenhuber & Poggio, 2000, 2002).

Something to Consider: How Do Neurons Become Specialized?

When researchers began describing neurons that were specialized to fire to specific stimuli, such as faces, places, and bodies, they naturally wondered how this specialization might have occurred. One possibility is that these neurons have become specialized by a process of biological evolution, so that people are born with selective neurons. Another possibility is that these neurons become specialized by a process involving people's experience as they perceive common objects in their environment.

Is Neural Selectivity Shaped by Evolution?

According to the **theory of natural selection**, genetically based characteristics that enhance an animal's ability to survive, and therefore reproduce, will be passed on to future generations. Thus, a person whose visual system contains neurons that fire to important things in the environment (such as faces) will be more likely to survive and pass on his or her characteristics than will a person whose visual system does not contain these specialized neurons. Through this evolutionary process, the visual system may have been shaped to contain neurons that respond to faces and other important perceptual information.

There is no question that evolution has shaped the functioning of the senses, just as it has shaped all the other physical and mental characteristics that have enabled us to survive as a species. We know that the visual system is not a "blank slate" at birth. Newborn monkeys have neurons that respond to the direction of movement and the relative depths of objects (Chino et al., 1997), and 3½-week-old monkeys possess orientation columns that are organized like the adult columns in Figure 4.20 (Hübener et al., 1995). Although we have less information about the neural structure of infant humans than of infant monkeys, we do know that babies prefer looking at pictures in which the parts are arranged to resemble a face compared to pictures in which the same parts are scrambled (Johnson et al., 1991; also see

Turati et al., 2002). It is likely that this behavior is caused by neurons that respond best to facelike patterns.

Although there is no question that the basic layout and functioning of all of the senses is the result of evolution, it is difficult to prove whether a particular capacity is "built in" by evolution or is the result of learning (Kanwisher, 2003). There is, however, a great deal of evidence that learning can shape the response properties of neurons that respond best to complex visual features.

How Neurons Can Be Shaped by Experience

Although it may be important for the visual system to have some specialized neurons at birth, it is also important that the visual system be able to adapt to the specific environment in which a person or animal lives. The nervous system can achieve this adaptation through a process that causes neurons to develop so that they respond best to the types of stimulation to which the person has been exposed. This is the process of experience-dependent plasticity introduced earlier in this chapter.

The idea of experience-dependent plasticity was first suggested by experiments with animals, such as the one in which kittens were raised in an environment that contained only verticals (Figure 4.12). The fact that most of the neurons in the kittens' cortex responded only to verticals after this experience is an example of experience-dependent plasticity. There is also evidence that experience causes changes in how neurons are tuned in the human cortex. For example, brain-imaging experiments have shown that there are regions in the human cortex specialized to respond to visual letters and word forms (Nobre et al., 1994). Because humans have been reading for only a few thousand years, this specialized responding could not have evolved but must have developed as people learned to read (Ungerleider & Pasternak, 2003).

Brain-imaging experiments have also demonstrated a shift in responding of neurons in the FFA due to training. Isabel Gauthier and coworkers (1999) used fMRI to determine the level of activity in the fusiform face area (FFA) in response to faces and to objects called Greebles—families of computer-generated "beings" that all have the same basic configuration but differ in the shapes of their parts (Figure 4.36a). Initially, the observers were shown both human faces and Greebles. The results for this part of the experiment, shown by the left pair of bars in Figure 4.36b, indicate that the FFA neurons responded poorly to the Greebles but well to the faces.

The participants were then trained in "Greeble recognition" for 7 hours over a 4-day period. After the training sessions, participants had become "Greeble experts," as indicated by their ability to rapidly identify many different Greebles by the names they had learned during the training. The right pair of bars in Figure 4.36b shows how becoming a Greeble expert affected the neural response in the

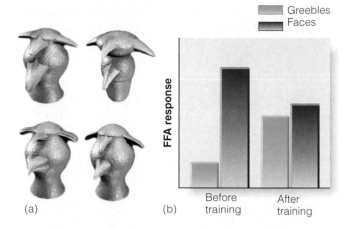

(a)   (b)

Figure 4.36 ❚ (a) Greeble stimuli used by Gauthier. Participants were trained to name each different Greeble. (b) Brain responses to Greebles and faces before and after Greeble training. *(Reprinted by permission from Macmillan Publishers Ltd, Copyright 1999: Nature Neuroscience, 2, 568–573. From Figure 1a, p. 569, from Gauthier, I., Tarr, M. J., Anderson, A. W., Skudlarski, P. L., & Gore, J. C., "Activation of the middle fusiform 'face area' increases with experience in recognizing novel objects,"1999.)*

participants' FFA. After the training, the FFA neurons responded about as well to Greebles as to faces.

Apparently, the FFA area of the cortex is an area that responds not just to faces but to other complex objects as well. The objects that the neurons respond to are established by experience with those objects. In fact, Gauthier has also shown that neurons in the FFA of people who are experts in recognizing cars or birds respond well not only to human faces but to cars (for the car experts) and to birds (for the bird experts; Gauthier et al., 2000). It is important to note that the function of the FFA is controversial: Some researchers agree with Gauthier's idea that the FFA is specialized to respond to complex objects that have become familiar through experience, and others believe that the FFA is specialized to respond specifically to faces. (See "If You Want to Know More #6" at the end of the chapter.)

Let's return to the question we posed at the beginning of this section: How do neurons become specialized? It seems that specialized tuning is at least partially the result of experience-dependent plasticity. This makes it possible for neurons to adapt their tuning to objects that are seen often and that are behaviorally important. Thus, evolution has apparently achieved exactly what it is supposed to achieve—it has created an area that is able to adapt to the specific environment in which an animal or human lives. According to this idea, if we moved to a new planet inhabited by Greebles or other strange-looking creatures, a place that contained landscapes and objects quite different from Earth's, our neurons that now respond well to Earth creatures and objects would eventually change to respond best to the creatures and environment of this new, and previously strange, environment (Gauthier et al., 1999).

TEST YOURSELF 4.2

1. How has ablation been used to demonstrate the existence of the ventral and dorsal processing streams? What is the function of these streams?
2. How has neuropsychology been used to show that one of the functions of the dorsal stream is to process information about coordinating vision and action? How do the results of a behavioral experiment involving the rod and frame illusion support this conclusion?
3. What is the evidence that there are modules for faces, places, and bodies? What is the evidence that stimuli like faces and places also activate a wide area of the cortex?
4. What is the evidence that the properties of selective neurons are determined by evolution? By experience?

THINK ABOUT IT

1. Cell A responds best to vertical lines moving to the right. Cell B responds best to 45-degree lines moving to the right. Both of these cells have an excitatory synapse with cell C. How will cell C fire to vertical lines? To 45-degree lines? (p. 78)

2. We have seen that the neural firing associated with an object in the environment does not necessarily look like, or resemble, the object. Can you think of situations that you encounter in everyday life in which objects or ideas are represented by things that do not exactly resemble those objects or ideas? (p. 86)

3. Ralph is hiking along a trail in the woods. The trail is bumpy in places, and Ralph has to avoid tripping on occasional rocks, tree roots, or ruts in the trail. Nonetheless, he is able to walk along the trail without constantly looking down to see exactly where he is placing his feet. That's a good thing because Ralph enjoys looking out at the woods to see whether he can spot interesting birds or animals. How can you relate this description of Ralph's behavior to the operation of the dorsal and ventral streams in the visual system? (p. 88)

4. Although most neurons in the striate cortex respond to stimulation of small areas of the retina, many neurons in the temporal lobe respond to areas that represent as much as half of the visual field (see "If You Want to Know More #4," below). What do you think the function of such neurons is? (p. 96)

5. We have seen that there are neurons that respond to complex shapes and also to environmental stimuli such as faces, bodies, and places. Which types of neurons do

Figure 4.37 ▌ "Howdy, pardner."

you think would fire to the stimulus in Figure 4.37? How would your answer to this question be affected if this stimulus were interpreted as a human figure? ("Howdy, pardner!") What role would top-down processing play in determining the response to a cactus-as-person stimulus? (p. 92)

IF YOU WANT TO KNOW MORE

1. *Seeing columns.* Location columns can be revealed by using a technique called *autoradiography,* in which a monkey injected with radioactive tracer views grating with a particular orientation. This makes it possible to see columns that were discovered using single-unit recording. (p. 85)

    Hubel, D. H., Wiesel, T. N., & Stryker, M. P. (1978). Anatomical demonstration of orientation columns in macaque monkey. *Journal of Comparative Neurology, 177,* 361–379.

2. *The origins of processing streams in the retina and LGN.* Experiments that determined how ablating specific areas of the LGN affected monkeys' behavior have shown that the dorsal and ventral streams can be traced back to the LGN and retina. (p. 89)

Schiller, P. H., Logothetis, N. K., & Charles, E. R. (1990). Functions of the colour-opponent and broad-band channels of the visual system. *Nature, 343,* 68–70.

3. *Another kind of specialized neuron.* Neurons called *bimodal neurons* respond to a visual stimulus presented near a place on a monkey's body, such as the face or the hand, and also to touching that part of the body. (p. 93)

    Graziano, M. S. A., & Gross, C. G. (1995). The representation of extrapersonal space: A possible role for bimodal, visual-tactile neurons. In M. S. Gazzaniga (Ed.), *The cognitive neurosciences* (pp. 1021–1034). Cambridge, MA: MIT Press.

4. *Wide-angle neurons.* There are maps of the retina in the striate cortex, and neurons in the striate cortex respond to stimulation of a small area of the retina. However, recording from neurons further "upstream" in the visual system, in places such as the temporal cortex, reveals that "maps" like those in the striate cortex no longer exist because neurons in these structures respond to stimulation of very large areas of the retina. (p. 95)

    Rolls, E. T. (1992). Neurophysiological mechanisms underlying face processing within and beyond the temporal cortical areas. *Philosophical Transactions of the Royal Society of London, 335B,* 11–21.

5. *Invariant neurons.* There are neurons at the far end of the ventral stream that continue to respond to objects even when these objects appear in different orientations or their size is changed. (p. 88)

    Perrett, D. I., & Oram, M. W. (1993). Neurophysiology of shape processing. *Image and Visual Computing, 11,* 317–333.

6. *Fusiform face area.* There is a controversy over the role of the fusiform face area: Some researchers believe it is specialized to respond to faces. Others believe it is specialized to respond to complex objects that we have had experience with; according to this view, the FFA responds to faces because we see lots of faces. (p. 95)

    Kanwisher, N. (2000). Domain specificity in face perception. *Nature, 3,* 759–763.

    Tarr, M. J., & Gauthier, I. (2000). FFA: A flexible fusiform area for subordinate-level visual processing automatized by expertise. *Nature, 3,* 764–769.

KEY TERMS

Ablation (p. 88)
Action pathway (p. 90)
Brain imaging (p. 82)
Complex cells (p. 78)
Contralateral eye (p. 76)
Contrast threshold (p. 79)

Cortical magnification factor (p. 82)
Dissociation (p. 89)
Dorsal pathway (p. 89)
Double dissociation (p. 89)
End-stopped cells (p. 79)

Experience-dependent plasticity (p. 80)
Extrastriate body area (EBA) (p. 93)
Feature detectors (p. 79)
Functional magnetic resonance imaging (fMRI) (p. 83)

MEDIA RESOURCES

The *Sensation and Perception* Book Companion Website

www.cengage.com/psychology/goldstein

See the companion website for flashcards, practice quiz questions, Internet links, updates, critical thinking exercises, discussion forums, games, and more!

CengageNOW

www.cengage.com/cengagenow

Go to this site for the link to CengageNOW, your one-stop shop. Take a pre-test for this chapter, and CengageNOW will generate a personalized study plan based on your test results. The study plan will identify the topics you need to review and direct you to online resources to help you master those topics. You can then take a post-test to help you determine the concepts you have mastered and what you will still need to work on.

Virtual Lab

Your Virtual Lab is designed to help you get the most out of this course. The Virtual Lab icons direct you to specific media demonstrations and experiments designed to help you visualize what you are reading about. The number beside each icon indicates the number of the media element you can access through your CD-ROM, CengageNOW, or WebTutor resource.

The following lab exercises are related to material in this chapter:

1. *The Visual Pathways* A drag-and-drop exercise that tests your knowledge of visual structures.

2. *Visual Cortex of the Cat* A classic 1972 film in which vision research pioneer Colin Blakemore demonstrates mapping of receptive fields of neurons in the cortex of the cat.

3. *Simple Cells in the Cortex* How the firing rate of a simple cortical cell depends on orientation of a stimulus.

4. *Complex Cells in the Cortex* How the firing rate of a complex cortical cell changes with orientation and direction of movement of a stimulus.

5. *Contrast Sensitivity* An experiment in which you measure your contrast sensitivity to grating patterns.

6. *Orientation Aftereffect* How adaptation to an oriented grating can affect the perception of orientation.

7. *Size Aftereffect* How adaptation to a grating can affect size perception.

8. *Development in the Visual Cortex* A classic 1973 film in which vision research pioneer Colin Blakemore describes his pioneering experiments that demonstrated how the properties of neurons in the kitten's cortex can be affected by the environment in which it is reared.

9. *Retinotopy Movie: Ring* How the cortex is activated as a ring shape expands. (Courtesy of Geoffrey Boynton.)

10. *Retinotopy Movie: Wedge* Record from an experiment demonstrating how the cortex is activated as a wedge rotates to different positions. (Courtesy of Geoffrey Boynton.)

11. *What and Where Streams* Drag-and-drop exercise to test your knowledge of the *what* and *where* pathways.

Chapter Contents

CHAPTER 5

Perceiving Objects and Scenes

OPPOSITE PAGE This painting by Robert Indiana, titled *The Great Love,* provides examples of how different areas of a picture can be perceived as figure and ground. At first you may see the red areas, spelling the word "Love," standing out as the figure. It is also possible, however, to see small green areas as arrows on a red background, or the blue shapes in the center as three figures on a red background.
© 2010 Morgan Art Foundation Ltd./Artists Rights Society (ARS), New York. Carnegie Museum of Art, Pittsburgh/Gift of the Women's Committee.

[VL] The Virtual Lab icons direct you to specific animations and videos designed to help you visualize what you are reading about. The number beside each icon indicates the number of the clip you can access through your CD-ROM or your student website.

Some Questions We Will Consider:

▌ Why do some perceptual psychologists say "The whole differs from the sum of its parts"? (p. 104)

▌ How do we distinguish objects from their background? (p. 108)

▌ How do "rules of thumb" help us in arriving at a perception of the environment? (p. 109)

▌ Why are even the most sophisticated computers unable to match a person's ability to perceive objects? (p. 119)

Sitting in the upper deck in PNC Park in Pittsburgh, Roger looks out over the city (Figure 5.1). On the left, he sees a group of about 10 buildings and can tell one building from another, even though they overlap. Looking straight ahead, he sees a small building in front of a larger one, and has no trouble telling that they are two separate buildings. Looking down toward the river, he notices a horizontal yellow band above the right field bleachers. It is obvious to him that this is not part of the ballpark but is located across the river.

All of Roger's perceptions come naturally to him and require little effort. However, what Roger achieves so easily is actually the end result of complex processes. We can gain some perspective on the idea that perception is complex and potentially difficult, by returning to the "science project" that we described at the beginning of Chapter 1 (review page 4).

This project posed the problem of designing a machine that can locate, describe, and identify all objects in the environment and, in addition, can travel from one point to another, avoiding obstacles along the way. This problem has attracted the interest of computer scientists for more than half a century. When computers became available in the 1950s and '60s, it was predicted that devices with capacities approaching human vision would be available within 10 or 15 years. As it turned out, the task of designing a computer that could equal human vision was much more difficult

Bruce Goldstein

Figure 5.1 ▌ It is easy to tell that there are a number of different buildings on the left and that straight ahead there is a low rectangular building in front of a taller building. It is also possible to tell that the horizontal yellow band above the bleachers is across the river. These perceptions are easy for humans, but would be difficult for a computer vision system.

than the computer scientists imagined; even now, the problem has still not been solved (Sinha et al., 2006).

One way to illustrate the complexity of the science project is to consider recent attempts to solve it. Consider, for example, the vehicles that were designed to compete in the "Urban Challenge" race that occurred on November 3, 2007, in Victorville, California. This race, which was sponsored by the Defense Advanced Research Project Agency (DARPA), required that vehicles drive for 55 miles through a course that resembled city streets, with other moving vehicles, traffic signals, and signs. The vehicles had to accomplish this feat on their own, with no human involvement other than entering global positioning coordinates of the course's layout into the vehicle's guidance system. Vehicles had to stay on course and avoid unpredictable traffic without any human intervention, based only on the operation of onboard computer systems.

The winner of the race is shown in Figure 5.2. "Boss," from Carnegie Mellon University, succeeded in staying on course and avoiding other cars while maintaining an average speed of 14 miles per hour. The vehicle from Stanford came in second, and the one from Virginia Tech came in third. Teams from MIT, Cornell, and the University of Pennsylvania also successfully completed the course out of a total of 11 teams that qualified for the final race.  [VL] 1

The feat of navigating through the environment, especially one that contains moving obstacles, is extremely impressive. However, even though these robotic vehicles can avoid obstacles along a defined pathway, they can't identify most of the objects they are avoiding. For example, even though "Boss" might be able to avoid an obstacle in the middle of the road, it can't tell whether the obstacle is "a pile of rocks" or "a bush."

Other computer-based machines have been designed specifically to recognize objects (as opposed to navigating a course). These machines can recognize some objects, but only after training on a limited set of objects. The machines can recognize faces, but only if the lighting is just right and the faces are viewed from a specific angle. The difficulty of computer face recognition is illustrated by the fact that systems designed to recognize faces at airport security checkpoints can accurately identify less than half of a group of specially selected faces (Sinha, 2002; also see Chella et al., 2000, and "If You Want to Know More," page 128, for more on computer perception).

Why Is It So Difficult to Design a Perceiving Machine?

We will now describe a few of the difficulties involved in designing a perceiving machine. Remember that the point of these descriptions is that although they pose difficulties for computers, our human "perceiving machine" solves these problems easily.

The Stimulus on the Receptors Is Ambiguous

When you look at the page of this book, the image cast by the page on your retina is ambiguous. It may seem strange to say that, because it is obvious that the page is rectangular, but consider Figure 5.3, which shows how the page is imaged on your retina. Viewed from straight on, the rectangular page creates a rectangular image on the retina. However, other objects, such as the tilted rectangle or slanted trapezoid, can also create the same image.

The fact that a particular image on the retina (or a computer vision machine's sensors) can be created by many different objects is called the inverse projection problem. Another way to state this problem is as follows: If we know an object's shape, distance, and orientation, we can determine the shape of the object's image on the retina. However, a particular image on the retina can be created by an infinite number of objects.

The ambiguity of the image on the retina is also illustrated by Figure 5.4a, which appears to be a circle of rocks. However, looking at these rocks from another viewpoint

Figure 5.2 ▌ The "Boss" robotic vehicle on a test run on a track at Robot City in Pittsburgh. Notice that there is no human driver. Navigation is accomplished by onboard computers that receive information from numerous sensors on the vehicle, each of which has a specialized task. Sensors mounted on the back of the roof are laser range scanners that point down to detect lane markings. Sensors on the roof rack point down crossroads to detect and track vehicles when attempting to merge with traffic. The black sensors on the hood at the front of the vehicle are multiplane, long-range laser scanners used for tracking vehicles. The two white sensors on the corners of the front bumper are short-range laser scanners used to detect and track nearby vehicles. The four rectangles in the grill are radar sensors. The white sensors are short-range, used for detecting obstacles near the vehicle. The black sensors are long-range, for tracking vehicles when Boss is moving quickly or considering turning across traffic.

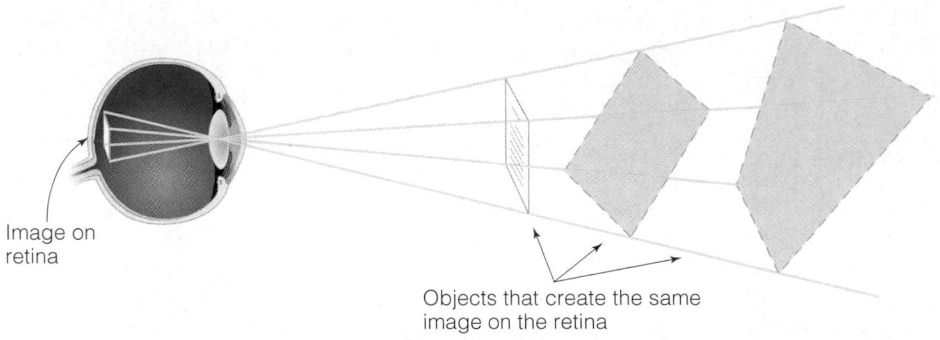

Image on retina

Objects that create the same image on the retina

Figure 5.3 ▌ The principle behind the inverse projection problem. The page of the book that is near the eye creates a rectangular image on the retina. However, this image could also have been created by the tilted square, by the trapezoid and by many other stimuli. This is why we say that the image on the retina is ambiguous.

Courtesy of Thomas Macaulay, Blackhawk Mountain School of Art, Blackhawk, CO

(a)   (b)

Figure 5.4 ▌ An environmental sculpture by Thomas Macaulay. (a) When viewed from exactly the right vantage point (the second-floor balcony of the Blackhawk Mountain School of Art, Black Hawk, Colorado), the stones appear to be arranged in a circle. (b) Viewing the stones from the ground floor reveals a truer indication of their configuration.

reveals that they aren't arranged in a circle after all (Figure 5.4b). Thus, just as a rectangular image on the retina can be created by trapezoid and other nonrectangular objects, a circular image on the retina can be created by objects that aren't circular. Although the example in Figure 5.4a leads human perceivers to the wrong conclusion about the rocks, this kind of confusion rarely occurs, because moving to another viewpoint reveals that the rocks aren't arranged in a circle.

These examples show that the information from a single view of an object can be ambiguous. Humans solve this problem by moving to different viewpoints, and by making use of knowledge they have gained from past experiences in perceiving objects.

Objects Can Be Hidden or Blurred

Sometimes objects are hidden or blurred. Can you find the pencil and eyeglasses in Figure 5.5? Although it might take a little searching, people can find the pencil in the foreground, and the glasses frame sticking out from behind the computer next to the scissors, even though only a small por-

tion of these objects is visible. People also easily perceive the book, scissors, and paper as single objects, even though they are partially hidden by other objects.

This problem of hidden objects occurs any time one object obscures part of another object. This occurs frequently in the environment, but people easily understand that the part of an object that is covered continues to exist, and they are able to use their knowledge of the environment to determine what is likely to be present.

People are also able to recognize objects that are not in sharp focus, such as the faces in Figure 5.6. See how many of these people you can identify, and then consult the answers on page 130. Despite the degraded nature of these images, people can often identify most of them, whereas computers perform poorly on this task (Sinha, 2002).

Objects Look Different From Different Viewpoints

Another problem facing any perception machine is that objects are often viewed from different angles. This means that the images of objects are continually changing, de-

Figure 5.5 ❚ A portion of the mess on the author's desk. Can you locate the hidden pencil (easy) and the author's glasses (hard)?

Figure 5.6 ❚ Who are these people? See bottom of page 130 for the answers. *(From Sinha, P. (2002). Recognizing complex patterns.* Nature Neuroscience, 5, *1093–1097. Reprinted by permission from Macmillan Publishers Ltd. Copyright 2002.)*

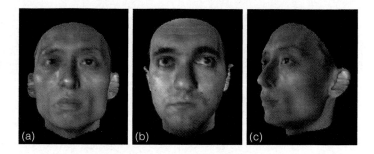

Figure 5.8 ❚ Which photographs are of the same person? *From Sinha, P. (2002). (Recognizing complex patterns.* Nature Neuroscience, 5, *1093–1097. Reprinted by permission from Macmillan Publishers Ltd. Copyright 2002.)*

pending on the angle from which they are viewed. Although humans continue to perceive the object in Figure 5.7 as the same chair viewed from different angles, this isn't so obvious to a computer. The ability to recognize an object seen from different viewpoints is called **viewpoint invariance**. People's ability to achieve viewpoint invariance enables them to identify the images in Figure 5.8a and c as being the same person, but a computer face recognition system would rate faces a and b as being more similar (Sinha, 2002).

The difficulties facing any perceiving machine illustrate that perception is more complex than it seems. But how do humans overcome these complexities? Early answers to this question were provided in the early 1900s by a group of psychologists who called themselves **Gestalt psychologists**—where *Gestalt,* roughly translated, means a whole configuration that cannot be described merely as the sum of its parts. We can appreciate the meaning of this definition by considering how Gestalt psychology began.

(a) (b) (c)

Figure 5.7 ❚ Your ability to recognize each of these views as being of the same chair is an example of viewpoint invariance.

The Gestalt Approach to Object Perception

We can understand the Gestalt approach by first considering an early attempt to explain perception that was proposed by Wilhelm Wundt, who established the first laboratory of scientific psychology at the University of Leipzig in 1879. Wundt's approach to psychology was called **structuralism**. One of the basic ideas behind structuralism was that perceptions are created by combining elements called **sensations**, just as each of the dots in the face in Figure 5.9 add together to create our perception of a face.

The idea that perception is the result of "adding up" sensations was disputed by the Gestalt psychologists, who offered, instead, the idea that *the whole differs from the sum of its parts.* This principle had its beginnings, according to a well-known story, in a train ride taken by psychologist Max Wertheimer in 1911 (Boring, 1942). Wertheimer got off the train to stretch his legs in Frankfurt and bought a toy stroboscope from a vendor who was selling toys on the train platform. The stroboscope, a mechanical device that created an illusion of movement by rapidly alternating two slightly different pictures, caused Wertheimer to wonder how the structuralist idea that experience is created from sensations could explain the illusion of movement he observed. We can understand why this question arose by looking at Figure 5.10a, which diagrams the principle behind the illusion of movement created by the stroboscope.

When two stimuli that are in slightly different positions are flashed one after another with the correct timing, movement is perceived between the two stimuli. This is an illusion called **apparent movement** because there is actually no movement in the display, just two stationary stimuli flashing on and off. How, wondered Wertheimer, can the movement that appears to occur between the two flashing stimuli be caused by sensations? After all, there is no stimulation in the space between the two stimuli, and therefore there are no sensations to provide an explanation for the movement. (A modern example of apparent movement is

Flash line on left | 50 ms of darkness | Flash line on right | Perception: movement from left to right

(a)

(b)

Figure 5.10 ▌ (a) Wertheimer's demonstration of apparent movement. (b) Moving electronic signs such as this one, in which the words are scrolling to the left, create the perception of movement by applying the principles of apparent movement studied by Wertheimer.

provided by electronic signs like the one in Figure 5.10b, which display moving advertisements or news headlines. The perception of movement in these displays is so compelling that it is difficult to imagine that they are made up of stationary lights flashing on and off.) VL 2

With his question about apparent movement as his inspiration, Wertheimer and two colleagues, Kurt Koffka and Ivo Kohler, set up a laboratory at the University of Frankfurt, called themselves Gestalt psychologists, and proceeded to do research and publish papers that posed serious problems for the structuralist idea that perceptions are created from sensations (Wertheimer, 1912). The following demonstration illustrates another phenomenon that is difficult to explain on the basis of sensations.

DEMONSTRATION

Making Illusory Contours Vanish

Consider the picture in Figure 5.11. If you see this as a cube like the one in Figure 5.11b floating in space in front of black circles, you probably perceive faint **illusory contours** that represent the edges of the cube (Bradley & Petry, 1977). These contours are called illusory because they aren't actually present in the physical stimulus. You can prove this to yourself by (1) placing your finger over the two black circles at the bottom or (2) imagining that the black circles are holes and that you are looking at the cube through these holes. Covering the circles or seeing the cube through the holes causes the illusory contours to either vanish or become more difficult to *see.* ▌

Figure 5.9 ▌ According to structuralism, a number of sensations (represented by the dots) add up to create our perception of the face.

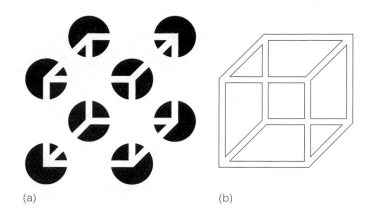

(a)   (b)

Figure 5.11 ▌ (a) This can be seen as a cube floating in front of eight discs or as a cube seen through eight holes. In the first case, the edges of the cube appear as illusory contours. (b) The cube without the black circles. *(Based on "Organizational Determinants of Subjective Contour: The Subjective Necker Cube," by D. R. Bradley and H. M. Petry, 1977, American Journal of Psychology, 90, 253–262. American Psychological Association.)*

When you made the contours vanish by placing your finger over the black circles, you showed that the contour was illusory and that our perception of one part of the display (the contours) is affected by the presence of another part (the black circles). The structuralists would have a hard time explaining illusory contours because there is no actual contour, so there can't be any sensations where the contour is perceived. **VL 3, 4**

Additional displays that are difficult to explain in terms of sensations are bistable figures, like the cube in Figure 5.11b, which switch back and forth as they are viewed, and illusions, in which perceptions of one part of a display are affected by another part. (See Virtual Labs 5–7.) Making the contours vanish by imagining that you are looking through black holes poses a similar problem for the structuralists. It is difficult to explain a perception that is present one moment and gone the next in terms of sensations, especially since the stimulus on your retina never changes. **VL 5-7**

Having rejected the idea that perception is built up of sensations, the Gestalt psychologists proposed a number of principles, which they called **laws of perceptual organization**.

The Gestalt Laws of Perceptual Organization

Perceptual organization involves the grouping of elements in an image to create larger objects. For example, some of the dark areas in Figure 5.12 become grouped to form a Dalmatian and others are seen as shadows in the background. Here are six of the laws of organization that the Gestalt psychologists proposed to explain how perceptual grouping such as this occurs. **VL 8**

Pragnanz *Pragnanz,* roughly translated from the German, means "good figure." The **law of pragnanz**, also called the **law of good figure** or the **law of simplicity**, is the central law of Gestalt psychology: *Every stimulus pattern is seen in such a way that the resulting structure is as simple as possible.* The familiar Olympic symbol in Figure 5.13a is an example of the law of simplicity at work. We see this display as five circles and not as a larger number of more complicated shapes such as the ones in Figure 5.13b. **VL 9**

Similarity Most people perceive Figure 5.14a as either horizontal rows of circles, vertical columns of circles, or both. But when we change the color of some of the columns, as in Figure 5.14b, most people perceive vertical columns of circles. This perception illustrates the **law of similarity**: *Similar things appear to be grouped together.* This law causes circles of the same color to be grouped together. Grouping

Figure 5.12 ▌ Some black and white shapes that become perceptually organized into a Dalmatian.

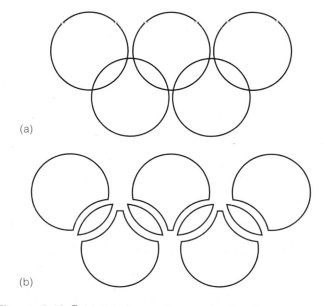

(a)

(b)

Figure 5.13 ▌ (a) This is usually perceived as five circles, not as the nine shapes in (b).

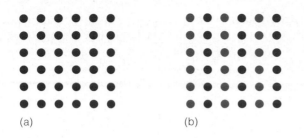

(a)   (b)

Figure 5.14 ▌ (a) Perceived as horizontal rows or vertical columns or both. (b) Perceived as vertical columns.

can also occur because of similarity of shape, [VL] **10** size, or orientation (Figure 5.15).

Grouping also occurs for auditory stimuli. For example, notes that have similar pitches and that follow each other closely in time can become perceptually grouped to form a melody. We will consider this and other auditory grouping effects when we describe organizational processes in hearing in Chapter 12.

Good Continuation In Figure 5.16 we see the wire starting at A as flowing smoothly to B. It does not go to C or D because those paths would involve making sharp turns and would violate the **law of good continuation:** *Points that, when connected, result in straight or smoothly curving lines are seen as belonging together, and the lines tend to be seen in such a way as to follow the smoothest path.* Another effect of good continuation is shown in the Celtic knot pattern in Figure 5.17. In this case, good continuation assures that we see a continuous interweaved pattern that does not appear to be broken into little pieces every time one strand overlaps another strand. Good continuation also helped us to perceive [VL] **11, 12** the smoothly curving circles in Figure 5.13a.

Proximity (Nearness) Our perception of Figure 5.18a as two pairs of circles illustrates the **law of proximity,** or **nearness:** *Things that are near each other appear to* [VL] **13** *be grouped together.*

Figure 5.15 ▌ What are they looking at? Whatever it is, Tiger Woods and Phil Mickelson have become perceptually linked because of the similar orientations of their arms, golf clubs, and bodies.

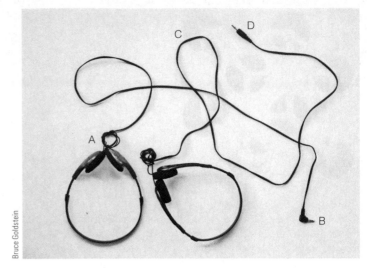

Bruce Goldstein

Figure 5.16 ▌ Good continuation helps us perceive two separate wires, even though they overlap.

Figure 5.17 ▌ Because of good continuation, we perceive this pattern as continuous interwoven strands.

Common Region Figure 5.18b illustrates the principle of common region: *Elements that are within the same region of space appear to be grouped together.* Even though the circles inside the ovals are farther apart than the circles that are next to each other in neighboring ovals, we see the circles inside the ovals as belonging together. This occurs because each oval is seen as a separate region of space (Palmer, 1992; Palmer & Rock, 1994). Notice that in this example common region overpowers proximity. Because the circles are in different regions, they do not group with each other, as they did in Figure 5.18a, but with circles in the same region.

Uniform Connectedness The principle of uniform connectedness states: *A connected region of visual properties, such as lightness, color, texture, or motion, is perceived as a single unit.* For example, in Figure 5.18c, the connected circles are perceived as grouped together, just as they were when they were in the same region in Figure 5.18b.

Synchrony The principle of synchrony states: *Visual events that occur at the same time are perceived as belonging together.* For example, the lights in Figure 5.18d that blink together are seen as belonging together.

Common Fate The law of common fate states: *Things that are moving in the same direction appear to be grouped together.* Thus, when you see a flock of hundreds of birds all flying

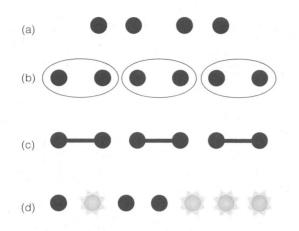

Figure 5.18 ▌ Grouping by (a) proximity; (b) common region; (c) connectedness; and (d) synchrony. Synchrony occurs when the yellow lights blink on and off together.

Figure 5.19 ▌ A flock of birds that are moving in the same direction are seen as grouped together. When a portion of the flock changes direction, their movement creates a new group. This illustrates the law of common fate.

together, you tend to see the flock as a unit, and if some birds start flying in another direction, this creates a new unit (Figure 5.19). Notice that common fate is like synchrony in that both principles are dynamic, but synchrony can occur without movement, and the elements don't have to change in the same direction as they do in common fate. V_L 14

Meaningfulness or Familiarity According to the law of familiarity, *things that form patterns that are familiar or meaningful are likely to become grouped together* (Helson, 1933; Hochberg, 1971). You can appreciate how meaningfulness influences perceptual organization by doing the following demonstration.

DEMONSTRATION

Finding Faces in a Landscape

Consider the picture in Figure 5.20. At first glance this scene appears to contain mainly trees, rocks, and water. But on closer inspection you can see some faces in the trees in the background, and if you look more closely, you can see that a

Figure 5.20 ▌ *The Forest Has Eyes* by Bev Doolittle (1984). Can you find 13 hidden faces in this picture? E-mail the author at bruceg@email.arizona.edu for the solution.

number of faces are formed by various groups of rocks. See if you can find all 13 faces hidden in this picture. ▌

Figure 5.21 ▌ A version of Rubin's reversible face–vase figure.

Some people find it difficult to perceive the faces at first, but then suddenly they succeed. The change in perception from "rocks in a stream" or "trees in a forest" to "faces" is a change in the perceptual organization of the rocks and the trees. The two shapes that you at first perceive as two separate rocks in the stream become perceptually grouped together when they become the left and right eyes of a face. In fact, once you perceive a particular grouping of rocks as a face, it is often difficult *not* to perceive them in this way—they have become permanently organized into a face. This is similar to the process we observed for the Dalmatian. Once we see the Dalmatian, it is difficult not to perceive it.

Perceptual Segregation: How Objects Are Separated From the Background

The Gestalt psychologists were also interested in explaining **perceptual segregation**, the perceptual separation of one object from another, as Roger did when he perceived each of the buildings in Figure 5.1 as separate from one another. The question of what causes perceptual segregation is often referred to as the problem of **figure–ground segregation**. When we see a separate object, it is usually seen as a **figure** that stands out from its background, which is called the **ground**. For example, you would probably see a book or papers on your desk as figure and the surface of your desk as ground. The Gestalt psychologists were interested in determining the properties of the figure and the ground and what causes us to perceive one area as figure and the other as ground.

What Are the Properties of Figure and Ground? One way the Gestalt psychologists studied the properties of figure and ground was by considering patterns like the one in Figure 5.21, which was introduced by Danish psychologist Edgar Rubin in 1915. This pattern is an example of **reversible figure–ground** because it can be perceived alternately either as two blue faces looking at each other, in front of a white background, or as a white vase on a blue background. Some of the properties of the figure and ground are:

- The figure is more "thinglike" and more memorable than the ground. Thus, when you see the vase as figure, it appears as an object that can be remembered later. However, when you see the same white area as ground, it does not appear to be an object and is therefore not particularly memorable. 〔VL〕 15

- The figure is seen as being in front of the ground. Thus, when the vase is seen as figure, it appears to be in front of the dark background (Figure 5.22a), and when the faces are seen as figure, they are on top of the light background (Figure 5.22b).

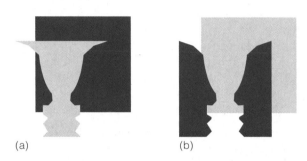

(a)   (b)

Figure 5.22 ▌ (a) When the vase is perceived as figure, it is seen in front of a homogeneous dark background. (b) When the faces are seen as figure, they are seen in front of a homogeneous light background.

- The ground is seen as unformed material and seems to extend behind the figure.

- The contour separating the figure from the ground appears to belong to the figure. This property of figure, which is called **border ownership**, means that, although figure and ground share a contour, the border is associated with the figure. Figure 5.23 illustrates border ownership for another display that can be perceived in two ways. If you perceive the display in Figure 5.23a as a light gray square (the figure) sitting on a dark background (the ground), then the border belongs to the gray square, as indicated by the dot in Figure 5.23b. But if you perceive the display as a black rectangle with a hole in it (the figure) through which you are viewing a gray surface (the ground), the border would be on the black rectangle, as shown in Figure 5.23c.

What Factors Determine Which Area Is Figure? What factors determine whether an area is perceived as figure or ground? Shaun Vecera and coworkers (2002) used the phenomenological method (see page 13) to show that regions in the lower part of a display are more likely to be perceived as figure than regions in the upper

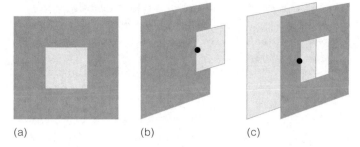

(a)　　　　　　(b)　　　　　　(c)

Figure 5.23 ▌ (a) This display can be perceived in two ways. (b) When it is perceived as a small square sitting on top of a dark background, the border belongs to the small square, as indicated by the dot. (c) When it is perceived as a large dark square with a hole in it, the border belongs to the dark square.

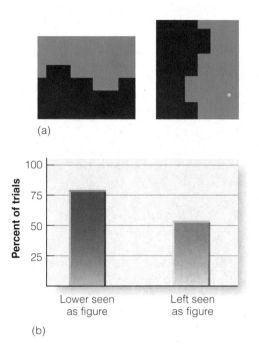

(a)

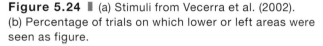

(b)

Figure 5.24 ▌ (a) Stimuli from Vecerra et al. (2002). (b) Percentage of trials on which lower or left areas were seen as figure.

part. They flashed stimuli like the ones in Figure 5.24a for 150 milliseconds (ms) and asked observers to indicate which area they saw as figure, the red area or the green area. The results, shown in Figure 5.24b, indicate that for the upper–lower displays, observers were more likely to perceive the lower area as figure, but for the left–right displays, they showed only a small preference for the left region. From this result, Vecera concluded that there is no left–right preference for determining figure, but there is a definite preference for seeing objects lower in the display as figure. The conclusion from this experiment is that the lower region of a display tends to be seen as figure.

Figure 5.25 illustrates four other factors that help determine which area will be seen as figure. In Figure 5.25a (symmetry), the symmetrical red areas on the left are seen as figure, as are the symmetrical yellow areas on the right.

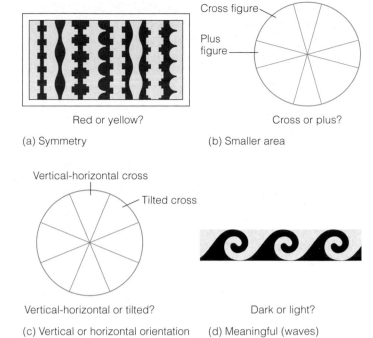

Figure 5.25 ▌ Examples of how (a) symmetry, (b) size, (c) orientation, and (d) meaning contribute to perceiving an area as figure.

In Figure 5.25b (smaller area), the smaller plus-shaped area is more likely to be seen as figure. In Figure 5.25c (vertical or horizontal areas), the vertical–horizontal cross tends to be seen as figure. In Figure 5.25d (meaningfulness), the fact that the dark areas look like waves increases the chances that this area will be seen as figure. **VL 16**

The Gestalt "Laws" as Heuristics

Although the Gestalt psychologists called their principles "laws of perceptual organization," most perceptual psychologists call them the Gestalt "principles" or "heuristics." The reason for rejecting the term *laws* is that the rules of perceptual organization and segregation proposed by the Gestalt psychologists don't make strong enough predictions to qualify as laws. Instead, the Gestalt principles are more accurately described as heuristics—rules of thumb that provide a best-guess solution to a problem. We can understand what heuristics are by comparing them to another way of solving a problem, called algorithms.

An **algorithm** is a procedure that is *guaranteed* to solve a problem. An example of an algorithm is the procedures we learn for addition, subtraction, and long division. If we apply these procedures correctly, we get the right answer every time. In contrast, a heuristic may not result in a correct solution every time. For example, suppose that you want to find a cat that is hiding somewhere in the house. An algorithm for doing this would be to systematically search every room in the house (being careful not to let the cat sneak past you!). If you do this, you will eventually find the cat, although it may take a while. A heuristic for finding the cat would be to first look in the places where the cat likes to hide. So you check under the bed and in the hall closet. This may not always lead to finding the cat, but if it does, it has the advantage of usually being faster than the algorithm.

We say the Gestalt principles are heuristics because, like heuristics, they are best-guess rules that work most of the time, but not necessarily all of the time. For example, consider the following situation in which the Gestalt laws might cause an incorrect perception: As you are hiking in the woods, you stop cold in your tracks because not too far ahead, you see what appears to be an animal lurking behind a tree (Figure 5.26a). The Gestalt laws of organization play a role in creating this perception. You see the two shapes to the left and right of the tree as a single object because of the Gestalt law of similarity (because both shapes are the same color, it is likely that they are part of the same object). Also, good continuation links these two parts into one because the line along the top of the object extends smoothly from one side of the tree to the other. Finally, the image resembles animals you've seen before. For all of these reasons, it is not surprising that you perceive the two objects as part of one animal.

Because you fear that the animal might be dangerous, you take a different path. As your detour takes you around the tree, you notice that the dark shapes aren't an animal after all, but are two oddly shaped tree stumps (Figure 5.26b). So in this case, the Gestalt laws have misled you.

The fact that heuristics are usually faster than algorithms helps explain why the perceptual system is designed to operate in a way that sometimes produces errors. Consider, for example, what the algorithm would be for determining what the shape in Figure 5.26a really is. It would involve walking around the tree, so you can see it from different angles and perhaps taking a closer look at the objects behind the tree. Although this may result in an accurate perception, it is slow and potentially risky (what if the shape actually *is* a dangerous animal?).

The advantage of our Gestalt-based rules of thumb is that they are fast, and correct most of the time. The reason

they work most of the time is that they reflect properties of the environment. For example, in everyday life, objects that are partially hidden often "come out the other side" (good continuation), and objects often have similar large areas of the same color (similarity). We will return to the idea that perception depends on what we know about properties of the environment later in the chapter.

Although the Gestalt approach dates back to the early 1900s, it is still considered an important way to think about perception. Modern researchers have done experiments like Vecera's (Figure 5.24) to study some of the principles of perceptual organization and segregation proposed by the Gestalt psychologists, and they have also considered issues in addition to organization and segregation. We will now describe a more recent approach to object perception called *recognition by components* that is designed to explain how we recognize objects.

Recognition-by-Components Theory

How do we recognize objects in the environment based on the image on the retina? Recognition-by-components (RBC) theory, which was proposed by Irving Biederman (1987), answers this question by proposing that our recognition of objects is based on features called geons, a term that stands for "geometric ions," because just as ions are basic units of molecules (see page 29), these geons are basic units of objects. Figure 5.27a shows a number of geons, which are shapes such as cylinders, rectangular solids, and pyramids. Biederman proposed 36 different geons and suggested that this number of geons is enough to enable us to mentally represent a large proportion of the objects that we can easily recognize. Figure 5.27b shows a few objects that have been constructed from geons.

To understand geons, we need to introduce the concept of **non-accidental properties (NAPs)**. NAPs are properties of *edges* in the retinal image that correspond to the

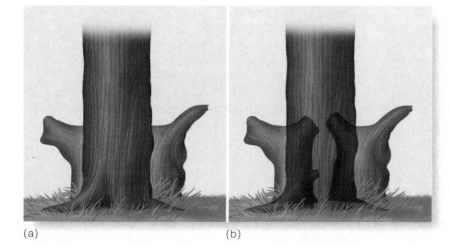

(a)   (b)

Figure 5.26 ▌ (a) What lurks behind the tree? (b) It is two strangely shaped tree stumps, not an animal!

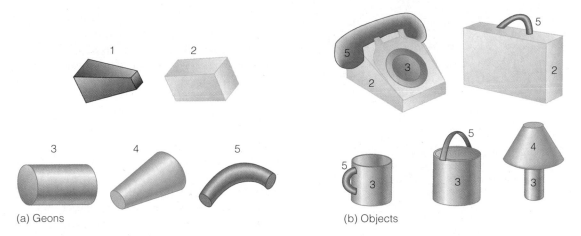

(a) Geons   (b) Objects

Figure 5.27 ▍ (a) Some geons. (b) Some objects created from these geons. The numbers on the objects indicate which geons are present. Note that recognizable objects can be formed by combining just two or three geons. Also note that the relations between the geons matter, as illustrated by the cup and the pail. *(Reprinted from "Recognition-by-Components: A Theory of Human Image Understanding," by I. Biederman, 1985,* Computer Vision, Graphics and Image Processing, 32, 29–73. Copyright © 1985, with permission from Elsevier.)

properties of *edges* in the three-dimensional environment. The following demonstration illustrates this characteristic of NAPs.

DEMONSTRATION

Non-Accidental Properties

Close one eye and look at a coin, such as a quarter, straight on, so your line of sight is perpendicular to the quarter, as shown in Figure 5.28a. When you do this, the edge of the quarter creates a curved image on the retina. Now tilt the quarter, as in Figure 5.28b. The edge of this tilted quarter still creates an image of a curved edge on the retina. Now tilt the quarter so you are viewing it edge-on, as in Figure 5.28c. When viewed in this way, the edge of the quarter creates an image of a straight edge on the retina. ▍

In this demonstration, the property of *curvature* is called a *non-accidental property,* because the only time it doesn't occur is when you view the quarter edge-on. Because this edge-on viewpoint occurs only rarely, it is called an **accidental viewpoint.** Thus, the vast majority of your views of circular objects result in a curved image on the retina. According to RBC, the image of a curved edge on the retina indicates the presence of a curved edge in the environment.

RBC proposes that a key property of geons is that each type of geon has a unique set of NAPs. For example, consider the rectangular-solid geon in Figure 5.29a. The NAP for this geon is three parallel straight edges. You can demonstrate the fact that these edges are NAPs by viewing a rectangular solid (such as a book) from different angles, as shown in Figure 5.30. When you do this, you will notice that most

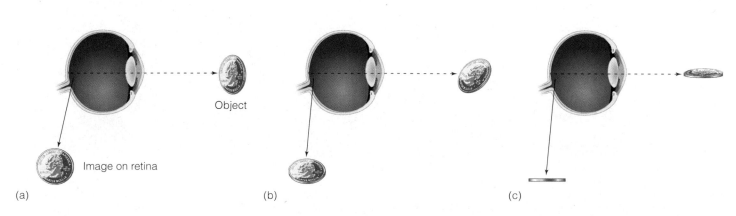

(a)   (b)   (c)

Figure 5.28 ▍ What happens to a quarter's image on the retina as it is tilted. Most views, such as (a) and (b), create a curved image on the retina. The rare accidental viewpoint shown in (c) creates an image of a straight line on the retina.

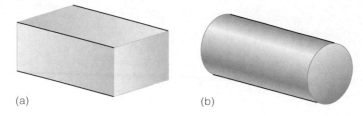

(a)

(b)

Figure 5.29 ❚ (a) Rectangular-solid geon. The highlighted three parallel edges are the non-accidental property for this geon. (b) Cylindrical geon. The highlighted two parallel edges are the non-accidental property of this geon.

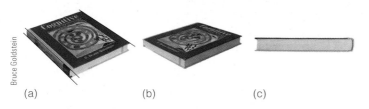

(a)

(b)

(c)

Figure 5.30 ❚ This book's non-accidental property (NAP) of three parallel edges are seen even when the book is viewed from different angles, as in (a) and (b). When viewed from an accidental viewpoint, as in (c), this NAP is not perceived.

of the time you can see three parallel straight edges, as in Figures 5.30a and b. Figure 5.30c shows what happens when you view the book from an accidental viewpoint. The three parallel edges are not visible from this viewpoint, just as the quarter's curvature was not visible when it was viewed from an accidental viewpoint.

The NAP for the cylinder geon in Figure 5.29b is two parallel straight edges, which you see as you view a cylindrical object such as a pencil or pen from different angles. Like the rectangular geon, the cylindrical geon has an accidental

viewpoint from which the NAP is not visible (what is the accidental viewpoint for the cylinder?).

The fact that each geon has a unique set of NAPs results in a property of geons called **discriminability**—each geon can be discriminated from other geons. The fact that NAPs are visible from most viewpoints results in another property of geons, *viewpoint invariance* (see page 103)—the geon can be identified when viewed from most viewpoints.

The main principle of recognition-by-components theory is that if we can perceive an object's geons, we can identify the object (also see Biederman & Cooper, 1991; Biederman, 1995). The ability to identify an object if we can identify its geons is called the **principle of componential recovery**. This principle is what is behind our ability to identify objects in the natural environment even when parts of the objects are hidden by other objects. Figure 5.31a shows a situation in which componential recovery can't occur because the visual noise is arranged so that the object's geons cannot be identified. Luckily, parts of objects are rarely obscured in this way in the natural environment, so, as we see in Figure 5.31b, we can usually identify geons and, therefore, are able to identify the object.

Another illustration of the fact that our ability to identify objects depends on our ability to identify the object's geons is shown by the tea kettle in Figure 5.32a. When we view it from the unusual perspective shown in Figure 5.32b, we can't identify some of its basic geons, and it is therefore more difficult to identify in Figure 5.32b than in Figure 5.32a.

RBC theory also states that we can recognize objects based on a relatively small number of geons. Biederman (1987) did an experiment to demonstrate this, by briefly presenting line drawings of objects with all of their geons and with some geons missing. For example, the airplane in Figure 5.33a, which has a total of 9 geons, is shown with only 3 of its geons in Figure 5.33b. Biederman found that

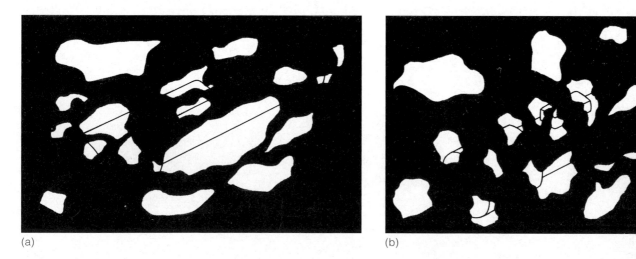

(a)

(b)

Figure 5.31 ❚ (a) It is difficult to identify the object behind the mask, because its geons have been obscured. (b) Now that it is possible to identify geons, the object can be identified as a flashlight. *(Reprinted from "Recognition-by-Components: A Theory of Human Image Understanding," by I. Biederman, 1985,* Computer Vision, Graphics and Image Processing, 32, 29–73. *Copyright © 1985, with permission from Elsevier.)*

Bruce Goldstein

(a)   (b)

Figure 5.32 ▌ (a) A familiar object. (b) The same object seen from a viewpoint that obscures most of its geons. This makes it harder to recognize the object.

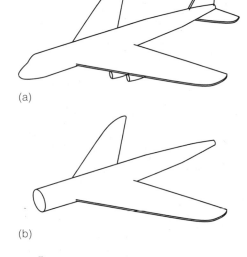

(a)

(b)

Figure 5.33 ▌ An airplane, as represented (a) by 9 geons and (b) by 3 geons. *(Reprinted from "Recognition-by-Components: A Theory of Human Image Understanding," by I. Biederman, 1985, Computer Vision, Graphics and Image Processing, 32, 29–73. Copyright © 1985, with permission from Elsevier.)*

their feathers or markings on their wings. Similarly, there are some things in the environment, such as clouds, that are difficult to create using geons (although even clouds are sometime arranged so that geons are visible, leading us to see "objects" in the sky).

The fact that there are things that RBC can't explain is not surprising because the theory was not meant to explain everything about object perception. For example, although edges play an important role in RBC, the theory is not concerned with the rapid processes that enable us to perceive these edges. It also doesn't deal with the processes involved in grouping objects (which the Gestalt approach does) or with how we learn to recognize different types of objects.

RBC does, however, provide explanations for some important phenomena, such as view invariance and the minimum information needed to identify objects. Some of the most elegant scientific theories are simple and provide partial explanations, leaving other theories to complete the picture. This is the case for RBC.

9-geon objects such as the airplane were recognized correctly about 78 percent of the time based on 3 geons and 96 percent of the time based on 6 geons. Objects with 6 geons were recognized correctly 92 percent of the time even when they were missing half their geons.

RBC theory explains many observations about shape-based object perception, but the idea that our perception of a complex object begins with the perception of features like geons is one that some students find difficult to accept. For example, one of my students who, having read the first four chapters of the book was apparently convinced that perception is a complex process, wrote, in reaction to reading about RBC theory, that "our vision is far too complex to be determined by a few geons."

This student's concern can be addressed in a few ways. First, there are factors in addition to geons that help us identify objects. For example, we might distinguish between two birds with the same shape on the basis of the texture of

TEST YOURSELF 5.1

1. What are some of the problems that make object perception difficult for computers but not for humans?
2. What is structuralism, and why did the Gestalt psychologists propose an alternative to this way of looking at perception?
3. How did the Gestalt psychologists explain perceptual organization?
4. How did the Gestalt psychologists describe figure–ground segregation?
5. What properties of a stimulus tend to favor perceiving an area as "figure"? Be sure you understand Vecera's experiment that showed that the lower region of a display tends to be perceived as figure.
6. How does RBC theory explain how we recognize objects? What are the properties of geons, and how do these properties enable us to identify objects from different viewpoints and identify objects that are partially hidden?

Perceiving Scenes and Objects in Scenes

So far we have been focusing on individual objects. But we rarely see objects in isolation. Just as we usually see actors in a play on a stage, we usually see objects within a scene (Epstein, 2005). A **scene** is a view of a real-world environment that contains (1) background elements and (2) multiple objects that are organized in a meaningful way relative to each other and the background (Epstein, 2005; Henderson & Hollingworth, 1999).

One way of distinguishing between objects and scenes is that objects are compact and are *acted upon,* whereas scenes are extended in space and are *acted within.* For example, if we are walking down the street and mail a letter, we would be *acting upon* the mailbox (an object) and *acting within* the street (the scene).

Perceiving the Gist of a Scene

Perceiving scenes presents a paradox. On one hand, scenes are often large and complex. However, despite this size and complexity, you can identify most scenes after viewing them for only a fraction of a second. This general description of the type of scene is called the **gist of a scene.** An example of your ability to rapidly perceive the gist of a scene is the way you can rapidly flip from one TV channel to another, yet still grasp the meaning of each picture as it flashes by—a car chase, quiz contestants, or an outdoor scene with mountains—even though you may be seeing each picture for a second or less. When you do this, you are perceiving the gist of each scene (Oliva & Torralba, 2006).

Research has shown that it is possible to perceive the gist of a scene within a fraction of a second. Mary Potter (1976) showed observers a target picture and then asked them to indicate whether they saw that picture as they viewed a sequence of 16 rapidly presented pictures. Her observers could do this with almost 100-percent accuracy even when the pictures were flashed for only 250 ms (milliseconds; 1/4 second). Even when the target picture was only specified by a description, such as "girl clapping," observers achieved an accuracy of almost 90 percent (Figure 5.34).

Another approach to determining how rapidly people can perceive scenes was used by Li Fei-Fei and coworkers (2007), who presented pictures of scenes for times ranging from 27 ms to 500 ms and asked observers to write a description of what they saw. This method of determining the observer's response is a nice example of the phenomenological method, described on page 13. Fei-Fei used a procedure called *masking* to be sure the observers saw the pictures for exactly the desired duration. **VL 17**

METHOD | **Using a Mask to Achieve Brief Stimulus Presentations**

To present a stimulus, such as a picture, for just 27 ms, we need to do more than just flash the picture for 27 ms, because the perception of any stimulus persists for about 250 ms after the stimulus is extinguished—a phenomenon called **persistence of vision.** Thus, a picture that is presented for 27 ms will be *perceived* as lasting about 275 ms. To eliminate the persistence of vision it is therefore necessary to flash a **masking stimulus,** usually a pattern of randomly oriented lines, immediately after presentation of the picture. This stops the persistence of vision and limits the time that the picture is perceived.

Typical results of Fei-Fei's experiment are shown in Figure 5.35. At brief durations, observers saw only light and dark areas of the pictures. By 67 ms they could identify some large objects (a person, a table), and when the duration was increased to 500 ms they were able to identify smaller objects and details (the boy, the laptop). For another picture, of an ornate 1800s living room, observers were able to identify the picture as a room in a house at 67 ms and to identify details, such as chairs and portraits, at 500 ms. Thus, the overall gist of the scene is perceived first, followed by perception of details and smaller objects within the scene.

What enables observers to perceive the gist of a scene so rapidly? Aude Oliva and Antonio Torralba (2001, 2006) propose that observers use information called **global image**

| Description | 250 ms | 250 ms | 250 ms |

Figure 5.34 ▌ Procedure for Potter's (1976) experiment. She first presented either a target photograph or, as shown here, a description, and then rapidly presented 16 pictures for 250 ms each. The observer's task was to indicate whether the target picture had been presented. In this example, only 3 of the 16 pictures are shown, with the target picture being the second one presented. On other trials, the target picture is not included in the series of 16 pictures.

27 ms	Looked like something black in the center with four straight lines coming out of it against a white background. (Subject: AM)
40 ms	The first thing I could recognize was a dark splotch in the middle. It may have been rectangular-shaped, with a curved top... but that's just a guess. (Subject: KM)
67 ms	A person, I think, sitting down or crouching. Facing the left side of the picture. We see their profile mostly. They were at a table or where some object was in front of them (to their left side in the picture). (Subject: EC)
500 ms	This looks like a father or somebody helping a little boy. The man had something in his hands, like a LCD screen or a laptop. They looked like they were standing in a cubicle. (Subject: WC)

Figure 5.35 ▌ Observers' descriptions of a photograph presented in Fei-Fei's (2007) experiment. Viewing durations are indicated on the left. *(From Fei-Fei, L., Iyer, A., Koch C., & Perona, P. (2007). What do we perceive in a glance of a real world scene? Journal of Vision, 7, 1–29, Figure 13. © ARVO.)*

features, which can be perceived rapidly and are associated with specific types of scenes. Some of the global image features proposed by Oliva and Torralba are:

- *Degree of naturalness.* Natural scenes, such as the beach and forest in Figure 5.36, have textured zones and undulating contours. Man-made scenes, such as the street, are dominated by straight lines and horizontals and verticals.

- *Degree of openness.* Open scenes, such as the beach, often have a visible horizon line and contain few objects. The street scene is also open, although not as much as the beach. The forest is an example of a scene with a low degree of openness.

- *Degree of roughness.* Smooth scenes (low roughness) like the beach contain fewer small elements. Scenes with high roughness like the forest contain many small elements and are more complex.

- *Degree of expansion.* The convergence of parallel lines, like what you see when you look down railroad tracks that appear to vanish in the distance, or in the street scene in Figure 5.36, indicates a high degree of expansion. This feature is especially dependent on the observer's viewpoint. For example, in the street scene, looking directly at the side of a building would result in low expansion.

- *Color.* Some scenes have characteristic colors, like the beach scene (blue) and the forest (green and brown). (Goffaux et al., 2005)

Global image features are *holistic* and *rapidly perceived.* They are properties of the scene as a whole and do not depend on time-consuming processes such as perceiving small details, recognizing individual objects, or separating one object from another. Another property of global image features is that they contain information that results in perception of a scene's structure and spatial layout. For example, the degree of openness and the degree of expansion refer directly to characteristics of a scene's layout, and naturalness also provides layout information that comes from knowing whether a scene is "from nature" or contains "human-made structures."

Global image properties not only help explain how we can perceive the gist of scenes based on features that can be seen in brief exposures, but also illustrate the following general property of perception: Our past experiences in perceiving properties of the environment plays a role in determining our perceptions. We learn, for example, that blue is associated with open sky, that landscapes are often green and smooth, and that verticals and horizontals are associated with buildings. Characteristics of the environment such as this, which occur frequently, are called **regularities in the environment**. We will now describe these regularities in more detail.

Regularities in the Environment: Information for Perceiving

Although observers make use of regularities in the environment to help them perceive, they are often unaware of the specific information they are using. This aspect of perception is similar to what occurs when we use language. Even though people easily string words together to create sentences in conversations, they may not know the rules of grammar that specify how these words are being combined.

Courtesy of Aude Oliva

Figure 5.36 ▌ Three scenes that have different global image features. See text for description.

Similarly, we easily use our knowledge of regularities in the environment to help us perceive, even though we may not be able to identify the specific information we are using. We can distinguish two types of regularities, *physical regularities* and *semantic regularities*.

Physical Regularities Physical regularities are regularly occurring physical properties of the environment. For example, there are more vertical and horizontal orientations in the environment than oblique (angled) orientations. This occurs in human-made environment (for example, buildings contain lots of horizontals and verticals) and also in natural environments (trees and plants are more likely to be vertical or horizontal than slanted) (Coppola et al., 1998). It is, therefore, no coincidence that people can perceive horizontals and verticals more easily than other orientations, an effect called the **oblique effect** (Appelle, 1972; Campbell et al., 1966; Orban et al., 1984).

Why should being exposed to more verticals and horizontals make it easier to see them? One answer to this question is that *experience-dependent plasticity,* introduced in Chapter 4 (see page 80), causes the visual system to have more neurons that respond best to these orientations. The fact that the visual system has a greater proportion of neurons that respond to verticals and horizontals has been demonstrated in experiments that have recorded from large numbers of neurons in the visual cortex of the monkey (R. L. Devalois et al., 1982; also see Furmanski & Engel, 2000, for evidence that the visual cortex in humans responds better to verticals and horizontals than to other orientations).

Another physical characteristic of the environment is that when one object partially covers another, the contour of the partially covered object "comes out the other side." If this sounds familiar, it is because it is an example of the Gestalt law of good continuation, which we introduced on page 106 and discussed in conjunction with our "creature" behind the tree on page 110 (Figure 5.26). Other Gestalt laws (or "heuristics") reflect regularities in the environment as well.

Consider, for example, the idea of uniform connectedness. Objects are often defined by areas of the same color or texture, so when an area of the image on the retina has the property of uniform connectedness, it is likely that this area arises from a single environmental shape (Palmer & Rock, 1994). Thus, uniformly connected regions are regularities in the environment, and the perceptual system is designed to interpret these regions so that the environment will be perceived correctly. The Gestalt heuristics are therefore based on the kinds of things that occur so often that we take them for granted. Another physical regularity is illustrated by the following demonstration.

DEMONSTRATION

Shape From Shading

What do you perceive in Figure 5.37a? Do some of the discs look as though they are sticking out, like parts of three-dimensional spheres, and others appear to be indentations? If you do see the discs in this way, notice that the ones that appear to be sticking out are arranged in a square. After observing this, turn the page over so the small dot is on the bottom. Does this change your perception? ▌

Figures 5.37b and c show that if we assume that light is coming from above (which is usually the case in the environment), then patterns like the circles that are light on the top would be created by an object that bulges out (Figure 5.37b), but a pattern like the circles that are light on the bottom would be created by an indentation in a surface (Figure 5.37c). The assumption that light is coming from above has been called the **light-from-above heuristic** (Kleffner & Ramachandran, 1992). Apparently, people make the light-from-above assumption because most light in our environment comes from above. This includes the sun, as well as most artificial light sources.

Another example of the light-from-above heuristic at work is provided by the two pictures in Figure 5.38. Figure 5.38a shows indentations created by people walking in the sand. But when we turn this picture upside down, as

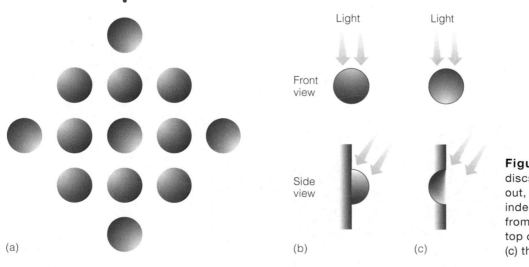

Figure 5.37 ▌ (a) Some of these discs are perceived as jutting out, and some are perceived as indentations. Why? Light coming from above would illuminate (b) the top of a shape that is jutting out and (c) the bottom of an indentation.

(a)　　　　　　　　　　(b)　　　　　　　　(c)

(a)   (b)

Figure 5.38 ▐ Why does (a) look like indentations in the sand and (b) look like mounds of sand? See text for explanation.

shown in Figure 5.38b, then the indentations in the sand become rounded mounds. [VL] **18–20**

It is clear from these examples of physical regularities in the environment that one of the reasons humans are able to perceive and recognize objects and scenes so much better than computer-guided robots is that our system is customized to respond to the physical characteristics of our environment. But this customization goes beyond physical characteristics. It also occurs because we have learned about what types of objects typically occur in specific types of scenes.

Semantic Regularities In language, *semantics* refers to the meanings of words or sentences. Applied to perceiving scenes, semantics refers to the meaning of a scene. This meaning is often related to the function of a scene—what happens within it. For example, food preparation, cooking, and perhaps eating occur in a kitchen; waiting around, buying tickets, checking luggage, and going through security checkpoints happens in airports. **Semantic regularities** are the characteristics associated with the functions carried out in different types of scenes.

One way to demonstrate that people are aware of semantic regularities is simply to ask them to imagine a particular type of scene or object, as in the following demonstration.

DEMONSTRATION

Visualizing Scenes and Objects

Your task in this demonstration is simple—visualize or simply think about the following scenes and objects:

1. An office
2. The clothing section of a department store
3. A microscope
4. A lion ▐

Most people who have grown up in modern society have little trouble visualizing an office or the clothing section of a department store. What is important about this ability, for our purposes, is that part of this visualization involves details within these scenes. Most people see an office as hav-

ing a desk with a computer on it, bookshelves, and a chair. The department store scene may contain racks of clothes, a changing room, and perhaps a cash register.

What did you see when you visualized the microscope or the lion? Many people report seeing not just a single object, but an object within a setting. Perhaps you perceived the microscope sitting on a lab bench or in a laboratory, and the lion in a forest or on a savannah or in a zoo.

An example of the knowledge we have of things that typically belong in certain scenes is provided by an experiment in which Andrew Hollingworth (2005) had observers study a scene, such as the picture of the gym in Figure 5.39 (but without the circles), that contained a target object, such

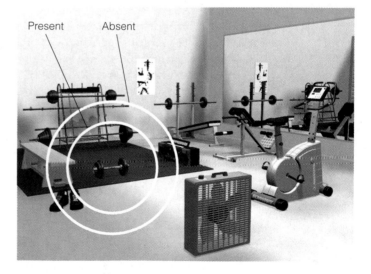

Figure 5.39 ▐ Hollingworth's (2005) observers saw scenes like this one (but without the circles). In this scene the target object is the barbell, although observers do not know this when they are viewing the scene. "Non-target" scenes are the same but do not include the target. The circles indicate the average error of observers' judgments of the position of the target object for trials in which they had seen the object in the scene (small circle) and trials in which the object had not appeared in the scene (larger circle). *(From A. Hollingsworth, 2005, Memory for object position in natural scenes. Visual Cognition, 12, 1003–1016. Reprinted by permission of the publisher, Taylor & Francis Ltd., http://www.tandf.co.uk/ journals.)*

as the barbell on the mat, or the same scene but without the target object, for 20 seconds. Observers then saw a picture of a target object followed by a blank screen, and were asked to indicate where the target object was in the scene (if they had seen the picture containing the target object) or where they would *expect* to see the target object in the scene (if they had seen the same picture but without the target object).

The results are indicated by the circles, which show the averaged error of observers' judgments for many different objects and scenes. The small circle shows that observers who saw the target objects accurately located their positions in the scene. The large circle shows that observers who had not seen the target objects were not quite as accurate but were still able to predict where the target objects would be. What this means for the gym scene is that observers were apparently able to predict where the barbell would appear based on their prior experience in seeing objects in gyms.

This effect of semantic knowledge on our ability to perceive was illustrated in an experiment by Stephen Palmer (1975), using stimuli like the picture in Figure 5.40. Palmer first presented a context scene such as the one on the left and then briefly flashed one of the target pictures on the right. When Palmer asked observers to identify the object in the target picture, they correctly identified an object like the loaf of bread (which is appropriate to the kitchen scene) 80 percent of the time, but correctly identified the mailbox or the drum (two objects that don't fit into the scene) only 40 percent of the time. Apparently Palmer's observers were using their knowledge about kitchens to help them perceive the briefly flashed loaf of bread.

The effect of semantic regularities is also illustrated in Figure 5.41, which is called "the multiple personalities of a blob" (Oliva & Torralba, 2007). The blob is perceived as different objects depending on its orientation and the context within which it is seen. It appears to be an object on a table in (b), a shoe on a person bending down in (c), and a car and a person crossing the street in (d), even though it is the same shape in all of the pictures.

Figure 5.41 ▌ What we expect to see in different contexts influences our interpretation of the identity of the "blob" inside the circles. *(Part (d) adapted from* Trends in Cognitive Sciences, *Vol. 11, 12, Oliva, A., and Torralba, A., The role of context in object recognition. Copyright 2007, with permission from Elsevier.)*

The Role of Inference in Perception

People use their knowledge of physical and semantic regularities such as the ones we have been describing to *infer* what is present in a scene. The idea that perception involves inference is nothing new; it was proposed in the 18th century by Hermann von Helmholtz (1866/1911) who was one of the preeminent physiologists and physicists of his day.

Helmholtz made many discoveries in physiology and physics, developed the ophthalmoscope (the device that an optometrist or ophthalmologist uses to look into your eye), and proposed theories of object perception, color vision, and hearing. One of his proposals about perception is a principle called the **theory of unconscious inference**, which states

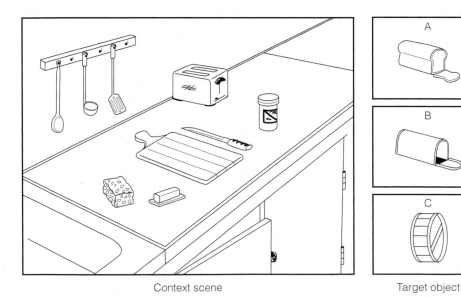

Context scene

Figure 5.40 ▌ Stimuli used in Palmer's (1975) experiment. The scene at the left is presented first, and the observer is then asked to identify one of the objects on the right.

Target object

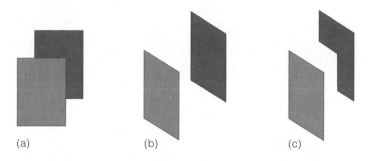

(a)   (b)   (c)

Figure 5.42 ∎ The display in (a) is usually interpreted as being (b) a blue rectangle in front of a red rectangle. It could, however, be (c) a blue rectangle and an appropriately positioned six-sided red figure.

that some of our perceptions are the result of unconscious assumptions we make about the environment.

The theory of unconscious inference was proposed to account for our ability to create perceptions from stimulus information that can be seen in more than one way. For example, what do you see in the display in Figure 5.42a? Most people perceive a blue rectangle in front of a red rectangle, as shown in Figure 5.42b. But as Figure 5.42c indicates, this display could have been caused by a six-sided red shape positioned either in front of or behind the blue rectangle. According to the theory of unconscious inference, we infer that Figure 5.42a is a rectangle covering another rectangle because of experiences we have had with similar situations in the past. A corollary of the theory of unconscious inference is the **likelihood principle**, which states that we perceive the object that is *most likely* to have caused the pattern of stimuli we have received.

One reason that Helmholtz proposed the likelihood principle is to deal with the ambiguity of the perceptual stimulus that we described at the beginning of the chapter. Helmholtz viewed the process of perception as being similar to the process involved in solving a problem. For perception, the task is to determine which object caused a particular pattern of stimulation, and this problem is solved by a process in which the observer brings his or her knowledge of the environment to bear in order to infer what the object might be. This process is unconscious, hence the term *unconscious inference*. (See Rock, 1983, for a modern version of this idea.)

Modern psychologists have quantified Helmholtz's idea of perception as inference by using a statistical technique called **Bayesian inference** that takes probabilities into account (Kersten et al., 2004; Yuille & Kersten, 2006). For example, let's say we want to determine how likely it is that it will rain tomorrow. If we know it rained today, then this increases the chances that it will rain tomorrow, because if it rains one day it is more likely to rain the next day. Applying reasoning like this to perception, we can ask, for example, whether a given object in a kitchen is a loaf of bread or a mailbox. Since it is more likely that a loaf of bread will be in a kitchen, the perceptual system concludes that bread is present. Bayesian statistics involves this type of reasoning, expressed in mathematical formulas that we won't describe here.

Revisiting the Science Project: Designing a Perceiving Machine

We are now ready to return to the science project (see pages 4 and 100) and to apply what we know about perception to the problem of designing a device that can identify objects in the environment. We can now see that one way to make our device more effective would be to program in knowledge about regularities in the environment. In other words, an effective "object perceiving machine" would be able to go beyond processing information about light, dark, shape, and colors that it might pick up with its sensors. It would also be "tuned" to respond best to regularities of the environment that are most likely to occur, and would be programmed to use this information to make inferences about what is out there.

Will robotic vision devices ever equal the human ability to perceive? Based on our knowledge of the complexities of perception, it is easy to say "no," but given the rapid advances that are occurring in the field of computer vision, it is not unreasonable to predict that machines will eventually be developed that approach human perceptual abilities. One reason to think that machines are gaining on humans is that present-day computers have begun incorporating humanlike inference processes into their programs. For example, consider CMU's vehicle "Boss," the winner of the "Urban Challenge" race (see page 101). One reason for Boss's success was that it was programmed to take into account common events that occur when driving on city streets.

Consider, for example, what happens when a human driver (like you) approaches an intersection. You probably check to see if you have a stop sign, then determine if other cars are approaching from the left or right. If they are approaching, you notice whether they have a stop sign. If they do, you might check to be sure they are slowing down in preparation for stopping. If you decide they might ignore their stop sign, you might slow down and prepare to take appropriate action. If you see that there are no cars coming, you proceed across the intersection. In other words, as you drive, you are constantly noticing what is happening and are taking into account your knowledge of traffic regulations and situations you have experienced in the past to make decisions about what to do.

The Boss vehicle is programmed to carry out a similar type of decision-making process to determine what to do when it reaches an intersection. It determines if another car is approaching by using its sensors to detect objects off to the side. It then decides whether an object is a car by taking its size into account and by using the rule "If it is moving, it is likely to be a car." Boss is also programmed to know that other cars should stop if they have a stop sign. Thus, the computer was designed both to sense what was out there and to go beyond simply sensing by taking knowledge into account to decide what to do at the intersection.

The problem for computer vision systems is that before they can compete with humans they have to acquire a great deal more knowledge. Present systems are programmed with just enough knowledge to accomplish specialized tasks like driving the course in the Urban Challenge. While Boss is programmed to determine where the street is and to always stay on the street, Boss can't always make good decisions about when it is safe to drive off-road. For example, Boss can't tell the difference between tall grass (which wouldn't pose much of a threat for off-road driving) and a field full of vertical spikes (which would be very unfriendly to Boss's tires) (C. Urmson, personal communication, 2007).[1]

To program the computer to recognize grass, it would be necessary to provide it with knowledge about grass such as "Grass is green," "Grass moves if it is windy," "Grass is flat and comes to a point." Once Boss has enough knowledge about grass to accurately identify it, then it can be programmed not to avoid it, and to drive off-road onto it if necessary. What all of this means is that while it is helpful to have lots of computing power, it is also nice to have knowledge about the environment. The human model of the perceiving machine has this knowledge, and uses it to perceive with impressive accuracy.

The Physiology of Object and Scene Perception

Thousands of experiments have been done to answer the question "What is the neural basis of object perception?" We have seen that object perception has many aspects, including perceptual organization, grouping, recognizing objects, and perceiving scenes and details within scenes. We first consider neurons that respond to perceptual grouping and figure–ground.

Neurons That Respond to Perceptual Grouping and Figure–Ground

Many years after the Gestalt psychologists proposed the laws of good continuation and similarity, researchers discovered neurons in the visual cortex that respond best to displays that reflect these principles of grouping. For example, Figure 5.43a shows a vertical line in the receptive field (indicated by the square) of a neuron in a monkey's striate cortex. The neuron's response to this single line is indicated by the left bar in Figure 5.43d. No firing occurs when lines are presented outside the square (Zapadia et al., 1995).

But something interesting happens when we add a field of randomly oriented lines, as in Figure 5.43b. These lines, which fall outside the neuron's receptive field, cause a decrease in how rapidly the neuron fires to the single vertical line. This effect of the stimuli that fall outside of the neuron's receptive field (which normally would not affect the neuron's firing rate), is called **contextual modulation**, because the context within which the bar appears affects the neuron's response to the bar.

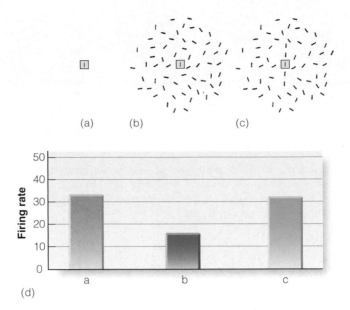

Figure 5.43 ▌ How a neuron in the striate cortex (V1) responds to (a) an oriented bar inside the neuron's receptive field (the small square); (b) the same bar surrounded by randomly oriented bars; (c) the bar when it becomes part of a group of vertical bars, due to the principles of similarity and good continuation. *(Adapted from Zapadia, M. K., Ito, M., Gilbert, C. G., & Westheimer, G. (1995). Improvement in visual sensitivity by changes in local context: Parallel studies in human observers and in V1 of alert monkeys.* Neuron, 15, *843–856. Copyright © 1995, with permission from Elsevier.)*

Figure 5.43c shows that we can increase the neuron's response to the bar by arranging a few of the lines that are outside the receptive field so that they are lined up with the line that is in the receptive field. When good continuation and similarity cause our receptive-field line to become perceptually grouped with these other lines, the neuron's response increases. This neuron is therefore affected by Gestalt organization even though this organization involves areas outside its receptive field.

Another example of how an area outside the receptive field can affect responding is shown in Figure 5.44. This neuron, in the visual cortex, responds well when leftward-slanted lines are positioned over the neuron's receptive field (indicated by the green bar in Figure 5.44a; Lamme, 1995). Notice that in this case we perceive the leftward slanting bars as a square on a background of right-slanted lines. However, when we replace the right-slanted "background" lines with left-slanted lines, as in Figure 5.44b, the neuron no longer fires.

Notice that when we replaced the right-slanted background lines with left-slanted lines the *stimulus* on the receptive field (left-slanted lines) did not change, but our *perception* of these lines changed from being part of a *figure* (in Figure 5.44a) to being part of the background (Figure 5.44b). This neuron therefore responds to right-slanted lines only when they are seen as being part of the figure. (Also see Qui & von der Heydt, 2005).

---

[1]Chris Urmson is Director of Technology, Tartan Racing Team, Carnegie Mellon University.

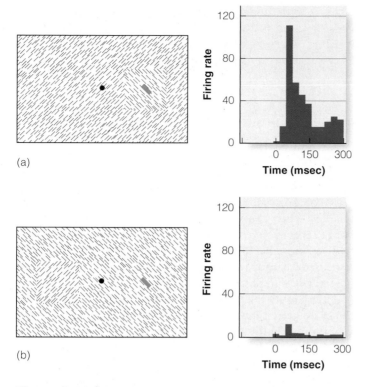

(a)

(b)

Figure 5.44 ▌ How a neuron in V1 responds to oriented lines presented to the neuron's receptive field (green rectangle). (a) The neuron responded when the bars on the receptive field are part of a figure, but there is no response when (b) the same pattern is not part of a figure. *Adapted from Lamme, V. A. F. (1995). The neurophysiology of figure–ground segregation in primary visual cortex.* Journal of Neuroscience, 15, *1605–1615.*

How Does the Brain Respond to Objects?

How are objects represented by the firing of neurons in the brain? To begin answering this question, let's review the basic principles of sensory coding we introduced in Chapters 2 and 4.

Review of Sensory Coding In Chapter 2 we described *specificity coding,* which occurs if an object is represented by the firing of a neuron that fires *only* to that object, and *distributed coding,* which occurs if an object is represented by the *pattern* of firing of a number of neurons. In Chapter 4 we introduced the idea that certain areas are specialized to process information about specific types of objects. We called these specialized areas *modules.* Three of these areas are the fusiform face area (FFA), for faces; the extrastriate body area (EBA), for bodies; and the parahippocampal place area (PPA), for buildings and places. Although neurons in these areas respond to specific types of stimuli, they aren't totally specialized, so a particular neuron that responds only to faces responds to a number of different faces (Tsao et al., 2006). Objects, according to this idea, are represented by distributed coding, so a specific face would be represented by the pattern of firing of a number of neurons that respond to faces.

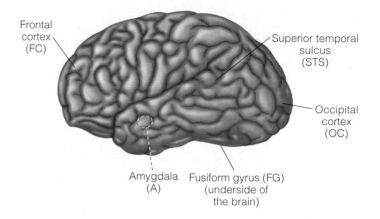

Figure 5.45 ▌ The human brain, showing some of the areas involved in perceiving faces. Some of the perceptual functions of these areas are: OC = initial processing; FG = identification; A = emotional reaction; STS = gaze direction; FC = atttractiveness. The amygdala is located deep inside the cortex, approximately under the ellipse.

We also noted that even though modules are specialized to process information about specific types of stimuli such as faces, places, and bodies, objects typically cause activity not only in a number of neurons within a module, but also in a number of different areas of the brain. Thus, a face might cause a large amount of activity in the FFA, but also cause activity in other areas as well. Firing is, therefore, distributed in two ways: (1) across groups of neurons within a specific area, and (2) across different areas in the brain.

More Evidence for Distributed Activity Across the Brain We begin our discussion where we left off in Chapter 4—with the idea that objects cause activity in a number of different brain areas. Faces provide one of the best examples of distributed representation across the brain. We know that the fusiform face area (FFA) is specialized to process information about faces, because the FFA responds to pictures of faces but not to pictures of other types of stimuli.

But perceiving a face involves much more than just looking at a face and identifying it as "a face," or even as "Bill's face." After you have identified a face as, say, your friend Bill, you may have an emotional reaction to Bill based on the expression on his face or on your past experience with him. You may notice whether he is looking straight at you or off to the side. You may even be thinking about how attractive (or unattractive) he is. Each of these reactions to faces has been linked to activity in different areas of the brain.

Figure 5.45 shows some of the areas involved in face perception. Initial processing of the face occurs in the occipital cortex, which sends signals to the fusiform gyrus, where visual information concerned with identification of the face is processed (Grill-Spector et al., 2004). Emotional aspects of the face, including facial expression and the observer's emotional reaction to the face, are reflected in activation of the amygdala, which is located within the brain (Gobbini & Haxby, 2007; Ishai et al., 2004).

Evaluation of where a person is looking is linked to activity in the superior temporal sulcus; this area is also involved in perceiving movements of a person's mouth as the person speaks (Calder et al., 2007; Puce et al., 1998). Evaluation of a face's attractiveness is linked to activity in the frontal area of the brain.

The fact that all, or most, of these factors come into play when we perceive a face has led to the conclusion that there is a distributed system in the cortex for perceiving faces (Haxby et al., 2000; Ishai, 2008). The activation caused by other objects is also distributed, with most objects activating a number of different areas in the brain (Shinkareva et al., 2008).

Connecting Neural Activity and Perception

The results we have been describing involved experiments in which a stimulus was presented and brain activity was measured. Other experiments have gone beyond simply observing which stimulus causes firing in specific areas to studying connections between brain activity and what a person or animal *perceives.*

One of these experiments, by Kalanit Grill-Spector and coworkers (2004), studied the question of how activation of the brain is related to whether a person recognizes an object by measuring brain activation as human observers identified pictures of the face of a well-known person—Harrison Ford. They focused on the fusiform face area (FFA). To locate the FFA in each person, they used a method called the region-of-interest (ROI) approach.

METHOD | Region-of-Interest Approach

One of the challenges of brain imaging research is that although maps have been published indicating the location of different areas of the brain, there is a great deal of variation from person to person in the exact location of a particular area. The **region-of-interest (ROI) approach** deals with this problem by pretesting people on the stimuli to be studied before running an experiment. For example, in the study we are going to describe, Grill-Spector located the FFA in each observer by presenting pictures of faces and nonfaces and noting the area that was preferentially activated by faces. Locating this ROI before doing the experiment enabled researchers to focus on the exact area of the brain that, *for each individual person,* was specialized to process information about faces.

Once Grill-Spector determined the location of the FFA for each observer, she presented stimuli as shown in Figure 5.46. On each trial, observers saw either (a) a picture of Harrison Ford, (b) a picture of another person's face, or (c) a random texture. Each of these stimuli was presented briefly (about 50 ms) followed immediately by a random-pattern mask, which limited the visibility of each stimulus to just 50 ms (see Method: Using a Mask to Achieve Brief Stimulus Presentations, page 114).

The observer's task in this experiment was to indicate, after presentation of the mask, whether the picture was "Harrison Ford," "another object," or "nothing." This is the "observer's response" in Figure 5.46. The results, based on presentation of 60 different pictures of Harrison Ford, 60 pictures of other faces, and 60 random textures, are shown in Figure 5.47. This figure shows the course of brain activation for the trials in which Harrison Ford's face was presented. The top curve (red) shows that activation was greatest when observers correctly identified the stimulus as Harrison Ford's face. The next curve shows that activation was less when they responded "other object" to Harrison Ford's face. In this case they detected the stimulus as a face but were not able to identify it as Harrison Ford's face. The lowest curve indicates that there was little activation when observers could not even tell that a face was presented.

Remember that all of the curves in Figure 5.47 represent the brain activity that occurred not when observers were responding verbally, but *during presentation* of Harrison Ford's face. These results therefore show that neural activity that occurs *as a person is looking at a stimulus* is determined not only by the stimulus that is presented, but also by how a person is processing the stimulus. A large neural response is associated with processing that results in the ability to *identify* the stimulus; a smaller response, with *detecting* the stimulus; and the absence of a response with missing the stimulus altogether.

Connections between neural responses and perception have also been determined by using a perceptual phenomenon called **binocular rivalry**: If one image is presented to the left eye and a different image is presented to the right eye, perception alternates back and forth between the two eyes. For example, if the sunburst pattern in Figure 5.48 is presented only to the left eye, and the butterfly is presented only to the right eye, a person would see the sunburst part of the time and the butterfly part of the time, but never both together.

D. L. Sheinberg and Nikos Logothetis (1997) presented a sunburst pattern to a monkey's left eye and a picture such as the butterfly or another animal or object to the monkey's right eye. To determine what the monkey was perceiving, they trained the monkey to pull one lever when it perceived the sunburst pattern and another lever when it perceived the butterfly. As the monkey was reporting what it was perceiving,

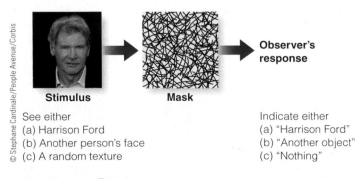

See either
(a) Harrison Ford
(b) Another person's face
(c) A random texture

Indicate either
(a) "Harrison Ford"
(b) "Another object"
(c) "Nothing"

© Stephane Cardinale/People Avenue/Corbis

Figure 5.46 ▌ Procedure for the Grill-Spector et al. (2004) experiment. See text for details.

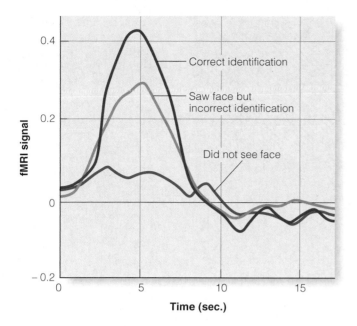

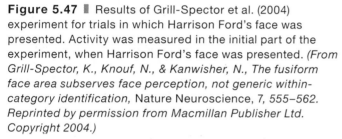

Figure 5.47 ▌ Results of Grill-Spector et al. (2004) experiment for trials in which Harrison Ford's face was presented. Activity was measured in the initial part of the experiment, when Harrison Ford's face was presented. *(From Grill-Spector, K., Knouf, N., & Kanwisher, N., The fusiform face area subserves face perception, not generic within-category identification,* Nature Neuroscience, 7, 555–562. *Reprinted by permission from Macmillan Publisher Ltd. Copyright 2004.)*

they simultaneously recorded the activity of a neuron in the inferotemporal (IT) cortex that had previously been shown to respond to the butterfly but not to the sunburst. The result of this experiment was straightforward: The cell fired vigorously when the monkey was perceiving the butterfly and ceased firing when the monkey was perceiving the sunburst.

Left eye
(Neuron doesn't fire when monkey sees this.)

Right eye
(Neuron fires when monkey sees this.)

Figure 5.48 ▌ Stimuli used by Sheinberg and Logothetis (1997). The "sunburst" stimulus was presented to the monkey's left eye and the butterfly to the right eye. See text for details. *(From Sheinberg, D. L., & Logothetis, N. K., The role of temporal cortical areas in perceptual organization,* Proceedings of the National Academy of Sciences, 94, *1997, pp. 3408–3413. Copyright © 1997 National Academy of Sciences, U.S.A. All rights reserved. Reproduced by permission.)*

Consider what happened in this experiment. The images on the monkey's retinas remained the same throughout the experiment—the sunburst was always positioned on the left retina, and the butterfly was always positioned on the right retina. The change in perception from "sunburst" to "butterfly" must therefore have been happening in the monkey's brain, and this experiment showed that these changes in perception were linked to changes in the firing of a neuron in the brain.

This binocular rivalry procedure has also been used to connect perception and neural responding in humans by using fMRI. Frank Tong and coworkers (1998) presented a picture of a person's face to one eye and a picture of a house to the other eye, by having observers view the pictures through colored glasses, as shown in Figure 5.49. The images are shown as overlapping in this figure, but because each eye

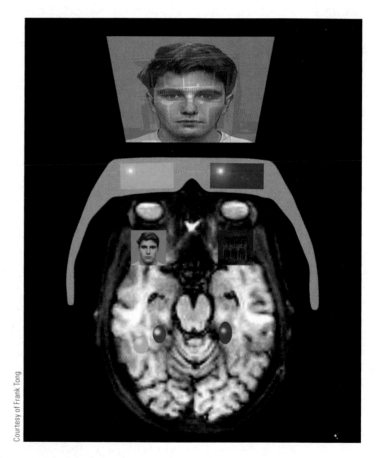

Figure 5.49 ▌ Observers in the Tong et al. (1998) experiment viewed the overlapping red house and green face through red-green glasses, so the house image was presented to the right eye and the face image to the left eye. Because of binocular rivalry, the observers' perception alternated back and forth between the face and the house. When the observers perceived the house, activity occurred in the parahippocampal place area (PPA), in the left and right hemispheres (red ellipses). When observers perceived the face, activity occurred in the fusiform face area (FFA) in the left hemisphere (green ellipse). *(From Tong, F., Nakayama, K., Vaughn, J. T., & Kanwisher, N., 1998, Binocular rivalry and visual awareness in human extrastriate cortex.* Neuron, 21, 753–759.)*

received only one of the images, binocular rivalry occurred. Observers perceived either the face alone or the house alone, and these perceptions alternated back and forth every few seconds.

Tong determined what the observers were perceiving by having them push a button when perceiving the house and another button when perceiving the face. As the observer's perception was flipping back and forth between the house and the face, Tong measured the fMRI response in the para-hippocampal place area (PPA) and the fusiform face area (FFA). When observers were perceiving the house, activity increased in the PPA (and decreased in the FFA); when they were perceiving the face, activity increased in the FFA (and decreased in the PPA). This result is therefore similar to what Sheinberg and Logothetis found in single neurons in the monkey. Even though the image on the retina remained the same throughout the experiment, activity in the brain changed, depending on what the person was experiencing.

Something to Consider: Models of Brain Activity That Can Predict What a Person Is Looking At

When you look at a scene, a pattern of activity occurs in your brain that represents the scene. When you look somewhere else, a new pattern occurs that represents the new scene. Is it possible to tell what scene a person is looking at by monitoring his or her brain activity? Some recent research has brought us closer to achieving this feat and has furthered our understanding of the connection between brain activity and perception.

Yakiyasui Kamitani and Frank Tong (2005) took a step toward being able to "decode" brain activity by measuring observers' fMRI response to grating stimuli—alternating black and white bars like the one in Figure 5.50a. They presented gratings with a number of different orientations (the one in Figure 5.50a slants 45 degrees to the right, for example) and determined the response to these gratings in a number of fMRI voxels. A *voxel* is a small cube-shaped area of the brain about 2 or 3 mm on each side. (The size of a voxel depends on the resolution of the fMRI scanner. Scanners are being developed that will be able to resolve areas smaller than 2 or 3 mm on a side.)

One of the properties of fMRI voxels is that there is some variability in how different voxels respond. For example, the small cubes representing voxels in Figure 5.50a show that the 45-degree grating causes slight differences in the responses of different voxels. A grating with a different orientation would cause a different pattern of activity in these voxels. By using the information provided by the responses of many voxels, Kamitani and Tong were able to create an "orientation decoder," which was able to determine what orientation a person was looking at based on the person's

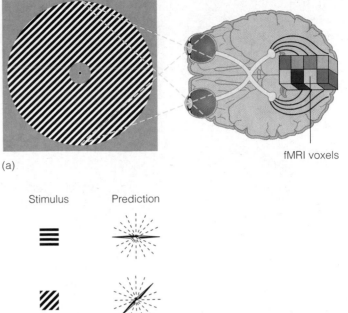

(a)

Stimulus   Prediction

(b)

Figure 5.50 ▮ (a) Observers in Kamitani and Tong's (2005) experiment viewed oriented gratings like the one on the left. The cubes in the brain represent the response of 8 voxels. The activity of 400 voxels was monitored in the experiment. (b) Results for two orientations. The gratings are the stimuli presented to the observer. The line on the right is the orientation predicted by the orientation decoder. The decoder was able to accurately predict when each of the 8 orientations was presented. *(From Kamitani, Y., & Tong, F., Decoding the visual and subjective contents of the human brain, Nature Neuroscience, 8, 679–685. Reprinted by permission of Macmillan Publishers Ltd. Copyright 2005.)*

brain activity. They created this decoder by measuring the response of 400 voxels in the primary visual cortex (V1) and a neighboring area called V2 to gratings with eight different orientations. They then carried out a statistical analysis on the patterns of voxel activity for each orientation to create an orientation decoder designed to analyze the pattern of activity recorded from a person's brain and predict which orientation the person was looking at.

Kaminiti and Tong demonstrated the predictive power of their orientation decoder by presenting oriented gratings to an observer and feeding the resulting fMRI response into the decoder, which predicted which orientation had been presented. The results, shown in Figure 5.50b, show that the decoder accurately predicted the orientations that were presented.

In another test of the decoder, Kaminiti and Tong presented two overlapping gratings, creating a lattice like the one in Figure 5.51, and asked their observers to pay attention to one of the orientations. Because attending to each orientation resulted in different patterns of brain activity, the decoder was able to predict which of the orientations the person was paying attention to. Think about what this means.

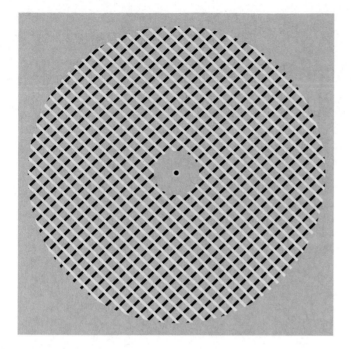

Figure 5.51 ‖ The overlapping grating stimulus used for Kaminiti and Tong's (2005) experiment, in which observers were told to pay attention to one of the orientations at a time. *(From Kamitani, Y., & Tong, F., Decoding the visual and subjective contents of the human brain,* Nature Neuroscience, *8, 679–685. Reprinted by permission of Macmillan Publishers Ltd. Copyright 2005.)*

Present 1,750 images

Measure response of each of the 500 voxels to all 1,750 images

One of the 500 voxels

Response properties of this voxel calculated based on its response to the images

Photos by Bruce Goldstein

Figure 5.52 ‖ The first part of the Kay et al. (2008) experiment, in which the scene decoder was created. They determined the response properties of 500 voxels in the striate cortex by measuring the response of each voxel as they presented 1,750 images to an observer. Three images like the ones Kay used are shown here. The cube represents one of the 500 voxels. The scene decoder was created by determining how each of the 500 voxels responded to an image's position in space, orientation, and level of detail.

If you were in Kaminiti and Tong's laboratory looking over their observer's shoulder as he or she was observing the overlapping gratings, you would have no way of knowing exactly what the person was perceiving. But by consulting the orientation decoder, you could find out which orientation the observer was focusing on. The orientation decoder essentially provides a window into the person's mind.

But what about stimuli that are more complex than oriented gratings? Kendrick Kay and coworkers (2008) have created a new decoder that can determine which photograph of a natural scene has been presented to an observer. In the first part of their experiment, they presented 1,750 black and white photographs of a variety of natural scenes to an observer and measured the activity in 500 voxels in the primary visual cortex (Figure 5.52). The goal of this part of the experiment was to determine how each voxel responds to specific features of the scene, such as the position of the image, the image's orientation, and the degree of detail in the image, ranging from fine details (like the two top images in Figure 5.52) to images with little detail (like the bottom image). Based on an analysis of the responses of the 500 voxels to the 1,750 images, Kay and coworkers created a scene decoder that was able to predict the voxel activity patterns that would occur in the brain in response to images of scenes.

To test the decoder, Kay and coworkers did the following (Figure 5.53): (1) They measured the brain activity pattern to a test image that had never been presented before (the lion in this example). (2) They presented this test image and 119 other new images to the decoder, which calculated the predicted voxel activity patterns (shown on the right) for each image. (3) They selected the pattern that most closely matched the actual brain activity elicited by the test image. When they checked to see if the image that went with this pattern was the same as the test image, they found that the decoder identified 92 percent of the images correctly for one observer, and 72 percent correctly for another observer. This is impressive because chance performance for 120 images is less than 1 percent. It is also impressive because the images

(1) Measure brain activity to test image.

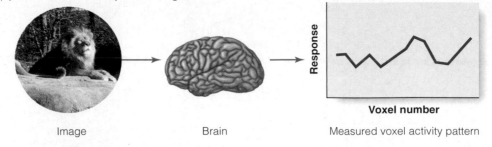

Image   Brain   Measured voxel activity pattern

(2) Present test image and 119 other images to the decoder.

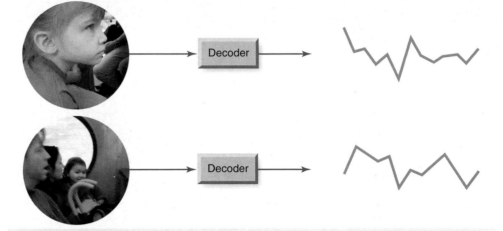

(3) Select the predicted voxel pattern that most closely matches the pattern for the test image.

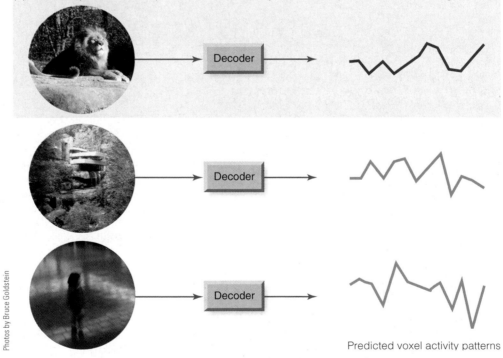

Predicted voxel activity patterns

Photos by Bruce Goldstein

Figure 5.53 ▌ To test their scene decoder, Kay and coworkers (2008) first (a) measured an observer's brain activity caused by the presentation of a test image that the observer had never seen, and then (b) used the decoder to predict the pattern of voxel activity for this test image and 119 other images. The highlighted pattern of voxel activity indicates that the decoder has correctly matched the predicted response to the test image with the actual brain activity generated by the test image that was measured in (a). In other words, the decoder was able to pick the correct image out of a group of 120 images as being the one that had been presented to the observer. *(Based on Kay, K. N., Naselaris, T., Prenger, R. J., & Gallant, J. L., Identifying natural images from human brain activity,* Nature, *7185, 352–355, Fig 1, top. Reprinted by permission from Macmillan Publisher Ltd. Copyright 2008.)*

presented were new ones, which the decoder had never been exposed to before.

Do these results mean that we can now use brain activity to "read minds," as suggested by some reports of this research that appeared in the popular press? These experiments do show that it is possible to identify information in the activity of the primary visual cortex that can predict which image *out of a group of images* a person is looking at. However, we are still not able to create, from a person's brain activity, a picture that corresponds to what the person is seeing. Nonetheless, this research represents an impressive step toward understanding how neural activity represents objects and scenes.

TEST YOURSELF 5.2

1. What is a "scene," and how is it different from an "object"?
2. What is the evidence that we can perceive the gist of a scene very rapidly? What information helps us identify the gist?
3. What are regularities in the environment? Give examples of physical regularities, and discuss how these regularities are related to the Gestalt laws of organization.
4. What are semantic regularities? How do semantic regularities affect our perception of objects within scenes? What is the relation between semantic regularities and the idea that perception involves inference? What did Helmholtz have to say about inference and perception? What is Bayesian inference, and how is it related to Helmholtz's ideas about inference?
5. What is a way to make a robotic vision device more effective? Why is there reason to think that machines are gaining on humans? What do computer vision systems have to do before they can compete with humans?
6. Describe research on (a) neurons that respond to perceptual grouping and to figure–ground; (b) the distributed nature of the representation of faces in the brain; and (c) connections between brain activity and perception (be sure you understand the "Harrison Ford" experiment and the two binocular rivalry experiments).
7. Describe how fMRI has been used to create "orientation decoders" and "scene decoders" that can predict how the brain will respond to (a) oriented gratings and (b) complex scenes.

THINK ABOUT IT

1. This chapter describes a number of perceptual heuristics, including the Gestalt "laws" and the light-from-above heuristic. Think of some other heuristics—either perceptual or from some other area—that help you solve problems quickly using "best guess" rules. (p. 109)
2. Consider this situation: We saw in Chapter 1 that top-down processing occurs when perception is affected by the observer's knowledge and expectations. Of course, this knowledge is stored in neurons and groups of neurons in the brain. In this chapter, we saw that there are neurons that have become tuned to respond to specific characteristics of the environment. We could therefore say that some knowledge of the environment is built into these neurons. Thus, if a particular perception occurs because of the firing of these tuned neurons, does this qualify as top-down processing? (p. 116)
3. Reacting to the results of the recent DARPA race, Harry says, "Well, we've finally shown that computers can perceive as well as people." How would you respond to this statement? (p. 119)
4. Biological evolution caused our perceptual system to be tuned to the Stone Age world in which we evolved. Given this fact, how well do we handle activities like downhill skiing or driving, which are very recent additions to our behavioral repertoire? (p. 115)
5. Vecera showed that regions in the lower part of a stimulus are more likely to be perceived as figure. How does this result relate to the idea that our visual system is tuned to regularities in the environment? (p. 108)
6. We are able to perceptually organize objects in the environment even when objects are similar, as in Figure 5.54. What perceptual principles are involved in perceiving two separate zebras? Consider both the Gestalt laws of organization and the geons of RBC theory. What happens when you cover the zebras' heads, so you see just the bodies? Do these priciples still work? Is there information in addition to what is proposed by the Gestalt laws and RBC theory that helps you perceptually organize the two zebras? (p. 105)
7. How did you perceive the picture in Figure 5.55 when you first looked at it? What perceptual assumptions in-

Figure 5.54 ∎ Which principles of organization enable us to tell the two zebras apart?

Figure 5.55 ❚ *The Scarf,* a drawing by Rita Ludden.

fluenced your response to this picture? (For example, did you make an assumption about how flowers are usually oriented in the environment?) (p. 118)

IF YOU WANT TO KNOW MORE

1. *Robotic vehicles.* To find out more about the DARPA race, go to www.grandchallenge.org or search for DARPA on the Internet. (p. 101)

2. *Perceiving figure and ground.* When you look at the vase–face pattern in Figure 5.21, you can perceive two blue faces on a white background or a white vase on a blue background, but it is difficult to see the faces and the vase simultaneously. It has been suggested that this occurs because of a heuristic built into the visual system that takes into account the unlikelihood that two adjacent objects would have the same contours and would line up perfectly. (p. 108)
   Baylis, G. C., & Driver, J. (1995). One-sided edge assignment in vision: I. Figure–ground segmentation and attention to objects. *Current Directions in Psychological Science 4,* 140–146.

3. *When does figure separate from ground?* The Gestalt psychologists proposed that figure must be separated from ground before it can be recognized. There is evidence, however, the meaning of an area can be recognized before it has become separated from the ground. This means that recognition must be occurring either before or at the same time as the figure is being separated from ground. (p. 108)
   Peterson, M. A. (1994). Object recognition processes can and do operate before figure–ground organization. *Current Directions in Psychological Science, 3,* 105–111.

4. *Global precedence.* When a display consists of a large object that is made up of smaller elements, what does the nervous system process first, the large object or the smaller elements? An effect called the *global precedence effect* suggests that the larger object is processed first. [VL] **21**
   Navon, D. (1977). Forest before trees: The precedence of global features in visual perception. *Cognitive Psychology, 9,* 353–383.

5. *Experience-dependent plasticity and object recognition.* A person's experience can shape both neural responding and behavioral performance related to the recognition of objects. (p. 116)
   Kourtzi, Z., & DiCarlo, J. J. (2006). Learning and neural plasticity in visual object recognition. *Current Opinion in Neurobiology, 16,* 152–158.

6. *Boundary extension effect.* When people are asked to remember a photograph of a scene, they tend to remember a wider-angle view than was shown in the original photograph. This suggests that visual mechanisms infer the existence of visual layout that occurs beyond the boundaries of a given view. There is evidence the parahippocampal place area may be involved in boundary extension. (p. 118)
   Intraub, H. (1997). The representation of visual scenes. *Trends in Cognitive Sciences, 1,* 217–222.
   Park, S., Intraub, H., Yi, D.-J., Widders, D., & Chun, M. M. (2007). Beyond the edges of view: Boundary extension in human scene-selective cortex. *Neuron 54,* 335–342.

7. *Identifying cognitive states associated with perceptions.* Research similar to that described in the Something to Consider section has used fMRI to identify different patterns of brain activation for tools and dwellings. (p. 124)
   Shinkareva, S. V., Mason, R. A., Malave, V. L., Wang, W., Mitchell, T. M., & Just, M. (2008). Using fMRI brain activation to identify cognitive states associated with perception of tools and dwellings. *PLoS ONE, 3*(1), e1394.

KEY TERMS

MEDIA RESOURCES

The *Sensation and Perception* Book Companion Website

www.cengage.com/psychology/goldstein

See the companion website for flashcards, practice quiz questions, Internet links, updates, critical thinking exercises, discussion forums, games, and more!

CengageNow

www.cengage.com/cengagenow

Go to this site for the link to CengageNOW, your one-stop shop. Take a pre-test for this chapter, and CengageNOW will generate a personalized study plan based on your test results. The study plan will identify the topics you need to review and direct you to online resources to help you master those topics. You can then take a post-test to help you determine the concepts you have mastered and what you will still need to work on.

Virtual Lab

Your Virtual Lab is designed to help you get the most out of this course. The Virtual Lab icons direct you to specific media demonstrations and experiments designed to help you visualize what you are reading about. The number beside each icon indicates the number of the media element you can access through your CD-ROM, CengageNOW, or WebTutor resource.

The following lab exercises are related to material in this chapter:

1. *Robotic Vehicle Navigation: DARPA Urban Challenge* A video showing the robotic car "Boss" as it navigates a course in California. (Courtesy of Tartan Racing, Carnegie Mellon University.)

2. *Apparent Movement* How the illusion of movement can be created between two flashing dots.

3. *Linear and Curved Illusory Contours* Examples of how characteristics of illusory contour display affects contours.

4. *Enhancing Illusory Contours* How adding components to a display can enhance illusory contours.

5. *Context and Perception: The Hering Illusion* How background lines can make straight parallel lines appear to curve outward.

6. *Context and Perception: The Poggendorf Illusion* How interrupting a straight line makes the segments of the line look as though they don't line up. (Courtesy of Michael Bach.)

7. *Ambiguous Reversible Cube* A stimulus that can be perceived in a number of different ways, and does strange things when it moves. (Courtesy of Michael Bach.)

8. *Perceptual Organization: The Dalmatian Dog* How a black-and-white pattern can be perceived as a Dalmatian. (Courtesy of Michael Bach.)

9. *Law of Simplicity or Good Figure* A situation in which the law of good figure results in an error of perception.

10. *Law of Similarity* How characteristics of a display cause grouping due to similarity.

11. *Law of Good Continuation* How good continuation influences perceptual organization.

12. *Law of Closure* The effect of adding small gaps to an object.

13. *Law of Proximity* How varying the distance between elements influences grouping.

14. *Law of Common Fate* Grouping that occurs due to common movement of stimulus elements.

15. *Real-World Figure–Ground Ambiguity* A reversible figure–ground display using a picture of a real vase.

16. *Figure–Ground Ambiguity* How changing the contrast of a painting influences figure–ground segregation.

17. *Perceiving Rapidly Flashed Stimuli* Some rapidly flashed stimuli like those used in the Fei-Fei experiment that investigated what people perceive when viewing rapidly flashed pictures. (Courtesy of Li Fei-Fei.)

18. *Rotating Mask 1* How our assumption about the three-dimensional shape of a face can create an error of perception. (Courtesy of Michael Bach.)

19. *Rotating Mask 2* Another example of a rotating mask, this one with a Charlie Chaplin mask. (Courtesy of Michael Bach.)

20. *Rotating Mask 3* Another rotating mask, this one with a nose ring! (Courtesy of Thomas Papathomas.)

21. *Global Precedence* An experiment to determine reaction times in response to large patterns and smaller elements that make up the larger patterns.

Answers for Figure 5.6. Faces from left to right: Prince Charles, Woody Allen, Bill Clinton, Saddam Hussein, Richard Nixon, Princess Diana.

Chapter Contents

CHAPTER 6

Visual Attention

OPPOSITE PAGE This photo of PNC Park shows a Pittsburgh Pirates game in progress and the city in the background. The yellow fixation dots and red lines indicate eye movements that show where one person looked in the first 3 seconds of viewing this picture. The eye movement record indicates that this person first looked just above the right field bleachers and then scanned the ball game. Another person might have looked somewhere else, depending on his or her interests and what attracted his or her attention.
Eye movement record courtesy of John Henderson. Photo by Bruce Goldstein.

VL The Virtual Lab icons direct you to specific animations and videos designed to help you visualize what you are reading about. The number beside each icon indicates the number of the clip you can access through your CD-ROM or your student website.

133

▌ Why do we pay attention to some parts of a scene but not to others? (p. 135)

▌ Do we have to pay attention to something to perceive it? (p. 137)

▌ Does paying attention to an object make the object "stand out"? (p. 142)

Look at the picture on the left, below (Figure 6.1) without looking to the right. Count the number of trees, and then immediately read the caption below the picture.

It is likely that you could describe the picture on the left much more accurately and in greater detail than the one on the right. This isn't surprising because you were looking directly at the trees on the left, and not at the hikers on the right. The point of this exercise is that as we shift our gaze from one place to another in our everyday perception of the environment, we are doing more than just "looking"; we are directing our attention to specific features of the environment in a way that causes these features to become more visible and deeply processed than those features that are not receiving our attention.

To understand perception as it happens in the real world, we need to go beyond just considering how we perceive isolated objects. We need to consider how observers seek out stimuli in scenes, how they perceive some things and not others, and how these active processes shape their perception of these objects and things around them.

As we describe the processes involved in attention in this chapter, we will continue our quest to understand perception as it occurs within the richness of the natural environment. We begin by considering why we pay attention to specific things in the environment. We consider some of the ways attention can affect perception and the idea that attention provides the "glue" that enables us to perceive a coherent, meaningful visual world. Finally, we will describe the connection between attention and neural firing.

Attention and Perceiving the Environment

In everyday life we often have to pay attention to a number of things at once, a situation called divided attention. For example, when driving down the road, you need to simultaneously attend to the other cars around you, traffic signals, and perhaps what the person in the passenger seat is saying, while occasionally glancing up at the rearview mirror. But there are limits to our ability to divide our attention. For example, reading your textbook while driving would most likely end in disaster. Although divided attention is something that does occur in our everyday experience, our main interest in this chapter will be selective attention—focusing on specific objects and ignoring others.

Why Is Selective Attention Necessary?

Why do we selectively focus on some things and ignore others? One possible answer is that we look at things that are interesting. Although that may be true, there is another, more basic, answer. You selectively focus on certain things in your environment because your visual system has been constructed to operate that way.

We can appreciate why attending to only a portion of the environment is determined by the way our visual system is constructed by returning to Ellen as she is walking in the woods (Figure 1.2). As she looks out at the scene before her, millions of her receptors are stimulated, and these receptors send signals out of the optic nerve and

Figure 6.1 ▌ How many trees are there? After counting the trees, and without moving your eyes from the picture, indicate how many of the first four hikers in the picture on the right (Figure 6.2) are males.

Figure 6.2 ▌ Although you may have noticed that this is an outdoor scene with people walking on a road, it is necessary to focus your attention on the lead hikers to determine if they are males or females.

toward the lateral geniculate nucleus (LGN) and visual cortex. The problem the visual system faces is that there is so much information being sent from Ellen's retina toward her brain that if the visual system had to deal with all of it, it would rapidly become overloaded. To deal with this problem, the visual system is designed to select only a small part of this information to process and analyze.

One of the mechanisms that help achieve this selection is the structure of the retina, which contains the all-cone fovea (see page 50). This area supports detail vision, so we must aim the fovea directly at objects we want to see clearly. In addition, remember that information imaged on the fovea receives a disproportionate amount of processing compared to information that falls outside of the fovea because of the magnification factor in the cortex (see page 82).

How Is Selective Attention Achieved?

One mechanism of selective attention is eye movements—scanning a scene to aim the fovea at places we want to process more deeply. As we will see in the following section, the eye is moving constantly to take in information from different parts of a scene. But even though eye movements are an important mechanism of selective attention, it is also important to acknowledge that there is more to attention than just moving the eyes to look at objects. We can pay attention to things that are not directly on our line of vision, as evidenced by the basketball player who dribbles down court while paying attention to a teammate off to the side, just before she throws a dead-on pass without looking. In addition, we can look directly at something without paying attention to it. You may have had this experience: While reading a book, you become aware that although you were moving your eyes across the page and "reading" the words, you have no idea what you just read. Even though you were looking at the words, you apparently were not paying attention.

What the examples of the basketball player and reader are telling us is that there is a *mental* aspect of attention that occurs in addition to eye movements. This connection between attention and what is happening in the mind was described more than 100 years ago by William James (1890/1981), in his textbook *Principles of Psychology*:

> Millions of items . . . are present to my senses which never properly enter my experience. Why? Because they have no interest for me. My experience is what I agree to attend to. . . . Everyone knows what attention is. It is the taking possession by the mind, in clear and vivid form, of one out of what seem several simultaneously possible objects or trains of thought. . . . It implies withdrawal from some things in order to deal effectively with others.

Thus, according to James, we focus on some things to the exclusion of others. As you walk down the street, the things you pay attention to—a classmate that you recognize, the "Don't Walk" sign at a busy intersection, and the fact that just about everyone except you seems to be carrying an umbrella—stand out more than many other things in the environment. One of our concerns in this chapter is to explain why attention causes some things to stand out more than others. The first step in doing this is to describe the eye movements that guide our eyes to different parts of a scene.

What Determines How We Scan a Scene?

The first task in the study of eye movements is to devise a way to measure them. Early researchers measured eye movements using devices such as small mirrors and lenses that were attached to the eyes, so the cornea had to be anesthetized (Yarbus, 1967). However, modern researchers use camera-based eye trackers, like the one in Figure 6.3. An eye tracker determines the position of the eye by taking pictures of the eye and noting the position of a reference point such as a reflection that moves as the eye moves (Henderson, 2003; Morimoto & Mimica, 2005).

Figure 6.4 shows eye movements that occurred when an observer viewed a picture of a fountain. Dots indicate **fixations**—places where the eye pauses to take in information about specific parts of the scene. The lines connecting the dots are eye movements called **saccades**. A person who is asked to simply view a scene typically makes about three fixations per second. [VL] 1

What determines where we fixate in a scene? The answer to this question is complicated because our looking behavior depends on a number of factors, including characteristics of the scene and the knowledge and goals of the observer.

Stimulus Salience Stimulus salience refers to characteristics of the environment that stand out because of physical properties such as color, brightness, contrast, or orientation. Areas with high stimulus salience are conspicuous, such as a brightly colored red ribbon on a green Christmas tree.

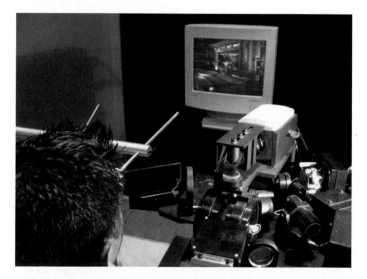

Figure 6.3 ▌ A person looking at a stimulus picture in a camera-based eye tracker. *(Reprinted from* Trends in Cognitive Sciences, 7, *Henderson, John M., 498–503, (2003), with permission from Elsevier.)*

First fixation

Figure 6.4 ▌ Scan path of a viewer while freely viewing a picture of a fountain in Bordeaux, France. Fixations are indicated by the yellow dots and eye movements by the red lines. Notice that this person looked preferentially at high-interest areas of the picture such as the statues and lights but ignored areas such as the fence and the sky. *(Reproduced with permission from John Henderson, University of Edinburgh.)*

Capturing attention by stimulus salience is a bottom-up process—it depends solely on the pattern of stimulation falling on the receptors. By taking into account three characteristics of the display in Figure 6.5a—color, contrast, and orientation—Derrick Parkhurst and coworkers (2002) created the **saliency map** in Figure 6.5b. To determine whether observers' fixations were controlled by stimulus saliency as indicated by the map, Parkhurst measured where people fixated when presented with various pictures. He found that the initial fixations were closely associated with the saliency map, with fixations being more likely on high-saliency areas.

But attention is not just based on what is bright or stands out. Cognitive factors are important as well. A number of cognitively based factors have been identified as important for determining where a person looks.

Knowledge About Scenes The knowledge we have about the things that are often found in certain types of scenes and what things are found together within a scene can help determine where we look. For example, consider how the observer scanned the ballpark in the chapter-opening picture facing page 133. Although we don't know the background of the particular person whose scanning records are shown, we can guess that this person may have used his or her knowledge of baseball to direct his or her gaze to the base runner leading off of first base and then to the shortstop and the runner leading off of second base. We can also guess that someone with no knowledge of baseball might scan the scene differently, perhaps even ignoring the players completely and looking at the city in the background instead.

You can probably think of other situations in which your knowledge about specific types of scenes might influ-

(a) Visual scene

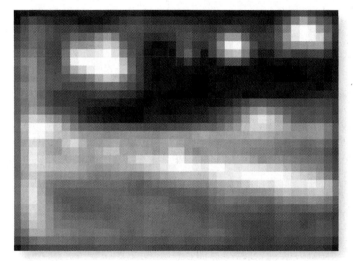

(b) Saliency map

Figure 6.5 ▌ (a) A visual scene. (b) Salience map of the scene determined by analyzing the color, contrast, and orientations in the scene. Lighter areas indicate greater salience. *(Reprinted from Vision Research, 42, Parkhurst, D., Law, K., and Niebur, E., 107–123, (2002), with permission from Elsevier.)*

ence where you look. You probably know a lot, for example, about kitchens, college campuses, automobile instrument panels, and shopping malls, and your knowledge about where things are usually found in these scenes can help guide your attention through each scene (Bar, 2004).

Nature of the Observer's Task Recently, light-weight, head-mounted eye trackers have been developed that make it possible to track a person's eye movements as he or she perform tasks in the environment. This device has enabled researchers to show that when a person is carrying out a task, the demands of the task override factors such as stimulus saliency. Figure 6.6 shows the fixations and eye movements that occurred as a person was making a peanut butter sandwich. The process of making the sandwich begins with the movement of a slice of bread from the bag to

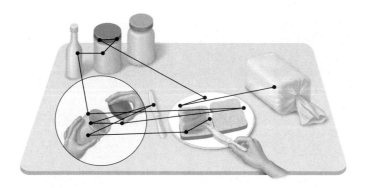

Figure 6.6 ▌ Sequence of fixations of a person making a peanut butter sandwich. The first fixation is on the loaf of bread. *(From Land, M. F., & Hayhoe, M. (2001). In what ways do eye movements contribute to everyday activities?* Vision Research, 41, *3559–3565.)*

the plate. Notice that this operation is accompanied by an eye movement from the bag to the plate. The peanut butter jar is then fixated, then lifted and moved to the front as its lid is removed. The knife is then fixated, picked up, and used to scoop the peanut butter, which is then spread on the bread (Land & Hayhoe, 2001). $\boxed{V_L}$2

The key finding of these measurements, and also of another experiment in which eye movements were measured as a person prepared tea (Land et al., 1999), was that the person fixated on few objects or areas that were irrelevant to the task and that eye movements and fixations were closely linked to the action the person was about to take. For example, the person fixated the peanut butter jar just before reaching for it (Hayhoe & Ballard, 2005).

Learning From Past Experience If a person has learned the key components of making a peanut butter sandwich, this learning helps direct attention to objects, such as the jar, the knife, and the bread, that are relevant to the task. Another example of a task that involves learning is driving. Hiroyuki Shinoda and coworkers (2001) measured observers' fixations and tested their ability to detect traffic signs as they drove through a computer-generated environment in a driving simulator. They found that the observers were more likely to detect stop signs positioned at intersections than those positioned in the middle of a block, and that 45 percent of the observers' fixations occurred close to intersections. In this example, the observer is using learning about regularities in the environment (stop signs are usually at corners) to determine when and where to look for stop signs.

It is clear that a number of factors determine how a person scans a scene. Salient characteristics may capture a person's initial attention, but cognitive factors become more important as the observer's knowledge of the meaning of the scene begins determining where he or she fixates. Even more important than *what* a scene is, is what the person is *doing* within the scene. Specific tasks, such as making a peanut butter sandwich or driving, exert strong control over where we look.

How Does Attention Affect Our Ability to Perceive?

Although there is no question that attention is a major mechanism of perception, there is evidence that we can take in some information even from places where we are not focusing our attention.

Perception Can Occur Without Focused Attention

A recent demonstration of perception without focused attention has been provided by Leila Reddy and coworkers (2007), who showed that we can take in information from a rapidly presented photograph of a face that is located off to the side from where we are attending. The procedure for Reddy's experiment is diagrammed in Figure 6.7. Observers looked at the + on the fixation screen (Figure 6.7a) and then saw the *central stimulus*—an array of five letters (Figure 6.7b). On some trials, all of the letters were the same; on other trials, one of the letters was different from the other four. Observers were instructed to keep looking at the center of the array of letters. $\boxed{V_L}$3

The letters were followed immediately by the *peripheral stimulus*—either a picture of a face or a disc that was half green and half red, flashed at a random position on the edge of the screen (Figure 6.7c). The face or disc was then followed by a mask, to limit the time it was visible (see Method: Using a Mask, page 114), and then the central letter stimulus and mask were turned off.

There were three conditions in this experiment. In all three conditions, the observers were instructed to look steadily at the middle of the letter display, where the + had appeared. The face or red–green disc stimulus was presented off to the side for about 150 ms, so there was no time to make eye movements. The three conditions were as follows:

1. *Central task condition.* The letters are flashed in the center of the screen, where the observer is looking. The observer's task is to indicate whether all of the letters are the same. A face or a red–green disc is presented off to the side, but these stimuli are not relevant in this condition.

2. *Peripheral task condition.* The letters are flashed, as in the central task condition, and observers are instructed to look at the center of the letters, but the letters are not relevant in this condition. The observer's task is to indicate whether a face flashed off to the side is male or female, or if a disc flashed off to the side is red–green or green–red.

3. *Dual task condition.* As in the other conditions, observers are always looking at the center of the letter display, but they are asked to indicate both (1) if all the letters in the middle are the same and (2) for the face stimulus, whether the face is a male or a female, or for the disc stimulus, whether it is red–green or green–red.

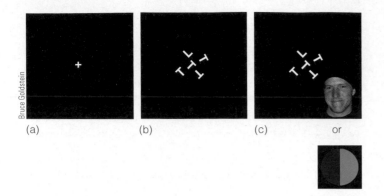

(a)   (b)   (c)   or

Figure 6.7 ▊ Procedure for the Reddy et al. experiment. See text for details. In (c) the peripheral stimulus was either the face or the red-green disc. *(Adapted from Reddy, L., Moradi, F., & Koch, C., 2007, Top-down biases win against focal attention in the fusiform face area, Neuroimage 38, 730–739. Copyright 2007, with permission from Elsevier.)*

One result of this experiment, which wasn't surprising, is that when observers only had to do one task at a time, they performed well. In the central task condition and in the peripheral task condition, performance was 80–90 percent on the letter task, the face task, or the disc task.

A result that was surprising is that in the dual task condition, in which observers had to do two tasks at once, performance on the faces was near 90 percent—just as high as it was for the peripheral task condition (Figure 6.8, left bar). These results indicate that it is possible to take in information about faces even when attention is not focused on the faces.

You could argue that it might be possible to pay some attention to the faces, even when images are presented

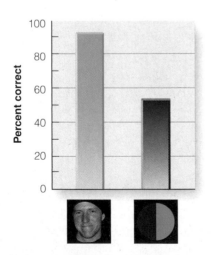

Figure 6.8 ▊ Results from the dual task condition of the Reddy and coworkers (2007) experiment. Observers were able to accurately indicate whether faces were male or female (left bar), but their performance dropped to near chance accuracy when asked to indicate whether a disc was red–green or green–red (right bar). *(Based on data from Reddy, L., Moradi, F., & Koch, C., 2007, Top-down biases win against focal attention in the fusiform face area, Neuroimage 38, 730–739. Copyright 2007, with permission from Elsevier.)*

briefly off to the side. But remember that in the dual task condition observers needed to focus on the letters to perform the letter task. Also, because they did not know exactly where the pictures would be flashed, they were not able to *focus* their attention on the discs or faces. Remember, also, that the stimuli were flashed for only 150 ms, so the observers were not able to make eye movements.

The observers' ability to tell whether the faces were male or female shows that some perception is possible even in the absence of focused attention. But although Reddy's observers performed with 80–90 percent accuracy for the faces in the dual task condition, performance on the red–green disc task dropped to 54 percent (chance performance would be 50 percent) in the dual task condition (Figure 6.8, right bar).

Why is it that the gender of a face can be detected without focused attention, but the layout of a red–green disc cannot? Reddy's experiment doesn't provide an answer to this question, but a place to start is to consider differences between the faces and the discs. Faces are meaningful, and we have had a great deal of experience perceiving them. There is also evidence that we initially process faces as a whole, without having to perceive individual features (Goffaux & Rossion, 2006). All of these factors—meaningfulness, experience, and perceiving as a whole—could make it possible to categorize faces as male or female without focusing attention directly on the face. Whatever mechanism is responsible for the difference in performance between faces and the red–green discs, there is no question that some types of information can be taken in without focused attention and some cannot. We will now look at some further demonstrations of situations in which perception depends on focused attention.

Perception Can Be Affected by a Lack of Focused Attention

Evidence that attention is necessary for perception is provided by a phenomenon called **inattentional blindness**—failure to perceive a stimulus that isn't attended, even if it is in full view.

Inattentional Blindness Arien Mack and Irvin Rock (1998) demonstrated inattentional blindness using the procedure shown in Figure 6.9. The observer's task is to indicate which arm of a briefly flashed cross is longer, the horizontal or the vertical. Then, on the inattention trial of the series, a small test object is flashed close to where the observer is looking, along with the cross. When observers were then given a recognition test in which they were asked to pick out the object from four alternatives, they were unable to indicate which shape had been presented. Just as paying attention to the letters in Reddy's (2007) experiment affected observers' ability to perceive the red–green disc, paying attention to the vertical and horizontal arms in Mack and Rock's experiment apparently made observers "blind" to the unattended geometric objects. VL 4

Mack and Rock demonstrated inattentional blindness using rapidly flashed geometric test stimuli. But other re-

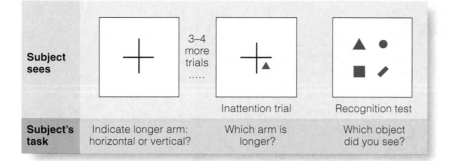

Figure 6.9 ▌ Inattentional blindness experiment. (a) Participants judge whether the horizontal or vertical arm is larger on each trial. (b) After a few trials, a geometric shape is flashed, along with the arms. (c) Then the participant is asked to pick which geometric stimulus was presented.

search has shown that similar effects can be achieved using more naturalistic stimuli that are presented for longer periods of time. Imagine looking at a display in a department store window. When you focus your attention on the display, you probably fail to notice the reflections on the surface of the window. Shift your attention to the reflections, and you become unaware of the display inside the window.

Daniel Simons and Christopher Chabris (1999) created a situation in which one part of a scene is attended and the other is not. They created a 75-second film that showed two teams of three players each. One team was passing a basketball around, and the other was "guarding" that team by following them around and putting their arms up as in a basketball game. Observers were told to count the number of passes, a task that focused their attention on one of the teams. After about 45 seconds, one of two events occurred. Either a woman carrying an umbrella or a person in a gorilla suit walked through the "game," an event that took 5 seconds.

After seeing the video, observers were asked whether they saw anything unusual happen or whether they saw anything other than the six players. Nearly half—46 percent—of the observers failed to report that they saw the woman or the gorilla. In another experiment, when the

gorilla stopped in the middle of the action, turned to face the camera, and thumped its chest, half of the observers still failed to notice the gorilla (Figure 6.10). These experiments demonstrate that when observers are attending to one sequence of events, they can fail to notice another event, even when it is right in front of them (also see Goldstein & Fink, 1981; Neisser & Becklen, 1975). If you would like to experience this demonstration for yourself (or perhaps try it on someone else), go to http://viscog.beckman.uiuc.edu/media/goldstein.html or Google "gorilla experiment."

Change Detection Following in the footsteps of the superimposed image experiments, researchers developed another way to demonstrate how a lack of focused attention can affect perception. Instead of presenting several stimuli at the same time, they first presented one picture, then another slightly different picture. To appreciate how this works, try the following demonstration.

DEMONSTRATION

Change Detection

When you are finished reading these instructions, look at the picture in Figure 6.11 for just a moment, and then turn the page and see whether you can determine what is different in Figure 6.12. Do this now. ▌

Figure 6.10 ▌ Frame from Simons and Chabris's (1999) "gorilla" experiment. (Figure provided by Daniel Simons. Simons, D. J., & Chabris, C. F. (1999). Gorillas in our midst: Sustained inattentional blindness for dynamic events. Perception, 28, 1059–1074.)

Bruce Goldstein

Figure 6.11 ▌ Stimulus for change blindness demonstration. See text.

Figure 6.12 ▌ Stimulus for change blindness demonstration.

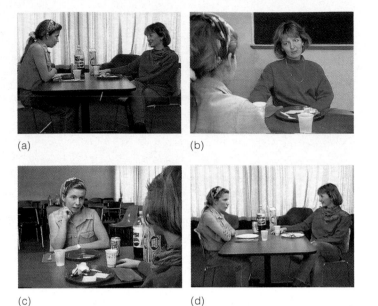

(a)　　　　　　　　　(b)

(c)　　　　　　　　　(d)

Figure 6.13 ▌ Frames from a video that demonstrates change blindness. The woman on the right is wearing a scarf around her neck in shots (a), (c), and (d), but not in shot (b). Also, the color of the plates changes from red in the first three frames to white in frame (d), and the hand position of the woman on the left changes between shots (c) and (d). *(From "Failure to Detect Changes to Attended Objects in Motion Pictures," by D. Levin and D. Simons, 1997,* Psychonomic Bulletin and Review, 4, *501–506.)*

Were you able to see what was different in the second picture? People often have trouble detecting the change even though it is obvious when you know where to look. (Try again, paying attention to the sign near the lower left portion of the picture.) Ronald Rensink and coworkers (1997) did a similar experiment in which they presented one picture, followed by a blank field, followed by the same picture but with an item missing, followed by the blank field, and so on. The pictures were alternated in this way until observers were able to determine what was different about the two pictures. Rensink found that the pictures had to be alternated back and forth a number of times before the difference was detected. ⟦VL⟧ **5–11**

This difficulty in detecting changes in scenes is called change blindness (Rensink, 2002). The importance of attention (or lack of it) in determining change blindness is demonstrated by the fact that when Rensink added a cue indicating which part of a scene had been changed, participants detected the changes much more quickly (also see Henderson & Hollingworth, 2003).

The change blindness effect also occurs when the scene changes in different shots of a film. Figure 6.13 shows successive frames from a video of a brief conversation between two women. The noteworthy aspect of this video is that changes take place in each new shot. In Shot (b), the woman's scarf has disappeared; in Shot (c), the other woman's hand is on her chin, although moments later, in Shot (d), both arms are on the table. Also, the plates change color from red in the initial views to white in Shot (d).

Although participants who viewed this video were told to pay close attention, only 1 of 10 participants claimed to notice any changes. Even when the participants were shown the video again and were warned that there would be changes in "objects, body position, or clothing," they noticed fewer than a quarter of the changes that occurred (Levin & Simons, 1997).

This blindness to change in films is not just a laboratory phenomenon. It occurs regularly in popular films, in which some aspect of a scene, which should remain the same, changes from one shot to the next, just as objects changed in the film shots in Figure 6.13. These changes in films, which are called *continuity errors,* are spotted by viewers who are looking for them, usually by viewing the film multiple times, but are usually missed by viewers in theaters who are not looking for these errors. You can find sources of continuity errors in popular films by Googling "continuity errors."

Change blindness is interesting not only because it illustrates the importance of attention for perception, but also because it is a counterintuitive result. When David Levin and coworkers (2000) told a group of observers about the changes that occurred in film sequences like the ones in Figure 6.13, and also showed them still shots from the film, 83 percent of the observers predicted that they would notice the changes. However, in experiments in which observers did not know which changes were going to occur, only 11 percent noticed the changes. Thus, even though people believe that they would detect such obvious changes, they fail to do so when actually tested.

One reason people think they would see the changes may be that they know from past experience that changes that occur in real life are usually easy to see. But there is an important difference between changes that occur in real life and those that occur in change detection experiments. Changes that occur in real life are often accompanied by motion, which provides a cue that indicates a change is occurring. For example, when a friend walks into a room, the person's motion attracts your attention. However, the appearance of a new object in a change detection experiment is not signaled by motion, so your attention is not attracted to the place where the object appears. The change detection experiments therefore show that when attention is disrupted, we miss changes.

To summarize this section, the answer to the question "How does attention affect our ability to perceive?" is that we can perceive some things, such as the gender of a face, without focused attention, but that focused attention is necessary for detecting many of the details within a scene and for detecting the details of specific objects in the scene.

Does Attention Enhance Perception?

William James, whose statement at the beginning of this chapter described attention as withdrawing from some things in order to deal effectively with others, did no experiments. Thus, many of the statements he made in his book *Principles of Psychology* were based purely on James's psychological insights. What is amazing about these insights is that many of them were correct. Consider, for example, James's idea that attending to a stimulus makes it more "clear and vivid." Although this idea may seem reasonable, it has only recently been confirmed experimentally. We will consider this evidence by first describing some experiments showing that paying attention increases our ability to react rapidly to a stimulus.

Effects of Attention on Information Processing

Michael Posner and coworkers (1978) were interested in answering the following question: Does attention to a specific location improve our ability to respond rapidly to a stimulus presented at that location? To answer this question, Posner used a procedure called precueing, as shown in Figure 6.14.

Posner's observers kept their eyes stationary throughout the experiment, always looking at the +. They first saw an arrow cue indicating on which side of the target a stimulus was likely to appear. In Figure 6.14a the cue indicates that they should focus their attention to the right. (Remember, they do this without moving their eyes.) The observer's task is to press a key as rapidly as possible when a target square is presented off to the side. The trial shown in Figure 6.14a is a *valid trial* because the square appears on the side indicated by the cue arrow. The location indicated by the arrow was

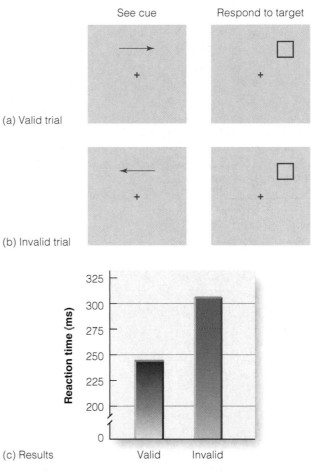

Figure 6.14 ▌ Procedure for (a) the valid task and (b) the invalid task in the Posner et al. (1978) precueing experiment; see text for details. (c) Results of the experiment: Average reaction time was 245 ms for valid trials but 305 ms for invalid trials. *(From Posner, M. I., Nissen, M. J., & Ogden, W. C., 1978, Attended and unattended processing modes: The role of set for spatial location. In H. L. Pick & I. J. Saltzman (Eds.), Modes of perceiving and processing information. Hillsdale, N.J.: Erlbaum.)*

valid 80 percent of the time. Figure 6.14b shows an *invalid trial*. The cue arrow indicates that the observer should attend to the left, but the target is presented on the right.

The results of this experiment, shown in Figure 6.14c, indicate that observers react more rapidly on valid trials than on invalid trials. Posner interpreted this result as showing that information processing is more effective at the place where attention is directed.

There is also evidence that when attention is directed to one place on an object, the enhancing effect of this attention spreads throughout the object. This idea was demonstrated in an experiment by Robert Egly and coworkers (1994), in which the observer first saw two side-by-side rectangles, as shown in Figure 6.15a. As the observer looked at the +, a cue signal was flashed at one location (A, B, C, or D). After the cue signal, a target was presented at one of the positions, and the observer responded as rapidly as possible (Figure 6.15b). Reaction time was fastest when the target appeared where the cue signal had been presented (at A in this example). Like Posner's experiment, this shows that paying attention to a location results in faster responding when a target is presented at that location.

But the most important result of this experiment is that observers responded faster when the target appeared at B, which is in the same rectangle as A, than when the target appeared at C, which is in the neighboring rectangle. Notice that B's advantage occurs even though B and C are the same distance from A. Apparently the enhancing effect of attention had spread within the rectangle on the right, so when the cue was at A, some enhancement occurred at B but not at C, which was just as close but was in a different object.

The same result occurs even when a horizontal bar is added to the display, as shown in Figure 6.16a (Moore et al., 1998). Even though the bar is covering the vertical rectangles, presenting the cue at A still results in enhancement at B. What this means is that enhancement still spreads throughout the object. This "spreading enhancement" may help us perceive partially obscured objects, such as our "animal" lurking behind the tree from Chapter 5 (Figure 6.16b).

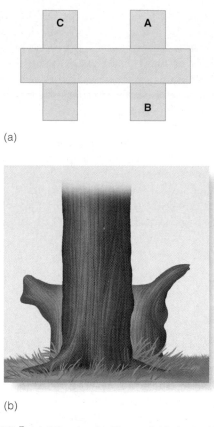

(a)

(b)

Figure 6.16 ❚ (a) Stimulus in Figure 6.15, but with a horizontal bar added (Moore et al., 1998). (b) Possible animal lurking behind a tree (see Chapter 5, p. 110).

Because the effects of attention spread behind the tree, our awareness spreads throughout the object, thereby enhancing the chances we will interpret the interrupted shape as being a single object. (Also see Baylis & Driver, 1993; Driver & Baylis, 1989, 1998; and Lavie & Driver, 1996, for more demonstrations of how attention spreads throughout objects.)

Does the finding that attention can result in faster reaction times show that attention can change the *appearance* of an object, as William James suggested? Not necessarily. It is possible that the target stimulus could *appear* identical in the valid and invalid trials, but that attention was enhancing the observer's ability to *press the button* quickly. Thus, to answer the question of whether attention affects an object's *appearance*, we need to do an experiment that measures the *perceptual response* to a stimulus rather than the *speed of responding* to the stimulus.

Effects of Attention on Perception

One possible way to measure the *perceptual response* to seeing a stimulus is shown in Figure 6.17a. An observer views two stimuli and is instructed to pay attention to one of them and decide whether this attended stimulus is brighter than the other, unattended, stimulus. The stimuli could be presented at different intensities from trial to trial, and the goal would be to determine whether observers report that

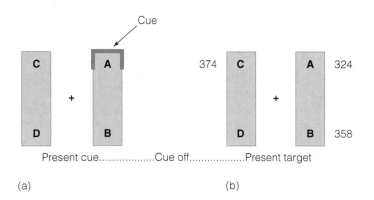

Cue

374   324

358

Present cue.................Cue off.................Present target

(a)   (b)

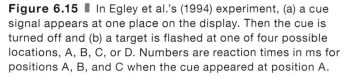

Figure 6.15 ❚ In Egley et al.'s (1994) experiment, (a) a cue signal appears at one place on the display. Then the cue is turned off and (b) a target is flashed at one of four possible locations, A, B, C, or D. Numbers are reaction times in ms for positions A, B, and C when the cue appeared at position A.

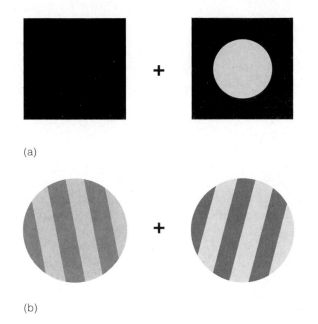

Figure 6.17 ▌ (a) Stimuli to measure how attention might affect perception. (b) A better procedure was devised by Carrasco et al. (2004), using grating stimuli.

the attended stimulus appears brighter when the two stimuli have the same intensity.

This procedure is a step in the right direction because it focuses on what the observer is *seeing* rather than on how fast the observer is reacting to the stimulus. But can we be sure that the observer is accurately reporting his or her perceptions? If the observer has a preconception that paying attention to a stimulus should make it stand out more, this might influence the observer to report that the attended stimulus appears brighter when, in reality, the two stimuli appear equally bright (Luck, 2004).

A recent study by Marissa Carrasco and coworkers (2004) was designed to reduce the possibility that bias could occur because of observers' preconceptions about how attention should affect their perception. Carrasco used grating stimuli with alternating light and dark bars, like the one in Figure 6.17b. She was interested in determining whether attention enhanced the *perceived contrast* between the bars. Higher perceived contrast would mean that there appeared to be an enhanced difference between the light and dark bars. However, instead of asking observers to judge the *contrast* of the stimuli, she instructed them to indicate the *orientation* of the grating that had the higher contrast. For the stimuli shown in the illustration, the correct response would be the grating on the right, because it has a slightly higher contrast than the one on the left. Thus, the observer had to first decide which grating had higher contrast and then indicate the orientation of that grating.

Notice that although the observer in this experiment had to decide which grating had higher contrast, they were asked to *report* the *orientation* of the grating. Having the observer focus on responding to orientation rather than to contrast reduced the chances that they would be influenced by their expectation about how attention should affect contrast.

Carrasco's observers kept their eyes fixed on the +. Just before the gratings were presented, a small dot was briefly flashed on the left or on the right to cause observers to shift their attention to that side. Remember, however, that just as in Posner's studies, observers continued to look steadily at the fixation cross. When the two gratings were presented, the observer indicated the orientation of the one that appeared to have more contrast.

Carrasco found that when there was a large difference in contrast between the two gratings, the attention-capturing dot had no effect. However, when two gratings were physically identical, observers were more likely to report the orientation of the one that was preceded by the dot. Thus, when two gratings were actually the same, the one that received attention appeared to have more contrast. More than 100 years after William James suggested that attention makes an object "clear and vivid," we can now say that we have good experimental evidence that attention does, in fact, enhance the appearance of an object. (Also see Carrasco, in press; Carrasco et al., 2006.)

Attention and Experiencing a Coherent World

We have seen that attending to an object brings it to the forefront of our consciousness and may even alter its appearance. Furthermore, not attending to an object can cause us to miss it altogether. We now consider yet another function of attention, one that is not obvious from our everyday experience. This function of attention is to help create **binding**, which is the process by which features—such as color, form, motion, and location—are combined to create our perception of a coherent object.

Why Is Binding Necessary?

We can appreciate why binding is necessary by remembering our discussion of modularity in Chapter 4, when we learned that separated areas of the brain are specialized for the perception of different qualities. In Chapter 4 we focused on the inferotemporal (IT) cortex, which is associated with perceiving forms. But there are also areas associated with motion, location, and possibly color (the exact location of a color area, if it exists, is still being researched) located at different places in the cortex.

Thus, when you see a red ball roll by, cells sensitive to the ball's shape fire in the IT cortex, cells sensitive to movement fire in the medial temporal (MT) cortex, and cells sensitive to color fire in other areas (Figure 6.18). But even though the ball's shape, movement, and color cause firing in different areas of the cortex, you don't perceive the ball as separated shape, movement, and color perceptions. You experience an integrated perception of a ball, with all of these components occurring together.

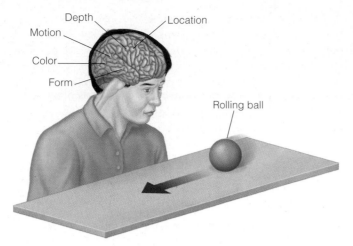

Figure 6.18 ▌ Any stimulus, even one as simple as a rolling ball, activates a number of different areas of the cortex. Binding is the process by which these separated signals are combined to create a unified percept.

This raises an important question: How do we combine all of these physically separated neural signals to achieve a unified perception of the ball? This question, which is called the **binding problem**, has been answered at both the behavioral and physiological levels. We begin at the behavioral level by describing feature integration theory, which assigns a central role to attention in the solution of the binding problem.

Feature Integration Theory

Feature integration theory, originally proposed by Anne Treisman and Garry Gelade (1980; also see Treisman, 1988, 1993, 1999), describes the processing of an object by the visual system as occurring in two stages (Figure 6.19).[1] The first stage is called the **preattentive stage** because it does not depend on attention. During this stage, which occurs so rapidly that we're not aware of it, an object is broken down into features such as color, orientation, and location.

The second stage is called the **focused attention stage** because it does depend on attention. In this stage, the features are recombined, so we perceive the whole object, not individual features.

Treisman links the process of binding that occurs in the focused attention stage to physiology by noting that an object causes activity in both the *what* and *where* streams of the cortex (see page 88). Activity in the *what* stream would include information about features such as color and form. Activity in the *where* stream would include information about location and motion. According to Treisman, attention is the "glue" that combines the information from the *what* and *where* streams and causes us to perceive all of the features of an object as being combined at a specific location.

---

[1] This is a simplified version of feature integration theory. For a more detailed description of the model, which also includes "feature maps" that code the location of each of an object's features, see Treisman (1999).

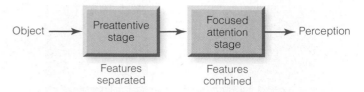

Figure 6.19 ▌ Flow diagram of Treisman's (1988) feature integration theory.

Let's consider how this might work for the object in Figure 6.20a. All of this object's features are registered as being located in the same area because this is the only object present. When we pay attention to the object, its features are all combined at that location, and we perceive the object. This process is simple because we are dealing with a single object at a fixed location. However, things become more complicated when we introduce multiple objects, as normally occurs in the environment.

When we consider multiple objects, numerous features are involved, and these features exist at many different locations (Figure 6.20b). The perceptual system's task is to associate each of these features with the object to which it belongs. Feature integration theory proposes that in order for this to occur, we need to focus our attention on each object in turn. Once we attend to a particular location, the features at that location are bound together and are associated with the object at that location.

What evidence supports the idea that focused attention is necessary for binding? One line of evidence, **illusory conjunctions**, is based on the finding that under some conditions, features associated with one object can become incorrectly associated with another object.

Illusory Conjunctions Illusory conjunctions were first demonstrated in an experiment by Treisman and Schmidt (1982), which used a stimulus display of four objects flanked by two black numbers, as shown in Figure 6.21. They flashed this display onto a screen for one-fifth of a second, followed by a random-dot masking field designed to eliminate any residual perception that might remain after the stimuli were turned off. Observers were told to report the black numbers first and then to report what they saw at each of the four locations where the shapes had been. Under these conditions, observers reported seeing illusory conjunctions on 18 percent of the trials. For example, after being presented with the display in Figure 6.21, in which the small triangle was red and the small circle was green, they might report seeing a small red circle and a small green triangle.

Although illusory conjunctions may seem like a phenomenon that would occur only in the laboratory, Treisman (2005) relates a situation in which she perceived illusory conjunctions in the environment. After thinking she'd seen a bald-headed man with a beard, she looked again and realized that she had actually seen two men—one bald and one with a beard—and had combined their features to create an illusory bald, bearded man.

(a)

(b)

Figure 6.20 ▌ (a) A single object. Binding features is simple in this case because all of the features are at one location. (b) When multiple objects with many features are present, binding becomes more complicated.

object among a number of other objects, such as looking for a friend in a crowd or trying to find Waldo in a "Where's Waldo?" picture (Handford, 1997). A type of visual search called a *conjunction search* has been particularly useful in studying binding.

DEMONSTRATION

Searching for Conjunctions

We can understand what a conjunction search is by first describing another type of search called a *feature search*. Before reading further, look at Figure 6.22, and find the horizontal line in (a) and the green horizontal line in (b). The search you carried out in Figure 6.22a was a **feature search** because the target can be found by looking for a single feature—"horizontal." In contrast, the search you carried out

Figure 6.21 ▌ Stimuli for Treisman and Schmidt's (1982) illusory conjunction experiment.

The reason illusory conjunctions occurred for the stimuli in Figure 6.21 is that these stimuli were presented rapidly, and the observers' attention was distracted from the target object by having them focus on the black numbers. Treisman and Schmidt found, however, that asking their observers to attend to the target objects eliminated the illusory conjunctions.

More evidence that supports the idea that illusory conjunctions are caused by a failure of attention is provided by studies of patient R.M., who had parietal lobe damage that resulted in a condition called **Balint's syndrome**. The crucial characteristic of this syndrome is an inability to focus attention on individual objects. According to feature detection theory, lack of focused attention would make it difficult for R.M. to combine features correctly, and this is exactly what happened. When R.M. was presented with two different letters of different colors, such as a red T and a blue O, he reported illusory conjunctions such as "blue T" on 23 percent of the trials, even when he was able to view the letters for as long as 10 seconds (Friedman-Hill et al., 1995; Reddy et al., 2006; Robertson et al., 1997).

Visual Search Another approach to studying the role of attention in binding has used a task called visual search. Visual search is something we do anytime we look for an

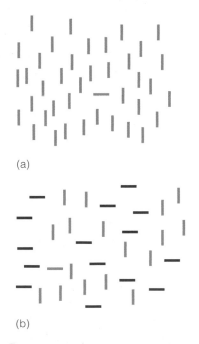

(a)

(b)

Figure 6.22 ▌ Find the horizontal line in (a) and then the green horizontal line in (b).

in Figure 6.22b was a **conjunction search** because it was necessary to search for a combination (or conjunction) of two or more features in the same stimulus—"horizontal" and "green." In Figure 6.22b, you couldn't focus just on green because there are vertical green lines, and you couldn't focus just on horizontal because there are horizontal red lines. You had to look for the *conjunction* of horizontal and green. ▌

Conjunction searches are useful for studying binding because finding the target in a conjunction search involves focusing attention at a specific location. To test the idea that attention to a location is required for a conjunction search, a number of researchers have tested the Balint's patient R.M. and have found that he cannot find the target when a conjunction search is required (Robertson et al., 1997). This is what we would expect, because of R.M's difficulty in focusing attention. R.M. can, however, find targets when only a feature search is required, as in Figure 6.22a, because attention-at-a-location is not required for this kind of search.

The link between the parietal lobe, which is damaged in patients with Balint's syndrome, and conjunction searches is also supported by the fact that other patients with parietal lobe damage also have difficulty performing conjunction searches (Ashbridge et al., 1999). In addition, carrying out a conjunction search activates the parietal lobe in people without brain damage (Shafritz et al., 2002). This connection between the parietal lobe and conjunction searches makes sense when we remember that the parietal lobe is the destination of the *where* stream, which is involved in determining the locations of objects.

In conclusion, behavioral evidence suggests that it is necessary to focus attention at a location in order to achieve binding. We will now consider how the binding problem has been approached physiologically.

The Physiological Approach to Binding

To solve the binding problem, the brain must combine information contained in neurons that are located in different places. For example, in the case of our rolling red ball, the brain must combine information from separate areas that are activated by form, color, and motion. Anatomical connections between these different areas enable neurons in these areas to communicate with one another (Gilbert & Wiesel, 1989; Lamme & Roelfesma, 2000). But what is it that they communicate?

One physiological solution to the binding problem, the **synchrony hypothesis**, states that when neurons in different parts of the cortex are firing to the same object, the pattern of nerve impulses in these neurons will be synchronized with each other. For example, consider the two "objects" in Figure 6.23—the woman and the dog. The image of the woman on the retina activates neurons in a number of different places in the visual cortex. The activity in two of the neurons activated by the woman is indicated by the blue firing records. The image of the dog activates other neurons,

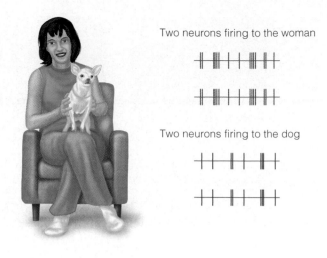

Figure 6.23 ▌ How synchrony can indicate which neurons are firing to the same object. See text for explanation. *(Based on Engel, A. K., Fries, P., Konig, P., Brecht, M., & Singer, W. (1999). Temporal binding, binocular rivalry, and consciousness.* Consciousness and Cognition, 8, *128–151.)*

which fire as indicated by the red records. Notice that the neurons associated with the woman have the same *pattern* of firing, and the neurons associated with the dog also have a common pattern of firing (but one that differs from the firing pattern associated with the woman). The similarity in the patterns of firing in each group of neurons is called **synchrony**. The fact that the two neurons activated by the woman have this property of synchrony tells the brain that these two neurons represent the woman; the same situation occurs for the neurons representing the dog.

Although attention is not a central part of the synchrony hypothesis, there is evidence that paying attention to a particular object may increase the synchrony among neurons representing that object (Engel et al., 1999). Perhaps further research will enable us to draw connections between the behavioral explanation of binding, which emphasizes the role of attention, and the physiological explanation, which emphasizes synchrony of neural firing. Note, however, that even though there is a great deal of physiological evidence that synchrony does occur in neurons that are associated with the same object (Brosch et al., 1997; Engel et al., 1999; Neuenschwander & Singer, 1996; Roskies, 1999), the synchrony hypothesis is not accepted by all researchers. More research is necessary to determine whether synchrony is, in fact, the signal that causes binding to occur.

The Physiology of Attention

How does attention affect neurons in the visual system? This question has attracted a great deal of research. We will focus here on one of the main conclusions from this research—that attention enhances the firing of neurons.

The results of a typical experiment are shown in Figure 6.24. Carol Colby and coworkers (1995) trained

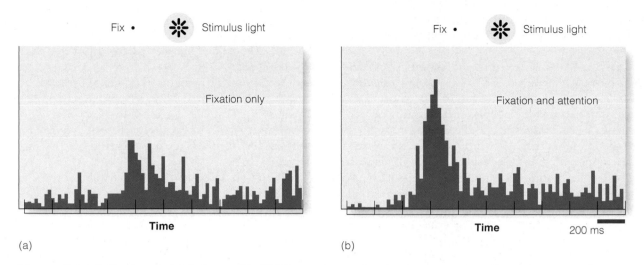

Fix • ✳ Stimulus light   Fix • ✳ Stimulus light

Fixation only   Fixation and attention

Time   Time   200 ms

(a)   (b)

Figure 6.24 ▊ The results of Colby et al.'s (1995) experiment showing how attention affects the responding of a neuron in a monkey's parietal cortex. The monkey always looked at the dot marked "Fix." A stimulus light was flashed within the circle off to the side. (a) Nerve firing when monkey was not paying attention to the light. (b) Nerve firing when monkey was paying attention to the light. *(Reprinted from Colby, C. L., Duhamel, J.-R, & Goldberg, M. E. (1995). Oculocentric spatial representation in parietal cortex. Cerebral Cortex, 5, 470–481. Copyright © 1995, with permission from Oxford University Press.)*

a monkey to continually look at the small fixation light marked "Fix." As the monkey looked at this light, a stimulus light was flashed at a location off to the right. In the *fixation only* condition (Figure 6.24a), the monkey's task was to release its hand from a bar when the *fixation light* was dimmed. In the *fixation and attention* condition (Figure 6.24b), the monkey continued looking at the fixation light but had to release the bar when the *stimulus light* was dimmed. Thus, in the *fixation and attention* condition, the monkey was looking straight ahead, but had to pay attention to the stimulus light located off to the side.

As the monkey was performing these tasks, Colby recorded from a neuron in the parietal cortex that fired to the stimulus light. The records in Figure 6.24 show that this neuron responded poorly to the flashing of the stimulus light in the *fixation only* condition, but responded well to the light in the *fixation and attention* condition. Because the monkey was always looking at the fixation light, the images of the fixation and stimulus lights were always the same on the monkey's retina. Thus, the greater response when the monkey was paying attention to the stimulus light must have been caused not by any change of the stimulus on the monkey's retina, but by the monkey's *attention* to the light. This means that the firing of a neuron depends on more than just the shape or size or orientation of a stimulus. It also depends on whether the animal is paying attention to the stimulus.

This enhancement of responding by attention has been demonstrated in many single-unit recording experiments on animals (Bisley & Goldberg, 2003; Moran & Desimone, 1985; Reynolds & Desimone, 2003) and also in brain imaging experiments on humans (Behrmann et al., 2004; Downar et al., 2001; Kastner et al., 1999). The single-unit

experiments show that although the enhancement effect occurs as early in the visual system as the striate cortex, V1, the effect becomes stronger at higher areas in the visual system (Figure 6.25). This makes sense because higher areas are more likely to reflect an observer's knowledge of characteristics of an object such as its meaning or behavioral significance (Gottlieb et al., 2002).

We can appreciate the connection between the behavioral significance of an object and attention by considering an experiment by Daniel Sheinberg and Nikos Logothetis

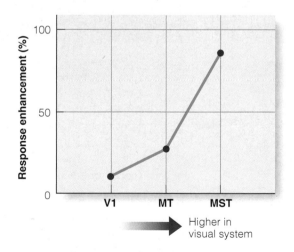

Higher in visual system

Figure 6.25 ▊ Enhancement of the rate of nerve firing caused by attention for neurons in areas V1, MT, and MST. Area MT is in the dorsal stream, and MST is further "downstream." *(Maunsell, J. H. R. (2004). The role of attention in visual cerebral cortex. In L. M. Chalupa & J. S. Werner (Eds.), The visual neurosciences (pp. 1538–1545). Cambridge, MA: MIT Press.)*

(2001), who recorded from neurons in a monkey's infero-temporal (IT) cortex (Figure 4.29) as the monkey was scanning a scene.

In the first part of the experiment, the monkeys were trained to move a lever to the left in response to pictures of some objects and to the right to pictures of other objects. These objects included people, animals, and views of human-made objects such as toys and drinking cups.

After the monkeys had learned the correct response to each picture, Sheinberg and Logothetis found IT neurons that responded to specific pictures. They found that if a neuron responded to a picture when it was presented alone on a blank field, it also responded to the picture when it was placed in an environmental scene. For example, a neuron that fired to a picture of an isolated parrot also fired when the parrot appeared on the roof of a church, as shown in Figure 6.26.

Having shown that the parrot on the roof causes an IT neuron to fire when the parrot is flashed within the neuron's receptive field, the next task was to determine whether the cell would fire when the monkey looked at the parrot while freely scanning the picture. The data below the picture in Figure 6.26 show the monkey's eye movements and when the monkey fixated on the parrot. Immediately after the monkey fixated the parrot, the neuron fired, and shortly after the neuron fired, the monkey moved the lever, indicating that it had identified the parrot. What's important about this result is that the neuron didn't fire when the monkey's gaze came very close to the parrot. It only fired once the monkey had *noticed* the parrot, as indicated by moving the lever.

Think about what this tells us about the connection between neural firing and perception. A particular scene may contain many different objects, and the brain contains many neurons that respond to those objects. But even though the retina is bombarded with stimuli that could, potentially, cause these neurons to fire, some of these neurons do not fire until a stimulus is *noticed*. This is another example of the fact that firing is not determined only by the image on the retina, but by how behaviorally significant the object is to the observer.

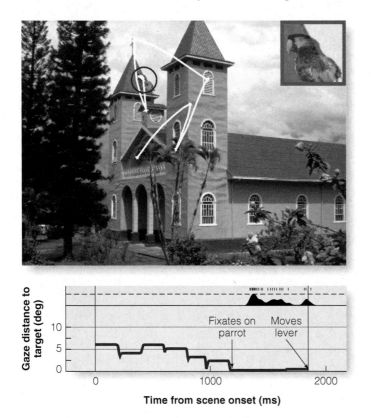

Figure 6.26 ▌ Top: scan path as a monkey looked for a target (the parrot on the roof). Just below picture: firing of an IT neuron as the monkey was looking. Bottom: graph showing how far the monkey's gaze was from the parrot. Notice that the neuron begins firing just after the monkey has fixated on the parrot (arrow), and shortly after this the monkey pulls the lever, indicating that it has identified the parrot (vertical line). *(From Sheinberg, D. L., & Logothetis, N. K. (2001). Noticing familiar objects in real world scenes: The role of temporal cortical neurons in natural vision. Journal of Neuroscience, 21, 1340–1350.)*

Something to Consider: Attention in Autism

Not only is attention important for detecting objects in the environment, as we have described above; it is also a crucial component of social situations. People pay attention not only to what others are saying, but also to their faces (Gullberg & Holmqvist, 2006) and to where they are looking (Kuhn & Land, 2006; Tatler & Kuhn, 2007), because these things provide information about the other person's thoughts, emotions, and feelings.

The link between attention and perceptions of social interactions becomes especially evident when we consider a situation in which that link is disturbed, as occurs in people with autism. Autism is a serious developmental disorder in which one of the major symptoms is the withdrawal of contact from other people. People with autism typically do not make eye contact with others and have difficulty telling what emotions others are experiencing in social situations.

Research has revealed many differences in both behavior and brain processes between autistic and nonautistic people (Grelotti et al., 2002, 2005). Ami Klin and coworkers (2003) note the following paradox: Even though people with autism can often solve reasoning problems that involve social situations, they cannot function when placed in an actual social situation. One possible explanation is differences in the way autistic people observe what is happening. Klin and coworkers (2003) demonstrated this by comparing eye fixations of autistic and nonautistic people as they watched the film *Who's Afraid of Virginia Woolf?*

Figure 6.27 shows fixations on a shot of George Segal's and Sandy Dennis's faces. The shot occurs just after the character in the film played by Richard Burton has smashed a bottle. The nonautistic observers fixated on Segal's eyes

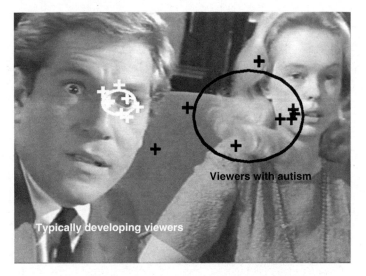

Figure 6.27 ▌ Where people look when viewing this image from the film *Who's Afraid of Virginia Woolf?* Nonautistic viewers: white crosses; autistic viewers: black crosses. *(From "The Enactive Mind, or From Actions to Cognition: Lessons From Autism," by A. Klin, W. Jones, R. Schultz, & F. Wolkmar,* Philosophical Transactions of the Royal Society of London B, *pp. 345–360. Copyright 2003. The Royal Society. Published online.)*

Figure 6.28 ▌ Scan paths for nonautistic viewers (white path) and autistic viewers (black path) in response to the picture and dialogue while viewing this shot from *Who's Afraid of Virginia Woolf? (From "The Enactive Mind, or From Actions to Cognition: Lessons From Autism," by A. Klin, W. Jones, R. Schultz, & F. Wolkmar,* Philosophical Transactions of the Royal Society of London B, *pp. 345–360. Copyright 2003. The Royal Society. Published online.)*

in order to access his emotional reaction, but the autistic observers looked near Sandy Dennis's mouth or off to the side.

Another difference between how autistic and nonautistic observers direct their attention is related to the tendency of nonautistic people to direct their eyes to the place where a person is pointing. Figure 6.28 compares the fixations of a nonautistic person (shown in white) and an autistic person (shown in black). In this scene, Segal's character points to the painting and asks Burton's character, "Who did the painting?" The nonautistic person follows the pointing movement from Segal's finger to the painting and then looks at Burton's face to await a reply. In contrast, the autistic observer looks elsewhere first, than back and forth between the pictures.

All of these results indicate that because of the way autistic people attend or don't attend to events as they unfold in a social situation, they may perceive the environment differently than normal observers. Autistic people look more at things, whereas nonautistic observers look at other people's actions and especially at their faces and eyes. Autistic observers therefore create a mental representation of a situation that does not include much of the information that nonautistic observers usually use in interacting with others.

Some recent experiments provide clues to physiological differences in attention between autistic and nonautistic people. Kevin Pelphrey and coworkers (2005) measured brain activity in the superior temporal sulcus (STS; see Figure 5.45), an area in the temporal lobe that has been shown to be sensitive to how other people direct their gaze in social situations. For example, the STS is strongly activated when a passerby makes eye contact with a person, but is more weakly activated if the passerby doesn't make eye contact (Pelphrey et al., 2004).

Pelphrey measured STS activity as autistic and nonautistic people watched an animated character's eyes move 1 second after a flashing checkerboard appeared (Figure 6.29a). The character either looked at the checkerboard (congruent condition) or in a direction away from the checkerboard (incongruent condition). To determine whether the observers saw the eye movements, Pelphrey asked his observers to press a button when they saw the character's eyes move. Both autistic and nonautistic observers performed this task with 99 percent accuracy.

But even though both groups of observers saw the character's eyes move, there was a large difference between how the STS responded in the two groups. The STS of the nonautistic observers was activated more for the incongruent situation, but the STS of the autistic observers was activated equally in the congruent and incongruent situations (Figure 6.29b).

What does this result mean? Since both groups saw the character's eyes move, the difference may have to do with how observers *interpreted* what the eye movements meant. Pelphrey suggests that there is a difference in autistic and nonautistic people's ability to read other people's *intentions*. The nonautistic observers expected that the character would look at the checkerboard, and when that didn't happen, this caused a large STS response. Autistic observers, on the other hand, may not have expected the observer to look at the checkerboard, so the STS responded in the same way to both the congruent and incongruent stimuli.

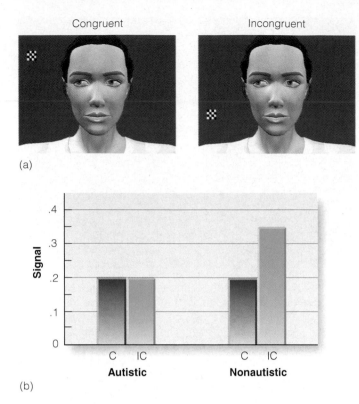

Congruent   Incongruent

(a)

(b)

Figure 6.29 ▌ (a) Observers in Pelphrey's (2005) experiment saw either the congruent condition, in which the animated character looked at the checkerboard 1 second after it appeared, or the incongruent condition, in which the character looked somewhere else 1 second after the checkerboard appeared. (b) Response of the STS in autistic and nonautistic observers to the two conditions: C = congruent; IC = incongruent. *(From Pelphrey, K. A., Morris, J. P., & McCarthy, G. (2005). Neural basis of eye gaze processing deficits in autism.* Brain, 128, *1038–1048. By permission of Oxford University Press.)*

The idea that neural responding may reflect cognitive factors, such as what people *expect* will happen in a particular situation, is something we will encounter again in the next chapter when we consider the connection between perception and how people interact with the environment.

THINK ABOUT IT

1. If salience is determined by characteristics of a scene such as contrast, color, and orientation, why might it be correct to say that paying attention to an object can increase its salience? (p. 136)

2. Art composition books often state that it is possible to arrange elements in a painting in a way that controls both what a person looks at in a picture and the order in which the person looks at things. An example of this would be the statement that when viewing Kroll's *Morning on the Cape* (Figure 6.30), the eye is drawn first to the woman with the books in the foreground, and then to the pregnant woman. But measurements of eye movements show that there are individual differences in the way people look at pictures. For example, E. H. Hess (1965) reported large differences between how men and women looked at the Kroll picture. Try showing this picture, and others, to people as suggested in the figure caption to see if you can observe these individual differences in picture viewing. (p. 135)

3. How is the idea of regularities of the environment that we introduced in Chapter 5 (see page 115) related to the cognitive factors that determine where people look? (p. 136)

4. Can you think of situations from your experience that are similar to the change detection experiments in that you missed seeing an object that became easy to see once you knew it was there? What do you think was behind your initial failure to see this object? (p. 139)

5. The "Something to Consider" section discussed differences between how autistic and nonautistic people

Figure 6.30 ▮ Leon Kroll, *Morning on the Cape.* Try showing this picture to a number of people for 1–2 seconds, and ask them what they notice first and what else they see. You can't determine eye scan patterns using this method, but you may gain some insight into differences in the way different people look at pictures.

direct their attention. Do you think differences in directing attention may also occur in nonautistic people? Can you think of situations in which you and another person perceived the same scene or event differently? (p. 148)

IF YOU WANT TO KNOW MORE

1. *Dividing attention.* Our ability to divide our attention among different tasks depends on the nature of the task and also on how well we have practiced specific tasks. The following two references describe (1) the idea that task difficulty determines our ability to divide our attention and (2) the finding that people who play video games may increase their ability to divide their attention among different tasks. (p. 134)

   Green, G. S., & Bavelier, D. (2003). Action video game modifies visual selective attention. *Nature, 423,* 534–537.

   Lavie, N. (1995). Perceptual load as a necessary condition for selective attention. *Journal of Experimental Psychology: Human Perception and Performance, 21,* 451–486.

2. *Eye movements.* The role of eye movements in determining attention is often studied by measuring the sequence of fixations that a person makes when freely viewing a picture. However, another important variable is how long a person looks at particular areas of a picture. Factors that determine the length of fixation may not be the same as those that determine the sequence of fixations. (p. 135)

   Henderson, J. M. (2003). Human gaze control during real-world scene perception. *Trends in Cognitive Sciences, 7,* 498–503.

3. *When does selection occur in selective attention?* A classic controversy in the field of attention is whether selective attention involves "early selection" or "late selection." Researchers in the "early selection" camp hold that when many messages are present, people select one to attend to based on physical characteristics of the message, such as a person's voice. Researchers in the "late selection" camp state that people don't select which message to attend until they have analyzed the meaning of the various messages that are present. (p. 135)

   Broadbent, D. E. (1958). *Perception and communication.* London: Pergamon.

   Luck, S. J., & Vecera, S. P. (2002). Attention. In H. Pashler & S. Yantis (Eds.), *Stevens' handbook of experimental psychology* (3rd ed., pp. 235–286). New York: Wiley.

   Treisman, A. M. (1964). Selective attention in man. *British Medical Bulletin, 20,* 12–16.

4. *Eye movements and reward systems.* The reward value of an element in a scene may help determine where people look. This idea is supported by evidence that looking at certain objects activates reward areas in the brain. (p. 135)

   Yue, X., Vessel, E. A., & Biederman, I. (2007). The neural basis of scene preferences. *Neuroreport, 18,* 525–529.

5. *Features and visual search.* Visual search has been used not only to study binding, as described in this chapter, but also to study how the match or mismatch between features in the target and the distractors can influence the ability to find the target. When a target has features that differ from those of the distractors, the target "pops out" and so is perceived immediately. However, when the target shares features with the

distractors, search takes longer. You can demonstrate this for yourself in Virtual Lab 12: Feature Analysis. (p. 144) **VL 12**

Treisman, A. (1986). Features and objects in visual processing. *Scientific American, 255,* 114B–125B.

Treisman, A. (1998). The perception of features and objects. In R. D. Wright (Ed.), *Visual attention* (pp. 26–54). New York: Oxford University Press.

6. *Emotion and attention.* There is evidence that emotion can affect attention in a number of ways, including the ability to detect stimuli and the appearance of objects. (p. 142)

Phelps, E. A., Ling, S., & Carrasco, M. (2006). Emotion facilitates perception and potentiates the perceptual benefits of attention. *Psychological Science, 17,* 292–299.

KEY TERMS

Attention (p. 134)
Autism (p. 148)
Balint's syndrome (p. 145)
Binding (p. 143)
Binding problem (p. 144)
Change blindness (p. 140)
Conjunction search (p. 146)
Divided attention (p. 134)

Feature integration theory (p. 144)
Feature search (p. 145)
Fixation (p. 135)
Focused attention stage (p. 144)
Illusory conjunction (p. 144)
Inattentional blindness (p. 138)
Preattentive stage (p. 144)
Precueing (p. 141)

Saccade (p. 135)
Saliency map (p. 136)
Selective attention (p. 134)
Stimulus salience (p. 135)
Synchrony (p. 146)
Synchrony hypothesis (p. 146)
Visual search (p. 145)

MEDIA RESOURCES
The *Sensation and Perception* Book Companion Website
www.cengage.com/psychology/goldstein

See the companion website for flashcards, practice quiz questions, Internet links, updates, critical thinking exercises, discussion forums, games, and more!

CengageNOW
CENGAGENOW™

www.cengage.com/cengagenow

Go to this site for the link to CengageNOW, your one-stop shop. Take a pre-test for this chapter, and CengageNOW will generate a personalized study plan based on your test results. The study plan will identify the topics you need to review and direct you to online resources to help you master those topics. You can then take a post-test to help you determine the concepts you have mastered and what you will still need to work on.

Virtual Lab
VL

Your Virtual Lab is designed to help you get the most out of this course. The Virtual Lab icons direct you to specific media demonstrations and experiments designed to help you visualize what you are reading about. The number beside each icon indicates the number of the media element you can access through your CD-ROM, CengageNOW, or WebTutor resource.

The following lab exercises are related to material in this chapter:

1. *Eye Movements While Viewing a Scene* Records of a person's fixations while viewing a picture of a scene. (Courtesy of John Henderson.)

2. *Task-Driven Eye Movements* Records of a head-mounted eye movement camera that show eye movements as a person makes a peanut butter and jelly sandwich. (Courtesy of Mary Hayhoe.)

3. *Perception Without Focused Attention* Some stimuli from Reddy's (2007) experiment in which she tested observers' ability to identify stimuli presented rapidly off to the side of the focus of attention. (Courtesy of Leila Reddy.)

4. *Inattentional Blindness Stimuli* The sequence of stimuli presented in an inattentional blindness experiment.

5. *Change Detection: Gradual Changes* Three images that test your ability to detect changes that happen slowly.

6. *Change Detection: Airplane* A test of your ability to determine the difference between two images that are flashed rapidly, separated by a blank field. (Courtesy of Ronald Rensink.)

7. *Change Detection: Farm* (Courtesy of Ronald Rensink.)

8. *Change Blindness: Harborside* (Courtesy of Ronald Rensink.)

9. *Change Detection: Money* (Courtesy of Ronald Rensink.)

10. *Change Detection: Sailboats* (Courtesy of Ronald Rensink.)

11. *Change Detection: Tourists* (Courtesy of Ronald Rensink.)

12. *Feature Analysis* A number of visual search experiments in which you can determine the function relating reaction time and number of distractors for a number of different types of targets and distractors.

Chapter Contents

CHAPTER 7

Taking Action

OPPOSITE PAGE The mechanisms that enable Lance Armstrong to negotiate this bend involve using both perceptual mechanisms that enable him to see what is happening around him, and action mechanisms that help him keep his bike upright and stay on course. These mechanisms work in concert with one another, with perception guiding action, and action, in turn, influencing perception.
(Steven E. Sutton/CORBIS)

[VL] The The Virtual Lab icons direct you to specific animations and videos designed to help you visualize what you are reading about. The number beside each icon indicates the number of the clip you can access through your CD-ROM or your student website.

Some Questions We Will Consider:

- What is the connection between perceiving and moving through the environment? (p. 156)
- What is the connection between somersaulting and vision? (p. 157)
- How do neurons in the brain respond when a person perceives an action and when the person watches someone else perceive the same action? (p. 168)
- Is it possible to control the position of a cursor on a computer screen by just thinking about where you want it to move? (p. 171)

Serena straps on her helmet for what she anticipates will be a fast, thrilling, and perhaps dangerous ride. As an employee of the Speedy Delivery Package Service, her mission is to deliver the two packages strapped to the back of her bicycle to an address 30 blocks uptown. Once on her bike, she weaves through traffic, staying alert to close calls with cars, trucks, pedestrians, and potholes. Seeing a break in traffic, she reaches down to grab her water bottle to take a quick drink before having to deal with the next obstacle. "Yes," Serena thinks, "I can multitask!" As she replaces the water bottle, she downshifts and keeps a wary eye out for the pedestrian ahead who looks as though he might decide to step off the curb at any moment.

Serena faces a number of challenges that involve both perception—using her sight and hearing to monitor what is happening in her environment—and action—staying balanced on her bike, staying on course, shifting gears, reaching for her water bottle. We have discussed some of these things in the last two chapters: perceiving a scene and individual objects within it, scanning the scene to shift attention from one place to another, focusing on what is important and ignoring what is not, and relying on prior knowledge about characteristics of the environment. This chapter builds on what we know about perceiving objects and scenes, and about paying attention, to consider the processes involved in being physically active within a scene and interacting with objects. In other words, we will be asking how perception operates as a person steps out (or rides a bike) into the world.

You might think that taking action in the world is a different topic than perception because it involves moving the body, rather than seeing or hearing or smelling things in the environment. However, the reality is that motor activity and perception are closely linked. We observed this link when we described how the ventral stream (temporal lobe) is involved in identifying objects and the dorsal stream (parietal lobe) is involved in locating objects and taking action. (Remember D.F. from Chapter 4, page 90, who had difficulty perceiving orientations because of damage to her temporal lobe but could "mail" a letter because her parietal lobe was not damaged.)

Our bicyclist's ability to balance, stay on course, grab her water bottle, and figure out what is going to happen ahead involves both perception and motor activity occurring together. How is this coordination achieved? Researchers have approached this question in a number of ways. An early and influential approach was proposed by J. J. Gibson, who founded the ecological approach to perception.

The Ecological Approach to Perception

The ecological approach to perception focuses on how perception occurs in the environment by (1) emphasizing the moving observer—how perception occurs as a person is moving through the environment—and (2) identifying information in the environment that the moving observer uses for perception.

The Moving Observer and Information in the Environment

The idea that we need to take the moving observer into account to fully understand perception does not seem very revolutionary today. After all, a good deal of our perception occurs as we are walking or driving through the environment. However, perception research in the 1950s and the decades that followed focused on testing stationary observers as they observed stimuli flashed on a screen.

It was in this era of the fixed-in-place observer that Gibson began studying how pilots land airplanes. In his first book, *The Perception of the Visual World* (1950), he reported that what we know about perception from testing people fixed in place in the laboratory cannot explain perception in dynamic environments that usually occur in everyday experience. The correct approach, suggested Gibson, is to look for information that moving observers use to help them carry out actions such as traveling toward a destination.

Gibson's approach to perception can be stated simply as "Look for information *in the environment* that provides *information for perception*." Information for perception, according to Gibson, is located not on the retina, but "out there" in the environment. He thought about information in the environment in terms of the optic array—the structure created by the surfaces, textures, and contours of the environment, and he focused on how movement of the observer causes changes in the optic array. According to this idea, when you look out from where you are right now, all of the surfaces, contours, and textures you see make up the optic array; if you get up and start walking, the changes that occur in the surfaces, contours, and textures provide information for perception.

One source of the information for perception that occurs as you move is optic flow—the movement of elements in a scene relative to the observer. For example, imagine driving through a straight tunnel. You see the opening of the tunnel as a small rectangle of light in the distance, and as your car hurtles forward, everything around you—the walls on the left and right, the ceiling above, and the road below—moves

Figure 7.1 ❚ The flow of the environment as seen through the front window of a car speeding across a bridge toward the destination indicated by the white dot. (The red object in the foreground is the hood of the car.) The flow is more rapid closer to the car, as indicated by the increased blur and the longer arrows. The flow occurs everywhere except at the white dot, which is the *focus of expansion* located at the car's destination at the end of the bridge.

past you in a direction opposite to the direction you are moving. This movement of the surroundings is the optic flow. Figure 7.1 shows the flow for a car driving across a bridge that has girders to the left and right and above. The arrows and the blur in the photograph indicate the flow. $\boxed{V_L}$ **1**

Optic flow has two characteristics: (1) the flow is more rapid near the moving observer, as indicated by the length of the arrows in Figure 7.1, and (2) there is no flow at the destination toward which the observer is moving, indicated by the small white dot in Figure 7.1. The different speed of flow—fast near the observer and slower farther away—is called the gradient of flow. According to Gibson, the gradient of flow provides information about the observer's speed. The absence of flow at the destination point is called the focus of expansion (FOE). Because the FOE is centered on the observer's destination, it indicates where the observer is heading.

Another characteristic of optic flow is that it produces invariant information. We introduced the idea of invariant information in Chapter 5, when we described the recognition-by-components approach to object perception (see page 112). We defined an invariant as a property that remains constant under different conditions. For Gibson, the key invariants are the properties that remain constant as an observer moves through the environment. Optic flow provides invariant information because it occurs no matter where the observer is, as long as he or she is moving. The focus of expansion is also invariant because it is always centered on where the person is heading.

Self-Produced Information

Another basic idea behind the ecological approach is self-produced information—an observer's movement provides information that the observer uses to guide further move-

ment. Another way to state this reciprocal relationship between movement and perception is that we need to perceive to move, and we also need to move to perceive (Figure 7.2). The optic flow that our observer produces by moving is an example of self-produced information. Another example is provided by somersaulting.

We can appreciate the problem facing a gymnast who wants to execute an airborne backward somersault by realizing that, within 600 ms, the gymnast must execute the somersault and then end in exactly the correct body configuration precisely at the moment that he or she hits the ground (Figure 7.3).

One way this could be accomplished is to learn to run a predetermined sequence of motions within a specific period of time. In this case, performance should be the same with eyes open or closed. However, Benoit Bardy and Makel Laurent (1998) found that expert gymnasts performed somersaults more poorly with their eyes closed. Films showed that when their eyes were open, the gymnasts appeared to be making in-the-air corrections to their trajectory. For example, a gymnast who initiated the extension of his or her body a little too late compensated by performing the rest of the movement more rapidly.

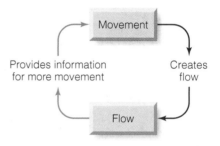

Figure 7.2 ❚ The relationship between movement and flow is reciprocal, with movement causing flow and flow guiding movement. This is the basic principle behind much of our interaction with the environment.

Figure 7.3 ❚ "Snapshots" of a somersault, starting on the left and finishing on the right. *(From Bardy, B. G., & Laurent, M. (1998). How is body orientation controlled during somersaulting?* Journal of Experimental Psychology: Human Perception and Performance, 24, 963–977. Copyright © 1998 by The American Physiological Society. Reprinted by permission.)*

Another interesting result was that closing the eyes did not affect the performance of novice somersaulters as much as it affected the performance of experts. Apparently, experts learn to coordinate their movements with their perceptions, but novices have not yet learned to do this. Therefore, when the novices closed their eyes, the loss of visual information had less effect than it did for the experts. Thus, somersaulting, like other forms of action, involves the regulation of action during the continuous flow of perceptual information.

The Senses Do Not Work in Isolation

Another of Gibson's ideas was that the senses do not work in isolation—that rather than considering vision, hearing, touch, smell, and taste in isolated categories, we should consider how each provides information for the same behaviors. One example of how a behavior originally thought to be the exclusive responsibility of one sense is also served by another one is provided by the sense of balance.

Your ability to stand up straight, and to keep your balance while standing still or walking, depends on systems that enable you to sense the position of your body. These systems include the vestibular canals of your inner ear and receptors in the joints and muscles. However, Gibson argued that information provided by vision also plays a role in keeping our balance. One way to illustrate the role of vision in balance is to see what happens when visual information isn't available, as in the following demonstration.

DEMONSTRATION

Keeping Your Balance

Keeping your balance is something you probably take for granted. Stand up. Raise one foot from the ground and stay balanced on the other. Then close your eyes and observe what happens. ▌

Did staying balanced become more difficult when you closed your eyes? Vision provides a frame of reference that

(a) Room swings toward person.

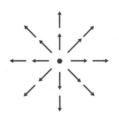

Flow when wall is moving toward person.

(b) Person sways back to compensate.

(c) When room swings away, person sways forward to compensate.

Flow when wall is moving away from person.

Figure 7.4 ▌ Lee and Aronson's swinging room. (a) Moving the room toward the observer creates an optic flow pattern associated with moving forward, so (b) the observer sways backward to compensate. (c) As the room moves away from the observer, flow corresponds to moving backward, so the person leans forward to compensate, and may even lose his or her balance. *(Based on Lee, D. N., & Aronson, E. (1974). Visual proprioceptive control of standing in human infants.* Perception and Psychophysics, 15, *529–532.)*

helps the muscles constantly make adjustments to help maintain balance.

The importance of vision in maintaining balance was demonstrated by David Lee and Eric Aronson (1974). Lee and Aronson placed 13- to 16-month-old toddlers in a "swinging room" (Figure 7.4). In this room, the floor was stationary, but the walls and ceiling could swing toward and away from the toddler. Figure 7.4a shows the room swaying toward the toddler. This movement of the wall creates the optic flow pattern on the right. Notice that this pattern is similar to the optic flow that occurs when moving forward, as when you are driving through a tunnel.

Because the flow is associated with moving forward, it creates the impression in the observer that he or she is swaying forward. This causes the toddler to sway back to compensate (Figure 7.4b). When the room moves away, as in Figure 7.4c, the flow pattern creates the impression of swaying backward, so the toddler sways forward to compensate. In Lee and Aronson's experiment, 26 percent of the toddlers swayed, 23 percent staggered, and 33 percent fell down!

Adults were also affected by the swinging room. If they braced themselves, "oscillating the experimental room through as little as 6 mm caused adult subjects to sway approximately in phase with this movement. The subjects were like puppets visually hooked to their surroundings and were unaware of the real cause of their disturbance" (Lee, 1980, p. 173). Adults who didn't brace themselves could, like the toddlers, be knocked over by their perception of the moving room.

The swinging room experiments show that vision is such a powerful determinant of balance that it can override the traditional sources of balance information provided by the inner ear and the receptors in the muscles and joints (see also C. R. Fox, 1990). In a developmental study, Bennett Berthenthal and coworkers (1997) showed that infants as young as 4 months old sway back and forth in response to movements of a room, and that the coupling of the room's movement and the swaying becomes closer with age. (See also Stoffregen et al., 1999, for more evidence that flow information can influence posture while standing still; and Warren et al., 1996, for evidence that flow is involved in maintaining posture while walking.)

Gibson's emphasis on the moving observer, on identifying information in the environment that observers use for perception, and on the importance of determining how people perceive in the natural environment was taken up by researchers that followed him. The next section describes some research designed to test Gibson's ideas about how people navigate through the environment.

Navigating Through the Environment

Gibson proposed that optic flow provides information about where a moving observer is heading. But do observers actually use this information in everyday life? Research

on whether people use flow information has asked observers to make judgments regarding their heading based on computer-generated displays of moving dots that create optic flow stimuli. The observer's task is to judge, based on optic flow stimuli, where he or she would be heading relative to a reference point such as the vertical line in Figures 7.5a and b. The flow in Figure 7.5a indicates movement directly toward the line, and the flow in Figure 7.5b indicates movement to the right of the line. Observers viewing stimuli such as this can judge where they are heading relative to the vertical line to within about 0.5 to 1 degree (Warren, 1995, 2004; also see Fortenbaugh et al., 2006; Li, 2006). $\boxed{V_L}$2

Other Strategies for Navigating

Although research has shown that flow information can be used to determine heading, there is also evidence that people use other information as well.

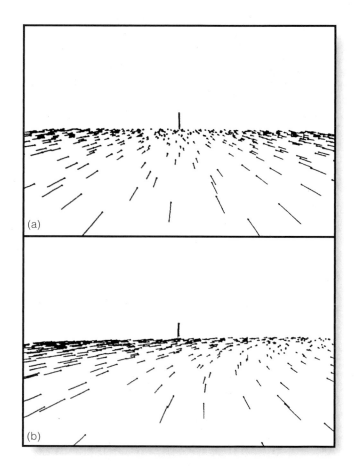

Figure 7.5 ▌ (a) Optic flow generated by a person moving straight ahead toward the vertical line on the horizon. The lengths of the lines indicate the person's speed. (b) Optic flow generated by a person moving in a curved path that is headed to the right of the vertical line. *(From Warren, W. H. (1995). Self-motion: Visual perception and visual control. In W. Epstein & S. Rogers (Eds.), Handbook of perception and cognition: Perception of space and motion (pp. 263–323). Copyright © 1965, with permission from Elsevier.)*

Driving Experiments To study what information people use to stay on course in an actual environmental situation, Michael Land and David Lee (1994) fitted an automobile with instruments to record the angle of the steering wheel and the speed, and measured where the driver was looking with a video eye tracker. According to Gibson, the focus of expansion provides information about the place toward which a moving observer is headed. However, Land and Lee found that although drivers look straight ahead while driving, they do not look directly at the focus of expansion (Figure 7.6a).

Land and Lee also studied where drivers look as they are negotiating a curve. This task poses a problem for the idea of focus of expansion because the driver's destination keeps changing as the car rounds the curve. Land and Lee found that when going around a curve, drivers don't look directly at the road, but look at the tangent point of the curve on the side of the road, as shown in Figure 7.6b. Because drivers don't look at the focus of expansion, which would be in the road directly ahead, Land and Lee suggested that drivers probably use information in addition to optic flow to determine their heading. An example of this additional information would be noting the position of the car relative to the lines in the center of the road or relative to the side of the road. (See also Land & Horwood, 1995; Rushton & Salvucci, 2001; Wann & Land, 2000; Wilkie & Wann, 2003, for more research on the information drivers use to stay on the road.)

Walking Experiments How do people navigate on foot? Apparently, an important strategy used by walkers (and perhaps drivers as well) that does not involve flow is the **visual direction strategy**, in which observers keep their body pointed toward a target. If they go off course, the target will drift to the left or right. When this happens, the walker can correct course to recenter the target (Fajen & Warren, 2003; Rushton et al., 1998).

Another indication that flow information is not always necessary for navigation is that we can find our way even when flow information is minimal, such as at night or in a snowstorm (Harris & Rogers, 1999). Jack Loomis and coworkers (Loomis et al., 1992; Philbeck, Loomis, & Beall, 1997) have demonstrated this by eliminating flow altogether, with a "blind walking" procedure in which people observe a target object located up to 12 meters away, then walk to the target with their eyes closed.

These experiments show that people are able to walk directly toward the target and stop within a fraction of a meter of it. In fact, people can do this even when they are asked to walk off to the side first and then make a turn and walk to the target, while keeping their eyes closed. Some records from these "angled" walks are shown in Figure 7.7, which depicts the paths taken when a person first walked

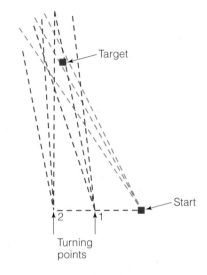

Figure 7.7 ▍ The results of a "blind walking" experiment (Philbeck et al., 1997). Participants looked at the target, which was 6 meters from the starting point, then closed their eyes and begin walking to the left. They turned either at point 1 or 2, keeping their eyes closed the whole time, and continued walking until they thought they had reached the target. *(From Philbeck, J. W., Loomis, J. M., & Beall, A. C., 1997, Visually perceived location is an invariant in the control of action.* Perception and Psychophysics, 59, *601–612. Adapted with permission.)*

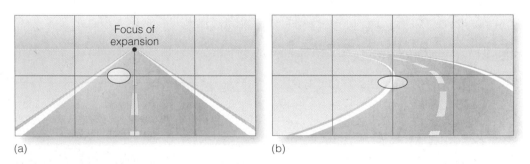

(a) (b)

Figure 7.6 ▍ Results of Land and Lee's (1994) experiment. The ellipses indicate where drivers were most likely to look while driving on (a) a straight road and (b) a curve to the left. *(Adapted by permission from Macmillan Publishers Ltd., from Sinai, M., Ooi Leng, T., & He, Z, Terrain influences the accurate judgment of distance,* Nature, 395, *497–500. Copyright 1998.)*

to the left from the "start" position and then was told to turn either at turn point 1 or 2 and walk to a target that was 6 meters away. The fact that the person stopped close to the target shows that we are able to accurately navigate short distances in the absence of any visual stimulation at all (also see Sun et al., 2004).

Gibson's ideas about identifying information in the environment that is available for perception plus the research we have described tell us something important about studying perception. One task is to determine what information is *available* for perception. This is what Gibson accomplished in identifying information such as optic flow and the focus of expansion. Another task is to determine what information is *actually used* for perception. As we have seen, optic flow can be used, but other sources of information are probably used as well. In fact, the information that is used may depend on the specific situation. Thus, as Serena speeds down the street on her bike, she may be using flow information provided by the parked cars "flowing by" on her right while simultaneously using the visual direction strategy to avoid potholes and point her bike toward her destination. In addition, she also uses auditory information, taking into account the sound of cars approaching from behind. Perception, as we have seen, involves multiple sources of information. This idea also extends to physiology. We will now consider how neurons and different areas of the brain provide information for navigation.

The Physiology of Navigation

The physiology of navigation has been studied both by recording from neurons in monkeys and by determining brain activity in humans.

Optic Flow Neurons Neurons that respond to optic flow patterns are found in the *medial superior temporal area* (MST) (Figure 7.8). Figure 7.9 shows the response of a neuron in MST that responded best to a pattern of dots that were expanding outward (Figure 7.9a) and another neuron that responded best to circular motions (Figure 7.9b; see also Duffy & Wurtz, 1991; Orban et al., 1992; Raffi et al., 2002; Regan & Cynader, 1979). What does the existence of these optic flow

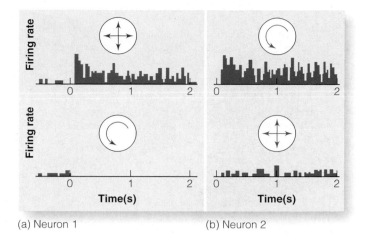

(a) Neuron 1   (b) Neuron 2

Figure 7.9 ▌ (a) Response of a neuron in the monkey's MST that responds with a high rate of firing to an expanding stimulus (top record) but that hardly fires to a stimulus that moves with a circular motion (bottom record) or with other types of motion (not shown). (b) Another neuron that responds best to circular movement (top) but does not respond well to an expanding pattern or other types of movement (bottom). *(From Graziano, M. S. A., Andersen, R. A., & Snowden, R. J. (1994). Tuning of MST neurons to spiral motions. Journal of Neuroscience, 14, 54–67.)*

neurons mean? We know from previous discussions that finding a neuron that responds to a specific stimulus is only the first step in determining whether this neuron has anything to do with perceiving that stimulus (see Chapter 4, p. 79; Chapter 5, p. 122). The next step is to demonstrate a connection between the neuron's response and behavior.

Kenneth Britten and Richard van Wezel (2002) demonstrated a connection between the response of neurons in MST and behavior by first training monkeys to indicate whether the flow of dots on a computer screen indicated movement to the left or right of straight ahead (Figure 7.10). Then, as monkeys were making that judgment, Britten and van Wezel electrically stimulated MST neurons that were tuned to respond to flow associated with a specific direction. When they did this, they found that the stimulation shifted the monkey's judgments toward the direction favored by the stimulated neuron.

For example, the blue bar in Figure 7.10b shows how a monkey responded to a flow stimulus before the MST was stimulated. The monkey judged this stimulus as moving to the left on about 60 percent of the trials and to the right on 40 percent of the trials. However, when Britten and van Wezel stimulated MST neurons that were tuned to respond to leftward movement, the monkey shifted its judgment so it made "leftward" judgments on more than 80 percent of the trials, as indicated by the red bar in Figure 7.10b. This link between MST firing and perception supports the idea that flow neurons do, in fact, help determine perception of the direction of movement.

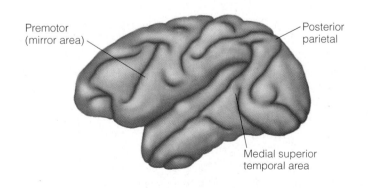

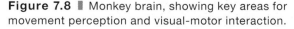

Figure 7.8 ▌ Monkey brain, showing key areas for movement perception and visual-motor interaction.

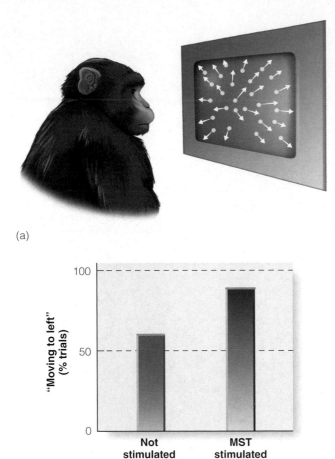

(a)

(b)

(a)

(b)

Figure 7.10 ▌ (a) A monkey watches a display of moving dots on a computer monitor. The dots indicate the flow pattern for movement slightly to the left of straight ahead, or slightly to the right. (b) Effect of microstimulation of the monkey's MST neurons that were tuned to respond to leftward movement. Stimulation (red bar) increases the monkey's judgment of leftward movement. *(Based on data from Britten, K. H., & van Wezel, R. J. A. (2002). Area MST and heading perception in macaque monkeys.* Cerebral Cortex, 12, *692–701.)*

Brain Areas for Navigation There is more to navigating through the environment than perceiving the direction of movement. An essential part of navigation is knowing what path to take to reach your destination. People often use landmarks to help them find their way. For example, although you may not remember the name of a specific street, you may remember that you need to turn right at the gas station on the corner.

In Chapter 4 (page 93; Figure 4.34a) we saw that there are neurons in the parahippocampal place area (PPA) that respond to buildings, the interiors of rooms, and other things associated with locations. We now return to the PPA, but instead of just describing neurons that respond to pictures of houses or rooms, we will describe some experiments that have looked at the connection between activity in the PPA and using landmarks to navigate through the environment.

Figure 7.11 ▌ (a) Scene from the "virtual town" viewed by Maguire et al.'s (1998) observers. (b) Plan of the town showing three of the paths observers took between locations A and B. Activity in the hippocampus and parietal lobe was greater for the accurate path (1) than for the inaccurate paths (2 and 3). *(From Maguire, E. A., Burgess, N., Donnett, J. G., Frackowiak, R. S. J., Frith, C. D., & O'Keefe, J., Knowing where, and getting there: A human navigation network,* Science, 280, *921–924, 1998. Copyright © 1998 by AAAS. Reprinted with permission from AAAS.)*

First, let's consider an experiment by Eleanor Maguire and coworkers (1998) in which observers viewed a computer screen to see a tour through a "virtual town" (Figure 7.11a). Observers first learned the town's layout, and then, as they were being scanned in a PET scanner, they were given the task of navigating from one point to another in the town (Figure 7.11b).

Maguire and coworkers found that navigating activated the right hippocampus and part of the parietal cortex. They also found that activation was greater when navigation between two locations, A and B, was accurate (path 1 in Figure 7.11b) than when it was inaccurate (paths 2 and 3). Based on these results, Maguire concluded that the hippocampus and portions of the parietal lobe form a "navigation network" in the human cortex.

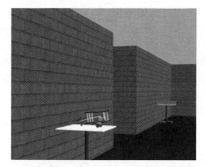 

(a) Toy at decision point   (b) Toy at nondecision point

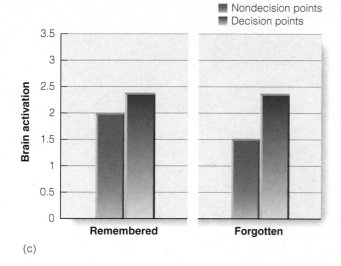

■ Nondecision points
■ Decision points

(c)

Figure 7.12 ▌ (a & b) Two locations in the "virtual museum" viewed by Janzen and van Turennouts's (2004) observers. (c) Brain activation during the recognition test for objects that had been located at decision points (red bars) and nondecision points (blue bars). *(Adapted by permission from Macmillan Publishers Ltd., from Janzen, G., & van Turennout, M., Selective neural representation of objects relevant for navigation,* Nature Neuroscience, 7, 673–677. Copyright 2004.)

But what about landmarks that people use to find their way through environments? Gabriele Janzen and Miranda van Turennout (2004) investigated the role of landmarks in navigation by having observers first study a film sequence that moved through a "virtual museum" (Figure 7.12). Observers were told that they needed to learn their way around the museum well enough to be able to guide a tour through it. Objects ("exhibits") were located along the hallway of this museum. *Decision-point objects,* like the object at (a), marked a place where it was necessary to make a turn. *Non-decision-point objects,* like the one at (b), were located at a place where a decision was not required.

After studying the museum's layout in the film, observers were given a recognition test while in an fMRI scanner. They saw objects that had been in the hallway and some objects they had never seen. Their brain activation was measured in the scanner as they indicated whether they remembered seeing each object. Figure 7.12c indicates activity in the right parahippocampal gyrus for objects the observers had seen as they learned their way through the museum. The left pair of bars, for objects that the observers remembered, indicates that activation was greater for decision-point objects than for non-decision-point objects. The right pair of bars indicates that the advantage for decision-point objects occurred even for objects that were not remembered during the recognition test.

Janzen and van Turennout concluded that the brain automatically distinguishes objects that are used as landmarks to guide navigation. The brain therefore responds not just to the object but also to how relevant that object is for guiding navigation. This means that the next time you are trying to find your way along a route that you have traveled before but aren't totally confident about, activity in your parahippocampal gyrus may automatically be "highlighting" landmarks that indicate where you should make that right turn, even though you may not remember having seen these landmarks before.

But what about situations in which a person is moving through a more realistic environment? Maguire and colleagues (1998) had previously shown how the brain responded as a person navigated from one place to another in a small "virtual town" (Figure 7.11). To increase both the realism and complexity of the navigation task, Hugo Spiers and Maguire (2006) used London taxi drivers as observers and gave them a task that involved navigating through the streets of central London. The taxi drivers operated an interactive computer game called "The Getaway" that accurately depicted the streets of central London as seen through the front window of a car, including all of the buildings and landmarks along the road and some pedestrians as well.

The drivers were given instructions, such as "Please take me to Big Ben," and carried out these instructions by using the computer game to drive toward the destination. In mid-route the instructions were changed ("Sorry, take me to the River Thames"), and later the drivers also heard an irrelevant statement that they might hear from a passenger in a real taxi ride ("I want to remember to post that letter").

The unique feature of this experiment is that the taxi drivers' brain activity was measured using fMRI during their trip. Also, immediately after the trip was over, the taxi drivers observed a playback of their trip and answered questions about what they were thinking at various points. This experiment therefore generated information about how the driver's brain was activated during the trip *and* what the driver was thinking about the driving task during the trip. The result, depicted in Figure 7.13, identifies connections between the drivers' thoughts and patterns of activity in the brain.

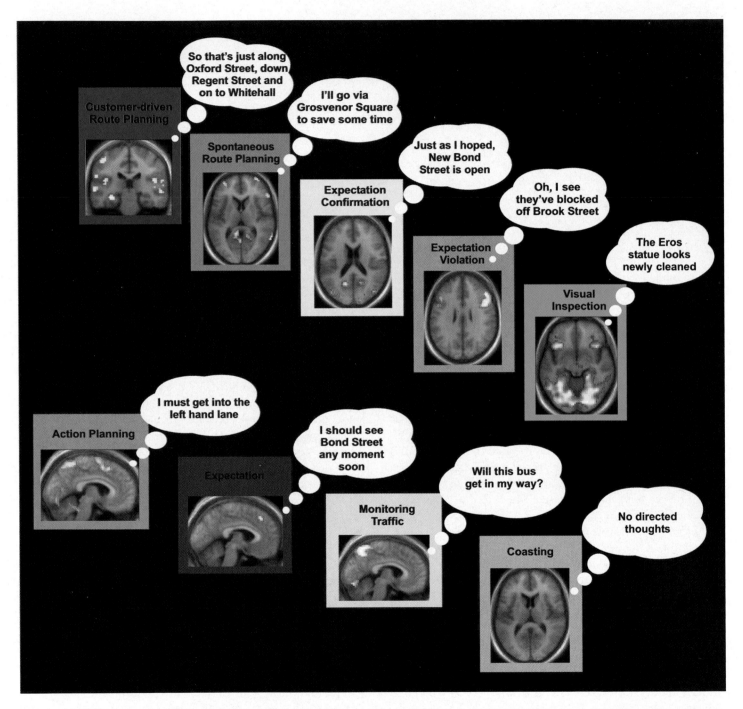

Figure 7.13 ▌ Patterns of brain activation in the taxi drivers in Spiers and Maguire's (2006) experiment. The descriptions above each picture indicate what event was happening at the time the brain was being scanned. For example, "customer-driven route planning" shows brain activity right after the passenger indicated the initial destination. The "thought bubbles" indicate the drivers' reports of what they were thinking at various points during the trip. *(Reprinted from Spiers, H. J., & Maguire, E. A., Thoughts, behaviour, and brain dynamics during navigation in the real world,* NeuroImage, 31, *1831. Copyright 2006, with permission from Elsevier.)*

One example of such a link is that the drivers' hippocampus and parahippocampal place area (PPA) were activated as the drivers were planning which route to take. Other structures were also activated during the trip, including the visual cortex and PPA, which responded as the taxi drivers visually inspected buildings along the way. Spiers and Maguire were thus able to link brain activation to specific navigation tasks.

Acting on Objects: Reaching and Grasping

So far, we have been describing how we move around in the environment. But our actions go beyond walking or driving. One of the major actions we take is reaching to pick something up, as Serena did on her bike ride, as she reached down, grabbed her water bottle, and raised it to her mouth. One of the characteristics of reaching and grasping is that it is usually directed toward specific objects, to accomplish a specific goal. We reach for and grasp doorknobs to open doors; we reach for a hammer to pound nails. An important approach to studying reaching and grasping, which originated with J. J. Gibson, starts with the idea that objects have a property called its *affordance,* which is related to the object's function.

Affordances: What Objects Are Used For

Remember that Gibson's ecological approach involves identifying information in the environment that provides information for perception. Earlier in the chapter we described information such as optic flow, which is created by movement of the observer. Another type of information that Gibson specified are affordances—information that indicates what an object is used for. In Gibson's (1979) words, "The affordances of the environment are what it *offers* the animal, what it *provides for* or *furnishes.*" A chair, or anything that is sit-on-able, affords sitting; an object of the right size and shape to be grabbed by a person's hand affords grasping; and so on.

What this means is that our response to an object does not only include physical properties, such as shape, size, color, and orientation, that might enable us to recognize the object; our response also includes information about how the object is used. For example, when you look at a cup, you might receive information indicating that it is "a round white coffee cup, about 5 inches high, with a handle," but your perceptual system would also respond with information indicating "can pick the cup up" and "can pour liquid into it." Information such as this goes beyond simply seeing or recognizing the cup, because it provides information that can guide our actions toward it. Another way of saying this is that "potential for action" is part of our perception of an object.

One way that affordances have been studied is by looking at the behavior of people with brain damage. As we have seen in other chapters, loss of function as a result of damage to one area of the brain can often reveal behaviors or mechanisms that were formerly not obvious. Glyn Humphreys and Jane Riddoch (2001) studied affordances by testing patient M.P., who had damage to his temporal lobe that impaired his ability to name objects.

M.P. was given a cue, either (1) the name of an object ("cup") or (2) an indication of the object's function ("an item you could drink from"). He was then shown 10 different objects and was told to press a key as soon as he found the object. The results of this testing showed that M.P. identified the object more accurately and rapidly when given the cue that referred to the object's function. Humphreys and Riddoch concluded from this result that M.P. was using his knowledge of an object's affordances to help find it.

Although M.P. wasn't reaching for these objects, it is likely that he would be able to use the information about the object's function to help him take action with respect to the object. In line with this idea, there are other patients with temporal lobe damage who cannot name objects, or even describe how they can be used, but who can pick them up and use them nonetheless.

Another study that demonstrated how an object's affordance can influence behavior was carried out by Guiseppi Di Pellegrino and coworkers (2005), who tested J.P., a woman who had a condition called *extinction,* caused by damage to her parietal lobe. A person with **extinction** can identify a stimulus in the right or left visual field if just one stimulus is presented. However, if two stimuli are presented, one on the left and one on the right, these people have trouble detecting the object on the left. For example, when Di Pellegrino briefly presented J.P. with two pictures of cups, one on the left and one on the right, she detected the right cup on 94 percent of the trials, but detected the left cup on only 56 percent of the trials (Figure 7.14a).

Extinction is caused by a person's inability to direct attention to more than one thing at a time. When only one object is presented, the person can direct his or her attention to that object. However, when two objects are presented, only the right object receives attention, so the left one is less likely to be detected. Di Pellegrino reasoned that if something could be done to increase attention directed toward the object on the left, then perhaps its detection would increase.

To achieve this, Di Pellegrino added a handle to the left cup, with the idea that this handle, which provides an affordance for grasping, might activate a system in the brain that is responsible for reaching and grasping. When he did this, detection of the cup increased to about 80 percent (Figure 7.14b). To be sure detection hadn't increased simply because the handle made the left cup stand out more, Di Pellegrino did a control experiment in which he presented the stimulus in Figure 7.14c, with the handle replaced by an easily distinguished mark. Even though the mark made the cup stand out as well as the handle, performance was only 50 percent. Di Pellegrino concluded from this result that (1) the presence of the handle, which provides an affordance for grasping, automatically activates a brain system that is responsible for reaching and grasping the handle, and (2) this activation increases the person's tendency to pay attention to the cup on the left. The results of experiments such as this one and Humphreys and Riddoch's study of patient M.P. support the idea that an object's potential for action is one of the properties represented when we perceive and recognize an object.

The Physiology of Reaching and Grasping

To study how neurons respond to reaching and grasping, it is necessary to record from the brain while an animal is awake and behaving (Milner & Goodale, 2006). Once procedures were developed that make it possible to record from awake, behaving animals (Evarts, 1966; Hubel, 1959; Jasper et al., 1958), researchers began studying how neurons in the brain respond as monkeys carry out tasks that involve reaching for objects.

One of the first discoveries made by these researchers was that some neurons in the parietal cortex that were silent when the monkey was not behaving began firing vigorously when the monkey reached out to press a button that caused the delivery of food (Hyvärinen & Poranen, 1974; Mountcastle et al., 1975). The most important aspect of this result is that the neurons fired only when the monkey was reaching *to achieve a goal* such as obtaining food. They didn't fire when the monkey made similar movements that were not goal-directed. For example, no response occurred to aggressive movements, even though the same muscles were activated as were activated during goal-directed movements.

The idea that there are neurons in the parietal cortex that respond to goal-directed reaching is supported by the discovery of neurons in the parietal cortex that respond before a monkey actually reaches for an object. Jeffrey Calton and coworkers (2002) trained monkeys to look at and reach for a blue square (Figure 7.15a). Then the square changed color to either green (which indicated that the monkey was to *look at* the next stimulus presented) or red (which indicated that the monkey was to *reach for* the next stimulus (Figure 7.15b). There was then a delay of about a second (Figure 7.15c), followed by presentation of a blue target at different positions around the red fixation stimulus (shown on top in Figure 7.15d). The monkey either *reached*

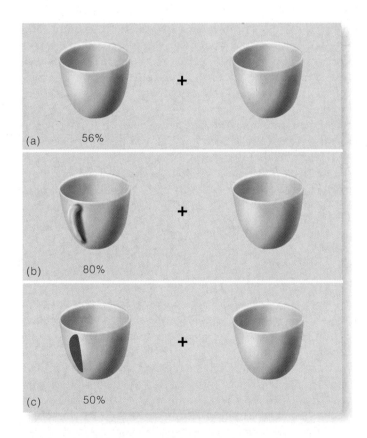

(a) 56%

(b) 80%

(c) 50%

Figure 7.14 ▌ Cup stimuli presented to Di Pellegrino et al.'s (2005) subject J.P. Numbers on the left indicate the percent of trials on which the left cup was detected (a) when the cups were the same; (b) when there was a handle on the left cup; and (c) when there was an easily visible mark on the left cup. *(Adapted from Di Pellegrino, G., Rafal, R, & Tipper, S. P., Implicitly evoked actions modulate visual selection: Evidence from parietal extinction, Current Biology, 15, 1470. Copyright 2005, with permission from Elsevier.)*

(a) Look at and reach
for blue square

(b) Square changes
to green or red

(c) Delay

(d) Target presented

(e) Reach for blue target
(top) or look at it (bottom)

Figure 7.15 ▌ Procedure of the Calton et al. (2002) experiment showing the delay period (shaded) during which brain activity increased when the monkey was planning to reach. See text for details. *(Adapted by permission from Macmillan Publishers, Ltd., from Calton, J. L., Dickenson, A. R., & Snyder, L. H., Non-spatial, motor-specific activation in posterior parietal cortex, Nature Neuroscience, 5, Fig. 1, p. 581. Copyright 2002.)*

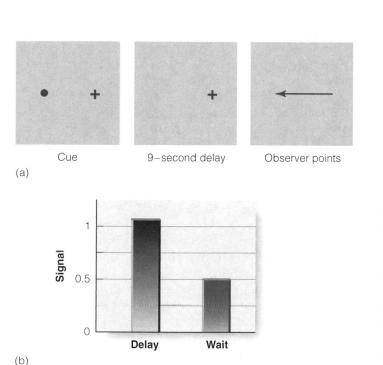

(a)

Cue   9–second delay   Observer points

(b)

Figure 7.16 ▌ Procedure for Connolly's (2003) experiment. (a) The observer looks at the fixation point (+), and the target (●) appears off to the side. (b) Activation of the PR during the 9-second delay or during a waiting period. See text for details.

for the blue target while still looking at the red fixation stimulus (Figure 7.15e, top) or *looked at* it by making an eye movement away from the fixation stimulus (Figure 7.15e, bottom). During this sequence, Calton recorded the activity of neurons in the monkey's parietal cortex.

The key data in this experiment were the neuron firings recorded during the delay period, when the monkey was waiting to either reach for a target or look at a target (Figure 7.15c). Calton found that the parietal neurons fired during this delay if the monkey was planning to reach, but did not fire if the monkey was planning to look. Neurons in the posterior parietal cortex (see Figure 7.8) that respond when a monkey is planning to reach, or is actually reaching, constitute the **parietal reach region (PRR)** (Snyder et al., 2000).

What about humans? Jason Connolly and coworkers (2003) did an experiment in which observers looking at a fixation point were given a cue indicating the location of a target; in Figure 7.16a, it is located off to the left. The cue then went off and the observers had to hold the target location in their mind during a 9-second delay period. When the delay was up, the fixation point disappeared and the observer pointed in the direction of the target, as indicated by the arrow. Activity in the PRR during the 9-second delay was measured using fMRI. In a control experiment, a 9-second waiting period occurred first, followed by the cue and the observer's pointing movement. Activity was measured during the waiting period for the control condition.

The results of this experiment, shown in Figure 7.16b, indicate that activity in the PRR was higher when the observers were holding a location in their mind during the 9-second delay than when they were simply waiting 9 seconds for the trial to begin. Connolly concluded from this result that the PRR in humans encodes information related to the observer's intention to make a movement to a specific location.

In the next section, we take our description of how the brain is involved in action one step further by showing that brain activity can be triggered not only by reaching for an object or by having the intention to reach for an object, but also by watching someone else reach for an object.

Observing Other People's Actions

We not only take action ourselves, but we regularly watch other people take action. This "watching others act" is most obvious when we watch other people's actions on TV or in a movie, but it also occurs any time we are around someone else who is doing something. One of the most exciting outcomes of research studying the link between perception and action was the discovery of neurons in the premotor cortex (Figure 7.8) called *mirror neurons*.

Mirroring Others' Actions in the Brain

In the early 1990s, Giacomo Rizzolatti and coworkers (2006; also see Gallese et al., 1996) were investigating how neurons in the monkey's premotor cortex fired as the monkey performed actions like picking up a toy or a piece of food. Their goal was to determine how neurons fired as the monkey carried out specific actions.

But as sometimes happens in science, they observed something they didn't expect. When one of the experimenters picked up a piece of food while the monkey was watching, neurons in the monkey's cortex fired. What was so unexpected was that the neurons that fired to observing the experimenter pick up the food were the same ones that had fired earlier when the monkey had itself picked up the food.

This initial observation, followed by many additional experiments, led to the discovery of **mirror neurons**—neurons that respond both when a monkey observes someone else (usually the experimenter) grasping an object such as food on a tray (Figure 7.17a) and when the monkey itself grasps the food (Figure 7.17b; Rizzolatti et al., 1996). They are called mirror neurons because the neuron's response to watching the experimenter grasp an object is similar to the response that would occur if the monkey were performing the action. Just looking at the food causes no response, and watching the experimenter grasp the food with a pair of pliers, as in Figure 7.17c, causes only a small response (Gallese et al., 1996; Rizzolatti, Forgassi, & Gallese, 2000).

Most mirror neurons are specialized to respond to only one type of action, such as grasping or placing an object somewhere. Although you might think that the monkey may have been responding to the anticipation of receiving food, the type of object made little difference. The neurons responded just as well when the monkey observed the experimenter pick up an object that was not food.

Consider what is happening when a mirror neuron fires in response to seeing someone else perform an action. This firing provides information about the characteristics of the action because the neuron's response to watching someone else perform the action is the same as the response that occurs when the observer performs the action. This means that one function of the mirror neurons might be to help understand another person's (or monkey's) actions and react appropriately to them (Rizzolatti & Arbib, 1998; Rizzolatti et al., 2000, 2006).

But what is the evidence that these neurons are actually involved in helping "understand" an action? The fact that a response occurs when the experimenter picks up the food with his hand but not with pliers argues that the neuron is not just responding to the pattern of motion. As further evidence that mirror neurons are doing more than just responding to a particular pattern of stimulation, researchers have discovered neurons that respond to sounds that are *associated with* actions. These neurons in the premotor cortex, called **audiovisual mirror neurons**, respond when a monkey performs a hand action *and* when it hears the sound associated with this action (Kohler et al., 2002). For example, the results in Figure 7.18 show the response of a neuron that fires (a) when the monkey sees and hears the experimenter break a peanut, (b) when the monkey just sees the experimenter break the peanut, (c) when the monkey just hears the sound of the breaking peanut, and (d) when the *monkey* breaks the peanut. What this means is that just *hearing* a peanut breaking or just *seeing* a peanut being broken causes activity that is also associated with the perceiver's *action* of breaking a peanut. These neurons are responding, therefore, to the characteristics of observed actions—in this case, what the action of breaking a peanut looks like and what it sounds like.

Another characteristic of action is the intention to carry out an action. We saw that there are neurons in the PRR that respond as a monkey or a human is planning on reaching for an object. We will now see that there is evidence for neurons that respond to *other people's* intentions to carry out an action.

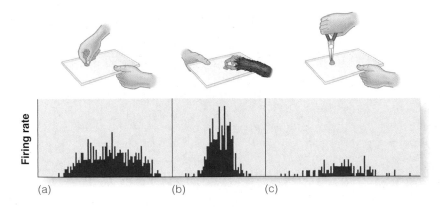

Figure 7.17 ▌ Response of a mirror neuron (a) to watching the experimenter grasp food on the tray; (b) when the monkey grasps the food; (c) to watching the experimenter pick up food with pliers. *(Reprinted from Rizzolatti, G., et al., Premotor cortex and the recognition of motor actions, Cognitive Brain Research, 3, 131–141. Copyright 2000, with permission from Elsevier.)*

Predicting People's Intentions

Let's return to Serena as she observes the pedestrian who looks as though he might step off the curb in front of her oncoming bike. As Serena observes this pedestrian, she is attempting to predict that person's *intentions*—whether or not he intends to step off the curb. What information do we use to predict others' intentions? Sometimes the cues can be obvious, such as watching the pedestrian start to step off the curb and then rapidly step back, indicating that he intended to step off the curb but suddenly decided not to. Cues can also be subtle, such as noticing where someone else is looking.

Andrea Pierno and coworkers (2006) studied the predictive power of watching where someone is looking by having observers view three different 4-second movies: (1) in the *grasping condition,* a person reaches and looks at a grasped target; (2) in the *gaze condition,* a person looks at target object; (3) in the *control condition,* the person does not look at the object or grasp it (Figure 7.19). Meanwhile, the observers' brain activity was being measured in a brain scanner. The researchers measured brain activity in a network of areas that Pierno has called the human *action observation system.* This system encompasses areas that contain mirror neurons, including the premotor cortex, as well as some other areas.

The results for the activity in two brain areas of the action observation system are shown in Figure 7.20. The activation is essentially the same in response to watching the person *grasp the ball* (grasp condition) and watching the person *look at the ball* (gaze condition). What this means, according to Pierno, is that seeing someone else look at the ball activates the observer's action observation system and therefore indicates the person's *intention* to grasp the ball. $\boxed{VL}$ 3

When we described the function of mirror neurons, we noted that these neurons might help us imitate the actions of others and that mirror neurons may also help us understand another person's actions and react appropriately to them. Pierno's experiment suggests that neurons in areas that contain mirror neurons and in some neighboring areas may help us predict what another person is thinking of doing, and therefore may help us predict what the person might do next.

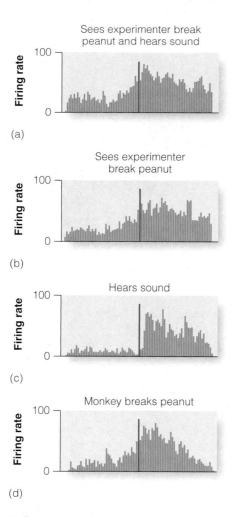

Figure 7.18 ▮ Response of an audiovisual mirror neuron to four different stimuli. *(From Kohler, E., et al., 2002, Hearing sounds, understanding actions: Action representation in mirror neurons. Science, 297, 846–848. Copyright © 2002 by AAAS. Reprinted with permission from AAAS.)*

(a) Grasp   (b) Gaze   (c) Control

Figure 7.19 ▮ Frames from the films shown to Pierno et al.'s (2006) observers: (a) grasping condition; (b) gaze condition; (c) control condition. *(From Pierno, A. C., et al., When gaze turns into grasp, Journal of Cognitive Neuroscience 18, 12.)*

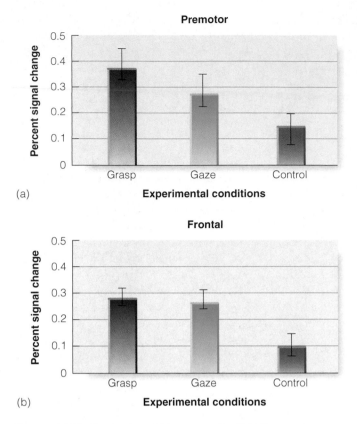

Figure 7.20 ▐ Results of Pierno et al.'s (2006) experiment showing the increase in brain activity that occurred for the three conditions shown in Figure 7.19 in (a) the premotor cortex and (b) an area in the frontal lobe.

Mirror Neurons and Experience

Does everybody have similar mirror neurons, or does activation of a person's mirror neurons depend on that person's past experiences? Beatriz Calvo-Merino and coworkers (2005, 2006) did an experiment to determine whether the response of mirror neurons is affected by a person's experience. They tested three groups of observers: (1) dancers professionally trained in ballet; (2) dancers professionally trained in capoeira dance (a Brazilian dance that includes some karate-like movements); and (3) a control group of nondancers. They showed these groups two videos, one showing standard ballet movements and the other showing standard capoeira movements (Figure 7.21).

Activity in the observer's premotor cortex, where many mirror neurons are located, was measured while the observers watched the films. The results, shown in Figure 7.22, indicate that activity in the PM cortex was greatest for the ballet dancers when they watched ballet and was greatest for the capoeira dancers when they watched capoeira. There was no difference for the nondancer control observers. Thus, even though all of the dancers saw the same videos, the mirror areas of their brains responded most when they watched actions that they had been trained to do. Apparently, mirror neurons are shaped by a person's experience. This means that each person has some mirror neurons that fire most strongly when they observe actions they have previously carried out (also see Catmur et al., 2007).

Figure 7.21 ▐ Sequence of frames from 3-second films shown to Calvo-Merino's (2005) observers: (a) ballet; (b) capoeira dancing. *(From Calvo-Merino, B., et al., Action observation and acquired motor skills: An fMRI study with expert dancers, Cerebral Cortex, August 2005, 15, No. 8, 1243–1249, Fig. 3, by permission of Oxford University Press.)*

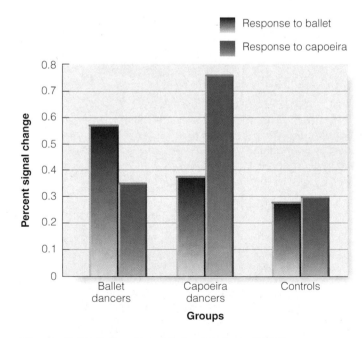

Figure 7.22 ▐ Results of Calvo-Merino's (2005) experiment, showing increase in activity in PM cortex. Red bars = response to ballet films; blue bars = response to capoeira films. *(From Calvo-Merino, B., et al., Action observation and acquired motor skills: An fMRI study with expert dancers, Cerebral Cortex, August 2005, 15, No. 8, 1243–1249, Fig. 3, Copyright © 2005, with permission from Oxford University Press.)*

Now that we are near the end of the chapter, you might look back and notice that much of the research we have described in the last few sections is very recent. The research on mirror neurons, which is just a little over a decade old, has resulted in proposals that these neurons have functions that include understanding other people's actions, reading people's intentions, helping imitate what they are doing, and understanding social situations (Rizzolatti et al., 2006).

But as amazing as these neurons and their proposed functions are, it is important to keep in mind that, because they have just recently been discovered, more research is needed before we can state with more certainty exactly what their function is. Consider that when feature detectors that respond to oriented moving lines were discovered in the 1960s, some researchers proposed that these feature detectors could explain how we perceive objects. With the information available at the time, this was a reasonable proposal. However, later, when neurons that respond to faces, places, and bodies were discovered, researchers revised their initial proposals to take these new findings into account. In all likelihood, a similar process will occur for these new neurons. Some of the proposed functions will be verified, but others may need to be revised. This evolution of thinking about what research results mean is a basic property not only of perception research, but of scientific research in general.

Something to Consider: Controlling Movement With the Mind

Moving a cursor on a computer screen by moving a mouse is a common example of coordination between perception and movement. This coordination involves the following sequence (Figure 7.23a):

1. The image of the cursor creates activity in visual areas of the brain, so the cursor is perceived.

2. Signals from visual areas are sent to the PRR, which calculates a motor plan that specifies the goal for movement of the person's hand that will cause the cursor to reach its desired location on the screen.

3. Signals from the PRR are sent to the motor area of the cortex.

4. Signals from the motor area are sent to the muscles.

5. The hand moves the mouse, which moves the cursor on the screen.

When the cursor moves, the process repeats, with movement on the screen creating new activity in the visual area of the brain (step 1) and the PRR (step 2). The PRR compares the new position of the cursor to the goal that was set in step 2, and if the movement is off course, the PRR recalculates the motor plan and resends it to the motor area

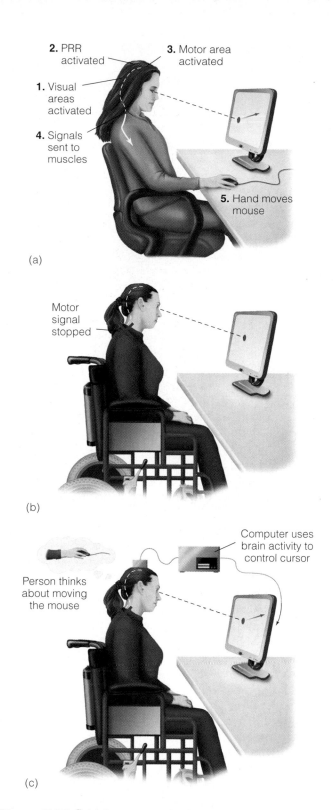

(a)

(b)

(c)

Figure 7.23 ▌ (a) Sequence of events that occur as person controls a cursor with a mouse. See text for details.
(b) Situation when there is spinal cord injury. The first three steps, in which the visual area, the PRR, and the motor area are activated, are the same as in (a). However, the injury, indicated by the X, stops the motor signal from reaching the arm and hand muscles, so the person is paralyzed.
(c) A neural prosthesis picks up signals from the PRR or motor area that are created as the person thinks about moving the mouse. This signal is then used to control the cursor.

(step 3). Signals from the motor area are sent to the muscles (step 4), the hand moves the mouse (step 5), and the process continues until the cursor has reached its goal location.

But what happens if, in Step 4, the signals can't reach the muscles—a situation faced by hundreds of thousands of people who are paralyzed because of spinal cord injury or other problems that prevent signals from traveling from the motor cortex to muscles in the hand (Figure 7.23b). Researchers are working to solve this problem by developing **neural prostheses**—devices that substitute for the muscles that move the mouse (Wolpaw, 2007). Figure 7.23c shows the basic principle. The first three steps of the sequence are the same as before. But the signal from the brain is sent, not to the muscles, but to a computer that transforms these signals into instructions to move the cursor, or in some cases to control a robotic arm that can grasp and manipulate objects.

One approach to developing a prosthesis has used signals from the motor cortex that normally would be sent to the muscles (Scott, 2006; Serruya et al., 2002; Taylor, 2002). For example, Leigh Hochberg and coworkers (2006) used this approach with a 25-year-old man (M.N.) who had been paralyzed by a knife wound that severed his spinal cord. The first step in designing the neural prosthesis was to determine activity in M.N.'s brain that would normally occur when he moved a computer mouse. To do this, Hochberg recorded activity with electrodes implanted in M.N.'s motor area while he imagined moving his hand as if we were using a computer mouse to move a cursor on a computer screen.

The activity recorded from M.N.'s motor cortex was analyzed to determine the connection between brain activity and cursor position. Eventually, enough data were collected and analyzed to enable the computer to read out a cursor position based on M.N.'s brain activity, and this readout was used to control the position of the cursor based on what M.N. was thinking. The test of this device was that M.N. was able to move the cursor to different places on the computer screen just by thinking about where he wanted the cursor to move (Figure 7.24). $\boxed{\text{VL}}$ **4**

Although the majority of research on neural prosthetics has focused on using activity in the motor area to control devices, another promising approach has used signals from the PRR (Andersen et al., 2004). Sam Musallam and coworkers (2004) showed that signals recorded from a monkey's PRR can be used to enable the monkey to move a cursor to different positions on a screen based only on its brain activity.

While these results are impressive, many problems remain to be solved before a device can become routinely available. One problem is that even under controlled laboratory conditions, using computer-analyzed brain activity to control movement is much less accurate and more variable than the control possible when signals are sent directly to the muscles. One reason for this variability is that signals are sent to the muscles in tens of thousands of neurons, and these signals contain all of the information needed to

Figure 7.24 ▌ Matthew Nagle (M.N.) shown controlling the location that is illuminated on a screen by imagining that he is moving a computer mouse. *(Courtesy of John Donoghue and Cyberkinetics Neurotechnology Systems, Inc.)*

achieve precise control of the muscles. In contrast, researchers developing neural prostheses are using signals from far fewer neurons and must determine which aspects of these signals are most effective for controlling movement. Thus, just as vision researchers have been working toward determining how nerve firing in visual areas of the brain represent objects and scenes (see Chapter 5, p. 124), so researchers developing neural prostheses are working toward determining how nerve firing in areas such as the PRR and motor cortex represent movement.

TEST YOURSELF 7.2

1. What is an affordance? Describe the results of two experiments on brain-damaged patients that illustrate the operation of affordances.
2. Describe the experiments that support the idea of a parietal reach region. Include monkey experiments that record from individual neurons (a) as a monkey reaches, and (b) as a monkey plans to reach; and (c) human brain scan experiments that study the brain activity associated with a person's intention to make a movement.
3. What are mirror neurons? Audiovisual mirror neurons? What are some of the potential functions of mirror neurons?
4. Describe the experiment that studied the idea that an action observation system responds to another person's intention to carry out an action.
5. What is the evidence that experience plays a role in the development of mirror neurons?
6. What is a neural prosthesis? Compare how a neural prosthesis can result in movement of a cursor on a computer screen to how an intact brain produces movement of a cursor.

Matthew McKee Photography

THINK ABOUT IT

1. We have seen that gymnasts appear to take visual information into account as they are in the act of executing a somersault. In the sport of synchronized diving, two people execute a dive simultaneously from two side-by-side diving boards. They are judged based on how well they execute the dive and how well the two divers are synchronized with each other. What environmental stimuli do you think synchronized divers need to take into account in order to be successful? (p. 157)

2. Can you identify specific environmental information that you use to help you carry out actions in the environment? This question is often particularly relevant to athletes. (p. 157)

3. It is a common observation that people tend to slow down as they are driving through long tunnels. Explain the possible role of optic flow in this situation. (p. 157)

4. What is the parallel between feeding brain activity into a computer to control movement and feeding brain activity into a computer to recognize scenes, as discussed in Chapter 5 (see page 125). (p. 171)

IF YOU WANT TO KNOW MORE

1. *Ecological psychology.* Ecological psychologists have studied many behaviors that occur in the natural environment. Here are a few papers that are associated with the ecological approach. Also, looking at recent issues of the journal *Ecological Psychology* will give you a feel for modern research by psychologists who identify themselves with the ecological approach. (p. 156)
   Lee, D. N., & Reddish, P. E. (1976). Plummeting gannets: A paradigm of ecological optics. *Nature, 293,* 293–294.
   Rind, F. C., & Simmons, P. J. (1999). Seeing what is coming: Building collision-sensitive neurons. *Trends in Neurosciences, 22,* 215–220.
   Schiff, W., & Detwiler, M. L. (1979). Information used in judging impending collision. *Perception, 8,* 647–658.

   Shaw, R. E. (2003). The agent–environment interface: Simon's indirect or Gibson's direct coupling? *Ecological Psychology, 15,* 37–106.
   Turvey, M. T. (2004). Space (and its perception): The first and final frontier. *Ecological Psychology, 16,* 25–29.

2. *Gibson's books.* J. J. Gibson described his approach in three books that explain his philosophy and approach in detail. (p. 156)
   Gibson, J. J. (1950). *The perception of the visual world.* Boston: Houghton Mifflin.
   Gibson, J. J. (1966). *The senses considered as perceptual systems.* Boston: Houghton Mifflin.
   Gibson, J. J. (1979). *The ecological approach to visual perception.* Boston: Houghton Mifflin.

3. *Motor area of brain activated when sounds are associated with actions.* Research has shown that the motor area of the cortex is activated when trained pianists hear music. This does not occur in nonpianists, presumably because the link between finger movements and sound is not present in these people. (p. 169)
   Haueisen, J., & Knosche, T. R. (2001). Involuntary motor activity in pianists evoked by music perception. *Journal of Cognitive Neuroscience, 136,* 786–792.

4. *Event perception.* Although people experience a continuously changing environment, they are able to divide this continuous stream of experience into individual events, such as preheating the oven, mixing the ingredients in a bowl, and putting the dough on a cookie sheet when baking cookies. Recent research has studied how people divide experience into events, and what is happening in the brain as they do. (p. 167)
   Kurby, C. A., & Zacks, J. M. (2007). Segmentation in the perception and memory of events. *Trends in Cognitive Sciences, 12,* 72–79.
   Zacks, J. M, Speer, N. K., Swallow, K. M., Braver, T. S., & Reynolds, J. R. (2007). Event perception: A mind-brain perspective. *Psychological Bulletin, 133,* 273–293.
   Zacks, J. M., & Swallow, K. M. (2007). Event segmentation. *Current Directions in Psychological Science, 16,* 80–84.

KEY TERMS

Affordance (p. 165)	Focus of expansion (FOE) (p. 157)	Optic array (p. 156)
Audiovisual mirror neuron (p. 168)	Gradient of flow (p. 157)	Optic flow (p. 156)
Ecological approach to perception (p. 156)	Invariant information (p. 157)	Parietal reach region (PRR) (p. 167)
Extinction (p. 165)	Mirror neuron (p. 168)	Self-produced information (p. 157)
	Neural prosthesis (p. 172)	Visual direction strategy (p. 160)

MEDIA RESOURCES

The *Sensation and Perception* Book Companion Website

www.cengage.com/psychology/goldstein

See the companion website flashcards, practice quiz questions, Internet links, updates, critical thinking exercises, discussion forums, games, and more!

CengageNow

www.cengage.com/cengagenow

Go to this site for the link to CengageNOW, your one-stop shop. Take a pre-test for this chapter, and CengageNOW will generate a personalized study plan based on your test results. The study plan will identify the topics you need to review and direct you to online resources to help you master those topics. You can then take a post-test to help you determine the concepts you have mastered and what you will still need to work on.

Virtual Lab

V_L

Your Virtual Lab is designed to help you get the most out of this course. The Virtual Lab icons direct you to specific media demonstrations and experiments designed to help you visualize what you are reading about. The number beside each icon indicates the number of the media element you can access through your CD-ROM, CengageNOW, or WebTutor resource.

The following lab exercises are related to the material in this chapter:

1. *Flow From Walking Down a Hallway* A computer-generated program showing the optic flow that occurs when moving through a patterned hallway. (Courtesy of William Warren.)

2. *Stimuli Used in Warren Experiment* Moving stimulus pattern seen by observers in William Warren's experiment. (Courtesy of William Warren.)

3. *Pierno Stimuli* Stimuli for the Pierno experiment. (Courtesy of Andrea Pierno.)

4. *Neural Prosthesis* Video showing a paralyzed person moving a cursor on a screen by mentally controlling the cursor's movement. (Courtesy of Cyberkinetics, Inc.)

Chapter Contents

CHAPTER 8

Perceiving Motion

OPPOSITE PAGE This stop-action photograph captures a sequence of positions of a bird as it leaves a tree branch. This picture represents the type of environmental motion that we perceive effortlessly every day. Although we perceive motion easily, the mechanisms underlying motion perception are extremely complex.
© Andy Rouse/Corbis

VL The Virtual Lab icons direct you to specific animations and videos designed to help you visualize what you are reading about. The number beside each icon indicates the number of the clip you can access through your CD-ROM or your student website.

Some Questions We Will Consider:

▌ Why do some animals freeze in place when they sense danger? (p. 179)

▌ How do films create movement from still pictures? (p. 180)

▌ When we scan or walk through a room, the image of the room moves across the retina, but we perceive the room and the objects in it as remaining stationary. Why does this occur? (p. 184)

Action fills our world. We are always taking action, either dramatically—as in Serena's bike ride in Chapter 7 (page 156) or a basketball player driving toward the basket—or routinely, as in reaching for a coffee cup or walking across a room. Whatever form action takes, it involves motion, and one of the things that makes the study of motion perception both fascinating and challenging is that we are not simply passive observers of the motion of others. We are often moving ourselves. Thus, we perceive motion when we are stationary, as when we are watching other people cross the street (Figure 8.1a), and we also perceive motion as we ourselves are moving, as might happen when we participate in a basketball game (Figure 8.1b). We will see in this chapter that both the "simple" case of a stationary observer perceiving motion and the more complicated case of a moving observer perceiving motion involve complex "behind the scenes" mechanisms.

Functions of Motion Perception

Motion perception has a number of different functions, ranging from providing us with updates about what is happening to helping us perceive things such as the shapes of objects and people's moods. Perhaps most important of all, especially for animals, the perception of motion is intimately linked to survival.

Motion Helps Us Understand Events in Our Environment

As you walk through a shopping mall, looking at the displays in the store windows, you are also observing other actions—a group of people engaged in an animated conversation, a salesperson rearranging piles of clothing and then walking over to the cash register to help a customer, a program on the TV in a restaurant that you recognize as a dramatic moment in a soap opera.

Much of what you observe involves information provided by motion. The gestures of the people in the group you observed indicate the intensity of their conversation; the motions of the salesperson indicate what she is doing and when she has shifted to a new task; and motion indicates, even in the absence of sound, that something

(a)

(b)

Figure 8.1 ▌ Motion perception occurs (a) when a stationary observer perceives moving stimuli, such as this couple crossing the street, and (b) when a moving observer, like this basketball player, perceives moving stimuli, such as the other players on the court.

important is happening in the soap opera (Zacks, 2004; Zacks & Swallow, 2007).

Our ability to use motion information to determine what is happening is an important function of motion perception that we generally take for granted. Motion perception is also essential for our ability to move through the environment. As we saw in Chapter 7 when we described how people "navigate" (see page 159), one source of information about where we are going and how fast we are moving is the way objects in the environment flow past us as we move. As a person moves forward, objects move relative to the person in the opposite direction. This movement, called *optic flow* (page 157), provides information about the walker's direction and speed. In Chapter 7 we discussed how we can use this information to help us stay on course.

But while motion provides information about what is going on and where we are moving, it provides information for more subtle actions as well. Consider, for example, the action of pouring water into a glass. As we perceive the water, we watch the level rise, and this helps us know when to stop pouring. We can appreciate the importance of this ability by considering the case of a 43-year-old woman who lost the ability to perceive motion when she suffered a stroke that damaged an area of her cortex involved in motion perception. Her condition, which is called **motion agnosia**, made it difficult for her to pour tea or coffee into a cup because the liquid appeared frozen, so she couldn't perceive the fluid rising in the cup and had trouble knowing when to stop pouring (Figure 8.2). It was also difficult for her to follow dialogue because she couldn't see motions of a speaker's face and mouth (Zihl et al., 1983, 1991).

But the most disturbing effect of her brain damage was the sudden appearance or disappearance of people and objects. People suddenly appeared or disappeared because she couldn't see them walking. Crossing the street presented serious problems because at first a car might seem far away, but then suddenly, without warning, it would appear very near. This disability was not just a social inconvenience, but enough of a threat to the woman's well-being that she rarely ventured outside into the world of moving—and sometimes dangerous—objects. This case of a breakdown in the ability to perceive motion provides a dramatic demonstration of the importance of motion perception in day-to-day life.

Motion Attracts Attention

As you try to find your friend among the sea of faces in the student section of the stadium, you realize that you have no idea where to look. But you suddenly see a person waving and realize it is your friend. The ability of motion to attract attention is called **attentional capture**. This effect occurs not only when you are consciously looking for something, but also while you are paying attention to something else. For example, as you are talking with a friend, your attention may suddenly be captured by something moving in your peripheral vision.

The fact that movement can attract attention plays an important role in animal survival. You have probably seen animals freeze in place when they sense danger. For example, if a mouse's goal is to avoid being detected by a cat, one thing it can do is to stop moving. Freezing in place not only eliminates the attention-attracting effects of movement, but it also makes it harder for the cat to differentiate between the mouse and its background.

Motion Provides Information About Objects

The idea that not moving can help an animal blend into the background is illustrated by the following demonstration. [VL] **1, 2**

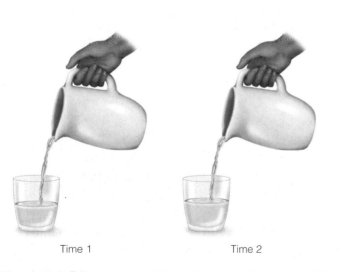

Time 1   Time 2

Figure 8.2 ▌ The woman with motion agnosia was not able to perceive the rising level as liquid was being poured into a glass.

DEMONSTRATION

Perceiving a Camouflaged Bird

For this demonstration, you will need to prepare stimuli by photocopying the bird and the hatched-line pattern in Figure 8.3. Then cut out the bird and the hatched pattern so they are separated. Hold the picture of the bird up against a window during the day. Turn the copy of the hatched pattern over so the pattern is facing out the window (the white side of the paper should be facing you) and place it over the bird. If the window is adequately illuminated by daylight, you should be able to see the hatched pattern. Notice how the presence of the hatched pattern makes it more difficult to see the bird. Then, slide the bird back and forth under the pattern, and notice what happens to your perception of the bird (from Regan, 1986). ▌

Figure 8.3 ▍ The bird becomes camouflaged when the random lines are superimposed on the bird. When the bird is moved relative to the lines, it becomes visible, an example of how movement enhances the perception of form. *(From Regan, D. (1986). Luminance contrast: Vernier discrimination.* Spatial Vision, 1, *305–318.)*

The stationary bird is difficult to see when covered by the pattern because the bird and the pattern are made up of similar lines. But as soon as all of the elements of the bird begin moving in the same direction, the bird becomes visible. What is happening here is that movement has perceptually organized all of the elements of the bird, so they create a figure that is separated from the background. This is why a mouse should stay stationary even if it is hidden by other objects, if it wants to avoid becoming perceptually organized in the cat's mind!

You might say, after doing the camouflaged bird demonstration, that although motion does make the bird easy to perceive amid the tangle of obscuring lines, this seems like a special case, because most of the objects we see are not camouflaged. But if you remember our discussion from Chapter 5 (p. 101) about how even clearly visible objects may be ambiguous, you can appreciate that moving relative to an object can help us perceive its shape more accurately. For example, moving around the "horse" in Figure 8.4 reveals that its shape is not exactly what you may have expected based on your initial view. Thus, our motion relative to objects is constantly adding to the information we have about the objects. This also happens when objects move relative to us, and a great deal of research has shown that observers perceive shapes more rapidly and accurately when an object is moving (Wexler et al., 2001). **VL** **3-7**

Studying Motion Perception

To describe how motion perception is studied, the first question we will consider is: When do we perceive motion?

When Do We Perceive Motion?

The answer to this question may seem obvious: We perceive motion when something moves across our field of view. Actual motion of an object is called **real motion**. Perceiving a car driving by, people walking, or a bug scurrying across a tabletop are all examples of the perception of real motion.

There are also a number of ways to produce the perception of motion that involve stimuli that are not moving. Perception of motion when there actually is none is called **illusory motion**. The most famous, and well-studied, type of illusory motion is called **apparent motion**. We introduced apparent motion in Chapter 5 when we told the story of Max Wertheimer, who showed that when two stimuli in slightly different locations are alternated with the correct timing, an observer perceives one stimulus moving back and forth smoothly between the two locations (Figure 8.5a). This perception is called apparent motion because there is no actual (or real) motion between the stimuli. This is the basis for the motion we perceive in movies, on television, and in moving signs that are used for advertising and entertainment (Figure 8.5b). **VL** **8-11**

Bruce Goldstein

(a) (b) (c)

Figure 8.4 ▍ Three views of a "horse." Moving around an object can reveal its true shape.

Induced motion occurs when motion of one object (usually a large one) causes a nearby stationary object (usually smaller) to appear to move. For example, the moon usually appears stationary in the sky. However, if clouds are moving past the moon on a windy night, the moon may appear to be racing through the clouds. In this case, movement of the larger object (clouds covering a large area) makes the smaller, but actually stationary, moon appear to be moving (Figure 8.6a). VL 12

Motion aftereffects occur after viewing a moving stimulus for 30 to 60 seconds and then viewing a stationary stimulus, which appears to move. One example of a motion aftereffect is the waterfall illusion (Figure 8.6b). If you look at a waterfall for 30 to 60 seconds (be sure it fills up only part of your field of view) and then look off to the side at part of the scene that is stationary, you will see everything you are looking at—rocks, trees, grass—appear to move up for a few seconds (Figure 8.6c). Motion aftereffects can also occur after viewing other kinds of motion. For example, viewing a rotating spiral that appears to move inward causes the apparent expansion of a stationary object. (See "If You Want to Know More," item 3, page 196, for a reference that discusses the mechanisms responsible for aftereffects.) VL 13–14

Researchers studying motion perception have investigated all of the types of perceived motion described above—and some others as well. Our purpose, however, is not to understand every type of motion perception but to understand some of the principles governing motion perception in general. To do this, we will focus on real motion and apparent motion.

Comparing Real and Apparent Motion

For many years, researchers treated the apparent motion created by flashing stationary objects or pictures and the real motion created by actual motion through space as though they were separate phenomena, governed by different mechanisms. However, there is ample evidence that these two types of motion have much in common. Consider, for example, an experiment by Axel Larsen and coworkers

(a)

(b)

Figure 8.5 ❚ Apparent motion (a) between these squares when they are flashed rapidly on and off; (b) on a moving sign. Our perception of words moving across a display such as this one is so compelling that it is often difficult to realize that signs like this are simply dots flashing on and off.

(a)   (b)   (c)

Figure 8.6 ❚ (a) Motion of the clouds induces the perception of motion in the stationary moon. (b) Observation of motion in one direction, such as occurs when viewing a waterfall, can cause (c) the perception of motion in the opposite direction when viewing stationary objects in the environment.

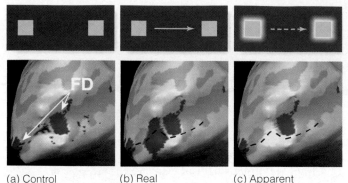

(a) Control   (b) Real   (c) Apparent

Figure 8.7 ▌ The three conditions in Larsen's (2006) experiment: (a) control; (b) real motion; and (c) apparent motion (flashing dots). Stimuli are shown on top, and the resulting brain activation below. In (c) the brain is activated in the space that represents the area between the two dots, indicating that movement was perceived even though no stimuli were present. *(Larsen, A., Madsen, K. H., Lund, T. E., & Bundesen, C., Images of illusory motion in primary visual cortex. Journal of Cognitive Neuroscience, 18, 1174–1180. © 2006 by the Massachusetts Institute of Technology.)*

(2006). Larsen presented three types of displays to a person in an fMRI scanner: (1) a *control condition,* in which two dots in slightly different positions were flashed simultaneously (Figure 8.7a); (2) a *real motion display,* in which a small dot moved back and forth (Figure 8.7b); and (3) an *apparent motion display,* in which dots were flashed one after another so that they appeared to move back and forth (Figure 8.7c).

Larsen's results are shown below the dot displays. The blue-colored area in Figure 8.7a is the area of visual cortex activated by the control dots, which are perceived as two dots simultaneously flashing on and off with no motion between them. Each dot activates a separate area of the cortex. In Figure 8.7b, the red indicates the area of cortex activated by real movement of the dot. In Figure 8.7c, the yellow indicates the area of cortex activated by the apparent motion display. Notice that the activation associated with apparent motion is similar to the activation for the real motion display. Two flashed dots that result in apparent motion activate the area of brain representing the space between the

positions of the flashing dots even though no stimulus was presented there.

Because of the similarities between the *perception* of real and apparent motion, and between the *brain mechanisms* associated with these two types of motion, researchers study both types of motion together and concentrate on discovering general mechanisms that apply to both. In this chapter, we will follow this approach as we look for general mechanisms of motion perception.

What We Want to Explain

Our goal is to understand how we perceive things that are moving. At first this may seem like an easy problem. For example, Figure 8.8a shows what Maria sees when she looks straight ahead as Jeremy walks by. Because she doesn't move her eyes, Jeremy's image sweeps across her retina. Explaining motion perception in this case seems straightforward because as Jeremy's image moves across Maria's retina, it stimulates a series of receptors one after another, and this stimulation signals Jeremy's motion.

Figure 8.8b shows what Maria sees when she follows Jeremy's motion with her eyes. In this case, Jeremy's image remains stationary on Maria's foveas as he walks by. This adds an interesting complication to explaining motion perception, because although Maria perceives Jeremy's motion, Jeremy's image remains stationary on her retina. This means that motion perception can't be explained just by considering what is happening on the retina.

Finally, let's consider what happens if Jeremy isn't present, and Maria decides to walk through the room (Figure 8.8c). When Maria does this, the images of the walls and objects in the room move across her retina, but Maria doesn't see the room or its contents as moving. In this case, there is motion across the retina, but no perception that objects are moving. This is another example of why we can't simply consider what is happening on the retina. Table 8.1 summarizes the three situations in Figure 8.8.

In the sections that follow, we will consider a number of different approaches to explaining motion perception, with the goal being to explain each of the situations in Table 8.1. We begin by considering an approach that focuses on how information in the environment signals motion.

TABLE 8.1 ▌ **Conditions for Perceiving and Not Perceiving Motion Depicted in Figure 8.8**

SITUATION	OBJECT MOVES?	OBSERVER	IMAGE ON OBSERVER'S RETINA	PERCEPTION
(a) Jeremy walks across room	Yes	Maria's eyes are stationary	Moves across retina as object moves	Object (Jeremy) moves
(b) Jeremy walks across room	Yes	Maria's eyes follow Jeremy as he moves	Stationary, because the image stays on the fovea	Object (Jeremy) moves
(c) Maria walks through the room	No, everything in the room is stationary	Maria is moving through the room	Moves across retina as Maria walks	Objects (the room and its contents) do not move

(a) Jeremy walks past Maria; Maria's eyes are stationary
   (creates local disturbance in optic array)

(b) Jeremy walks past Maria; Maria follows him with her eyes
   (creates local disturbance in optic array)

(c) Maria walks through the scene
   (creates global optic flow)

Figure 8.8 | Three motion situations: (a) Maria is stationary and observes Jeremy walking past; (b) Maria follows Jeremy's movement with her eyes; (c) Maria walks through the room.

Motion Perception: Information in the Environment

From the three examples in Figure 8.8, we saw that motion perception can't be explained by considering just what is happening on the retina. So, what if we ignore the retina altogether and focus instead on information "out there" in the environment that signals motion? That is exactly what J. J. Gibson, who founded the ecological approach to perception, did.

In Chapter 7 we noted that Gibson's approach involves looking for information in the environment that provides information for perception (see page 156). This information for perception, according to Gibson, is located not on the retina but "out there" in the environment. He thought about information in the environment in terms of the **optic array**—the structure created by the surfaces, textures, and contours of the environment—and he focused on how movement of the observer causes changes in the optic array. Let's see how this works by returning to Jeremy and Maria in Figure 8.8.

In Figure 8.8a, when Jeremy walks across Maria's field of view, portions of the optic array become covered as he walks by and then are uncovered as he moves on. This result is called a **local disturbance in the optic array**. A local disturbance in the optic array occurs when one object moves relative to the environment, covering and uncovering the stationary background. According to Gibson, this local disturbance in the optic array provides information that Jeremy is moving relative to the environment.

In Figure 8.8b, Maria follows Jeremy with her eyes. Remember that Gibson doesn't care what is happening on the retina. Even though Jeremy's image is stationary on the retina, the same local disturbance information that was available when Maria was keeping her eyes still remains available when she is moving her eyes, and this local disturbance information indicates that Jeremy is moving.

In Figure 8.8c, when Maria walks through the environment, something different happens: As Maria moves, everything around her moves. The walls, the window, the trashcan, the clock, and the furniture all move relative to Maria as she walks through the scene. The fact that everything moves at once is called **global optic flow**; this signals that Maria is moving but that the environment **VL 15** is stationary.

In identifying information in the environment that signals what is moving and what is not, the ecological approach provides a nice solution to the problem that we can't explain how we perceive movement in some situations based just on what is happening on the retina. However, this explanation does not consider what is happening physiologically. We will now consider that.

Neural Firing to Motion Across the Retina

Whereas the ecological approach focuses on environmental information, the physiological approach to motion perception focuses on determining the connection between neural firing and motion perception. First, let's return to the case of the observer looking straight ahead at something moving across the field of view, as in Figure 8.8a. As we will now see, even this "simple" case is not so simple.

Motion of a Stimulus Across the Retina: The Aperture Problem

How can we explain how neural firing signals the direction that an object is moving? One possible answer to this question is that as the stimulus sweeps across the retina, it activates directionally selective neurons in the cortex that respond to oriented bars that are moving in a specific direction (see Chapter 4, page 78). This is illustrated in Figure 8.9, which shows a bar sweeping across a neuron's receptive field.

Although this appears to be a straightforward solution to signaling the direction an object is moving, it turns out that the response of single directionally selective neurons does not provide sufficient information to indicate the direction in which an object is moving. We can understand why this is so by considering how a directionally selective neuron would respond to movement of a vertically oriented pole like the one being carried by the woman in Figure 8.10.

We are going to focus on the pole, which is essentially a bar with an orientation of 90 degrees. The circle repre-

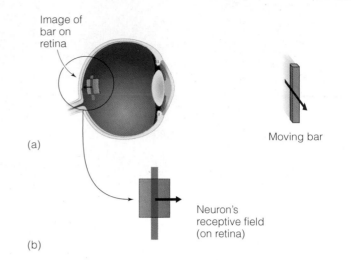

Figure 8.9 ▌ (a) The rectangle area at the back of the eye represents the receptive field of a neuron in the cortex that responds to movement of vertical bars to the right. (b) When the image of the vertical bar sweeps across the receptive field, the neuron in the cortex fires.

Figure 8.10 ▌ The pole's overall motion is horizontal to the right (blue arrows). The circle represents the area in Maria's field of view that corresponds to the receptive field of a cortical neuron. The pole's motion across the receptive field (which is located on Maria's retina) is also horizontal to the right (red arrows).

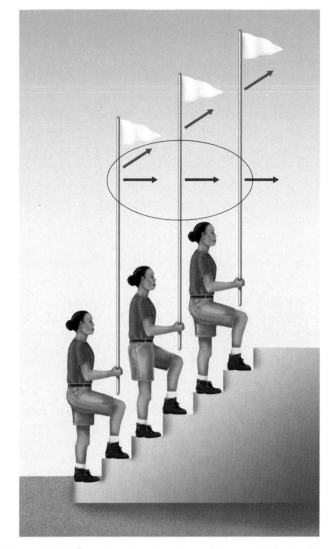

Figure 8.11 ▌ In this situation the pole's overall motion is up and to the right (blue arrows). The pole's motion across the receptive field, however, remains horizontal to the right (red arrows), as in Figure 8.10. Thus, the receptive field "sees" the same motion whether the overall motion is horizontal or up and to the right.

DEMONSTRATION

Motion of a Bar Across an Aperture

Make a small aperture, about 1 inch in diameter, by creating a circle with the fingers of your left hand, as shown in Figure 8.12 (or you can create a circle by cutting a hole in a piece of paper). Then orient a pencil vertically, and move the pencil from left to right behind the circle, as in Figure 8.12a. As you do this, focus on the direction that the *front edge* of the pencil appears to be moving across the aperture. Now, again holding the pencil vertically, position the pencil below the circle, as shown in Figure 8.12b, and move it up behind the aperture at a 45-degree angle (being careful to keep its orientation vertical). Again, notice the direction in which the *front edge* of the pencil appears to be moving across the aperture. ▌ $\boxed{V_L}$ **16, 17**

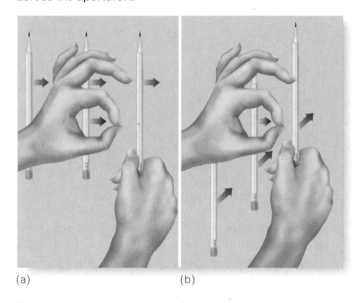

(a)   (b)

Figure 8.12 ▌ Moving a pencil across an aperture. See text for details.

sents the area of the receptive field of a complex neuron in the cortex that responds when a vertically oriented bar moves to the right across the neuron's receptive field. Figure 8.10 shows the pole entering the receptive field. As the pole moves to the right, it moves across the receptive field in the direction indicated by the red arrow, and the neuron fires.

But what happens if the woman climbs some steps? Figure 8.11 shows that as she walks up the steps she and the pole are now moving up and to the right (blue arrow). We know this because we can see the woman and the flag moving up. But the neuron, which only sees movement through the narrow view of its receptive field, only receives information about the rightward movement. You can appreciate this by noting that movement of the pole across the receptive field appears the same when the pole is moving to the right (red arrow) and when it is moving up and to the right (blue arrow). You can demonstrate this for yourself by doing the following demonstration.

If you were able to focus only on what was happening inside the aperture, you probably noticed that the direction that the front edge of the pencil was moving appeared the same whether the pencil was moving horizontally to the right or up and to the right. In both cases, the front edge of the pencil moves across the aperture horizontally. Another way to state this is that the movement of an edge across an aperture occurs *perpendicular to the direction in which the edge is oriented.* Because the pencil in our demonstration was oriented vertically, motion through the aperture was horizontal. Because motion of the edge was the same in both situations, a single directionally selective neuron would fire similarly in both situations, so the activity of this neuron would not provide accurate information about the direction of the pencil's motion.

The fact that viewing only a small portion of a larger stimulus can result in misleading information about the direction in which the stimulus is moving is called the

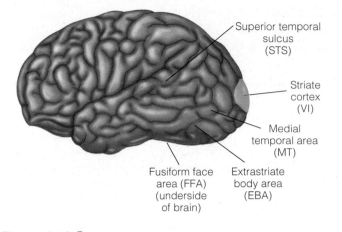

Figure 8.13 ❚ Human brain, showing the location of a number of the structures we will be discussing in this chapter. MT = medial temporal cortex (motion perception); VI = striate cortex (primary visual receiving area); STS = superior temporal sulcul (biological motion); FFA = fusiform face area (face perception); EBA = extrastriate body area (perceiving bodies).

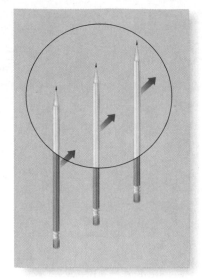

Figure 8.14 ❚ The circle represents a neuron's receptive field. When the pencil is moved up and to the right, as shown, movement of the tip of the pencil provides information indicating that the pencil is moving up and to the right.

aperture problem. The visual system appears to solve the aperture problem by pooling the responses of a number of neurons like our complex cell. One place this may occur is the medial temporal (MT) cortex, a nucleus in the dorsal (*where* or *action*) stream, which contains a large number of directionally selective neurons and which we will see is important for movement perception. Figure 8.13 shows the location of MT cortex.

Evidence that the MT may be involved in pooling the responses from a number of neurons was provided by an experiment by Christopher Pack and Richard Born (2001), in which they determined how neurons in the monkey's MT cortex responded to moving oriented lines like the pole or our pencil. They found that the MT neurons' initial response to the stimulus, at about 70 msec after the stimulus was presented, was determined by the orientation of the bar. Thus the neuron responded in the same way to a vertical bar moving horizontally to the right and a vertical bar moving up and to the right (red arrows in Figure 8.12). However, 140 ms after presentation of the moving bars, the neurons began responding to the *actual* direction in which the bars were moving (blue arrows in Figure 8.12). Apparently, MT neurons receive signals from a number of neurons in the striate cortex and then combine these signals to determine the actual direction of motion.

Can you think of another way a neuron might indicate that the pole in Figure 8.11 is moving up and to the right? One of my students tried the demonstration in Figure 8.12 and noticed that when he followed the directions for the demonstration, the edge of the pencil did appear to be moving horizontally across the aperture, whether the pencil was moving to the right or up and to the right. However, when he moved the pencil so that he could see its tip moving through the aperture, as in Figure 8.14, he could tell that the pencil was moving up. Thus, a neuron could use

information about the end of a moving object (such as the tip of the pencil) to determine its direction of motion. As it turns out, neurons that could signal this information, because they respond to the ends of moving objects, have been found in the striate cortex (Pack et al., 2003).

What all of this means is that the "simple" situation of an object moving across the visual field as an observer looks straight ahead is not so simple because of the aperture problem. The visual system apparently can solve this problem (1) by using information from neurons in the MT cortex that pool the responses of a number of directionally selective neurons, and (2) by using information from neurons in the striate cortex that respond to the movement of the ends of objects (also see Rust et al., 2006; Smith et al., 2005; Zhang & Britten, 2006).

Motion of Arrays of Dots on the Retina

The bar stimuli used in the research we have been describing are easy to detect. But what about stimuli that are more difficult to detect? One tactic used in perception research is to determine how the perceptual system responds to stimuli that we are just able to detect. We have described experiments such as this in Chapter 3 (measuring spectral sensitivity curves, dark adaptation, and visual acuity), Chapter 5 (determining how well people can detect briefly presented stimuli), and Chapter 6 (determining how attention affects the perception of contrast between bars in a grating). We will now describe some experiments using a type of movement stimulus that makes it possible to vary how difficult it is to determine the direction of motion.

Neural Firing and the Perception of Moving-Dot Stimuli William Newsome and coworkers (1989) used a computer to create moving-dot displays in which the direction of motion of individual dots can be varied. Figure 8.15a represents a display in which all of the dots are moving in random directions. Newsome used the term **coherence** to indicate the degree to which the dots move in the same direction. When the dots are all moving in random directions, much like the "snow" you see when your TV set is tuned between channels, coherence is 0 percent. Figure 8.15b represents a coherence of 50 percent, as indicated by the darkened dots, which means that at any point in time half of the dots are moving in the same direction. Figure 8.15c represents 100 percent coherence, which means that all of the dots are moving in the same direction.

Newsome and coworkers used these stimuli to determine the relationship between (1) a monkey's ability to judge the direction in which dots were moving and (2) the response of a neuron in the monkey's MT cortex. They found that as the dots' coherence increased, two things happened: (1) the monkey judged the direction of motion more accurately, and (2) the MT neuron fired more rapidly. The monkey's behavior and the firing of the MT neurons were so closely related that the researchers could predict one from the other. For example, when the dots' coherence was 0.8 percent, the monkey was not able to judge the direction of the dots' motion and the neuron's response did not differ appreciably from its baseline firing rate. But at a coherence of 12.8 percent, the monkey judged the direction of the dots that were moving together correctly on virtually every trial, and the MT neuron always fired faster than its baseline rate. $\boxed{V_L}$ **18**

These experiments are important because by simultaneously measuring the response of MT neurons and the monkey's perception, Newsome directly measured the relationship between physiology and perception (relationship PH2 in the perceptual cycle in Figure 8.16). This is in contrast to most of the experiments we have described in this book so far, which have measured relationship PH1, the relationship between stimuli and the physiological response. For example, remember Hubel and Wiesel's (1959, 1965) experiments from Chapter 4, which showed that moving bars cause neurons in the cortex to fire (see page 78). These experiments provided important information about neurons in the cortex, but did not provide any direct information about the connection between these neurons and perception.

The simultaneous measurement of neural firing and perception is extremely difficult because before the recording experiments can begin, monkeys must be trained for months to indicate the direction in which they perceive the dots moving. Only after this extensive behavioral training can the monkey's perception and neural firing be measured simultaneously. The payoff, however, is that relationship PH2 is measured *directly,* instead of having to be *inferred* from measurements of the relationship between stimuli and perception (PP) and between stimuli and physiological responding (PH1).

Effect of Lesioning and Microstimulation Measuring perception and the firing of neurons in the MT cortex simultaneously is one way of showing that the MT cortex is important for motion perception. The role of the MT cortex has also been studied by determining how the perception of motion is affected by (1) lesioning

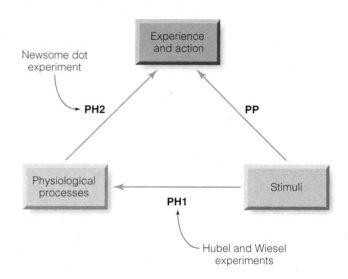

Figure 8.16 ▮ The perceptual cycle from Chapter 1. Newsome measured relationship PH2 by simultaneously recording from neurons and measuring the monkey's behavioral response. Other research we have discussed, such as Hubel and Wiesel's receptive field studies, have measured relationship PH1.

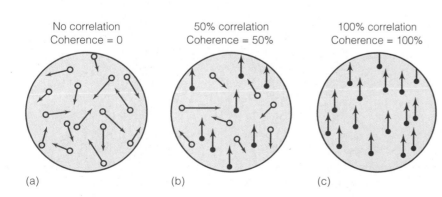

Figure 8.15 ▮ Moving-dot displays used by Newsome, Britten, and Movshon (1989). These pictures represent moving-dot displays that were created by a computer. Each dot survives for a brief interval (20–30 microseconds), after which it disappears and is replaced by another randomly placed dot. Coherence is the percentage of dots moving in the same direction at any point in time. *(From Newsome, W. T., & Paré, E. B. (1988). A selective impairment of motion perception following lesions of the middle temporal visual area (MT).* Journal of Neuroscience, 8, 2201–2211.)

(destroying) some or all of the MT cortex or (2) electrically stimulating neurons in the MT cortex.

A monkey with an intact MT cortex can begin detecting the direction dots are moving when coherence is as low as 1–2 percent. However, after the MT is lesioned, the coherence must be 10–20 percent before monkeys can begin detecting the direction of motion. (Newsome & Paré, 1988; also see Movshon & Newsome, 1992; Newsome et al., 1995; Pasternak & Merigan, 1994). This provides further evidence linking the firing of MT neurons to the perception of the direction of motion. Another way this link between MT cortex and motion perception has been studied is by electrically stimulating neurons in the MT cortex using a technique called *microstimulation*.

METHOD ▌ Microstimulation

Microstimulation is achieved by lowering a small wire electrode into the cortex and passing a weak electrical charge through the tip of the electrode. This weak shock stimulates neurons that are near the electrode tip and causes them to fire, just as they would if they were being stimulated by neurotransmitter released from other neurons.

Remember from Chapter 4 that neurons are organized in orientation columns in the cortex, with neurons in the same column responding best to one specific orientation (page 85). Taking advantage of this fact, Movshon and Newsome (1992) used microstimulation to activate neurons in a column that responded best to a particular direction of motion while a monkey was judging the direction of dots that were moving in a different direction.

When they applied the stimulation, the monkey suddenly shifted its judgment toward the direction signaled by the stimulated neurons. For example, when the monkey was judging the motion of dots that were moving horizontally to the right (Figure 8.17a) and a column of MT neurons that preferred downward motion was stimulated, the monkey began responding as though the dots were moving downward and to the right (Figure 8.17b). The fact that stimulating the MT neurons shifted the monkey's perception of the direction of movement provides more evidence linking MT neurons and motion perception.

(a) No stimulation

(b) Stimulation

Figure 8.17 ▌ (a) A monkey judges the motion of dots moving horizontally to the right. (b) When a column of neurons that prefer downward motion is stimulated, the monkey judges the same motion as being downward and to the right.

TEST YOURSELF 8.1

1. Describe four different functions of motion perception.
2. Describe four different situations that can result in motion perception. Which of these situations involves real motion, and which involve illusions of motion?

3. What is the evidence that real motion and apparent motion may involve similar mechanisms?
4. Describe the ecological approach to motion perception. What is the advantage of this approach? (Give a specific example of how the ecological approach can explain the situations in Figure 8.8b and c.)
5. Describe the aperture problem—why the response of individual directionally selective neurons does not provide sufficient information to indicate the direction of motion. Also describe two ways that the brain might solve the aperture problem.
6. Describe the series of experiments that used moving dots as stimuli and (a) recorded from neurons in the MT cortex, (b) lesioned the MT cortex, and (c) stimulated neurons in the MT cortex. What do the results of these experiments enable us to conclude about the role of the MT cortex in motion perception?

Taking Eye Motions Into Account: The Corollary Discharge

Up until now we have been considering the situation like the one in Figure 8.8a, in which a stationary person, keeping his or her eyes still, watches a moving stimulus. But in real life we often move our eyes to follow a moving stimulus, as in Figure 8.8b. Remember that when Maria did this, she perceived Jeremy as moving even though his image remained on the same place on her retina.

How does the perceptual system indicate that the stimulus is moving, even though there is no movement on the retina? The answer, according to *corollary discharge theory,* is that the perceptual system uses a signal called the *corollary discharge* to take into account the fact that the observer's eye is moving (von Holst, 1954).

Corollary Discharge Theory

Imagine you are watching someone walk past by keeping your head stationary but following the person with your eyes, so the image of the moving person remains on the same place on your retinas. Your eyes move because **motor signals (MS)** are being sent from the motor area of your brain to your eye muscles (Figure 8.18a). According to corollary discharge theory, another neural signal, called the **corollary discharge signal (CDS)**, splits off from the motor signal. The corollary discharge signal, which occurs anytime a motor signal is sent to the eye muscles, indicates that a signal has been sent from the brain to move the eye. The corollary discharge signal reaches a hypothetical structure called the **comparator**, which relays information back to the brain that the eye is moving (Figure 8.18b). Basically, what corollary discharge theory says is that if there is no movement of an image across the retina, but the comparator is receiving information indicating that the eye is moving, then the observer perceives motion.

The beauty of corollary discharge theory is that it can also deal with the situation in which the observer's eye remains stationary and a stimulus moves across the observer's field of view (Figure 8.19a). It does this by proposing that the comparator not only receives the CDS, but also receives the signal that occurs when an image moves across the retina. This movement activates the retinal receptors and sends a signal out the optic nerve that we will call the **image displacement signal (IDS)** because it occurs when a stimulus is displaced across the retina.

According to corollary discharge theory, when the IDS reaches the comparator, the comparator sends a signal to the brain that results in the perception of motion (Figure 8.19b). Corollary discharge theory is therefore a fairly simple idea, which can be summarized by saying that the perception of movement occurs if the comparator receives either (1) a sig-

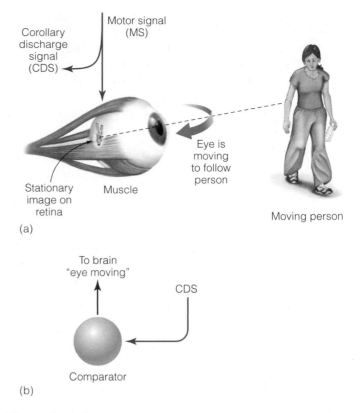

(a)

(b)

Figure 8.18 ▮ According to the corollary discharge model, (a) when a motor signal (MS) is sent to the eye muscles, so the eye can follow a moving object, a corollary discharge signal (CDS) splits off from the motor signal. (b) When the CDS reaches the comparator, it sends a signal to the brain that the eye is moving, and motion is perceived.

nal that the eye is moving (CDS) or (2) a signal that an image is being displaced across the retina (IDS).

But what happens if both a CDS *and* an IDS reach the comparator simultaneously? This would occur if you were to move your eyes to inspect a stationary scene, as in Figure 8.19c. In this case, a CDS is generated because the eye is moving, and an IDS is generated because images of the scene are sweeping across the retina. According to corollary discharge theory, when both the CDS and IDS reach the comparator simultaneously, no signal is sent to the brain, so no motion is perceived. In other words, if an image is moving across the retina, but the CDS indicates that this movement of the image is being caused by movements of the eyes, then no motion is perceived.

Upon hearing this explanation, students often wonder where the comparator is located. The answer is that the comparator is most likely not located in one specific place in the brain, but may involve a number of different structures. Similarly, the corollary discharge signal probably originates from a number of different places in the brain (Sommer & Crapse, in press; Sommer & Wurtz, 2008). The important thing, for our purposes, is that corollary discharge theory proposes that the visual system takes into account information about both stimulation of the receptors and movement

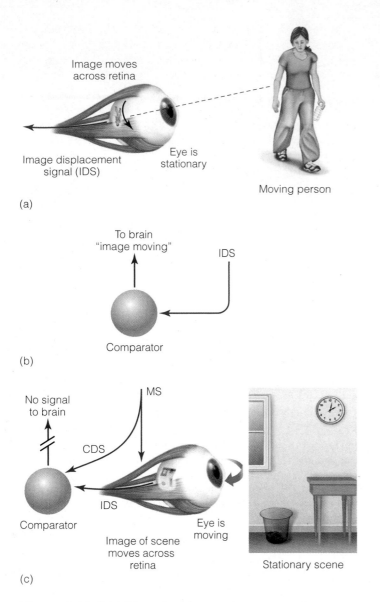

(a)

(b)

(c)

Figure 8.19 ▮ (a) When a stationary observer watches a moving object, movement of the image across the retina creates an image displacement signal (IDS). (b) When the IDS reaches the comparator, it sends a signal to the brain, and motion is perceived. (c) If both a CDS and IDS reach the comparator simultaneously, as would occur if a person is scanning a stationary scene, then no signal is sent to the brain, and no motion is perceived.

of the eye to determine our perception of motion. And although we can't pinpoint exactly where the CDS and comparator are located, there is both behavioral and physiological evidence that supports the theory.

Behavioral Demonstrations of Corollary Discharge Theory

Here are two demonstrations that enable you to create situations in which motion perception occurs even though there is no motion across the retina.

DEMONSTRATION

Eliminating the Image Displacement Signal With an Afterimage

Illuminate the circle in Figure 8.20 with your desk lamp and look at it for about 60 seconds. Then go into your closet (or a completely dark room) and observe what happens to the circle's afterimage (blink to make it come back if it fades) as you look around. Notice that the afterimage moves in synchrony with your eye motions (Figure 8.21). ▮

Figure 8.20 ▮ Afterimage stimulus.

Eye moves in dark

Bleached patch stays stationary on retina as eye moves

Figure 8.21 ▮ When the eye moves in the dark, the image remains stationary (the bleached area on the retina), but a corollary discharge signal is sent to the comparator, so the afterimage appears to move.

Why does the afterimage appear to move when you move your eyes? The answer cannot be that an image is moving across your retina because the circle's image always remains at the same place on the retina. (The circle's image on the retina has created a circular area of bleached visual pigment, which remains in the same place no matter where the eye is looking.) Without motion of the stimulus across the retina, there is no image displacement signal. However, a corollary discharge signal accompanies the motor signals sent to your eye muscles as you move your eyes, as in Figure 8.18a. Thus, only the corollary discharge signal reaches the comparator, and you see the afterimage move.

DEMONSTRATION

Seeing Motion by Pushing on Your Eyelid

Pick a point in the environment and keep looking at it while *very gently* pushing back and forth on the side of your eyelid, as shown in Figure 8.22. As you do this, you will see the scene move. ▮

Figure 8.22 ▮ Why is this woman smiling? Because when she pushes on her eyelid while keeping her eye fixed on one place, she sees the world jiggle.

Why do you see motion when you push on your eyeball? Lawrence Stark and Bruce Bridgeman (1983) did an experiment in which they instructed observers to keep looking at a particular point while pushing on their eyelid. Because the observers were paying strict attention to the instructions ("Keep looking at that point!"), the push in their eyelid didn't cause their eyes to move. This lack of movement occurred because the observer's eye muscles were pushing back against the force of the finger to keep the eye in place. According to corollary discharge theory, the motor signal sent to the eye muscles to hold the eye in place created a corollary discharge signal, which reached the comparator alone, as in

Figure 8.18b, so Stark and Bridgeman's observers saw the scene move (also see Bridgeman & Stark, 1991; Ilg, Bridgeman, & Hoffmann, 1989). (See "Think About It" #3 on page 196 for a question related to this explanation.)

These demonstrations support the central idea proposed by corollary discharge theory that there is a signal (the corollary discharge) that indicates when the observer moves, or tries to move, his or her eyes. (Also see "If You Want to Know More" #5, at the end of the chapter, for another demonstration). When the theory was first proposed, there was little physiological evidence to support it, but now there is a great deal of physiological evidence for the theory.

Physiological Evidence for Corollary Discharge Theory

In both of our demonstrations, there was a corollary discharge signal but no image displacement signal. What would happen if there was *no* corollary discharge but there *was* an image displacement signal? That is apparently what happened to R.W., a 35-year-old male who experienced vertigo (dizziness) anytime he moved his eyes or experienced motion when he looked out the window of a moving car.

A brain scan revealed that R.W. had lesions in an area of his cortex called the medial superior temporal area (MST), which is just above the MT cortex (Figure 8.13). Behavioral testing of R.W. also revealed that as he moved his eyes, the stationary environment appeared to move with a velocity that matched the velocity with which he was moving his eyes (Haarmeier et al., 1997). Thus, when he moved his eyes, there was an IDS, because images were moving across his retina, but the damage to his brain had apparently eliminated the CDS. Because only the IDS reached the comparator, R.W. saw motion when there actually was none.

Other physiological evidence for the theory comes from experiments that involve recording from neurons in the monkey's cortex. Figure 8.23 shows the response recorded

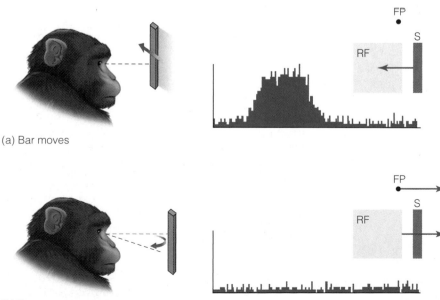

(a) Bar moves

(b) Eye moves

Figure 8.23 ▮ Responses of a real-motion neuron in the extrastriate cortex of a monkey. In both cases, a bar sweeps across the neuron's receptive field. (a) The neuron fires when the bar moves to the left across the retina. (b) The neuron doesn't fire when the eye moves to the right past the bar. *(Adapted from Galletti, C., & Fattori, P. (2003). Neuronal mechanisms for detection of motion in the field of view.* Neuropsychologia, 41, *1717–1727.)*

from a motion-sensitive neuron in the monkey's extrastriate cortex. This neuron responds strongly when the monkey looks steadily at the fixation point (FP) as a moving bar sweeps across the cell's receptive field (Figure 8.23a), but does not respond when the monkey follows a moving fixation point with its eyes and the bar remains stationary (Figure 8.23b; Galletti & Fattori, 2003).

This neuron is called a **real-motion neuron** because it responds only when the stimulus moves and doesn't respond when the eye moves, even though the stimulus on the retina—a bar sweeping across the cell's receptive field—is the same in both situations. This real-motion neuron must be receiving information like the corollary discharge, which tells the neuron when the eye is moving. Real-motion neurons have also been observed in many other areas of the cortex (Battaglini, Galletti, & Fattori, 1996; Robinson & Wurtz, 1976), and more recent research has begun to determine where the corollary discharge is acting in the brain (Sommer & Wurtz, 2006; Wang et al., 2007).

Perceiving Biological Motion

One of the most common and important types of motion we perceive is the movement of people. We watch other people's movements not only to see where they are going but also to determine their intentions, what they are doing, and perhaps also their moods and feelings.

Although information about people's actions, intentions, and moods can be determined from many types of cues, including facial expressions and what they are saying, this information can also be obtained based solely on motion information (Puce & Perrett, 2003). This was demonstrated by Gunnar Johansson (1973, 1975), who created **point-light walker** stimuli by placing small lights on people's joints and then filming the patterns created by these lights when people worked and carried out other actions in the dark (Figure 8.24). When the person wearing the lights is stationary, the lights look like a meaningless pattern. However, as soon as the person starts walking, with arms and legs swinging back and forth and feet moving in flattened arcs, first one leaving the ground and touching down, and then the other, the lights are immediately perceived as being caused by a walking person. This motion of a person or other living organism is called biological motion. VL 20,21

Brain Activation by Point-Light Walkers

The perception of the point-light walker stimulus as a person is seen walking is an example of how movement can create perceptual organization, because the movement transforms dots that appear unrelated into a pattern that is almost immediately seen as a meaningful figure. One reason we are particularly good at perceptually organizing the

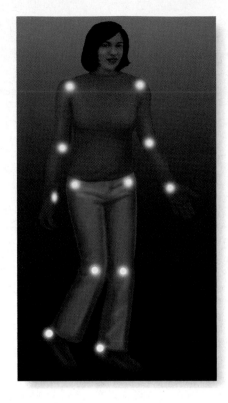

Figure 8.24 ▌ A person wearing lights for a biological motion experiment. In the actual experiment, the room is totally dark, and only the lights can be seen.

complex motion of an array of moving dots into the perception of a walking person is that we see biological motion all the time. Every time you see a person walking, running, or behaving in any way that involves movement, you are seeing biological motion. Our ability to easily organize biological motions into meaningful perceptions led some researchers to suspect that there may be an area in the brain that responds to biological motion, just as there are areas such as the extrastriate body area (EBA) and fusiform face area (FFA) that are specialized to respond to bodies and faces, respectively (Figure 8.13).

Emily Grossman and Randolph Blake (2001) provided evidence supporting the idea of a specialized area in the brain for biological motion by measuring observers' brain activity as they viewed the moving dots created by a point-light walker (Figure 8.25a) and as they viewed dots that moved similarly to the point-light walker dots, but were scrambled so they did not result in the impression of a person walking (Figure 8.25b). They found that activity in a small area in the superior temporal sulcus (STS; see Figure 8.13) was greater for biological motion than for scrambled motion in all eight of their observers. In another experiment, Grossman and Blake (2002) showed that other regions, such as the FFA, were activated more by biological motion than by scrambled motion, but that activity in the EBA did not distinguish between biological and scrambled motion. Based on these results, they concluded that there is a network of areas, which includes the STS and FFA, that are specialized for the perception of biological motion (also see Pelphrey et al., 2003).

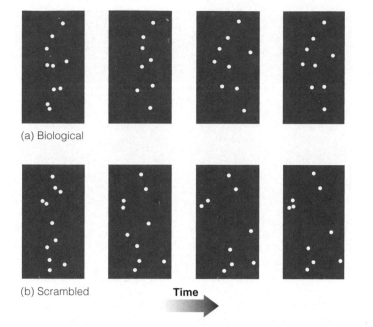

(a) Biological

(b) Scrambled

Time

Figure 8.25 ▮ Frames from the stimuli used by Grossman and Blake (2001). (a) Sequence from the point-light walker stimulus. (b) Sequence from the scrambled point-light stimulus.

Linking Brain Activity and the Perception of Biological Motion

One of the principles we have discussed in this book is that just showing that a structure responds to a specific type of stimulus does not prove that the structure is involved in *perceiving* that stimulus. Earlier in the chapter we described how Newsome used a number of different methods to show that MT cortex is specialized for the perception of motion. In addition to showing that MT cortex is *activated* by motion, he also showed that *perception* of motion is decreased by lesioning MT cortex and is influenced by stimulating neurons in MT cortex. Directly linking brain processes and perception enabled Newsome to conclude that the MT cortex is important for the perception of motion.

Just as Newsome showed that disrupting operation of the MT cortex decreases a monkey's ability to perceive the direction of moving dots, Emily Grossman and coworkers (2005) showed that disrupting operation of the STS in humans decreases the ability to perceive biological motion. Newsome disrupted operation of the monkey's MT cortex by lesioning that structure. Because Grossman's experiments were on humans, she used a more gentle and temporary method of disrupting brain activity—a procedure called *transcranial magnetic stimulation*.

METHOD ▮ Transcranial Magnetic Stimulation (TMS)

One way to investigate whether an area of the brain is involved in determining a particular function is to remove that part of the brain in animals or study cases of brain

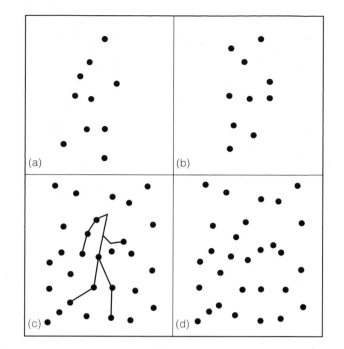

Figure 8.26 ▮ (a) Biological motion stimulus; (b) scrambled stimulus; (c) stimulus from a, with "noise" added (dots corresponding to the walker are indicated by lines, which were not seen by the observer); (d) how the stimulus appears to the observer. *(From Grossman, E. D., Batelli, L., & Pascual-Leone, A. (2005). Repetitive TMS over posterior STS disrupts perception of biological motion.* Vision Research, 45, 2847–2853.)

damage in humans. Of course, we cannot purposely remove a portion of a person's brain, but it is possible to temporarily disrupt the functioning of a particular area by applying a pulsating magnetic field using a stimulating coil placed over the person's skull. A series of pulses presented to a particular area of the brain for a few seconds decreases or eliminates brain functioning in that area for seconds or minutes. A participant's behavior is tested while the brain area is deactivated. If the behavior is disrupted, researchers conclude that the deactivated area of the brain is causing that behavior.

The observers in Grossman's (2005) experiment viewed point-light stimuli for activities such as walking, kicking, and throwing (Figure 8.26a), and they also viewed scrambled point-light displays (Figure 8.26b). Their task was to determine whether a display was biological motion or scrambled motion. This is normally an extremely easy task, but Grossman made it more difficult by adding extra dots to create "noise" (Figure 8.26c and d). The amount of noise was adjusted for each observer so that they could distinguish between biological and scrambled motion with 71 percent accuracy.

The key result of this experiment was that presenting TMS to the area of the STS that is activated by biological motion caused a significant decrease in the observers' ability to perceive biological motion. TMS stimulation of other motion-sensitive areas, such as the MT cortex, had no effect on the perception of biological motion. From this result, Grossman concluded that normal functioning of the "biological motion" area, STS, is necessary for perceiving biological motion. This conclusion is also supported by studies that have shown that people who have suffered damage to this area have trouble perceiving biological motion (Battelli et al., 2003). What all of this means is that biological motion is more than just "motion"—it is a special type of motion that is served by specialized areas of the brain.

Something to Consider: Going Beyond the Stimulus

We have seen that the brain responds to a number of different types of stimuli, including moving bars, moving dots, and moving people. But is our perception of motion determined solely by automatic responding to different types of stimuli? There is evidence that the meaning of a stimulus and the knowledge people have gained from their past experiences in perceiving motion can influence both the perception of motion and the activity of the brain. One example of how meaning and knowledge influence perception and brain activity is provided by a phenomenon called *implied motion.*

Implied Motion

Look at the picture in Figure 8.27. Most people perceive this picture as a "freeze frame" of an action—dancing—that involves motion. It is not hard to imagine the person's dress and feet moving to a different position in the moments following the situation depicted in this picture. A situation such as this, in which a still picture depicts a situation involving motion, is called **implied motion**.

Jennifer Freyd (1983) did an experiment involving implied motion pictures by briefly showing observers pictures that depicted a situation involving motion, such as a person jumping off of a low wall. After a pause, she showed her observers either (1) the same picture; (2) a picture slightly forward in time (the person who had jumped off the wall was closer to the ground); or (3) a picture slightly backward in time (the person was further from the ground). The observers' task was to indicate, as quickly as possible, whether the second picture was the same as or different from the first picture.

Freyd predicted that her observers would "unfreeze" the implied motion depicted in the picture, and therefore anticipate the motion that was going to occur in a scene. If this occurred, observers might "remember" a picture as depicting a situation that occurred slightly later in time. For the picture of the person jumping off the wall, that would mean the observers might remember the person as being closer to

Figure 8.27 ▌ A picture that creates implied motion, because people assume that the dress is in motion, and perhaps the dancer's feet as well. *(Painting by Julie Tvaruzek.)*

the ground than he was in the initial picture. Freyd's results confirmed this prediction, because observers took longer to decide whether the "time-forward" picture was different from the original picture.

The idea that the motion depicted in a picture tends to continue in the observers' mind is called **representational momentum** (David & Senior, 2000; Freyd, 1983). Representational momentum is an example of experience influencing perception because it depends on our knowledge of the way situations involving motion typically unfold.

Catherine Reed and Norman Vinson (1996) studied the effect of experience on representational momentum by presenting a sequence of pictures, as in Figure 8.28. Each picture was seen as a still picture because the sequence was presented slowly enough so that no apparent motion occurred. Thus, any motion that did occur was implied by the positions and meanings of the objects in the pictures. After the third picture, which was called the *memory picture,* the observer saw the *test picture.* The test picture could appear in the same position as the memory picture or slightly lower or slightly higher. The observer's task was to indicate as quickly as possible whether the test picture was in the same position as the memory picture.

Reed and Vinson wanted to determine whether the meaning of a picture had any effect on representational momentum, so they used pictures with different meanings. Figure 8.28a shows *rocket pictures,* and Figure 8.28b shows *weight pictures.* They found that the rocket pictures showed a greater representational momentum effect than the weight pictures. That is, observers were more likely to say that the test picture of the rocket that appeared in a position *higher* than the memory picture was in the *same position* as the memory picture. Reed and Vinson therefore concluded that the representational momentum effect is affected by a person's expectations about the motion of an object and

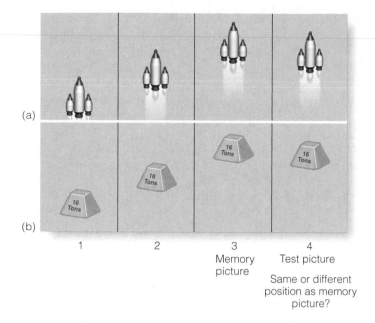

(a)

(b)

1 2 3 4

Memory picture

Test picture

Same or different position as memory picture?

Figure 8.28 ▌ Stimuli used by Reed and Vinson (1996) to demonstrate the effect of experience on representational momentum. In this example, the test pictures are lower than the memory picture. On other trials, the rocket or weight would appear in the same position as or higher than the memory picture.

that learned properties of objects (that rockets go up, for example) contributes to these expectations (Vinson & Reed, 2002).

If implied motion causes an object to continue moving in a person's mind, then it would seem reasonable that this continued motion would be reflected by activity in the brain. When Zoe Kourtzi and Nancy Kanwisher (2000) measured the fMRI response in areas MT and MST to pictures like the ones in Figure 8.29, they found that the area of the brain that responds to actual motions also responds to *pictures* of motion and that implied-motion pictures (IM) caused a greater response than non-implied-motion pictures (No-IM), rest pictures (R), or house pictures (H). Thus, activity occurs in the brain that corresponds to the continued motion that implied-motion pictures create in a person's mind (also see Lorteije et al., 2006; Senior et al., 2000).

Apparent Motion

The effect of a person's past experience on motion perception has also been determined using apparent motion displays. Remember that apparent motion occurs when one stimulus is flashed, followed by another stimulus at a slightly different position (see Figure 8.5). When V. S. Ramachandran and Stuart Anstis (1986) flashed the two dots on the left in Figure 8.30a followed by the single dot on the right, their observers saw the top dot move horizontally to the right and the bottom one move diagonally, so both dots appeared to move to the dot on the right (Figure 8.30b). But adding a square, as in Figure 8.30c, caused a change in this perception. Now observers perceived both dots as moving horizon-

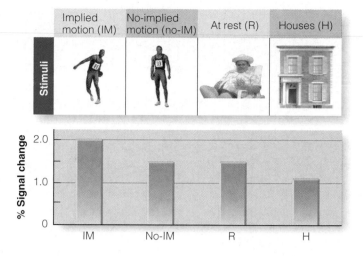

Figure 8.29 ▌ Examples of pictures used by Kourtzi and Kanwisher (2000) to depict implied motion (IM), no implied motion (no-IM), at rest (R), and a house (H). The height of the bar below each picture indicates the average fMRI response of the MT cortex to that type of picture. *(From Kourtzi, Z., & Kanwisher, N., Activation in human MT/MST by static images with implied motion, Journal of Cognitive Neuroscience, 12, 1, January 2000, 48–55. © 2000 by Massachusetts Institute of Technology. All rights reserved. Reproduced by permission.)*

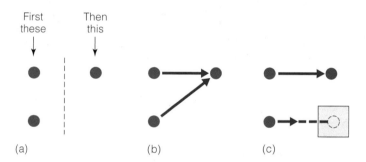

First these Then this

(a) (b) (c)

Figure 8.30 ▌ Stimuli from the Ramachandran and Anstis (1986) experiment. (a) The initial stimulus condition. Both dots move to the position of the dot on the right. (b) Placing a square in the position shown changes the perception of the movement of the lower dot, which now moves to the right and under the square.

tally to the right, with the bottom dot sliding behind the square. According to Ramachandran and Anstis, this perception occurs because of our past experience in seeing objects disappear behind other objects. VL 22-25

VL 22-25

TEST YOURSELF 8.2

1. Describe the corollary discharge model. In your description, indicate (1) what the model is designed to explain; (2) the three types of signals—motor signal, corollary discharge signal, and image displacement signal; and (3) when these signals cause motion perception when reaching the comparator, and when

they do not cause motion perception when reaching the comparator.

2. What is biological motion, and how has it been studied using point-light displays?

3. Describe the experiments that have shown that an area in the STS is specialized for perceiving biological motion.

4. What is implied motion, and what does it tell us about the role of experience in perceiving motion? Describe Ramachandran and Anstis' apparent motion experiment.

THINK ABOUT IT

1. We perceive real motion when we see things that are physically moving, such as cars on the road and people on the sidewalk. But we also see motion on TV, in movies, on our computer screens, and in electronic displays such as those in Las Vegas or Times Square. How are images presented in these situations in order to result in the perception of motion? (This may require some research.) (p. 180)

2. In this chapter, we described a number of principles that also hold for object perception (Chapter 5). Find examples from Chapter 5 of the following (page numbers are for this chapter):

   • There are neurons that are specialized to respond to specific stimuli. (p. 187)

   • More complex stimuli are processed in higher areas of the cortex. (p. 186)

   • Top-down processing and experience affect perception. (p. 194)

   • There are parallels between physiology and perception. (pp. 187, 193)

3. Stark and Bridgeman explained the perception of movement that occurs when pushing gently on the eyelid by a corollary discharge generated when muscles are pushing back to counteract the push on the side of the eye. What if the push on the eyelid causes the eye to move, and the person sees the scene move? How would perception of the scene's movement in this situation be explained by corollary discharge theory? (p. 191)

4. In the "Something to Consider" section, we stated that the representational momentum effect shows how knowledge can affect perception. Why could we also say that representational momentum illustrates an interaction between perception and memory? (p. 194)

IF YOU WANT TO KNOW MORE

1. *Perceiving events.* People are able to segment the ongoing stream of behavior into individual events, such as when the salesperson in the mall first was sorting clothes and then moved to check people out at the cash register. New research has shown that motion is central to perceiving different events in our environment. (p. 178)

   Zacks, J. M. (2004). Using movement and intentions to understand simple events. *Cognitive Science, 28,* 979–1008.

   Zacks, J. M., & Swallow, K. M. (2007). Event segmentation. *Current Directions in Psychological Science, 16,* 80–84.

2. *Effect of early experience on motion perception.* When kittens are raised in an environment that is illuminated by flashing lights, they lose the ability to detect the direction of moving stimuli. Experience in perceiving motion is necessary in order for motion perception to develop.

   Pasternak, T. (1990). Vision following loss of cortical directional selectivity. In M. A. Berkley & W. C. Stebbins (Eds.), *Comparative perception* (Vol. 1, pp. 407–428). New York: Wiley.

3. *Motion aftereffects and the brain.* After viewing a waterfall, a rotating spiral, or moving stripes, an illusion of motion called a motion aftereffect occurs. These effects have been linked to activity in the brain. (p. 181)

   Anstis, S. M., Verstraten, F. A. J., & Mather, G. (1998). The motion aftereffect: A review. *Trends in Cognitive Science, 2,* 111–117.

4. *New research on the corollary discharge signal.* When neurons in an area in the monkey's thalamus are deactivated by a chemical injection, the monkeys have trouble locating objects after moving their eyes because of a disruption in the corollary discharge that signals when the eyes are moving. (p. 191)

   Sommer, M., & Wurtz, R. H. (2006). Influence of the thalamus on spatial visual processing in frontal cortex. *Nature, 444,* 374–376.

5. *Eliminating the image movement signal by paralysis.* Experiments have been done in which a person has been temporarily paralyzed by a drug injection. When the person tries to move his or her eyes, a motor signal (MS) and corollary discharge signal (CDS) are sent from the brain, but no image displacement signal (IDS) occurs because the person can't actually move the eyes. Corollary discharge theory predicts that the person should see the environment move, which is what happens. (p. 191)

   Matin, L., Picoulet, E., Stevens, J., Edwards, M., & McArthur, R. (1982). Oculoparalytic illusion:

Visual-field dependent spatial mislocations by humans partially paralyzed by curare. *Science, 216,* 198–201.

6. *Cats perceive biological motion.* The perception of biological motion is not restricted to humans. There is evidence that cats can perceive it as well. (p. 192)
Blake, R. (1993). Cats perceive biological motion. *Psychological Science, 4,* 54–57.

7. *Motions of face and body as social signals.* Motion of faces and bodies provide information that can be used to decode complex social signals. Neurons on the superior temporal sulcus (STS) play a role in perceiving this motion. (p. 193)
Puce, A., & Perrett, D. (2003). Electrophysiology and brain imaging of biological motion. *Philosophical Transactions of the Royal Society of London, 358,* 435–445.

KEY TERMS

Aperture problem (p. 186)
Apparent motion (p. 180)
Attentional capture (p. 179)
Biological motion (p. 192)
Coherence (p. 187)
Comparator (p. 189)
Corollary discharge signal (CDS) (p. 189)
Global optic flow (p. 184)

Illusory motion (p. 180)
Image displacement signal (IDS) (p. 189)
Implied motion (p. 194)
Induced motion (p. 181)
Local disturbance in the optic array (p. 183)
Microstimulation (p. 188)
Motion aftereffect (p. 181)

Motion agnosia (p. 179)
Motor signal (MS) (p. 189)
Optic array (p. 183)
Point-light walker (p. 192)
Real motion (p. 180)
Real-motion neuron (p. 192)
Representational momentum (p. 194)
Waterfall illusion (p. 181)

MEDIA RESOURCES

The *Sensation and Perception* Book Companion Website

www.cengage.com/psychology/goldstein

See the companion website for flashcards, practice quiz questions, Internet links, updates, critical thinking exercises, discussion forums, games, and more!

CengageNOW

www.cengage.com/cengagenow

Go to this site for the link to CengageNOW, your one-stop shop. Take a pre-test for this chapter, and CengageNOW will generate a personalized study plan based on your test results. The study plan will identify the topics you need to review and direct you to online resources to help you master those topics. You can then take a post-test to help you determine the concepts you have mastered and what you will still need to work on.

Virtual Lab

VL

Your Virtual Lab is designed to help you get the most out of this course. The Virtual Lab icons direct you to specific media demonstrations and experiments designed to help you visualize what you are reading about. The number beside each icon indicates the number of the media element you can access through your CD-ROM, CengageNOW, or WebTutor resource.

The following lab exercises are related to the material in this chapter:

1. *Motion Providing Organization: The Hidden Bird* How movement can cause an image to stand out from a complex background. (Courtesy of Michael Bach.)

2. *Perceptual Organization: The Dalmatian Dog* How a black-and-white pattern can be perceived as a Dalmatian. (Courtesy of Michael Bach.)

3. *Motion Parallax and Object Form* How the image of an object changes when it is viewed from different angles.

4. *Shape From Movement* How movement of some dots in a field of dots can create perception of an object.

5. *Form and Motion* How moving dot patterns can create the perception of three-dimensional forms. Click on "parameters" to set up this demonstration.

6. *Motion Reference* How the presence of two moving "reference" dots can influence the perceived movement of another dot that is moving between them.

7. *Motion Binding* Like the Motion Reference demonstration, this illustrates how adding an object to a display can influence how we perceive motion. (Courtesy of Michael Bach.)

8. *The Phi Phenomenon, Space, and Time* How the perception of apparent motion created by flashing two spheres depends on the distance and time interval between the spheres.

9. *Illusory Contour Motion* How alternating two displays that contain illusory contours can result in perception of a moving contour.

10. *Apparent Movement and Figural Selection* How movement is perceived when vertical and horizontal rectangles are flashed in different positions.

11. *Motion Capture* How dots on a surface are "captured" by apparent movement of that surface.

12. *Induced Movement* How the perception of movement can be influenced by movement of the background.

13. *Waterfall Illusion* How viewing a moving horizontal grating can cause an aftereffect of motion.

14. *Spiral Motion Aftereffect* How viewing a rotating spiral can cause an aftereffect of motion that is opposite to the direction of rotation.

15. *Flow From Walking Down a Hallway* Global optical flow. (Courtesy of William Warren.)

16. *Aperture Problem* (Wenderoth) A demonstration of why viewing movement through an aperture poses a problem for motion perception. (Courtesy of Peter Wenderoth.)

17. *Barberpole Illusion* (Wenderoth) A version of the aperture problem with an elongated aperture. (Courtesy of Peter Wenderoth.)

18. *Cortical Activation by Motion* Video showing how motion activates areas outside the primary visual receiving area. (Courtesy of Geoffrey Boynton.)

19. *Corollary Discharge Model* How the corollary discharge model operates for movement of objects and movement of the observer.

20. *Biological Motion 1* Shows how biological motion stimuli for a human walker change when gender, weight, and mood are varied. (Courtesy of Nikolaus Troje.)

21. *Biological Motion 2* Illustrates biological motion stimuli for humans, cats, and pigeons and what happens when these stimuli are inverted, scrambled, and masked. (Courtesy of Nikolaus Troje.)

22. *Motion and Introduced Occlusion* How placing your finger over an apparent movement display can influence the perception of an object's motion.

23. *Field Effects and Apparent Movement* How introducing an occluder in an apparent-movement display can influence the perception of an object's motion.

24. *Line-Motion Effect* An illusion of motion that is created by directing attention to one location and then flashing a line. (Courtesy of Peter Wenderoth.)

25. *Context and Apparent Speed* How the perceived speed of a bouncing ball changes when it is near a border.

Chapter Contents

CHAPTER 9

Perceiving Color

OPPOSITE PAGE The multicolored facades of buildings in the La Placita Village in downtown Tucson, Arizona, which houses the Chamber of Commerce and corporate offices.
Bruce Goldstein

▐V̄L̄▐ The Virtual Lab icons direct you to specific animations and videos designed to help you visualize what you are reading about. The number beside each icon indicates the number of the clip you can access through your CD-ROM or your student website.

Some Questions We Will Consider:

▪ What does someone who is "color-blind" see? (p. 211)

▪ Why do we perceive blue dots when a yellow flash bulb goes off? (p. 214)

▪ What colors does a honeybee perceive? (p. 224)

Color is one of the most obvious and pervasive qualities in our environment. We interact with it every time we note the color of a traffic light, choose clothes that are color coordinated, or appreciate the colors of a painting. We pick favorite colors (blue is the most favored; Terwogt & Hoeksma, 1994), we associate colors with emotions (we turn purple with rage, red with embarrassment, green with envy, and feel blue; Terwogt & Hoeksma, 1994; Valdez & Mehribian, 1994), and we imbue colors with special meanings (for example, red signifies danger; purple, royalty; green, ecology). But for all of our involvement with color, we sometimes take it for granted, and—just as with our other perceptual abilities—we may not fully appreciate color unless we lose our ability to experience it. The depth of this loss is illustrated by the case of Mr. I, a painter who became color-blind at the age of 65 after suffering a concussion in an automobile accident.

> In March of 1986, the neurologist Oliver Sacks[1] received an anguished letter from Mr. I, who, identifying himself as a "rather successful artist," described how ever since he had been involved in an automobile accident, he had lost his ability to experience colors, and he exclaimed with some anguish, that "My dog is gray. Tomato juice is black. Color TV is a hodge-podge. . . ."
>
> In the days following his accident, Mr. I became more and more depressed. His studio, normally awash with the brilliant colors of his abstract paintings, appeared drab to him, and his paintings, meaningless. Food, now gray, became difficult for him to look at while eating; and sunsets, once seen as rays of red, had become streaks of black against the sky.

Mr. I's color blindness was caused by cortical injury after a lifetime of experiencing color, whereas most cases of total color blindness or of color deficiency (partial color blindness, which we'll discuss in more detail later in this chapter) occur at birth because of the genetic absence of one or more types of cone receptors. Most people who are born color-blind are not disturbed by their lack of color perception, because they have never experienced color. However, some of their reports, such as the darkening of reds, are similar to Mr. I's. People with total color blindness often echo Mr. I's complaint that it is sometimes difficult to distinguish one object from another, as when his brown dog, which he could easily see silhouetted against a light-colored road, became very difficult to perceive when seen against irregular foliage.

Eventually, Mr. I overcame his strong psychological reaction and began creating striking black-and-white pictures. But his account of his color-blind experiences provides an impressive testament to the central place of color in our everyday lives. (See Heywood et al., 1991; Nordby, 1990; Young et al., 1980; and Zeki, 1990, for additional descriptions of cases of complete color blindness.)

In this chapter, we consider color perception in three parts. We first consider some basic facts about color perception, and then focus on two questions: (1) What is the connection between color perception and the firing of neurons? (2) How do we perceive the colors and lightness of objects in the environment under changing illumination?

Introduction to Color

Why do we perceive different colors? We will begin answering this question by first speculating about some of the functions that color serves in our lives and in the lives of monkeys. We will then look at how we describe our experience of color and how this experience is linked to the properties of light.

What Are Some Functions of Color Vision?

Color adds beauty to our lives, but it does more than that. Color serves important signaling functions, both natural and contrived by humans. The natural and human-made world provides many color signals that help us identify and classify things. I know the rock on my desk contains copper by the rich blue vein that runs through it; I know a banana is ripe when it has turned yellow; and I know to stop when the traffic light turns red.

In addition to its signaling function, color helps facilitate perceptual organization, the process we discussed in Chapter 5 (p. 105) by which small elements become grouped perceptually into larger objects. Color perception greatly facilitates the ability to tell one object from another and especially to pick out objects within scenes, an ability crucial to the survival of many species. Consider, for example, a monkey foraging for fruit in the forest or jungle. A monkey with good color vision easily detects red fruit against a green background (Figure 9.1a), but a color-blind monkey would find it more difficult to find the fruit (Figure 9.1b). Color vision thus enhances the contrast of objects that, if they didn't appear colored, would appear more similar.

This link between good color vision and the ability to detect colored food has led to the proposal that monkey and human color vision may have evolved for the express purpose of detecting fruit (Mollon, 1989, 1997; Sumner & Mollon, 2000; Walls, 1942). This suggestion sounds reasonable when we consider the difficulty color-blind human observers have when confronted with the seemingly simple task of picking berries. Knut Nordby (1990), a totally color-

---

[1] Dr. Sacks, well known for his elegant writings describing interesting neurological cases, came to public attention when he was played by Robin Williams in the 1995 film *Awakenings*.

(a)   (b)

Figure 9.1 ▌ (a) Red berries in green foliage. (b) These berries become more difficult to detect without color vision.

blind visual scientist who sees the world in shades of gray, described his experience as follows: "Picking berries has always been a big problem. I often have to grope around among the leaves with my fingers, feeling for the berries by their shape" (p. 308). If Nordby's experience, which is similar to Mr. I's difficulty in seeing his dog against foliage, is any indication, a color-blind monkey would have difficulty finding berries or fruit and might be less likely to survive than monkeys with color vision.

Our ability to perceive color not only helps us detect objects that might otherwise be obscured by their surroundings; it also helps us recognize and identify things we can see easily. James W. Tanaka and L. M. Presnell (1999) demonstrated this by asking observers to identify objects like the ones in Figure 9.2, which appeared either in their normal colors, like the yellow banana, or in inappropriate colors, like the purple banana. The result was that observers recognized the appropriately colored objects more rapidly and accurately. Thus, knowing the colors of familiar objects helps us to recognize these objects (Tanaka et al., 2001). (Remember from Chapter 5, page 115, that color also helps us process complex scenes.)

What Colors Do We Perceive?

We can describe all the colors we can perceive by using the terms *red, yellow, green, blue,* and their combinations

Figure 9.2 ▌ Normally colored fruit and inappropriately colored fruit. *(From Tanaka, J. W., Weiskopf, D., & Williams, P. The role of color in high-level vision.* Trends in Cognitive Sciences, 5, *211–215. Copyright 2001, with permission from Elsevier.)*

(Abramov & Gordon, 1994; Hurvich, 1981). When people are presented with many different colors and are asked to describe them, they can describe all of them when they are allowed to use all four of these terms, but they can't when one of these terms is omitted. Other colors, such as orange, violet, purple, and brown, are not needed to achieve these descriptions (Fuld et al., 1981; Quinn et al., 1988). Color researchers therefore consider red, yellow, green, and blue to be basic colors (Backhaus, 1998).

Figure 9.3 shows the four basic colors arranged in a circle, so that each is perceptually similar to the one next to it. The order of the four basic colors in the color circle— blue, green, yellow, and red—matches the order of the colors in the visible spectrum, shown in Figure 9.4, in which the short-wavelength end of the spectrum is blue, green is in the middle of the spectrum, and yellow and red are at the long-wavelength end of the spectrum. The color circle also contains the colors brown and purple, which are called *extraspectral colors* because they do not appear in the spectrum. Brown is actually a mixture of either red, orange, or yellow with black, and purple is created by mixing red and blue.

Although the color circle is based on four colors, there are more than four colors in the circle. In fact, people can discriminate between about 200 different colors across the length of the visible spectrum (Gouras, 1991). Furthermore, we can create even more colors by changing the intensity to make colors brighter or dimmer, or by adding white to change a color's saturation. White is equal amounts

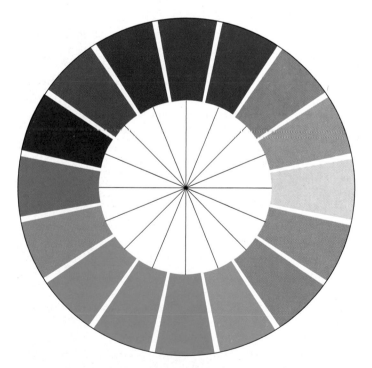

Figure 9.3 ▌ The color circle. Colors are arranged by placing perceptually similar colors next to each other so that the four basic colors are positioned at 12, 3, 6, and 9 o'clock on the circle. *(From Leo M. Hurvich,* Color Vision, *1981. Reprinted by permission of Dr. Leo M. Hurvich.)*

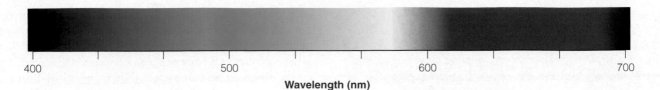

400   500   600   700

Wavelength (nm)

Figure 9.4 ▌ The visible spectrum.

of all wavelengths across the spectrum, and adding white decreases a color's saturation. For example, adding white to the deep red at the top of the color circle makes it become pink, which is a less saturated (or desaturated) form of red.

By changing the wavelength, the intensity, and the saturation, we can create about a million or more different discriminable colors (Backhaus, 1998; Gouras, 1991). But although we may be able to discriminate millions of colors, we encounter only a fraction of that number in everyday experience. The paint chips at the paint store total less than a thousand, and the *Munsell Book of Colors,* once the color "bible" for designers, contained 1,225 color samples (Wysecki & Stiles, 1965). The Pantone Matching System in current use by graphic artists has about 1,200 color choices.

Having described the different colors we can perceive, we now turn to the question of how these colors come about. What causes us to perceive a tomato as red or a banana as yellow? Our first answer to this question is that these colors are related to the wavelength of light.

Color and Wavelength

The first step in understanding how our nervous system creates our perception of color is to consider the visible spectrum in Figure 9.4. When we introduced this spectrum in Chapter 3 (page 44), we saw that the perception of color is associated with the physical property of wavelength. The spectrum stretches from short wavelengths (400 nm) to long wavelengths (700 nm), and bands of wavelengths within this range are associated with different colors. Wavelengths from about 400 to 450 nm appear violet; 450 to 490 nm, blue; 500 to 575 nm, green; 575 to 590 nm, yellow; 590 to 620 nm, orange; and 620 to 700 nm, red.

Reflectance and Transmission The colors of *light* in the spectrum are related to their wavelengths, but what about the colors of *objects*? The colors of objects are largely determined by the wavelengths of light that are *reflected* from the objects into our eyes. This is illustrated in Figure 9.5, which shows **reflectance curves**—plots of the percentage of light reflected versus wavelength—for a number of objects. Notice that black paper and white paper both reflect all wavelengths equally across the spectrum, but blue, green, and yellow paint and a tomato reflect some wavelengths but not others.

When some wavelengths are reflected more than others—as for the colored paints and the tomato—we call

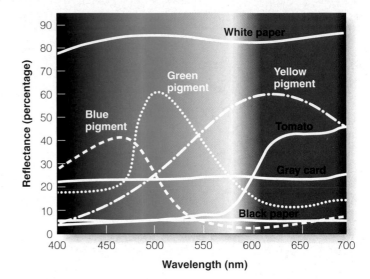

Figure 9.5 ▌ Reflectance curves for surfaces that appear white, gray, and black, and for blue, green and yellow pigments. *(Adapted from Clulow, F. W. (1972). Color: Its principles and their applications. New York: Morgan & Morgan.)*

TABLE 9.1 ▌ **Relationship Between Predominant Wavelengths Reflected and Color Perceived**

WAVELENGTHS REFLECTED	PERCEIVED COLOR
Short	Blue
Medium	Green
Long	Red
Long and medium	Yellow
Long, medium, and short	White

these **chromatic colors**, or **hues**.[2] This property of reflecting some wavelengths more than others, which is a characteristic of chromatic colors, is called **selective reflection**. Table 9.1 indicates the relationship between the wavelengths reflected and the color perceived. When light reflection is similar across the full spectrum—that is, contains no

---

[2] The term *hue* is rarely used in everyday language. We usually say "The color of the fire engine is red" rather than "The hue (or chromatic color) of the fire engine is red." Therefore, throughout the rest of this book, we will use the word *color* to mean "chromatic color" or "hue," and we will use the term *achromatic color* to refer to white, gray, or black.

hue—as in white, black, and all the grays between these two extremes, we call these colors **achromatic colors**.

Most colors in the environment are created by the way objects selectively reflect some wavelengths. But in the case of things that are transparent, such as liquids, plastics, and glass, chromatic color is created by **selective transmission**, meaning that only some wavelengths pass through the object or substance. For example, cranberry juice selectively transmits long-wavelength light and appears red, whereas limeade selectively transmits medium-wavelength light and appears green.

The idea that the color we perceive depends largely on the wavelengths of light that are reflected into our eye provides a way to explain what happens when we mix different colors together. We will describe two ways of mixing colors: mixing lights and mixing paints.

Mixing Lights If a light that appears blue is projected onto a white surface and a light that appears yellow is superimposed onto the blue, the area that is superimposed is perceived as white (Figure 9.6). Although this result may surprise you if you have ever mixed blue and yellow paints to create green, we can understand why this occurs by considering the wavelengths that the mixture of blue and yellow lights reflect into the eye. Because the two spots of light are projected onto a white surface, all of the wavelengths that hit the surface are reflected into an observer's eye (see the reflectance curve for white paper in Figure 9.5). The blue spot consists of a band of short wavelengths; when it is projected alone, the short-wavelength light is reflected into the observer's eyes (Table 9.2). Similarly, the yellow spot consists of medium and long wavelengths, so when presented alone, these wavelengths are reflected into the observer's eyes. The key to understanding what happens when colored lights are superimposed is that *all of the light that is reflected from the surface by each light when alone is also reflected when the lights are*

	TABLE 9.2 ∎ Mixing Blue and Yellow Lights (Additive Color Mixture)		

Parts of the spectrum that are reflected from a white surface for blue and yellow spots of light projected onto the surface. Wavelengths that are reflected are highlighted.

	WAVELENGTHS		
	SHORT	**MEDIUM**	**LONG**
Spot of blue light	Reflected	No Reflection	No Reflection
Spot of yellow light	No Reflection	Reflected	Reflected
Overlapping blue and yellow spots	Reflected	Reflected	Reflected

superimposed. Thus, where the two spots are superimposed, the light from the blue spot and the light from the yellow spot are still reflected into the observer's eye. The added-together light therefore contains short, medium, and long wavelengths, which results in the perception of white. Because mixing lights involves adding up the wavelengths of each light in the mixture, mixing lights is called [VL] 1 **additive color mixture**.

Mixing Paints We can appreciate why we see different colors when mixing paints than when mixing lights by considering the blobs of paint in Figure 9.7. The blue blob absorbs long-wavelength light and reflects some short-wavelength light and some medium-wavelength light (see the reflectance curve for "blue pigment" in Figure 9.5). The yellow blob absorbs short-wavelength light and reflects some medium- and long-wavelength light (see the reflectance curve for "yellow pigment" in Figure 9.5).

The key to understanding what happens when colored paints are mixed together is that *when mixed, both paints still absorb the same wavelengths they absorbed when alone, so the only wavelengths reflected are those that are reflected by both paints in common.* Because medium wavelengths are the only ones reflected by both paints in common, a mixture of blue and

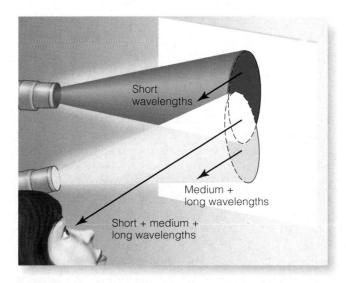

Figure 9.6 ∎ Color mixing with light. Superimposing a blue light and a yellow light creates the perception of white in the area of overlap. This is additive color mixing.

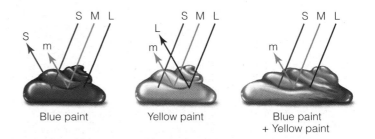

Figure 9.7 ∎ Color mixing with paint. Mixing blue paint and yellow paint creates a paint that appears green. This is subtractive color mixture.

TABLE 9.3	Mixing Blue and Yellow Paints (Subtractive Color Mixture)		
Parts of the spectrum that are absorbed and reflected by blue and yellow paint. Wavelengths that are reflected are highlighted for each paint. Light that is usually seen as green is the only light that is reflected in common by both paints.			
	WAVELENGTHS		
	SHORT	MEDIUM	LONG
Blob of blue paint	Reflects all	Reflects some	Absorbs all
Blob of yellow paint	Absorbs all	Reflects some	Reflects some
Mixture of blue and yellow blobs	Absorbs all	Reflects some	Absorbs all

yellow paints appears green (Table 9.3). Because each blob of paint absorbs wavelengths and these wavelengths are still absorbed by the mixture, mixing paints is called **subtractive color mixture**. The blue and yellow blobs subtract all of the wavelengths except some that are associated with green.

The reason that our blue and yellow mixture results in green is that both paints reflect a little green (see the overlap between the blue and yellow pigment curves in Figure 9.5). If our blue paint had reflected only short wavelengths and our yellow paint had reflected only medium and long wavelengths, these paints would reflect no color in common, so mixing them would result in little or no reflection across the spectrum, and the mixture would appear black. It is rare, however, for paints to reflect light in only one region of the spectrum. Most paints reflect a broad band of wavelengths. If paints didn't reflect a range of wavelengths, then many of the color-mixing effects of paints that we take for granted would not occur.

We can summarize the connection between wavelength and color as follows:

- Colors of light are associated with wavelengths in the visible spectrum.

- The colors of objects are associated with which wavelengths are *reflected* (for opaque objects) or *transmitted* (for transparent objects).

- The colors that occur when we mix colors are also associated with which wavelengths are reflected into the eye. Mixing lights causes more wavelengths to be reflected (each light *adds* wavelengths to the mixture); mixing paints causes fewer wavelengths to be reflected (each paint *subtracts* wavelengths from the mixture).

We will see later in the chapter that things other than the wavelengths reflected into our eye can influence color

perception. For example, our perception of an object's color can be influenced by the background on which the object is seen. But for now our main goal is to focus on the connection between wavelength and color.

Wavelengths Do Not Have Color!

After establishing that our perception of color is closely linked to wavelength, how can the title of this section—that wavelengths don't have color—be true? Our explanation begins with the following statement by Isaac Newton.

> The Rays to speak properly are not coloured. In them there is nothing else than a certain Power and Disposition to stir up a Sensation of this or that Colour. . . . So Colours in the Object are nothing but a Disposition to reflect this or that sort of Rays more copiously than the rest. . . . (*Optiks*, 1704)

Newton's idea is that the colors that we see in response to different wavelengths are not contained in the rays of light themselves. Instead, *these colors are created by our perceptual system*. What this means is that although we can relate specific colors to specific wavelengths, the connection between wavelength and the experience we call "color" is an arbitrary one. Light rays are simply energy, and there is nothing intrinsically "blue" about short wavelengths or "red" about long wavelengths. Looking at it this way, color is not a property of wavelength but is the brain's way of informing us what wavelengths are present.

We can appreciate the role of the nervous system in creating color experience by considering that people like Mr. I see no colors, even though they are receiving the same stimuli as people with normal color vision. Also, many animals perceive either no color or a greatly reduced palette of colors compared to humans. This occurs not because they receive different kinds of light energy than humans, but because their nervous system processes wavelength information differently and doesn't transform wavelength information into the perception of color.

The question of exactly how the nervous system accomplishes the transformation from wavelengths into the experience of color has not been answered. Rather than try to answer the extremely difficult question of how the nervous system creates experiences (see "The Mind–Body Problem," Chapter 2, p. 39), researchers have instead focused on the question of how the nervous system determines which wavelengths are present. We will now consider two theories of color vision that deal with that question. Both of these theories were proposed in the 1800s based on behavioral data, and both are basically correct. As we will see, the physiological evidence to support them didn't become available until more than 100 years after they were originally proposed.

We will consider each of the theories in turn, first describing the behavioral evidence on which the theory was based and then describing the physiological evidence that became available later.

Trichromatic Theory of Color Vision

The trichromatic theory of color vision, which states that color vision depends on the activity of three different receptor mechanisms, was proposed by two eminent 19th-century researchers, Thomas Young (1773–1829) and Hermann von Helmholtz (1821–1894). They based their theory on the results of a psychophysical procedure called *color matching*.

Behavioral Evidence for the Theory

In Helmholtz's **color-matching experiments**, observers adjusted the amounts of three different wavelengths of light mixed together in a "comparison field" until the color of this mixture matched the color of a single wavelength in a "test field." For example, an observer might be asked to adjust the amount of 420-nm, 560-nm, and 640-nm light in a comparison field until the field matched the color of a 500-nm light presented in the test field (Figure 9.8). (Any three wavelengths can be used, as long as any of them can't be matched by mixing the other two.) The key findings of these color-matching experiments were as follows:

1. By correctly adjusting the proportions of *three* wavelengths in the comparison field, it was possible to match any wavelength in the test field.

2. People with normal color vision cannot match all wavelengths in the spectrum with only two wavelengths. For example, if they were given only the 420-nm and 640-nm lights to mix, they would be unable to match certain colors. People who are color deficient, and therefore can't perceive all colors in the spectrum, can match the colors of all wavelengths in the spectrum by mixing only two other wavelengths.

The Theory: Vision Is Trichromatic

Thomas Young (1802) proposed the trichromatic theory of color vision based on the finding that people with normal

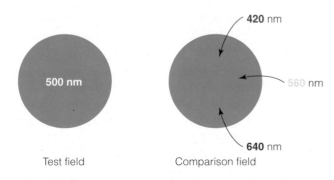

Figure 9.8 ▌ In a color-matching experiment, the observer adjusts the amount of three wavelengths in one field (right) until it matches the color of the single wavelength in another field (left).

color vision need at least three wavelengths to match any wavelength in the test field. This theory was later championed and refined by Helmholtz (1852) and is therefore also called the **Young-Helmholtz theory of color vision**. The central idea of the theory is that color vision depends on three receptor mechanisms, each with different spectral sensitivities. (Remember from Chapter 3 that spectral sensitivity indicates the sensitivity to wavelengths across the visible spectrum, as shown in Figure 3.22.)

According to this theory, light of a particular wavelength stimulates the three receptor mechanisms to different degrees, and the pattern of activity in the three mechanisms results in the perception of a color. Each wavelength is therefore represented in the nervous system by its own pattern of activity in the three receptor mechanisms.

Physiology of Trichromatic Theory

More than a century after the trichromatic theory was first proposed, physiological research identified the three receptor mechanisms proposed by the theory.

Cone Pigments Physiological researchers who were working to identify the receptor mechanisms proposed by trichromatic theory asked the following question: Are there three mechanisms, and if so, what are their physiological properties? This question was answered in the 1960s, when researchers were able to measure the absorption spectra of three different cone visual pigments, with maximum absorption in the short- (419-nm), middle- (531-nm), and long-wavelength (558-nm) regions of the spectrum (S, M, and L in Figure 9.9; P. K. Brown & Wald, 1964; Dartnall et al., 1983; Schnapf et al., 1987). All visual pigments are made up of a large protein component called opsin and a small light-sensitive component called retinal (see Chapter 3, page 48). Differences in the structure of the long opsin part of the pigments are responsible for the three different absorption spectra (Nathans et al., 1986).

Cone Responding and Color Perception If color perception is based on the pattern of activity of these three receptor mechanisms, we should be able to determine which colors will be perceived if we know the response of each of the receptor mechanisms. Figure 9.10 shows the relationship between the responses of the three kinds of receptors and our perception of color. In this figure, the responses in the S, M, and L receptors are indicated by the size of the receptors. For example, blue is signaled by a large response in the S receptor, a smaller response in the M receptor, and an even smaller response in the L receptor. Yellow is signaled by a very small response in the S receptor and large, approximately equal responses in the M and L receptors. White is signaled by equal activity in all of the receptors. VL 2, 3

Thinking of wavelengths as causing certain patterns of receptor responding helps us to predict which colors should result when we combine lights of different colors. We have already seen that combining blue and yellow lights results

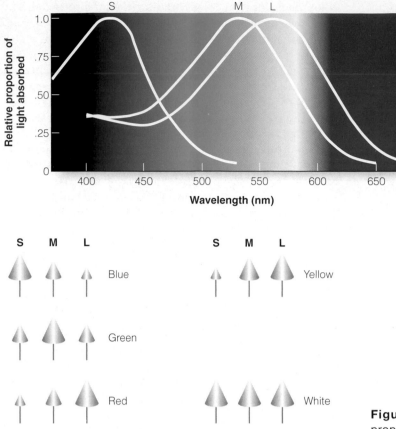

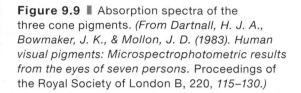

Figure 9.9 ▮ Absorption spectra of the three cone pigments. *(From Dartnall, H. J. A., Bowmaker, J. K., & Mollon, J. D. (1983). Human visual pigments: Microspectrophotometric results from the eyes of seven persons. Proceedings of the Royal Society of London B, 220, 115–130.)*

Figure 9.10 ▮ Patterns of firing of the three types of cones to different colors. The size of the cone symbolizes the size of the receptor's response.

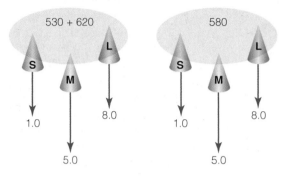

Figure 9.11 ▮ Principle behind metamerism. The proportions of 530- and 620-nm lights in the field on the left have been adjusted so that the mixture appear identical to the 580-nm light in the field on the right. The numbers indicate the responses of the short-, medium-, and long-wavelength receptors. Because there is no difference in the responses of the two sets of receptors, the two fields are perceptually indistinguishable.

in white. The patterns of receptor activity in Figure 9.10 show that blue light causes high activity in the S receptors and that yellow light causes high activity in the M and L receptors. Thus, combining both lights should stimulate all three receptors equally, which is associated with the perception of white.

Now that we know that our perception of colors is determined by the pattern of activity in different kinds of receptors, we can explain the physiological basis behind the color-matching results that led to the proposal of trichromatic theory. Remember that in a color-matching experiment, a wavelength in one field is matched by adjusting the proportions of three different wavelengths in another field (Figure 9.8). This result is interesting because the lights in the two fields are physically different (they contain different wavelengths) but they are perceptually identical (they look the same). This situation, in which two physically different stimuli are perceptually identical, is called **metamerism**, and the two identical fields in a color-matching experiment are called **metamers**.

The reason metamers look alike is that they both result in the same pattern of response in the three cone receptors. For example, when the proportions of a 620-nm red light and a 530-nm green light are adjusted so the mixture matches the color of a 580-nm light, which looks yellow, the

two mixed wavelengths create the same pattern of activity in the cone receptors as the single 580-nm light (Figure 9.11). The 530-nm green light causes a large response in the M receptor, and the 620-nm red light causes a large response in the L receptor. Together, they result in a large response in the M and L receptors and a much smaller response in the S receptor. This is the pattern for yellow and is the same as the pattern generated by the 580-nm light. Thus, even though the lights in these two fields are *physically different,* the two lights result in identical physiological responses and so are identical, as far as the visual system is concerned.

Are Three Receptor Mechanisms Necessary for Color Vision? According to trichromatic theory, a light's wavelength is signaled by the pattern of activity of three receptor mechanisms. But do we need three different mechanisms to see colors? The answer to this question is that color vision is possible with two receptor types but not with one. Let's first consider why color vision does not occur with just one receptor type.

We can understand why color vision is not possible with just one receptor type by considering how Jay, who has just one type of receptor, which contains a single visual pigment, perceives the dresses worn by two women, Mary and Barbara. Mary and Barbara have just purchased dresses from the "Monochromatic Dress Company," which specializes in dresses that reflect only one wavelength. (Such dresses don't exist, but let's assume they do, for the purposes of this example.) Mary's dress reflects only 550-nm light, and Barbara's reflects only 590-nm light.

Let's assume that Mary's and Barbara's dresses are illuminated by spotlights that are adjusted so that each dress reflects 1,000 photons of light into Jay's eye. (Remember from page 49 in Chapter 3 that a photon is a small packet of light energy, and that a visual pigment molecule is activated if it absorbs one photon.) To determine how this light affects the pigment in Jay's receptor, we refer to the absorption spectrum of Jay's pigment, shown in Figure 9.12a. This absorption spectrum indicates the fraction of light at each wavelength that the pigment absorbs.

By taking into account the amount of light present (1,000 photons) and the absorption spectrum, we can see that 100 photons of the 550-nm light from Mary's dress are absorbed by Jay's visual pigment (1,000 × 0.10 = 100) (Figure 9.12b), and 50 photons of the 590-nm light from Barbara's dress are absorbed (1,000 × 0.05 = 50) (Figure 9.12c). Because each photon of light activates one visual pigment molecule, and each activated molecule increases the receptor's electrical response, this means that Mary's dress generates a larger signal in Jay's retina than Barbara's dress.

At this point you might say that Jay's single pigment did, in fact, enable him to distinguish Mary's dress from Barbara's dress. However, if we increase the intensity of

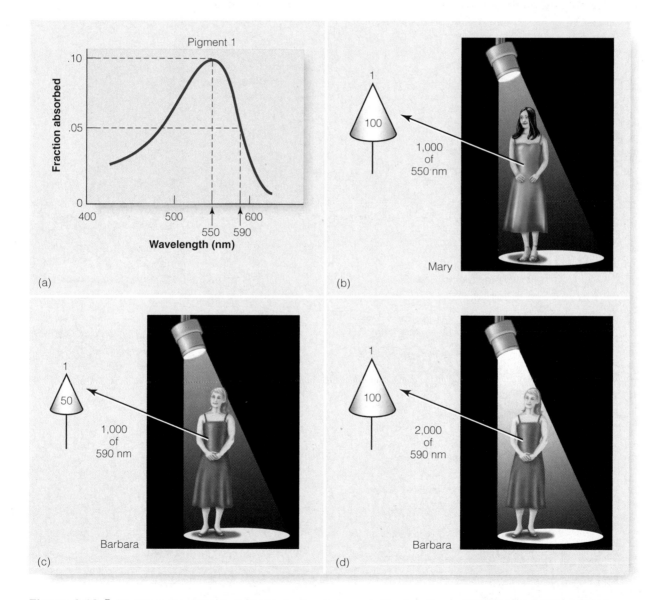

Figure 9.12 ▌ (a) Absorption spectrum of Jay's visual pigment. The fractions of 550-nm and 590-nm lights absorbed are indicated by the dashed lines. (b) The size of the cone indicates activation caused by the reflection of 1,000 photons of 550-nm light by Mary's dress. (c) The activation caused by the reflection of 1,000 photons of 590-nm light by Barbara's dress. (d) The activation caused by the reflection of 2,000 photons of 590-nm light from Barbara's dress. Notice that the cone response is the same in (b) and (d).

the spotlight on Barbara's dress so that 2,000 photons of 590-nm light are reflected into Jay's eyes, his pigment absorbs 100 photons of 590-nm light; now 100 pigment molecules are activated—the same as were activated by Mary's dress when illuminated by the dimmer light (Figure 9.12d). (Notice that it doesn't matter if the light absorbed by the pigment is 550-nm light or 590-nm light. Once a photon is absorbed, no matter what its wavelength, it has the same effect on the visual pigment.) Thus, by adjusting the intensity of the light, we can cause Mary's and Barbara's dresses to have exactly the same effect on Jay's pigment. Therefore, Jay cannot tell the difference between the two dresses based on the wavelengths they reflect.

Another way to state this result is that a person with only one visual pigment can match any wavelength in the spectrum by adjusting the *intensity* of any other wavelength.

Thus, by adjusting the intensity appropriately, Jay can make the 550-nm and 590-nm lights (or any other wavelengths) look identical. Furthermore, Jay will perceive all of these wavelengths as shades of gray.

How can the nervous system tell the difference between Mary and Barbara's dresses, no matter what the light intensity? The answer to this question is that adding a second pigment makes it possible to distinguish between wavelengths *independent of light intensity*. We can see why this is so by considering Dan, who has two visual pigments, pigment 1, which is the same as Jay's pigment, and pigment 2, which has an absorption spectrum that indicates that the fraction of light absorbed for 550-nm is 0.05 and the fraction for 590-nm is 0.01 (Figure 9.13a).

Figure 9.13b shows that when Mary's dress is illuminated by the dim light, 100 molecules of pigment 1 are acti-

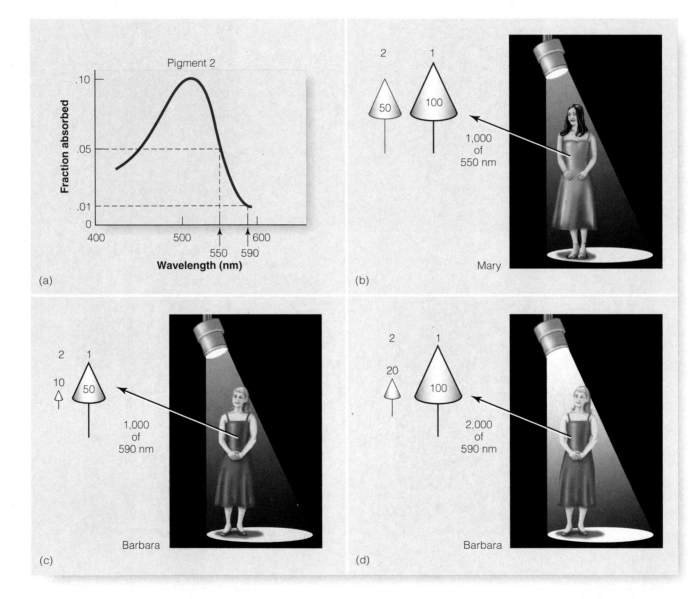

Figure 9.13 ▌ The same as Figure 9.12, but with a second pigment added. (a) Absorption spectrum of pigment 2, with the fraction absorbed by 550-nm and 590-nm indicated by the dashed lines. (b) Response of the two types of cones when they absorb light from Mary's dress. The response of cone 1 is on the right. (c) Response caused by light reflected from Barbara's dress at the same intensity. (d) Response from Barbara's dress at a higher intensity. Notice that the cone response is different in (b) and (d).

vated, as before, and 50 molecules of pigment 2 are activated ($1,000 \times 0.05 = 50$). Figure 9.13c shows that for Barbara's dress, 50 molecules of pigment 1 are activated, as before, and 10 molecules of pigment 2 are activated ($1,000 \times 0.01 = 10$).

Thus, when both Mary and Barbara are illuminated by the dim light, their dresses activate the receptors differently, just as occurred in the single-pigment example. But when we increase the illumination on Barbara, as we did before, we see that the pattern of receptor activation caused by Barbara's dress is still different from the pattern for Mary's dress (Figure 9.13d). Adding the second pigment causes Mary's and Barbara's dresses to have different effects, even when we change the illumination. So color vision becomes possible when there are two pigments.

Notice that the *ratios* of response caused by the two pigments are the same for a particular wavelength, no matter what the intensity. The ratio for the 550-nm light is always 2 to 1, and the ratio for the 590-nm light is always 5 to 1. Thus, the visual system can use this ratio information to determine the wavelength of any light. This is what trichromatic theory proposes when it states that color perception depends on the pattern of activity in three receptor mechanisms.

As we will see when we consider color deficiency in the next section, there are people with just two types of cone pigment. These people, called *dichromats,* do see colors, just as our calculations predict, but they see fewer colors than people with three visual pigments, who are called trichromats. The addition of a third pigment, although not necessary for creating color vision, increases the number of colors that can be seen across the visual spectrum.

TEST YOURSELF 9.1

1. What are the various functions of color vision?
2. What physical characteristic is most closely associated with color perception? How is this demonstrated by differences in reflection of different objects?
3. Describe additive color mixture and subtractive color mixture. How can the results of these two types of color mixing be related to the wavelengths that are reflected into an observer's eyes?
4. Describe trichromatic theory and the experiments on which it was based. How does this theory explain the results of color-matching experiments?
5. Describe how trichromatic theory is based on cone pigments and how the code for color can be determined by the activity of the cones.
6. What are metamers, and how can our perception of metamers be explained by the code for color described above?
7. Why is color vision possible when there are only two different cone pigments but not possible when there is just one pigment? What is the effect on color vision of having three pigments rather than just two?

Color Deficiency

It has long been known that some people have difficulty perceiving certain colors. We have described the case of Mr. I, who lost his ability to see color due to brain damage. However, most problems with color vision involve only a partial loss of color perception, called **color deficiency**, and are associated with problems with the receptors in the retina.

In a famous early report of color deficiency, the well-known 18th-century chemist John Dalton (1798/1948) described his own color perceptions as follows: "All crimsons appear to me to consist chiefly of dark blue: but many of them seem to have a tinge of dark brown. I have seen specimens of crimson, claret, and mud, which were very nearly alike" (p. 102).

Dalton's descriptions of his abnormal color perceptions led to the early use of the term *Daltonism* to describe color deficiency. We now know that there are a number of different types of color deficiency. This has been determined by color vision tests like the ones shown in Figure 9.14a, which are called Ishihara plates. In this example, people with normal color vision see a "74," but people with a form of red–green color deficiency might see something like the depiction in Figure 9.14b, in which the "74" is not visible. Another way to determine the presence of color deficiency is by using the color-matching procedure to determine the minimum number of wavelengths needed to match any other wavelength in the spectrum. This procedure has revealed the following three types of color deficiency: $\boxed{\text{VL} \; 4}$

1. A **monochromat** can match any wavelength in the spectrum by adjusting the intensity of any other wavelength. Thus, a monochromat needs only one wavelength to match any color in the spectrum and sees only in shades of gray. Jay, from our example in Figure 9.12, is a monochromat.

2. A dichromat needs only two wavelengths to match all other wavelengths in the spectrum. Dan, from Figure 9.13, is a dichromat.

3. An anomalous trichromat needs three wavelengths to match any wavelength, just as a normal trichromat does. However, the anomalous trichromat mixes these wavelengths in different proportions from a trichromat, and an anomalous trichromat is not as good as a trichromat at discriminating between wavelengths that are close together.

Once we have determined whether a person's vision is color deficient, we are still left with the question: What colors does a person with color deficiency see? When I pose this question in my class, a few students suggest that we can answer it by pointing to objects of various colors and asking a color deficient person what he sees. (Most color deficient people are male; see page 212.) This method does not really tell us what the person perceives, however, because a color deficient person may say "red" when we point to a strawberry simply because he has learned that people call

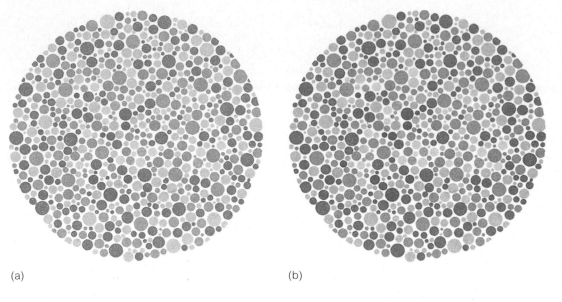

Figure 9.14 ▍(a) Ishihara plate for testing color deficiency. A person with normal color vision sees a "74" when the plate is viewed under standardized illumination. (b) Ishihara plate as perceived by a person with a form of red–green color deficiency.

(a)

(b)

strawberries "red." It is quite likely that the color deficient person's experience of "red" is very different from the experience of the person without color deficiency. For all we know, he may be having an experience similar to what a person without deficient color vision would call "yellow."

To determine what a dichromat perceives, we need to locate a **unilateral dichromat**—a person with trichromatic vision in one eye and dichromatic vision in the other. Both of the unilateral dichromat's eyes are connected to the same brain, so this person can look at a color with his dichromatic eye and then determine which color it corresponds to in his trichromatic eye. Although unilateral dichromats are extremely rare, the few who have been tested have helped us determine the nature of a dichromat's color experience (Alpern et al., 1983; Graham et al., 1961; Sloan & Wollach, 1948). Let's now look at the nature of the color experience of both monochromats and dichromats.

Monochromatism

Monochromatism is a rare form of color blindness that is usually hereditary and occurs in only about 10 people out of 1 million (LeGrand, 1957). Monochromats usually have no functioning cones; therefore, their vision has the characteristics of rod vision in both dim and bright lights. Monochromats see everything in shades of lightness (white, gray, and black) and can therefore be called **color-blind** (as opposed to dichromats, who see some chromatic colors and therefore should be called color deficient).

In addition to a loss of color vision, people with hereditary monochromatism have poor visual acuity and are so sensitive to bright lights that they often must protect their eyes with dark glasses during the day. The rod system is not designed to function in bright light and so becomes overloaded in strong illumination, creating a perception of glare. VL 5

Dichromatism

Dichromats experience some colors, though a lesser range than trichromats. There are three major forms of dichromatism: protanopia, deuteranopia, and tritanopia. The two most common kinds, protanopia and deuteranopia, are inherited through a gene located on the X chromosome (Nathans et al., 1986).

Males (XY) have only one X chromosome, so a defect in the visual pigment gene on this chromosome causes color deficiency. Females (XX), on the other hand, with their two X chromosomes, are less likely to become color deficient, because only one normal gene is required for normal color vision. These forms of color vision are therefore called sex-linked because women can carry the gene for color deficiency without being color deficient themselves, and they can pass the condition to their male offspring. Thus, many more men than women are dichromats. As we describe what the three types of dichromats perceive, we use as our reference points Figures 9.15d and 9.16d, which show how a trichromat perceives a bunch of colored paper flowers and the visible spectrum, respectively. VL 6

- Protanopia affects 1 percent of males and 0.02 percent of females and results in the perception of colors shown in Figure 9.15a. A protanope perceives short-wavelength light as blue, and as wavelength is increased, the blue becomes less and less saturated until, at 492 nm, the protanope perceives gray (Figure 9.16a). The wavelength at which the protanope perceives gray is called the **neutral point**. At wavelengths above the neutral point, the protanope perceives yellow, which becomes increasingly saturated as wavelength is increased, until at the long-wavelength end of the spectrum the protanope perceives a saturated yellow.

- Deuteranopia affects about 1 percent of males and 0.01 percent of females and results in the perception

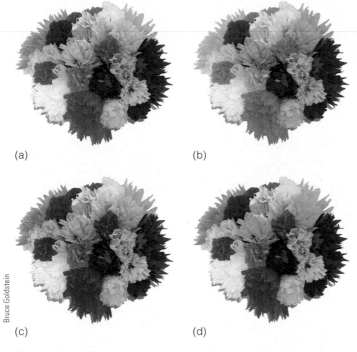

(a)   (b)

(c)   (d)

Figure 9.15 ▌ How colored paper flowers appear to (a) protanopes; (b) deuteranopes; (c) tritanopes; and (d) trichromats. *(Color processing courtesy of John Carroll.)*

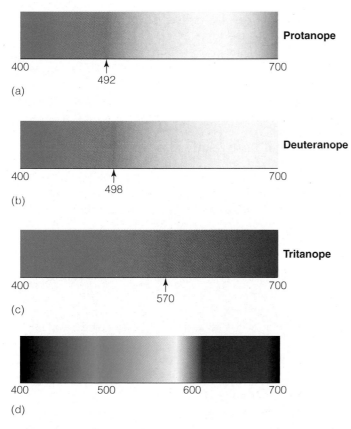

Figure 9.16 ▌ How the visible spectrum appears to (a) protanopes; (b) deuteranopes; (c) tritanopes; and (d) trichromats. The number indicates the wavelength of the neutral point.

of color in Figure 9.15b. A deuteranope perceives blue at short wavelengths, sees yellow at long wavelengths, and has a neutral point at about 498 nm (Figure 9.16b) (Boynton, 1979).

- Tritanopia is very rare, affecting only about 0.002 percent of males and 0.001 percent of females. A tritanope sees colors as in Figure 9.15c, and sees the spectrum as in Figure 9.16c—blue at short wavelengths, red at long wavelengths, and a neutral point at 570 nm (Alpern et al., 1983). VL 7

Physiological Mechanisms of Receptor-Based Color Deficiency

What are the physiological mechanisms of color deficiency? Most monochromats have no color vision because they have just one type of cone or no cones. Dichromats are missing one visual pigment, with the protanope missing the long-wavelength pigment and the deuteranope missing the medium-wavelength pigment (W. A. H. Rushton, 1964). Because of the tritanope's rarity and because of the low number of short-wavelength cones even in normal retinas, it has been difficult to determine which pigment tritanopes are missing, but they are probably missing the short-wavelength pigment.

Genetic research has identified differences in the genes that determine visual pigment structure in trichromats and dichromats (Nathans et al., 1986). Based on this research, it has also been suggested that anomalous trichromats probably match colors differently from normal trichromats and have more difficulty discriminating between some wavelengths because their M and L pigment spectra have been shifted so they are closer together (Neitz et al., 1991).

Opponent-Process Theory of Color Vision

Although trichromatic theory explains a number of color vision phenomena, including color matching and color mixing, and some facts about color deficiency, there are some color perceptions it cannot explain. These color perceptions were demonstrated by Ewald Hering (1834–1918), another eminent physiologist who was working at about the same time as Helmholtz. Hering used the results of phenomenological observations, in which stimuli were presented and observers described what they perceived, to propose the **opponent-process theory of color vision**. This theory states that color vision is caused by opposing responses generated by blue and yellow and by red and green.

Behavioral Evidence for the Theory

You can make some phenomenological observations similar to Hering's by doing the following demonstrations.

DEMONSTRATION

The Colors of the Flag

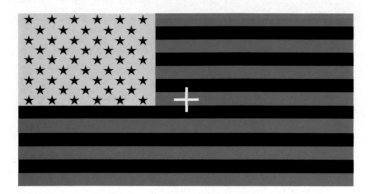

Figure 9.17 | Stimulus for afterimage demonstration.

Look at the cross at the center of the strangely colored American flag in Figure 9.17 for about 30 seconds. If you then look at a piece of white paper and blink, the image you see, which is called an *afterimage,* has colors that probably match the red, white, and blue of the American flag. Notice that the green area of the flag in Figure 9.17 created a red afterimage, and the yellow area created a blue afterimage. VL 8

Although Hering didn't use a strangely colored flag to create afterimages, he did observe that viewing a green field generates a red afterimage, and viewing a yellow field creates a blue afterimage. He also observed the opposite—viewing green causes a red afterimage, and viewing blue causes a yellow afterimage. You can demonstrate that this works both ways by looking at the center of Figure 9.18 for 30 seconds and then looking at a white surface and noticing how

Figure 9.18 | Color matrix for afterimage and simultaneous contrast demonstrations.

red and green, and blue and yellow, have changed places. (Note that the colors associated with long wavelengths—red and yellow—are on the right in the figure, and switch to the left in the afterimage.) Based on observations such as these, Hering proposed that red and green are paired and blue and yellow are paired. Here is another demonstration that illustrates this pairing.

DEMONSTRATION

Afterimages and Simultaneous Contrast

Cut out a 1/2-inch square of white paper and place it in the center of the green square in Figure 9.18. Cover the other squares with white paper and stare at the center of the white square for about 30 seconds. Then look at a white background and blink to observe the afterimage. What color is the outside area of the afterimage? What color is the small square in the center? Repeat your observations on the red, blue, and yellow squares in Figure 9.18. █

When you made your observations using the green square, you probably confirmed your previous observation that green and red are paired because the afterimage corresponding to the green area of the original square is red. But the color of the small square in the center also shows that green and red are paired: Most people see a green square inside the red afterimage. This green afterimage is due to **simultaneous color contrast,** an effect that occurs when surrounding an area with a color changes the appearance of the surrounded area. In this case, the red afterimage surrounds a white area and causes the white area to appear green. Table 9.4 summarizes this result and the results that occur when we repeat this demonstration on the other squares. All of these results show a clear pairing of red and green and of blue and yellow. VL 9

TABLE 9.4   Results of Afterimage and Simultaneous Contrast Demonstration

ORIGINAL SQUARE	COLOR OF OUTSIDE AFTERIMAGE	COLOR OF INSIDE AFTERIMAGE
Green	Red	Green
Red	Green	Red
Blue	Yellow	Blue
Yellow	Blue	Yellow

DEMONSTRATION

Visualizing Colors

This demonstration involves visualizing colors. Start by visualizing the color red, with your eyes either opened or closed, whichever works best for you. Attach this color to a specific object such as a fire engine, if that makes your visualizing easier. Now visualize a reddish-yellow and then a reddish-green. Which of these two combinations is easier to visualize? Now do the same thing for blue. Visualize a pure blue, then a bluish-green and a bluish-yellow. Again, which of these combinations is easier to visualize? ▮

Most people find it easy to visualize a bluish-green or a reddish-yellow, but find it difficult (or impossible) to visualize a reddish-green or a bluish-yellow. In other experiments, in which observers were shown patches of color and were asked to estimate the percentages of blue, green, yellow, and red in each patch, they rarely reported seeing blue and yellow or red and green at the same time (Abramov & Gordon, 1994), just as the results of the visualization demonstration would predict.

The above observations, plus Hering's observation that people who are color-blind to red are also color-blind to green, and that people who can't see blue also can't see yellow, led to the conclusion that red and green are paired and that blue and yellow are paired. Based on this conclusion, Hering proposed the opponent-process theory of color vision (Hering, 1878, 1905, 1964).

The Theory: Vision Is an Opponent Process

The basic idea underlying Hering's theory is shown in Figure 9.19. He proposed three mechanisms, each of which responds in opposite ways to different intensities or wavelengths of light. The Black (−) White (+) mechanism responds positively to white light and negatively to the absence of light. Red (+) Green (−) responds positively to red and negatively to green, and Blue (−) Yellow (+) responds negatively to blue and positively to yellow. Although Hering's phenomenological observations supported his theory, it wasn't until many years later that modern physiological research showed that these colors do cause physiologically opposite responses.

The Physiology of Opponent-Process Vision

Modern physiological research, which has measured the response of single neurons to different wavelengths, has pro-vided physiological evidence for neurons that respond in opposite ways to blue and yellow and to red and green.

Opponent Neurons In the 1950s and '60s researchers began finding opponent neurons in the retina and lateral geniculate nucleus that responded with an excitatory response to light from one part of the spectrum and with an inhibitory response to light from another part (R. L. DeValois, 1960; Svaetichin, 1956). For example, the left column of Figure 9.20 shows records for a neuron that responds to short-wavelength light with an increase in firing and to long-wavelength light with a decrease in firing. (Notice that firing decreases to below the level of spontaneous activity.) This neuron is called a B+ Y− neuron because the wavelengths that cause an increase in firing are in the blue part of the spectrum, and the wavelengths that cause a decrease are in the yellow part of the spectrum.

The right column of Figure 9.20 shows records for an R+ G− neuron, which increases firing to light in the red part of the spectrum and decreases firing to light in the green part of the spectrum. There are also B− Y+ and G+ R− neurons (R. L. DeValois et al., 1966).

How Opponent Responding Can Be Created by Three Receptors The discovery of opponent neurons provided physiological evidence for opponent process theory to go with the three different cone pigments of trichromatic theory. This evidence, which was not available in the 1800s, showed modern researchers that both trichromatic and opponent-process theories are correct and that each one describes physiological mechanisms at different places in the visual system. Figure 9.21 shows how this works.

Trichromatic theory describes what is happening at the beginning of the visual system, in the receptors of the retina. Each wavelength causes a different ratio of response in the three different kinds of cone receptors, and it takes a minimum of three wavelengths to match any wavelength

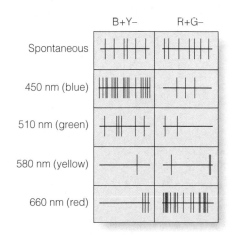

Figure 9.20 ▮ Responses of B+ Y− and R+ G− opponent cells in the monkey's lateral geniculate nucleus. *(From DeValois, R. L., & Jacobs, G. H. (1968). Primate color vision. Science, 162, 533–540.)*

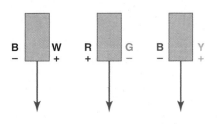

Figure 9.19 ▮ The three opponent mechanisms proposed by Hering.

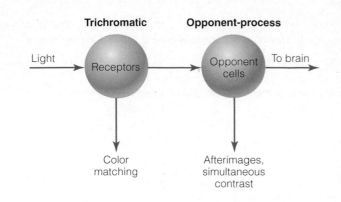

Figure 9.21 ▌ Our experience of color is shaped by physiological mechanisms, both in the receptors and in opponent neurons.

in the spectrum. Opponent-process theory describes events later in the visual system. Opponent neurons are responsible for perceptual experiences such as afterimages and simultaneous contrast.

Figure 9.22 shows two neural circuits in which the cones are wired in a way that creates two kinds of opponent neurons. In circuit 1, the short-wavelength cone sends an excitatory signal to the ganglion cell, and the medium- and long-wavelength cones pool their activity and then send inhibitory signals to this cell. (The bipolar cells have been omitted to simplify the circuits.) This creates a B+ Y− opponent neuron because stimulation of the short-wavelength cone increases firing and stimulation of the medium- or long-wavelength cones decreases firing. In circuit 2, the medium-wavelength cone sends excitatory signals and the long-wavelength cone sends inhibitory signals to the ganglion cell. This creates a G+ R− opponent neuron, in which stimulation of the medium-wavelength cone causes an increase in firing and stimulation of the long-wavelength cone causes a decrease in firing.

The important thing about these two circuits is that their responses are determined both by the wavelengths to which the receptors respond best and by the arrangement

of inhibitory and excitatory synapses. Another way to describe this is that processing for color vision takes place in two stages: First, the receptors respond with different patterns to different wavelengths (trichromatic theory), and then other neurons integrate the inhibitory and excitatory signals from the receptors (opponent-process theory). ▭ **10–12**

Why Are Opponent Neurons Necessary? Our neural circuit shows that wavelengths can be signaled in two ways: (1) by trichromatic signals from the receptors, and (2) by opponent signals in later neurons. But why are two different ways of signaling wavelength necessary? Specifically, since the firing pattern of the three types of cone receptors contains enough information to signal which wavelength has been presented, why is this information

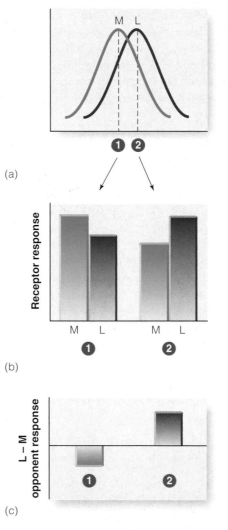

Figure 9.23 ▌ (a) Response curves for the M and L receptors. (b) Bar graph indicating the size of the responses generated in the receptors by wavelengths 1 (left pair of bars) and 2 (right pair). (c) Bar graph showing the opponent response of the R+ G− cell to wavelengths 1 and 2. The response to 1 is inhibitory, and the response to 2 is excitatory.

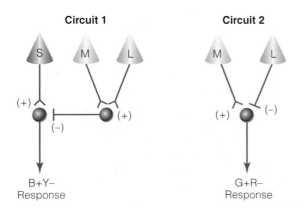

Figure 9.22 ▌ Neural circuit showing how the blue–yellow and red–green mechanisms can be created by excitatory and inhibitory inputs from the three types of cone receptors.

changed into opponent responses? The answer to this question is that opponent responding provides a way of specifying wavelengths that may be clearer and more efficient than the ratio of the cone receptor responses.

To understand how this works, let's consider how the two cones in Figure 9.23a respond to two wavelengths, labeled 1 and 2. Figure 9.23b shows that when wavelength 1 is presented, receptor M responds more than receptor L, and when wavelength 2 is presented, receptor L responds more than receptor M. Although we can tell the difference between the responses to these two wavelengths, the two pairs of bars in Figure 9.23b look fairly similar. But taking the difference between the response of the L cone and the response of the M cone, enables us to tell the difference between wavelengths 1 and 2 much more easily (Figure 9.23c). Thus, the information contained in the firing of opponent cells transmits information about wavelength more efficiently than the information contained in the receptor response (Buchsbaum & Gottschalk, 1983).

Color in the Cortex

How is color represented in the cortex? One possible answer is that there is a specific area in the cortex, a specialized "color center," that processes information about color (Livingstone & Hubel, 1988; Zeki, 1983a, 1983b). **Cerebral achromatopsia**, color blindness due to damage to the cortex, supports this idea. Although Mr. I's cerebral achromatopsia meant that he could no longer see color, he still had excellent visual acuity and could still see form and movement. This absence of color perception, while other visual functions remained relatively normal, supports the idea that an area specialized for color perception had been damaged.

However, when researchers record from neurons in the cortex, a different picture emerges. They find cortical neurons that respond to just some wavelengths in the spectrum, and some neurons that have opponent responses in many areas of the cortex, including the striate cortex (V1) and other areas in the ventral processing stream (Figure 4.27). But these neurons that respond to color also usually respond to specific forms and orientations (Lennie et al., 1990; Leventhal et al., 1995; Shein & Desimone, 1990). Also, many of the wavelength-selective neurons in the area originally designated as the "color module" respond to white, leading some researchers to question the idea that these neurons determine our perception of color (Gordon & Abramov, 2001; also see Girard et al., 2002; Heywood & Cowey, 1998; Hinkle & Connor, 2002).

Taken together, the evidence seems to show that there may not be a single "module" for color vision (Engel et al., 1997; Gegenfurtner, 2001; Zeki & Marini, 1998). Thus, color vision presents an example of distributed processing in the cortex, with a number of areas being involved in processing wavelength information and creating color perception (Gegenfurtner, 2003; Solomon & Lennie, 2007).

Discovering the cortical mechanism for color perception is complicated because there are two issues involved in determining how the cortex processes color information: (1) Where is *information about wavelength* processed? (2) Where is the *perception of color* determined? You might think these are equivalent questions because color is determined largely by wavelength. However, there are people who can use information about wavelength but can't see colors. An example is M.S., who suffered from cerebral achromatopsia due to an illness that left his cone pigments intact but damaged his cortex (Stoerig, 1998). Although he was able to use wavelength information being sent to the brain by the cones, he could not see color. For example, he could detect the line separating two adjacent fields consisting of different wavelengths, even though they both appeared the same shade of gray.

Apparently, what is happening for M.S. is that wavelength information is being processed by the undamaged area of his brain, but this information is not being transformed into the experience of color, presumably because of damage to another area. Understanding how color perception occurs in the brain, therefore, involves determining both how wavelength information is processed and how further processing of this information creates the experience of color (Cowey & Heywood, 1997; Solomon & Lennie, 2007).

TEST YOURSELF 9.2

1. What is color deficiency? How can it be detected using the procedure of color mixing? How can we determine how a color deficient person perceives different wavelengths?
2. How is color deficiency caused by (a) problems with the receptors? (b) damage to the cortex?
3. Describe opponent-process theory, including the observations on which it is based and the physiological basis of this theory.
4. What is the evidence that a number of areas in the cortex are involved in color vision? Why is it important to distinguish between processing information about wavelength and perceiving color?

Perceiving Colors Under Changing Illumination

It is midday, with the sun high in the sky, and as you are walking to class you notice a classmate who is wearing a green sweater. Then, a few minutes later, as you are sitting in class, you again notice the same green sweater. The fact that the sweater appears green both outside under sunlight and inside under artificial indoor illumination may not seem particularly remarkable. After all, the sweater *is* green,

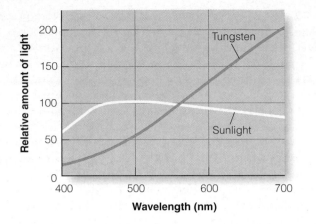

Figure 9.24 ▮ The wavelength distribution of sunlight and of light from a tungsten light bulb. *(From Judd, D. B., MacAdam, D. L., & Wyszecki, G. (1964). Spectral distribution of typical daylight as a function of correlated color temperature.* Journal of the Optical Society of America, 54, *1031–1040.)*

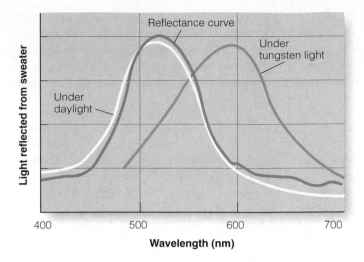

Figure 9.25 ▮ Reflectance curve of sweater, and light reflected from sweater when illumination by tungsten light and white light.

isn't it? However, when we consider the interaction between the illumination and the properties of the sweater, we can appreciate that your perception of the sweater as green, both outside and inside, represents a remarkable achievement of the visual system. This achievement is called **color constancy**—we perceive the colors of objects as being relatively constant even under changing illumination.

We can appreciate why color constancy is an impressive achievement by considering the interaction between illumination, such as sunlight or lightbulbs, and the reflection properties of an object, such as the green sweater. First, let's consider the illumination. Figure 9.24 shows the wavelengths that are contained in sunlight and the wavelengths that are contained in light from a lightbulb. The sunlight contains approximately equal amounts of energy at all wavelengths, which is a characteristic of white light. The bulb contains much more energy at long wavelengths. This wavelength distribution is sometimes called "tungsten" light because it is produced by the tungsten filament inside old-style lightbulbs (which are in the process of being replaced with screw-in "twisty" fluorescent lightbulbs). This large amount of long-wavelength light is why the tungsten bulb looks slightly yellow.

Now consider the interaction between the wavelengths produced by the illumination and the wavelengths reflected from the green sweater. The reflectance curve of the sweater is indicated by the green line in Figure 9.25. It reflects mostly medium-wavelength light, as we would expect of something that is green.

The actual light that is reflected from the sweater depends on both its reflectance curve and the illumination that reaches the sweater and is then reflected from it. To determine the wavelengths that are actually reflected from the sweater, we multiply the reflectance curve by the amount of light provided by the illumination source (sunlight or tungsten) at each wavelength. This calculation indicates that the sweater reflects more long-wavelength light when it is seen

under tungsten illumination (orange line) than when it is seen under sunlight (white line). The fact that we still see the sweater as green even though the wavelength composition of the reflected light differs under different illuminations is color constancy. Without color constancy, the color we see would depend on how the sweater was being illuminated (Delahunt & Brainard, 2004). Luckily, color constancy works, so we can refer to objects as having a particular well-defined color. You can demonstrate color constancy to yourself by doing the following demonstration.

DEMONSTRATION

Color Perception Under Changing Illumination

View the color circle of Figure 9.3 so it is illuminated by natural light by taking it outdoors or illuminating it with light from a window. Then illuminate it with the tungsten lightbulb of your desk lamp. Notice whether the colors change and, if so, how much they change. ▮

In this demonstration, you may have noticed some change in color as you changed the illumination, but the change was probably much less than we would predict based on the change in the wavelength distribution of the light. Even though the wavelengths reflected from a blue object illuminated by long-wavelength-rich tungsten light can match the wavelengths reflected by a yellow object illuminated by sunlight (Jameson, 1985), our perception of color remains relatively constant with changing illumination. As color vision researcher Dorthea Jameson puts it, "A blue bird would not be mistaken for a goldfinch if it were brought indoors" (1985, p. 84). (Note, however, that color constancy breaks down under extreme kinds of illumination such as sodium vapor lamps that emit narrow bands of wavelengths.)

Researchers still do not completely understand why color constancy occurs; however, it is likely that it is caused by a number of things working together. We will consider some of these things, beginning with chromatic adaptation.

Chromatic Adaptation

One reason why color constancy occurs lies in the results of the following demonstration.

DEMONSTRATION

Adapting to Red

Illuminate Figure 9.26 with a bright light from your desk lamp; then, with your left eye near the page and your right eye closed, look at the field with your left eye for about 30 to 45 seconds. Then look at various colored objects in your environment, first with your left eye and then with your right. ∎

Figure 9.26 ∎ Red adapting field.

This demonstration shows that color perception can be changed by **chromatic adaptation**—prolonged exposure to chromatic color. Adaptation to the red light selectively bleaches your long-wavelength cone pigment, which decreases your sensitivity to red light and causes you to see the reds and oranges viewed with your left (adapted) eye as less saturated and bright than those viewed with the right eye.

We can understand how chromatic adaptation contributes to color constancy by realizing that when you walk into a room illuminated with tungsten light, the eye adapts to the long-wavelength-rich light, which decreases your eye's sensitivity to long wavelengths. This decreased sensitivity causes the long-wavelength light reflected from objects to have less effect than before adaptation, and this compensates for the greater amount of long-wavelength tungsten light that is reflected from everything in the room. Because of this adaptation, the tungsten illumination has only a small effect on your perception of color.

The idea that chromatic adaptation is responsible for color constancy has been tested in an experiment by Keiji Uchikawa and coworkers (1989). Observers viewed isolated patches of colored paper under three different conditions (Figure 9.27): (a) *baseline:* paper and observer illuminated by white light; (b) *observer not adapted:* paper illuminated by red light, observer by white (the illumination of the object is changed, but the observer is not chromatically adapted); and (c) *observer adapted to red:* both paper and observer illuminated by red light (the illumination of the object is changed, and the observer is chromatically adapted).

The results from these three conditions are shown above each condition. In the *baseline condition,* a green paper is perceived as green. In the *observer not adapted condition,* the observer perceives the paper's color as being shifted toward the red. Thus, color constancy does not occur in this condition. But in the *observer adapted to red condition,* perception is shifted only slightly to the red, so it appears more yellowish. Thus, the chromatic adaptation has created **partial color constancy**—the perception of the object is shifted after adaptation, but not as much as when there was no adaptation. This means that the eye can adjust its sensitivity to

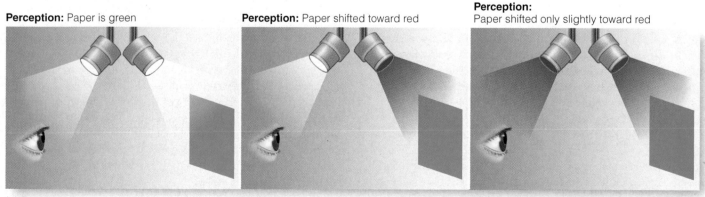

Perception: Paper is green

Perception: Paper shifted toward red

Perception:
Paper shifted only slightly toward red

(a) Baseline

(b) Observer not adapted

(c) Observer adapted to red

Figure 9.27 ∎ The three conditions in Uchikawa et al.'s (1989) experiment. See text for details.

different wavelengths to keep color perception approximately constant as illumination changes.

The Effect of the Surroundings

An object's perceived color is affected not only by the observer's state of adaptation, but also by the object's surroundings, as shown by the following demonstration.

DEMONSTRATION

Color and the Surroundings

Illuminate the green quadrant of Figure 9.18 with tungsten light, and then look at the square through a small hole punched in a piece of paper so that all you see through the hole is part of the green area. Now repeat this observation while illuminating the same area with daylight from your window. ▌

When the surroundings are masked, most people perceive the green area to be slightly more yellow under the tungsten light than in daylight, which shows that color constancy works less well when the surroundings are masked. A number of investigators have shown that color constancy works best when an object is surrounded by objects of many different colors, a situation that often occurs when viewing objects in the environment (E. H. Land, 1983, 1986; E. H. Land & McCann, 1971).

The surroundings help us achieve color constancy because the visual system—in ways that are still not completely understood—uses the information provided by the way objects in a scene are illuminated to estimate the characteristics of the illumination and to make appropriate corrections. (For some theories about exactly how the presence of the surroundings enhances color constancy, see Brainard & Wandell, 1986; E. H. Land, 1983, 1986; Pokorny et al., 1991.)

Memory and Color

Another thing that helps achieve color constancy is our knowledge about the usual colors of objects in the environment. This effect on perception of prior knowledge of the typical colors of objects is called **memory color**. Research has shown that because people know the colors of familiar objects, like a red stop sign, or a green tree, they judge these familiar objects as having richer, more saturated colors than unfamiliar objects that reflect the same wavelengths (Jin & Shevell, 1996; Ratner & McCarthy, 1990).

In a recent experiment, Thorsten Hansen and coworkers (2006) demonstrated an effect of memory color by presenting observers with pictures of fruits with characteristic colors, such as lemons, oranges, and bananas, against a gray background. Observers also viewed a spot of light against the same gray background. When the intensity and wavelength of the spot of light were adjusted so the spot was physically the same as the background, observers reported that the spot appeared the same gray as the background. But when the intensity and wavelength of the fruits were set to be physically the same as the background, observers reported that the fruits appeared slightly colored. For example, a banana that was physically the same as the gray background appeared slightly yellowish, and an orange looked slightly orange. This led Hansen to conclude that the observer's knowledge of the fruit's characteristic colors actually changed the colors they were experiencing. This effect of memory on our experience of color may help us accurately perceive the colors of familiar objects under different illuminations and so makes a small contribution to color constancy (Jin & Shevell, 1996).

Lightness Constancy

We not only perceive chromatic colors like red and green as remaining relatively constant, even when the illumination changes; we perceive achromatic colors, like white, gray, and black, as remaining fairly constant as well. Thus, we perceive a Labrador retriever as black when it is inside under dim illumination, and it remains black even when it runs out of the house into bright sunlight.

Consider what is happening in this situation. The Labrador retriever lying on the rug in the living room is illuminated by a 100-watt lightbulb in the overhead light fixture. Some of the light that hits the retriever's black coat is reflected, and we see the coat as black. When the dog goes outside into bright sunlight, much more light hits its coat, and therefore much more light is reflected. But the dog still appears black. Even though more light is reflected, the perception of the shade of achromatic color (white, gray, and black), which we call **lightness**, remains the same. The fact that we see whites, grays, and blacks as staying about the same shade under different illuminations is called **lightness constancy**.

The visual system's problem is that the amount of light reaching the eye from an object depends on two things: (1) the illumination—the *total amount of light* that is striking the object's surface—and (2) the object's **reflectance**—the *proportion of this light* that the object reflects into our eyes. When lightness constancy occurs, our perception of lightness is determined not by the illumination hitting an object, but by the object's reflectance. Objects that look black reflect about 5 percent of the light. Objects that look gray reflect about 10 to 70 percent of the light (depending on the shade of gray); and objects that look white, like the paper in this book, reflect 80 to 95 percent of the light. Thus, our perception of an object's lightness is related not to the *amount* of light that is reflected from the object, which can change depending on the illumination, but to the *percentage* of light reflected from the object, which remains the same no matter what the illumination.

You can appreciate the existence of lightness constancy by imagining a checkerboard illuminated by room light, like the one in Figure 9.28. Let's assume that the white

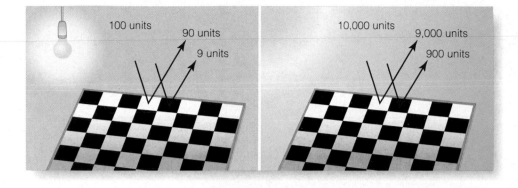

Figure 9.28 ▌ A black-and-white checkerboard illuminated by (a) tungsten light and (b) sunlight.

squares have a reflectance of 90 percent, and the black squares have a reflectance of 9 percent. If the light intensity inside the room is 100 units, the white squares reflect 90 units and the black squares reflect 9 units. Now, if we take the checkerboard outside into bright sunlight, where the intensity is 10,000 units, the white squares reflect 9,000 units of light, and the black squares reflect 900 units. But even though the black squares when outside reflect much more light than the white squares did when the checkerboard was inside, the black squares still look black. Your perception is determined by the reflectance, not the amount of light reflected. What is responsible for lightness constancy? There are a number of possible causes.

Intensity Relationships: The Ratio Principle

One observation about our perception of lightness is that when an object is illuminated evenly—that is, when the illumination is the same over the whole object, as in our checkerboard example—then lightness is determined by the *ratio* of reflectance of the object to the reflectance of surrounding objects. According to the **ratio principle**, as long as this ratio remains the same, the perceived lightness will remain the same (Jacobson & Gilchrist, 1988; Wallach, 1963). For example, consider one of the black squares in the checkerboard. The ratio of a black square to the surrounding white squares is 9/90 = 0.10 under low illuminations and 900/9,000 = 0.10 under high illuminations. Because the ratio of the reflectances is the same, our perception of the lightness remains the same.

The ratio principle works well for flat, evenly illuminated objects like our checkerboard. However, things get more complicated in three-dimensional scenes, which are usually illuminated unevenly.

Lightness Perception Under Uneven Illumination

If you look around, you will probably notice that the illumination is not even over the entire scene, as was the case for our two-dimensional checkerboard. The illumination in three-dimensional scenes is usually uneven because of shadows cast by one object onto another or because one part of

an object faces the light and another part faces away from the light. For example, in Figure 9.29, in which a shadow is cast across a wall, it is necessary to determine whether the changes in appearance we see across the wall are due to differences in the properties of different parts of the wall or to differences in the way the wall is illuminated.

The problem for the perceptual system is that it has to somehow take the uneven illumination into account. One way to state this problem is that the perceptual system needs to distinguish between *reflectance edges* and *illumination edges*. A **reflectance edge** is an edge where the reflectance of two surfaces changes. The border between areas *a* and *c* in Figure 9.29 is a reflectance edge because they are made of different materials that reflect different amounts of light. An **illumination edge** is an edge where the lighting changes. The border between *a* and *b* is an illumination edge because area a is receiving more light than area b, which is in shadow.

Some explanations for how the visual system distinguishes between these two types of edges have been proposed (see Adelson, 1999; Gilchrist, 1994; and Gilchrist et al., 1999, for details). The basic idea behind these explanations is that the perceptual system uses a number of sources of information to take the illumination into account. Let's look at a few of these sources of information.

The Information in Shadows In order for lightness constancy to work, the visual system needs to be able to take the uneven illumination created by shadows into account. It must determine that this change in illumination caused by a shadow is due to an illumination edge and not due to a reflectance edge. Obviously, the visual system usually succeeds in doing this because although the light intensity is reduced by shadows, you don't usually see shadowed areas as gray or black. For example, in the case of the wall in Figure 9.30, you assume that the shadowed and unshadowed areas are bricks with the same lightness, but that less light falls on some areas than on others. (See "Think About It" #4 on page 225 for another example of an image of a tree on a wall.)

How does the visual system know that the change in intensity caused by the shadow is an illumination edge and not a reflectance edge? One thing the visual system may take into account is the shadow's meaningful shape. In this

Figure 9.29 ❙ This unevenly illuminated wall contains both reflectance edges (between *a* and *c*) and illumination edges (between *a* and *b*). The perceptual system must distinguish between these two types of edges to accurately perceive the actual properties of the wall, as well as other parts of the scene.

Figure 9.30 ❙ Shadow of a tree.

particular example, we know that the shadow was cast by a tree, so we know it is the illumination that is changing, not the color of the bricks on the wall. Another clue is provided by the nature of the shadow's contour, as illustrated by the following demonstration.

DEMONSTRATION

The Penumbra and Lightness Perception

Place an object, such as a cup, on a white piece of paper on your desk. Then illuminate the cup at an angle with your desk lamp and adjust the lamp's position to produce a shadow with a slightly fuzzy border, as in Figure 9.31a. (Generally, moving the lamp closer to the cup makes the border get fuzzier.) The fuzzy border at the edge of the shadow is called the shadow's penumbra. Now take a marker and draw a thick line, as shown in Figure 9.31b, so you can no longer see the penumbra. What happens to your perception of the shadowed area inside the black line? ❙

Covering the penumbra causes most people to perceive a change in the appearance of the shadowed area. Apparently, the penumbra provides information to the visual system that the dark area next to the cup is a shadow, so the edge between the shadow and the paper is an illumination edge. However, masking off the penumbra eliminates that information, so the area covered by the shadow is seen as a change in reflectance. In this demonstration, lightness con-

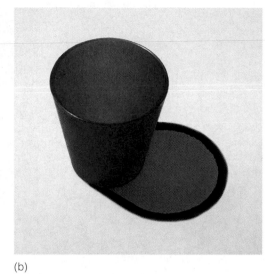

Bruce Goldstein

(a)   (b)

Figure 9.31 ▮ (a) A cup and its shadow. (b) The same cup and shadow with the penumbra covered by a black border.

stancy occurs when the penumbra is present, but does not occur when it is masked.

The Orientation of Surfaces The following demonstration provides an example of how information about the orientation of a surface affects our perception of lightness.

DEMONSTRATION

Perceiving Lightness at a Corner

Stand a folded index card on end so that it resembles the outside corner of a room, and illuminate it so that one side is illuminated and the other is in shadow. When you look at the corner, you can easily tell that both sides of the corner are made of the same white material but that the nonilluminated side is shadowed (Figure 9.32a). In other words, you perceive the edge between the illuminated and shadowed "walls" as an illumination edge.

Now create a hole in another card and, with the hole a few inches from the corner of the folded card, view the corner with one eye about a foot from the hole (Figure 9.32b). If, when viewing the corner through the hole, you perceive the corner as a flat surface, your perception of the left and right surfaces will change. ▮

In this demonstration, the illumination edge you perceived at first became transformed into an erroneous perception of a reflectance edge. The erroneous perception occurs because viewing the shaded corner through a small hole eliminated information about the conditions of illumination and the orientation of the corner. In order for lightness constancy to occur, it is important that the visual system have adequate information about the conditions of illumination. Without this information, lightness constancy can break down. $\boxed{V_L}$ **13–16**

How Images Are Perceptually Organized Figure 9.33 provides an example of how lightness perception can be affected by the way elements are perceptually organized (Anderson & Winawer, 2005). The four disks on the left are identical to the four disks on the right in terms of how much light is reflected from the disks. To

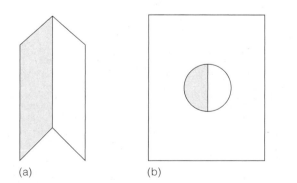

(a)   (b)

Figure 9.32 ▮ Viewing a shaded corner. (a) Illuminate a folded card so one side is illuminated and the other is in shadow. (b) View the folded card through a small hole so the two sides of the corner are visible, as shown.

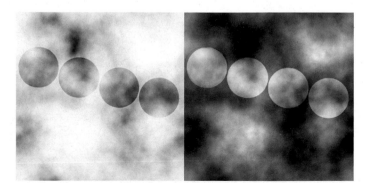

Figure 9.33 ▮ (a) Four dark discs partially covered by a white mist; (b) four light discs partially covered by a dark mist. The discs are identical in (a) and (b). *(Anderson, B. L., & Winawer, J. (2005). Image segmentation and lightness perception.* Nature, 434, *79–83.)*

prove this to yourself, mask the surroundings by viewing each disk through a hole punched in a piece of paper.

Despite being *physically* identical, the disks on the left appear dark and the ones on the right appear light. This is because the visual system organizes the dark areas differently in the two displays. In the display on the left, the dark areas within the circles are seen as belonging to dark disks that are partially obscured by a light "mist." In the display on the right, the same dark areas inside the circles are seen as belonging to dark "mist" that is partially obscuring white disks. Thus, the way the various parts of the display are perceptually organized influences our perception of lightness. (See "If You Want to Know More" #4 at the end of the chapter for some additional examples of how our perception of lightness can be affected by characteristics of a display.) VL 17

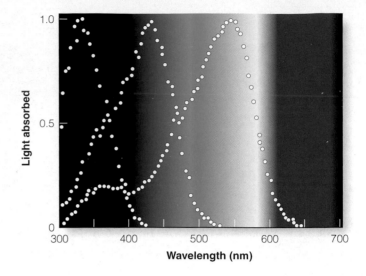

Figure 9.34 ▮ Absorption spectra of honeybee visual pigments.

Something to Consider: Experiences That Are Created by the Nervous System

At the beginning of the chapter we introduced the idea that wavelengths themselves aren't colored but that our experience of color is created by our nervous system. We can appreciate that color isn't the only perceptual quality that is created by the nervous system by considering our experience of hearing sounds. We will see in Chapter 11 that our experience of hearing is caused by pressure changes in the air. But why do we perceive rapid pressure changes as high pitches (like the sound of a piccolo) and slower pressure changes as low pitches (like a tuba)? Is there anything intrinsically "high-pitched" about rapid pressure changes? Or consider the sense of smell. We perceive some substances as "sweet" and others as "rancid," but where is the "sweetness" or "rancidity" in the molecular structure of the substances that enter the nose? Again, the answer is that these perceptions are not in the molecular structures. They are created by the action of the molecular structures on the nervous system.

We can better understand the idea that some perceptual qualities—such as color, pitch, or smell—are created by our nervous system by considering animals that can perceive energy that humans can't perceive at all. For example, Figure 9.34 shows the absorption spectra of a honeybee's visual pigments. The pigment that absorbs short-wavelength light enables the honeybee to see short wavelengths that can't be detected by humans (Menzel & Backhaus, 1989; Menzel et al., 1986). What "color" do you think bees perceive at 350 nm, which you can't see? You might be tempted to say "blue" because humans see blue at the short-wavelength end of the spectrum, but you really have no way of knowing what the honeybee is seeing, because, as Newton stated, "The Rays . . . are not coloured" (see page 206). There is no color in the wavelengths, so the bee's nervous system creates its experience of color. For all we know, the honeybee's experience of color at short wavelengths is quite different from ours, and may also be different for wavelengths in the middle of the spectrum that humans and honeybees can both see.

One of the themes of this book has been that our experience is filtered through our nervous system, so the properties of the nervous system can affect what we experience. For example, in Chapter 3 (page 58) we saw that the way the rods and cones converge onto other neurons results in high sensitivity for rod vision and good detail vision for cone vision. The idea we have introduced here, that the nervous system creates the way we experience the *qualities* of color, sound, taste, and smell, adds another dimension to the idea that properties of the nervous system can affect what we experience. Experience is not only *shaped* by the nervous system, as in the example of rod and cone vision, but—in cases such as color vision, hearing, taste, and smell—the very essence of our experience is *created* by the nervous system.

TEST YOURSELF 9.3

1. What is color constancy? Describe three factors that help achieve color constancy.
2. What is lightness constancy? Describe the factors that are responsible for lightness constancy.
3. What does it mean to say that color is created by the nervous system?

THINK ABOUT IT

1. A person with normal color vision is called a trichromat. This person needs to mix three wavelengths to match all other wavelengths and has three cone pigments. A person who is color deficient is called a dichromat. This person needs only two wavelengths to match

all other wavelengths and has only two operational cone pigments. A tetrachromat needs four wavelengths to match all other wavelengths and has four cone pigments. If a trichromat were to meet a tetrachromat, would the tetrachromat think that the trichromat was color deficient? How would the tetrachromat's color vision be "better than" the trichromat's? (p. 207)

2. When we discussed color deficiency, we noted the difficulty in determining the nature of a color deficient person's color experience. Discuss how this is related to the idea that color experience is a creation of our nervous system. (p. 211)

Bruce Goldstein

Figure 9.35 ▌ Are these shadows on the wall, or paintings of trees?

3. When you walk from outside, which is illuminated by sunlight, to inside, which is illuminated by tungsten illumination, your perception of colors remains fairly constant. But under some illuminations, such as streetlights called "sodium-vapor" lights that sometimes illuminate highways or parking lots, colors do seem to change. Why do you think color constancy would hold under some illuminations, but not others? (p. 218)

4. Look at the photograph in Figure 9.35. Are the edges between the dark areas and the lighter areas reflectance edges or illumination edges? What characteristics of the dark area did you take into account in determining your answer? (Compare this picture to the one in Figure 9.30) (p. 221)

5. We have argued that the link between wavelength and color is created by our nervous system. What if you met a person whose nervous system was wired differently than yours, so he experienced the entire spectrum as "inverted," as shown in Figure 9.36, with short wavelengths perceived as red and long wavelengths perceived as blue? Can you think of a way to determine whether this person's perception of color is different from yours? (p. 224)

6. The "Something to Consider" section pointed out that properties of color, sound, taste, and smell are created by the nervous system. Do you think the same thing holds for perceptions of shape ("I see a square shape") or distance ("that person appears to be 10 feet away)? (Hint: Think about how you might determine the *accuracy* of a person's color perception or taste perception, and the accuracy of their shape perception or distance perception.) (p. 224)

IF YOU WANT TO KNOW MORE

1. **The adaptive nature of animal coloration.** Some birds have bright plumage to attract mates. This could be dangerous if these colors also made these birds more obvious to predators. It has been shown that Swedish songbirds reflect light in the ultraviolet area of the spectrum, which other songbirds can see. However, these wavelengths are not very conspicuous to potential predators. (p. 202)

   Hastad, O., Victorsson, J., & Odeen, A. (2005). Differences in color vision make passerines less conspicuous in the eyes of their predators. *Proceedings of the National Academy of Sciences, 102*, 6391–6394.

Figure 9.36 ▌ In this "inverted" spectrum, short wavelengths appear red and long wavelengths appear blue.

2. **Color vision in animals.** What does your cat or dog see? Are there animals other than humans that have trichromatic vision? Are there animals that have better color vision than humans? (p. 211)

Jacobs, G. H. (1993). The distribution and nature of colour vision among the mammals. *Biological Review, 68,* 413–471.

Jacobs, G. H. (in press). Color vision in animals. In E. B. Goldstein (Ed.), *Sage encyclopedia of perception.* Thousand Oaks, CA: Sage.

Neitz, J., Geist, T., & Jacobs, G. H. (1989). Color vision in the dog. *Visual Neuroscience, 3,* 119–125.

Varela, F. J., Palacios, A. G., & Goldsmith, T. H. (1993). Color vision of birds. In H. P. Zeigler & H.-J. Bishof (Eds.), *Vision, brain and behavior in birds* (pp. 77–98). Cambridge, MA: MIT Press.

3. **The strength of opponent color mechanisms.** The strengths of the blue, yellow, red, and green mechanisms shown in Virtual Labs 10–12 were determined using a psychophysical procedure. (p. 215)

Hurvich, L. (1981). *Color vision.* Sunderland, MA: Sinauer Associates.

Hurvich, L. M., & Jameson, D. (1957). An opponent-process theory of color vision. *Psychological Review, 64,* 384–404.

4. **Lightness perception in three-dimensional displays.** At the end of the chapter, we saw that our perception of lightness depends on a number of things in addition to the amount of light reflected from objects. Figure 9.37 is another example of this because the intensity distributions are identical in both displays. This display shows that surface curvature can affect lightness displays. Other displays have been created that show how lightness depends on the perception of surface layout. (p. 224)

Knill, D. C., & Kersten, D. (1991). Apparent surface curvature affects lightness perception. *Nature, 351,* 228–230.

Adelson, E. H. (1999). Light perception and lightness illusions. In M. Gazzaniga (Ed.), *The new cognitive neurosciences* (pp. 339–351). Cambridge, MA: MIT Press.

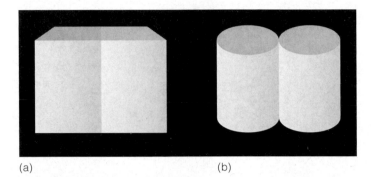
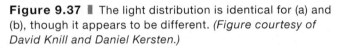

(a)   (b)

Figure 9.37 ▌ The light distribution is identical for (a) and (b), though it appears to be different. *(Figure courtesy of David Knill and Daniel Kersten.)*

KEY TERMS

Achromatic color (p. 205)	Ishihara plates (p. 211)	Reflectance (p. 220)
Additive color mixture (p. 205)	Lightness (p. 220)	Reflectance curves (p. 204)
Anomalous trichromat (p. 211)	Lightness constancy (p. 220)	Reflectance edge (p. 221)
Cerebral achromatopsia (p. 217)	Memory color (p. 220)	Saturation (p. 203)
Chromatic adaptation (p. 219)	Metamer (p. 208)	Selective reflection (p. 204)
Chromatic color (p. 204)	Metamerism (p. 208)	Selective transmission (p. 205)
Color-blind (p. 212)	Monochromat (p. 211)	Simultaneous color contrast (p. 214)
Color constancy (p. 218)	Neutral point (p. 212)	Subtractive color mixture (p. 206)
Color deficiency (p. 211)	Opponent neurons (p. 215)	Trichromat (p. 211)
Color-matching experiment (p. 207)	Opponent-process theory of color vision (p. 213)	Trichromatic theory of color vision (p. 207)
Desaturated (p. 204)	Partial color constancy (p. 219)	Tritanopia (p. 213)
Deuteranopia (p. 212)	Penumbra (p. 222)	Unilateral dichromat (p. 212)
Dichromat (p. 211)	Protanopia (p. 212)	Young-Helmholtz theory of color vision (p. 207)
Hue (p. 204)	Ratio principle (p. 221)	
Illumination edge (p. 221)		

MEDIA RESOURCES

The *Sensation and Perception* Book Companion Website

www.cengage.com/psychology/goldstein

See the companion website for flashcards, practice quiz questions, Internet links, updates, critical thinking exercises, discussion forums, games, and more!

CengageNOW

www.cengage.com/cengagenow

Go to this site for the link to CengageNOW, your one-stop shop. Take a pre-test for this chapter, and CengageNOW will generate a personalized study plan based on your test results. The study plan will identify the topics you need to review and direct you to online resources to help you mas-

ter those topics. You can then take a post-test to help you determine the concepts you have mastered and what you will still need to work on.

Virtual Lab

VL

Your Virtual Lab is designed to help you get the most out of this course. The Virtual Lab icons direct you to specific media demonstrations and experiments designed to help you visualize what you are reading about. The number beside each icon indicates the number of the media element you can access through your CD-ROM, CengageNOW, or WebTutor resource.

The following lab exercises are related to the material in this chapter:

1. *Color Mixing* Mixing colored lights. (Ignore the "Color Space" on the right).

2. *Cone Response Profiles and Hue* How the relative response of each type of cone changes across the visible spectrum.

3. *Cone Response Profiles and Perceived Color* Relative cone responses for colors arranged in the color circle.

4. *Color Arrangement Test* A color vision test that involves placing colors that appear similar next to each other.

5. *Rod Monochromacy* How the spectrum appears to a rod monochromat.

6. *Dichromacy* How removing one type of cone affects color perception.

7. *Missing Blue–Yellow Channel* Which colors are most likely to be confused by a tritanope?

8. *"Oh Say Can You See" Afterimage Demonstration* An American flag afterimage that illustrates the opponent nature of afterimages.

9. *Mixing Complementary Colors* How mixing blue and yellow, and red and green, results in gray when mixed in the correct proportions.

10. *Strength of Blue–Yellow Mechanisms* The strength of blue and yellow components of the blue–yellow opponent mechanism across the spectrum.

11. *Strength of Red–Green Mechanism* The strength of the red and green components of the red–green opponent mechanism across the spectrum.

12. *Opponent-Process Coding of Hue* The strengths of opponent mechanisms across the spectrum (combining the blue–yellow and red–green demonstrations).

13. *Checker-Shadow Illusion* How interpretation of a display as a three-dimensional scene can affect our judgment of the lightness of a surface. (Courtesy of Michael Bach.)

14. *Corrugated Plaid Illusion 1* Another demonstration of how interpretation of a display as three-dimensional can affect our perception of lightness. (Courtesy of Edward Adelson.)

15. *Corrugated Plaid Illusion 2* Another version of this illusion. (Courtesy of Michael Bach.)

16. *Impossible Steps* How the three-dimensional interpretation of a display can change a reflectance edge into an illumination edge. (Courtesy of Edward Adelson.)

17. *Troxler Effect* How vision fades when contours are blurred.

Chapter Contents

CHAPTER 10

Perceiving Depth and Size

OPPOSITE PAGE This scene near the California coast illustrates how the sizes of objects relative to one another can provide information about an object's size. The size of the house in the lower part of the picture indicates that the surrounding trees are extremely tall. The sizes of objects in the field of view can also provide information about depth. The smallness of the trees on the top of the hill suggests that the hill is far away.
Bruce Goldstein

[VL] The Virtual Lab icons direct you to specific animations and videos designed to help you visualize what you are reading about. The number beside each icon indicates the number of the clip you can access through your CD-ROM or your student website.

Some Questions We Will Consider:

▌ How can we see far into the distance based on the flat image on the retina? (p. 230)

▌ Why do we see depth better with two eyes than with one eye? (p. 235)

▌ Why don't people appear to shrink in size when they walk away? (p. 244)

You can easily tell that this book is about 18 inches away and, when you look up at the scene around you, that other objects are located at distances ranging from your nose (very close!) to across the room, down the street, or even as far as the horizon, depending on where you are. What's amazing about this ability to see the distances of objects in your environment is that your perception of these objects, and the scene as a whole, is based on a two-dimensional image on your retina.

We can begin to appreciate the problem of perceiving depth based on two-dimensional information on the retina by focusing on two points on the retina, N and F, shown in Figure 10.1. These points represent where rays of light have been reflected onto the retina from the tree, which is near (N) and the house, which is farther away (F). If we look just at these places on the retina, we have no way of knowing how far the light has traveled to reach points N and F. For all we know, the light stimulating either point on the retina could have come from 1 foot away or from a distant star. Clearly, we need to expand our view beyond single points on the retina to determine where objects are located in space.

When we expand our view from two isolated points to the entire retinal image, we increase the amount of infor-mation available to us because now we can see the images of the house and the tree. However, because this image is two-dimensional, we still need to explain how we get from the flat image on the retina to the three-dimensional per-ception of the scene. One way researchers have approached this problem is to ask what information is contained in this two-dimensional image that enables us to perceive depth in the scene. This is called the **cue approach to depth perception.**

The cue approach to depth perception focuses on identifying information in the retinal image that is corre-lated with depth in the scene. For example, when one object partially covers another object, as the tree in the foreground in Figure 10.1 covers part of the house, the object that is partially covered must be at a greater distance than the object that is covering it. This situation, which is called **occlusion,** is a signal, or cue, that one object is in front of another. According to cue theory, we learn the connection between this cue and depth through our previous expe-rience with the environment. After this learning has oc-curred, the association between particular cues and depth becomes automatic, and when these depth cues are pres-ent, we experience the world in three dimensions. A number of different types of cues that signal depth in a scene have been identified. We can divide these cues into three major groups:

1. *Oculomotor.* Cues based on our ability to sense the po-sition of our eyes and the tension in our eye muscles.

2. *Monocular.* Cues that work with one eye.

3. *Binocular.* Cues that depend on two eyes.

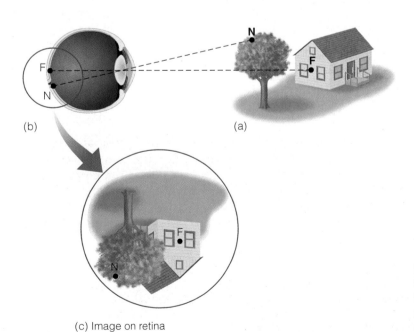

(b)

(a)

(c) Image on retina

Figure 10.1 ▌ (a) The house is farther away than the tree, but (b) the images of points F on the house and N on the tree both fall on the two-dimensional surface of the retina, so (c) these two points, considered by themselves, do not tell us the distances to the house and the tree.

Oculomotor Cues

The **oculomotor cues** are created by (1) convergence, the inward movement of the eyes that occurs when we look at nearby objects, and (2) accommodation, the change in the shape of the lens that occurs when we focus on objects at various distances. The idea behind these cues is that we can *feel* the inward movement of the eyes that occurs when the eyes converge to look at nearby objects, and we feel the tightening of eye muscles that change the shape of the lens to focus on a nearby object. You can experience the feelings in your eyes associated with convergence and accommodation by doing the following demonstration. $\boxed{VL}$ 1

DEMONSTRATION

Feelings in Your Eyes

Look at your finger as you hold it at arm's length. Then, as you slowly move your finger toward your nose, notice how you feel your eyes looking inward and become aware of the increasing tension inside your eyes.

The feelings you experience as you move your finger closer are caused by (1) the change in convergence angle as your eye muscles cause your eyes to look inward, as in Figure 10.2a, and (2) the change in the shape of the lens as the eye accommodates to focus on a near object (Figure 3.3). If you move your finger farther away, the lens flattens, and your eyes move away from the nose until they are both looking straight ahead, as in Figure 10.2b. Convergence and accommodation indicate when an object is close and are useful up to a distance of about arm's length, with convergence being the more effective of the two (Cutting & Vishton, 1995; Mon-Williams & Tresilian, 1999; Tresilian et al., 1999).

Monocular Cues

Monocular cues work with only one eye. They include accommodation, which we have described under oculomotor cues; pictorial cues, which is depth information that can be depicted in a two-dimensional picture; and movement-based cues, which are based on depth information created by movement.

Pictorial Cues

Pictorial cues are sources of depth information that can be depicted in a picture, such as the illustrations in this book or the image on the retina (Goldstein, 2001).

Occlusion We have already described the depth cue of occlusion. Occlusion occurs when one object hides or partially hides another from view. The partially hidden object is seen as being farther away, so the mountains in Figure 10.3 are perceived as being farther away than the hill. Note that occlusion does not provide information about an object's absolute distance; it only indicates relative distance. We know that the object that is partially covered is farther away than another object, but from occlusion alone we can't tell how much farther.

Relative Height According to the cue of **relative height**, objects that are below the horizon and have their bases higher in the field of view are usually seen as being more distant. Notice how this applies to the two motorcycles in Figure 10.3. The base of the far motorcycle (where its tires touch the road) is higher in the picture than the base of the near motorcycle. When objects are *above* the horizon, like the clouds, being *lower* in the field of view indicates more distance. There is also a connection between an observer's gaze and distance. Looking straight out at an object high in the visual field, near the horizon, indicates greater depth than looking down, as you would for an object lower in the visual field (Ooi et al., 2001).

Relative Size According to the cue of **relative size**, when two objects are of equal size, the one that is farther away will take up less of your field of view than the one that is closer. This cue depends, to some extent, on a person's knowledge of physical sizes—for example, that the two telephone poles in Figure 10.3 are about the same size, as are the two motorcycles.

Perspective Convergence When parallel lines extend out from an observer, they are perceived as converging—becoming closer together—as distance increases. This

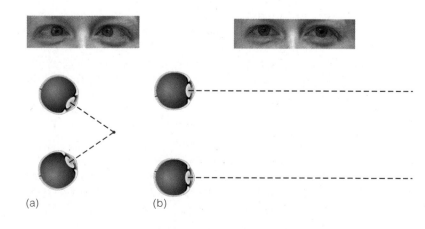

Figure 10.2 ▌ (a) Convergence of the eyes occurs when a person looks at something that is very close. (b) The eyes look straight ahead when the person observes something that is far away.

Bruce Goldstein

Figure 10.3 ▌ A scene in Tucson, Arizona, containing a number of depth cues: occlusion (the cactus occludes the hill, which occludes the mountain); perspective convergence (the sides of the road converge in the distance); relative size (the far motorcycle and telephone pole are smaller than the near ones); and relative height (the far motorcycle is higher in the field of view; the far cloud is lower).

perceptual coming-together of parallel lines, which is illustrated by the road in Figure 10.3, is called **perspective convergence**.

Familiar Size We use the cue of **familiar size** when we judge distance based on our prior knowledge of the sizes of objects. We can apply this idea to the coins in Figure 10.4. If you are influenced by your knowledge of the actual size of dimes, quarters, and half-dollars, you would probably say that the dime is closer than the quarter. An experiment by William Epstein (1965) shows that under certain conditions, our knowledge of an object's size influences our perception of that object's distance. The stimuli in Epstein's experiment were equal-sized photographs of a dime, a quarter, and a half-dollar, which were positioned the same distance from an observer. By placing these photographs in a darkened room, illuminating them with a spot of light, and having subjects view them with one eye, Epstein created the illusion that these pictures were real coins.

When the observers judged the distance of each of the coin photographs, they estimated that the dime was closest, the quarter was farther than the dime, and the half-dollar was the farthest of them all. The observers' judgments

Figure 10.4 ▌ Drawings of the stimuli used in Epstein's (1965) familiar-size experiment. The actual stimuli were photographs that were all the same size as a real quarter.

were influenced by their knowledge of the sizes of real dimes, quarters, and half-dollars. This result did not occur, however, when the observers viewed the scene with both eyes, because the use of two eyes provided information indicating the coins were at the same distance. The cue of familiar size is therefore most effective when other information about depth is absent (see also Coltheart, 1970; Schiffman, 1967).

Atmospheric Perspective Atmospheric perspective occurs when more distant objects appear less sharp and often have a slight blue tint. The farther away an object is, the more air and particles (dust, water droplets, airborne pollution) we have to look through, making objects that are farther away look less sharp and bluer than close objects. Figure 10.5 illustrates atmospheric perspective. The details in the foreground are sharp and well defined, but as we look out at the rocks, details become less and less visible as we look farther into the distance.

If, instead of viewing these hills, you were standing on the moon, where there is no atmosphere, and hence no atmospheric perspective, far craters would look just as clear as near ones. But on Earth, there is atmospheric perspective, with the exact amount depending on the nature of the atmosphere. An example of how atmospheric perspective depends on the nature of the atmosphere occurred when one of my friends took a trip from Philadelphia to Montana. He started walking toward a mountain that appeared to be perhaps a two- or three-hour hike away but found after three hours of hiking that he was still far from the mountain. Because my friend's perceptions were "calibrated" for Philadelphia, he found it difficult to accurately estimate distances in the clearer air of Montana, so a mountain that would have looked three hours away in Philadelphia was more than six hours away in Montana!

Figure 10.5 ▍ A scene on the coast of Maine showing the effect of atmospheric perspective.

Figure 10.6 ▍ A texture gradient in Death Valley, California.

Texture Gradient Another source of depth information is the texture gradient: Elements that are equally spaced in a scene appear to be more closely packed as distance increases, as with the textured ground in the scene in Figure 10.6. Remember that according to the cue of relative size, more distant objects take up less of our field of view. This is exactly what happens to the faraway elements in the texture gradient.

Shadows Shadows that are associated with objects can provide information regarding the locations of these objects. Consider, for example, Figure 10.7a, which shows seven spheres and a checkerboard. In this picture, the location of the spheres relative to the checkerboard is unclear. They could be resting on the surface of the checkerboard, or floating above it. But adding shadows, as shown in Figure 10.7b, makes the spheres' locations clear—the ones on the left are resting on the checkerboard, and the ones on the right are floating above it. This illustrates how shadows can help determine the location of objects (Mamassian et al., 1998).

(a)

(b)

Figure 10.7 ▍ (a) Where are the spheres located in relation to the checkerboard? (b) Adding shadows makes their location clear. *(Courtesy of Pascal Mamassion.)*

Shadows also enhance the three-dimensionality of objects. For example, shadows make the circles in Figure 10.7 appear spherical, and help define some of the contours in the mountains in Figure 10.3. In the middle of the day, when the sun is directly overhead and there are no shadows, the mountains appear almost flat. VL 2

Motion-Produced Cues

All of the cues we have described so far work if the observer is stationary. If, however, we decide to take a walk, new cues emerge that further enhance our perception of depth. We will describe two different motion-produced cues: (1) motion parallax and (2) deletion and accretion.

Motion Parallax Motion parallax occurs when, as we move, nearby objects appear to glide rapidly past us, but more distant objects appear to move more slowly. Thus, when you look out the side window of a moving car or train, nearby objects appear to speed by in a blur, whereas objects on the horizon may appear to be moving only slightly.

We can understand why motion parallax occurs by noting how the image of a near object (the tree in Figure 10.8a) and a far object (the house in Figure 10.8b) move across the retina as the eye moves from position 1 to position 2. First let's consider the tree: Figure 10.8a shows that when the eye moves to position 2, the tree's image moves all the way across the retina from T_1 to T_2, as indicated by the dashed arrow. Figure 10.8b shows that the house's image moves a shorter distance, from H_1 to H_2. Because the image of the near object travels a large distance across the retina, it appears to move rapidly as the observer moves. The image of the far object travels a much smaller distance across the retina, so it appears to move more slowly as the observer moves.

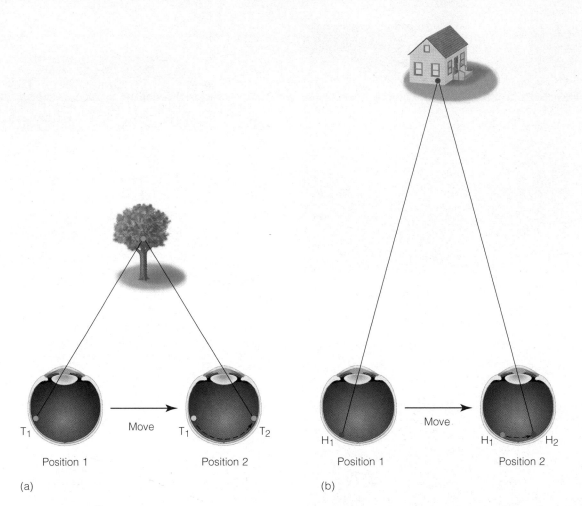

Position 1   Move   Position 2

(a)

Position 1   Move   Position 2

(b)

Figure 10.8 ▌ Eye moving past (a) a nearby tree; (b) a faraway house. Notice how the image of the tree moves farther on the retina than the image of the house.

Motion parallax is one of the most important sources of depth information for many animals. The information provided by motion parallax has also been used to enable human-designed mechanical robots to determine how far they are from obstacles as they navigate through the environment (Srinivasan & Venkatesh, 1997). Motion parallax is also widely used to create an impression of depth in cartoons and video games.

Deletion and Accretion As an observer moves sideways, some things become covered, and others become uncovered. Try the following demonstration.

DEMONSTRATION

Deletion and Accretion

Close one eye. Position your hands out as shown in Figure 10.9, so your right hand is at arm's length and your left hand at about half that distance, just to the left of the right hand. Then as you look at your right hand, move your head sideways to the left and then back again, keeping your hands still. As you move your left hand will appear to move back and forth, covering and uncovering your right hand. Covering the right hand is *deletion*. Uncovering is *accretion*. ▌

Figure 10.9 ▌ Position of the hands for deletion and accretion demonstration.

Deletion and accretion are related to both motion parallax and overlap because they occur when overlapping surfaces appear to move relative to one another. They are especially effective for detecting the differences in the depths of two surfaces (Kaplan, 1969).

Our discussion so far has described a number of the cues that contribute to our perception of depth. As shown in Table 10.1, these cues work over different distances, some only at close range (accommodation and convergence), some at close and medium ranges (motion parallax), some at long range (atmospheric perspective), and some at the whole range of depth perception (occlusion and relative size; Cutting & Vishton, 1995). For example, we can appreciate how occlusion operates over a wide range of distances by noticing how this cue works over a distance of a few inches for the cactus flower in Figure 10.10a, and over a distance of many miles for the scene in Figure 10.10b.

TABLE 10.1 ∎ Range of Effectiveness of Different Depth Cues

DEPTH INFORMATION	0–2 METERS	2–20 METERS	ABOVE 30 METERS
Occlusion	✓	✓	✓
Relative size	✓	✓	✓
Accommodation and convergence	✓		
Motion parallax	✓	✓	
Relative height		✓	✓
Atmospheric perspective			✓

Source: Based on Cutting & Vishton, 1995.

Binocular Depth Information

In addition to the cues we have described so far, there is one other important source of depth information—the differences in the images received by our two eyes. Because our eyes view the world from positions that are about 6 cm apart in the average adult, this difference in the viewpoint of the two eyes creates the cue of binocular disparity.

Binocular Disparity

Binocular disparity is the difference in the images in the left and right eyes. The following demonstration illustrates this difference.

DEMONSTRATION

Two Eyes: Two Viewpoints

Close your right eye. Hold your finger vertically about 6 inches in front of you and position it so it is partially covering an object in the distance. Look directly at the distant object with your left eye, then close your left eye and look directly at the distant object with your right eye. When you switch eyes, how does the position of your finger change relative to the far object? ∎

When you switched from looking with your left eye to your right, you probably noticed that your finger appeared to move to the left relative to the far object. Figure 10.11 diagrams what happened on your retinas. The green line in Figure 10.11a shows that when the left eye was open, the images of the finger and far object both fell on the same place on the retina. This occurred because you were looking right at both objects, so their images would fall on the foveas. The green lines in Figure 10.11b show that when the right eye was open, the image of the far object still fell on the fovea

(a)

(b)

Figure 10.10 ∎ (a) Occlusion operating on a small scale: the flower near the center occludes the cactus, so the flower appears closer. (b) Occlusion operating on a larger scale: The green shrubbery occludes the river; the buildings in Pittsburgh occlude one another; the city occludes the hills in the far distance. Occlusion indicates only that one object is closer than another object. What other depth cues make us aware of the actual distances in this scene?

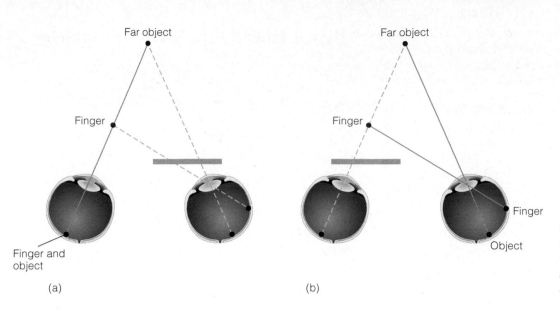

Finger

Far object

Finger

Far object

Finger and
object

(a)

Finger

Object

(b)

Figure 10.11 ▌ Location of images on the retina for the "Two Eyes: Two Viewpoints" demonstration. See text for explanation.

because you were looking at it, but the image of the finger was now off to the side.

The difference between the images in the left and right eyes shown in Figure 10.11 creates binocular disparity. To describe how disparity works, we need to introduce the idea of **corresponding retinal points**—the places on each retina that would overlap if one retina could be slid on top of the other. In Figure 10.12, we see that the two foveas, marked F,

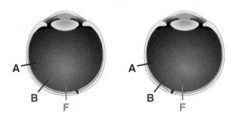

Figure 10.12 ▌ Corresponding points on the two retinas. To determine corresponding points, imagine that one eye is slid on top of the other one.

fall on corresponding points, and that the two A's and the two B's also fall on corresponding points. VL 3

To take the idea of corresponding points into the real world, let's consider the lifeguard in Figure 10.13a, who is looking directly at Frieda. The dashed line that passes through Harry, Frieda, and Susan is part of the **horopter**, which is an imaginary surface that passes through the point of fixation and indicates the location of objects that fall on corresponding points on the two retinas. In this example, Frieda is the point of fixation because the lifeguard is looking directly at her, and so her image falls on the foveas, which are corresponding points, indicated by F in Figure 10.13b. Because Harry and Susan are also on the horoptor, their images, indicated by H and S also fall on corresponding points.

Figure 10.14 shows where Carole's image falls on the lifeguard's retinas when he is looking at Frieda. Frieda's image falls on corresponding points F_L and F_R. Carole's images fall on **noncorresponding points** C_L in the left

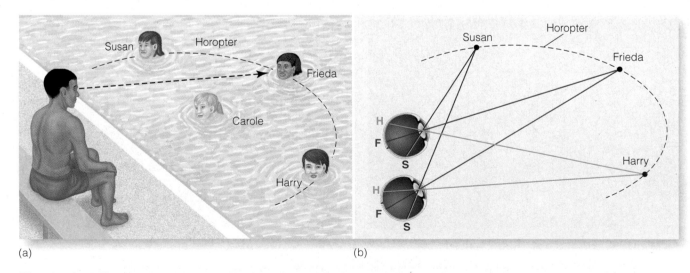

(a)

(b)

Figure 10.13 ▌ (a) When the lifeguard looks at Frieda, the images of Frieda, Susan, and Harry fall on corresponding points on the lifeguard's retinas. (b) The locations of the images of Susan, Frieda, and Harry on the lifeguard's retinas.

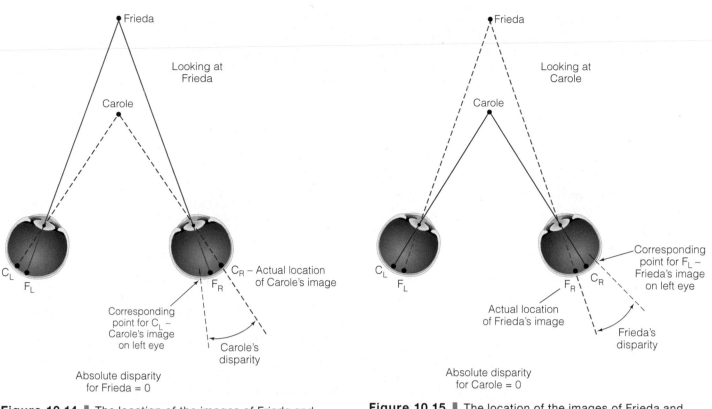

Figure 10.14 ▍ The location of the images of Frieda and Carole in the lifeguard's eyes when the lifeguard is looking at Frieda. Because Carole is not located on the horopter, her images fall on noncorresponding points. The absolute angle of disparity is the angle between the point on the right eye that corresponds to Carole's image on the left eye (C_L), and the point where the image actually falls (C_R).

Figure 10.15 ▍ The location of the images of Frieda and Carole in the lifeguard's eyes when the lifeguard is looking at Carole. Because Frieda is not located on the horopter, her images fall on noncorresponding points. The absolute angle of disparity is the angle between the point on the right eye that corresponds to Frieda's image on the left eye (F_L), and the point where the image actually falls (F_R).

eye and C_R in the right eye. Note that if you slid the retinas on top of each other, point C_L would not overlap with point C_R. The difference between where Carole's image falls on the right eye (C_R) and the corresponding point is called the **angle of disparity**. Carole's angle of disparity, which in this example is about 26 degrees, is the *absolute angle of disparity,* or simply the absolute disparity for Carole's image when the lifeguard is looking at Frieda. [VL 4]

Absolute disparity is important because it provides information about the distances of objects. The amount of absolute disparity indicates how far an object is from the horopter. Greater disparity is associated with greater distance from the horopter. Thus, if Carole were to swim toward the lifeguard while the lifeguard kept looking at Frieda, the angle of disparity of Carole's image on the lifeguard's retina would increase. (Notice that as Carole approaches, the dashed red lines in Figure 10.14 would move outward, creating greater disparity.)

One of the properties of absolute disparity is that it changes every time the observer changes where he or she is looking. For example, if the lifeguard decided to shift his fixation from Frieda to Carole, as shown in Figure 10.15, the absolute disparity for Carole's images at C_L and C_R would become zero, because they would fall on the lifeguard's foveas. But Frieda's images are no longer on corresponding

points, and when we determine the disparity of her images, it turns out to be about 26 degrees.[1]

What this means is that the absolute disparity of every object in an observer's visual field is constantly changing as the observer looks around. When we consider that a person makes as many as 3 fixations per second when scanning a scene and that every new fixation establishes a new horopter, this means that the absolute disparities for every object in a scene have to be constantly recalculated.

There is, however, disparity information that remains the same no matter where an observer looks. This information is called relative disparity—the difference between two objects' absolute disparities. We can see how this works by comparing the situations in Figures 10.14 and 10.15. We saw in Figure 10.14 that when the lifeguard is looking at Frieda, her absolute disparity is zero, and Carole's is about 26 degrees. The relative disparity for Carole and Frieda is therefore 26 degrees (the difference between 0 and 26 degrees).

When the lifeguard shifts his fixation to Carole, as shown in Figure 10.15, her absolute disparity becomes 0 degrees, and Frieda's becomes about 26 degrees. As before, the

[1]The disparities in the real world are much smaller than the large disparities in these pictures, because in the environment, objects are much farther away relative to the spacing between the eyes.

relative disparity is 26 degrees. Although both Carol's and Frieda's absolute disparities changed when the lifeguard shifted his fixation from Frieda to Carol, the *difference between them* remained the same. The same thing happens for all objects in the environment. As long as the objects stay in the same position relative to an observer, the difference in their disparities remains the same, no matter where the observer looks. Thus, relative disparity, which remains constant, offers an advantage over absolute disparity, which changes as a person looks around. As we will see below, there is evidence that both absolute and relative disparity information is represented by neural activity in the visual system.

Connecting Disparity Information and the Perception of Depth

We have seen that both absolute and relative disparity information contained in the images on the retinas provides information indicating an object's distance from an observer. Notice, however, that our description of disparity has focused on *geometry*—where an object's images fall on the retina—but has not mentioned *perception,* the observer's experience of an object's depth or its relation to other objects in the environment. We now consider the relationship between disparity and what observers perceive. To do this we introduce stereopsis—the impression of depth that results from information provided by binocular disparity.

An example of stereopsis is provided by the depth effect achieved by the stereoscope, a device introduced by the physicist Charles Wheatstone (1802–1875), which produces a convincing illusion of depth by using two slightly different pictures. This device, extremely popular in the 1800s and reintroduced as the View Master in the 1940s, presents two photographs that are made with a camera with two lenses separated by the same distance as the eyes. The result is two slightly different views, like those shown in Figure 10.16. The stereoscope presents the left picture to the left eye and the right picture to the right eye. This creates the same binocular disparity that occurs when a person views the scene naturally, so that slightly different images appear in the left and right eyes. In this next demonstration, the binocular disparity created by two pictures creates a perception of depth.

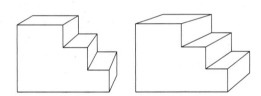

VL 5–7

DEMONSTRATION

Binocular Depth From a Picture, Without a Stereoscope

Place a 4 × 6 card vertically, long side up, between the stairs in Figure 10.17, and place your nose against the card so that you are seeing the left-hand drawing with just your left eye and the right-hand drawing with just your right eye. (Blink back and forth to confirm this separation.) Then relax and wait for the two drawings to merge. When the drawings form a single image, you should see the stairs in depth, just as you would if you looked at them through a stereoscope. ▮

Figure 10.17 ▮ See text for instructions for viewing these stairs.

(a) Left eye image

(b) Right eye image

Bruce Goldstein

Figure 10.16 ▮ The two images of a stereoscopic photograph. The difference between the two images, such as the distances between the front cactus and the window in the two views, creates retinal disparity. This creates a perception of depth when the left image is viewed by the left eye and the right image is viewed by the right eye.

The principle behind the stereoscope is also used in 3-D movies. The left-eye and right-eye images are presented simultaneously on the screen, slightly displaced from one another, to create disparity. These images can be presented separately to the left and right eyes by coloring one red and the other green and viewing the film through glasses with a red filter for one eye and a green filter for the other eye (Figure 10.18). Another way to separate the images is to create the left and right images from polarized light—light waves that vibrate in only one direction. One image is polarized so its vibration is vertical, and the other is polarized so its vibration is horizontal. Viewing the film through polarizing lenses, which let vertically polarized light into one eye and horizontally polarized light into the other eye, creates the disparity that results in three-dimensional perception.

Our conclusion that disparity creates stereopsis seems to be supported by the demonstration above, which shows that we perceive depth when two slightly displaced views are presented to the left and right eyes. However, this demonstration alone doesn't prove that disparity creates a perception of depth because images such as those in Figure 10.16 also contain potential depth cues, such as occlusion and relative height, which could contribute to our perception of depth. In order to show that disparity alone can result in depth perception, Bela Julesz (1971) created a stimulus called the *random-dot stereogram,* which contained no pictorial cues. **VL 8**

By creating stereoscopic images of random-dot patterns, Julesz showed that observers can perceive depth in displays that contain no depth information other than disparity. Two such random-dot patterns, which constitute a **random-dot stereogram**, are shown in Figure 10.19. These patterns were constructed by first generating two identical random-dot patterns on a computer and then shifting a square-shaped section of the dots one or more units to the side. In the stereogram in Figure 10.19a, a section of dots on the right pattern has been shifted one unit to the right. This shift is too subtle to be seen in these dot patterns, but we can understand how it is accomplished by looking at the diagrams below the dot patterns (Figure 10.19b). In these

Figure 10.18 ▌ A scene in a movie theater in the 1950s, when three-dimensional movies were first introduced. The glasses create different images in the left and right eyes, and the resulting disparity leads to a convincing impression of depth.

(a)

(b)

1	0	1	0	1	0	0	1	0	1
1	0	0	1	0	1	0	1	0	0
0	0	1	1	0	1	1	0	1	0
0	1	0	A	A	B	B	1	0	1
1	1	1	B	A	B	A	0	0	1
0	0	1	A	A	B	A	0	1	0
1	1	1	B	B	A	B	1	0	1
1	0	0	1	1	0	1	1	0	1
1	1	0	0	1	1	0	1	1	1
0	1	0	0	0	1	1	1	1	0

1	0	1	0	1	0	0	1	0	1
1	0	0	1	0	1	0	1	0	0
0	0	1	1	0	1	1	0	1	0
0	1	0	Y	A	A	B	B	0	1
1	1	1	X	B	A	B	A	0	1
0	0	1	X	A	A	B	A	1	0
1	1	1	Y	B	B	A	B	0	1
1	0	0	1	1	0	1	1	0	1
1	1	0	0	1	1	0	1	1	1
0	1	0	0	0	1	1	1	1	0

Figure 10.19 ▌ (a) A random-dot stereogram. (b) The principle for constructing the stereogram. See text for explanation.

diagrams, the black dots are indicated by 0's, A's, and X's and the white dots by 1's, B's, and Y's. The A's and B's indicate the square-shaped section where the shift is made in the pattern. Notice that the A's and B's are shifted one unit to the right in the right-hand pattern. The X's and Y's indicate areas uncovered by the shift that must be filled in with new black dots and white dots to complete the pattern.

The effect of shifting one section of the pattern in this way is to create disparity. When the two patterns are presented simultaneously to the left and the right eyes in a stereoscope, observers perceive a small square floating above the background. Because binocular disparity is the only depth information present in these stereograms, disparity alone must be causing the perception of depth.

Psychophysical experiments, particularly those using Julesz's random-dot stereograms, show that retinal disparity creates a perception of depth. But before we can fully understand the mechanisms responsible for depth perception, we must answer one more question: How does the visual system match the parts of the images in the left and right eyes that correspond to one another? This is called the **correspondence problem**, and as we will see, it has still not been fully explained.

The Correspondence Problem

Let's return to the stereoscopic images of Figure 10.16. When we view this image in a stereoscope, we see different parts of the image at different depths because of the disparity between images on the left and right retinas. Thus, the cactus and the window appear to be at different distances when viewed through the stereoscope because they create different amounts of disparity. But in order for the visual system to calculate this disparity, it must compare the images of the cactus on the left and right retinas and the images of the window on the left and right retinas. This is the correspondence problem. How does the visual system match up the images in the two eyes?

A possible answer to this question is that the visual system may match the images on the left and right retinas on the basis of the specific features of the objects. For example, the upper-left window pane on the left could be matched with the upper-left pane on the right, and so on. Explained in this way, the solution seems simple: Most things in the world are quite discriminable from one another, so it is easy to match an image on the left retina with the image of the same thing on the right retina. But what about images in which matching similar points would be extremely difficult, as with Julesz's random-dot stereogram?

You can appreciate the problem involved in matching similar parts of a stereogram by trying to match up the points in the left and right images of the stereogram in Figure 10.19. Most people find this to be an extremely difficult task, involving switching their gaze back and forth between the two pictures and comparing small areas of the pictures one after another. But even though matching similar features on a random-dot stereogram is much more difficult and time-consuming than matching features in the real world, the visual system somehow matches similar parts of the two stereogram images, calculates their disparities, and creates a perception of depth. A number of proposals, all too complex to describe here, have been put forth to explain how the visual system solves the correspondence problem, but a totally satisfactory answer has yet to be proposed (see Blake & Wilson, 1991; Menz & Freeman, 2003; Ohzawa, 1998; Ringbach, 2003).

Depth Information Across Species

Humans make use of a number of different sources of depth information in the environment. But what about other species? Many animals have excellent depth perception. Cats leap on their prey; monkeys swing from one branch to the next; a male housefly follows a flying female, maintaining a constant distance of about 10 cm; and a frog accurately jumps across a chasm (Figure 10.20).

There is no doubt that many animals are able to judge distances in their environment, but what depth information do they use? A survey of mechanisms used by different animals reveals that animals use the entire range of cues described in this chapter. Some animals use many cues, and others rely on just one or two.

To make use of binocular disparity, an animal must have eyes that have overlapping visual fields. Thus, animals such as cats, monkeys, and humans that have **frontal eyes** (Figure 10.21a), which result in overlapping fields of view, can use disparity to perceive depth. Animals with **lateral eyes**, such as the rabbit (Figure 10.21b), do not have overlapping visual fields and therefore cannot use disparity to perceive depth. Note, however, that in sacrificing binocular disparity, animals with lateral eyes gain a wider field of

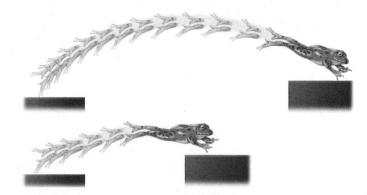

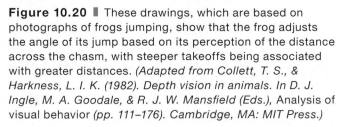

Figure 10.20 ❚ These drawings, which are based on photographs of frogs jumping, show that the frog adjusts the angle of its jump based on its perception of the distance across the chasm, with steeper takeoffs being associated with greater distances. *(Adapted from Collett, T. S., & Harkness, L. I. K. (1982). Depth vision in animals. In D. J. Ingle, M. A. Goodale, & R. J. W. Mansfield (Eds.), Analysis of visual behavior (pp. 111–176). Cambridge, MA: MIT Press.)*

view—something that is extremely important for animals that need to constantly be on the lookout for predators.

The pigeon is an example of an animal with lateral eyes that are placed so the visual fields of the left and right eyes overlap only in a 35-degree area surrounding the pigeon's beak. This overlapping area, however, happens to be exactly where pieces of grain would be located when the pigeon is pecking at them, and psychophysical experiments have shown that the pigeon does have a small area of binocular depth perception right in front of its beak (McFadden, 1987; McFadden & Wild, 1986).

Movement parallax is probably insects' most important method of judging distance, and they use it in a number of different ways (Collett, 1978; Srinivasan & Venkatesh, 1997). For example, the locust uses a "peering" response—moving its body from side to side to create movement of its head—as it observes potential prey. T. S. Collett (1978) measured a locust's "peering amplitude"—the distance of this side-to-side

(a)

(b)

Figure 10.21 ▍ (a) Frontal eyes such as those of the cat have overlapping fields of view that provide good depth perception. (b) Lateral eyes such as those of the rabbit provide a panoramic view but poorer depth perception.

sway—as it observed prey at different distances, and found that the locust swayed more when targets were farther away. Since more distant objects move less across the retina than nearer objects for a given amount of observer movement (Figure 10.8), a larger sway would be needed to cause the image of a far object to move the same distance across the retina as the image of a near object. The locust may therefore be judging distance by noting how much sway is needed to cause the image to move a certain distance across its retina (also see Sobel, 1990).

The above examples show how depth can be determined from different sources of information in light. But bats, some of which are blind to light, use a form of energy we usually associate with sound to sense depth. Bats sense objects by using a method similar to the sonar system used in World War II to detect underwater objects such as submarines and mines. Sonar, which stands for sound navigation and ranging, works by sending out pulses of sound and using information contained in the echoes of this sound to determine the location of objects. Donald Griffin (1944) coined the term **echolocation** to describe the biological sonar system used by bats to avoid objects in the dark.

Bats emit pulsed sounds that are far above the upper limit of human hearing, and they sense objects' distances by noting the interval between when they send out the pulse and when they receive the echo (Figure 10.22). Since they

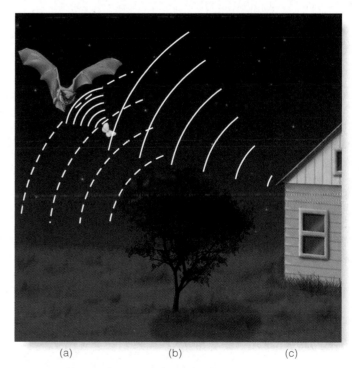
(a)　　　　(b)　　　　(c)

Figure 10.22 ▍ When a bat sends out its pulses, it receives echoes from a number of objects in the environment. This figure shows the echoes received by the bat from (a) a moth located about half a meter away; (b) a tree, located about 2 meters away; and (c) a house, located about 4 meters away. The echoes from each object return to the bat at different times, with echoes from more distant objects taking longer to return. The bat locates the positions of objects in the environment by sensing how long it takes the echoes to return.

use sound echoes to sense objects, they can avoid obstacles even when it is totally dark (Suga, 1990). Although we don't have any way of knowing what the bat experiences when these echoes return, we do know that the timing of these echoes provides the information the bat needs to locate objects in its environment. (Also see von der Emde et al., 1998, for a description of how electric fish sense depth based on "electrolocation.") From the examples we have described, we can see that animals use a number of different types of information to determine depth, with the type of information used depending on the animal's specific needs and on its anatomy and physiological makeup.

The Physiology of Depth Perception

Most of the research on the physiology of depth perception has concentrated on looking for neurons that signal information about binocular disparity. But neurons have also been found that signal the depth indicated by pictorial depth cues.

Neurons That Respond to Pictorial Depth

Ken-Ichino Tsutsui and coworkers (2002, 2005) studied the physiology of neurons that respond to the depth indicated by texture gradients by having monkeys match stimuli like the ones in Figure 10.23 to three-dimensional displays created by stereograms. The results showed that monkeys perceive the pattern in Figure 10.23a as slanting to the right, 10.23b as flat, and 10.23c as slanting to the left.

The records below the texture gradient patterns are the responses of a neuron in an area in the parietal cortex that had been associated with depth perception in other studies. This neuron does not fire to the right-slanting gradient, or to a flat pattern, but does fire to the left-slanting gradient. Thus, this neuron fires to a display in which depth is indicated by the pictorial depth cues of texture gradients. This neuron also responds when depth is indicated by disparity,

so it is tuned to respond to depth whether it is determined by pictorial depth cues or by binocular disparity. (Also see Sereno et al., 2002, for a description of a neuron that responds to the depth cue of motion parallax.)

Neurons That Respond to Binocular Disparity

One of the most important discoveries about the physiology of depth perception was the finding that there are neurons that are tuned to respond to specific amounts of disparity (Barlow et al., 1967; Hubel & Wiesel, 1970). The first research on these neurons described neurons in the striate cortex (V1) that responded to absolute disparity. These neurons are called **binocular depth cells** or **disparity-selective cells**. A given cell responds best when stimuli presented to the left and right eyes create a specific amount of absolute disparity. Figure 10.24 shows a disparity tuning curve for one of these neurons (Uka & DeAngelis, 2003). This particular neuron responds best when the left and right eyes are stimulated to create an absolute disparity of about 1 degree. Further research has shown that there are also neurons higher up in the visual system that respond to relative disparity (Parker, 2007) (see page 237).

Connecting Binocular Depth Cells and Depth Perception

Just because disparity-selective neurons fire best to a specific angle of disparity doesn't prove that these neurons have anything to do with depth perception. To show that binocular depth cells are actually involved in depth perception, we need to demonstrate a connection between disparity and behavior.

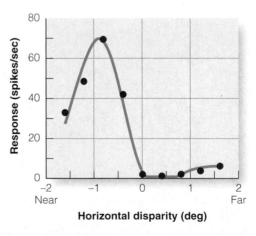

Figure 10.24 ▌ Disparity tuning curve for a neuron sensitive to absolute disparity. This curve indicates the neural response that occurs when stimuli presented to the left and right eyes create different amounts of disparity. *(From Uka, T., & DeAngelis, G. C. (2003). Contribution of middle temporal area to coarse depth discrimination: Comparison of neuronal and psychophysical sensitivity.* Journal of Neuroscience, 23, *3515–3530.)*

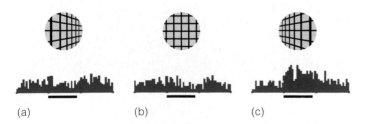

(a) (b) (c)

Figure 10.23 ▌ Top: gradient stimuli. Bottom: response of neurons in the parietal cortex to each gradient. *(From Tsutsui, K. I., Sakata, H., Naganuma, T., & Taira, M. (2002). Neural correlates for perception of 3D surface orientation from texture gradient.* Science, 298, *402–412; Tsutsui, K. I., Tiara, M., & Sakata, H. (2005). Neural mechanisms of three-dimensional vision.* Neuroscience Research, 51, *221–229.)*

Randolph Blake and Helmut Hirsch (1975) demonstrated this connection by doing a selective rearing experiment that resulted in the elimination of binocular neurons. (See Chapter 4, page 80, for another example of a selective rearing experiment.) They reared cats so that their vision was alternated between the left and right eyes every other day during the first 6 months of their lives. After this 6-month period of presenting stimuli to just one eye at a time, Blake and Hirsch recorded from neurons in the cat's cortex and found that (1) these cats had few binocular neurons, and (2) they were not able to use binocular disparity to perceive depth. Thus, eliminating binocular neurons eliminates stereopsis and confirms what everyone suspected all along—that disparity-selective neurons are responsible for stereopsis (also see Olson & Freeman, 1980).

Another technique that has been used to demonstrate a link between neural responding and depth perception is microstimulation (see Method: Microstimulation in Chapter 8, page 188). Microstimulation is achieved by inserting a small electrode into the cortex and passing an electrical charge through the electrode to activate the neurons near the electrode (M. R. Cohen & Newsome, 2004). Neurons that are sensitive to the same disparities tend to be organized in clusters, so stimulating one of these clusters activates a group of neurons that respond best to a specific disparity.

Gregory DeAngelis and coworkers (1998) trained a monkey to indicate the depth created by presenting images with different absolute disparities to the left and right eyes. Presumably, the monkey perceived depth because the disparate images on the monkey's retina activated disparity-selective neurons in the cortex. But what would happen if microstimulation were used to activate a different group of disparity-selective neurons? DeAngelis and coworkers stimulated disparity-selective neurons that were tuned to a disparity different from what was indicated by the images on the retina. When they did this, the monkey shifted its depth judgment toward the disparity signaled by the stimulated neurons (Figure 10.25).

DeAngelis' experiment provides another demonstration of a connection between disparity-selective neurons and depth perception. (This result is like the result we described on page 188 in Chapter 8, in which stimulating neurons that preferred specific directions of movement shifted a monkey's perception toward that direction of movement.) In addition, brain-imaging experiments on humans show that a number of different areas are activated by stimuli that create binocular disparity (Backus et al., 2001; Kwee et al., 1999; Ts'o et al., 2001). Experiments on monkeys have determined that neurons sensitive to absolute disparity are found in the primary visual receiving area, and neurons sensitive to relative disparity are found higher in the visual system, in the temporal lobe and other areas. Apparently, depth perception involves a number of stages of processing that begins in the primary visual cortex and extends to many different areas in both the ventral and dorsal streams (Parker, 2007).

Figure 10.25 ❚ DeAngeles and coworkers (1998) stimulated neurons in the monkey's cortex that were sensitive to a particular amount of disparity, while the monkey was observing a random-dot stereogram. This stimulation shifted perception of the dots from position 1 to position 2.

TEST YOURSELF 10.1

1. What is the basic problem of depth perception, and how does the cue approach deal with this problem?
2. What monocular cues provide information about depth in the environment?
3. What is binocular disparity? What is the difference between absolute disparity and relative disparity? How are absolute and relative disparity related to the depths of objects in a scene? What is the advantage of relative disparity?
4. What is stereopsis? What is the evidence that disparity creates stereopsis?
5. What does perception of depth from a random-dot stereogram demonstrate?
6. What is the correspondence problem? Has this problem been solved?
7. What kinds of information do other species use to perceive depth? How does the information they use depend on the animals' sensory systems?
8. What is the relationship between the firing of neurons in the cortex and depth perception? Be sure to distinguish between (a) experiments that demonstrated a connection between neurons that respond to depth *information* and (b) experiments that demonstrate a connection between neural responding and depth *perception.*
9. Where does the neural processing for depth perception occur in the brain?

Perceiving Size

We discuss size perception in this chapter because our perception of size can be affected by our perception of depth. This link between size perception and depth perception is graphically illustrated by the following example.

Whiteout—one of the most treacherous weather conditions possible for flying—can arise quickly and unexpectedly. As Frank pilots his helicopter across the Antarctic wastes, blinding light, reflected down from thick cloud cover above and up from the pure white blanket of snow below, makes it difficult to see the horizon, details on the surface of the snow, or even up from down. He is aware of the danger because he has known pilots dealing with similar conditions who flew at full power directly into the ice. He thinks he can make out a vehicle on the snow far below, and he drops a smoke grenade to check his altitude. To his horror, the grenade falls only three feet before hitting the ground. Realizing that what he thought was a truck was actually a discarded box, Frank pulls back on the controls and soars up, his face drenched in sweat, as he comprehends how close he just came to becoming another whiteout fatality.

This account is based on descriptions of actual flying conditions at an Antarctic research base. It illustrates that our ability to perceive an object's size can sometimes be drastically affected by our ability to perceive the object's distance. A small box seen close up can, in the absence of accurate information about its distance, be misperceived as a large truck seen from far away (Figure 10.26). The idea that we can misperceive size when accurate depth information is not present was demonstrated in a classic experiment by A. H. Holway and Edwin Boring (1941).

Figure 10.26 ▌ When a helicopter pilot loses the ability to perceive distance, due to "whiteout," a small box that is close can be mistaken for a truck that is far away.

The Holway and Boring Experiment

Observers in Holway and Boring's experiment sat at the intersection of two hallways and saw a luminous *test circle* when looking down the right hallway and a luminous *comparison circle* when looking down the left hallway (Figure 10.27). The comparison circle was always 10 feet from the observer, but the test circles were presented at distances ranging from 10 feet to 120 feet. The observer's task on each trial was to adjust the diameter of the comparison circle on the left to match their perception of the size of the test circle on the right.

An important feature of the test stimuli in the right corridor was that they all cast exactly the same-sized image on the retina. We can understand how this was accomplished by introducing the concept of visual angle.

What Is Visual Angle? Visual angle is the angle of an object relative to the observer's eye. Figure 10.28a shows how we determine the visual angle of a stimulus (a person, in this example) by extending lines from the person to the lens of the observer's eye. The angle between the lines is the visual angle. Notice that the visual angle depends both on the size of the stimulus and on its distance from the observer, so when the person moves closer, as in Figure 10.28b, the visual angle becomes larger.

The visual angle tells us how large the object will be on the back of the eye. There are 360 degrees around the entire circumference of the eyeball, and an object with a visual angle of 1 degree would take up 1/360 of this circumference—about 0.3 mm in an average-sized adult eye. One way to get a feel for visual angle is to fully extend your arm and look at your thumb, as the woman in Figure 10.29 is doing. The approximate visual angle of the width of the thumb at arm's length is 2 degrees. Thus, an object that is exactly covered by the thumb held at arm's length, such as the iPod in Figure 10.29, has a visual angle of approximately 2 degrees.

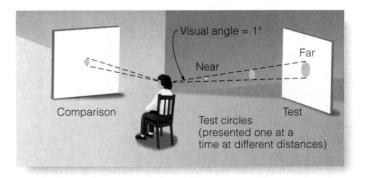

Figure 10.27 ▌ Setup of Holway and Boring's (1941) experiment. The observer changes the diameter of the comparison circle in the left corridor to match his or her perception of the size of test circles presented in the right corridor. Each test circle has a visual angle of 1 degree and is presented separately. This diagram is not drawn to scale. The actual distance of the far test circle was 100 feet.

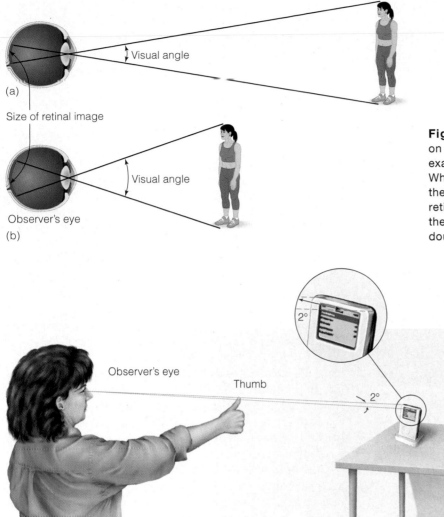

(a)

Size of retinal image

Visual angle

Observer's eye

(b)

Figure 10.28 ▌ (a) The visual angle depends on the size of the stimulus (the woman in this example) and its distance from the observer. (b) When the woman moves closer to the observer, the visual angle and the size of the image on the retina increase. This example shows how halving the distance between the stimulus and the observer doubles the size of the image on the retina.

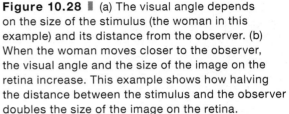

Observer's eye

Thumb

2°

Figure 10.29 ▌ The "thumb" method of determining the visual angle of an object. When the thumb is at arm's length, whatever it covers has a visual angle of about 2 degrees. The woman's thumb covers the width of her iPod, so the visual angle of the iPod, from the woman's point of view, is 2 degrees. Note that the visual angle will change if the distance between the woman and the iPod changes.

This "thumb technique" provides a way to determine the approximate visual angle of any object in the environment. It also illustrates an important property of visual angle: A small object that is near (like the thumb) and a larger object that is far (like the iPod) can have the same visual angle. This is illustrated in Figure 10.30, which shows a photograph taken by Jennifer, a student in my sensation and perception class. To take this picture, Jennifer adjusted the distance between her fingers so that the Eiffel Tower just fit between them. When she did this, the space between her fingers had the same visual angle as the Eiffel Tower.

How Holway and Boring Tested Size Perception in a Hallway The idea that objects with different sizes can have the same visual angle was used in the creation of the test circles in Holway and Boring's experiment. You can see from Figure 10.27 that small circles were positioned close to the observer and larger circles were positioned farther away, and that all of the circles had a visual angle of 1 degree. Objects with the same visual angle create the same-sized image on the retina, so all of the test circles had the same-sized image on the observers' retinas, no matter where in the hallway they were located.

In the first part of Holway and Boring's experiment, many depth cues were available, including binocular disparity, motion parallax, and shading, so the observer could easily judge the distance of the test circles. The results, indicated by line 1 in Figure 10.31, show that even though all of the retinal images were the same size, observers based their judgments on the physical sizes of the circles. When they viewed a large test circle that was located far away (far circle in Figure 10.27), they made the comparison circle large (point F in Figure 10.31); when they viewed a small test circle that was located nearby (near circle in Figure 10.27), they made the comparison circle small (point N in Figure 10.31). The observers' adjustment of the comparison circle to match the physical size of the test circles means that they were accurately judging the physical sizes of the circles.

Holway and Boring then determined how accurate the observers' judgments would be when they eliminated depth information. They did this by having the observer view the test circles with one eye, which eliminated binocular disparity (line 2 in Figure 10.31); then by having the observer view the test circles through a peephole, which eliminated motion parallax (line 3); and finally by adding drapes to the

Figure 10.30 ▌ The visual angle between the two fingers is the same as the visual angle of the Eiffel Tower.

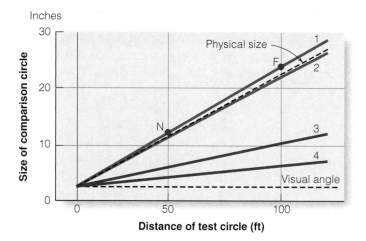

Figure 10.31 ▌ Results of Holway and Boring's (1941) experiment. The dashed line marked "Physical size" is the result that would be expected if the observers adjusted the diameter of the comparison circle to match the actual diameter of each test circle. The line marked "Visual angle" is the result that would be expected if the observers adjusted the diameter of the comparison circle to match the visual angle of each test circle.

hallway to eliminate shadows and reflections (line 4). The results of these experiments indicate that as it became harder to determine the distance of the test circles, the observer's perception of the sizes of the circles became inaccurate.

Eliminating depth information made it more difficult to judge the physical sizes of the circles. Without depth information, the perception of size was determined not by the actual size of an object but by the size of the object's image on the observer's retina. Because all of the test circles in Holway and Boring's experiment had the same retinal size, they were judged to be about the same size once depth information was eliminated. Thus, the results of this experiment indicate that size estimation is based on the actual sizes of objects when there is good depth information (blue lines), but that size estimation is strongly influenced by the object's visual angle when depth information is eliminated (red lines).

An example of size perception that is determined by visual angle is our perception of the sizes of the sun and the moon, which, due to a cosmic coincidence, have the same visual angle. The fact that they have identical visual angles becomes most obvious during an eclipse of the sun. Although we can see the flaming corona of the sun surrounding the moon, as shown in Figure 10.32, the moon's disk almost exactly covers the disk of the sun.

If we calculate the visual angles of the sun and the moon, the result is 0.5 degrees for both. As you can see in Figure 10.32, the moon is small (diameter 2,200 miles) but close (245,000 miles from Earth), whereas the sun is large (diameter 865,400 miles) but far away (93 million miles from Earth). Even though these two celestial bodies are vastly different in size, we perceive them to be the same size because, as we are unable to perceive their distance, we base our judgment on their visual angles.

In yet another example, we perceive objects viewed from a high-flying airplane as very small. Because we have no way of accurately estimating the distance from the airplane to the ground, we perceive size based on objects' visual angles, which are very small because we are so high up.

Size Constancy

The examples just described all demonstrate a link between our perception of size and our perception of depth, with good depth perception favoring accurate size perception. And even though our perception of size is not always totally accurate (Gilinsky, 1951), it is good enough to cause psychologists to propose the principle of size constancy. This principle states that our perception of an object's size remains relatively constant, even when we view an object from different distances, which changes the size of the object's image on the retina.

To introduce the idea of size constancy to my perception class, I ask someone in the front row to estimate my height when I am standing about 3 feet away. Their guess is usually accurate, around 5 feet 9 inches. I then take one large step back so I am now 6 feet away and ask the person to estimate my height again. It probably doesn't surprise you that the second estimate of my height is about the same as the first. The point of this demonstration is that even though my image on the person's retina becomes half as large when I step

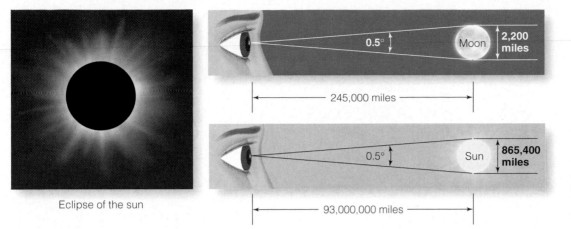

Eclipse of the sun

Figure 10.32 ▌ The moon's disk almost exactly covers the sun during an eclipse because the sun and the moon have the same visual angle.

back to 6 feet (Figure 10.28), I do not appear to shrink to less than 3 feet tall, but still appear to be my normal size. This perception of size as remaining constant no matter what the viewing distance is size constancy. The following demonstration illustrates size constancy in another way.

DEMONSTRATION

Perceiving Size at a Distance

Hold a quarter between the fingertips of each hand so you can see the faces of both coins. Hold one coin about a foot from you and the other at arm's length. Observe the coins with both of your eyes open and note their sizes. Under these conditions, most people perceive the near and far coins as being approximately the same size. Now close one eye, and holding the coins so they appear side-by-side, notice how your perception of the size of the far coin changes so that it now appears smaller than the near coin. This demonstrates how size constancy is decreased under conditions of poor depth information. ▌

Size Constancy as a Calculation The link between size constancy and depth perception has led to the proposal that size constancy is based on a mechanism called size–distance scaling that takes an object's distance into account (Gregory, 1966). Size–distance scaling operates according to the equation $S = K (R \times D)$, where S is the object's perceived size, K is a constant, R is the size of the retinal image, and D is the perceived distance of the object. (Since we are mainly interested in R and D, and K is a scaling factor that is always the same, we will omit K in the rest of our discussion).

According to the size–distance equation, as a person walks away from you, the size of the person's image on your retina (R) gets smaller, but your perception of the person's distance (D) gets larger. These two changes balance each other, and the net result is that you perceive the person's size (S) as remaining constant.

DEMONSTRATION

Size–Distance Scaling and Emmert's Law

You can demonstrate size–distance scaling to yourself by looking back at Figure 8.20 in Chapter 8 (page 190). Look at the center of the circle for about 60 seconds. Then look at the white space to the side of the circle and blink to see the circle's afterimage. Before the afterimage fades, also look at a wall far across the room. You should see that the size of the afterimage depends on where you look. If you look at a distant surface, such as the far wall of the room, you see a large afterimage that appears to be far away. If you look at a near surface, such as the page of this book, you see a small afterimage that appears to be close. ▌

Figure 10.33 illustrates the principle underlying the effect you just experienced, which was first described by Emmert in 1881. Staring at the circle bleached a small circular area of visual pigment on your retina (see page 55). This bleached area of the retina determined the retinal size of the afterimage and remained constant no matter where you were looking.

The perceived size of the afterimage, as shown in Figure 10.33, is determined by the distance of the surface against which the afterimage is viewed. This relationship between the apparent distance of an afterimage and its perceived size is known as Emmert's law: The farther away an afterimage appears, the larger it will seem. This result follows from our size–distance scaling equation, $S = R \times D$. The size of the bleached area of pigment on the retina (R) always stays the same, so that increasing the afterimage's distance (D) increases the magnitude of $R \times D$. We therefore perceive the size of the afterimage (S) as larger when it is viewed against the far wall.

Other Information for Size Perception Although we have been stressing the link between size constancy and depth perception and how size–distance scaling works, other sources of information in the environment also help achieve size constancy. One source of information

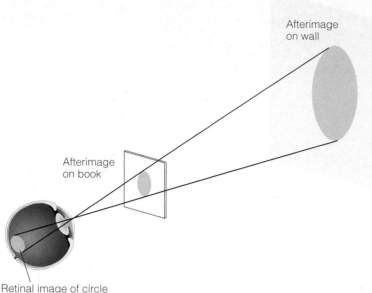

Afterimage
on wall

Afterimage
on book

Retinal image of circle
(bleached pigment)

Figure 10.33 ▌ The principle behind the observation that the size of an afterimage increases as the afterimage is viewed against more distant surfaces.

for size perception is relative size. We often use the sizes of familiar objects as a yardstick to judge the size of other objects, as in Figure 10.34, in which the size of the woman indicates that the wheel is very large. (Also see the chapter opening picture, facing page 229, in which the size of the house indicates that the trees are very tall.) This idea that our perception of the sizes of objects can be influenced by the sizes of nearby objects explains why we often fail to appreciate how tall basketball players are, when all we see for comparison are other basketball players. But as soon as a person of average height stands next to one of these players, the player's true height becomes evident.

Another source of information for size perception is the relationship between objects and texture information on the ground. We saw that a texture gradient occurs when elements that are equally spaced in a scene appear to be more closely packed as distance increases (Figure 10.6). Figure 10.35 shows two cylinders sitting on a texture gradient formed by a cobblestone road. Even if we have trouble perceiving the depth of the near and far cylinders, we can

Bruce Goldstein

Figure 10.34 ▌ The size of this wheel becomes apparent when it can be compared to an object of known size, such as the person. If the wheel were seen in total isolation, it would be difficult to know that it is so large.

Bruce Goldstein

Figure 10.35 ▌ Two cylinders resting on a texture gradient. According to Gibson (1950), the fact that the bases of both cylinders cover the same number of units on the gradient indicates that the bases of the two cylinders are the same size.

tell that they are the same size because their bases both cover the same portion of a paving stone.

Visual Illusions

Visual illusions fascinate people because they demonstrate how our visual system can be "tricked" into seeing inaccurately (Bach & Poloschek, 2006). We have already described a number of types of illusions: Illusions of lightness include Mach bands (page 64), in which small changes in lightness are seen near a border even though no changes are present in the physical pattern of light; simultaneous contrast (page 66) and White's illusion (page 67), in which two physically identical fields can appear different; and the Hermann grid (page 63), in which small gray spots are seen that aren't there in the light. Attentional effects include change blindness (page 139), in which two alternating scenes appear similar even though there are differences between them. Illusions of motion are those in which stationary stimuli are perceived as moving (page 180).

We will now describe some illusions of size—situations that lead us to misperceive the size of an object. We will see that some explanations of these illusions involve the connection we have described between the perception of size and the perception of depth. We will also see that some of the most familiar illusions have yet to be fully explained.

A good example of this situation is provided by the Müller-Lyer illusion.

The Müller-Lyer Illusion

In the Müller-Lyer illusion, the right vertical line in Figure 10.36 appears to be longer than the left vertical line, even though they are both exactly the same length (measure them). It is obvious by just looking at these figures that one line appears longer than the other, but you can measure how much longer the right line appears by using the simple matching procedure described in the following demonstration. [VL]9

DEMONSTRATION

Measuring the Müller-Lyer Illusion

The first step in measuring the Müller-Lyer illusion is to create a "standard stimulus" by drawing a line 30 millimeters long on an index card and adding outward-going fins, as in the right figure in Figure 10.36. Then, on separate cards, create "comparison stimuli" by drawing lines that are 28, 30, 32, 34, 36, 38, and 40 millimeters long with inward-going fins, as in the left figure. Then ask your observer to pick the comparison stimulus that most closely matches the length of the standard stimulus. The difference in length between the standard stimulus and the comparison stimulus chosen by your observer (typically between 10 percent and 30 percent) defines the

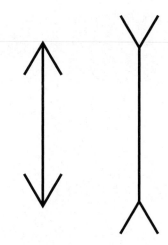

Figure 10.36 ❙ The Müller-Lyer illusion. Both lines are actually the same length.

size of the illusion. Try this procedure on a number of people to see how variable it is. ❙

Misapplied Size Constancy Scaling Why does the Müller-Lyer display cause a misperception of size? Richard Gregory (1966) explains the illusion on the basis of a mechanism he calls **misapplied size constancy scaling**. He points out that size constancy normally helps us maintain a stable perception of objects by taking distance into account (as expressed in the size–distance scaling equation). Thus, size constancy scaling causes a 6-foot-tall person to appear 6 feet tall no matter what his distance. Gregory proposes, however, that the very mechanisms that help us maintain stable perceptions in the three-dimensional world sometimes create illusions when applied to objects drawn on a two-dimensional surface.

We can see how misapplied size constancy scaling works by comparing the left and right lines in Figure 10.36 to the left and right lines that have been superimposed on the corners in Figure 10.37. Gregory suggests that the fins on the right line in Figure 10.37 make this line look like part of an inside corner, and that the fins on the left line make this line look like part of an outside corner. Because inside corners appear to "recede" and outside corners "jut out," our size–distance scaling mechanism treats the inside corner as if it is farther away, so the term D in the equation $S = R \times D$ is larger and this line therefore appears longer. (Remember that the retinal sizes, R, of the two lines are the same, so perceived size, S, is determined by the perceived distance, D.)

At this point, you could say that although the Müller-Lyer figures may remind Gregory of inside and outside corners, they don't look that way to you (or at least they didn't until Gregory told you to see them that way). But according to Gregory, it is not necessary that you be consciously aware that these lines can represent three-dimensional structures; your perceptual system unconsciously takes the depth information contained in the Müller-Lyer figures into account, and your size–distance scaling mechanism adjusts the perceived sizes of the lines accordingly.

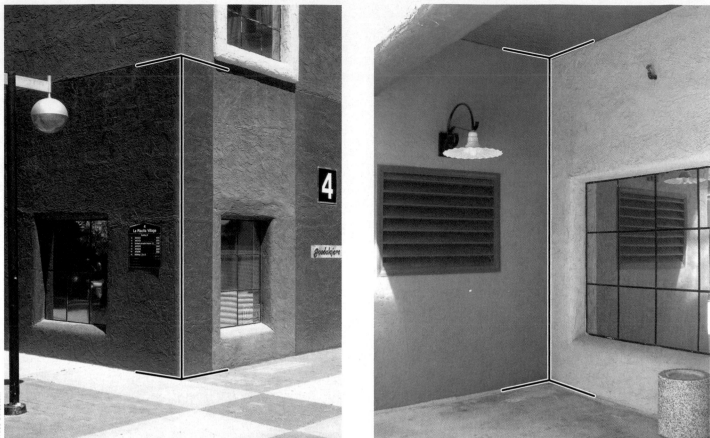

Figure 10.37 ▌ According to Gregory (1966), the Müller-Lyer line on the left corresponds to an outside corner, and the line on the right corresponds to an inside corner. Note that the two vertical lines are the same length (measure them!).

Bruce Goldstein

Gregory's theory of visual illusions has not, however, gone unchallenged. For example, figures like the dumbbells in Figure 10.38, which contain no obvious perspective or depth, still result in an illusion. And Patricia DeLucia and Julian Hochberg (1985, 1986, 1991; Hochberg, 1987) have shown that the Müller-Lyer illusion occurs for a three-dimensional display like the one in Figure 10.39, in which it is obvious that the spaces between the two sets of fins are not at different depths. (Measure distances *x* and *y* to convince yourself that they are the same.) You can experience this effect for yourself by doing the following demonstration.

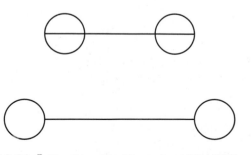

Figure 10.38 ▌ The "dumbbell"' version of the Müller-Lyer illusion. As in the original Müller-Lyer illusion, the two straight lines are actually the same length.

DEMONSTRATION
The Müller-Lyer Illusion With Books

Pick three books that are the same size and arrange two of them with their corners making a 90-degree angle and standing in positions A and B, as shown in Figure 10.39. Then, without using a ruler, position the third book at position C, so that distance *x* appears to be equal to distance *y*. Check your placement, looking down at the books from the top and from

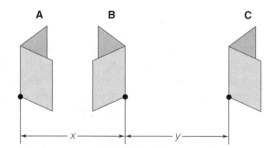

Figure 10.39 ▌ A three-dimensional Müller-Lyer illusion. The 2-foot-high wooden "fins" stand on the floor. Although the distances *x* and *y* are the same, distance *y* appears larger, just as in the two-dimensional Müller-Lyer illusion.

other angles as well. When you are satisfied that distances *x* and *y* appear about equal, measure the distances with a ruler. How do they compare? ▮

If you set distance *y* so that it was smaller than distance *x*, this is exactly the result you would expect from the two-dimensional Müller-Lyer illusion, in which the distance between the outward-going fins appears enlarged compared to the distance between the inward-going fins. You can also duplicate the illusion shown in Figure 10.39 with your books by using your ruler to make distances *x* and *y* equal. Then, notice how the distances actually appear. The fact that we can create the Müller-Lyer illusion by using three-dimensional stimuli such as these, along with demonstrations like the dumbbell in Figure 10.38, is difficult for Gregory's theory to explain.

Conflicting Cues Theory R. H. Day (1989, 1990) has proposed the conflicting cues theory, which states that our perception of line length depends on two cues: (1) the actual length of the vertical lines, and (2) the overall length of the figure. According to Day, these two conflicting cues are integrated to form a compromise perception of length. Because the overall length of the right figure in Figure 10.36 is larger due to its outward-oriented fins, the vertical line appears larger.

Another version of the Müller-Lyer illusion, shown in Figure 10.40, results in the perception that the space between the dots is greater in the lower figure than in the upper figure, even though the distances are actually the same. According to Day's conflicting cues theory, the space in the lower figure appears greater because the overall extent of the figure is greater. Notice that conflicting cues theory can also be applied to the dumbbell display in Figure 10.38. Thus, although Gregory believes that depth information is involved in determining illusions, Day rejects this idea and says that cues for length are what is important. Let's now look at some more examples of illusions and the mechanisms that have been proposed to explain them.

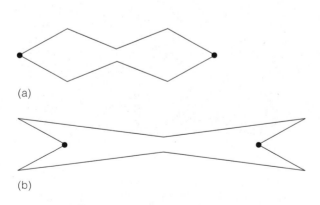

Figure 10.40 ▮ An alternate version of the Müller-Lyer illusion. We perceive that the distance between the dots in (a) is less than the distance in (b), even though the distances are the same.

The Ponzo Illusion

In the Ponzo (or railroad track) illusion, shown in Figure 10.41, both animals are the same size on the page, and so have the same visual angle, but the one on top appears longer. According to Gregory's misapplied scaling explanation, the top animal appears larger because of depth information provided by the converging railroad tracks that make the top animal appear farther away. Thus, just as in the Müller-Lyer illusion, the scaling mechanism corrects for this apparently increased depth (even though there really isn't any, because the illusion is on a flat page), and we perceive the top animal to be larger. (Also see Prinzmetal et al., 2001; Shimamura & Prinzmetal, 1999, for another explanation of the Ponzo illusion.) [VL] **10, 11**

The Ames Room

The Ames room causes two people of equal size to appear very different in size (Ittleson, 1952). In Figure 10.42, you can see that the woman on the right looks much taller than the woman on the left. This perception occurs even though both women are actually about the same height. The reason for this erroneous perception of size lies in the construction of the room. The shapes of the wall and the windows at the rear of the room make it look like a normal rectangular room when viewed from a particular observation point; however, as shown in the diagram in Figure 10.43, the Ames room is

William Vann/www.edupic.net

Figure 10.41 ▮ The Ponzo (or railroad track) illusion. The two animals are the same length on the page (measure them), but the far one appears larger. *(Courtesy of Mary Bravo.)*

Figure 10.42 ▌ The Ames room. Both women are actually the same height, but the woman on the right appears taller because of the distorted shape of the room.

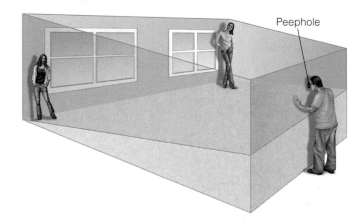

Peephole

Figure 10.43 ▌ The Ames room, showing its true shape. The woman on the left is actually almost twice as far from the observer as the one on the right; however, when the room is viewed through the peephole, this difference in distance is not seen. In order for the room to look normal when viewed through the peephole, it is necessary to enlarge the left side of the room.

actually shaped so that the left corner of the room is almost twice as far from the observer as the right corner.

What's happening in the Ames room? The construction of the room causes the woman on the left to have a much smaller visual angle than the one on the right. We think that we are looking into a normal rectangular room at two women who appear to be at the same distance, so we perceive the one with the smaller visual angle as shorter. We can understand why this occurs by returning to our size–distance scaling equation, $S = R \times D$. Because the *perceived* distance (D) is the same for the two women, but the size of the retinal image (R) is smaller for the woman on the left, her perceived size (S) is smaller.

Another explanation for the Ames room is based not on size–distance scaling, but on relative size. The relative size explanation states that our perception of the size of the two women is determined by how they fill the distance between the bottom and top of the room. Because the woman on the right fills the entire space and the woman on the left occupies only a little of it, we perceive the woman on the right as taller (Sedgwick, 2001).

The Moon Illusion

You may have noticed that when the moon is on the horizon, it appears much larger than when it is higher in the sky. This enlargement of the horizon moon compared to the elevated moon, shown in Figure 10.44, is called the moon illusion. When I discuss this in class, I first explain that visual angles of the horizon moon and elevated moon are the same. This must be so because the moon's physical size (2,200 miles in diameter) and distance from Earth (245,000 miles) are constant throughout the night; therefore, the moon's visual angle must be constant. (If you are still skeptical, photograph the horizon and the elevated moons with a digital camera. When you compare the two images, you will find that the diameters in the resulting two pictures are identical. Or you can view the moon through a quarter-inch-diameter hole held at about arm's length. For most people, the moon just fits inside this hole, wherever it is in the sky.)

Once students are convinced that the moon's visual angle remains the same throughout the night, I ask why they think the moon appears larger on the horizon. One common response is "When the moon is on the horizon, it appears closer, and that is why it appears larger." When I ask why it appears closer, I often receive the explanation "Because it

Figure 10.44 ▌ An artist's conception of the how the moon is perceived when it is on the horizon and when it is high in the sky. Note that the visual angle of the horizon moon is depicted as larger than the visual angle of the moon high in the sky. This is because the picture is simulating the illusion. In the environment, the visual angles of the two moons are the same.

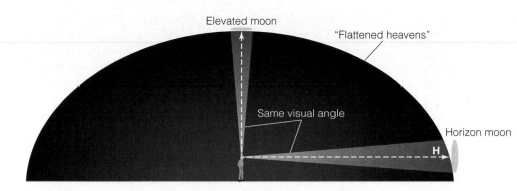

Figure 10.45 ▌ When observers are asked to consider the sky as a surface and to compare the distance to the horizon (H) and the distance to the top of the sky on a clear moonless night, they usually say that the horizon appears farther away. This results in the "flattened heavens" shown here.

appears larger." But saying "It appears larger because it appears closer, and it appears closer because it appears larger" is clearly a case of circular reasoning that doesn't really explain the moon illusion.

One explanation that isn't circular is called the apparent distance theory. This theory does take distance into account, but in a way opposite to our hypothetical student's explanation. According to apparent distance theory, the moon on the horizon appears more distant because it is viewed across the filled space of the terrain, which contains depth information; but when the moon is higher in the sky, it appears less distant because it is viewed through empty space, which contains little depth information.

The idea that the horizon is perceived as farther away than the sky overhead is supported by the fact that when people estimate the distance to the horizon and the distance to the sky directly overhead, they report that the horizon appears to be farther away. That is, the heavens appear "flattened" (Figure 10.45).

The key to the moon illusion, according to apparent distance theory, is that both the horizon and the elevated moons have the same visual angle, but because the horizon moon is seen against the horizon, which appears farther than the zenith sky, it appears larger. This follows from the size–distance scaling equation, $S = R \times D$, because retinal size, R, is the same for both locations of the moon (remember that the visual angle is always the same), so the moon that appears farther away will appear larger. This is the principle we invoked to explain why an afterimage appears larger if it is viewed against a faraway surface in the Emmert's law demonstration.

Just as the near and far afterimages in the Emmert's law demonstration have the same visual angles, so do the horizon and the elevated moons. The afterimage that appears on the wall far across the room simulates the horizon moon; the circle appears farther away, so your size–distance scaling mechanism makes it appear larger. The afterimage that is viewed on a close surface simulates the elevated moon; the circle appears closer, so your scaling mechanism makes it appear smaller (King & Gruber, 1962).

Lloyd Kaufman and Irvin Rock (1962a, 1962b) have done a number of experiments that support the apparent distance theory. In one of their experiments, they showed that when the horizon moon was viewed over the terrain, which made it seem farther away, it appeared 1.3 times larger than the elevated moon; however, when the terrain was masked off so that the horizon moon was viewed through a hole in a sheet of cardboard, the illusion vanished (Kaufman & Rock, 1962a, 1962b; Rock & Kaufman, 1962).

Some researchers, however, are skeptical of the apparent distance theory. They question the idea that the horizon moon appears farther, as shown in the flattened heavens effect in Figure 10.45, because some observers see the horizon moon as floating in space in front of the sky (Plug & Ross, 1994).

Another theory of the moon illusion is the angular size contrast theory, which states that the moon appears smaller when it is surrounded by larger objects. Thus, when the moon is elevated, the large expanse of sky surrounding it makes it appear smaller. However, when the moon is on the horizon, less sky surrounds it, so it appears larger (Baird et al., 1990).

Even though scientists have been proposing theories to explain the moon illusion for hundreds of years, there is still no agreement on an explanation (Hershenson, 1989). Apparently a number of factors are involved, in addition to the ones we have considered here, including atmospheric perspective (looking through haze on the horizon can increase size perception), color (redness increases perceived size), and oculomotor factors (convergence of the eyes, which tends to occur when we look toward the horizon and can cause an increase in perceived size; Plug & Ross, 1994). Just as many different sources of depth information work together to create our impression of depth, many different factors may work together to create the moon illusion, and perhaps the other illusions as well. $\boxed{\text{VL}}$ **12–16**

Something to Consider: Distance Perception and Perceived Effort

Imagine the following situation: You are hiking in the woods with a friend. You have agreed to take turns carrying a heavy backpack, and it is your turn. In the distance you see the small lake where you plan to set up camp. Just as you are thinking that it is pretty far to the lake, your friend says, "There's the lake. It's pretty close."

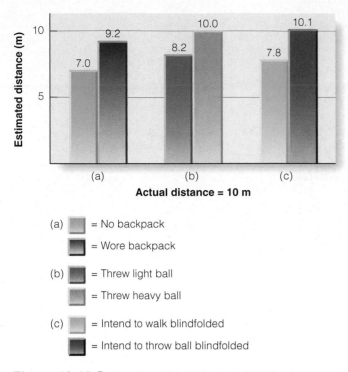

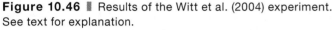

Figure 10.46 ❚ Results of the Witt et al. (2004) experiment. See text for explanation.

The idea that wearing a heavy backpack may make things appear more distant has been confirmed in the laboratory, by having people judge the distance to various targets while wearing a heavy backpack and while not wearing a backpack (Proffitt et al., 2003). The people in this experiment did not have to walk the distances wearing the backpack; they just wore the backpack while making their distance estimates. The result, in Figure 10.46a, shows that people estimated the distance as farther when wearing the backpack.

To test the idea that judging distance might depend on the effort that people believe is associated with a particular distance, Janice Witt and coworkers (2004) had participants throw balls to targets ranging from 4 to 10 meters away. After they had thrown either a light ball or a heavy ball, participants estimated the distances to the targets. The results for the 10-meter target, shown in Figure 10.46b, indicate that distance estimates were larger after throwing the heavy ball.

Finally, here's an additional twist to these findings: Apparently, distance judgments are determined not only by the amount of effort people actually exert, but their *expectation* that they will have to exert some effort. This was demonstrated by dividing participants who had previously thrown heavy balls into two groups. One group was told that they were going to have to throw the balls at the targets while blindfolded, and the other group was told that they were going to have to walk to the targets while blindfolded. Because throwing heavy balls involves more effort than walking, we

might expect that the group that was told they would be throwing would estimate the distance as greater than those who were told they would be walking. The results, in Figure 10.46c, indicate that this is what happened. Apparently just thinking about expending effort over a distance can increase people's judgment of distance.

What all of this adds up to is that distance perception depends not only on optical information, such as monocular and binocular depth cues, but also on actions we intend to perform and the effort associated with these actions. This is consistent with our discussion in Chapter 7 (Taking Action), in which we saw how perception and action are closely linked.

TEST YOURSELF 10.2

1. Describe the Holway and Boring experiment. What do the results of this experiment tell us about how size perception is influenced by depth perception?
2. What are some examples of situations in which our perception of an object's size is determined by the object's visual angle? Under what conditions does this occur?
3. What is size constancy, and under what conditions does it occur?
4. What is size–distance scaling? How does it explain size constancy?
5. Describe two other types of information (other than depth) that can influence our perception of size.
6. Describe how illusions of size, such as the Müller-Lyer illusion, the Ponzo illusion, the Ames room, and the moon illusion, can be explained in terms of size–distance scaling.
7. What are some problems with the size–distance scaling explanation of (a) the Müller-Lyer illusion and (b) the moon illusion? What alternative explanations have been proposed?
8. What does it mean to say that the perception of distance depends not only on optical information but also on perceived effort?

THINK ABOUT IT

1. Texture gradients are said to provide information for depth perception because elements in a scene become more densely packed as distance increases. The classic example of a texture gradient is a tiled floor, like the one in Figure 10.47, which has regularly spaced elements. But regularly spaced elements are more the exception than the rule in the environment. Make an informal survey of your environment, both inside and outside, and decide (1) whether texture gradients are

Figure 10.47 ▌ Texture gradients in a hallway in the Versailles Palace in France. How prevalent is texture gradient information in the environment in general?

present in your environment and (2) if you think the principle behind texture gradients could contribute to the perception of depth even if the texture information in the environment is not as obvious as the information in Figure 10.47. (p. 233)

2. How could you determine the contribution of binocular vision to depth perception? One way would be to close one eye and notice how this affects your perception. Try this, and describe any changes you notice. Then devise a way to quantitatively measure the accuracy of depth perception that is possible with two-eyed and one-eyed vision. (p. 235)

3. One of the triumphs of art is creating the impression of depth on a two-dimensional canvas. Go to a museum or look at pictures in an art book, and identify the depth information that helps increase the perception of depth in these pictures. You may also notice that you perceive less depth in some pictures, especially abstract ones. In fact, some artists purposely create pictures that are per-

ceived as "flat." What steps do these artists have to take to accomplish this? (p. 231)

IF YOU WANT TO KNOW MORE

1. *Perception of spatial layout can affect the perception of lightness.* A classic early paper showed that our perception of light and dark can be strongly influenced by our perception of the locations of surfaces in space. (p. 231)

   Gilchrist, A. L. (1977). Perceived lightness depends on perceived spatial arrangement. *Science, 195,* 185–187.

2. *Achieving stereopsis after decades without it.* Neurologist Oliver Sachs gives an account of a woman who had been unable to achieve stereopsis for decades because of a condition that prevented coordination of her left and right eyes. He describes how, through therapy that included wearing prisms and doing eye exercises, she was able to achieve stereopsis and an enhanced perception of depth. (p. 238)

   Sacks, O. (2006, June 19). Stereo Sue. *New Yorker,* 64–73.

3. *How depth cues are combined in the brain.* Our perception of depth is determined by a combination of different cues working together. The experiments described in the following article show which brain structures may be involved in combining these cues. (p. 242)

   Welchman, A. E., Deubelius, A., Conrad, V., Bülthoff, H. H., & Kourtzi, Z. (2005). 3D shape perception from combined depth cues in human visual cortex. *Nature Neuroscience, 8,* 820–827.

4. *Information about depth and size in the primary visual cortex.* The mechanism responsible for how depth perception can influence our perception of an object's size was originally thought to be located in higher areas of the visual system, where size and depth information were combined. Recent research has shown that this process may occur as early as the primary visual cortex. (p. 242)

   Murray, S. O., Boyaci, H., & Kersten, D. (2006). The representation of perceived angular size in human primary visual cortex. *Nature Neuroscience, 9,* 429–434.

   Sterzer, P., & Rees, G. (2006). Perceived size matters. *Nature Neuroscience, 9,* 302–304.

5. *Action and depth perception.* Actions such as locomotion, eye and hand movements, and the manipulation of objects can influence our perception of three-dimensional space and an object's shape. (p. 253)

   Wexler, M., & van Boxtel, J. J. A. (2005). Depth perception by the active observer. *Trends in Cognitive Sciences, 9,* 431–438.

KEY TERMS

Absolute disparity (p. 237)
Accretion (p. 234)
Ames room (p. 251)
Angle of disparity (p. 237)
Angular size contrast theory (p. 253)
Apparent distance theory (p. 253)
Atmospheric perspective (p. 232)
Binocular depth cell (p. 242)
Binocular disparity (p. 235)
Conflicting cues theory (p. 251)
Correspondence problem (p. 240)
Corresponding retinal points (p. 236)
Cue approach to depth perception (p. 230)
Deletion (p. 234)

Disparity-selective cell (p. 242)
Echolocation (p. 241)
Emmert's law (p. 247)
Familiar size (p. 232)
Frontal eyes (p. 240)
Horopter (p. 236)
Lateral eyes (p. 240)
Misapplied size constancy scaling (p. 249)
Monocular cue (p. 231)
Moon illusion (p. 252)
Motion parallax (p. 233)
Müller-Lyer illusion (p. 249)
Noncorresponding points (p. 236)
Occlusion (p. 230)

Oculomotor cue (p. 231)
Perspective convergence (p. 232)
Pictorial cue (p. 231)
Ponzo illusion (p. 251)
Random-dot stereogram (p. 239)
Relative disparity (p. 237)
Relative height (p. 231)
Relative size (p. 231)
Size constancy (p. 246)
Size–distance scaling (p. 247)
Stereopsis (p. 238)
Stereoscope (p. 238)
Texture gradient (p. 233)
Visual angle (p. 244)

MEDIA RESOURCES

The *Sensation and Perception* Book Companion Website

www.cengage.com/psychology/goldstein

See the companion website for flashcards, practice quiz questions, Internet links, updates, critical thinking exercises, discussion forums, games, and more!

CengageNOW

www.cengage.com/cengagenow

Go to this site for the link to CengageNOW, your one-stop shop. Take a pre-test for this chapter, and CengageNOW will generate a personalized study plan based on your test results. The study plan will identify the topics you need to review and direct you to online resources to help you master those topics. You can then take a post-test to help you determine the concepts you have mastered and what you will still need to work on.

Virtual Lab

V_L

Your Virtual Lab is designed to help you get the most out of this course. The Virtual Lab icons direct you to specific media demonstrations and experiments designed to help you visualize what you are reading about. The number beside each icon indicates the number of the media element you can access through your CD-ROM, CengageNOW, or WebTutor resource.

The following lab exercises are related to the material in this chapter:

1. *Convergence* Shows how convergence of the eyes depends on an object's distance.

2. *Shape From Shading* How the shadows that result from illumination can help define the shape of a rotating three-dimensional object.

3. *The Horopter and Corresponding Points* How corresponding points on the two eyes can be determined by sliding one eye over the other. How the angle of convergence changes with different distances of fixation.

4. *Disparity and Retinal Location* How disparity changes as one object is moved closer to the eye as a person fixates on another object.

5. *Pictures* Some "classic" stereograms of photographs. Red–green glasses required.

6. *Outlines* Stereogram of a Necker cube. Red–green glasses required.

7. *Depth Perception* An experiment in which you can determine how your perception of depth changes with the amount of binocular disparity. Red–green glasses required.

8. *Random-Dot Stereogram* How the perception of depth can be created by random-dot stereograms. Red–green glasses required.

9. *The Müller-Lyer Illusion* Measure the effect of the Müller-Lyer illusion with both inward and outward fins.

10. *The Ponzo Illusion* Measure the size of the Ponzo (railroad track) illusion.

11. *Size Perception and Depth* How perspective cues can cause two "monsters" to appear different in size.

12. *Horizontal–Vertical Illusion* Measure the size of the horizontal–vertical illusion.

13. *Zollner Illusion* How context can affect the perceived orientation of parallel lines.

14. *Context and Perception: The Hering Illusion* How background lines can make straight parallel lines appear to curve outward.

15. *Context and Perception: The Poggendorf Illusion* How interrupting a straight line makes the segments of the line look as though they don't line up. (Courtesy of Michael Bach.)

16. *Poggendorf Illusion* Measure the size of the Poggendorf illusion.

Also see VL2 (Measuring Illusions) in Chapter 1.

Space Shuttle launch ground zero (150) — 150

Military jet on runway (140) — 140

Pain threshold (130) — 130

Rock concert in front row (120) — 120

— 110

Loud basketball or hockey crowd (100) — 100

— 90

Heavy traffic (80) — 80

— 70

Normal conversation (60) — 60

— 50

Library (40) — 40

— 30

Whisper at 5 feet (20) — 20

— 10

Threshold of hearing (0) — 0 dB

Chapter Contents

CHAPTER 11

Sound, the Auditory System, and Pitch Perception

OPPOSITE PAGE We hear sounds ranging from a quite whisper to the roar of a rocket blasting off. The graph shows how this range of sound stimuli can be plotted using a measure called decibels (dB), which is described in the chapter.
© Roger Ressmeyer/CORBIS

V̄L̄ The Virtual Lab icons direct you to specific animations and videos designed to help you visualize what you are reading about. The number beside each icon indicates the number of the clip you can access through your CD-ROM or your student website.

Some Questions We Will Consider:

▌ If a tree falls in the forest and no one is there to hear it, is there a sound? (p. 261)

▌ What is it that makes sounds high pitched or low pitched? (p. 265)

▌ How do sound vibrations inside the ear lead to the perception of different pitches? (p. 273)

▌ How are sounds represented in the auditory cortex? (p. 280)

Hearing has an extremely important function in my life. I was born legally blind, so although I can see, my vision is highly impaired and is not correctable. Even though I am not usually shy or embarrassed, sometimes I do not want to call attention to myself and my disability. . . . There are many methods that I can use to improve my sight in class, like sitting close to the board or copying from a friend, but sometimes these things are impossible. Then I use my hearing to take notes. . . . My hearing is very strong. While I do not need my hearing to identify people who are very close to me, it is definitely necessary when someone is calling my name from a distance. I can recognize their voice, even if I cannot see them.

This statement, written by one of my students, Jill Robbins, illustrates a special effect hearing has had on her life. The next statement, by student Eileen Lusk, illustrates her reaction to temporarily losing her ability to hear.

In an experiment I did for my sign language class, I bandaged up my ears so I couldn't hear a sound. I had a signing interpreter with me to translate spoken language. The two hours that I was "deaf" gave me a great appreciation for deaf people and their culture. I found it extremely difficult to communicate, because even though I could read the signing, I couldn't keep up with the pace of the conversation. . . . Also, it was uncomfortable for me to be in that much silence. Knowing what a crowded cafeteria sounds like and not being able to hear the background noise was an uncomfortable feeling. I couldn't hear the buzzing of the fluorescent light, the murmur of the crowd, or the slurping of my friend's Coke (which I usually object to, but which I missed when I couldn't hear it). I saw a man drop his tray, and I heard nothing. I could handle the signing, but not the silence.

You don't have to bandage up your ears for two hours to appreciate what hearing adds to your life. Just close your eyes for a few minutes, observe the sounds you hear, and notice what they tell you about your environment. What most people experience is that by listening closely they become aware of many events in the environment that without hearing they would not be aware of at all.

As I sit here in my office in the psychology department, I hear things that I would be unaware of if I had to rely only on my sense of vision: people talking in the hall; a car passing by on the street below; and an ambulance, siren blaring, heading up the hill toward the hospital. If it weren't for hearing, my world at this particular moment would be limited to what I can see in my office and the scene directly outside my window. Although the silence might make it easier to concentrate on writing this book or studying my lecture notes, without hearing I would be unaware of many of the events in my environment.

Our ability to hear events that we can't see serves an important signaling function for both animals and humans. For an animal living in the forest, the rustle of leaves or the snap of a twig may signal the approach of a predator. For humans, hearing provides signals such as the warning sound of a smoke alarm or an ambulance siren, the distinctive high-pitched cry of a baby who is distressed, or telltale noises that signal problems in a car engine.

But hearing has other functions, too. On the first day of my perception class, I ask my students which sense they would choose to keep if they had to pick between hearing and vision. Two of the strongest arguments for keeping hearing instead of vision are music and speech. Many of my students wouldn't want to give up hearing because of the pleasure they derive from listening to music, and they also realize that speech is important because it facilitates communication between people.

Helen Keller, who was both deaf and blind, stated that she felt being deaf was worse than being blind because blindness isolated her from things, but deafness isolated her from people. Being unable to hear people talking creates an isolation that makes it difficult to relate to hearing people and sometimes makes it difficult even to know what is going on. To appreciate this last point, try watching a dramatic program on television with the sound turned off. You may be surprised at how little, beyond physical actions and perhaps some intense emotions, you can understand about the story.

Our goal in this chapter is to describe the basic mechanisms responsible for our ability to hear. We begin by describing the nature of sound and how we experience both laboratory-produced sounds and naturally occurring sounds in the environment. We then consider the physiology behind our perception of pitch, starting with how structures in the ear respond to sound and then how different parts of the brain respond to sound.

As you read this chapter, you will see important differences between vision and hearing, especially when we consider the complex path that the sound stimulus must negotiate in order to reach the receptors. You will also see similarities, especially in the cortex, where there is evidence for *what* and *where* streams in the auditory system that are similar to the *what* and *where* streams we have described for vision.

The Sound Stimulus

The first step in understanding hearing is to define what we mean by *sound* and to show how we measure the characteristics of sound. One way to answer the question "What is sound?" is to consider the following question: *If a tree falls in the forest and no one is there to hear it, would there be a sound?*

This question is useful because it shows that we can use the word **sound** in two different ways. Sometimes *sound* refers to a physical stimulus, and sometimes it refers to a perceptual response. The answer to the question about the tree depends on which of the following definitions of sound we use.

■ *Physical definition:* Sound is *pressure changes* in the air or other medium.

Answer to the question: "Yes," because the falling tree causes pressure changes whether or not someone is there to hear them.

■ *Perceptual definition:* Sound is the *experience* we have when we hear.

Answer to the question: "No," because if no one is in the forest, there would be no experience.

This difference between physical and perceptual is important to be aware of as we discuss hearing in this chapter and the next two. Luckily, it is usually easy to tell from the context in which the terms are used whether "sound" refers to the physical stimulus or to the experience of hearing. For example, "the sound of the trumpet pierced the air" refers to the experience of sound, but "the sound's level was 10 decibels" refers to sound as a physical stimulus. We will first describe sound as a physical stimulus and then describe sound as a perceptual experience.

Sound as Pressure Changes

A sound stimulus occurs when the movements or vibrations of an object cause pressure changes in air, water, or any other elastic medium that surrounds the object. Let's begin by considering your radio or stereo system's loudspeaker, which is really a device for producing vibrations to be transmitted to the surrounding air. People have been known to turn up the volume control on their stereos so high that vibrations can be felt through a neighbor's wall, but even at lower levels the vibrations are there.

The speaker's vibrations affect the surrounding air, as shown in Figure 11.1a. When the diaphragm of the speaker moves out, it pushes the surrounding air molecules together, a process called *condensation,* which causes a slight increase in the density of molecules near the diaphragm. This increased density results in a local increase in the air pressure that is superimposed on the atmospheric pressure. When the speaker diaphragm moves back in, air molecules spread out to fill in the increased space, a process called *rarefaction.* The decreased density of air molecules caused by rarefaction causes a slight decrease in air pressure. By repeating this process many hundreds or thousands of times a second, the speaker creates a pattern of alternating high- and low-pressure regions in the air as neighboring air molecules affect each other. This pattern of air pressure changes, which travels through air at 340 meters per second (and through water at 1,500 meters per second), is called a **sound wave.**

You might get the impression from Figure 11.1a that this traveling sound wave causes air to move outward from the speaker into the environment. What is actually happening is analogous to the ripples created by a pebble dropped into a still pool of water (Figure 11.1b). As the ripples move outward from the pebble, the water at any particular place moves up and down. This becomes obvious when you realize that the ripples would cause a toy boat to bob up and

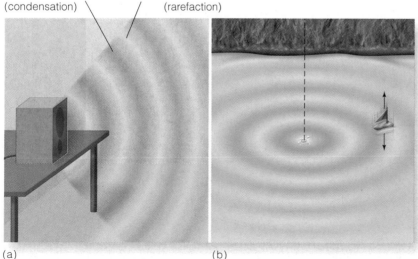

Increase in pressure (condensation)   Decrease in pressure (rarefaction)

(a)   (b)

Figure 11.1 ▌ (a) The effect of a vibrating speaker diaphragm on the surrounding air. Dark areas represent regions of high air pressure, and light areas represent areas of low air pressure. (b) When a pebble is dropped into still water, the resulting ripples appear to move outward. However, the water is actually moving up and down, as indicated by movement of the boat. A similar situation exists for the sound waves produced by the speaker in (a).

down—not to move outward. Similarly, although *air pressure changes* move outward from the speaker, the *air molecules* at each location move back and forth, but stay in about the same place. What is transmitted is the pattern of increases and decreases in pressure that eventually reach the listener's ear. (Note that this is different from what occurs when waves are pounding on a beach. In that case, water moves in and back; in contrast to our boat in the pond, a small boat near the shore could be carried ashore on an incoming wave.)

Pressure Changes: Pure Tones

To describe the pressure changes associated with sound, we will first focus on a simple kind of sound wave called a pure tone. A pure tone occurs when pressure changes in the air occur in a pattern described by a mathematical function called a *sine wave,* as shown in Figure 11.2. Tones with this pattern of pressure changes are occasionally found in the environment. A person whistling or the high-pitched notes produced by a flute are close to pure tones. Tuning forks, which are designed to vibrate with a sine-wave motion, also produce pure tones. For laboratory studies of hearing, computers generate pure tones that cause a speaker diaphragm to vibrate in and out with a sine-wave motion. This vibration can be described by noting its amplitude—the size of the pressure change and its frequency—the number of times per second that the pressure changes repeat.

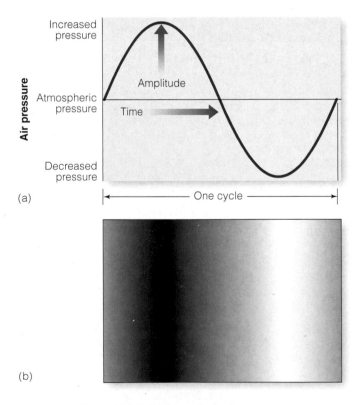

(a)

(b)

Figure 11.2 ▌ (a) Plot of sine-wave pressure changes for a pure tone. (b) Pressure changes are indicated, as in Figure 11.1, by darkening (pressure increased relative to atmospheric pressure) and lightening (pressure decreased relative to atmospheric pressure).

Amplitude One way to specify a sound's amplitude would be to indicate the difference in pressure between the high and low peaks of the sound wave. Figure 11.3 shows three pure tones with different amplitudes. The physical property of amplitude is associated with our experience of loudness, with higher amplitudes associated with louder sounds.

The range of amplitudes we can encounter in the environment is extremely large, as shown in Table 11.1, which shows the relative amplitudes of some environmental sounds. We can dramatize the size of the range of amplitudes as follows: If the pressure change plotted in the middle record of Figure 11.3, in which the sine wave is about 1/2-inch high on the page, represented the amplitude associated with a sound we can just barely hear, then to plot the graph for a very loud sound, such as you might hear at a rock concert, you would need to make the sine wave several miles high! Since this is somewhat impractical, auditory researchers have devised a unit of sound called the decibel,

TABLE 11.1 ▌ **Relative Amplitudes and Decibels for Environmental Sounds**

SOUND	RELATIVE AMPLITUDE	DECIBELS (DB)
Barely audible (threshold)	1	0
Leaves rustling	10	20
Quiet residential community	100	40
Average speaking voice	1,000	60
Express subway train	100,000	100
Propeller plane at takeoff	1,000,000	120
Jet engine at takeoff (pain threshold)	10,000,000	140

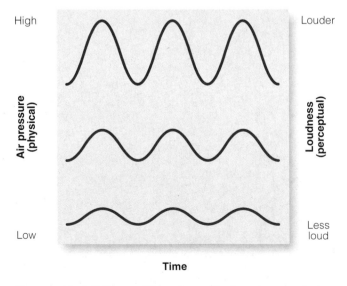

Figure 11.3 ▌ Three different amplitudes of a pure tone. Larger amplitude is associated with the perception of greater loudness.

which converts the large range of sound pressure into [VL] 1 a more manageable scale.

The following equation is used to convert sound pressure into decibels:

$$dB - 20 \times \text{logarithm}(p/p_o)$$

where dB stands for decibels, p is the sound pressure of the stimulus, and p_o is a standard sound pressure, usually set at 20 micropascals, where a pascal is a unit of pressure and 20 micropascals is a pressure near the threshold for human hearing. We can use this equation to calculate the decibels for a 20 micropascal tone ($p = 20$) as follows:

$$dB = 20\log(p/p_o) = 20\log(20/20) = 20 \times (\log 1)$$
$$= 20 \times (0) = 0 \text{ dB SPL}$$

(Note: log of 1 = 0)

Adding the notation SPL, for **sound pressure level**, indicates that we have used the standard pressure of 20 micropascals as p_o in our calculation. In referring to the decibels or sound pressure of a sound stimulus, the term **level** or **sound level** is usually used.

Now let's calculate dB for two higher pressure levels. First, we multiply pressure by 10, so $p = 200$:

$$dB = 20\log(p/p_o) = 20\log(200/20) = 20(\log 10)$$
$$= 20(1) = 20 \text{ dB SPL}$$

(Note: log 10 = 1)

Notice that *multiplying* pressure by 10 *adds* 20 dB. Now let's multiple by 10 again, so $p = 2,000$:

$$dB = 20\log(p/p_o) = 20\log(2,000/20) = 20(\log 100)$$
$$= 20(2) = 40 \text{ dB SPL}$$

(Note: log 100 = 2)

Notice that multiplying pressure by 10 again adds another 20 dB.

Because multiplying pressure by 10 only adds 20 dB, a large increase in amplitude causes a much smaller increase in dB. The right column of Table 11.1 shows that a range of amplitudes from 1 to 10,000,000 results in a range of decibels from 0 to 140.

Frequency Frequency, the other characteristic of a pure tone, is illustrated in Figure 11.4, which shows three different frequencies. Frequency, the number of cycles per second the change in pressure repeats, is the physical measure associated with our perception of pitch, with higher frequencies associated with higher pitches.

Frequency is indicated in units called **Hertz (Hz)**, in which 1 Hz is 1 cycle per second. Thus, the middle stimulus in Figure 11.4, which repeats five times in a second would be a 5-Hz tone. As we will see, humans can perceive frequencies ranging from about 20 Hz to 20,000 Hz.

Pure tones are important because they are simple and because they have been used extensively in auditory research. Pure tones are, however, rare in the environment. Sounds in the environment, such as those produced by musical instruments, people speaking, and the various sounds

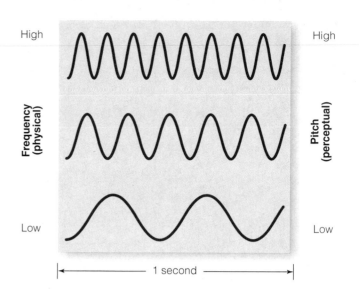

Figure 11.4 ❚ Three different frequencies of a pure tone. Higher frequencies are associated with the perception of higher pitches.

produced by nature and machines, have waveforms that are more complex than the pure tone's sine-wave pattern of pressure changes.

Pressure Changes: Complex Tones

To describe complex tones, we will focus on sounds created by musical instruments (in Chapter 13 we will consider sound produced when people speak). Figure 11.5a shows the waveform of a complex tone that would be created by a musical instrument. Notice that the waveform repeats. For example, the waveform in Figure 11.5a repeats four times. This property of repetition means that this complex tone, like a pure tone, is a *periodic tone*. The repetition rate of a complex tone is called the **fundamental frequency** of the tone.

An important property of periodic complex tones is that they consist of a number of pure tones. Because of this, we can "build" a complex tone by using a technique called **additive synthesis**, in which a number of sine-wave components are added together to create the complex tone. The starting point for creating a complex tone by additive synthesis is a single pure tone, like the one in Figure 11.5b, which has a frequency equal to the complex tone's fundamental frequency. The frequency of this fundamental is 200 Hz. We then add to the fundamental additional pure tones, each of which has a frequency that is a multiple of the fundamental. For the 200-Hz fundamental, the frequency of the second tone is 400 Hz (Figure 11.5c), the frequency of the third tone is 600 Hz (Figure 11.5d), and the fourth is 800 Hz (Figure 11.5e). These additional tones are higher **harmonics** of the tone. Adding the fundamental (also called the **first harmonic**) and the higher harmonics results in the waveform of the complex tone.

Another way to represent the harmonic components of a complex tone is by **frequency spectra**, shown on the right

Waveforms **Frequency spectra**

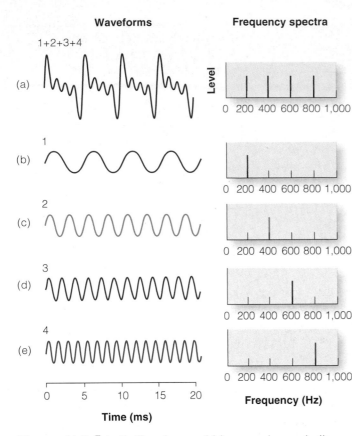

1+2+3+4

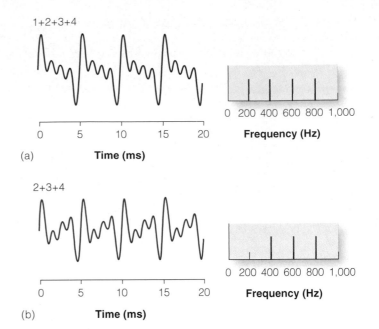

Figure 11.5 ▌ Left: Waveforms of (a) a complex periodic sound with a fundamental frequency of 200 Hz; (b) fundamental (first harmonic) = 200 Hz; (c) second harmonic = 400 Hz; (d) third harmonic = 600 Hz; (e) fourth harmonic = 800 Hz. Right: Frequency spectra for the tones on the left. *(Adapted from Plack, 2005.)*

Figure 11.6 ▌ (a) The complex tone from Figure 11.5a, with its frequency spectrum; (b) the same tone with its first harmonic removed. *(Adapted from Plack, 2005.)*

of Figure 11.5. The position of each line on the horizontal axis indicates the harmonic's frequency, and the height of the line indicates the harmonic's amplitude. Frequency spectra provide a way of indicating a complex tone's fundamental frequency and harmonics without drawing the tone's waveform.

Figure 11.6 shows what happens if we remove the first harmonic of a complex tone. The tone in Figure 11.6a is the one from Figure 11.5a, which has a fundamental frequency of 200 Hz. The tone in Figure 11.6b is the same tone with the first harmonic (200 Hz) removed. Note that removing a harmonic changes the tone's waveform, but that the repetition rate remains the same. Even though the fundamental is no longer present, the repetition rate, which is still 200 Hz, indicates the frequency of the harmonic.

You may wonder why the repetition rate remains the same even though the fundamental has been removed. Looking at the frequency spectrum on the right, we can see that the distance between harmonics equals the fundamental frequency. When the fundamental is removed, this spacing remains, so there is still information in the waveform indicating the frequency of the fundamental. In the following section, we will see that since a tone's pitch (perceiving a tone as "high" or "low") is related to repetition rate, removing

the fundamental does not change the tone's pitch, but the changed waveform does affect our perception of other qualities of the tone.

Perceiving Sound

As we described the physical characteristics of the sound stimulus, we mentioned the connection between amplitude (physical) and loudness (perceptual) (Figure 11.3) and between frequency (physical) and pitch (perceptual) (Figure 11.4). Let's now look more closely at the perceptual qualities of sound.

Loudness

Loudness is the quality most closely related to the amplitude or sound pressure, which is also called the level of an auditory stimulus. Thus, decibels are often associated with loudness, as shown in Table 11.1, which indicates that a sound with zero decibels is just barely detectable and 120 dB is extremely loud.

Figure 11.7 shows the relationship between decibels and loudness for a pure tone, determined by S. S. Stevens's magnitude estimation procedure (see Chapter 1, page 16). In this experiment, loudness was judged relative to a standard of a 1,000-Hz tone at 40 dB, which was assigned a value of 1. Thus, a tone that sounds 10 times louder than this standard would be judged to have a loudness of 10. This curve indicates that increasing the sound level by 10 dB almost (but not quite) doubles the sound's loudness. VL 2

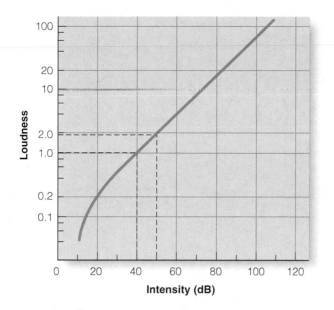

Figure 11.7 ▌ Loudness of a 1,000-Hz tone as a function of intensity, determined using magnitude estimation. The dashed lines show that increasing the intensity by 10 dB almost doubles the loudness. *(Adapted from Gulick, Gescheider, & Frisina, 1989.)*

Although decibels and loudness are related, it is important to distinguish between them. Decibels are a *physical measure,* whereas loudness is *psychological.* To appreciate the physical nature of dB, all you have to do is look back at the equation that indicates how dB are calculated. Notice that decibels are defined in terms of *pressure,* not perception.

Pitch

Pitch, the perceptual quality we describe as "high" or "low" is defined as *the attribute of auditory sensation in terms of which sounds may be ordered on a musical scale* (Bendor & Wang, 2005). We have seen that pitch is most closely related to the physical property of frequency. Low fundamental frequencies are associated with low pitches (like the sound of a tuba), and high fundamental frequencies are associated with high pitches (like the sound of a piccolo).

Tone height is the perceptual experience of increasing pitch that accompanies increases in a tone's fundamental frequency. Starting at the lowest note on the piano, at the left end of the keyboard (fundamental frequency = 27.5 Hz), and moving to the right toward the highest note (fundamental = 4,166 Hz) creates the perception of increasing tone height (Figure 11.8). [VL]3

In addition to the increase in tone height that occurs as we move from the low to the high end of the piano keyboard, something else happens: the letters of the notes A, B, C, D, E, F, and G repeat, and we notice that notes with the same letter sound similar. Because of this similarity, we say that notes with the same letter have the same **tone chroma.** Every time we pass the same letter on the keyboard, we have gone up an interval called an **octave.** Tones separated by octaves have the same tone chroma. For example, each of the A's in Figure 11.8, indicated by the arrows, has the same tone chroma.

Interestingly, notes with the same chroma have fundamental frequencies that are multiples of one another. Thus, A_1 has a fundamental frequency of 27.5 Hz, A_2's is 55 Hz, A_3's is 110 Hz, and so on. Somehow this doubling of frequency for each octave results in similar perceptual experiences. Thus, a male with a low-pitched voice and a female with a high-pitched voice can be regarded as singing "in unison," even when their voices are separated by an octave or more.

We have been describing how pitch is associated with fundamental frequency, but let's consider what happens when the fundamental frequency is not present in a complex tone. Remember, from Figure 11.6, that removing the first harmonic changes a tone's waveform but not its repetition rate and that because the tone's repetition rate remains the same, the tone's pitch remains the same. The pitch, therefore, is determined not by the *presence* of the fundamental frequency, but by information, such as the spacing of the harmonics and the repetition rate of the waveform, that *indicates* the fundamental frequency.

The constancy of pitch, even when the fundamental or other harmonics are removed, is called the **effect of the missing fundamental,** and the pitch that we perceive in tones, and that has had harmonics removed, is called **periodicity pitch.** We will see soon, when we discuss a quality of tones called *timbre,* that although removing the fundamental does not affect a tone's pitch, it does cause a tone to sound different, just as an oboe and a trumpet that are playing the same note sound different. [VL]4,5

The phenomenon of periodicity pitch has a number of practical consequences. Consider, for example, what happens when you listen to someone talking to you on the telephone. Even though the telephone does not reproduce frequencies below about 300 Hz, we hear the low pitch of a male voice, which contains frequencies below 300 Hz, because of periodicity pitch created by higher harmonics (Truax, 1984).

The Range of Hearing

Just as we see light only within only a narrow band of wavelengths called the visible spectrum, we hear sound only within a specific range of frequencies, called the **range of hearing.**

The Audibility Curve The human range of hearing is depicted by the green curve in Figure 11.9. This is the **audibility curve,** which indicates the threshold for hearing determined by free-field presentation (listening to a loudspeaker) versus frequency. This curve indicates that the range of hearing is between about 20 Hz and 20,000 Hz and that we are most sensitive (the threshold for hearing is lowest) at frequencies between 2,000 and 4,000 Hz, which happens to be the range of frequencies that is most important for understanding speech. [VL]6

The light green area above the audibility curve is called the **auditory response area** because we can hear tones

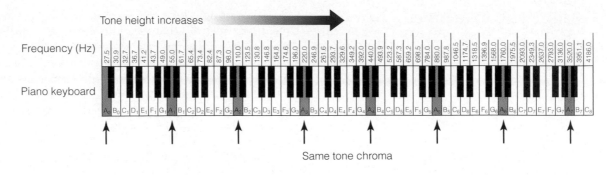

Figure 11.8 ▌ A piano keyboard, indicating the frequency associated with each key. Moving up the keyboard to the right increases frequency and tone height. Notes with the same letter, like the A's (arrows), have the same tone chroma.

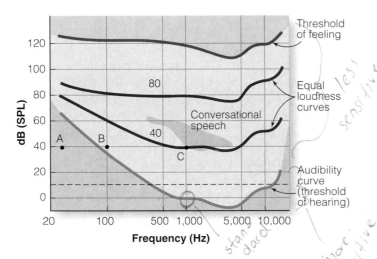

Figure 11.9 ▌ The audibility curve and the auditory response area. Hearing occurs in the light green area between the audibility curve (the threshold for hearing) and the upper curve (the threshold for feeling). Tones with combinations of dB and frequency that place them in the light red area below the audibility curve cannot be heard. Tones above the threshold of feeling result in pain. Where the dashed line at 10 dB traverses the auditory response area indicates which frequencies can be heard at 10 dB SPL. *(From Fletcher & Munson, 1933.)*

that fall within this area. At intensities below the audibility curve, we can't hear a tone. For example, we wouldn't be able to hear a 30-Hz tone at 40 dB SPL (point A). The upper boundary of the auditory response area is the curve marked "threshold of feeling." Tones with these high amplitudes are the ones we can "feel"; they can become painful and can cause damage to the auditory system.

Although humans hear frequencies between about 20 and 20,000 Hz, other animals can hear frequencies outside the range of human hearing. Elephants can hear stimuli below 20 Hz. Above the high end of the human range, dogs can hear frequencies above 40,000 Hz, cats can hear above 50,000 Hz, and the upper range for dolphins extends as high as 150,000 Hz.

Loudness Depends on Sound Pressure and Frequency The audibility curve and auditory response area indicate the loudness of pure tones depends not only on sound pressure but also on frequency. We can appreciate how loudness depends on frequency by comparing the loudness of two tones that have the same dB level but different frequencies. For example, point B in Figure 11.9 indicates where a 40-dB SPL 100-Hz tone is located in the response area, and point C indicates where a 40-dB SPL 1,000-Hz tone is located.

We can tell that these two tones would have very different loudnesses by considering their location relative to the audibility curve. The 100-Hz tone is located just above the audibility curve, so it is just above threshold and would just barely be heard. However, the 1,000-Hz tone is far above threshold, well into the auditory response area, so it would be much louder than the 100-Hz tone. Thus, to determine the loudness of any tone we need to know both its dB level *and* its frequency.

Another way to understand the relationship between loudness and frequency is by looking at the **equal loudness curves** in Figure 11.9. These curves indicate the number of decibels that create the same perception of loudness at different frequencies. An equal loudness curve is determined by presenting a standard tone of one frequency and dB level and having a listener adjust the level of tones with frequencies across the range of hearing to match the loudness of the standard. For example, the curve marked 40 in Figure 11.9 was determined by matching the loudness of frequencies across the range of hearing to the loudness of a 1,000-Hz 40-dB SPL tone. Similarly, the curve marked 80 was determined by matching the loudness of different frequencies to a 1,000-Hz 80-dB SPL tone.

Notice that the audibility curve and the equal loudness curve marked 40 bend up at high and low frequencies, but the equal loudness curve marked 80 is flat between 30 and 5,000 Hz, meaning that tones at a level of 80 dB are equally loud between these frequencies. The difference between the relatively flat 80 curve and the upward-bending curves at lower decibel levels explains something that happens as you adjust the volume control on your stereo system.

If you are playing music at a fairly high level—say, 80 dB SPL—you should be able to easily hear each of the frequencies in the music because, as the equal loudness curve for 80 indicates, all frequencies between about 20 Hz and 5,000 Hz sound equally loud at this level. However, when you turn the level down to 10 dB SPL, all frequencies don't sound equally loud. In fact, from the audibility curve in Figure 11.9 we can see that frequencies below about 400 Hz (the bass notes) and above about 12,000 Hz (the treble notes) are inaudible at 10 dB. (Notice that the dashed 10-dB line crosses the audibility curve at about 400 Hz and 12,000 Hz.) This means that frequencies lower than 400 Hz and higher than 12,000 Hz are not audible at 10 dB.

Being unable to hear very low and very high frequencies at low dB levels means that when you play music softly you won't hear the very low or very high frequencies. To compensate for this, some stereo receivers have a button labeled "loudness" which boosts the level of very high and very low frequencies when the volume control is turned down. (There are also *loudness* settings on some MP3 players.) This enables you to hear these frequencies even when the music is soft.

Timbre

Another perceptual quality of tones, in addition to pitch and loudness, is timbre (pronounced TIM-ber or TAM-ber). Timbre is the quality that distinguishes between two tones that have the same loudness, pitch, and duration, but still sound different. For example, when a flute and a bassoon play the same note with the same loudness, we can still tell the difference between these two instruments. We might describe the sound of the flute as *clear* or *mellow* and the sound of the bassoon as *nasal* or *reedy*. When two tones have the same loudness, pitch, and duration, but sound different, this difference is a difference in timbre.

Timbre is closely related to the harmonic structure of a tone. In Figure 11.10, frequency spectra indicate the harmonics of a guitar, a bassoon, and an alto saxophone playing the note G$_3$ with a fundamental frequency of 196 Hz. Both the relative strengths of the harmonics and the number of harmonics are different in these instruments. For example, the guitar has more high-frequency harmonics than either the bassoon or the alto saxophone. Although the frequencies of the harmonics are always multiples of the fundamental frequency, harmonics may be absent, as is true of some of the high-frequency harmonics of the bassoon and the alto saxophone.

The difference in the harmonics of different instruments is one factor that causes musical instruments to have different timbres. Timbre also depends on the time course of the tone's attack (the buildup of sound at the beginning of the tone) and on the time course of the tone's decay (the decrease in sound at the end of the tone). Thus, it is easy to tell the difference between a tape recording of a high note played on the clarinet and a recording of the same note played on the flute when the attack, the decay, and the sustained portion of the tone are heard. It is, however, difficult

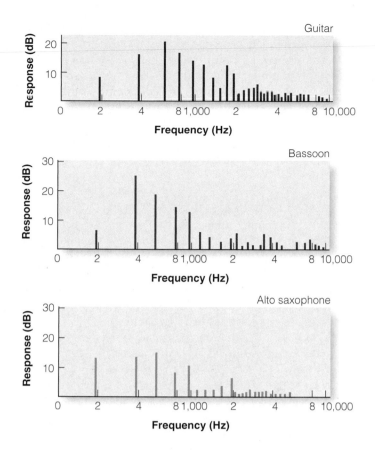

Figure 11.10 ▌ Frequency spectra for a guitar, a bassoon, and an alto saxophone playing a tone with a fundamental frequency of 196 Hz. The position of the lines on the horizontal axis indicates the frequencies of the harmonics, and their height indicates their intensities. *(From Olson, 1967.)*

to distinguish between the same instruments when the tone's attack and decay are eliminated by erasing the first and last 1/2-second of the recording (Berger, 1964; also see Risset & Mathews, 1969). **VL 7,8**

Another way to make it difficult to distinguish one instrument from another is to play an instrument's tone backward. Even though this does not affect the tone's harmonic structure, a piano tone played backward sounds more like an organ than a piano because the tone's original decay has become the attack and the attack has become the decay (Berger, 1964; Erickson, 1975). Thus, timbre depends both on the tone's steady-state harmonic structure and on the time course of the attack and decay of the tone's harmonics. **VL 9**

The sounds we have been considering so far—pure tones and the tones produced by musical instruments—are all periodic sounds. That is, the pattern of pressure changes repeats, as in the tone in Figure 11.5a. There are also aperiodic sounds, which have sound waves that do not repeat. Examples of aperiodic sounds would be a door slamming shut, people talking, and noises such as the static on a radio not tuned to a station. The sounds produced by these events are more complex than musical tones, but many of these sound stimuli can also be analyzed into a number of simpler frequency components. We will describe how we perceive speech stimuli in Chapter 13. We will focus in this chapter on pure tones and musical tones because these sounds are the ones that have been used in most of the basic research on the operation of the auditory system. In the next section, we will begin considering how the sound stimuli we have been describing are processed by the auditory system so that we can experience sound.

The Ear

The auditory system must accomplish three basic tasks before we can hear. First, it must deliver the sound stimulus to the receptors. Second, it must transduce this stimulus from pressure changes into electrical signals, and third, it must process these electrical signals so they can indicate qualities of the sound source such as pitch, loudness, timbre, and location.

We begin our description of how the auditory system accomplishes these tasks by focusing on the ear, at the beginning of the auditory system. Our first question, "How does energy from the environment reach the receptors?" takes us on a journey through what Diane Ackerman (1990) has described as a device that resembles "a contraption some ingenious plumber has put together from spare parts." An overall view of this "contraption" is shown in Figure 11.11. The ear is divided into three divisions: outer, middle, and inner. We begin with the outer ear.

The Outer Ear

When we talk about ears in everyday conversation, we are usually referring to the pinnae, the structures that stick out from the sides of the head. Although this most obvious part of the ear is important in helping us determine the location of sounds and is of great importance for those who wear eyeglasses, it is the part of the ear we could most easily do without. The major workings of the ear are found within the head, hidden from view.

Sound waves first pass through the outer ear, which consists of the pinna and the auditory canal (Figure 11.11). The auditory canal is a tubelike structure about 3 cm long in adults that protects the delicate structures of the middle ear from the hazards of the outside world. The auditory canal's 3-cm recess, along with its wax, protects the delicate tympanic membrane, or eardrum, at the end of the canal and helps keep this membrane and the structures in the middle ear at a relatively constant temperature.

In addition to its protective function, the outer ear has another effect: to enhance the intensities of some sounds by means of the physical principle of resonance. Resonance occurs in the auditory canal when sound waves that are reflected back from the closed end of the auditory canal interact with sound waves that are entering the canal. This interaction reinforces some of the sound's frequencies, with the frequency that is reinforced the most being determined by the length of the canal. The frequency reinforced the most is called the resonant frequency of the canal.

We can appreciate how the resonant frequency depends on the length of the canal by noting how the tone produced by blowing across the top of a soda bottle changes as we drink more soda. Drinking more soda increases the length of the air path inside the bottle, which decreases the resonant frequency, and this creates a lower-pitched tone. Measurements of the sound pressures inside the ear indicate that the resonance that occurs in the auditory canal has a slight amplifying effect on frequencies between about 1,000 and 5,000 Hz.

The Middle Ear

When airborne sound waves reach the tympanic membrane at the end of the auditory canal, they set it into vibration, and this vibration is transmitted to structures in the middle ear, on the other side of the tympanic membrane. The middle ear is a small cavity, about 2 cubic centimeters in volume, which separates the outer and inner ears (Figure 11.12). This cavity contains the ossicles, the three smallest bones in the body. The first of these bones, the malleus (also known

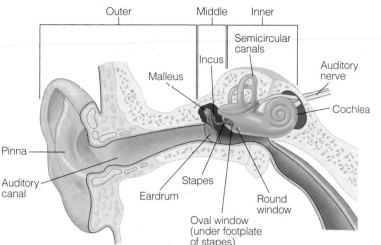

Figure 11.11 ▎ The ear, showing its three subdivisions—outer, middle, and inner. *(From Lindsay & Norman, 1977.)*

as the *hammer*), is set into vibration by the tympanic membrane, to which it is attached, and transmits its vibrations to the incus (or *anvil*), which, in turn, transmits its vibrations to the stapes (or *stirrup*). The stapes then transmits its vibrations to the inner ear by pushing on the membrane covering the **oval window.**

Why are the ossicles necessary? We can answer this question by noting that both the outer ear and middle ear are filled with air, but the inner ear contains a watery liquid that is much denser than the air (Figure 11.13). The mismatch between the low density of the air and the high density of this liquid creates a problem: pressure changes in the air are transmitted poorly to the much denser liquid. This mismatch is illustrated by the difficulty you would have hearing people talking to you if you were underwater and they were above the surface.

If vibrations had to pass directly from the air in the middle ear to the liquid in the inner ear, less than 1 percent of the vibrations would be transmitted (Durrant & Lovrinic, 1977). The ossicles help solve this problem in two ways: (1) by concentrating the vibration of the large tympanic membrane onto the much smaller stapes, which increases the pressure by a factor of about 20 (Figure 11.14a); and (2) by being hinged to create a lever action that creates an effect similar to what happens when a fulcrum is placed under a board, so pushing down on the long end of the board makes it possible to lift a heavy weight on the short end (Figure 11.14b). We can appreciate the effect of the ossicles by noting that in patients whose ossicles have been damaged beyond surgical repair, it is necessary to increase the sound by a factor of 10 to 50 to achieve the same hearing as when the ossicles were functioning.

Not all animals require the concentration of pressure and lever effect provided by the ossicles in the human. For example, there is only a small mismatch between the density of water, which transmits sound in a fish's environment, and the liquid inside the fish's ear. Thus, fish have no outer or middle ear.

The middle ear also contains the **middle-ear muscles,** the smallest skeletal muscles in the body. These muscles are attached to the ossicles, and at very high sound intensities they contract to dampen the ossicle's vibration, thereby protecting the structures of the inner ear against potentially painful and damaging stimuli.

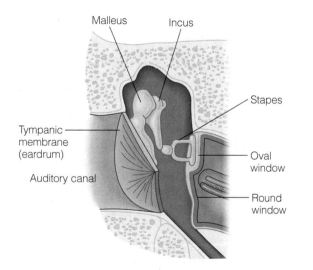

Figure 11.12 ▎ The middle ear. The three bones of the middle ear transmit the vibrations of the tympanic membrane to the inner ear.

Figure 11.13 ▎ Environments inside the outer, middle, and inner ears. The fact that liquid fills the inner ear poses a problem for the transmission of sound vibrations from the air of the middle ear.

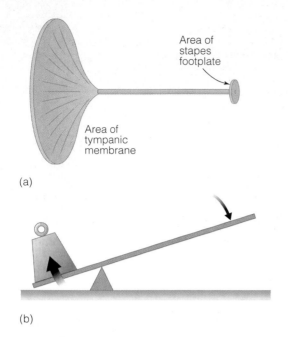

(a)

(b)

Figure 11.14 ▌ (a) A diagrammatic representation of the tympanic membrane and the stapes, showing the difference in size between the two. (b) How lever action can amplify a small force, presented on the right, to lift the large weight on the left. The lever action of the ossicles amplifies the sound vibrations reaching the tympanic inner ear. *(Adapted from Schubert, 1980.)*

The Inner Ear

The main structure of the **inner ear** is the liquid-filled **cochlea**, the snail-like structure shown in green in Figure 11.11, and shown partially uncoiled in Figure 11.15a. The liquid inside the cochlea is set into vibration by the movement of the stapes against the oval window. We can see the structure inside the cochlea more clearly by imagining how it would appear if uncoiled to form a long straight tube (Figure 11.15b). The most obvious feature of the uncoiled cochlea is that the upper half, called the *scala vestibuli,* and the lower half, called the *scala tympani,* are separated by a structure called the **cochlear partition**. This partition extends almost the entire length of the cochlea, from its base near the stapes to its apex at the far end. Note that this diagram is not drawn to scale and so doesn't show the cochlea's true proportions. In reality, the uncoiled cochlea would be a cylinder 2 mm in diameter and 35 mm long.

We can best see the structures within the cochlear partition by taking a cross section cut of the cochlea, as shown in Figure 11.15b, and looking at the cochlea end-on and in cross section, as in Figure 11.16a. When we look at the cochlea in this way, we see that the cochlear partition contains a large structure called the **organ of Corti**. Figure 11.16b shows the following key structures of the organ of Corti.

■ The hair cells, shown in red in Figure 11.16b, and in Figure 11.17, which is a view looking down on the

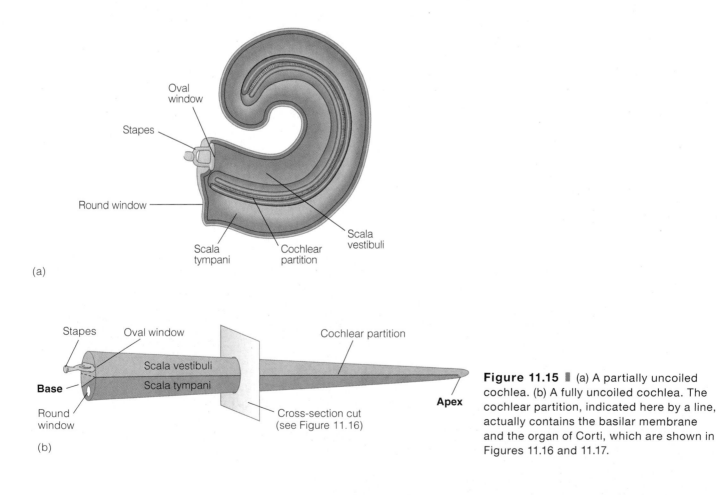

(a)

(b)

Figure 11.15 ▌ (a) A partially uncoiled cochlea. (b) A fully uncoiled cochlea. The cochlear partition, indicated here by a line, actually contains the basilar membrane and the organ of Corti, which are shown in Figures 11.16 and 11.17.

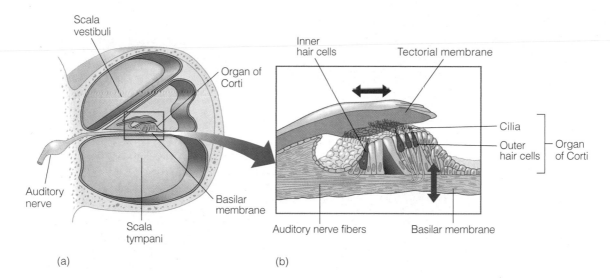

Figure 11.16 ▌ (a) Cross section of the cochlea. (b) Close-up of the organ of Corti, showing how it rests on the basilar membrane. Arrows indicate the motions of the basilar membrane and tectorial membrane that are caused by vibration of the cochlear partition. *(Adapted from Denes & Pinson, 1993.)*

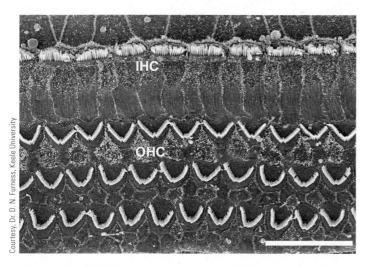

Figure 11.17 ▌ Electron micrograph looking down on the organ of Corti of a mouse. Note the one row of inner hair cells (IHC) and three rows of outer hair cells (OHC). The white structures are hair cell cilia.

organ of Corti, are the receptors for hearing. The **cilia**, which protrude from the tops of the cells, are where the sound acts to produce electrical signals. There are two types of hair cells, the **inner hair cells** and the **outer hair cells**. There are about 3,500 inner hair cells and 12,000 outer hair cells in the human ear (Møller, 2000).

- The **basilar membrane** supports the organ of Corti and vibrates in response to sound.

- The **tectorial membrane** extends over the hair cells.

One of the most important events in the auditory process is the bending of the cilia of the inner hair cells, which are responsible for transduction—the conversion of the vibrations caused by the sound stimulus into electrical signals. As we will see later, the major role of the outer hair cells is to increase the vibration of the basilar membrane.

The cilia bend because the in-and-out movement of the stapes creates pressure changes in the liquid inside the cochlea that sets the cochlear partition into an up-and-down motion, as indicated by the blue arrow in Figure 11.16b. This up-and-down motion of the cochlear partition causes two effects: (1) it sets the organ of Corti into an up-and-down vibration, and (2) it causes the tectorial membrane to move back and forth, as shown by the red arrow. These two motions cause the cilia of the inner hair cells to bend because of their movement against the surrounding liquid and affects the outer hair cells because some of the cilia are in contact with the tectorial membrane (Dallos, 1996).

Figure 11.18 shows what happens when the cilia bend. Movement in one direction (Figure 11.18a) opens channels in the membrane, and ions flow into the cell. Remember from our description of the action potential in Chapter 2 (see page 28) that electrical signals occur in neurons when ions flow across the cell membrane. The ion flow in the inner hair cells has the same effect, creating electrical signals that result in the release of neural transmitter from the inner hair cell. $\boxed{V_L}$ **10**

When the cilia bend in the other direction (Figure 11.18b), the ion channels close, so electrical signals are not generated. Thus, the back-and-forth bending of the hair cells causes alternating bursts of electrical signals (when the cilia bend in one direction) and no electrical signals (when the cilia bend in the opposite direction).

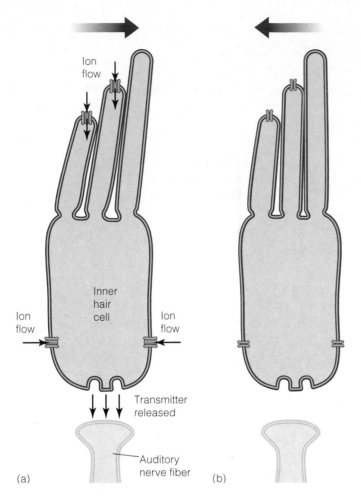

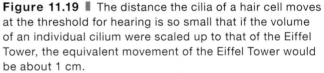

Figure 11.18 ▌ (a) Movement of hair cilia in one direction opens ion channels in the hair cell, which results in the release of neurotransmitter onto an auditory nerve fiber. (b) Movement in the opposite direction closes the ion channels, so there is no ion flow and no transmitter release.

Figure 11.19 ▌ The distance the cilia of a hair cell moves at the threshold for hearing is so small that if the volume of an individual cilium were scaled up to that of the Eiffel Tower, the equivalent movement of the Eiffel Tower would be about 1 cm.

The amount the cilia of the inner hair cells must bend to cause an electrical signal is extremely small. At the threshold for hearing, cilia movements as small as 100 trillionths of a meter (100 picometers) can generate a response in the hair cell. To give you an idea of just how small a movement this is, consider that if we were to increase the size of a cilium so it was as big as the 325-meter high Eiffel Tower, the movement of the cilia would translate into a movement of the pinnacle of the Eiffel Tower of only 1 cm (Figure 11.19; Hudspeth, 1983, 1989).

Given the small amount of movement needed to hear a sound, it isn't surprising that the auditory system can detect extremely small pressure changes. In fact, the auditory system can detect pressure changes so small that they cause the eardrum to move only 10^{-11} cm, a dimension that is less than the diameter of a hydrogen atom (Tonndorf & Khanna, 1968), and the auditory system is so sensitive that the air pressure at threshold in the most sensitive range of hearing is only 10 to 15 dB above the air pressure generated by the random movement of air molecules. This means that

if our hearing were much more sensitive than it is now, we would hear the background hiss of colliding air molecules!

The Representation of Frequency in the Cochlea

One of the major goals of research on hearing has been to understand the physiological mechanisms behind our perception of pitch. Because our perception of pitch is closely linked to a tone's frequency, a great deal of research has focused on determining how frequency is represented by the firing of neurons in the auditory system. The classic research on this problem was done by Georg von Békésy, who won the Nobel Prize in physiology and medicine in 1961 for his research on the physiology of hearing.

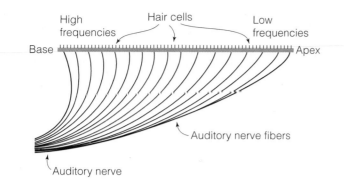

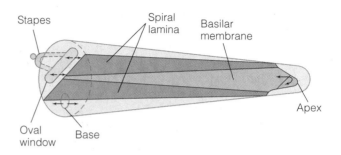

Figure 11.20 ▍ Hair cells all along the cochlea send signals to nerve fibers that combine to form the auditory nerve. According to place theory, low frequencies cause maximum activity at the apex end of the cochlea, and high frequencies cause maximum activity at the base. Activation of the hair cells and auditory nerve fibers indicated in red would signal that the stimulus is in the middle of the frequency range for hearing.

Békésy's Place Theory of Hearing

Békésy proposed the place theory of hearing, which states that the frequency of a sound is indicated by the place along the cochlea at which nerve firing is highest. Figure 11.20 represents the basilar membrane, which stretches from the base of the cochlea, near the vibrating stapes, to the apex, near the end of the cochlea. There are hair cells associated with each place along the basilar membrane and auditory nerve fibers associated with the hair cells.

According to place theory, low frequencies cause maximum activity in the hair cells and auditory nerve fibers at the apex end of the basilar membrane, and high frequencies cause maximum activity in hair cells and auditory nerve fibers at the base of the membrane. Thus, the frequency of a tone is indicated by the *place* along the basilar membrane at which auditory nerve fibers are activated.

Békésy came to this conclusion by determining how the basilar membrane vibrated in response to different frequencies. He determined this in two ways: (1) by actually observing the vibration of the basilar membrane and (2) by building a model of the cochlea that took into account the physical properties of the basilar membrane.

Békésy observed the vibration of the basilar membrane by boring a hole in cochleas taken from animal and human cadavers, presenting different frequencies of sound, and observing the membrane's vibration by using a technique similar to that used to create "stop-action" photographs of high-speed events, which enabled him to see the membrane's position at different points in time (Békésy, 1960). He found that the vibrating motion of the basilar membrane is similar to the motion that occurs when one person holds the end of a rope and "snaps" it, sending a wave traveling down the rope. This traveling wave motion of the basilar membrane is shown in Figure 11.21.

Békésy also determined how the basilar membrane vibrates by analyzing its structure. In this analysis he took

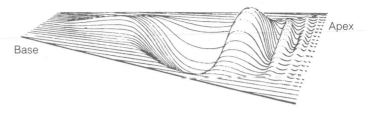

Figure 11.21 ▍ A perspective view showing the traveling wave motion of the basilar membrane. This picture shows what the membrane looks like when the vibration is "frozen" with the wave about two thirds of the way down the membrane. *(From Tonndorf, 1960.)*

Figure 11.22 ▍ A perspective view of an uncoiled cochlea, showing how the basilar membrane gets wider at the apex end of the cochlea. The spiral lamina is a supporting structure that makes up for the basilar membrane's difference in width at the base and the apex ends of the cochlea. *(From Schubert, 1980.)*

note of two important facts: (1) the base of the basilar membrane (the end located nearest the stapes) is three or four times narrower than the apex of the basilar membrane (the end of the membrane located at the far end of the cochlea; Figure 11.22); and (2) the base of the membrane is about 100 times stiffer than the apex. Using this information, Békésy constructed models of the cochlea that revealed that the pressure changes in the cochlea cause the basilar membrane to vibrate in a traveling wave.

Figure 11.23 shows the traveling wave caused by a pure tone, at three successive moments in time. The solid horizontal line represents the basilar membrane at rest. Curve 1 shows the position of the basilar membrane at one moment during its vibration, and curves 2 and 3 show the positions of the membrane at two later moments. From these curves we can see that over a period of time most of the membrane vibrates, but that some parts vibrate more than others. The envelope of the traveling wave, which is indicated by the dashed line, indicates the maximum displacement that the traveling wave causes at each point along the membrane. This maximum displacement is important because the amount that the hair cell's cilia move depends on how far the basilar membrane is displaced. Therefore, hair cells located near the place where the basilar membrane vibrates the most will be stimulated the most strongly, and the nerve fibers associated with these hair cells will therefore fire the most strongly.

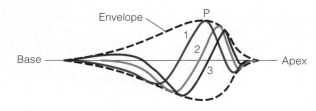

Figure 11.23 ▮ Vibration of the basilar membrane, showing the position of the membrane at three instants in time, indicated by the blue, green, and red lines, and the envelope of the vibration, indicated by the black dashed line. P indicates the peak of the basilar membrane vibration. *(From Békésy, 1960.)*

Békésy's (1960) observations of the basilar membrane's vibrations led him to conclude that the envelope of the traveling wave of the basilar membrane has two important properties:

1. The envelope has a peak amplitude at one point on the basilar membrane. The envelope of Figure 11.23 indicates that point P on the basilar membrane is displaced the most by the traveling wave. Thus, the hair cells near point P will send out stronger signals than those near other parts of the membrane.

2. The position of this peak on the basilar membrane is a function of the frequency of the sound. We can see in Figure 11.24, which shows the envelopes of vibration for stimuli ranging from 25 to 1,600 Hz, that low frequencies cause maximum vibration near the apex. High frequencies cause less of the membrane to vibrate, and the maximum vibration is near the base. (One way to remember this relationship is to imagine low-frequency waves as being long waves that reach farther.)

Evidence for Place Theory

Békésy's linking of the place on the cochlea with the frequency of the tone has been confirmed by measuring the electrical response of the cochlea and of individual hair cells and auditory nerve fibers. For example, placing disc electrodes at different places along the length of the cochlea and measuring the electrical response to different frequencies results in a **tonotopic map**—an orderly map of frequencies along the length of the cochlea (Culler et al., 1943). This result, shown in Figure 11.25, confirms the idea that the apex of the cochlea responds best to low frequencies and the base responds best to high frequencies. More precise electrophysiological evidence for place coding is provided by determining that auditory nerve fibers that signal activity at different places on the cochlea respond to different frequencies.

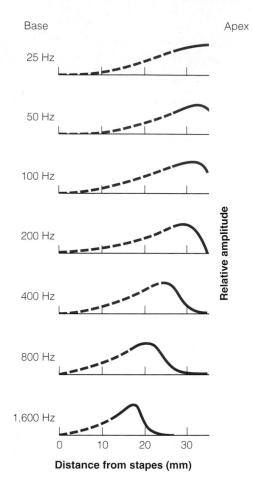

Figure 11.24 ▮ The envelope of the basilar membrane's vibration at frequencies ranging from 25 to 1,600 Hz, as measured by Békésy (1960). These envelopes were based on measurements of damaged cochleas. The envelopes are more sharply peaked in healthy cochleas.

METHOD ▮ **Neural Frequency Tuning Curves**

Each hair cell and auditory nerve fiber responds to a narrow range of frequencies. This range is indicated by each neuron's **frequency tuning curve**. This curve is determined by presenting pure tones of different frequencies and measuring how many decibels are necessary to cause the neuron to fire. This decibel level is the threshold for that frequency. Plotting the threshold for each frequency results in frequency tuning curves like the ones in Figure 11.26. The arrow under each curve indicates the frequency to which the neuron is most sensitive. This frequency is called the **characteristic frequency** of the particular auditory nerve fiber.

The frequency tuning curves in Figure 11.26 were recorded from auditory nerve fibers that originated at different places along the cochlea. As we would expect from Békésy's place theory, the fibers originating near the base of the cochlea have high characteristic frequencies, and those originating near the apex have low characteristic frequencies.

The idea that the frequency of a tone is represented by the firing of fibers located at specific places along the cochlea has also been supported by the results of psychophysical experiments that make use of the phenomenon of auditory masking. **Auditory masking** occurs in everyday experience any time your ability to hear a sound is decreased by the presence of other sounds. For example, if you are standing on the street having a conversation with a friend and the sound of a passing bus makes it difficult to hear what your friend is saying, the sound of the bus has *masked* the sound of your friend's voice.

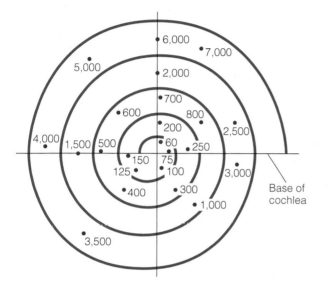

Figure 11.25 ▊ Tonotopic map of the guinea pig cochlea. Numbers indicate the location of the maximum electrical response for each frequency. *(From Culler, E. A., Coakley, J. D., Lowy, K., & Gross, N., A revised frequency map of the Guinea pig cochlea, American Journal of Psychology, 56, 1943, 475–500, figure 11. Copyright © 1943 by the Board of Trustees of the University of Illinois. Used with the permission of the University of Illinois.)*

METHOD ▌ Auditory Masking

In the laboratory, an auditory masking experiment is carried out using the procedure diagramed in Figure 11.27. First, the threshold intensity is determined at a number of frequencies, by presenting test tones (blue arrows) and determining the lowest intensity for each test tone that can just be heard (Figure 11.27a). Then, an intense masking stimulus (red arrow) is presented at one frequency. This stimulus, which corresponds to the passing bus in the example above, makes it more difficult to hear the low-intensity test tones. While the masking stimulus is sounding, the thresholds for all of the test tones are re-determined (Figure 11.27b). The increased sizes of some of the arrows indicates that the intensity of the test tones must be increased to hear them. Typically, the presence of the masking tone causes the largest increase in threshold for test tones at or near the masking tone's frequency, but the effect does spread to test tones that are above and below the masking tone's frequency.

Figure 11.28 shows the results of a masking experiment in which the masking tone contained frequencies between 365 and 455 Hz (Egan & Hake, 1950). The height of the curve indicates how much the intensity of the test tone had to be increased to be heard. Notice that the thresholds for frequencies near the masking tone are raised the most. Also notice that this curve is not symmetrical. That is, the masking effect spreads more to high frequencies than to low frequencies. $\boxed{V_L}$ **12**

We can relate the larger effect of masking on high-frequency tones to the vibration of the basilar membrane by looking at Figure 11.29, which reproduces the vibration patterns from Figure 11.24 caused by 200- and 800-Hz test tones and a 400-Hz masking tone. We can see how a 400-Hz masking tone would affect the 200- and 800-Hz tones by noting how their vibration patterns overlap. Notice that the pattern for the 400-Hz tone, which is shaded,

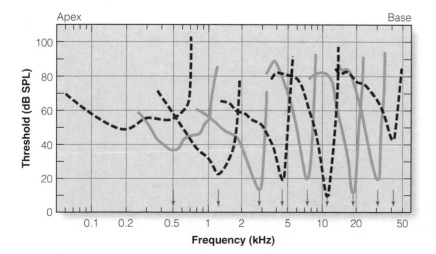

Figure 11.26 ▊ Frequency tuning curves of cat auditory nerve fibers. The characteristic frequency of each fiber is indicated by the arrows along the frequency axis. The frequency scale is in kilohertz (kHz), where 1 kHz = 1,000 Hz. *(From Palmer, A. R., Physiology of the cochlear nerve and cochlear nucleus, British Medical Bulletin on Hearing, 43, 1987, 838–855, by permission of Oxford University Press.)*

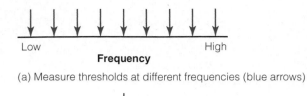

Low — Frequency — High

(a) Measure thresholds at different frequencies (blue arrows)

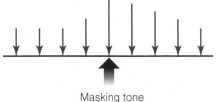

Masking tone

(b) Remeasure thresholds with the masking tone present

Figure 11.27 ❚ The procedure for a masking experiment. (a) Threshold is determined across a range of frequencies. Each blue arrow indicates a frequency where the threshold is measured. (b) The threshold is redetermined at each frequency (blue arrows) in the presence of a masking stimulus (red arrow). The larger blue arrows indicate that the intensities must be increased to hear these test tones when the masking tone is present.

almost totally overlaps the pattern for the higher-frequency 800-Hz tone, but does not overlap the peak vibration of the lower-frequency 200-Hz tone. We would therefore expect the masking tone to interfere more with the 800-Hz tone than with the 200-Hz tone, and this greater interference is what causes the greater masking effect at higher frequencies. Thus, Békésy's description of the envelope of the basilar membrane's vibration predicts the masking function in Figure 11.28.

All of the results we have described—(1) description of the traveling wave, (2) tonotopic maps on the cochlea, (3) frequency tuning curves, and (4) masking experiments—support the link between frequency and activation of specific places along the basilar membrane. The way the cochlea separates frequencies along its length has been described

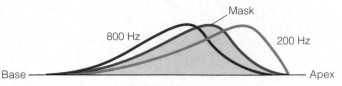

Base — Apex

Figure 11.29 ❚ Vibration patterns caused by 200- and 800-Hz test tones, and the 400-Hz mask (shaded), taken from basilar membrane vibration patterns in Figure 11.24. Notice that the vibration caused by the masking tone overlaps the 800-Hz vibration more than the 200-Hz vibration.

as an acoustic prism (Fettiplace & Hackney, 2006). Just as a prism separates white light, which contains all wavelengths in the visible spectrum, into its components, the cochlea separates frequencies entering the ear into activity along different places on the basilar membrane. This property of the cochlea is particularly important when considering complex tones that contain many frequencies.

How the Basilar Membrane Vibrates to Complex Tones

To show how the basilar membrane responds to complex tones, we return to our discussion of musical tones from page 263. Remember that musical tones consist of a fundamental frequency and harmonics that are multiples of the fundamental.

Research that has measured how the basilar membrane responds to complex tones shows that the basilar membrane vibrates to the fundamental and to each harmonic, so there are peaks in the membrane's vibration that correspond to each harmonic. Thus, a complex tone with a number of harmonics (Figure 11.30a), will cause peak vibration of the basilar membrane at places associated with the frequency of each harmonic (Figure 11.30b) (Hudspeth, 1989). The acoustic prism idea therefore describes how the cochlea

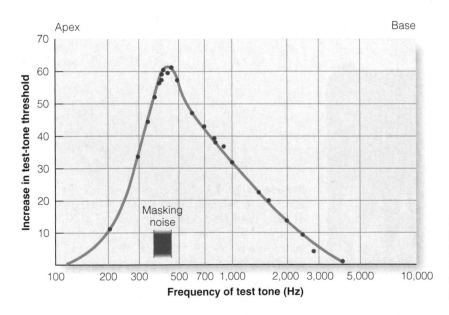

Figure 11.28 ❚ Results of Egan and Hake's (1950) masking experiment. The threshold increases the most near the frequencies of the masking noise, and the masking effect spreads more to high frequencies than to low frequencies. *(From Egan & Hake, 1950.)*

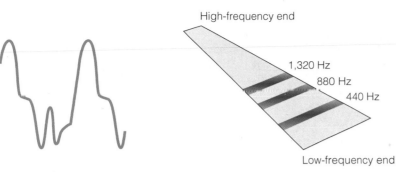

(a) Complex tone
(440, 880, 1,320 Hz harmonics)

(b) Basilar membrane

High-frequency end

1,320 Hz

880 Hz

440 Hz

Low-frequency end

Figure 11.30 ▌ (a) Waveform of a complex tone consisting of three harmonics. (b) Basilar membrane. The shaded areas indicate locations of peak vibration associated with each harmonic in the complex tone.

sorts each of the harmonics of a musical tone onto different places along the basilar membrane.

Updating Békésy

While the basic idea behind Békésy's place theory has been confirmed by many experiments, some results were difficult to explain based on the results of Békésy's original experiments. Consider, for example, Békésy's picture of how the basilar membrane vibrates to different frequencies in Figure 11.24. A problem with these curves is that two nearby frequencies would cause overlapping and almost identical patterns of vibration. Yet psychophysical experiments show that we can distinguish small differences in frequency. For example, Békésy's vibration patterns for 400 and 405 Hz are almost identical, but we can distinguish between these two frequencies.

The explanation for this discrepancy is that Békésy made his measurements of basilar membrane vibration in cochleas isolated from animal and human cadavers. When modern researchers measured the basilar membrane's vibration in live cochleas using techniques more sensitive than the ones available to Békésy, they found that the peak vibration for a particular frequency is much more sharply localized than Békésy had observed, so there is less overlap between the curves for nearby frequencies (Johnstone & Boyle, 1967; Khanna & Leonard, 1982; Narayan et al., 1998).

These new measurements explained our ability to distinguish between small differences in frequency, but they also posed a new question: Why does the basilar membrane vibrate more sharply in healthy cochleas? The answer is that the outer hair cells expand and contract in response to the vibration of the basilar membrane, and this expansion and contraction, which only occurs in live cochleas, amplifies and sharpens the vibration of the basilar membrane.

Figure 11.31 shows how this works. When vibration of the basilar membrane causes the cilia of the outer hair cells to bend in one direction, this causes the entire outer hair cell to elongate, which pushes on the basilar membrane (Figure 11.31a). Bending in the other direction causes the hair cells to contract, which pulls on the basilar membrane (Figure 11.31b). This pushing and pulling increases the motion of the basilar membrane and sharpens its response to

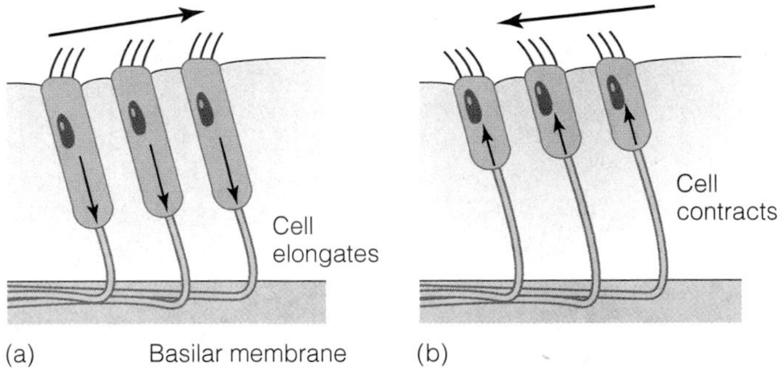

Cell elongates

Cell contracts

(a)

Basilar membrane

(b)

Figure 11.31 ▌ The outer hair cells (a) elongate when cilia bend in one direction; (b) contract when the cilia bend in the other direction. This results in an amplifying effect on the motion of the basilar membrane. The difference between elongated and contracted lengths is exaggerated in this figure.

specific frequencies. For this reason, the action of the outer hair cells is called the **cochlear amplifier**. $\boxed{V_L}$ **13**

The importance of the outer hair cell's amplifying effect is illustrated by the frequency tuning curves in Figure 11.32. The solid blue curve shows the frequency tuning of a cat's auditory nerve fiber with a characteristic frequency of about 8,000 Hz. The dashed red curve shows what happened when the outer hair cells were destroyed by a chemical that attacked the outer hair cells but left the inner hair cells intact. It now takes much higher intensities to get the fiber to respond, especially in the frequency range to which the fiber originally responded best (Fettiplace & Hackney, 2006; Liberman & Dodds, 1984).

How the Timing of Neural Firing Can Signal Frequency

We have been focusing on the idea that frequency is signaled by *which* fibers in the cochlea fire to a tone. But frequency can also be signaled by *how* the fibers fire. Remember from Figure 11.18 that inner hair cells respond when their cilia bend in one direction and stop responding when the cilia bend in the opposite direction. Figure 11.33 shows how the bending of the cilia follows the increases and decreases in the pressure of a pure tone sound stimulus. When the pressure increases, the cilia bend to the right and firing occurs. When the pressure decreases, the cilia bend to

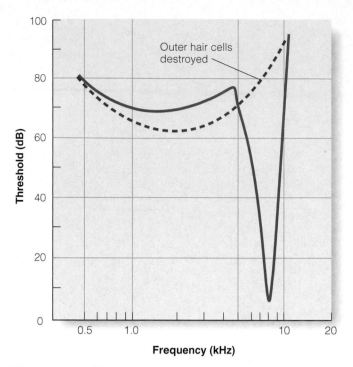

Figure 11.32 ▌ Effect of OHC damage on frequency tuning curve. The solid blue curve is the frequency tuning curve of a neuron with a characteristic frequency of about 8,000 Hz. The dashed red curve is the tuning curve for the same neuron after the outer hair cells were destroyed by injection of a chemical. *(Adapted from Fettiplace & Hackney, 2006.)*

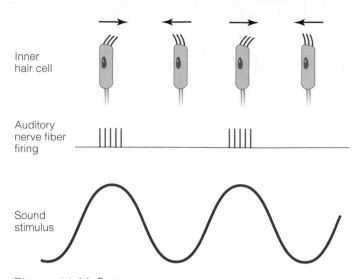

Figure 11.33 ▌ How hair cell activation and auditory nerve fiber firing are synchronized with pressure changes of the stimulus. The auditory nerve fiber fires when the cilia are bent to the right. This occurs at the peak of the sine-wave change in pressure.

the left and no firing occurs. This means that the hair cells fire in synchrony with the rising and falling pressure of the sound stimulus. For high-frequency tones, a hair cell may not fire every time the pressure increases because it needs to rest after it fires (see *refractory period,* Chapter 2, page 30). But when the cell does fire, it fires at the peak of the sound stimulus.

This property of firing at the same place in the sound stimulus is called **phase locking**. When the firing of a number of auditory nerve fibers is phase locked to the stimulus, they fire in bursts separated by silent intervals, and the timing of these bursts matches the frequency of the stimulus. Thus, the rate of bursting of auditory nerve fibers provides information about the frequency of the sound stimulus.

The connection between the frequency of a sound stimulus and the timing of the auditory nerve fiber firing is called **temporal coding**. Measurements of the pattern of firing for auditory nerve fibers indicate that phase locking occurs up to a frequency of about 4,000 Hz.

From the research we have described, we can conclude that frequency is coded in the cochlea and auditory nerve based both on which fibers are firing (place coding) and on the timing of nerve impulses in auditory nerve fibers (temporal coding). Place coding is effective across the entire range of hearing, and temporal coding up to 4,000 Hz, the frequency at which phase locking stops operating. This information for frequency originates in the inner hair cells

and their auditory nerve fibers. In the next section we will consider how hearing is affected if the hair cells or auditory nerve fibers are damaged.

Hearing Loss Due to Hair Cell Damage

The audibility curve in Figure 11.9 is the average curve for people with normal hearing. There are, however, a number of ways that hearing loss can occur, and this is reflected in changes in the audibility function. Hearing loss can occur for a number of reasons: (1) blockage of sound from reaching the receptors, called **conductive hearing loss**; (2) damage to the hair cells, and (3) damage to the auditory nerve or the brain. Hearing loss due to damage to the hair cells, auditory nerve, or brain is called **sensorineural hearing loss**. We will focus on hearing loss caused by hair cell damage. $\boxed{V_L}$ **14**

We have already seen that damage to the outer hair cells can have a large effect on hearing. Inner hair cell damage, as we would expect, also causes a large effect, with hearing loss occurring for the frequencies corresponding to the frequencies signaled by the damaged hair cells. The most common form of sensorineural hearing loss is presbycusis, which means "old hearing." (Remember that the equivalent term for vision is *presbyopia,* or "old eye." See page 46.)

Presbycusis The loss of sensitivity associated with presbycusis, which is greatest at higher frequencies, accompanies aging and affects males more severely than females. Figure 11.34 shows the progression of loss as a function of age. Unlike the visual problem of presbyopia, which is an inevitable consequence of aging, presbycusis is apparently caused by factors in addition to aging, since people in preindustrial cultures, who have not been exposed to the noises that accompany industrialization or to drugs that could

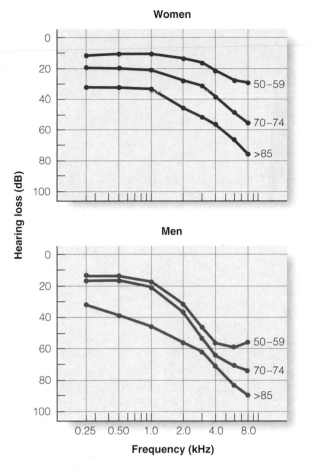

Figure 11.34 ▮ Hearing loss associated with presbycusis as a function of frequency for groups of women and men of various ages. Losses are expressed relative to hearing for a group of young persons with normally functioning auditory systems, which is assigned a value of 0 at each frequency. *(Adapted from Dubno, in press.)*

damage the ear, often do not experience large decreases in high-frequency hearing in old age. This may be why males, who historically have been exposed to more workplace noise than females, as well as to noises associated with hunting and wartime, experience a greater presbycusis effect.

Noise-Induced Hearing Loss Noise-induced hearing loss occurs when loud noises cause degeneration of the hair cells. This degeneration has been observed in examinations of the cochleas of people who have worked in noisy environments and have willed their ear structures to medical research. Damage to the organ of Corti is often observed in these cases. For example, examination of the cochlea of a man who worked in a steel mill indicated that his organ of Corti had collapsed and no receptor cells remained (J. Miller, 1974). More controlled studies, of animals that are exposed to loud sounds, provide further evidence that high-intensity sounds can damage or completely destroy inner hair cells (Liberman & Dodds, 1984).

Because of the danger to hair cells posed by workplace noise, the United States Occupational Safety and Health Agency (OSHA) has mandated that workers not be exposed to sound levels greater than 85 decibels for an 8-hour work shift. But in addition to workplace noise hazards, other sources of intense sound can cause hearing loss due to hair cell damage.

If you turn up the volume on your MP3 player, you are exposing yourself to what hearing professionals call leisure noise. Other sources of leisure noise are activities such as recreational gun use, riding motorcycles, playing musical instruments, and working with power tools. A number of studies have demonstrated hearing loss in people who listen to MP3 players (Peng et al., 2007), play in rock/pop bands (Schmuziger et al., 2006), use power tools (Dalton et al., 2001), and attend sports events (Hodgetts & Liu, 2006). The amount of hearing loss depends on the level of sound intensity and the duration of exposure. Given the high levels of sound that occur in these activities, such as the levels above 90 dB that can occur for the three hours of a hockey game (Figure 11.35) and levels as high as 90 db while using power tools in woodworking, it isn't surprising that both temporary and permanent hearing losses are associated with these leisure activities.

The potential for hearing loss from listening to music at high volume on MP3 players for extended periods of time cannot be overemphasized, because at their highest settings MP3 players reach levels of 100 dB or higher—far above OSHA's recommended maximum of 85 dB. This has led Apple Computer to add a setting to iPods that limits the maximum volume, and also to develop a device that can monitor playing time and listening levels and can either gradually reduce maximum sound levels or provide a warning signal when playing time and sound intensity have reached potentially damaging levels. (This feature was not in use, however, at the time this was written.)

One suggestion for minimizing the potential for hearing damage is to follow this simple rule, proposed by James Battey, Jr., director of the National Institute on Deafness and Other Communication Disorders: If you can't hear someone talking to you at arm's length, turn down the music ("More Noise Than Signal," 2007). If you can't bring yourself to turn down the volume, another thing that would help is to take a 5-minute break from listening at least once an hour!

TEST YOURSELF 11.2

1. Describe the structure of the ear, focusing on the role that each component plays in transmitting the vibrations that enter the outer ear to the auditory receptors in the inner ear.
2. Describe Békésy's place theory of hearing and the physiological and psychophysical evidence that supports his theory. Be sure you understand the following: tonotopic map, frequency tuning curve, auditory masking.
3. What does it mean to say that the basilar membrane is an acoustic prism?

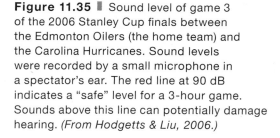

Figure 11.35 ▌ Sound level of game 3 of the 2006 Stanley Cup finals between the Edmonton Oilers (the home team) and the Carolina Hurricanes. Sound levels were recorded by a small microphone in a spectator's ear. The red line at 90 dB indicates a "safe" level for a 3-hour game. Sounds above this line can potentially damage hearing. *(From Hodgetts & Liu, 2006.)*

---

4. How can the frequency of a sound be signaled by the *timing* of nerve firing? Be sure you understand phase locking.
5. What is the connection between hair cell damage and hearing loss? Exposure to occupational or leisure noise and hearing loss?

Central Auditory Processing

So far we have been focusing on how the ear creates electrical signals in hair cells and fibers of the auditory nerve. But perception does not occur in the ear or in the auditory nerve. Just as for vision, we need to follow signals from the receptors to more central structures in order to understand perception.

Pathway From the Cochlea to the Cortex

The auditory nerve carries the signals generated by the inner hair cells away from the cochlea and toward the auditory receiving area in the cortex. Figure 11.36 shows the pathway the auditory signals follow from the cochlea to the auditory cortex. Auditory nerve fibers from the cochlea synapse in a sequence of subcortical structures—structures below the cerebral cortex. This sequence begins with the **cochlear nucleus** and continues to the **superior olivary nuclei** in the brain stem, which consists of a number of subdivisions that serve different functions, the **inferior colliculus** in the midbrain, and the **medial geniculate nucleus** in the thalamus. (Meanwhile, signals from the retina are synapsing in the nearby lateral geniculate nucleus in the thalamus.)

From the medial geniculate nucleus, fibers continue to the primary **auditory receiving area (A1)**, in the temporal lobe of the cortex. If you have trouble remembering this

sequence of structures, remember the acronym SONIC MG (a very fast sports car), which represents the three structures between the cochlear nucleus and the auditory cortex, as follows: SON = superior olivary nuclei; IC = inferior colliculus; MG = medial geniculate nucleus.

A great deal of processing occurs as signals travel through the subcortical structures along the pathway from the cochlea to the cortex. Some of this processing can be related to perception. For example, processing in the superior olivary nuclei is important for determining auditory localization—where a sound appears to originate in space (Litovsky et al., 2002)—and it has been suggested that one of the functions of subcortical structures in general is to respond to individual features of complex stimuli (Frisina, 2001; Nelken, 2004). There has been a tremendous amount of research on these subcortical structures, but we will focus on what happens once the signals reach the cortex.

Auditory Areas in the Cortex

As we begin discussing the auditory areas of the cortex, some of the principles we will describe may seem familiar because many of them are similar to principles we introduced in our description of the visual system in Chapters 3 and 4. Most of the discoveries about the auditory areas of the cortex are fairly recent compared to discoveries about the visual areas, so in some cases discoveries about the auditory cortex that are being made today are similar to discoveries that were made about the visual system 10 or 20 years earlier. For example, you may remember that it was initially thought that most visual processing occurred in the primary visual receiving area (V1), but beginning in the 1970s, it became obvious that other areas were also important for visual processing.

Recently it has been discovered that a similar situation occurs for hearing. At first most research focused on the primary auditory receiving area (A1) in the temporal lobe

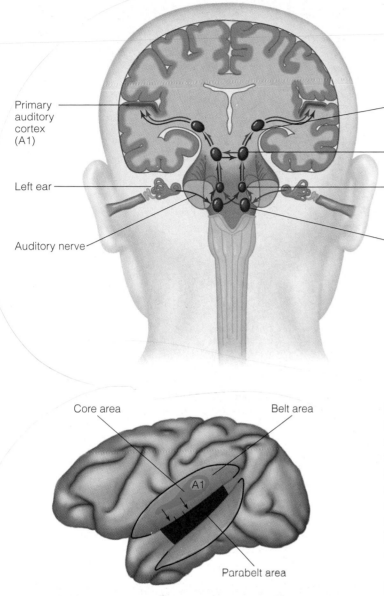

Primary auditory cortex (A1)

Left ear

Auditory nerve

Medial geniculate nucleus

Inferior colliculus

Superior olivary nuclei

Cochlear nucleus

Figure 11.36 ▌ Diagram of the auditory pathways. This diagram is greatly simplified, as numerous connections between the structures are not shown. Note that auditory structures are bilateral—they exist on both the left and right sides of the body—and that messages can cross over between the two sides. *(Adapted from Wever, 1949.)*

Core area

Belt area

A1

Parabelt area

Figure 11.37 ▌ The three main auditory areas in the cortex are the core area, which contains the primary auditory receiving area (A1), the belt area, and the parabelt area. Signals, indicated by the arrows, travel from core, to belt, to parabelt. The dark lines show where the temporal lobe was pulled back to show areas that would not be visible from the surface. *(From Kaas, Hackett, & Tramo, 1999.)*

(Figure 11.37). But now additional areas have been discovered that extend auditory areas in the cortex beyond A1. Research on the monkey describes cortical processing as starting with a core area, which includes the primary auditory cortex (A1) and some nearby areas. Signals then travel to an area surrounding the core, called the belt area, and then to the parabelt area (Kaas et al., 1999; Rauschecker, 1997, 1998).

One of the properties of these auditory areas is hierarchical processing—signals are first processed in the core and then travel to the belt and then to the parabelt. One

finding that supports this idea is that the core area can be activated by simple sounds, such as pure tones, but areas outside the core require more complex sounds, such as auditory noise that contains many frequencies, human vocalizations, and monkey "calls" (Wissinger et al., 2001). The fact that areas outside the auditory core require complex stimuli is similar to the situation in the visual system in which neurons in the visual cortex (V1) respond to spots or oriented lines, but neurons in the temporal lobe respond to complex stimuli such as faces and landmarks (Figures 4.33 and 4.35).

In addition to discovering an expanded area in the temporal lobe that is devoted to hearing, recent research has shown that other parts of the cortex also respond to auditory stimuli (Figure 11.38; Poremba et al., 2003). What is particularly interesting about this picture of the brain is that some areas in the parietal and frontal lobes are activated by both visual and auditory stimuli. Some of this overlap between the senses occurs in areas associated with the *what* and *where* streams for vision (Ungerleider & Mishkin, 1982); interestingly enough, *what* and *where* streams, indicated by the arrows in Figure 11.38, have recently been discovered in the auditory system.

What and *Where* Streams for Hearing

Piggybacking on visual research of the 1970s that identified *what* and *where* streams in the visual system (see page 88), evidence began accumulating in the late 1990s for the existence of *what* and *where* streams for hearing (Kaas & Hackett, 1999; Romanski et al., 1999). The *what,* or *ventral,* stream (green arrow) starts in the anterior (front) part of the core and belt, and extends to the prefrontal cortex. The *where,* or

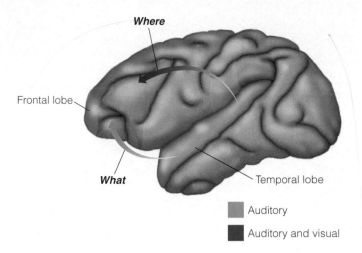

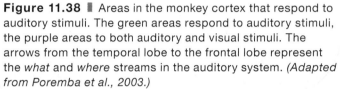

Auditory

Auditory and visual

Figure 11.38 ▌ Areas in the monkey cortex that respond to auditory stimuli. The green areas respond to auditory stimuli, the purple areas to both auditory and visual stimuli. The arrows from the temporal lobe to the frontal lobe represent the *what* and *where* streams in the auditory system. *(Adapted from Poremba et al., 2003.)*

dorsal, stream (red arrow) starts in the posterior (rear) part of the core and belt, and extends to the parietal cortex and the prefrontal cortex (Figure 11.38). The *what* stream is responsible for identifying sounds, and the *where* stream for locating sounds.

Some of the first evidence supporting the idea of *what* and *where* streams for hearing came from experiments that showed that neurons in the *anterior* of the core and belt responded to the sound pattern of a stimulus, and neurons in the *posterior* of the core and belt responded to the location of the stimulus (Rauschecker & Tian, 2000; Tian et al., 2001).

Cases of human brain damage also support the *what/where* idea (Clarke et al., 2002). For example, Figure 11.39a shows the areas of the cortex that are damaged in J.G., a 45-year-old man with temporal lobe damage caused by a head injury, and E.S., a 64-year-old woman with parietal and frontal lobe damage caused by a stroke. Figure 11.39b shows that J.G. can locate sounds, but his recognition is poor, whereas E.S. can recognize sounds, but her ability to locate them is poor. Thus, J.G.'s *what* stream is damaged, and E.S's *where* stream is damaged.

The *what/where* division is also supported by brain scan experiments. Figure 11.40 shows areas of cortex that are more strongly activated by recognizing pitch (a *what* task) in green and areas that are more strongly activated by detecting a location (a *where* task) in red (Alain et al., 2001). Notice that pitch processing causes greater activation in ventral parts of the brain (anterior temporal cortex), and sound localization causes greater activity in dorsal regions (parietal cortex and frontal cortex). (Also see Meader et al., 2001; Wissinger et al., 2001.) Thus, evidence from animal recording, the effects of brain damage, and brain scanning supports the idea that different areas of the brain are activated for identifying sounds and for localizing sounds (also see Lomber & Malhotra, 2008).

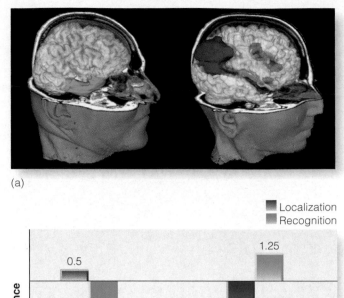

(a)

(b)

Figure 11.39 ▌ (a) Colored areas indicate brain damage for J.G. (left) and E.S. (right). (b) Performance on recognition test (green bar) and localization test (red bar). *(Clarke, S., Thiran, A. B., Maeder, P., Adriani, M., Vernet, O., Regli, L., Cuisenaire, O., & Thiran, J.-P., What and where in human auditory systems: Selective deficits following focal hemispheric lesions, Experimental Brain Research, 147, 2002, 8–15.)*

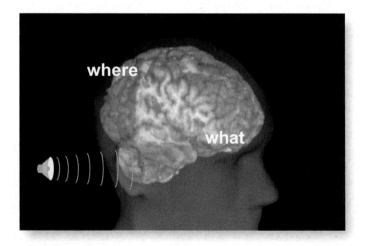

Figure 11.40 ▌ Areas associated with *what* (green) and *where* (red) auditory functions as determined by brain imaging. *(Alain, C., Arnott, S. R., Hevenor, S., Graham, S., & Grady, C. L. (2001). "What" and "where" in the human auditory systems. Proceedings of the National Academy of Sciences, 98, 12301–12306. Copyright 2001 National Academy of Sciences, U.S.A.)*

Pitch and the Brain

What are the brain mechanisms that determine pitch, and where are they located? We have already seen that the frequencies of pure tones are mapped along the length of the cochlea, with low frequencies represented at the apex and higher frequencies at the base (Figure 11.25). This tonotopic map also occurs in the structures along the pathway from the cochlea to the cortex, and in the primary auditory receiving area, A1. Figure 11.41 shows the tonotopic map in the monkey cortex, which shows that neurons that respond best to low frequencies are located to the left, and neurons that respond best to higher frequencies are located to the right (Kosaki et al., 1997; also see Reale & Imig, 1980; Schreiner & Mendelson, 1990).

Linking Physiological Responding and Perception

Just because neurons that respond best to specific frequencies are organized into maps on the cortex doesn't mean that these neurons are responsible for pitch perception. As we noted for vision, we need to go beyond mapping a system's physiological characteristics to demonstrate a link between physiology and perception. Just as finding neurons in the visual cortex that respond to oriented bars does not mean that these neurons are responsible for our perception of the bars, finding neurons in the auditory cortex that respond to specific frequencies doesn't mean that these neurons are responsible for our perception of pitch. What is necessary in both cases is to demonstrate links between the physiological processes and perception.

Mark Tramo and coworkers (2002) studied a patient they called A, who had suffered extensive damage to his auditory cortex on both sides of the brain due to two successive strokes. The green bars in Figure 11.42 show that A's ability to judge the duration of sounds and the orientation of lines was normal, but the red bars show that his ability to judge the direction of frequency change (high to low or low to high) and to detect differences in pitch were much worse than normal. This result, which shows that damage to the auditory cortex affects the ability to discriminate between frequencies, led Tramo to conclude that the auditory cortex is important for discriminating between different frequencies.

Another approach that has been used to study the link between pitch and the brain is to find neurons in the brain that respond to both pure tones and complex tones that differ in their harmonics but have the same pitch. Remember from page 264 that the pitch of a complex tone is determined by information about the tone's fundamental frequency; even when the fundamental or other harmonics are removed, the repetition rate of a stimulus remains the same, so the perception of the tone's pitch remains the same.

Daniel Bendor and Xiaoqin Wang (2005) did this experiment on a marmoset, a primate that has a range of hearing similar to that of humans. When they recorded from single neurons in an area just outside the primary auditory cortex and in nearby areas, they found some neurons that responded similarly to complex tones with the same fundamental frequency, but with different harmonic structures. For example, Figure 11.43a shows the frequency spectra for a tone with a fundamental frequency of 182 Hz. In the top record, the tone contains the fundamental frequency and the second and third harmonics; in the second record, harmonics 4–6 are present; and so on, until at the bottom, only harmonics 12–14 are present. The important thing about these stimuli is that even though they contain different frequencies (for example, 182, 364, and 566 Hz in the top record; 2,184, 2,366, and 2,548 Hz in the bottom record), they are all perceived as having a pitch corresponding to the 182-Hz fundamental.

The corresponding cortical response records (Figure 11.43b) show that these stimuli all caused an increase in firing. To demonstrate that this firing occurred only when information about the 182-Hz fundamental frequency was present, Bendor and Wang showed that the neuron responded well to a 182-Hz tone presented alone, but not to any of the harmonics when they were presented alone. These cortical neurons, therefore, responded only to stimuli associated with the 182-Hz tone, which is associated with a specific pitch. Because of this, Bendor and Wang call these neurons **pitch neurons**.

The two types of evidence we have just described—research showing that damage to the auditory cortex affects

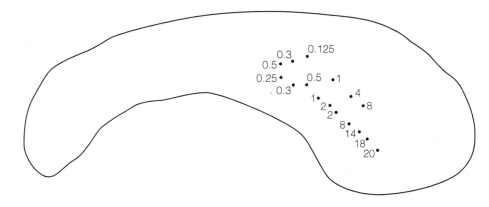

Figure 11.41 ▌ The outline of the core area of the monkey auditory cortex, showing the tonotopic map on the primary auditory receiving area, A1, which is located within the core. The numbers represent the characteristic frequencies (CF) of neurons in thousands of Hz. Low CFs are on the left, and high CFs are on the right. *(Adapted from Kosaki et al., 1997.)*

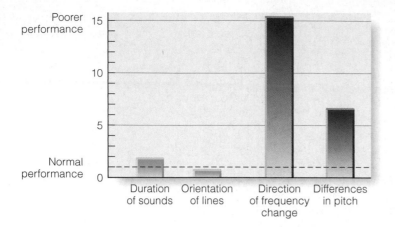

Figure 11.42 ▌ Performance of patient A, with auditory cortex damage, on four tasks. See text for details. *(Based on data from Tramo et al., 2002.)*

the ability to discriminate between frequencies, and the discovery of pitch neurons that respond to stimuli associated with a specific pitch even if these stimuli have different harmonics—both support the idea that the auditory cortex is important for the perception of pitch.

How the Auditory Cortex Is Shaped by Experience

In Chapter 4 we described how the phenomenon of experience-dependent plasticity operates in the visual system. We described the Greeble experiments, which showed that training people to recognize Greebles increased the neural response to Greebles in the fusiform face area (FFA; see page 94). An example of experience-dependent plasticity in the auditory system is provided by experiments that show that training that involves a particular frequency increases the space devoted to that frequency in A1. Gregg Recanzone and coworkers (1993) demonstrated this by training owl monkeys to discriminate between two frequencies near 2,500 Hz. After the training had produced a large improvement in the monkey's ability to tell the difference between frequencies, a tonotopic map of A1 was determined (Recanzone et al., 1993). The results indicate that compared to a monkey that had no discrimination training (Figure 11.44a), the trained monkey (Figure 11.44b) had much more space devoted to neurons that respond best to 2,500 Hz.

Experience-dependent plasticity for hearing has also been demonstrated for humans. Christo Pantev and co-workers (1998) showed that musical training enlarges the area of auditory cortex that responds to piano tones. They compared the cortical response to piano tones of musicians who had been playing their instruments for 12 to 28 years to the response of people who had never played an instrument. The results indicated that 25 percent more cortex was activated in musicians than in nonmusicians. Another study has shown that electrical activity elicited from the auditory areas of professional musicians is twice as strong as the activity elicited from the auditory areas of nonmusicians (Schneider et al., 2002).

Thus, just as visual areas of the brain are shaped by training with visual stimuli, auditory areas are shaped by training with auditory stimuli. Perhaps the most striking demonstration of shaping-by-training is an experiment by Jonathan Fritz and coworkers (2003), which showed how rapidly experience-dependent plasticity can occur for hearing. They demonstrated this by recording from neurons in the ferret while the animals were involved in an auditory task.

Figure 11.45a is a plot that shows how a neuron in the ferret's auditory cortex responds to different frequencies before training. In this plot, red and yellow indicates increased firing in response to sound, green indicates an average level of firing, and blue indicates decreased firing in response to sound. Thus, this plot indicates how the neuron responds to frequencies between 2,000 and 16,000 Hz (ver-

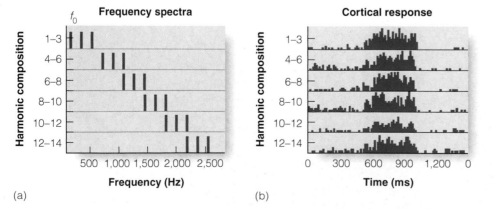

(a) (b)

Figure 11.43 ▌ Records from a pitch neuron recorded from the marmoset auditory cortex. (a) Frequency spectra for tones with a fundamental frequency of 182 Hz. Each tone contains three harmonic components of the 182-Hz fundamental frequency. (b) Response of the neuron to each stimulus. *(Adapted from Bendor & Wang, 2005.)*

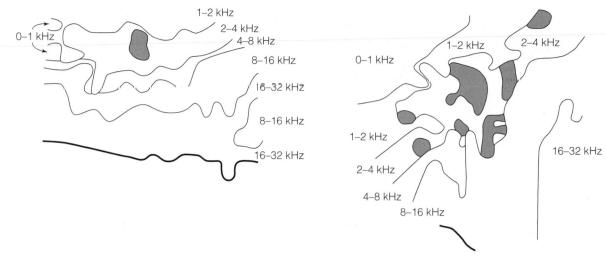

(a) Normal owl monkey   (b) Monkey trained on 2,500 Hz task

Figure 11.44 | (a) Tonotopic map of the owl monkey's primary auditory receiving area (A1), showing areas that contain neurons with the characteristic frequencies indicated. The blue area contains neurons with CF = 2,500 Hz. (b) Tonotopic map of an owl monkey that was trained to discriminate between frequencies near 2,500 Hz. The blue areas indicate that after training more of the cortex responds best to 2,500 Hz. *(From Recanzone et al., 1993.)*

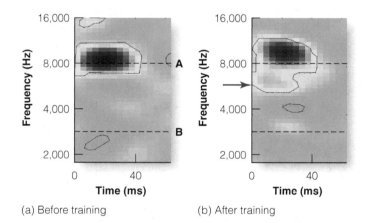

(a) Before training   (b) After training

Figure 11.45 | Response of a neuron in the ferret auditory cortex. (a) before training; (b) after training. See text for details. *(Reprinted by permission from Macmillan Publishers Ltd.: Fritz, J., Shamma, S., Elhilali, M., & Klein, D., Rapid task-related plasticity of spectrotemporal receptive fields in primary auditory cortex, Nature Neuroscience, 6, 1216–1223. Copyright 2003.)*

tical axis) at various times after the tone is presented (horizontal axis). For example, look at the dashed line labeled A in Figure 11.45a. Looking at the far left, we can see that just after an 8,000-Hz tone is presented, firing rate increases and then continues at a high rate for 40 ms. In contrast, the dashed line labeled B indicates that this neuron's firing rate is unaffected when a 3,000-Hz tone is presented.

Once Fritz and coworkers had determined the characteristics of a particular neuron, they trained the ferret to lick a water spout as it was hearing a series of complex sounds and to stop licking when it heard a pure tone. Thus,

in a particular block of trials the ferret was learning to be ready to respond to a particular frequency of pure tone.

After just a few trials in which the ferret responded to the pure tone, they remeasured the neuron's response function and obtained the plot in Figure 11.45b. The frequency of the training tone is indicated by the arrow. If we look directly to the right of this arrow, we can see that the neuron's response profile has changed so that its firing rate now increases to this frequency (indicated by yellow), whereas before training it remained about the same (indicated by green). Thus, just a small amount of training caused the neuron to become tuned to respond better to this frequency. What is amazing about this result is not only how rapidly it occurred, but that in many neurons the effect lasted for hours after the training. The auditory system, therefore, shapes its neurons to respond better to environmental stimuli that are behaviorally important to the animal.

Something to Consider: Cochlear Implants—Where Science and Culture Meet

Deafness, which affects about 600,000 people in the United States, is most often caused by damage to the hair cells in the cochlea. When this occurs, hearing aids are ineffective because the damaged hair cells cannot convert the amplified sound provided by the hearing aid into electrical signals. A solution to this problem has been provided by a device called a cochlear implant, in which electrodes are inserted in the cochlea to create hearing by electrically stimulating

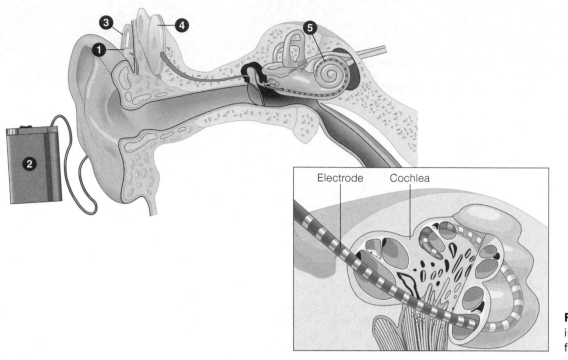

Figure 11.46 | Cochlear implant device. See text for details.

the cell bodies of auditory nerve fibers that are distributed along the length of the cochlea.

The Technology

The cochlear implant bypasses the damaged hair cells and stimulates auditory nerve fibers directly. The following are the basic components of a cochlear implant (Figure 11.46):

- The microphone (1), worn behind the person's ear, receives the sound signal, transforms it into electrical signals, and sends these signals to the sound processor.

- The sound processor (2), which looks like a small transistor radio, shapes the signal generated by the microphone to emphasize the information needed for the perception of speech by splitting the range of frequencies received by the microphone into a number of frequency bands. These signals are sent, in the form of an electrical code, from the processor to the transmitter. Newer versions of cochlear implants now package the entire sound processor in what looks like a behind-the-ear hearing aid.

- The transmitter (3), held in place by a magnet just behind the ear, transmits the coded signals received from the processor through the skin to the receiver.

- The receiver (4) is surgically mounted on the mastoid bone, beneath the skin. It picks up the coded signals from the transmitter and converts the code into signals that are sent to electrodes implanted inside the cochlea (5). These electrodes stimulate auditory nerve fibers at different places along the cochlea.

The implant makes use of the observation that there is a tonotopic map of frequencies on the cochlea, with high frequencies represented by activity near the base of the cochlea and low frequencies represented by activity at the apex of the cochlea. The most widely used implants therefore have a multichannel design that typically uses 22 electrodes to stimulate the cochlea at different places along its length, depending on the frequencies in the stimuli received by the microphone. Stimulation of the cochlea causes signals to be sent the auditory area of the cortex, and hearing results.

What does a person using this system hear? The answer to this question depends on the person. Most people with a cochlear implant are able to recognize a few everyday sounds, such as horns honking, doors closing, and water running. In addition, many people are able to perceive speech. In the best cases, people can perceive speech on the telephone, but it is more common for cochlear-implant recipients to use the sounds perceived from their implant in conjunction with speech reading, the observation of lip and face movements. In one test, 24 people scored 54 percent on a test of speech reading alone and 83 percent when speech reading was combined with sound from the implant. In addition, the implant enabled people to track speech much more rapidly—16 words per minute using speech reading alone and 44 words per minute with speech reading plus the implant (A. A. Brown et al., 1987; Owens, 1989). In another test it was found that deaf children who received a cochlear implant before the age of 5 were able to learn to produce speech more easily than children who received the implant when they were older (Tye-Murray et al., 1995).

According to the U.S. Food and Drug Administration, as of 2006 more than 112,000 people worldwide had received cochlear implants. The best results occur for people who were able to perceive speech before they became deaf. These people are most likely to understand speech with the aid of the implant because they already know how to connect the sounds of speech with specific meanings. Thus, these people's ability to perceive speech often improves with time, as 15-17 they again learn to link sounds with meanings.

The development of cochlear implants is an impressive demonstration of how basic research yields practical benefits. The technology of cochlear implants, which has made it possible to bring deaf adults and children into the world of hearing (Kiefer et al., 1996; Tye-Murray et al., 1995), is the end result of research that demonstrated the link between a sound's frequency and the firing of neurons in the cochlea and auditory nerve fibers.

The Controversy

Many deaf people have had strong negative emotions about cochlear implants. It might be hard for a hearing person to understand why. "After all," a hearing person might say, "don't cochlear implants offer an opportunity for deaf people to enter the world of the hearing?" But many deaf people see statements like this as part of the problem. To people in the deaf community, the cochlear implant is a symbol of the hearing world's desire to "fix" deaf people, even though deaf people can communicate perfectly well with sign language and have a rich and functioning culture that is every bit as vibrant and fulfilling as other cultures that are based on ethnicity or nationality. Thus, many in the deaf community, especially parents who are deaf and have deaf children, see the widespread use of cochlear implants, particularly in young children, as a threat to the existence of their culture, and in 1991 the National Association of the Deaf condemned the use of implants in children (CBS News, 2001; "Growing Up Different," 2001; Edwards, in press).

In addition to the cultural issue, there is also the fear that a young child receiving an implant will be handicapped in terms of language development if receiving the implant causes him or her to avoid learning to sign. The problem is that the sounds provided by the implant generally do not replace the richness of language that is available to someone who is a fluent signer, and early experience with language is important not only for communication, but for cognitive development in general.

This controversy about cochlear implants was highlighted in 2001 by an award-winning documentary called *The Sound and the Fury*. The controversy still continues; however, it may be cooling somewhat. The National Association of the Deaf, which opposed implants in 1991, changed its stand in 2000, issuing a statement that the deaf world "welcomes all individuals regardless of race, religion, ethnic background, socioeconomic status, cultural orientation, mode of communication, preferred language use, hearing status, educational background, and use of technologies." The statement also stresses that "implanted children are still deaf" and should be encouraged to develop both speech and sign skills accordingly (Edwards, in press). Reasons for this shift include improvements in cochlear implant technology and an increased awareness that a child who is exposed to both oral English and American Sign Language may be able to function in both hearing and deaf worlds without changing the child's positive identification as a deaf person.

THINK ABOUT IT

1. One of the principles that we introduced in studying vision is how perception can be determined by activity at all levels in the visual system, from receptors to the brain. What are some examples of this principle for the sense of hearing? (pp. 275, 283)

2. Presbycusis usually begins with loss of high-frequency hearing and gradually involves lower frequencies. From what you know about cochlear function, can you explain why the high frequencies are more vulnerable to damage? (p. 278)

3. Which auditory streams—*what, where,* or a combination of the two—would be involved in the following: (1) finding an object dropped in the dark based on hearing it roll across the rug and onto the floor; (2) recognizing a friend's voice on the telephone; (3) listening to music through headphones; (4) following the sound of an ambulance as it speeds down the street with its siren blaring. (p. 281)

IF YOU WANT TO KNOW MORE

1. *Activation of auditory cortex by vision.* Deaf people use the visual sense to help them understand speech, by speech reading. It has been shown that speech reading

activates the auditory cortex. Another example of one sense being activated by stimulation usually associated with another sense is that the visual cortex is activated when blind people use touch to read Braille. (p. 282)

Calvert, G. A., et al. (1997). Activation of auditory cortex during silent lipreading. *Science, 276,* 593–596.

Sadato, N., et al. (1996). Activation of the primary visual cortex by Braille reading blind subjects. *Nature, 380,* 526–528.

2. *Cross-modal experience: synaesthesia.* One of the most intriguing connections between the senses is a phenomenon called synaesthesia, in which presentation of stimuli from one sense can cause an experience associated with another sense. An example of this would be seeing light in response to sound.

Marks, L. (1975). On colored-hearing synaesthesia: Cross-modal translations of sensory dimensions. *Psychological Bulletin, 82,* 303–331.

Paulesu, E., et al. (1995). The physiology of colored hearing. *Brain, 118,* 661–676.

3. *Losing one sense can hurt another one.* There is evidence that deafness reduces performance on visual attention tasks and that a cochlear implant can improve both hearing and visual attention. (p. 285)

Quittner, A. L., et al. (1994). The impact of audition on the development of visual attention. *Psychological Science, 5,* 347–353.

KEY TERMS

Additive synthesis (p. 263)
Amplitude (p. 262)
Apex of the cochlea (p. 270)
Attack (p. 267)
Audibility curve (p. 265)
Auditory canal (p. 268)
Auditory masking (p. 274)
Auditory receiving area (A1) (p. 280)
Auditory response area (p. 265)
Base of the cochlea (p. 270)
Basilar membrane (p. 271)
Belt area (p. 281)
Characteristic frequency (p. 274)
Cilia (p. 271)
Cochlea (p. 270)
Cochlear amplifier (p. 277)
Cochlear implant (p. 285)
Cochlear nucleus (p. 280)
Cochlear partition (p. 270)
Conductive hearing loss (p. 278)
Core area (p. 281)
Decay (p. 267)
Decibel (p. 262)
Eardrum (p. 268)
Effect of the missing fundamental (p. 265)
Envelope of the traveling wave (p. 273)

Equal loudness curve (p. 266)
First harmonic (p. 263)
Frequency (p. 262)
Frequency spectrum (p. 263)
Frequency tuning curve (p. 274)
Fundamental frequency (p. 263)
Hair cells (p. 270)
Harmonics (p. 263)
Hertz (Hz) (p. 263)
Hierarchical processing (p. 281)
Incus (p. 269)
Inferior colliculus (p. 280)
Inner ear (p. 270)
Inner hair cells (p. 271)
Leisure noise (p. 279)
Level (p. 263)
Loudness (p. 264)
Malleus (p. 268)
Medial geniculate nucleus (p. 280)
Middle ear (p. 268)
Middle-ear muscles (p. 269)
Noise-induced hearing loss (p. 279)
Octave (p. 265)
Organ of Corti (p. 270)
Ossicles (p. 268)
Outer ear (p. 268)
Outer hair cells (p. 271)
Oval window (p. 269)

Parabelt area (p. 281)
Periodicity pitch (p. 265)
Phase locking (p. 278)
Pinna (p. 268)
Pitch (p. 265)
Pitch neuron (p. 283)
Place theory of hearing (p. 273)
Presbycusis (p. 278)
Pure tone (p. 262)
Range of hearing (p. 265)
Resonance (p. 268)
Resonant frequency (p. 268)
Sensorineural hearing loss (p. 278)
Sound (p. 261)
Sound level (p. 263)
Sound pressure level (SPL) (p. 263)
Sound wave (p. 261)
Stapes (p. 269)
Subcortical structure (p. 280)
Superior olivary nuclei (p. 280)
Tectorial membrane (p. 271)
Temporal coding (p. 278)
Timbre (p. 267)
Tone chroma (p. 265)
Tone height (p. 265)
Tonotopic map (p. 274)
Traveling wave (p. 273)
Tympanic membrane (p. 268)

MEDIA RESOURCES

The *Sensation and Perception* Book Companion Website

www.cengage.com/psychology/goldstein

See the companion website for flashcards, practice quiz questions, Internet links, updates, critical thinking exercises, discussion forums, games, and more!

CengageNOW

www.cengage.com/cengagenow

Go to this site for the link to CengageNOW, your one-stop shop. Take a pre-test for this chapter, and CengageNOW will generate a personalized study plan based on your test results. The study plan will identify the topics you need to review and direct you to online resources to help you mas-

ter those topics. You can then take a post-test to help you determine the concepts you have mastered and what you will still need to work on.

Virtual Lab

Your Virtual Lab is designed to help you get the most out of this course. The Virtual Lab icons direct you to specific media demonstrations and experiments designed to help you visualize what you are reading about. The number beside each icon indicates the number of the media element you can access through your CD-ROM, CengageNOW, or WebTutor resource.

The following lab exercises are related to material in this chapter:

1. *Decibel Scale* Demonstrates how loudness increases for a 10 dB increase in decibels.

2. *Loudness Scaling* Do a magnitude estimation experiment to determine the relationship between dB and loudness.

3. *Tone Height and Tone Chroma* A demonstration of tone height and tone chroma.

4. *Periodicity Pitch: Eliminating the Fundamental and Lower Harmonics* How your perception of a tone changes as harmonics are removed.

5. *Periodicity Pitch: St. Martin's Chimes With Harmonics Removed* How your perception of a melody changes as harmonics are removed.

6. *Frequency Response of the Ear* Shows how our ability to hear a tone that is always at the same dB level depends on its frequency.

7. *Harmonics of a Gong* A demonstration that enables you to hear each of the individual harmonics that make up the sound produced by a gong.

8. *Effect of Harmonics on Timbre* How adding harmonics to a tone changes the quality of the sound.

9. *Timbre of a Piano Tone Played Backward* How presenting piano tones backward (so the end of the tone comes first and the beginning come last) affects our perception of the tone's quality.

10. *Cochlear Mechanics: Cilia Movement* How the hair-cell cilia move back and forth in response to the sound stimulus. (Courtesy of Stephen Neely.)

11. *Cochlear Mechanics: Traveling Waves* How the basilar membrane vibrates in response to two different frequencies. (Courtesy of Stephen Neely.)

12. *Masking High and Low Frequencies* How a high-frequency test tone and a low-frequency test tone are affected by a masking tone.

13. *Cochlear Mechanics: Cochlear Amplifier* How changes in length of the outer hair cells amplify the vibration of the basilar membrane.

14. *Hearing Loss* How mild and moderate levels of hearing loss affect the perception of some common sounds. (Courtesy of Phonak, Inc.)

15. *Cochear Implant: Environmental Sounds* How a person with a cochlear implant perceives some common environmental sounds. (Courtesy of Sensimetrics Corporation.)

16. *Cochlear Implant: Music* How a person with a cochlear implant perceives music. (Courtesy of Sensimetrics Corporation.)

17. *Cochlear Implant: Speech* How a person with a cochlear implant perceives speech. (Courtesy of Sensimetrics Corporation.)

Chapter Contents

CHAPTER 12

Sound Localization and the Auditory Scene

OPPOSITE PAGE The band U2 performing at the opening of the 2002 Grammy awards at the Staples Center in Los Angeles. Our perception of music depends on the nature of the sound stimuli produced by musical instruments and the human voice, the acoustics of the venue where the music is being played, and the physiological functioning of the auditory system.
© Reuters/CORBIS

V̲L̲ The Virtual Lab icons direct you to specific animations and videos designed to help you visualize what you are reading about. The number beside each icon indicates the number of the clip you can access through your CD-ROM or your student website.

Some Questions We Will Consider:

▌ What makes it possible to tell where a sound is coming from in space? (p. 292)

▌ When we are listening to a number of musical instruments playing at the same time, how can we perceptually separate the sounds coming from the different instruments? (p. 299)

▌ Why does music sound better in some concert halls than in others? (p. 305)

You are in a small club, listening to a trio. The vocalist/ guitar is directly in front of you, the bass guitar to the right, and the keyboard to the left. You note that the sound seems more "spacious" in person than when you listen to it on your MP3 player, and even with your eyes closed you can easily locate the singer directly ahead, the bass guitar on the right, and the keyboard on the left.

In this chapter, we will consider how you are able to judge where sounds are coming from, even with your eyes closed. We will first describe the auditory stimuli and then how the auditory system processes these stimuli. We will also consider another aspect of your listening experience: your ability to hear the sounds produced by each of the musicians separately—even as they play together—and how you are able to make auditory sense of the sounds you hear in the environment. Finally, we will consider how your listening experience is affected by whether you are listening inside a room or outside.

Auditory Localization

When you perceive objects located at different positions based on their sounds, you are experiencing **auditory space**. Auditory space extends around your head in all directions, existing wherever there is a sound. To experience auditory space, close your eyes and notice the sounds around you, paying particular attention to the directions and distances of these sounds. Unless you are in an extremely quiet environment, you will probably be able to perceive objects (a computer humming, for example) and events (people talking, cars driving by) located at various positions in space.

These feats of locating objects in space based on their sound are examples of **auditory localization**. To study this ability to localize sounds, researchers have determined how well people can locate the position of a sound in three dimensions: the **azimuth**, which extends from left to right (Figure 12.1); **elevation**, which extends up and down; and the **distance** of the sound source from the listener. In this chapter, we will focus on the azimuth and elevation. The following demonstration will give you an idea of how well people can determine the azimuth and elevation of a sound source.

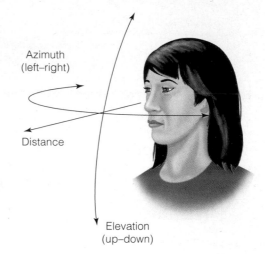

Figure 12.1 ▌ The three directions used for studying sound localization: azimuth (left-right); elevation (up-down); and distance.

DEMONSTRATION

Sound Localization

Have a friend close her eyes. Say that you are going to rattle your keys at various places around her head and that she should point to where the sound is coming from. Do this by varying the azimuth (left to right) and elevation (up and down) of the sound, and include some sounds both in front of and behind her head. Note how accurate she is for sounds in various locations. After you are through, ask your friend if she found some locations harder to judge than others. (There is substantial variability among different listeners in their ability to localize sounds, so you may want to try this on a few people.) ▌

Figure 12.2 shows an apparatus used to test sound localization, which makes it possible to present sounds at 227 different places on a sphere surrounding the listener. Controlled measurements of localization indicate that sounds directly in front are easiest to localize and sounds off to the side and behind the head are harder to localize (Carlile et al., 1997; Middlebrooks & Green, 1991).

The problems the auditory system faces in determining locations are formidable. We can appreciate one of the problems by comparing the information available for vision and for hearing in Figure 12.3. Visual information for the relative locations of the bird and the cat is contained in the images of the bird and the cat on the surface of the retina. But the ear is different. The bird's "tweet" and the cat's "meow" stimulate the cochlea based on their sound frequencies, and as we saw in Chapter 11, the place that is activated in the cochlea provides information that determines the sound's pitch and timbre. Because the place activated on the cochlea does not indicate a sound's location, the auditory system

Figure 12.2 ❙ In this sound localization tester at Wright-Patterson AFB in Dayton, Ohio, the listener is surrounded by 227 loudspeakers. *(Courtesy of Marc Ericson, Wright-Patterson Air Force Base, Dayton, OH.)*

must use other information to determine location. The information it uses involves **location cues** that are created by the way sound interacts with the listener's head and ears.

Binaural Cues for Sound Location

There are two **binaural cues**: *interaural time difference* and *interaural level difference*. Both are based on a comparison of the sound signals reaching the left and right ears. Sounds that are off to the side reach one ear before the other and are louder at one ear than the other.

Interaural Time Difference The interaural time difference (ITD) is based on the fact that there is a difference in when a sound reaches the left and right ears (Figure 12.4). If the source is located directly in front of the listener, at A, the distance to each ear is the same, and the sound reaches the left and right ears simultaneously. However, if a source is located off to the side, at B, the sound reaches the right ear before it reaches the left ear. Because the ITD becomes larger as sound sources are located more to the side, the magnitude of the ITD can be used as a cue to determine a sound's location. Behavioral research, in which listeners judge sound locations as ITD is varied, indicate that ITD is an effective cue for location of low-frequency sounds (Wightman & Kistler, 1997, 1998).

Interaural Level Difference The other binaural cue, **interaural level difference (ILD)**, is based on the difference in the sound pressure level (or just "level") of the sound

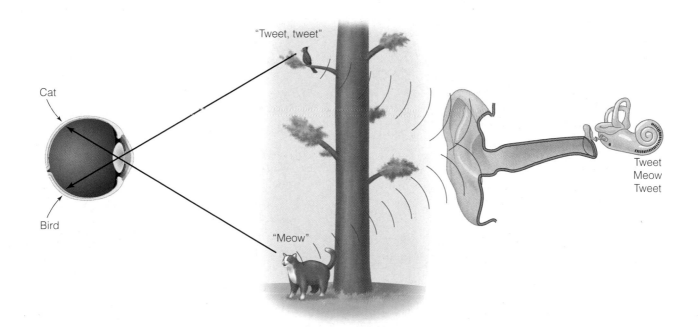

Figure 12.3 ❙ Comparing location information for vision and hearing. *Vision:* The bird and the cat are at different locations and are imaged on different places on the retina. *Hearing:* The frequencies in the sounds from the bird and the cat are spread out over the cochlea, with no regard to the locations of the bird and the cat.

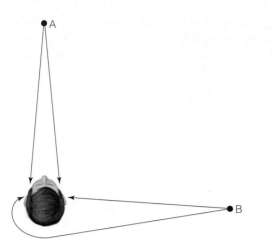

Figure 12.4 ▌ The principle behind interaural time difference (ITD). The tone directly in front of the listener, at A, reaches the left and the right ears at the same time. However, when the tone is off to the side, at B, it reaches the listener's right ear before it reaches the left ear.

reaching the two ears. A difference in level between the two ears occurs because the head creates a barrier that reduces the intensity of sounds that reach the far ear. This reduction of intensity at the far ear occurs for high-frequency sounds, but not for low-frequency sounds. [VL] 1

We can understand why an ILD occurs for high frequencies but not for low frequencies by drawing an analogy between sound waves and water waves. Consider, for example, a situation in which small ripples in the water are approaching the boat in Figure 12.5a. Because the ripples are small compared to the boat, they bounce off the side of the boat and go no further. Now imagine the same ripples approaching the cattails in Figure 12.5b. Because the distance between the ripples is large compared to the cattails, the ripples are hardly disturbed and continue on their way. These two examples illustrate that an object can have a large effect on the wave if it is larger than the distance between the waves, but has a small effect if its size is smaller than the distance between the waves.

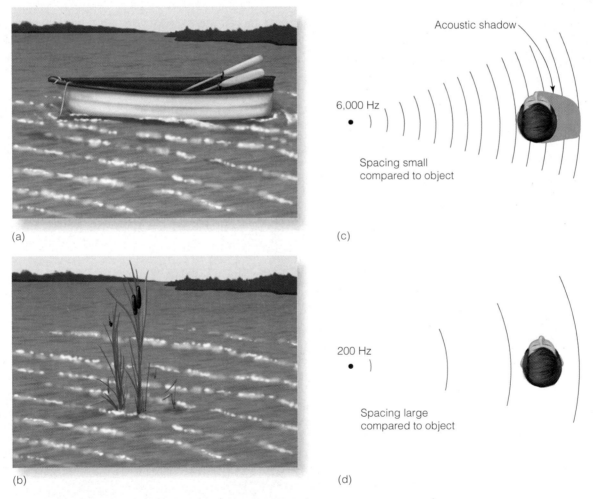

Figure 12.5 ▌ Why interaural level difference (ILD) occurs for high frequencies but not for low frequencies. (a) When water ripples are small compared to an object, such as this boat, they are stopped by the object. (b) The same ripples are large compared to the cattails, so they are unaffected by the cattails. (c) The spacing between high-frequency sound waves is small compared to the head. The head interferes with the sound waves, creating an acoustic shadow on the other side of the head. (d) The spacing between low-frequency sound waves is large compared to the person's head, so the sound is unaffected by the head.

When we apply this principle to sound waves interacting with a listener's head, we find that high-frequency sound waves (which are small compared to the size of the head) are disrupted by the head (Figure 12.5c), but that low-frequency waves are not (Figure 12.5d). This disruption of high-frequency sound waves creates a decrease in sound intensity on the far side of the head, called the **acoustic shadow** (Figure 12.5c).

This effect of frequency on the interaural level difference has been measured by using small microphones to record the intensity of the sound reaching each ear in response to a sound source located at different positions relative to the head (Figure 12.6). The results show that the level is affected only slightly by changes in location for low frequencies, but that the level is greatly affected by location for higher frequencies.

Using Binaural Cues for Perceiving Azimuth Locations When we consider ITD and ILT together, we see that they complement each other. ITD provides information about the location of low-frequency sounds, and ILD provides information about the location of high-frequency sounds.

ITD and ILD provide information that enables people to judge location along the azimuth coordinate, but provide ambiguous information about the elevation of a sound source. You can demonstrate why this is so by considering a sound source located directly in front of your face at arm's length, which would be equidistant from your left and right ears, so ITD and ILD would be zero. If you now increase the sound source's elevation by moving it straight up so it is above your head, it is still equidistant from the two ears, so both ITD and ILD are still zero.

Thus, the ITD and ILD can be the same at a number of different elevations, and therefore can't reliably indicate the elevation of the sound source. Similar ambiguous information is provided when the sound source is off to the side. These places of ambiguity are illustrated by the **cone of confusion** shown in Figure 12.7. All points on this cone have the same ILD and ITD. For example, points A and B would result in the same ILD and ITD because they are both the same distance from the left ear and from the right ear. Similar situations occur for other points on the cone.

The ambiguous nature of the information provided by ITD and ILD at different elevations means that another source of information is needed to locate sounds along the elevation coordinate. This information is provided by a **monaural cue**—a cue that depends on information from only one ear.

Monaural Cue for Localization

The primary monaural cue for localization is called a **spectral cue**, because the information for localization is contained in differences in the distribution (or spectrum) of frequencies that reach the ear from different locations. These differences are caused by the fact that before the sound stimulus enters the auditory canal, it is reflected from the head and within the various folds of the pinnae. The effect of this interaction with the head and pinnae has been measured by placing small microphones inside a listener's ears and comparing frequencies from sounds that are coming from different directions.

This effect is illustrated in Figure 12.8, which shows the frequencies picked up by the microphone when a broadband sound (one containing many frequencies) is presented at elevations of 15 degrees above the head and 15 degrees below the head. Sounds coming from these two locations would result in the same ITD and ILD, because they are the same distance from the left and right ears, but differences

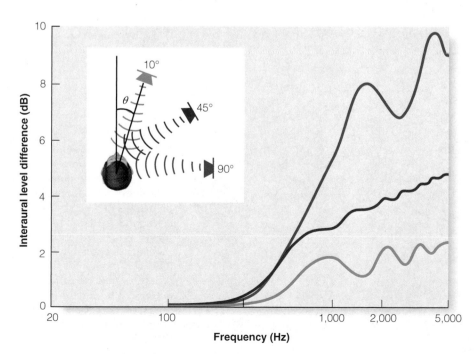

Figure 12.6 ❚ The three curves indicate interaural level difference (ILD) as a function of frequency for three different sound source locations. Note that the ILD is greater for locations farther to the side and is greater for all three locations at higher frequencies. *(Adapted from Hartmann, 1999.)*

Figure 12.7 ▍ The "cone of confusion." There are many pairs of points on this cone that have the same left-ear distance and right-ear distance and so result in the same ILD and ITD.

in the way the sounds bounce around within the pinna create different frequency spectra for the two locations (King et al., 2001).

The importance of the pinna for determining elevation has been demonstrated by showing that smoothing out the nooks and crannies of the pinnae with molding compound makes it difficult to locate sounds along the elevation coordinate (Gardner & Gardner, 1973). (You can investigate for yourself the effect of the pinnae on judging elevation by repeating the sound localization demonstration from earlier in the chapter while your listener folds over his or her pinnae.)

The idea that localization can be affected by using a mold to change the inside contours of the pinnae was also demonstrated by Paul Hofman and coworkers (1998). They determined how localization changes when the mold is worn for several weeks, and then what happens when the mold is removed. The results for one listener's localization performance measured before the mold was inserted are shown in Figure 12.9a. Sounds were presented at positions indicated by the intersections of the blue grid. Average localization performance is indicated by the red grid. The overlap between the two grids indicates that localization was accurate.

After measuring initial performance, Hofman fitted his listeners with molds that altered the shape of the pinnae and therefore changed the spectral cue. Figure 12.9b shows that localization performance is poor for the elevation coordinate immediately after the mold is inserted, but locations can still be judged at locations along the azimuth coordinate. This is exactly what we would expect if binaural cues are used for judging azimuth location and spectral cues are responsible for judging elevation locations.

Hofman continued his experiment by retesting localization as his listeners continued to wear the molds. You can see from Figure 12.9c and d that localization performance improved, until by 19 days localization had become reasonably accurate. Apparently, the person had learned, over a period of weeks, to associate new spectral cues to different directions in space.

What do you think happened when the molds were removed? It would be logical to expect that once adapted to the new set of spectral cues created by the molds, localization performance would suffer when the molds were removed. However, as shown in Figure 12.9e, localization remained excellent immediately after removal of the ear molds. Apparently, training with the molds created a new set of correlations between spectral cues and location, but the old correlation was still there as well. One way this could occur is if different sets of neurons were involved in responding to each set of spectral cues, just as separate brain areas are involved in processing different languages in people who speak more than one language (King et al., 2001; Wightman & Kistler, 1998; also see Van Wanrooij & Van Opstal, 2005).

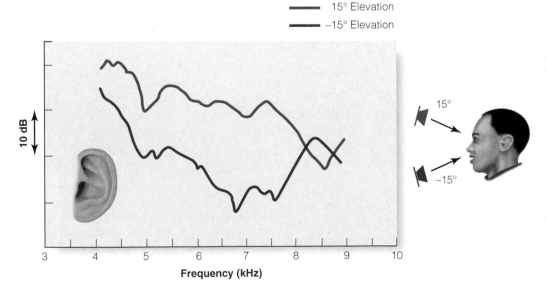

Figure 12.8 ▍ Frequency spectra recorded by a small microphone inside the listener's right ear for the same broadband sound coming from two different locations. The difference in the pattern when the sound is 15 degrees above the head and 15 degrees below the head is caused by the way different frequencies bounce around within the pinna after entering it from different angles. *(Adapted from Plack, 2005, Figure 9.11. Ear photo by Bruce Goldstein.)*

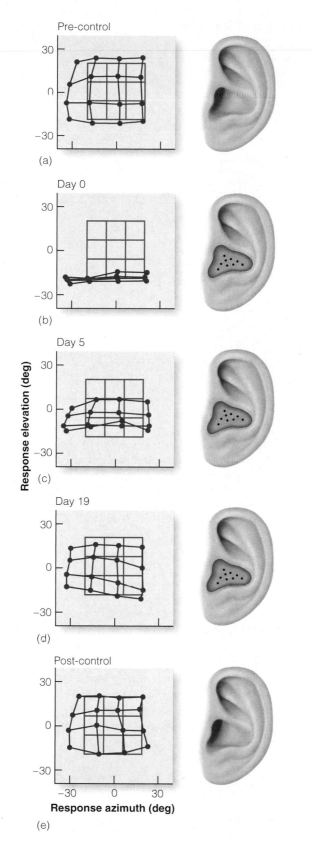

Figure 12.9 ▌ How localization changes when a mold is placed in the ear. See text for explanation. *(Reprinted from King, A. J., Schnupp, J. W. H., & Doubell, T. P., The shape of ears to come: Dynamic coding of auditory space, Trends in Cognitive Sciences, 5, 261–270. Copyright 2001, with permission from Elsevier.)*

We have seen that each type of cue works best for different frequencies and different coordinates. ITDs and ILDs work for judging azimuth location, with ITD best for low frequencies and ILD for high frequencies. Spectral cues work best for judging elevation, especially at higher frequencies. These cues work together to help us locate sounds. In real-world listening, we also move our heads, which provides additional ITD, ILD, and spectral information that helps minimize the effect of the cone of confusion (Figure 12.7) and helps locate continuous sounds. Vision also plays a role in sound localization, as when you hear talking and see a person making gestures and lip movements that match what you are hearing. Thus, the richness of the environment and our ability to actively search for information often help us zero in on a sound's location.

The Physiology of Auditory Localization

Having identified the cues that are associated with where a sound is coming from, we now ask how the information in these cues is represented in the nervous system. We describe two different answers to this question, both focusing on ITD. One answer proposes that there are neurons that are narrowly tuned to respond best to a specific ITD. The other answer proposes that there are neurons that are broadly tuned to ITD.

Narrowly Tuned ITD Neurons

The idea that there are neurons that respond best to a specific ITD has been suggested by experiments that have found neurons in the inferior colliculus and superior olivary nuclei that respond to a narrow range of ITDs. Figure 12.10 shows the ITD tuning curves for narrowly tuned neurons. The neurons associated with the curves on the left (blue) fire when sound reaches the left ear first, and the ones on the right (red) fire when sound reaches the right ear first. This type of responding, in which a specific ITD activates neurons tuned to that ITD is a form of specificity coding (see Chapter 2, page 36).

An ingenious explanation for how these neurons might work was proposed by Lloyd Jeffress (1948). The Jeffress model starts with the idea that there are a series of neurons that each respond best to a specific ITD. These neurons are wired so that they each receive signals from the two ears, as shown in Figure 12.11. Signals from the left ear arrive along the blue axon, and signals from the right ear arrive along the red axon.

If the sound source is directly in front of the listener, so the sound reaches the left and right ears simultaneously, then signals from the left and right ears start out together, as shown in Figure 12.11a. As each signal travels along its axon, it stimulates each neuron in turn. At the beginning of the journey, neurons receive signals from only the left ear

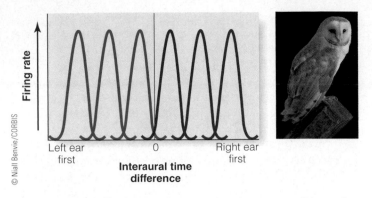

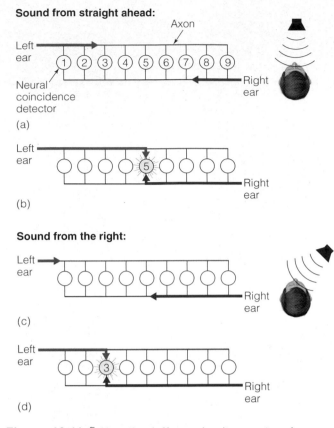

Figure 12.10 ❚ ITD tuning curves for six neurons that each respond to a narrow range of ITDs. The neurons on the left respond when sound reaches the left ear first. The ones on the right respond when sound reaches the right ear first. Neurons such as these have been recorded from the barn owl and other animals. *Adapted from McAlpine, 2005.*

(neurons 1, 2, 3) or the right ear (neurons 9, 8, 7), but not both, and they do not fire. But when the signals both reach neuron 5 together, that neurons fires (Figure 12.11b). This neuron and the others in this circuit are called *coincidence detectors*, because they only fire when both signals arrive at the neuron simultaneously. The firing of neuron 5 indicates that ITD = 0.

If the sound comes from the right, similar events occur, but the signal from the right ear has a head start, as shown in Figure 12.11c. These signals reach neuron 3 simultaneously (Figure 12.11d), so this neuron fires. This neuron, therefore, detects ITDs that occur when the sound is coming from a specific location on the right. The other neurons in the circuit fire to locations corresponding to other ITDs.

Broadly Tuned ITD Neurons

Recent research on the gerbil indicates that localization can also be based on neurons that are broadly tuned, as shown in Figure 12.12a (McAlpine, 2005). According to this idea, there are neurons in the gerbil's right hemisphere that respond best when sound is coming from the left and neurons in the left hemisphere that respond when sound is coming from the right. The location of a sound is indicated by the ratio of responding of these two types of broadly tuned neurons. For example, a sound from the left would cause the pattern of response shown in the left pair of bars in Figure 12.12b; sounds straight ahead, by the middle pair of bars; and sounds to the right, by the far right bars.

This type of coding resembles the distributed coding model we described in Chapter 2, in which information in the nervous system is based on the pattern of neural responding. This is, in fact, how the visual system signals different wavelengths of light, as we saw when we discussed color vision in Chapter 9, in which wavelengths are signaled by the pattern of response of three different cone pigments (Figure 9.10).

Figure 12.11 ❚ How the Jeffress circuit operates. Axons transmit signals from the left ear (blue) and right ear (red) to neurons, indicated by circles. (a) Sound in front: signals start in left and right channels simultaneously. (b) Signals meet at neuron 5, causing it to fire. (c) Sound to the right: signal starts in the right channel first. (d) Signals meet at neuron 3, causing it to fire.

We have seen that there is evidence for both narrowly tuned ITD neurons and broadly tuned ITD neurons. Both types of neurons can potentially provide information regarding the location of low-frequency sounds. Exactly which of these mechanisms, or perhaps a combination of the two, works in different animals is being studied by auditory researchers. In addition to determining that the firing of single neurons can provide information for localization, researchers have also determined that there are specific areas of the cortex that are involved in auditory localization. This research is described in Chapter 11 (see "*What* and *Where* Streams for Hearing," page 281).

TEST YOURSELF 12.1

1. How is auditory space described in terms of three coordinates?
2. How well can people localize sounds that are in front, to the side, and in back?
3. What is the basic difference between determining the location of a sound source and determining the location of a visual object?

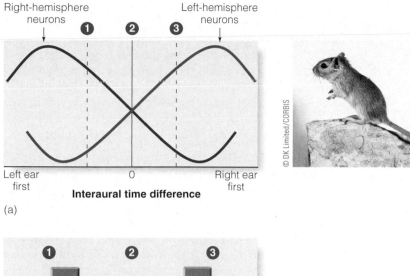

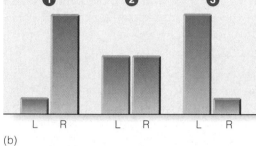

(a)

(b)

Figure 12.12 ▌ (a) ITD tuning curves for broadly tuned neurons. The left curve represents the tuning of neurons in the right hemisphere; the right curve is the tuning of neurons in the left hemisphere; (b) patterns of response of the broadly tuned neurons for stimuli coming from the left (ITD indicated by line 1), in front (ITD indicated by line 2), and from the right (ITD indicated by line 3). Neurons such as this have been recorded from the gerbil. *(Adapted from McAlpine, 2005.)*

4. Describe the binaural cues for localization. Indicate the frequencies and directions relative to the listener for which the cues are effective.
5. Describe the monaural cue for localization.
6. How is auditory space represented physiologically in single neurons? Describe the two different types of neural coding that have been proposed.

Perceptually Organizing Sounds in the Environment

So far we have been describing how single tones are localized in space. But we rarely hear just a single tone (unless you are a subject in a hearing experiment!). Our experience usually involves hearing a number of sounds simultaneously. This poses a problem for the auditory system: How can it separate one sound from another?

Consider, for example, a situation in which you are listening to music in the old-fashioned way, with "stereo" turned off so all of the music is coming from a single speaker. By doing this, you have eliminated the location information usually supplied by binaural cues, so the sound of all of the instruments appears to be coming from the speaker in front of you. But even though you have eliminated information about location, you can still make out the vocalist, the guitar, and the keyboard. "Well, of course," you might think. "After all, each of the instruments makes different sounds."

This is a good example of a situation in which our perceptual system enables us to effortlessly solve a perceptual problem that is actually extremely complex. We can appreciate why this is a complex problem by considering how the sounds coming from the loudspeaker affect vibration of the basilar membrane and therefore activation of the auditory nerve fibers.

Figure 12.13 shows the sound stimuli created by the vocalist and two instruments and the output of the loudspeaker. The problem for our auditory system is that although each sound source produces its own signal, all of the signals are combined when they are broadcast by the loudspeaker and enter the listener's ear. Each of the frequencies in this signal causes the basilar membrane to vibrate, but just as in the case of the bird and the cat in Figure 12.3, in which there was no information on the cochlea for the locations of the two sounds, there is also no information on the cochlea about which vibration is created by which instrument. We now consider how the auditory system solves this problem.

Auditory Scene Analysis

A problem similar to the one above occurs when you are talking to a friend at a noisy party. Even though the sounds produced by your friend's conversation are mixed together on your cochlea with the sounds produced by all of the other people's conversations, plus perhaps music, the sound of the refrigerator door slamming, and glasses clinking, you are somehow able to separate what your friend is saying from all of the other sounds. The array of sound sources in the environment is called the **auditory scene**, and the

Figure 12.13 ▌ Each musician produces a sound stimulus, and all three sounds are combined in the output of the loudspeaker.

process by which you separate the stimuli produced by each of the sources in the scene into separate perceptions is called **auditory scene analysis** (Bregman, 1990, 1993; Darwin, 1997; Yost, 2001). The auditory system's problem is deciding which frequency components belong together to form each sound in the auditory scene.

It might seem as though one way to analyze an auditory scene into its separate components would be to use information about where each source is coming from. According to this idea, you can separate your friend's voice and the slamming of the refrigerator door because your friend is standing nearby and the sound of the refrigerator door is coming from the next room. The sound sources' positions in space can potentially help you separate the sources from one another, but the fact that you can still hear separate instruments when you listen to a recording played through a single speaker means that the auditory system must also use other information to analyze an auditory scene into separate sound sources (Yost, 1997). We can describe this information in terms of **principles of auditory grouping**, and we will use music to illustrate these principles.

Principles of Auditory Grouping

In Chapter 5, we introduced the idea that the visual system uses a number of different heuristics, proposed by the Gestalt psychologists and modern researchers, to determine which elements of a visual scene belong together. We saw that these heuristics are based on properties of visual stimuli

that usually occur in the environment (see page 116). Now, as we turn to the sense of hearing, we will see that a similar situation exists for auditory stimuli. There are a number of heuristics that help us perceptually organize elements of an auditory scene, and these heuristics are based on how sounds usually originate in the environment. For example, if two sounds start at different times, it is likely that they came from different sources. This is called **onset time**. Let's look at some additional principles that aid in grouping.

Location Sounds created by a particular source usually come from one position in space or from a slowly changing location. Anytime two sounds are separated in space, the cue of location helps us separate them perceptually. In addition, when a source moves, it typically follows a continuous path rather than jumping erratically from one place to another. For example, this continuous movement of sound helps us perceive the sound from a passing car as originating from a single source.

Similarity of Timbre and Pitch Sounds that have the same timbre or pitch range are often produced by the same source. For example, if we are listening to two instruments with different ranges such as a flute and a trombone, the timbre of the flute and trombone stay the same no matter what notes they are playing. (The flute continues to sound like a flute, and the trombone sounds like a trombone.) Similarly, the flute tends to play in a high pitch range, and the trombone plays in a low range. $\boxed{V_L}$2

Composers made use of grouping by similarity of pitch long before psychologists began studying it. Composers in the Baroque period (1600–1750) knew that when a single instrument plays notes that alternate rapidly between high and low tones, the listener perceives two separate melodies, with the high notes perceived as being played by one instrument and the low notes as being played by another. An excerpt from a composition by J. S. Bach that uses this device is shown in Figure 12.14. When this passage is played rapidly, the low notes sound as though they are a melody played by one instrument, and the high notes sound like a different melody played by another instrument. This ability to separate different sound sources, which musicians call *implied polyphony* or *compound melodic line,* is an example of what psychologists call **auditory stream segregation** (see Bregman, 1990; Darwin, in press; Jones & Yee, 1993; Yost & Sheft, 1993).

Albert Bregman and Jeffrey Campbell (1971) demonstrated auditory stream segregation based on pitch by alternating high and low tones, as shown in the sequence in Figure 12.15. When the high-pitched tones were slowly alternated with the low-pitched tones, as in Figure 12.15a, the tones were heard in one stream, one after another: Hi-Lo-Hi-Lo-Hi-Lo, as indicated by the dashed line. But when the tones were alternated very rapidly, the high and low tones became perceptually grouped into two auditory streams so that the listener perceived two separate streams of sound, one high-pitched and one low-pitched, occurring simultaneously (Figure 12.15b; see Heise & Miller, 1951, and

Figure 12.14 ▌ Four measures of a composition by J. S. Bach (Choral Prelude on *Jesus Christus unser Heiland*, 1739). When played rapidly, the upper notes become perceptually grouped, and the lower notes become perceptually grouped, a phenomenon called *auditory stream segregation*.

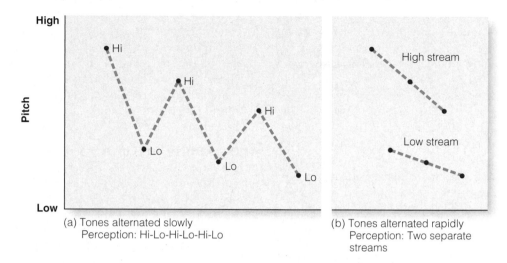

(a) Tones alternated slowly
Perception: Hi-Lo-Hi-Lo-Hi-Lo

(b) Tones alternated rapidly
Perception: Two separate streams

Figure 12.15 ▌ (a) When high and low tones are alternated slowly, auditory stream segregation does not occur, so the listener perceives alternating high and low tones. (b) Faster alternation results in segregation into high and low streams.

Miller & Heise, 1950, for an early demonstration of auditory stream segregation). [VL] **3, 4**

This grouping of tones into streams by similarity of pitch is also demonstrated by an experiment done by Bregman and Alexander Rudnicky (1975). The listener is first presented with two standard tones, X and Y (Figure 12.16a). When these tones are presented alone, it is easy to perceive their order (XY or YX). However, when these tones are sandwiched between two distractor (D) tones (Figure 12.16b), it becomes very hard to judge their order. The name *distractor tones* is well chosen: they distract the listener, making it difficult to judge the order of tones X and Y. [VL] **5**

But the distracting effect of the D tones can be eliminated by adding a series of captor (C) tones (Figure 12.16c).

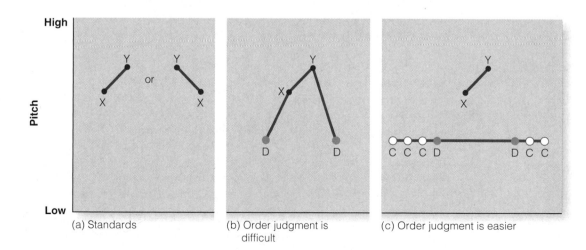

(a) Standards

(b) Order judgment is difficult

(c) Order judgment is easier

Figure 12.16 ▌ Bregman and Rudnicky's (1975) experiment. (a) The standard tones X and Y have different pitches. (b) The distractor (D) tones group with X and Y, making it difficult to judge the order of X and Y. (c) The addition of captor (C) tones with the same pitch as the distractor tones causes the distractor tones to form a separate stream (grouping by similarity), making it easier to judge the order of tones X and Y. *(Based on Bregman & Rudnicky, 1975.)*

These tones work as "captors" because they have the same pitch as the distractors, so they capture the distractors and form a stream that separates the distractors from tones X and Y. The result is that X and Y are perceived as one stream and the distractors as another stream, making it much easier to perceive the order of X and Y.

Figure 12.17 provides another demonstration of grouping by similarity. Figure 12.17a shows two streams of sound, one a series of similar repeating notes (red), and the other, a scale that goes up (blue). Figure 12.17b shows how this stimulus is perceived if the tones are presented fairly rapidly. At first the two streams are separated, so listeners simultaneously perceive the same note repeating and a scale. However, when the frequencies of the two stimuli become similar, something interesting happens. Grouping by similarity of frequency occurs, and perception changes to a back-and-forth "galloping" between the tones of the two streams. Then, as the scale continues upward and the frequencies become more separated, the two sequences are again perceived as separated. $\boxed{VL}$ 6

A final example of how similarity of pitch causes grouping is an effect called the **scale illusion**, or **melodic channeling**. Diana Deutsch (1975, 1996) demonstrated this effect by presenting two sequences of notes simultaneously through earphones, one to the right ear and one to the left (Figure 12.18a). Notice that the notes presented to each ear jump up and down and do not create a scale. However, Deutsch's listeners perceived smooth sequences of notes in each ear, with the higher notes in the right ear and the lower ones in the left ear (Figure 12.18b). Even though each ear received both high and low notes, grouping by similarity of pitch caused listeners to group the higher notes in the right

ear (which started with a high note) and the lower notes in the left ear (which started with a low note).

The scale illusion highlights an important property of perceptual grouping. Most of the time, the principles of auditory grouping help us to accurately interpret what is happening in the environment. It is most effective to perceive similar sounds as coming from the same source because this is what usually happens in the environment. In Deutsch's experiment, the perceptual system applies the principle of grouping by similarity to the artificial stimuli presented through earphones and makes the mistake of assigning similar pitches to the same ear. But most of the time, when psychologists aren't controlling the stimuli, sounds with similar frequencies tend to be produced by the same sound source, so the auditory system usually uses pitch to correctly $\boxed{VL}$ **7, 8** determine where sounds are coming from.

Proximity in Time We have already seen that sounds that stop and start at different times tend to be produced by different sources. If you are listening to one instrument playing and then another one joins in later, you know that two sources are present because of the cue of onset time. Another time cue is based on the fact that sounds that occur in rapid progression tend to be produced by the same source. We can illustrate the importance of timing in stream segregation by returning to our examples of grouping by similarity. Before stream segregation by similarity of timbre or pitch can occur, tones with similar timbres or frequencies have to occur close together in time. If the tones are too far

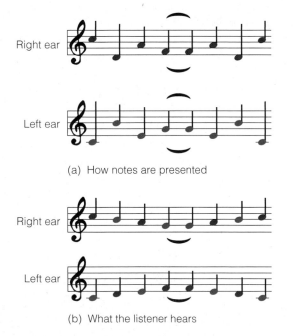

(a) How notes are presented

(b) What the listener hears

Figure 12.18 ❙ (a) These stimuli were presented to a listener's right ear (red) and left ear (blue) in Deutsch's (1975) scale illusion experiment. Notice how the notes presented to each ear jump up and down. (b) What the listener hears: Although the notes in each ear jump up and down, the listener perceives a smooth sequence of notes in each ear. This effect is called the scale illusion, or melodic channeling. *(Adapted from Deutsch, 1975.)*

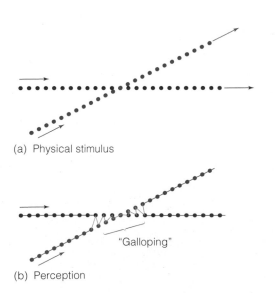

(a) Physical stimulus

"Galloping"

(b) Perception

Figure 12.17 ❙ (a) Two sequences of stimuli: a series of similar notes (red) and a scale (blue). (b) Perception of these stimuli: Separate streams are perceived when they are far apart in frequency, but when the frequencies are in the same range, the tones appear to jump back and forth between stimuli.

apart in time, as in Figure 12.15a, segregation will not occur, even when the tones are similar in pitch.

Auditory Continuity Sounds that stay constant or that change smoothly are often produced by the same source. This property of sound leads to a principle that resembles the Gestalt principle of good continuation for vision (see page 106). Sound stimuli with the same frequency or smoothly changing frequencies are perceived as continuous even when they are interrupted by another stimulus (Deutsch, 1999). **VL 9**

Richard Warren and coworkers (1972) demonstrated auditory continuity by presenting bursts of tone interrupted by gaps of silence (Figure 12.19a). Listeners perceived these tones as stopping during the silence. But when Warren filled in the gaps with noise (Figure 12.19b), listeners perceived the tone as continuing behind the noise (Figure 12.19c). This demonstration is analogous to the demonstration of visual good continuation illustrated by the Celtic knot pattern in Figure 5.17. Just as the strands that make up the pattern are perceived as continuous even though they overlap one another, a tone can be perceived as continuous even though it is interrupted by bursts of noise.

Experience The effect of past experience on the perceptual grouping of auditory stimuli can be demonstrated by presenting the melody of a familiar song, as in Figure 12.20a. These are the notes for the song "Three Blind Mice," but

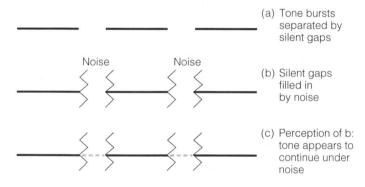

Figure 12.19 ▌ A demonstration of auditory continuity, using tones.

with the notes jumping from one octave to another. When people first hear these notes, they find it difficult to identify the song. But once they have heard the song as it was meant to be played (Figure 12.20b), they can follow the melody in the octave-jumping version shown in Figure 12.20a.

This is an example of the operation of a **melody schema**—a representation of a familiar melody that is stored in a person's memory. When people don't know that a melody is present, they have no access to the schema and therefore have nothing with which to compare the unknown melody. But when they know which melody is present, they compare what they hear to their stored schema and perceive the melody (Deutsch, 1999; Dowling & Harwood, 1986). **VL 10, 11**

Each of the principles of auditory grouping that we have described provides information about the number and identity of sources in the auditory environment. But each principle alone is not foolproof, and basing our perceptions on just one principle can lead to error—as in the case of the scale illusion, which is purposely arranged so that similarity of pitch dominates our perception. Thus, in most naturalistic situations, we base our perceptions on a number of these cues working together. This is similar to the situation we described for visual perception, in which our perception of objects depends on a number of organizational principles working together and our perception of depth depends on a number of depth cues working together. **VL 12**

Hearing Inside Rooms

So far in this chapter and also in Chapter 11, we have seen that our perception of sound depends on various properties of the sound, including its frequency, sound level, location in space, and relation to other sounds. But we have left out the fact that in our normal everyday experience we hear sounds in a specific setting, such as a small room, a large auditorium, or outside. As we consider this aspect of hearing, we will see why we perceive sounds differently when we are outside and inside, and how our perception of

(a)

(b)

Figure 12.20 ▌ "Three Blind Mice": (a) jumping octave version; (b) normal version.

sound quality is affected by specific properties of indoor environments.

Figure 12.21 shows how the nature of the sound reaching your ears depends on the environment in which you hear the sound. If you are listening to someone playing a guitar on an outside stage, some of the sound you hear reaches your ears after being reflected from the ground or objects like trees, but most of the sound travels directly from the sound source to your ears (Figure 12.21a). If, however, you are listening to the same guitar in an auditorium, then a large proportion of the sound bounces off the auditorium's walls, ceiling, and floor before reaching your ears (Figure 12.21b). The sound reaching your ears directly, along path a, is called direct sound; the sound reaching your ears later, along paths like b, c, and d, is called indirect sound.

The fact that sound can reach our ears directly from where the sound is originating and indirectly from other locations creates a potential problem because the listener is receiving a sequence of sounds, coming from many directions and reaching the ears at slightly different times. Nonetheless, we generally perceive the sound as coming from only one location. We can understand why this occurs by considering the results of research in which listeners were presented with sounds originating from two different locations.

Perceiving Two Sounds That Reach the Ears at Different Times

Research on sound reflections and the perception of location has usually simplified the problem by having people listen to sounds coming from two speakers separated in space, as shown in Figure 12.22. The speaker on the left is the *lead speaker*, and the one on the right as the *lag speaker*. If a sound is presented in the lead speaker followed by a long delay (fractions of a second), and then a sound is presented in the lag speaker, listeners typically hear two separate sounds—one from the left (lead) followed by one from the right (lag). But when the delay between the lead and lag sounds is much shorter, something different happens. Even though the sound is coming from both speakers, listeners hear the sound as coming only from the lead speaker. This situation, in which the sound appears to originate from the lead speaker, is called the **precedence effect** because we perceive the sound as coming from the source that reaches our ears first (Litovsky et al., 1997, 1999; Wallach, Newman, & Rosenzweig, 1949).   VL 13

The precedence effect governs most of our indoor listening experience. The indirect sounds reflected from the walls have a lower level than the direct sound and reach our ears with delays of about 5 to 10 ms for small rooms, and with larger delays for larger rooms like concert halls. The operation of the precedence effect means that we generally perceive sound as coming from its source, rather than from

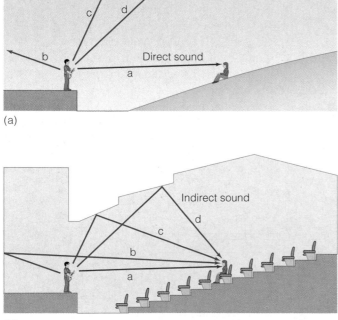

(a)

(b)

Figure 12.21 ▌ (a) When you hear a sound outside, you hear mainly direct sound (path a). (b) When you hear a sound inside a room, you hear both direct sound (path a) and indirect sound (paths b, c, and d) that is reflected from the walls, floor, and ceiling of the room.

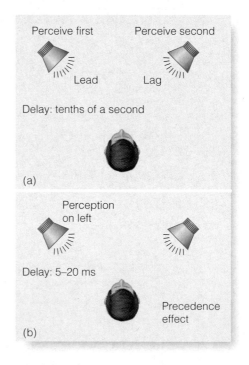

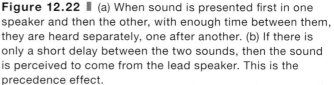

Figure 12.22 ▌ (a) When sound is presented first in one speaker and then the other, with enough time between them, they are heard separately, one after another. (b) If there is only a short delay between the two sounds, then the sound is perceived to come from the lead speaker. This is the precedence effect.

many different directions at once. You can demonstrate the precedence effect to yourself by doing the following demonstration.

DEMONSTRATION

The Precedence Effect

To demonstrate the precedence effect, set the controls on your stereo system so that both speakers play the same sounds, and position yourself between the speakers so that you hear the sound coming from a point between both speakers. Then move a small distance to the left or right. When you do this, does the sound appear to be coming from only the nearer speaker? ▌

You perceive the sound as coming from the nearer speaker because the sound from the nearer speaker is reaching your ears first, just as in Figure 12.22b, in which there was a short delay between the sounds presented by the two speakers. But even though you hear the sound as coming from the near speaker, this doesn't mean that you aren't hearing the far speaker. The sound from the far speaker changes the quality of the sound, giving it a fuller, more expansive quality (Blauert, 1997; Yost & Guzman, 1996). You can demonstrate this by positioning yourself closer to one speaker and having a friend disconnect the other speaker. When this happens, you will notice a difference in the quality of the sound.

Architectural Acoustics

Having solved the location problem for sounds heard in rooms, we now consider how properties of the room can affect the quality of the sound we hear. When we studied vision, we saw that our perception of light depends not only on the nature of the light source but also on what happens to the light between the time it leaves its source and the time it enters our eyes. When light passes through haze on its way from an object to our eyes, the object may seem bluer or fuzzier than it would if the haze were not there. Similarly, our perception of sound also depends not only on the sound produced at the source, but also on how the sounds are reflected from the walls and other surfaces in a room.

Architectural acoustics, the study of how sounds are reflected in rooms, is largely concerned with how indirect sound changes the quality of the sounds we hear in rooms. The major factor affecting indirect sound is the amount of sound absorbed by the walls, ceiling, and floor of the room. If most of the sound is absorbed, then there are few sound reflections and little indirect sound. If most of the sound is reflected, then there are many sound reflections and a large amount of indirect sound. Another factor affecting indirect sound is the size and shape of the room. This determines how sound hits surfaces and the directions in which it is reflected.

The amount and duration of indirect sound produced by a room is expressed as **reverberation time**—the time it takes for the sound to decrease to 1/1000th of its original pressure (or a decrease in level by 60 dB). If the reverberation time of a room is too long, sounds become muddled because the reflected sounds persist for too long. In extreme cases, such as cathedrals with stone walls, these delays are perceived as echoes, and it may be difficult to accurately localize the sound source. If the reverberation time is too short, music sounds "dead," and it becomes more difficult to produce high-intensity sounds. VL 14

Acoustics in Concert Halls Because of the relationship between reverberation time and perception, acoustical engineers have tried to design concert halls in which the reverberation time matches the reverberation time of halls that are renowned for their good acoustics, like Symphony Hall in Boston and the Concertgebouw in Amsterdam, which have reverberation times of about 2.0 seconds. However, an "ideal" reverberation time does not always predict good acoustics. This is illustrated by the problems associated with the design of New York's Philharmonic Hall. When it opened in 1962, Philharmonic Hall had a reverberation time close to the ideal of 2.0 seconds. Even so, the hall was criticized for sounding as though it had a short reverberation time, and musicians in the orchestra complained that they could not hear each other. These criticisms resulted in a series of alterations to the hall, made over many years, until eventually, when none of the alterations proved satisfactory, the entire interior of the hall was destroyed, and the hall was completely rebuilt in 1992. It is now called Avery Fisher Hall.

The experience with Philharmonic Hall, plus new developments in the field of architectural acoustics, has led architectural engineers to consider factors in addition to reverberation time in designing concert halls. Some of these factors have been identified by Leo Beranek (1996), who showed that the following physical measures are associated with how music is perceived in concert halls:

- *Intimacy time:* The time between when sound arrives directly from the stage and when the first reflection arrives. This is related to reverberation, but involves just comparing the time between the direct sound and the first reflection, rather than the time it takes for many reflections to die down.

- *Bass ratio:* The ratio of low frequencies to middle frequencies that are reflected from walls and other surfaces.

- *Spaciousness factor:* The fraction of all of the sound received by a listener that is indirect sound.

To determine the optimal values for these physical measures, acoustical engineers measured them in 20 opera houses and 25 symphony halls in 14 countries. By comparing their measurements with ratings of the halls by conductors and music critics, they confirmed that the best concert halls had reverberation times of about 2 seconds; they

Figure 12.23 ▌ Interior of the Walt Disney Concert Hall in Los Angeles. The performance space is located near the center of the hall.

found that 1.5 seconds was better for opera houses, with the shorter time being necessary to enable people to clearly hear the singers' voices. They also found that intimacy times of about 20 ms and high bass ratios and spaciousness factors were associated with good acoustics (Glanz, 2000). When these factors have been taken into account in the design of new concert halls, the result has been acoustics rivaling the best halls in the world, such as the Walt Disney Concert Hall in Los Angeles (Figure 12.23).

In designing Walt Disney Hall, the architects paid attention not only to how the shape, configuration, and materials of the walls and ceiling would affect the acoustics, but also to the absorption properties of the cushions on each of the 2,273 seats. One problem that often occurs in concert halls is that the acoustics depend on the number of people attending a performance, because people absorb sound. Thus, a hall with good acoustics when full could echo when there are too many empty seats. To deal with this problem, the seat cushions were designed to have the same absorption properties as an "average" person. This means that the hall has the same acoustics when empty or full. This is a great advantage to musicians, who usually rehearse in an empty hall.

Acoustics in Classrooms Although the acoustics of glamorous performance spaces such as concert halls receive a great deal of attention, acoustics often receive little attention in the design of lecture halls or classrooms. The ideal reverberation time for a small classroom is about 0.4–0.6 seconds and for an auditorium, about 1.0–1.5 seconds. These are less than the 2.0-second optimum for concert halls because the goal is not to create a rich musical sound, but to create an environment in which students can hear what the teacher is saying. Even though the ideal reverberation time for classrooms is under 0.6 seconds, many classrooms have reverberation times of 1 second or more (Acoustical Society of America, 2000).

But classrooms face other problems as well. While the main sound present in a concert hall is created by the performers, there are often many sounds in addition to the lecture in a classroom. These sounds, called *background noise,* include noisy ventilation systems, students talking in class (when they aren't supposed to!), and noise from the hall and adjacent classrooms. The presence of background noise has led to the use of **signal-to-noise (S/N) ratio** in designing classrooms. The S/N ratio is the level of the teacher's voice in dB minus the level of the background noise in the room. Ideally, the S/N ratio is +10 to +15 dB or more. At S/N ratios below this, students may have trouble hearing what the teacher is saying.

Our foray into concert halls and classrooms has taken us quite far from basic research on things like localization cues and auditory scene analysis that we discussed at the beginning of the chapter. But to totally understand how we hear, we need to consider not only basic perceptual mechanisms that are most often studied in the laboratory, but also how we hear in natural environments under real-world conditions.

Something to Consider: Interactions Between Vision and Hearing

The division of this book into separate chapters for each sense might give the impression that the senses operate independently of one another. This impression would, of course, be erroneous because we rarely just hear sound, see visual stimuli, or smell odors, in isolation. Perception, as it occurs in the natural environment, involves interactions among all the senses. We will now look at a few examples of some interactions between hearing and vision.

In general, there is overlap between where a sound seems to be coming from and where we see the source of this sound. You hear the annoying person talking behind you at a concert and turn around to see that the person is, in fact, located just about where you would have predicted. But sometimes vision and hearing provide discrepant information, as when the sound is produced at one place but you see the apparent sound source somewhere else. A familiar example of this phenomenon occurs in movie theaters when an actor's dialogue is produced by a speaker located on the right side of the screen while the image of the actor who is talking is located in the center of the screen, many feet away. When this happens, we hear the sound coming from its seen location (the image at the center of the screen) rather than from where it is actually produced (the speaker to the right of the screen). This effect is called **visual capture,** or the **ventriloquism effect**—sound appears to be coming from the apparent visual source of the sound, even if it actually originates from another location. Note that because virtually all theaters have stereophonic sound, the match between sound position and characters on the screen is at least partially caused by the binaural cues we described earlier in the chapter. But before the advent of stereophonic sound, the ventriloquism effect alone caused movie viewers to perceive sound as originating from places on the screen rather than from off to the side.

There are other situations in which sound and visual stimuli appear to have the same location, even though sound is coming from one place and the visual stimulus is located somewhere else. Another example of visual capture occurs when a sound that would normally be perceived as moving from left to right is heard while a person is viewing a visual stimulus that is moving from right to left; in this case, both sound and visual stimuli appear to be moving from right to left (Soto-Faraco et al., 2002, 2004).

Visual capture is important because it reflects the way we usually experience stimuli in the environment. Another illustration of this connection is shown in Figure 12.24. Robert Sekuler and coworkers (1997) presented an animated display that showed two identical objects moving diagonally, one from left to right and the other from right to left, crossing in the middle. Eighty-eight percent of Sekuler's observers perceived these objects as moving past each other and continuing their straight-line motion, as shown in Figure 12.24a. The other 12 percent of observers perceived the objects as contacting each other and bouncing off in opposite directions, as shown in Figure 12.24b. However, when Sekuler added a brief "click" sound just when the objects ap-

peared adjacent to each other, 63 percent perceived them as colliding and bouncing off in opposite directions. As was the case for visual capture, in which vision influenced hearing, this example, in which hearing influences vision, also seems to reflect the way we normally perceive events in the environment. When a sound occurs just as two moving objects become adjacent to one another, this usually means that a collision has occurred to cause the sound (also see Shams et al., 2000; Ecker & Heller, 2005). VL 15–17

TEST YOURSELF 12.2

1. What is auditory scene analysis, and why is it a "problem" for the auditory system?
2. What are the basic principles of auditory grouping that help us achieve auditory scene analysis? Be sure you understand the following experiments: Bregman and Campbell (Figure 12.15); Bregman and Rudnicky (Figure 12.16); "galloping" crossing streams (Figure 12.17); scale illusion (Figure 12.18); auditory continuity (Figure 12.19), and melody schema (Figure 12.20).
3. Why would music played outdoors sound different from music played indoors?
4. What is the precedence effect, and what does it do for us perceptually?
5. What are some basic principles of architectural acoustics that have been developed to help design concert halls? What are some special problems in designing classrooms?
6. Describe the following demonstrations of the way that vision and hearing can interact: (1) vision influencing sound (visual capture); (2) sound influencing perception of visual collision. What do these demonstrations tell us about the relationship between what we perceive and what usually occurs in the environment?

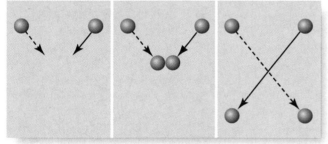

(a) Objects appear to pass by each other

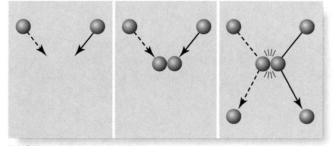

(b) Objects appear to collide

12.24 ❙ Two conditions in the Sekuler et al. (1999) experiment showing successive positions of two balls that were presented so they appeared to be moving. (a) No sound condition: The two balls were perceived to pass each other and continue moving in a straight-line motion. (b) Click added condition: Observers were more likely to see the balls as colliding.

THINK ABOUT IT

1. What are some situations in which (a) you use one sense in isolation, and (b) the combined use of two or more senses is necessary to accomplish a task? (p. 292)

2. We can perceive space visually, as we saw in the chapter on depth perception, and through the sense of hearing, as we have described in this chapter. How are these two ways of perceiving space similar and different? (p. 293)

3. How is object recognition in vision like stream segregation in hearing? (p. 300)

4. How good are the acoustics in your classrooms? Can you hear the professor clearly? Does it matter where you sit? Are you ever distracted by noises from inside or outside the room? (p. 306)

IF YOU WANT TO KNOW MORE

1. *The physiology of auditory grouping.* New research is looking at how the brain separates sounds. (p. 299)
   Carlyon, R. P. (2004). How the brain separates sounds. *Trends in Cognitive Sciences, 8,* 465–471.

2. *Multimodal cells.* One way the brain may coordinate information for different senses in order to create a unified perception of objects and events in the environment is through areas of the brain that are activated by more than one sense. (pp. 282, 287, 306)
   Bushara, K. O., et al. (2003). Neural correlates of cross-modal bonding. *Nature Neuroscience, 6,* 190–195.

3. *Loss of one sense can enhance another one.* Although losing one sense can sometimes hurt another one (see page 288), the opposite can also occur, so that when one sense is lost or reduced, performance by the other senses become enhanced. The physiological basis for this appears to be that the remaining senses take over cortical area from the lost one.
   Rauschecker, J. P., & Korte, M. (1993). Auditory compensation for early blindness in cat cerebral cortex. *Journal of Neuroscience, 13,* 4538–4548.

4. *Auditory looming.* Looming occurs in vision when an object that is headed in your direction becomes larger and larger in your field of view. Auditory looming occurs when you hear an approaching sound source become louder and louder.
   Ghazanfar, A. A., Neuhoff, J. G., & Logothetis, N. K. (2002). Auditory looming perception in rhesus monkeys. *Proceedings of the National Academy of Sciences, 99,* 15755–15757.
   Seifritz, E., et al., (2002). Neural processing of auditory looming in the human brain. *Current Biology, 12,* 2147–2151.

5. *Change deafness.* Just as we can fail to notice when changes occur in a visual stimulus (p. 139), we also sometimes fail to notice changes in sound stimuli.
   Eramudugolla, R., et al. (2005). Directed attention eliminates "change deafness" in complex auditory scenes. *Current Biology, 15,* 1108–1113.
   Vitevitch, M. S. (2003). Change deafness: The inability to detect changes between two voices. *Journal of Experimental Psychology: Human Perception and Performance, 29,* 333–342.

KEY TERMS

Acoustic shadow (p. 295)
Architectural acoustics (p. 305)
Auditory localization (p. 292)
Auditory scene (p. 299)
Auditory scene analysis (p. 300)
Auditory space (p. 292)
Auditory stream segregation (p. 300)
Azimuth coordinate (p. 292)
Binaural cue (p. 293)
Cone of confusion (p. 295)
Direct sound (p. 304)

Distance coordinate (p. 292)
Elevation coordinate (p. 292)
Indirect sound (p. 304)
Interaural level difference (ILD) (p. 293)
Interaural time difference (ITD) (p. 293)
Location cue (p. 293)
Melodic channeling (p. 302)
Melody schema (p. 303)
Monaural cue (p. 295)

Onset time (p. 300)
Precedence effect (p. 304)
Principles of auditory grouping (p. 300)
Reverberation time (p. 305)
Scale illusion (p. 302)
Signal-to-noise (S/N) ratio (p. 306)
Spectral cue (p. 295)
Ventriloquism effect (p. 306)
Visual capture (p. 306)

MEDIA RESOURCES

The *Sensation and Perception* Book Companion Website

www.cengage.com/psychology/goldstein

See the companion website for flashcards, practice quiz questions, Internet links, updates, critical thinking exercises, discussion forums, games, and more!

CengageNOW

www.cengage.com/login

Go to this site for the link to CengageNOW, your one-stop shop. Take a pre-test for this chapter, and CengageNOW will generate a personalized study plan based on your test results. The study plan will identify the topics you need to review and direct you to online resources to help you master those topics. You can then take a post-test to help you determine the concepts you have mastered and what you will still need to work on.

Virtual Lab

Your Virtual Lab is designed to help you get the most out of this course. The Virtual Lab icons direct you to specific media demonstrations and experiments designed to help you visualize what you are reading about. The number beside each icon indicates the number of the media element you can access through your CD-ROM, CengageNOW, or WebTutor resource.

The following lab exercises are related to material in this chapter:

1. *Interaural Level Difference as a Cue for Sound Localization* How the relative loudness of two tones presented in different speakers determines the perceived location of the tone.

2. *Grouping by Similarity of Timbre: The Wessel Demonstration* How similarity of timbre can change the perceived organization of a series of tones, if the tones are presented fast enough.

3. *Grouping by Pitch and Temporal Closeness* How our perception of groups of three tones changes as the tones are presented more rapidly. A demonstration of auditory stream segregation.

4. *Effect of Repetition on Grouping by Pitch* How the grouping observed in the "Grouping by Pitch and Temporal Closeness" demonstration can be affected by repeating the sequences.

5. *Captor Tone Demonstration* The stimuli used in Bregman and Rudnicky's captor tone experiment.

6. *Grouping by Similarity of Pitch* How the perceptual organization of two sequences of tones changes when their pitches approach each other.

7. *Octave Illusion* Perceptual grouping of sounds in the left and right ears. (Courtesy of Diana Deutsch.)

8. *Chromatic Scale Illusion* Another demonstration of perceptual grouping of sounds in the left and right ears. (Courtesy of Diana Deutsch.)

9. *Auditory Good Continuation* How we hear a tone as continuous when spaces are filled in with noise.

10. *Melody Schema* How perception of a melody can be influenced by playing its notes in different octaves, and by knowledge of the melody. (Courtesy of Diana Deutsch.)

11. *Perceiving Interleaved Melodies* How when two melodies are "interleaved," it becomes easier to hear both when the separation between their tones is increased.

12. *Layering Naturalistic Sounds* How we are able to hear different environmental sounds as being produced by different sound sources, even when they are presented at the same time.

13. *The Precedence Effect* How perception of sound location depends on the lag between sounds presented by two different speakers.

14. *Reverberation Time* How increasing a tone's reverberation time changes its perceived quality.

15. *Sound and Vision 1: Crossing or Colliding Balls* How sound can influence perception of the path of two moving balls. (Courtesy of Robert Sekuler.)

16. *Sound and Vision 2: Rolling Ball* How sound can affect perception of the path of a rolling ball. (Courtesy of Laurie Heller.)

17. *Sound and Vision 3: Flashing Dot* How sound can affect perception of a flashing dot. (Courtesy of Ladan Shams.)

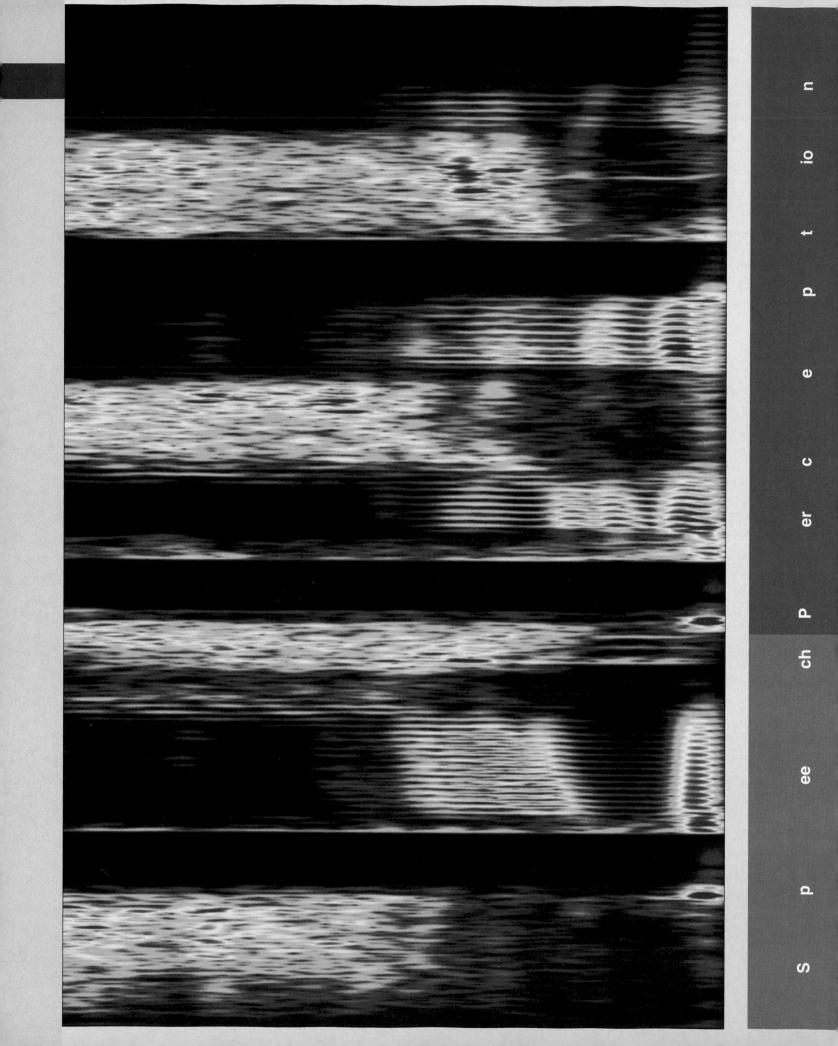

Chapter Contents

CHAPTER 13

Speech Perception

OPPOSITE PAGE This pattern is a speech spectrogram, which represents the sound energy from speaking the words *speech perception*. Spectrograms are usually displayed as black on a white background, with frequency indicated on one axis and speech sounds on the other axis. See page 312 for more details on speech spectrograms.
Original spectrogram (before colorizing) courtesy of David Pisoni, Luis Hernandez, and Tessa Bent.

[VL] The Virtual Lab icons direct you to specific animations and videos designed to help you visualize what you are reading about. The number beside each icon indicates the number of the clip you can access through your CD-ROM or your student website.

Some Questions We Will Consider:

■ Can computers perceive speech as well as humans? (p. 312)

■ Does each word that we hear have a unique pattern of air pressure changes associated with it? (p. 315)

■ Why does an unfamiliar foreign language often sound like a continuous stream of sound, with no breaks between words? (p. 320)

■ Are there specific areas in the brain that are responsible for perceiving speech? (p. 323)

Although we perceive speech easily under most conditions, beneath this ease lurks processes as complex as those involved in perceiving the most complicated visual scenes. One way to appreciate this complexity is to consider attempts to use computers to recognize speech. Many companies now use computer speech recognition systems to provide services such as booking tickets, automated banking, and computer technical support. But if you've ever used one of these systems, it is likely that a friendly computer voice has told you "I can't understand what you said" on more than one occasion.

Computer speech recognition is constantly improving, but it still can't match people's ability to recognize speech. Computers perform well when a person speaks slowly and clearly, and when there is no background noise. However, humans can perceive speech under a wide variety of conditions, including the presence of various background noises, sloppy pronunciation, speakers with different dialects and accents, and the often chaotic give-and-take that routinely occurs when people talk with one another (Sinha, 2002; Zue & Glass, 2000).

This chapter will help you appreciate the complex perceptual problems posed by speech and will describe research that has helped us begin to understand how the human speech perception system has solved some of these problems.

The Speech Stimulus

We began describing sound in Chapter 11 by introducing pure tones—simple sine-wave patterns with different amplitudes and frequencies. We then introduced musical tones consisting of a number of pure tones, called harmonics, with frequencies that are multiples of the tone's fundamental frequency. The sounds of speech increase the complexity one more level. We can still describe speech in terms of frequencies, but also in terms of the abrupt starts and stops, silences and noises that occur as speakers form words. And it is these words that add an important dimension to speech—the meanings that speakers create by saying these words, and by stringing them together into sentences. This meaning influences perception of the incoming stimuli, so that what we perceive depends not only on the physical

sound stimulus, but also on cognitive processes that help us interpret what we are hearing. We begin by describing the physical sound stimulus, called the *acoustic signal*.

The Acoustic Signal

Speech sounds are produced by the position or the movement of structures within the vocal apparatus, which produce patterns of pressure changes in the air called the **acoustic stimulus**, or the **acoustic signal**. The acoustic signal for most speech sounds is created by air that is pushed up from the lungs past the vocal cords and into the vocal tract. The sound that is produced depends on the shape of the vocal tract as air is pushed through it. The shape of the vocal tract is altered by moving the **articulators**, which include structures such as the tongue, lips, teeth, jaw, and soft palate (Figure 13.1).

Let's first consider the production of vowels. Vowels are produced by vibration of the vocal cords, and the specific sounds of each vowel are created by changing the overall shape of the vocal tract. This change in shape changes the resonant frequency of the vocal tract and produces peaks of pressure at a number of different frequencies (Figure 13.2). The frequencies at which these peaks occur are called formants.

Each vowel sound has a characteristic series of formants. The first formant has the lowest frequency; the second formant is the next highest; and so on. The formants for the vowel /ae/ (the vowel sound in the word *had*) are shown on a **sound spectrogram** in Figure 13.3. The sound spectrogram indicates the pattern of frequencies and intensities over time that make up the acoustic signal. Frequency is

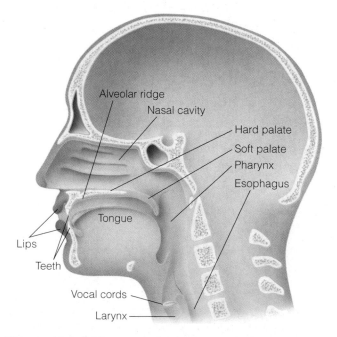

Figure 13.1 ▌ The vocal tract includes the nasal and oral cavities and the pharynx, as well as components that move, such as the tongue, lips, and vocal cords.

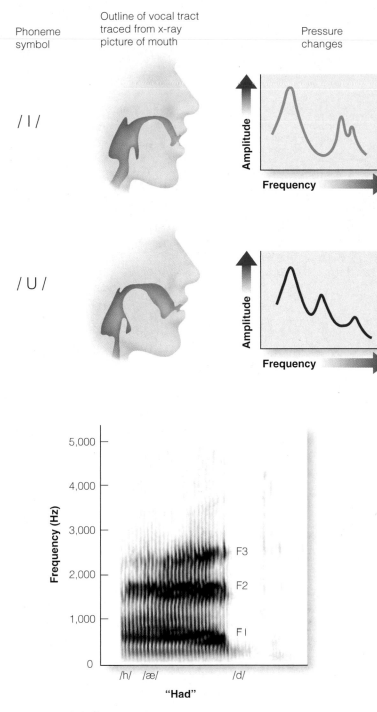

Phoneme symbol	Outline of vocal tract traced from x-ray picture of mouth	Pressure changes

/ I /

/ U /

Figure 13.2 ▌ Left: The shape of the vocal tract for the vowel sounds /I/ and /u/. Right: The amplitude of the pressure changes produced for each vowel. The peaks in the pressure changes are the formants. Each vowel sound has a characteristic pattern of formants that is determined by the shape of the vocal tract for that vowel. *(From Denes, P. B., & Pinson, E. N.,* The speech chain, *2nd ed. Copyright © 1993 by W. H. Freeman and Company. Used with permission.)*

Figure 13.3 ▌ Spectrogram of the word *had* showing the first (F1), second (F2), and third (F3) formants for the vowel sound /ae/. *(Spectrogram courtesy of Kerry Green.)*

indicated on the vertical axis and time on the horizontal axis; intensity is indicated by darkness, with more darkness indicating greater intensity. From Figure 13.3 we can see that formants are concentrations of energy at specific frequencies, with the sound /ae/ having formants at 500, 1,700, and 2,500 Hz. The vertical lines in the spectrogram are pressure oscillations caused by vibrations of the vocal cord.

Consonants are produced by a constriction, or closing, of the vocal tract. To illustrate how different consonants are produced, let's focus on the sounds /d/ and /f/ (speech sounds are indicated by setting them off with slashes). Make these sounds, and notice what your tongue, lips, and teeth are doing. As you produce the sound /d/, you place your tongue against the ridge above your upper teeth (the alveolar ridge of Figure 13.1) and then release a slight rush of air as you move your tongue away from the alveolar ridge (try it). As you produce the sound /f/, you place your bottom lip against your upper front teeth and then push air between the lips and the teeth.

These movements of the tongue, lips, and other articulators create patterns of energy in the acoustic signal that we can observe on the sound spectrogram. For example, the spectrogram for the sentence "Roy read the will," shown in Figure 13.4, shows aspects of the signal associated with vowels and consonants. The three horizontal bands marked F1, F2, and F3 are the three formants associated with the /e/ sound of *read*. Rapid shifts in frequency preceding or following formants are called **formant transitions** and are associated with consonants. For example, T2 and T3 are formant transitions associated with the /r/ of *read*.

We have described the physical characteristics of the *speech stimulus*. To understand *speech perception*, we need to consider the basic units of speech.

Basic Units of Speech

Our first task in studying speech perception is to separate speech sounds into manageable units. What are these

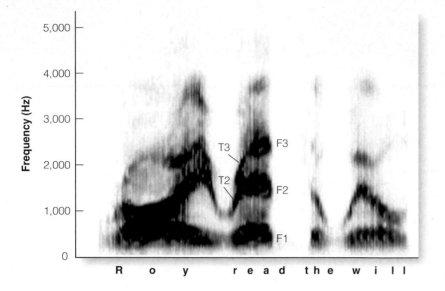

Figure 13.4 ❚ Spectrogram of the sentence "Roy read the will," showing formants F1, F2, and F3, and formant transitions T2 and T3. *(Spectrogram courtesy of Kerry Green.)*

units? The flow of a sentence? A particular word? A syllable? The sound of a letter? A sentence is too large a unit for easy analysis, and some letters have no sounds at all. Although there are arguments for the idea that the syllable is the basic unit of speech (Mehler, 1981; Segui, 1984), most speech research has been based on a unit called the **phoneme**. A phoneme is the shortest segment of speech that, if changed, would change the meaning of a word. Consider the word *bit*, which contains the phonemes /b/, /i/, and /t/. We know that /b/, /i/, and /t/ are phonemes because we can change the meaning of the word by changing each phoneme individually. Thus, *bit* becomes *pit* if /b/ is changed to /p/, it becomes *bat* if /i/ is changed to /a/, and it becomes *bid* if /t/ is changed to /d/.

The phonemes of American English, listed in Table 13.1, are represented by phonetic symbols that stand for speech sounds. This table shows phonemes for 13 vowel sounds and 24 consonant sounds. Your first reaction to this table may be that there are more vowels than the standard set you learned in grade school (a, e, i, o, u, and sometimes y). But some vowels can have more than one pronunciation, so there are more vowel sounds than vowel letters. For example, the vowel *o* sounds different in *boat* and *hot*, and the vowel *e* sounds different in *head* and *heed*. Phonemes, therefore, refer not to letters but to speech sounds that serve to distinguish the meaning of what people say.

Because different languages use different sounds, the number of phonemes varies across languages. Although there are only 11 phonemes in Hawaiian, as many as 47 have been identified in American English and up to 60 in some African languages. Thus, phonemes are defined in terms of the sounds that are used to create words in a specific language.

It might seem that, having identified the phoneme as the basic unit of speech, we could describe speech perception in terms of strings of phonemes. According to this idea, we perceive a series of sounds called phonemes, which create syllables that combine to create words. These syllables and words appear strung together one after another like beads

TABLE 13.1 ❚ **Major Consonants and Vowels of English and Their Phonetic Symbols**

CONSONANTS				VOWELS	
p	*p*ull	s	*s*ip	i	h*ee*d
b	*b*ull	z	*z*ip	I	h*i*d
m	*m*an	r	*r*ip	e	b*ai*t
w	*w*ill	š	*sh*ould	ε	h*ea*d
f	*f*ill	ž	plea*s*ure	æ	h*a*d
v	*v*et	č	*ch*op	u	wh*o*'d
θ	*th*igh	ǰ	*g*yp	U	p*u*t
ð	*th*at	y	*y*ip	ʌ	b*u*t
t	*t*ie	k	*k*ale	o	b*oa*t
d	*d*ie	g	*g*ale	ɔ	b*ou*ght
n	*n*ear	h	*h*ail	a	h*o*t
l	*l*ear	ŋ	si*ng*	ə	s*o*fa
				ɨ	m*a*ny

There are other American English phonemes in addition to those shown here, and specific symbols may vary depending on the source.

on a string. For example, we perceive the phrase "perception is easy" as the sequence of units "per-sep-shun-iz-ee-zee." But although perceiving speech may seem to be just a matter of processing a series of discrete sounds that are lined up one after another, the actual situation is much more complex.

Rather than following one another, with the signal for one sound ending and then the next beginning, like letters on a page, signals for neighboring sounds overlap one another. In addition, the pattern of air pressure changes for a particular word can vary greatly depending on whether the speaker is male or female, young or old, speaks rapidly or slowly, or has an accent.

The Variable Relationship Between Phonemes and the Acoustic Signal

The main problem facing researchers trying to understand speech perception is that there is a variable relationship between the acoustic signal and the sounds we hear. In other words, a particular acoustic signal can produce a number of different sounds. Let's consider some of the sources of this variability.

Variability From Context

The acoustic signal associated with a phoneme changes depending on its context. For example, look at Figure 13.5, which shows spectrograms for the sounds /di/ and /du/. These are smoothed hand-drawn spectrograms that show the two most important characteristics of the sounds: the formants (shown in red) and the formant transitions (shown in blue). Because formants are associated with vowels, we know that the formants at 200 and 2,600 Hz are the acoustic signal for the vowel /i/ in /di/ and that the formants at 200 and 600 Hz are the acoustic signal for the vowel /u/ in /du/.

Because the formants are the acoustic signals for the vowels, the formant transitions that precede the formants must be the signal for the consonant /d/. But notice that the formant transitions for the second (higher-frequency) formants of /di/ and /du/ are different. For /di/, the formant transition starts at about 2,200 Hz and rises to about 2,600 Hz. For /du/, the formant transition starts at about 1,100 Hz and falls to about 600 Hz. Thus, even though we perceive the same /d/ sound in /di/ and /du/, the formant transitions, which are the acoustic signals associated with these sounds, are very different.

This effect of context occurs because of the way speech is produced. The articulators are constantly moving as we talk, so the shape of the vocal tract for a particular phoneme is influenced by the shapes for the phonemes that both precede it and follow it. This overlap between the articulation of neighboring phonemes is called **coarticulation**. You can demonstrate coarticulation to yourself by noting how you produce phonemes in different contexts. For example, say *bat* and *boot*. When you say *bat*, your lips are unrounded, but when you say *boot*, your lips are rounded, even during the initial /b/ sound. Thus, even though the /b/ is the same in both words, you articulate each differently. In this example, the articulation of /oo/ in *boot* overlaps the articulation of /b/, causing the lips to be rounded even before the /oo/ sound is actually produced.

The fact that we perceive the sound of a phoneme as the same even though the acoustic signal is changed by coarticulation is an example of *perceptual constancy*. This term may be familiar to you from our observations of constancy phenomena in the sense of vision, such as color constancy (we perceive an object's chromatic color as constant even when the wavelength distribution of the illumination changes) and size constancy (we perceive an object's size as constant even when the size of its image changes on our retina). Perceptual constancy in speech perception is similar. We perceive the sound of a particular phoneme as constant even when the phoneme appears in different contexts that change its acoustic signal.

Variability From Different Speakers

People say the same words in a variety of different ways. Some people's voices are high pitched, and some are low pitched; people speak with accents; some talk extremely rapidly, and others speak e-x-t-r-e-m-e-l-y s-l-o-w-l-y. These wide variations in speech mean that for different speakers, a particular phoneme or word can have very different acoustic signals.

Speakers also introduce variability by their sloppy pronunciation. For example, say the following sentence at the speed you would use in talking to a friend: "This was a best buy." How did you say "best buy"? Did you pronounce the /t/ of best, or did you say "bes buy"? What about "She is a bad girl"? While saying this rapidly, notice whether your tongue hits the top of your mouth as you say the /d/ in bad. Many people omit the /d/ and say "ba girl." Finally, what about "Did you go to the store?" Did you say "did you" or "dijoo"? You have your own ways of producing various words and phonemes, and other people have theirs. Analysis of how people actually speak has determined that there are 50 different ways to produce the word "the" (Waldrop, 1988).

That people do not usually articulate each word individually in conversational speech is reflected in the spectrograms in Figure 13.6. The spectrogram in Figure 13.6a is for the question "What are you doing?" spoken slowly and distinctly; the spectrogram in Figure 13.6b is for the same question taken from conversational speech, in which "What are you doing?" becomes "Whad'aya doin'?" This difference shows up clearly in the spectrogram, which indicates that although the first and last words (*what* and *doing*) create similar patterns in the two spectrograms, the pauses between words are absent or are much less obvious in the

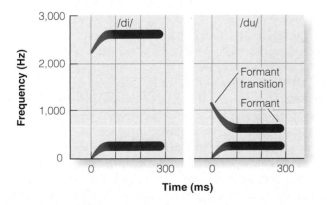

Figure 13.5 ▌ Hand-drawn spectrograms for /di/ and /du/. *(From Liberman et al., 1967.)*

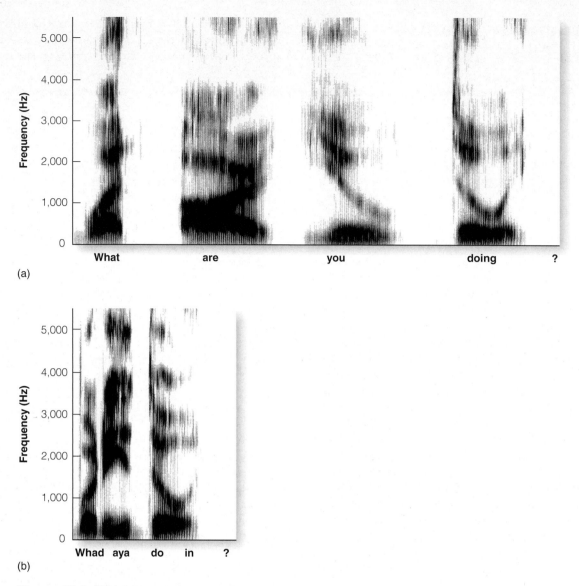

(a)

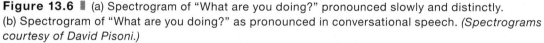

(b)

Figure 13.6 ▌ (a) Spectrogram of "What are you doing?" pronounced slowly and distinctly. (b) Spectrogram of "What are you doing?" as pronounced in conversational speech. *(Spectrograms courtesy of David Pisoni.)*

spectrogram of Figure 13.6b, and the middle of this spectrogram is completely changed, with a number of speech sounds missing.

The variability in the acoustic signal caused by coarticulation, different speakers, and sloppy pronunciation creates a problem for the listener, who must somehow transform the information contained in this highly variable acoustic signal into familiar words. In the next section we will consider some of the ways the speech perception system deals with the variability problem.

Information for Phoneme Perception

One way the speech perception system deals with the variability problem is by simplifying what we hear through a process called *categorical perception.*

Categorical Perception

While looking for connections between the speech signal and speech perception, researchers discovered a phenomenon called **categorical perception**—a wide range of acoustic signals results in perception of a limited number of categories of sounds. We will use a specific example to explain what this means. ▐V*L*▌ **1**

The example we will describe involves varying a characteristic of the acoustic signal called **voice onset time** (VOT). Voice onset time is the time delay between when a sound begins and when the vocal cords begin vibrating. We can illustrate this delay by comparing the spectrograms for the sounds /da/ and /ta/ in Figure 13.7. We can see from these spectrograms that the time between the beginning of the sound /da/ and the beginning of the vocal cord vibrations (indicated by the presence of vertical stripes in the spectrogram) is 17 ms for /da/ and 91 ms for /ta/. Thus, /da/ has a short VOT, and /ta/ has a long VOT.

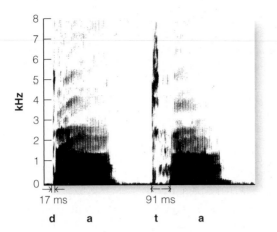

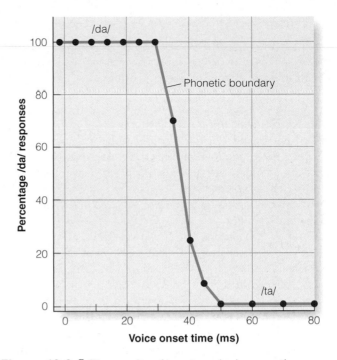

Figure 13.7 ▮ Spectrograms for /da/ and /ta/. The voice onset time—the time between the beginning of the sound and the onset of voicing—is indicated at the beginning of the spectrogram for each sound. *(Spectrograms courtesy of Ron Cole.)*

By using computers, researchers have created sound stimuli in which the VOT is varied in small steps from short to long. When they vary VOT, using stimuli like the ones in Figure 13.7, and ask listeners to indicate what sound they hear, the listeners report hearing only one or the other of the two phonemes, /da/ or /ta/, even though a large number of stimuli with different VOTs are presented.

This result is shown in Figure 13.8 (Eimas & Corbit, 1973). At short VOTs, listeners report that they hear /da/, and they continue reporting this even when the VOT is increased. But when the VOT reaches about 35 ms, their perception abruptly changes, so at VOTs above 40 ms, they report hearing /ta/. The VOT when the perception changes from /da/ to /ta/ is called the **phonetic boundary**. The key result of the categorical perception experiment is that even though the VOT is changed continuously across a wide range, the listener perceives only two categories: /da/ on one side of the phonetic boundary and /ta/ on the other side.

Once we have demonstrated categorical perception using the procedure above, we can run a *discrimination test*, in which we present two stimuli with different VOTs and ask the listener whether they sound the same or different. When we present two stimuli separated by a VOT of 25 ms that are on the same side of the phonetic boundary, such as stimuli with VOTs of 0 and 25 ms, the listener says they sound the same (Figure 13.9). However, when we present two stimuli that are separated by the same difference in VOT but are on the opposite side of the phonetic boundary, such as stimuli with VOTs of 25 and 50 ms, the listener says they sound different. The fact that all stimuli on the same side of the phonetic boundary are perceived as the same category is an example of perceptual constancy. If this constancy did not exist, we would perceive different sounds every time we changed the VOT. Instead, we experience one sound on each side of the phonetic boundary. This simplifies our perception of phonemes and helps us more easily perceive the wide variety of sounds in our environment.

Figure 13.8 ▮ The results of a categorical perception experiment indicate that /da/ is perceived for VOTs to the left of the phonetic boundary, and that /ta/ is perceived at VOTs to the right of the phonetic boundary. *(From Eimas & Corbit, 1973.)*

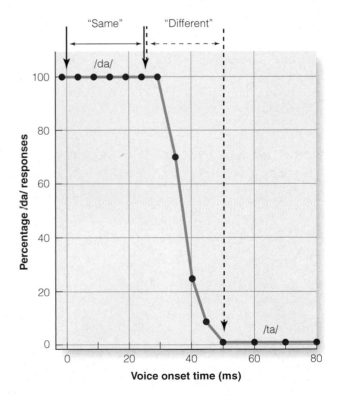

Figure 13.9 ▮ In the discrimination part of a categorical perception experiment, two stimuli are presented, and the listener indicates whether they are the same or different. The typical result is that two stimuli with VOTs on the same side of the phonetic boundary (VOT = 0 and 25 ms; solid arrows) are judged to be the same, and two stimuli on different sides of the phonetic boundary (VOT = 25 ms and 50 ms; dashed arrows) are judged to be different.

Information Provided by the Face

Another property of speech perception is that it is **multimodal**; that is, our perception of speech can be influenced by information from a number of different senses. One illustration of how speech perception can be influenced by visual information is shown in Figure 13.10. At first our listener hears the sounds /ba-ba/ coming from the speakers. But when visual stimulation is added in the form of a videotape showing a person making the lip movements for the sound /ga-ga/, our listener begins hearing the sound /da-da/. Despite the fact that the listener is still receiving the acoustic signal for /ba-ba/, his perception is shifted, so he hears /da-da/. **VL** 2, 3

This effect is called the **McGurk effect**, after the person who first described it (McGurk & MacDonald, 1976). It illustrates that although auditory information is the major source of information for speech perception, visual information can also exert a strong influence on what we hear. This influence of vision on speech perception is called **audiovisual speech perception**. The McGurk effect is one example of audiovisual speech perception. Another example is the way people routinely use information provided by the speaker's lip movements to help understand speech in a noisy environment (also see Sumby & Pollack, 1954).

The link between vision and speech has also been shown to have a physiological basis. Gemma Calvert and coworkers (1997) used fMRI to measure brain activity as observers watched a silent videotape of a person making mouth movements for saying numbers. Observers silently repeated the numbers as they watched, so this task was similar to what people do when they read lips. In a control condition, observers watched a static face while silently repeating numbers. A comparison of the brain activity in these two conditions showed that watching the lips move activated an area in the auditory cortex that is also activated when people are perceiving speech. Perhaps, suggests Calvert, the fact that the same areas are activated for lipreading and speech perception may be a neural mechanism behind the McGurk effect.

The link between speech perception and face perception was demonstrated in another way by Katharina von Kriegstein and coworkers (2005), who measured fMRI activation as listeners were carrying out a number of tasks involving sentences spoken by familiar speakers (people who also worked in the laboratory) and unfamiliar speakers (people they had never heard before).

Just listening to speech activated the superior temporal sulcus (STS; see Figure 8.13), an area that had been associated in previous studies with speech perception (Belin et al., 2000). But when listeners were asked to carry out a task that involved paying attention to the sounds of familiar voices, the fusiform face area (FFA) was also activated. In contrast, paying attention to the sounds of unfamiliar voices did not activate the FFA. Apparently, what is happening is that when people hear a voice that they associate with a specific person, this activates areas not only for perceiving speech but also for perceiving faces. The link between perceiving speech and perceiving faces, which has been demonstrated in both behavioral and physiological experiments, provides information that helps us deal with the variability of phonemes (also see Hall et al., 2005, and Wassenhove et al., 2005, for more on the link between observing someone speaking and perceiving speech).

Information From Our Knowledge of Language

A large amount of research has shown it is easier to perceive phonemes that appear in a meaningful context. Philip Rubin, M. T. Turvey, and Peter Van Gelder (1976) showed that meaning enhances a listener's ability to recognize phonemes by presenting a series of short words, such as *sin, bat*, and *leg*, or nonwords, such as *jum, baf*, and *teg*, and asking listeners to respond by pressing a key as rapidly as possible whenever they heard a sound that began with /b/. On average, participants took 631 ms to respond to the nonwords and 580 ms to respond to the real words. Thus, when a phoneme is at the beginning of a real word, it is identified about 8 percent faster than when it is at the beginning of a meaningless syllable.

The effect of meaning on the perception of phonemes was demonstrated in another way by Richard Warren (1970), who had participants listen to a recording of the sentence "The state governors met with their respective legislatures convening in the capital city." Warren replaced the first /s/ in "legislatures" with the sound of a cough and told his subjects that they should indicate where in the sentence the cough occurred. None of the participants identified the correct position of the cough, and, even more significantly, none noticed that the /s/ in "legislatures" was missing.

Figure 13.10 ▌ The McGurk effect. The woman's lips are moving as if she is saying /ga-ga/, but the actual sound being presented is /ba-ba/. The listener reports hearing the sound /da-da/. If the listener closes his eyes, so that he no longer sees the woman's lips, he hears /ba-ba/. Thus, seeing the lips moving influences what the listener hears.

This effect, which Warren called the **phonemic restoration effect**, was experienced even by students and staff in the psychology department who knew that the /s/ was missing.

Warren not only demonstrated the phonemic restoration effect but also showed that it can be influenced by the meaning of words following the missing phoneme. For example, the last word of the phrase "There was time to *ave..." (where the * indicates the presence of a cough or some other sound) could be "shave," "save," "wave," or "rave," but participants heard the word "wave" when the remainder of the sentence had to do with saying good-bye to a departing friend.

The phonemic restoration effect was used by Arthur Samuel (1981) to show that speech perception is determined both by the nature of the acoustic signal (bottom-up processing) and by context that produces expectations in the listener (top-down processing). Samuel demonstrated bottom-up processing by showing that restoration is better when a masking sound, such as the hissing sound produced by a TV set tuned to a nonbroadcasting channel, and the masked phoneme sound similar. Thus, phonemic restoration is more likely to occur for a phoneme such as /s/, which is rich in high-frequency acoustic energy, if the mask also contains a large proportion of high-frequency energy. What happens in phonemic restoration, according to Samuel, is that before we actually perceive a "restored" sound, its presence must be confirmed by the presence of a sound that is similar to it. If the white-noise mask contains frequencies that make it sound similar to the phoneme we are expecting, phonemic restoration occurs, and we are likely to hear the phoneme. If the mask does not sound similar, phonemic restoration is less likely to occur (Samuel, 1990).

Samuel demonstrated top-down processing by showing that longer words increase the likelihood of the phonemic restoration effect. Apparently, participants used the additional context provided by the long word to help identify the masked phoneme. Further evidence for the importance of context is Samuel's finding that more restoration occurs for a real word such as *prOgress* (where the capital letter indicates the masked phoneme) than for a similar pseudoword such as *crOgress* (Samuel, 1990; also see Samuel, 1997, 2001, for more evidence that top-down processing is involved in phonemic restoration).

TEST YOURSELF 13.1

1. Describe the speech stimulus. Be sure you understand what phonemes are and how the acoustic signal can be displayed using a sound spectrogram to reveal formants and formant transitions.
2. What are two sources of variability that affect the relationship between the acoustic signals and the sounds we hear? Be sure you understand coarticulation.
3. What is categorical perception? Be sure you understand how it is measured and what it illustrates.

4. What is the McGurk effect, and what does it illustrate about how speech perception can be influenced by visual information? What physiological evidence demonstrates a link between visual processing and speech perception?
5. Describe evidence that shows how perceiving phonemes is influenced by the context in which they appear. Describe the phonemic restoration effect and the evidence for both bottom-up and top-down processing in creating this effect.

Information for Spoken Word Perception

We have seen that there is not a one-to-one relation between the acoustic signals and our perception of phonemes. We now show how this lack of one-to-one correspondence also occurs for perceiving words.

Information From Sentence Context

Just as the perception of phonemes is aided by the meanings of words, the perception of words can be aided by the sentences in which they occur.

Perceiving Words In Sentences One way to illustrate how being in a sentence can influence word perception is to show that words can be read even when they are degraded, as in the following demonstration.

DEMONSTRATION

Perceiving Degraded Sentences

Read the following sentences:

1. M*R* H*D * L*TTL* L*MB I*S FL**C* W*S WH*T* *S SN*W
2. TH* S*N *S N*T SH*N*NG T*D**
3. S*M* W**DS *R* EA*I*R T* U*D*R*T*N* T*A* *T*E*S ▌

Your ability to read the sentences, even though up to half of the letters have been eliminated, was aided by your knowledge of English words, how words are strung together to form sentences, and perhaps, in the first example, your familiarity with the nursery rhyme (Denes & Pinson, 1993).

A similar effect of meaningfulness also occurs for spoken words. An early demonstration of how meaningfulness makes it easier to perceive spoken words was provided by George Miller and Steven Isard (1963), who showed that words are more intelligible when heard in the context of a grammatical sentence than when presented as items in a list of unconnected words. They demonstrated this by creating three kinds of stimuli: (1) normal grammatical sentences, such as *Gadgets simplify work around the house*; (2) anomalous sentences that follow the rules of grammar but make no sense, such as *Gadgets kill passengers from the eyes*; and (3) ungrammatical strings of words, such as *Between gadgets highways passengers the steal*.

Miller and Isard used a technique called shadowing, in which they presented these sentences to subjects through earphones and asked them to repeat aloud what they were hearing. The participants reported normal sentences with an accuracy of 89 percent, but their accuracy fell to 79 percent for the anomalous sentences and 56 percent for the ungrammatical strings. The differences among the three types of stimuli became even greater when the listeners heard the stimuli in the presence of a background noise. For example, at a moderately high level of background noise, accuracy was 63 percent for the normal sentences, 22 percent for the anomalous sentences, and only 3 percent for the ungrammatical strings of words. This result tells us that when words are arranged in a meaningful pattern, we can perceive them more easily. But most people don't realize it is their knowledge of the nature of their language that helps them fill in sounds and words that might be difficult to hear. For example, our knowledge of permissible word structures tells us that ANT, TAN, and NAT are all permissible sequences of letters in English, but that TQN or NQT cannot be English words.

A similar effect of meaning on perception also occurs because our knowledge of the rules of grammar tells us that "There is no time to question" is a permissible English sentence, but "Question, no time there is" is not permissible or, at best, is extremely awkward (unless you are Yoda, who says this in *Star Wars, Episode III: Revenge of the Sith*). Because we mostly encounter meaningful words and grammatically correct sentences, we are continually using our knowledge of what is permissible in our language to help us understand what is being said. This becomes particularly important when listening under less than ideal conditions, such as in noisy environments or when the speaker's voice quality or accent is difficult to understand (see also Salasoo & Pisoni, 1985).

Perceiving Breaks Between Words Just as we effortlessly see objects when we look at a visual scene, we usually have little trouble perceiving individual words when conversing with another person. But when we look at the speech signal, we see that the acoustic signal is continuous, with either no physical breaks in the signal or breaks that don't necessarily correspond to the breaks we perceive between words (Figure 13.11). The perception of individual words in a conversation is called speech segmentation.

The fact that there are usually no spaces between words becomes obvious when you listen to someone speaking a foreign language. To someone who is unfamiliar with that language, the words seem to speed by in an unbroken string. However, to a speaker of that language, the words seem separated, just as the words of your native language seem separated to you. We somehow solve the problem of speech segmentation and divide the continuous stream of the acoustic signal into a series of individual words.

The fact that we can perceive individual words in conversational speech, even though there are no breaks in the speech signal, means that our perception of words is not based only on the energy stimulating the receptors. One thing that helps us tell when one word ends and another begins is knowledge of the meanings of words. The link between speech segmentation and meaning is illustrated in the following demonstration.

DEMONSTRATION

Organizing Strings of Sounds

Read the following words: Anna Mary Candy Lights Since Imp Pulp Lay Things. Now that you've read the words, what do they mean? ▊

If you think this is a list of unconnected words beginning with the names of two women, Anna and Mary, you're right; but read this series of words out loud speaking rapidly and ignoring the spaces between the words on the page. When you do this, can you hear a connected sentence that does *not* begin with the names Anna and Mary? (For the answer, see page 327—but don't peek until you've tried reading the words rapidly.)

If you succeeded in creating a new sentence from the series of words, you did so by changing the perceptual organization of the sounds, and this change was achieved by your

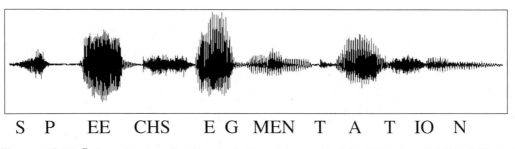

S   P   EE   CHS   E G   MEN   T   A   T   IO   N

Figure 13.11 ▊ Sound energy for the words "speech segmentation." Notice that it is difficult to tell from this record where one word ends and the other begins. *(Speech signal courtesy of Lisa Saunders.)*

knowledge of the meaning of the sounds. Just as the perceptual organization of the forest scene in Figure 5.20 depended on seeing the rocks as meaningful patterns (faces), your perception of the new sentence depended on knowing the meanings of the sounds you created when you said these words rapidly.

Another example of how meaning and prior knowledge or experience are responsible for organizing sounds into words is provided by these two sentences.

- Jamie's mother said, "Be a *big girl* and eat your vegetables."

- The thing *Big Earl* loved most in the world was his car.

"Big girl" and "Big Earl" are both pronounced the same way, so hearing them differently depends on the overall meaning of the sentence in which these words appear. This example is similar to the familiar "I scream, you scream, we all scream for ice cream" that many people learn as children. The sound stimuli for "I scream" and "ice cream" are identical, so the different organizations must be achieved by the meaning of the sentence in which these words appear.

While segmentation is aided by knowing the meanings of words and making use of the context in which these words occur, listeners use other information as well to achieve segmentation. As we learn a language, we learn that certain sounds are more likely to follow one another within a word, and other sounds are more likely to be separated by the space between two words. For example, consider the words *pretty baby*. In English it is likely that *pre* and *ty* will be in the same word (***pre-tty***) and that *ty* and *ba* will be separated by a space so will be in two different words (pre***ty ba***by). Thus, the space in the phrase *prettybaby* is most likely to be between *pretty* and *baby*.

Psychologists describe the way sounds follow one another in language in terms of **transitional probabilities**—the chances that one sound will follow another sound. Every language has transitional probabilities for different sounds, and as we learn a language, we not only learn how to say and understand words and sentences, but we also learn about the transitional probabilities in that language. The process of learning about transitional probabilities and about other characteristics of language is called **statistical learning**. Research has shown that infants as young as 8 months of age are capable of statistical learning.

Jennifer Saffran and coworkers (1996) carried out an early experiment that demonstrated statistical learning in young infants. Figure 13.12a shows the design of this experiment. During the learning phase of the experiment, the infants heard four nonsense "words" such as *bidaku, padoti, golabu,* and *tupiro*, which were combined in random order to create two minutes of continuous sound. An example of part of a string created by combining these words is *bidaku***padoti**golabu**tupiro**padoti**bidaku*. . . . In this string, every other word is printed in boldface in order to help you pick out the words. However, when the infants heard these strings, all the words were pronounced with the same intonation, and

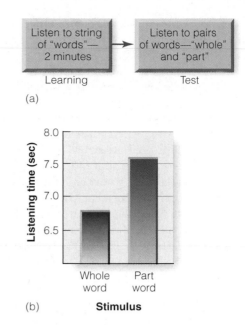

(a)

(b) **Stimulus**

Figure 13.12 ▌ (a) Design of the experiment by Saffran and coworkers (1996), in which infants listened to a continuous string of nonsense syllables and were then tested to see which sounds they perceived as belonging together. (b) The results indicated that infants listened longer to the "part-word" stimuli.

there were no breaks between the words to indicate where one word ended and the next one began. VL 4

Because the words were presented in random order and with no spaces between them, the two-minute string of words the infants heard sounds like a jumble of random sounds. However, there was information within the string of words in the form of transitional probabilities, which the infants could potentially use to determine which groups of sounds were words. The transitional probabilities between two syllables that appeared *within* a word was always 1.0. For example for the word *bidaku*, when /bi/ was presented, /da/ always followed it. Similarly, when /da/ was presented, /ku/ always followed it. In other words, these three sounds always occurred together and in the same order, to form the word *bidaku*. However, the transitional probabilities between the *end* of one word and the *beginning* of another was only 0.33. For example, there was a 33-percent chance that the last sound, /ku/ from *bidaku* would be followed by the first sound, /pa/, from *padoti*, a 33-percent chance that it would be followed by /tu/ from *tupiro*, and a 33-percent chance it would be followed by /go/ from *golabu*.

If Saffran's infants were sensitive to transitional probabilities, they would perceive stimuli like *bidaku* or *padoti* as words, because the three syllables in these words are linked by transitional probabilities of 1.0. In contrast, stimuli like *tibida* (the end of *padoti* plus the beginning of *bidaku*) would not be perceived as words, because the components were not linked.

To determine whether the infants did, in fact, perceive stimuli like *bidaku* and *padoti* as words, the infants were tested by being presented with pairs of three-syllable stimuli. One of the stimuli was a "word" that had been presented before, such as *padoti*. This was the "whole-word" test stimulus. The other stimulus was created from the end of one word and the beginning of another, such as *tibida*. This was the "part-word" test stimulus.

The prediction was that the infants would choose to listen to the part-word test stimuli longer than to the whole-word stimuli. This prediction was based on previous research that showed that infants tend to lose interest in stimuli that are repeated, and so become familiar, but pay more attention to novel stimuli that they haven't experienced before. Thus, if the infants perceived the whole-word stimuli as words that had been repeated over and over during the two-minute learning session, they would pay less attention to these familiar stimuli than to the more novel part-word stimuli that they had not perceived as being words.

Saffran measured how long the infants listened to each sound by presenting a blinking light near the speaker where the sound was coming from. When the light attracted the infant's attention, the sound began, and it continued until the infant looked away. Thus, the infant controlled how long they heard each sound by how long they looked at the light.

Figure 13.12b shows that the infants did, as predicted, listen longer to the part-word stimuli. These results are impressive, especially because the infants had never heard the words before, they heard no pauses between words, and they had only listened to the strings of words for two minutes. From results such as these, we can conclude that the ability to use transitional probabilities to segment sounds into words begins at an early age.

Information From Speaker Characteristics

When you're having a conversation, hearing a lecture, or listening to dialogue in a movie, you usually focus on determining the meaning of what is being said. But as you are taking in these messages, you are also, perhaps without realizing it, taking in characteristics of the speaker's voice. These characteristics, called **indexical characteristics**, carry information about speakers such as their age, gender, place of origin, emotional state, and whether they are being sarcastic or serious. Consider, for example, the following joke:

> A linguistics professor was lecturing to his class one day. "In English," he said, "a double negative forms a positive. In some languages, though, such as Russian, a double negative is still a negative. However, there is no language wherein a double positive can form a negative." A voice from the back of the room piped up, "Yeah, right."

This joke is humorous because "Yeah, right" contains two positive words that, despite the linguistics professor's

statement, produce a negative statement that most people who know contemporary English usage would interpret as "I disagree." The point of this example is not just that "Yeah, right" can mean "I disagree," but that the meaning of this phrase is determined by our knowledge of current English usage and also (if we were actually listening to the student's remark) by the speaker's tone of voice, which in this case would be highly sarcastic.

The speaker's tone of voice is one factor that helps listeners determine the meaning of what is being said. But most research on indexical characteristics has focused on how speech perception is influenced by the speaker's identity. Thomas Palmeri, Stephen Goldinger, and David Pisoni (1993) demonstrated the effect of speaker identity by presenting listeners with a sequence of words. After each word, listeners indicated whether the word was a new word (this was the first time it appeared) or an old word (it had appeared previously in the sequence). They found that listeners reacted more rapidly and were more accurate when the same speaker said all of the words than when different speakers said the words. This means that listeners are taking in two levels of information about the word: (1) its meaning and (2) characteristics of the speaker's voice.

From the results of this experiment and the others we have discussed, we can conclude that speech perception depends both on the bottom-up information provided by the acoustic signal and on the top-down information provided by the meanings of words and sentences, the listener's knowledge of the rules of grammar, and information that the listener has about characteristics of the speaker's voice (Figure 13.13).

We can appreciate the interaction between the acoustic signal for speech and the meaning of speech when we realize that although we use the meaning to help us to understand the acoustic signal, the acoustic signal is the starting point for determining the meaning. Look at it this way: There may be enough information in my sloppy handwriting so that a

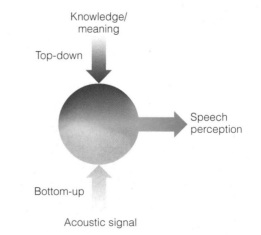

Figure 13.13 ▌ Speech perception is the result of top-down processing (based on knowledge and meaning) and bottom-up processing (based on the acoustic signal) working together.

person using bottom-up processing can decipher it solely on the basis of the squiggles on the page, but my handwriting is much easier to decipher when, by using top-down processing, the person takes the meanings of the words into account. And just as previous experience in hearing a particular person's voice makes it easier to understand that person later, previous experience in reading my handwriting would make it easier to read the squiggles on the page. Speech perception apparently works in a similar way. Although most of the information is contained in the acoustic signal, taking meaning and indexical properties into account [VL]5 makes understanding speech much easier.

Speech Perception and the Brain

Investigation of the physiological basis for speech perception stretches back to at least the 19th century, but considerable progress has been made only recently in understanding the physiological foundations of speech perception and spoken word recognition.

Cortical Location of Speech Perception

Based on their studies of brain-damaged patients, 19th-century researchers Paul Broca and Carl Wernicke showed that damage to specific areas of the brain causes language problems, called aphasias (Figure 13.14). There are numerous forms of aphasia, with the specific symptoms depending on the area damaged and extent of the damage. Patients with damage to Broca's area in the frontal lobe have a condition called Broca's aphasia. They have labored and stilted speech and can only speak in short sentences. They are, however, capable of comprehending what others are saying. Patients with damage to Wernicke's area in the temporal lobe have Wernicke's aphasia. They can speak fluently, but what they say is extremely disorganized and not meaningful. These patients have great difficulty understanding what other people are saying. In the most extreme form of Wernicke's aphasia, the person has a condition called word deafness, in which he or she cannot recognize words, even though the ability to hear pure tones remains intact (Kolb & Whishaw, 2003).

Modern research has gone beyond localizing speech production and perception in these two areas through further studies of brain damaged patients (see Method: Dissociations in Neuropsychology, Chapter 4, page 89) and by using brain imaging to locate areas in the brain related to speech. An example of a finding from neuropsychology is that some patients with damage to the parietal lobe have difficulty discriminating between syllables (Blumstein et al., 1977; Damasio & Damasio, 1980). Although we might expect that difficulty in discriminating between syllables would make it difficult to understand words, some patients who have trouble discriminating syllables can still under-

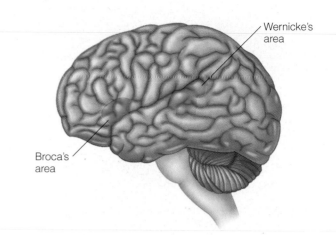

Figure 13.14 ▮ Broca's and Wernicke's areas were identified in early research as being specialized for language production and comprehension.

stand words (Micelli et al., 1980). Results such as these illustrate the complex relationship between brain functioning and speech perception.

Brain imaging studies have yielded results that are easier to understand. For example, Pascal Belin and coworkers (2000) used fMRI to locate a "voice area" in the superior temporal sulcul (STS) that is activated more by human voices than by other sounds. This area is part of the ventral processing stream for hearing that we described in Chapter 11 (see page 281). In describing the cortical organization for hearing in Chapter 11, we saw that the ventral stream is involved in identifying sounds, and the dorsal stream is involved in locating sounds (Figure 11.38). Piggybacking on this dual-stream idea for hearing, a dual-stream model of speech perception has proposed a ventral stream starting in the temporal lobe that is responsible for recognizing speech, and a dorsal stream starting in the parietal lobe that is responsible for linking the acoustic signal to the movements used to produce speech (Figure 13.15; Hickock & Poeppel, 2007).

You may notice similarities between this scheme and the dorsal/ventral system for vision that we described in Chapter 4 (page 88). The visual ventral stream is responsible for identifying objects ("what") and the dorsal stream for locating or taking action toward objects ("where/how"). The idea of dual streams has therefore been proposed for vision, for hearing, and for perceiving speech.

What all of this means is that the cortical mechanisms for perceiving speech are distributed throughout the cortex. This is similar to the situation we described for perceiving faces in Chapter 5 (page 121). We saw that perceiving faces involves many aspects, including identifying the face, reading expressions, noting where the face is looking, and evaluating the face's attractiveness, and that mechanisms for face perception are therefore distributed across many areas. There are also a number of different aspects to speech perception, as it is influenced by cognitive factors such as the meaning of words, the context of sentences, and familiarity

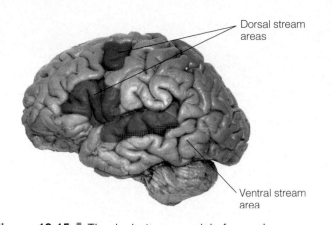

Dorsal stream areas

Ventral stream area

Figure 13.15 ▮ The dual-stream model of speech perception proposes a ventral pathway that is responsible for recognizing speech and a dorsal pathway that links the acoustic signal and motor movements. The blue areas are associated with the dorsal pathway; the yellow area with the ventral pathway. The red and green areas are also involved in the analysis of speech stimuli. *(Adapted from Hickock & Poeppel, 2007.)*

with a speaker's voice; it is linked to vision; and it can have a strong emotional component. It is not surprising, therefore, that perceiving speech involves many interconnected areas of the cortex.

Experience-Dependent Plasticity

Another example of the connection between brain functioning and speech perception is provided by the phenomenon of *experience-dependent plasticity*. We saw in Chapter 4 that experience-dependent plasticity occurs when the brain's ability to respond to specific stimuli is shaped by experience. For example, for vision, raising kittens in an environment consisting entirely of vertical lines causes the kitten's brain to contain neurons that respond only to verticals (page 80); and for hearing, training owl monkeys to discriminate between two different frequencies increases the space in the cortex devoted to those frequencies (Chapter 11, page 284).

The effect of experience-dependent plasticity on speech perception is illustrated by how the sounds infants are exposed to influence (1) their ability to hear certain sounds when they are older, and (2) how their brain responds to these sounds. We begin by considering what very young infants can perceive, and then consider what happens when they get older.

Young infants in all cultures can tell the difference between sounds that create all of the speech sounds used in the world's languages, but by the age of 1, they have lost the ability to distinguish between some of these sounds (Kuhl, 2000). The classic example of this phenomenon is provided by Japanese children and adults. Six-month-old Japanese children can tell the difference between the /r/ and /l/ used in American English just as well as American children can. However, by 12 months, Japanese children can no longer do this, leading to difficulty distinguishing between words

like *lent* and *rent*. Over the same period, American children become better at telling the difference between these two sounds (Kuhl et al., 1997; Strange, 1995).

Evidence supporting the idea that the physiological mechanism responsible for this early shift in speech perception is likely to involve experience-dependent plasticity has been provided by Maritza Rivera-Gaxiola and coworkers (2005), who recorded electrical potentials from the surface of the cortex of 7- and 11-month-old American infants from English-speaking households in response to pairs of sounds that sound the same to adult English-speakers but are perceived as different by adult Spanish-speakers. At 7 months of age, the electrical response to these two sounds was different in the English-speaking children, but by 11 months of age, the response had become the same.

This result provides a physiological parallel to the experience of young Japanese children described earlier. A pair of sounds can be perceived as different or can cause different physiological responses at an early age, but if the child doesn't have experience discriminating between the two sounds, then the child loses the ability to tell the difference between the two sounds, and physiological responses to the sounds become the same. Apparently, the brain is shaped by experience to respond to sounds that are used in the particular language that the child is learning.

Something to Consider: Speech Perception and Action

An important characteristic of speech is that we not only perceive it, but we also produce it. This close link between perceiving speech and producing it led Alvin Liberman and coworkers (1963, 1967) to propose a theory called the **motor theory of speech perception**. Motor theory proposed that speech has special status as an auditory stimulus, which involves special processing mechanisms not shared by other auditory stimuli. We won't discuss this idea further (see "If You Want to Know More" item 2, page 326), but we will consider another proposal of motor theory: Hearing a particular speech sound activates motor mechanisms controlling the movement of the articulators responsible for producing sounds, and activation of these motor mechanisms activates additional mechanisms that enables us to *perceive* the sound.

When motor theory was first proposed in the 1960s, it was extremely controversial. In the decades that followed, the theory stimulated a large number of experiments, some obtaining results that supported the theory, and others obtaining results that argued against it. Details of the theory were revised in response to some of these results (Liberman & Mattingly, 1989).

Present-day speech researchers are less concerned with whether the details of motor theory are correct and more concerned with evidence from a number of recent experiments that supports the idea that there are, in fact, links between speech perception and motor mechanisms. One of the results supporting this idea is the discovery of mirror neurons. In Chapter 7 we saw that mirror neurons in monkeys respond both when the monkey carries out an action and when the monkey sees someone else carry out the action. A type of mirror neuron related to hearing is called *audiovisual mirror neurons*. These neurons fire when a monkey *carries out an action* that produces a sound (like breaking a peanut) and when the monkey *hears the sound* (the sound of a breaking peanut) that results from the action (Kohler, 2002; see Chapter 7, page 168). Interestingly, mirror neurons that have been studied in the monkey are found in an area roughly equivalent to Broca's area in humans; for this reason, some researchers have proposed a close link between mirror neurons and language (Arbib, 2001).

But is there any evidence directly linking *perceiving* speech and *producing* speech in humans? K. D. Watkins and coworkers (2003) provided some evidence for this link by using transcranial magnetic stimulation (TMS) to activate the area of the motor cortex that controls movements of the face (see Method: Transcranial Magnetic Stimulation, Chapter 8, page 193). When they stimulated this area, they were able to detect small responses, called motor-evoked potentials (MEP), from the lips (Figure 13.16a). This wasn't surprising because stimulating this area of the motor cortex should cause movement potentials in the lips. But what was significant was that the MEP response became larger when the person either listened to speech or watched someone else's lip movements (Figure 13.16b).

Watkins also did other experiments that showed that this MEP enhancement occurs only for structures such as the lips, which are part of the motor system for producing speech. Based on these results, he suggested (1) that perhaps mirror neurons are involved and (2) that his result is consistent with the idea proposed by motor theory that hearing a speech sound activates motor mechanisms for perceiving the sound. Whatever the implications of Watkins' results and the results of research on mirror neurons, there is no question that our statement on page 156 of Chapter 7, that motor activity and perception are closely linked, holds not only for vision, but for perceiving speech as well.

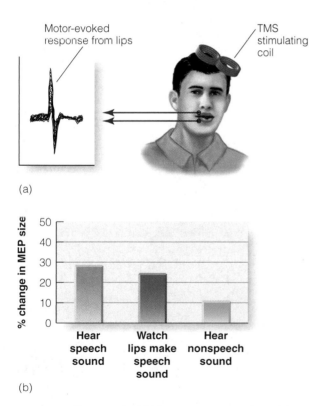

(a)

(b)

Figure 13.16 ▌ The transcranial magnetic stimulation experiment that provides evidence for a link between speech perception and production in humans. See text for details. *(Reprinted from Watkins, K. E., Strafella, A. P., & Paus, T., Seeing and hearing speech excites the motor system involved in speech production,* Neuropsychologia, 41, *989–994. Copyright 2003, with permission from Elsevier.)*

TEST YOURSELF 13.2

1. What is the evidence that meaning can influence phoneme perception?
2. What is the evidence that meaning can influence word perception?
3. How do speaker characteristics influence speech perception?
4. Describe evidence for both bottom-up and top-down processing in speech perception.
5. What did Broca and Wernicke discover about the physiology of speech perception?
6. Describe the following evidence that is relevant to the physiology of speech perception: (1) determining the brain's response to speech stimuli; (2) the change in speech perception abilities that takes place during the first year of life.
7. What is the link between perception and motor responding that is proposed by the motor theory. Describe how the results of research on mirror neurons and transcranial magnetic stimulation are related to motor theory.

THINK ABOUT IT

1. How well can computers recognize speech? You can research this question by getting on the telephone with a computer. Dial a service such as the one that books movie tickets, and then instead of going out of your way to talk slowly and clearly, try talking in a normal conversational voice (but talk clearly enough so a human would still understand you), and see whether you can determine the limits of the computer's ability to understand speech. (p. 312)

2. How do you think your perception of speech would be affected if the phenomenon of categorical perception did not exist? (p. 316)

IF YOU WANT TO KNOW MORE

1. *Tadoma: "hearing" with touch.* People who are both deaf and blind can figure out what people are saying by using a procedure called Tadoma, which involves touching a person's face while he or she is speaking. (p. 318)

   Reed, C. M., Durlach, N. I., Braida, L. D., & Schultz, M. C. (1982). Analytic study of the Tadoma method: Identification of consonants and vowels by an experienced Tadoma user. *Journal of Speech and Hearing Research, 25,* 108–116.

2. *Is speech special?* This is a controversy in which some researchers (many of whom are proponents of the motor theory of speech perception) argue that speech perception involves special mechanisms not shared by other auditory mechanisms, and another group of researchers hold that speech perception is served by the same mechanisms that enable us to hear other types of auditory stimuli. (p. 324)

   Fowler, C. A., & Rosenblum, L. D. (1990). Duplex perception: A comparison of monosyllables and slamming doors. *Journal of Experimental Psychology: Human Perception and Performance, 17,* 816–828.

   Trout, J. D. (2003). Biological specializations for speech: What can the animals tell us? *Current Directions in Psychological Science, 5,* 155–159.

3. *The connection between speech and music.* There is evidence that speech and music involve different brain mechanisms, but there is also evidence that they may have some mechanisms in common.

   Patel, A. D. (2008). *Music, language, and the brain.* New York: Oxford University Press.

   Patel, A. D., & Daniele, J. R. (2003). An empirical comparison of rhythm in language and music. *Cognition, 87,* B35–B45.

   Peretz, I., & Hyde, K. L. (2003). What is specific to music processing? Insights from congenital amusia. *Trends in Cognitive Sciences, 7,* 362–367.

4. *Brain mechanisms linking language and action.* Hearing statements referring to different parts of the body, such as the face, arms, or legs, activates areas of the brain associated with speech and also areas associated with moving that part of the body. (p. 324)

   Pulvermuller, F. (2005). Brain mechanisms linking language and action. *Nature Reviews Neuroscience, 6,* 576–582.

5. *Approaches to the study of speech perception.* A number of different theoretical approaches to studying speech perception have been proposed. It has also been suggested that our knowledge of the mechanisms of speech perception could be enhanced by studying speech perception within the more general framework of auditory science that we described in Chapters 11 and 12.

   Diehl, R. L., Lotto, A. J., & Holt, L. L. (2004). Speech perception. *Annual Review of Psychology, 55,* 149–179.

   Holt, L. L., & Lotto, A. J. (2008). Speech perception within an auditory cognitive science framework. *Current Directions in Psychological Science, 17,* 42–46.

KEY TERMS

Acoustic signal (p. 312)
Acoustic stimulus (p. 312)
Aphasia (p. 323)
Articulator (p. 312)
Audiovisual speech perception (p. 318)
Broca's aphasia (p. 323)
Broca's area (p. 323)
Categorical perception (p. 316)
Coarticulation (p. 315)
Dual-stream model of speech perception (p. 323)

Formant (p. 312)
Formant transitions (p. 313)
Indexical characteristic (p. 322)
McGurk effect (p. 318)
Motor theory of speech perception (p. 324)
Multimodal (p. 318)
Phoneme (p. 314)
Phonemic restoration effect (p. 319)
Phonetic boundary (p. 317)
Shadowing (p. 320)

Sound spectrogram (p. 312)
Speech segmentation (p. 320)
Statistical learning (p. 321)
Transitional probabilities (p. 321)
Voice onset time (VOT) (p. 316)
Wernicke's aphasia (p. 323)
Wernicke's area (p. 323)
Word deafness (p. 323)

MEDIA RESOURCES

The *Sensation and Perception* Book Companion Website

www.cengage.com/psychology/goldstein

See the companion website for flashcards, practice quiz questions, Internet links, updates, critical thinking exercises, discussion forums, games, and more!

CengageNOW
CENGAGENOW

www.cengage.com/cengagenow

Go to this site for the link to CengageNOW, your one-stop shop. Take a pre-test for this chapter, and CengageNOW will generate a personalized study plan based on your test results. The study plan will identify the topics you need to review and direct you to online resources to help you mas-

ter those topics. You can then take a post-test to help you determine the concepts you have mastered and what you will still need to work on.

Virtual Lab

VL

Your Virtual Lab is designed to help you get the most out of this course. The Virtual Lab icons direct you to specific media demonstrations and experiments designed to help you visualize what you are reading about. The number beside each icon indicates the number of the media element you can access through your CD-ROM, CengageNOW, or WebTutor resource.

The following lab exercises are related to material in this chapter:

1. *Categorical Perception* How perception of a tone suddenly changes from one category to another as the characteristics of a tone are slowly changed over a wide range.

2. *The McGurk Effect* How seeing a person's lips move can influence what we hear.

3. *Speechreading* How perceiving someone speaking can make it easier to understand what they are saying. (Courtesy of Sensimetrics Corporation.)

4. *Statistical Learning Stimuli* A sample of the string of nonsense words used in the Saffran experiment.

5. *Phantom Words* How listening to a repeating sound can result in the perception of words. (Courtesy of Diana Deutsch.)

Answer to question on page 320:
An American delights in simple playthings.

Chapter Contents

CHAPTER 14

The Cutaneous Senses

OPPOSITE PAGE The fingers of a person reading Braille. Scanning the fingers over the raised Braille dots is an example of detecting details with touch.
Terry Vine/Getty Images

VL The Virtual Lab icons direct you to specific animations and videos designed to help you visualize what you are reading about. The number beside each icon indicates the number of the clip you can access through your CD-ROM or your student website.

Some Questions We Will Consider:

■ Are there specialized receptors in the skin for sensing different tactile qualities? (p. 331)
■ What is the most sensitive part of the body? (p. 332)
■ Is it possible to reduce pain with your thoughts? (p. 343)

When asked which sense they would choose to lose, if they had to lose either vision, hearing, or touch, some people pick touch. This is understandable given the high value we place on seeing and hearing, but making a decision to lose the sense of touch would be a serious mistake, because although people who are blind or deaf can get along quite well, people with a rare condition that results in losing the ability to feel sensations though the skin often suffer constant bruises, burns, and broken bones in the absence of the warnings provided by touch and pain (Melzack & Wall, 1988; Rollman, 1991; Wall & Melzack, 1994).

But losing the sense of touch does more than increase the chance of injury. It also makes it difficult to interact with the environment because of the loss of feedback from the skin that accompanies many actions. As I type this, I hit my computer keys with just the right amount of force, because I can feel pressure when my fingers hit the keys. Without this feedback, typing and other actions that receive feedback from touch would become much more difficult. Experiments in which subjects have had their hands temporarily anesthetized have shown that the resulting loss of feeling causes them to apply much more force than necessary when carrying out tasks with their fingers and hands (Avenanti et al., 2005; Monzée et al., 2003).

A particularly dramatic case that involved losing the ability to sense with the skin, as well as the closely related ability to sense the movement and positions of the limbs, is that of Ian Waterman, a 17-year-old apprentice butcher, who in May 1971 contracted what at first appeared to be a routine case of the flu (Cole, 1995; Robles-De-La-Torre, 2006). He anticipated returning to work after recovering; however, instead of improving, his condition worsened, with an initial tingling sensation in his limbs becoming a total loss of the ability to feel touch below the neck. Ian's doctors, who were initially baffled by his condition, eventually determined that an autoimmune reaction had destroyed most of the neurons that transmitted signals from his skin, joints, tendons, and muscles to his brain. The loss of the ability to feel skin sensations meant that Ian couldn't feel his body when lying in bed, which resulted in a frightening floating sensation, and he often used inappropriate force when grasping objects—sometimes gripping too tightly, and sometimes dropping objects because he hadn't gripped tightly enough.

As difficult as losing sensations from his skin made Ian's life, destruction of the nerves from his muscles, tendons, and joints caused an even more serious problem. The destruction of these nerves eliminated Ian's ability to sense the position of his arms, legs, and body. This is something we take for granted. When you close your eyes, you can tell where your hands and legs are relative to each other and to your body. But Ian had lost this ability, so even though he could move, because the nerves conducting signals from his brain to his muscles were unaffected, he avoided moving, because not knowing where his limbs were made it difficult to control them.

Eventually, after many years of practice, Ian was able to sit, stand, and even carry out movements and tasks such as writing. Ian was able to do these things not because his sensory nerves had recovered (they remained irreversibly damaged), but because he had learned to use his sense of vision to constantly monitor the positions of his limbs and body. Imagine, for a moment, what it would be like to have to constantly look at your hands, arms, legs, and body, so you could tell where they were and make the necessary muscular adjustments to maintain your posture and carry out actions. Ian described the extreme and constant effort needed to do this as making his life like "running a daily marathon" (Cole, 1995).

Ian's problems were caused by a breakdown of his **somatosensory system**, which includes (1) the **cutaneous senses**, which are responsible for perceptions such as touch and pain that are usually caused by stimulation of the skin; (2) **proprioception**, the ability to sense the position of the body and limbs; and (3) **kinesthesis**, the ability to sense the movement of the body and limbs. In this chapter we will focus on the cutaneous senses, which, it should be pointed out, are important not only for activities like grasping objects and protecting against damage to the skin, but also for motivating sexual activity.

When we recognize that the perceptions we experience through our skin are crucial for carrying out everyday activities, protecting ourselves from injury, and motivating sexual activity, we can see that these perceptions are crucial to our survival and to the survival of our species. We could, in fact, make a good case for the idea that perceptions felt through the skin and our ability to sense the positions and movements of our limbs are more important for survival than those provided by vision and hearing. We begin our consideration of the cutaneous senses by focusing on the skin.

Overview of the Cutaneous System

In this section we will describe some basic facts about the anatomy and functioning of the various parts of the cutaneous system.

The Skin

Comel (1953) called the skin the "monumental facade of the human body" for good reason. It is the heaviest organ in the human body, and, if not the largest (the surface areas of the gastrointestinal tract or of the alveoli of the lungs exceed the surface area of the skin), it is certainly the most obvious, especially in humans, whose skin is not obscured by fur or large amounts of hair (Montagna & Parakkal, 1974). **1**

In addition to its warning function, the skin also prevents body fluids from escaping and at the same time protects us by keeping bacteria, chemical agents, and dirt from penetrating our bodies. Skin maintains the integrity of what's inside and protects us from what's outside, but it also provides us with information about the various stimuli that contact it. The sun's rays heat our skin, and we feel warmth; a pinprick is painful; and when someone touches us, we experience pressure or other sensations.

Our main experience with the skin is its visible surface, which is actually a layer of tough dead skin cells. (Try sticking a piece of cellophane tape onto your palm and pulling it off. The material that sticks to the tape is dead skin cells). This layer of dead cells is part of the outer layer of skin, which is called the epidermis. Below the epidermis is another layer, called the dermis (Figure 14.1). It is in these two layers that we find the mechanoreceptors, receptors that respond to mechanical stimulation such as pressure, stretching, and vibration.

Mechanoreceptors

Many of the tactile perceptions that we feel from stimulation of the skin can be traced to the four types of mechanoreceptors that are located in the epidermis and the dermis.

We can distinguish between these receptors by their distinctive structures and by how fibers associated with the receptors respond to stimulation. Two mechanoreceptors, the Merkel receptor and the Meissner corpuscle, are located close to the surface of the skin, near the epidermis. Figure 14.1 shows their structure and firing in response to a pressure stimulus that is presented and then removed (blue line). The Merkel receptor fires continuously, as long as the stimulus is on; the Meissner corpuscle fires only when the stimulus is first applied and when it is removed. The type of perception associated with the Merkel receptor is sensing fine details, and with the Meissner corpuscle, controlling handgrip.

The other two mechanoreceptors, the Ruffini cylinder and Pacinian corpuscle, are located deeper in the skin (Figure 14.2). The Ruffini cylinder responds continuously to stimulation, and the Pacinian corpuscle responds when the stimulus is applied and removed. The Ruffini cylinder is associated with perceiving stretching of the skin, the Pacinian corpuscle with sensing rapid vibrations and fine texture.

Pathways From Skin to Cortex

Nerve fibers from receptors in the skin travel in bundles called peripheral nerves that enter the spinal cord through the dorsal root (Figure 14.3). The nerve fibers then go up the spinal cord along two major pathways: the medial lemniscal pathway and the spinothalamic pathway. Just as

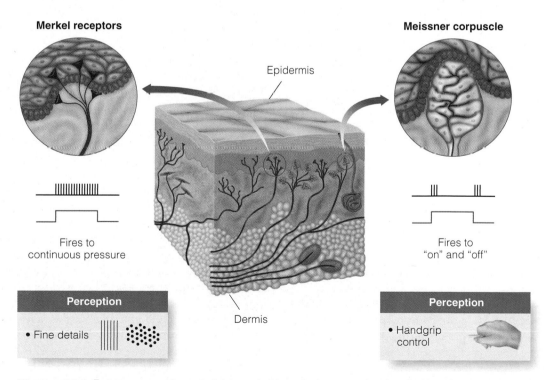

Merkel receptors

Meissner corpuscle

Epidermis

Fires to continuous pressure

Fires to "on" and "off"

Dermis

Perception
• Fine details

Perception
• Handgrip control

Figure 14.1 ▌ A cross section of glabrous (without hairs or projections) skin, showing the layers of the skin and the structure, firing properties, and perceptions associated with the Merkel receptor and Meissner corpuscle—two mechanoreceptors that are near the surface of the skin.

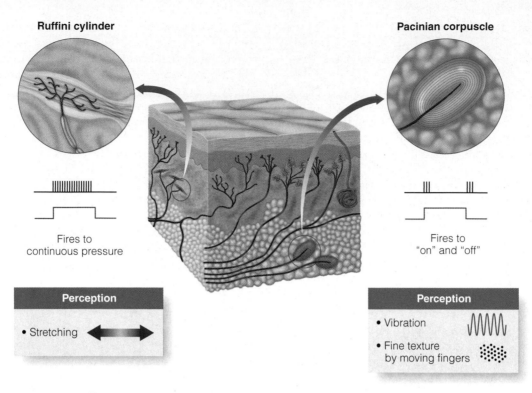

Ruffini cylinder

Fires to
continuous pressure

Perception

• Stretching

Pacinian corpuscle

Fires to
"on" and "off"

Perception

• Vibration

• Fine texture
by moving fingers

Figure 14.2 ▌ A cross section of glabrous skin, showing the structure, firing properties, and perceptions associated with the Ruffini cylinder and the Pacinian cropuscle—two mechanoreceptors that are deeper in the skin.

parallel pathways in the visual and auditory systems serve different perceptual functions, so it is with the cutaneous system. The lemniscal pathway has large fibers that carry signals related to sensing the positions of the limbs (proprioception) and perceiving touch. The spinothalamic pathway consists of smaller fibers that transmit signals related to temperature and pain. The case of Ian Waterman illustrates this separation in function, because although he lost the ability to feel touch and to sense the positions of his limbs (lemniscal pathway), he was still able to sense pain and temperature (spinothalamic pathway).

Fibers from both pathways cross over to the other side of the body during their upward journey to the thalamus. Most of these fibers synapse in the ventrolateral nucleus in the thalamus, but some synapse in other thalamic nuclei. (Remember that fibers from the retina and the cochlea also synapse in the thalamus, in the *lateral geniculate nucleus* for vision and the *medial geniculate nucleus* for hearing.) Because the signals in the spinal cord have crossed over to the opposite side of the body on their way to the thalamus, signals originating from the left side of the body reach the thalamus in the right hemisphere of the brain, and signals from the right side of the body reach the left hemisphere.

Maps of the Body on the Cortex

From the thalamus, signals travel to the somatosensory receiving area (S1) in the parietal lobe of the cortex and possibly also to the secondary somatosensory cortex (S2) (Rowe et al., 1996; Turman et al., 1998; Figure 14.4b). Signals also travel between S1 and S2 and from S1 and S2 to additional somatosensory areas.

An important characteristic of the somatosensory cortex is that it is organized into maps that correspond to locations on the body. The existence of a map of the body on S1, the primary somatosensory receiving area, was determined in a classic series of investigations carried out by neurosurgeon Wilder Penfield while operating on awake patients who were having brain surgery to relieve symptoms of epilepsy (Penfield & Rasmussen, 1950). When Penfield stimulated points on S1 and asked patients to report what they perceived, they reported sensations such as tingling and touch on various parts of their body. Penfield found that stimulating the ventral part of S1 (lower on the parietal lobe) caused sensations on the lips and face, stimulating higher on S1 caused sensations in the hands and fingers, and stimulating the dorsal S1 caused sensations in the legs and feet.

The resulting body map, shown in Figure 14.4a, is called the **homunculus**, Latin for "little man." The homunculus shows that some areas on the skin are represented by a disproportionately large area of the brain. The area devoted to the thumb, for example, is as large as the area devoted to the entire forearm. This result is analogous to the magnification factor in vision (see page 82), in which receptors in the fovea, which are responsible for perceiving

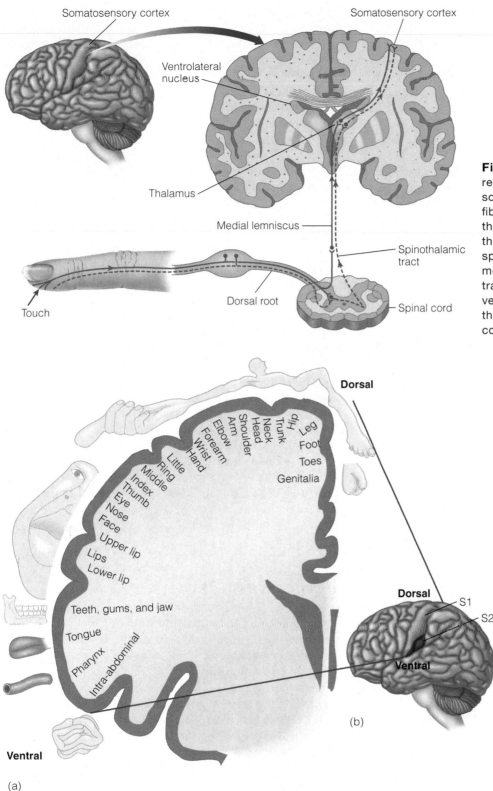

Figure 14.3 ▌ The pathway from receptors in the skin to the somatosensory receiving area of the cortex. The fiber carrying signals from a receptor in the finger enters the spinal cord through the dorsal root and then travels up the spinal cord along two pathways: the medial lemniscus and the spinothalamic tract. These pathways synapse in the ventrolateral nucleus of the thalamus and then send fibers to the somatosensory cortex in the parietal lobe.

Figure 14.4 ▌ (a) The sensory homunculus on the somatosensory cortex. Parts of the body with the highest tactile acuity are represented by larger areas on the cortex. (b) The somatosensory cortex in the parietal lobe. The primary somatosensory area, S1 (light shading), receives inputs from the ventrolateral nucleus of the thalamus. The secondary somatosensory area, S2 (dark shading), is partially hidden behind the temporal lobe. (*Adapted from Penfield & Rasmussen, 1950.*)

visual details, are allotted a disproportionate area on the visual cortex. Similarly, parts of the body such as the fingers, which are used to detect details through the sense of touch, are allotted a disproportionate area on the somatosensory cortex (Duncan & Boynton, 2007). A similar body map also occurs in the secondary somatosensory cortex (S2).

The Plasticity of Cortical Body Maps

One of the basic principles of cortical organization is that the cortical representation of a particular function can become larger if that function is used often. We introduced this principle, which is called *experience-dependent plasticity*, in Chapter 4, when we described how rearing kittens in a vertical environment caused most of the neurons in their visual cortex to respond best to vertical orientations (see page 80) and how training humans to recognize shapes called Greebles caused the fusiform face area of the cortex to respond more strongly to Greeble stimuli (see page 94). Similarly, in the sense of hearing, we saw that training owl monkeys to discriminate between two frequencies of sound increased the area of cortex devoted to these frequencies (see Chapter 11, page 284).

Most of the early experiments that demonstrated experience-dependent plasticity were carried out in the somatosensory system. In one of these early experiments, William Jenkins and Michael Merzenich (1987) showed that increasing stimulation of a specific area of the skin causes an expansion of the cortical area receiving signals from that area of skin. When they measured the cortical areas devoted to each of a monkey's fingers and trained monkeys to complete a task that involved the extensive use of a particular location on one fingertip, they obtained the results shown in Figure 14.5. Comparison of the cortical maps of the fingertip measured just before the training and 3 months later shows that the area representing the stimulated fingertip was greatly expanded after the training. Thus, the cortical area representing part of the fingertip, which is large to begin with, becomes even larger when the area receives a large amount of stimulation.

In most animal experiments, like the one we just described, the effect of plasticity is determined by measuring how special training affects the brain. An experiment that measured this effect in humans determined how training affected the brains of musicians. Consider, for example, players of stringed instruments. A right-handed violin player bows with the right hand and uses the fingers of his or her left hand to finger the strings. One result of this tactile experience is that these musicians have a greater than normal cortical representation for the fingers on their left hand (Elbert et al., 1995). Just as in the monkeys, plasticity has created more cortical area for parts of the body that have been used more.

What this plasticity means is that while we can specify the general area of the cortex that represents a particular part of the body, the exact size of the area representing each part of the body is not totally fixed. Now that we have described the basic structures involved in sensing with the skin, we will consider the mechanisms behind four types of perception: (1) perceiving details, (2) perceiving vibration, (3) perceiving texture, and (4) perceiving objects.

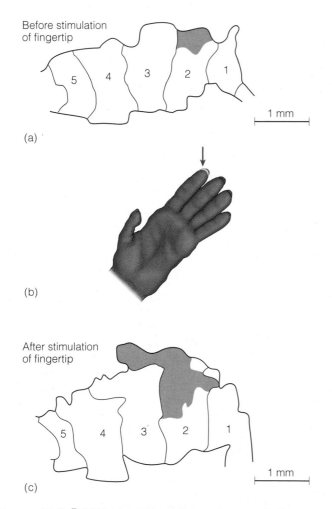

Figure 14.5 ▌ (a) Each numbered zone represents the area in the somatosensory cortex that corresponds to one of a monkey's five fingers. The shaded area on the zone for finger 2 is the part of the cortex that represents the small area on the tip of the finger shown in (b). (c) The shaded region shows how the area representing the fingertip increased in size after this area was heavily stimulated over a 3-month period. *(From Merzenich, M. M., Reconzone, G., Jenkins, W. M., Allard, T. T., & Nudo, R. J., Cortical representational plasticity. In P. Rakic and W. Singer (Eds.), Neurobiology of neocortex, pp. 42–67, figure 1. Copyright © 1988 John Wiley & Sons. Reproduced by permission of M. M. Merzenich.)*

Perceiving Details

One of the most impressive examples of perceiving details with the skin is provided by Braille, the system of raised dots that enables blind people to read with their fingertips (Figure 14.6). A Braille character consists of a cell made up of from one to six dots. Different arrangements of dots and blank spaces represent letters of the alphabet, as shown; additional characters represent numbers, punctuation marks, and common speech sounds and words.

Experienced Braille readers can read at a rate of about 100 words per minute, slower than the rate for visual reading, which averages about 250 to 300 words per minute, but impressive nonetheless when we consider that a Braille reader transforms an array of raised dots into information that goes far beyond simply feeling sensations on the skin.

The ability of Braille readers to identify patterns of small raised dots based on the sense of touch depends on tactile detail perception. The first step in describing research on tactile detail perception is to consider how researchers have measured our capacity to detect details of stimuli presented to the skin.

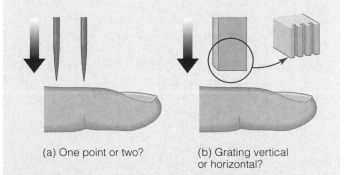

Figure 14.6 ▌ The Braille alphabet consists of raised dots in a 2 x 3 matrix. The large dots indicate the location of the raised dot for each letter. Blind people read these dots by scanning them with their fingertips.

METHOD ▌ Measuring Tactile Acuity

Just as there are a number of different kinds of eye charts for determining a person's visual acuity, there are a number of ways to measure a person's **tactile acuity**—the ability to detect details on the skin. The classic method of measuring tactile acuity is the **two-point threshold**, the minimum separation between two points on the skin that when stimulated is perceived as two points (Figure 14.7a). The two-point threshold is measured by gently touching the skin with two points, such as the points of a drawing compass, and having the person indicate whether he or she feels one point or two.

The two-point threshold was the main measure of acuity in most of the early research on touch. Recently, however, other methods have been introduced. **Grating acuity** is measured by pressing a grooved stimulus like the one in Figure 14.7b onto the skin and asking the person to indicate the orientation of the grating. Acuity is measured by determining the narrowest spacing for which orientation can be accurately judged. Finally, acuity can also be measured by pushing raised patterns such as letters onto the skin and determining the smallest sized pattern or letter that can be identified (Cholewaik & Collins, 2003; Craig & Lyle, 2001, 2002).

(a) One point or two? (b) Grating vertical or horizontal?

Figure 14.7 ▌ Methods for determining tactile acuity: (a) two-point threshold; (b) grating acuity.

As we consider the role of both receptor mechanisms and cortical mechanisms in determining tactile acuity, we will see that there are a number of parallels between the cutaneous system and the visual system.

Receptor Mechanisms for Tactile Acuity

The properties of the receptors are one of the things that determines what we experience when the skin is stimulated. We will illustrate this by first focusing on the connection between the Merkel receptor and associated fibers and tactile acuity. We have indicated that the Merkel receptor is sensitive to details. Figure 14.8a shows how the fiber associated with a Merkel receptor fires in response to a grooved stimulus pushed into the skin. Notice that the firing of the fiber reflects the pattern of the grooved stimuli. This indicates that the firing of the Merkel receptor's fiber signals details (Johnson, 2002; Phillips & Johnson, 1981). For comparison, Figure 14.8b shows the firing of the fiber associated with the Pacinian corpuscle. The lack of match between the grooved pattern and the firing indicates that this receptor is not sensitive to the details of patterns that are pushed onto the skin.

It is not surprising that there is a high density of Merkel receptors in the fingertips, because the fingertips are the parts of the body that are most sensitive to details (Vallbo & Johansson, 1978). The relationship between locations on the body and sensitivity to detail has been studied psychophysically by measuring the two-point threshold on different parts of the body. Try this yourself by doing the following demonstration.

DEMONSTRATION

Comparing Two-Point Thresholds

To measure two-point thresholds on different parts of the body, hold two pencils side by side (or better yet, use a

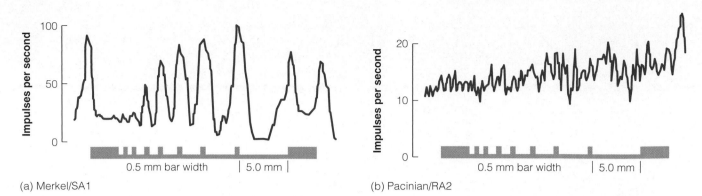

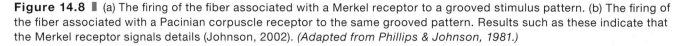

(a) Merkel/SA1

(b) Pacinian/RA2

Figure 14.8 ▌ (a) The firing of the fiber associated with a Merkel receptor to a grooved stimulus pattern. (b) The firing of the fiber associated with a Pacinian corpuscle receptor to the same grooved pattern. Results such as these indicate that the Merkel receptor signals details (Johnson, 2002). *(Adapted from Phillips & Johnson, 1981.)*

drawing compass) so that their points are about 12 mm (0.5 in.) apart; then touch both points simultaneously to the tip of your thumb and determine whether you feel two points. If you feel only one, increase the distance between the pencil points until you feel two; then note the distance between the points. Now move the pencil points to the underside of your forearm. With the points about 12 mm apart (or at the smallest separation you felt as two points on your thumb), touch them to your forearm and note whether you feel one point or two. If you feel only one, how much must you increase the separation before you feel two? ▌

A comparison of grating acuity on different parts of the hand shows that better acuity is associated with less spacing between Merkel receptors (Figure 14.9). But receptor spacing can't be the whole story, because although tactile acuity is better on the tip of the index finger than on the tip of the little finger, the spacing between Merkel receptors is the same on all the fingertips. This means that while receptor spacing is part of the answer, the cortex also plays a role in determining tactile acuity (Duncan & Boynton, 2007).

Cortical Mechanisms for Tactile Acuity

Just as there is a parallel between the density of receptors in the skin and tactile acuity, there is also a parallel between the representation of the body in the brain and the acuity at different locations on the body. Figure 14.10 indicates the two-point threshold measured on different parts of the male body. By comparing these two-point thresholds to how different parts of the body are represented in the brain (Figure 14.4a), we can see that regions of high acuity, like the fingers and lips, are represented by larger areas on the cortex. As we mentioned earlier, "magnification" of the representation on the brain of parts of the body such as the fingertips parallels the magnification factor in vision (page 82). The map of the body on the brain is enlarged to provide the extra neural

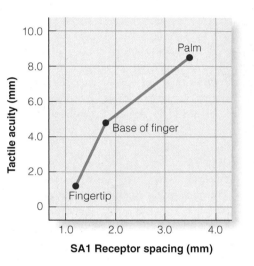

Figure 14.9 ▌ Correlation between density of Merkel receptors and tactile acuity. *(From Craig & Lyle, 2002.)*

processing that enables us to accurately sense fine details with our fingers and other parts of the body.

Another way to demonstrate the connection between cortical mechanisms and acuity is to determine the receptive fields of neurons in different parts of the cortical homunculus. Remember that the receptive field for a neuron in the visual system is *the area on the retina that, when stimulated, influences the firing rate of the neuron*. The receptive field for a neuron in the cutaneous system is *the area on the skin that, when stimulated, influences the firing rate of the neuron*.

From Figure 14.11, which shows the sizes of receptive fields from cortical neurons that receive signals from a monkey's fingers (Figure 14.11a), hand (Figure 14.11b), and arm (Figure 14.11c), we can see that cortical neurons representing parts of the body with better acuity, such as the fingers, have smaller receptive fields. This means that two points that are close together on the fingers might fall on receptive fields that don't overlap (as indicated by the two arrows in Figure 14.11a) and so would cause neurons that are separated in the cortex to fire (Figure 14.11d). However,

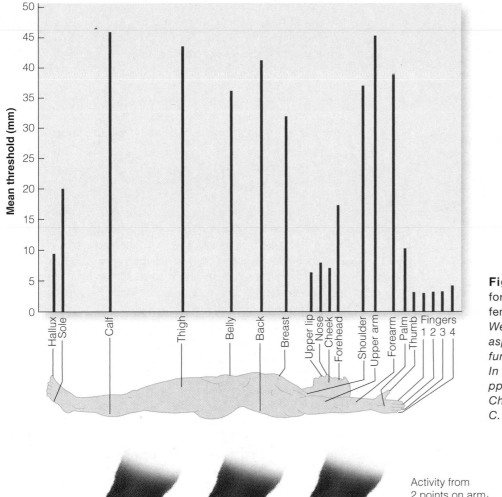

Figure 14.10 ▌ Two-point thresholds for males. Two-point thresholds for females follow the same pattern. *(From Weinstein, S., Intensive and extensive aspects of tactile sensitivity as a function of body part, sex, and laterality. In D. R. Kenshalo (Ed.), The skin senses, pp. 206, 207. Copyright © 1968 by Charles C. Thomas. Courtesy of Charles C. Thomas, Publishers, Springfield, IL.)*

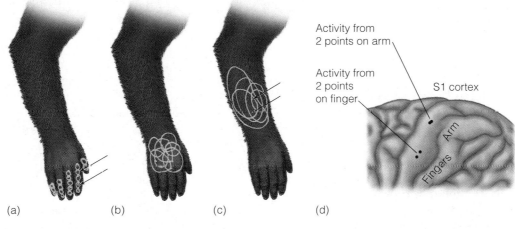

Figure 14.11 ▌ Receptive fields of monkey cortical neurons that fire (a) when the fingers are stimulated; (b) when the hand is stimulated; and (c) when the arm is stimulated. (d) Stimulation of two nearby points on the finger causes separated activation in the finger area of the cortex, but stimulation of two nearby points on the arm causes overlapping activation in the arm area of the cortex. *(From Kandel, E. R., & Jessell, T. M., Touch. In E. R. Kandel, J. H. Schwartz, & T. M. Jessell (Eds.), Principles of neural science, 3rd ed., figure 26-8a. Copyright © 1991 Appleton & Lange, Norwalk, CT. Reprinted with permission of McGraw-Hill Companies.)*

the same separation of points when applied to the arm are likely to fall on receptive fields that overlap (see arrows in Figure 14.11c), and so could cause neurons that are not separated in the cortex to fire. Thus, having small receptive fields of neurons receiving signals from the fingers translates into more separation on the cortex, which enhances the ability to feel two close-together points on the skin as two separate points.

Perceiving Vibration

The skin is capable of detecting not only spatial details of objects, but other qualities as well. When you place your hands on mechanical devices that are producing vibration, such as a car, a lawnmower, or an electric toothbrush, you can sense these vibrations with your fingers and hands.

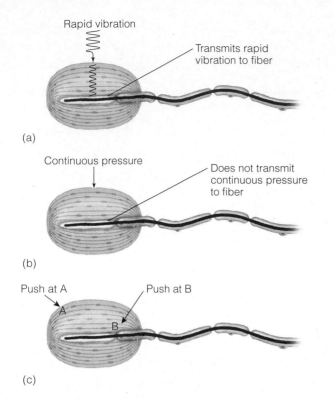

(a)

(b)

(c)

Figure 14.12 ▮ (a) When a vibrating pressure stimulus is applied to the Pacinian corpuscle, it transmits these pressure vibrations to the nerve fiber. (b) When a continuous pressure stimulus is applied to the Pacinian corpuscle, it does not transmit the continuous pressure to the fiber. (c) Lowenstein determined how the fiber fired to stimulation of the corpuscle (at A) and to direct stimulation of the fiber (at B). *(From Lowenstein, W. R., Biological transducers, p. 103. Copyright © 1960 by Scientific American, Inc. All rights reserved. Reproduced with permission.)*

The mechanoreceptor that is primarily responsible for sensing vibration is the Pacinian corpuscle (PC). One piece of evidence linking the PC to vibration is that recording from fibers associated with the PC shows that these fibers respond poorly to slow or constant pushing, but respond well to high rates of vibration.

Why do the PC fibers fire well to rapid vibration? The answer to this question is that the presence of the PC determines which pressure stimuli actually reach the fiber. The PC, which consists of a series of layers, like an onion, with fluid between each layer, transmits rapidly applied pressure, like vibration, to the nerve fiber, as shown in Figure 14.12a, but does not transmit continuous pressure, as shown in Figure 14.12b. Thus, the corpuscle causes the fiber to receive rapid changes in pressure, but not to receive continuous pressure.

If the PC does not transmit continuous pressure to the fiber, then presenting continuous pressure to the PC should cause no response in the fiber. This is exactly what Werner Lowenstein (1960) observed in a classic experiment, in which he showed that when pressure was applied to the corpuscle (at A in Figure 14.12c), the fiber responded when the pressure was first applied and when it was removed, but did

not respond to continuous pressure. But when Lowenstein dissected away the corpuscle and applied pressure directly to the fiber (at B in Figure 14.12c), the fiber fired to the continuous pressure. Lowenstein concluded from this result that properties of the corpuscle cause the fiber to respond poorly to continuous stimulation, such as sustained pressure, but to respond well to changes in stimulation that occur at the beginning and end of a pressure stimulus or when stimulation is changing rapidly, as occurs in vibration.

Perceiving Texture

When you touch an object or run your fingers over the object, you can sense textures ranging from coarse (the spacing of the teeth of a comb) to fine (the surface of the page of this book). Research on texture perception tells an interesting story, which extends from 1925 to the present and which illustrates how psychophysics can be used to understand perceptual mechanisms. ▮VL▮2

In 1925, David Katz proposed that our perception of texture depends on both spatial cues and temporal cues. **Spatial cues** are caused by relatively large surface elements, such as bumps and grooves, that can be felt both when the skin moves across the surface elements and when it is pressed onto the elements. These cues result in feeling different shapes, sizes, and distributions of these surface elements. An example of spatial cues is perceiving a coarse texture such as Braille dots or the texture you feel when you touch the teeth of a comb.

Temporal cues occur when the skin moves across a textured surface like fine sandpaper. This cue provides information in the form of vibrations that occur as a result of the movement over the surface. Temporal cues are responsible for our perception of fine texture that cannot be detected unless the fingers are moving across the surface.

Although Katz proposed that texture perception is determined by both spatial and temporal cues, research on texture perception has, until recently, focused on spatial cues. However, recent experiments by Mark Hollins and coworkers (2000, 2001, 2002) have provided evidence that temporal cues are responsible for our perception of fine textures. Hollins called Katz's proposal that there are two types of receptors involved in texture perception the **duplex theory of texture perception**.

Hollins and Ryan Risner (2000) presented evidence for the role of temporal cues by showing that when participants touch surfaces without moving their fingers and judge "roughness" using the procedure of magnitude estimation (see Chapter 1, page 16), they sense little difference between two fine textures (particle sizes of 10 and 100 μm; Figure 14.13a). However, when participants are allowed to move their fingers across the surface, they are able to detect the difference between the fine textures (Figure 14.13b). Thus, movement, which generates vibration as the skin scans a surface, makes it possible to sense the roughness of fine surfaces.

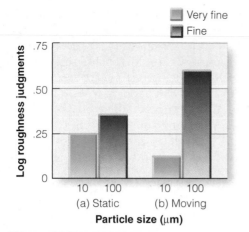

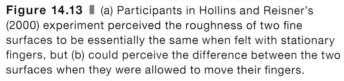

Figure 14.13 ▮ (a) Participants in Hollins and Reisner's (2000) experiment perceived the roughness of two fine surfaces to be essentially the same when felt with stationary fingers, but (b) could perceive the difference between the two surfaces when they were allowed to move their fingers.

Additional evidence for the role of vibration in sensing fine textures was provided by using the selective adaptation procedure we introduced in Chapter 4 (see page 79). This procedure involves presenting a stimulus that adapts a particular type of receptor and then testing to see how inactivation of that receptor by adaptation affected perception. Hollins and coworkers (2001) used this procedure by presenting two adaptation conditions. The first condition was 10-Hz (10 vibrations per second) adaptation, in which the skin was vibrated with a 10-Hz stimulus for 6 minutes. This frequency of adaptation was picked to adapt the Meissner corpuscle, which responds to low frequencies. The second condition was 250-Hz adaptation. This frequency was picked to adapt the Pacinian corpuscle, which responds to high frequencies.

Following each type of adaptation, participants ran their fingers over two fine textures—a "standard" texture and a "test" texture. The participant's task was to indicate which texture was finer. Because there were two surfaces, chance performance would be 50 percent, as indicated by the dashed line in Figure 14.14. The results indicate that participants could tell the difference between the two textures when they had not been adapted or had received the 10-Hz adaptation. However, after they had been adapted to the 250-Hz vibration, they were unable to tell the difference between two fine textures, as indicated by their chance performance. Thus, adapting the Pacinian corpuscle receptor, which is responsible for perceiving vibration, eliminates the ability to sense fine textures by moving the fingers over a surface. These results and the results of other experiments (Hollins et al., 2002) support the duplex theory of perception—the perception of coarse textures is determined by spatial cues and fine textures by temporal (vibration) cues.

Additional evidence for the role of temporal cues in perceiving texture has been provided by research that shows that vibrations are important for perceiving textures not only when people explore a surface directly with their

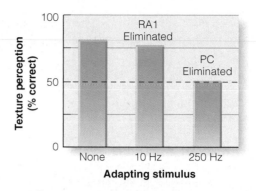

Figure 14.14 ▮ Eliminating the action of fibers associated with the Meissner corpuscle by adaptation to a 10-Hz vibration had no effect on perception of a fine texture, but eliminating the action of the Pacinian corpuscle by adapting to a 250-Hz vibration eliminated the ability to sense the fine textures. *(Data from Hollins et al., 2001.)*

fingers, but also when they make contact with a surface indirectly, through the use of tools. You can experience this yourself by doing the following demonstration.

DEMONSTRATION

Perceiving Texture With a Pen

Turn your pen over (or cap it) so you can use it as a "probe" (without writing on things!). Hold the pen at one end and move the other end over something smooth, such as this page. As you do this, notice that you can sense the smoothness of the page, even though you are not directly touching it. Then, try the same thing on a rougher surface, such as a rug, fabric, or concrete. ▮

Your ability to detect differences in texture by running a pen (or some other "tool," such as a stick) over a surface is determined by vibrations transmitted through the tool to your skin (Klatzky et al., 2003). The most remarkable thing about perceiving texture with a tool is that what you perceive is not the vibrations, but the texture of the surface, even though you are feeling the surface remotely, with the tip of the tool (Carello & Turvey, 2004).

TEST YOURSELF 14.1

1. Describe the four types of mechanoreceptors in the skin, indicating their appearance, where they are located, and the type of perception associated with each receptor.
2. Where is the cortical receiving area for touch, and what does the map of the body on the cortical receiving area look like? How can this map be changed by experience?

Perceiving Objects

Imagine that you and a friend are at the seashore. Your friend knows something about shells from the small collection he has accumulated over the years, so as an experiment you decide to determine how well he can identify different types of shells by using his sense of touch alone. When you blindfold your friend and hand him a snail shell and a crab shell, he has no trouble identifying the shells as a snail and a crab. But when you hand him shells of different types of snails that are very similar, he finds that identifying the different types of snails is much more difficult.

Geerat Vermij, blind at the age of 4 from a childhood eye disease, and currently Distinguished Professor of Geology at the University of California at Davis, describes his experience when confronted with a similar task. His experience occurred when he was being interviewed by Edgar Boell, who was considering Vermeij's application for graduate study in the biology department at Yale. Boell took Vermeij to the museum, introduced him to the curator, and handed him a shell. Here is what happened next, as told by Vermeij (1997):

> "Here's something. Do you know what it is?" Boell asked as he handed me a specimen.
>
> My fingers and mind raced. Widely separated ribs parallel to outer lip; large aperture; low spire; glossy; ribs reflected backward. "It's a Harpa," I replied tentatively. "It must be Harpa major." Right so far.
>
> "How about this one?" inquired Boell, as another fine shell changed hands. Smooth, sleek, channeled suture, narrow opening; could be any olive. "It's an olive. I'm pretty sure it's Oliva sayana, the common one from Florida, but they all look alike."
>
> Both men were momentarily speechless. They had planned this little exercise all along to call my bluff. Now that I had passed, Boell had undergone an instant metamorphosis. Beaming with enthusiasm and warmth, he promised me his full support. (pp. 79–80)

Vermeij was admitted to graduate study at Yale, graduated with a PhD in evolutionary biology, and is now a world-renowned expert on marine mollusks. His ability to identify objects and their features by touch is an example of **active touch**—touch in which a person actively explores an object, usually with fingers and hands. Active touch contrasts with **passive touch**, which occurs when touch stimuli are applied to the skin, as when two points are pushed onto the skin to determine the two-point threshold. The following demonstration compares the ability to identify objects using active touch and passive touch.

DEMONSTRATION

Identifying Objects

Ask another person to select five or six small objects for you to identify. Close your eyes and have the person place an object in your hand. Your job is to identify the object by touch alone, by moving your fingers and hand over the object. As you do this, be aware of what you are experiencing: your finger and hand movements, the sensations you are feeling, and what you are thinking. Do this for three objects. Then hold out your hand, keeping it still, with fingers outstretched, and let the person move each of the remaining objects around on your hand, moving their surfaces and contours across your skin. Your task is the same as before: to identify the object and to pay attention to what you are experiencing as the object is moved across your hand. ▮

You may have noticed that in the active condition, in which you moved your fingers across the object, you were much more involved in the process and had more control over what parts of the objects you were exposed to. In the active part of the demonstration, you were engaging in **haptic perception**—perception in which three-dimensional objects are explored with the hand.

Identifying Objects by Haptic Exploration

Haptic perception provides a particularly good example of a situation in which a number of different systems are interacting with each other. As you manipulated the objects in the first part of the demonstration above, you were using three distinct systems to arrive at your goal of identifying the objects: (1) the sensory system, which was involved in detecting cutaneous sensations such as touch, temperature, and texture and the movements and positions of your fingers and hands; (2) the motor system, which was involved in moving your fingers and hands; and (3) the cognitive system, which was involved in thinking about the information provided by the sensory and motor systems.

Haptic perception is an extremely complex process because the sensory, motor, and cognitive systems must all work together. For example, the motor system's control of finger and hand movements is guided by cutaneous feelings in the fingers and the hands, by your sense of the positions of the fingers and hands, and by thought processes that determine what information is needed about the object in order to identify it.

These processes working together create an experience of active touch that is quite different from the experience of passive touch. J. J. Gibson (1962), who championed the importance of movement in perception (see Chapters 7 and 8), compared the experience of active and passive touch by noting that we tend to relate passive touch to the sensation experienced in the skin, whereas we relate active touch to the object being touched. For example, if someone pushes a pointed object into your skin, you might say, "I feel a pricking sensation on my skin"; if, however, you push on the tip of the pointed object yourself, you might say, "I feel a

pointed object" (Kruger, 1970). Thus, for passive touch you experience stimulation of the skin, and for active touch you experience the objects you are touching.

Psychophysical research has shown that people can accurately identify most common objects within 1 or 2 seconds (Klatzky, Lederman, & Metzger, 1985). When Susan Lederman and Roberta Klatzky (1987, 1990) observed participants' hand movements as they made these identifications, they found that people use a number of distinctive movements, which the researchers called **exploratory procedures (EPs)**, and that the types of EPs used depend on the object qualities the participants are asked to judge.

Figure 14.15 shows four of the EPs observed by Lederman and Klatzky. People tend to use just one or two EPs to determine a particular quality. For example, people use mainly lateral motion and contour following to judge texture, and they use enclosure and contour following to judge exact shape.

The Physiology of Tactile Object Perception

What is happening physiologically as we explore an object with our fingers and hands? Researchers have tried to answer this question by recording from mechanoreceptor fibers in the skin, from neurons in the somatosensory cortex, and from neurons in the parietal and frontal lobes.

In order for the brain to control everyday tasks, such as screwing a lid on a bottle, it needs to have access to information about the size and contour of the lid, and the amount of force needed to grasp the lid. This information is provided by receptors within the body that indicate the position of the joints and by mechanoreceptors in the skin that indicate the textures and contours of the lid.

The information for indicating the contours of the lid is signaled by the pattern of firing of a large number of mechanoreceptors. This is illustrated by the response profiles in Figure 14.16, which indicate how fibers in the fingertips

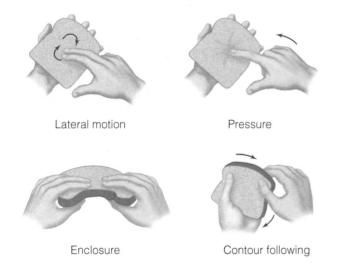

Lateral motion   Pressure

Enclosure   Contour following

Figure 14.15 ▌ Some of the exploratory procedures (EPs) observed by Lederman and Klatzky as participants identified objects. *(From Lederman & Klatzky, 1987.)*

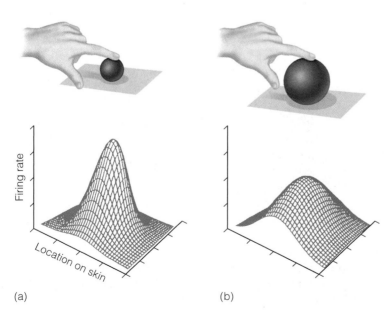

(a)   (b)

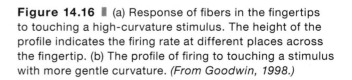

Figure 14.16 ▌ (a) Response of fibers in the fingertips to touching a high-curvature stimulus. The height of the profile indicates the firing rate at different places across the fingertip. (b) The profile of firing to touching a stimulus with more gentle curvature. *(From Goodwin, 1998.)*

respond to contact with two different spheres, one with high curvature relative to the fingertip (Figure 14.16a) and one that is more gently curved (Figure 14.16b). In both cases, the receptors right at the point where the fingers contact the sphere respond the most, and ones farther away fire less, but the *pattern* of response is different in the two cases. It is this overall pattern that provides information to the brain about the curvature of the sphere (Goodwin, 1998).

As we move from mechanoreceptor fibers in the fingers toward the brain, we see that neurons become more specialized. This is similar to what occurs in the visual system. Neurons in the ventral posterior nucleus, which is the tactile area of the thalamus, have center-surround receptive fields that are similar to the center-surround receptive fields in the lateral geniculate nucleus, which is the visual area of the thalamus (Mountcastle & Powell, 1959; Figure 14.17).

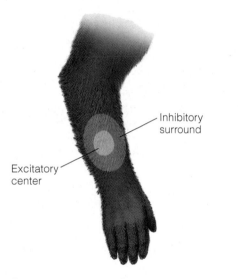

Figure 14.17 ▌ An excitatory-center, inhibitory-surround receptive field of a neuron in a monkey's thalamus.

In the cortex, we find some neurons with center-surround receptive fields and others that respond to more specialized stimulation of the skin. Figure 14.18 shows stimuli that cause neurons in the monkey's somatosensory cortex to fire. There are neurons that respond to specific orientations (Figure 14.18a) and neurons that respond to movement across the skin in a specified direction (Figure 14.18b; Hyvärinen & Poranen, 1978; also see Costanzo & Gardner, 1980; Romo et al., 1998; Warren et al., 1986).

There are also neurons in the monkey's somatosensory cortex that respond when the monkey grasps a specific object (Sakata & Iwamura, 1978). For example, Figure 14.19 shows the response of one of these neurons. This neuron responds when the monkey grasps the ruler but does not respond when the monkey grasps a cylinder or a sphere (see also Iwamura, 1998).

Cortical neurons are affected not only by the properties of the object, but also by whether or not the perceiver is paying attention. Steven Hsiao and coworkers (1993, 1996) recorded the response of neurons in areas S1 and S2 to raised letters that were scanned across a monkey's finger. In the tactile-attention condition, the monkey had to perform a task that required focusing its attention on the letters being presented to its fingers. In the visual-attention condition, the monkey had to focus its attention on an unrelated visual stimulus. The results, shown in Figure 14.20, show that even though the monkey is receiving exactly the same stimulation on its fingertips in both conditions, the response is larger for the tactile-attention condition. Thus, stimulation of the receptors may trigger a response, but the size of the response can then be affected by processes such as attention, thinking, and other actions of the perceiver.

If the idea that events other than stimulation of the receptors can affect perception sounds familiar, it is because similar situations occur in vision (see pages 10, 118) and

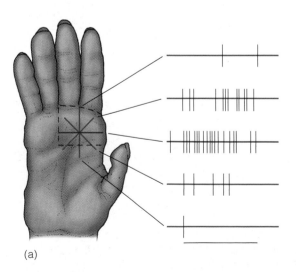

(a)

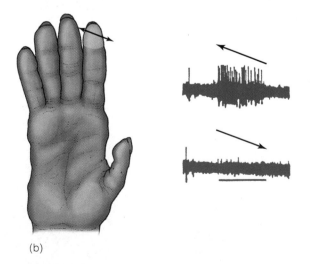

(b)

Figure 14.18 ▌ Receptive fields of neurons in the monkey's somatosensory cortex. (a) This neuron responds best when a horizontally oriented edge is presented to the monkey's hand. (b) This neuron responds best when a stimulus moves across the fingertip from right to left. *(From Hyvärinen & Poranen, 1978.)*

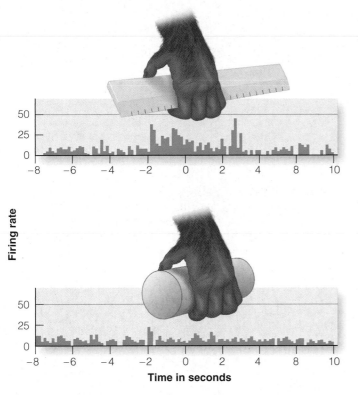

Figure 14.19 ▌ The response of a neuron in a monkey's parietal cortex that fires when the monkey grasps a ruler but that does not fire when the monkey grasps a cylinder. The monkey grasps the objects at time = φ. *(From Sakata & Iwamura, 1978.)*

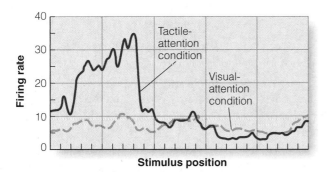

Figure 14.20 ▌ Firing rate of a neuron in area S1 of a monkey's cortex to a letter being rolled across the fingertips. The neuron responds only when the monkey is paying attention to the tactile stimulus. *(From Hsiao, O'Shaughnessy, & Johnson, 1993.)*

hearing (page 229). A person's active participation makes a difference in perception, not just by influencing what stimuli stimulate the receptors but by influencing the processing that occurs once the receptors are stimulated. This is perhaps most clearly demonstrated for the experience of pain, which is strongly affected by processes in addition to stimulation of the receptors.

Pain

As we mentioned at the beginning of this chapter, pain functions to warn us of potentially damaging situations and therefore helps us avoid or deal with cuts, burns, and broken bones. People born without the ability to feel pain might become aware that they are leaning on a hot stove burner only by smelling their burning flesh, or might be unaware of broken bones, infections, or internal injuries—situations that could easily be life-threatening (Watkins & Maier, 2003). The signaling function of pain is reflected in the following definition, from the International Association for the Study of Pain: "Pain is an unpleasant sensory and emotional experience associated with actual or potential tissue damage, or described in terms of such damage" (Merskey, 1991).

Joachim Scholz and Clifford Woolf (2002) distinguish three different types of pain. **Nociceptive pain** is pain caused by activation of receptors in the skin called **nociceptors**. There are a number of different kinds of nociceptors, which respond to different stimuli—heat, chemical, severe pressure, and cold (Figure 14.21). **Inflammatory pain** is caused by damage to tissues and inflammations to joints or by tumor cells. **Neuropathic pain** is caused by lesions or other damage to the nervous system. Examples of neuropathic pain are carpal tunnel syndrome, which is caused by repetitive tasks such as typing; spinal cord injury; and brain damage due to stroke. We will focus on nociceptive pain. Our discussion will include not only pain that is caused by stimulation of nociceptors in the skin, but also mechanisms that affect the perception of nociceptive pain, and even some examples of pain that can occur when the skin is not stimulated at all.

Questioning the Direct Pathway Model of Pain

We begin our discussion of pain by considering how early researchers thought about pain, and how these early ideas began changing in the 1960s. In the 1950s and early 1960s, pain was explained by the **direct pathway model**. According to this model, pain occurs when nociceptor receptors in the skin are stimulated and send their signals to the brain. Pain, according to the direct pathway model, is caused by signals sent directly from the skin to the brain (Melzack & Wall, 1965). But in the 1960s, some researchers began noting examples such as the following, which showed that pain can be affected by factors in addition to stimulation of the skin.

Pain Can Be Affected by a Person's Mental State H. K. Beecher (1959) observed that most American soldiers wounded at the Anzio beachhead "entirely denied pain from their extensive wounds or had so little that they did not want any medication to relieve it" (p. 165). One reason for this was that the soldier's wounds had a positive aspect: they provided escape from a hazardous battlefield to

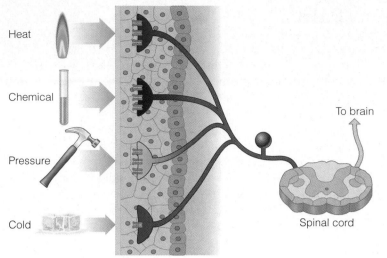

Heat

Chemical

Pressure

Cold

To brain

Spinal cord

Figure 14.21 ❙ Nociceptive pain is created by activation of nociceptors in the skin that respond to different types of stimulation. Signals from the nociceptors are transmitted to the spinal cord and then from the dorsal root of the spinal cord along pathways that lead to the brain.

the safety of a behind-the-lines hospital. The soldiers therefore reacted differently to wounds they received in battle than they would probably have reacted if they had received the same wounds in civilian life.

Pain Can Occur When There Is No Stimulation of the Skin   One of the most interesting and mystifying phenomena in perception is the phantom limb, in which people who have had a limb amputated continue to experience the limb (Figure 14.22). This perception is so convincing that amputees have been known to try stepping off a bed onto phantom feet or legs, or to attempt lifting a cup with a phantom hand. For many, the limb moves with the body, swinging while walking. But perhaps most interesting of all, it not uncommon for amputees to experience pain in the phantom limb (Jensen & Nikolajsen, 1999; Katz & Gagliese, 1999; Melzack, 1992; Ramachandran & Hirstein, 1998).

One idea about what causes pain in the phantom limb is that signals are sent from the stump that remains after amputation or from a remaining part of the limb. However, researchers noted that cutting the nerves that used to transmit signals from the limb to the brain does not eliminate the phantom or the pain and concluded that the pain must originate not in the skin, but in the brain.

Pain Can Be Affected by a Person's Attention   The perception of pain can increase if perception is focused on it, or decreased if it is ignored. Examples of this effect of attention on pain were noted in the 1960s (Melzack & Wall, 1965). Here is a recent description of such a situation, as reported by a student in my class:

> I remember being around five or six years old, and I was playing Nintendo when my dog ran by and pulled the wire out of the game system. When I got up to plug the wire back in I stumbled and banged my forehead on the radiator underneath the living room window. I got back up and staggered over to the Nintendo and plugged the controller back into the port, thinking nothing of my little fall. . . . As I resumed play-

Figure 14.22 ❙ Phantom limb. The lighter part of the arm represents the phantom limb—an extremity that is not physically present, but which the person perceives as existing.

> ing the game, all of a sudden I felt liquid rolling down my forehead, and reached my hand up to realize it was blood. I turned and looked into the mirror on the closet door to see a gash running down my forehead with blood pouring from it. All of a sudden I screamed out, and the pain hit me. My mom came running in, and took me to the hospital to get stitches. (Ian Kalinowski)

The important message of this description is that Ian's pain occurred not when he was injured, but when he *realized* he was injured. The fact that he didn't experience pain until he saw the gash in his head is consistent with evidence that was available in the 1960s that indicated that pain cannot be explained just based on stimulation of the skin.

To explain observations like these, Ronald Melzack and Patrick Wall (1965) proposed a mechanism called the *gate control model* of pain. Although this model was proposed more than 40 years ago, the basic principles behind it are still valid today.

The Gate Control Model

The **gate control model** begins with the idea that pain signals enter the spinal cord from the body and are then transmitted from the spinal cord to the brain. In addition, the model proposes that there are additional pathways that influence the signal sent from the spinal cord to the brain. The central idea behind the theory is that the signals from these additional pathways can act to open or close a *gate*, located in the spinal cord, which determines the strength of the signal leaving the spinal cord. $\boxed{V_L}$3

Figure 14.23 shows the circuit that Melzack and Wall (1965) proposed. The gate control system consists of cells in the spinal cord called the **substantia gelatinosa** (Figure 14.23a). These cells are represented by SG− and SG+ in the gate control circuit in Figure 14.23b. We can understand how this circuit functions by considering the following facts about its operation.

Input to the gate control system occurs along three pathways:

- *S-fibers.* The **small-diameter fibers (S-fibers)** are associated with nociceptors—fibers or receptors that fire to damaging and potentially painful stimuli. Activity in the S-fibers increases the activity of the **transmis**

sion cell (T-cell). The intensity of pain is determined by the amount of T-cell activity, with more activity resulting in more pain. You can see how this works by following the paths along which signals from the S-fibers travel and noting that all of the synapses are excitatory. Thus, signals from S-fibers always excite T-cells, and therefore increase pain.

- *L-fibers.* The **large-diameter fibers (L-fibers)** carry information about nonpainful tactile stimulation. An example of this type of stimulus would be signals sent from rubbing the skin. Activity in the L-fibers can send inhibition to the T-cells. This occurs because signals that pass through SG (dashed line) activate an inhibitory synapse. This closes the gate, which decreases T-cell activity and decreases pain.

- *Central control.* These fibers, which contain information related to cognitive functions such as expectation, attention, and distraction, carry signals down from the cortex. As with the L-fibers, activity coming down from the brain also closes the gate, decreases T-cell activity, and decreases pain.

Since the introduction of the gate control model in 1965, researchers have determined that the neural circuits that control pain are much more complex than what was proposed in the original model (Perl & Kruger, 1996; Sufka & Price, 2002). Nonetheless, the idea proposed by the model—that the perception of pain is determined by a balance between input from nociceptors in the skin and nonnociceptive activity from the skin and the brain—stimulated research that provided a great deal of additional evidence for the idea that the perception of pain is influenced by more than just stimulation of the skin (Fields & Basbaum, 1999; Sufka & Price, 2002; Turk & Flor, 1999; Weissberg, 1999). We will now consider some examples of how cognition can influence the perception of pain.

Cognition and Pain

Modern research has shown that pain can be influenced by what a person expects, how the person directs his or her attention, the type of distracting stimuli that are present, and suggestions made under hypnosis (Wiech et al., 2008). $\boxed{V_L}$4

Expectation In a hospital study in which surgical patients were told what to expect and were instructed to relax to alleviate their pain, the patients requested fewer painkillers following surgery and were sent home 2.7 days earlier than patients who were not provided with this information. Studies have also shown that a significant proportion of patients with pathological pain get relief from taking a **placebo**, a pill that they believe contains painkillers but that, in fact, contains no active ingredients (Finniss & Benedetti, 2005; Weisenberg, 1977).

Shifting Attention My student's descriptions of his Nintendo experience is an example of how pain is affected by attention. This effect of attention on pain has been used

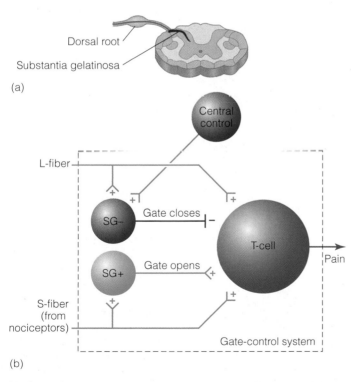

Figure 14.23 ▌ (a) Cross section of the spinal cord showing fibers entering through the dorsal root and the location of the substantia gelatinosa. (b) The circuit proposed by Melzack and Wall (1965, 1988) in their gate control model of pain perception. See text for details.

in hospitals as a tool to alleviate pain using virtual reality techniques. Consider, for example, the case of James Pokorny, who had received third-degree burns over 42 percent of his body when the fuel tank of the car he was repairing exploded. While having his bandages changed at the University of Washington Burn Center, he wore a black plastic helmet with a computer monitor inside, on which he saw a virtual world of multicolored, three-dimensional graphics. This world placed him in a virtual kitchen that contained a virtual spider, and he was able to chase the spider into the sink so he could grind it up with a virtual garbage disposal (Robbins, 2000).

The point of this "game" was to reduce Pokorny's pain by shifting his attention from the bandages to the virtual reality world. Pokorny reports that "you're concentrating on different things, rather than your pain. The pain level went down significantly." Studies of other patients indicate that burn patients using this virtual reality technique experienced much greater pain reduction than patients in a control group who were distracted by playing video games (Hoffman et al., 2000).

Content of Emotional Distraction An experiment by Minet deWied and Marinis Verbaten (2001) shows how the content of distracting materials can influence pain perception. The stimuli they used were pictures that had been previously rated as being positive (sports pictures and attractive females), neutral (household objects, nature, and people), or negative (burn victims and accidents). Male participants looked at the pictures as one of their hands was immersed in cold (2°C) water. They were told to keep the hand immersed for as long as possible but to withdraw the hand when it began to hurt.

The results, shown in Figure 14.24, indicate that the length of time the participants kept their hands in the water depended on the content of the pictures, with longer times associated with more positive pictures. Because the participants' ratings of the intensity of their pain—made immediately after removing their hands from the water—was the same for all three groups, deWied and Verbaten concluded that the content of the pictures influenced the time it took to reach the same pain level in the three groups.

Hypnosis Experiences of pain can be induced by hypnotic suggestion (Barber & Hahn, 1964; Dudley et al., 1966; Whalley & Oakley, 2003). Stuart Derbyshire and coworkers (2004) did an experiment in which they attached a thermal stimulator to the palm of a subject's hand. In the physically induced pain (PI) condition, heat pulses were delivered through the stimulator. In the hypnotically induced pain (HI) condition, subjects received suggestions that painful heat was presented through the stimulator (which was actually inactivated during this condition). In a control group, hypnotized subjects were told that the stimulator was turned off (which was accurate information) and that they should just imagine that heat was increasing at the stimulator. Subjects in all three conditions rated their pain experience on a scale from 0 (no pain) to 10 (extreme pain).

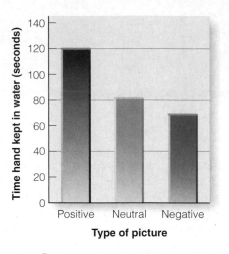

Figure 14.24 ▮ The results of deWied and Verbaten's (2001) experiment showing that participants kept their hands in cold water longer when looking at positive pictures than when looking at neutral or negative pictures.

Average pain ratings were 5.7 in the PI condition and 2.8 in the HI condition. A few subjects in the control ("imagine") condition reported feeling some heat, but none reported feeling pain. These results confirm previous research that showed that pain can be induced hypnotically. But Derbyshire went beyond simply asking people to rate physically produced and hypnotically produced pain, by using fMRI to measure his subject's brain activation as they were making their pain estimates. Figure 14.25 shows the areas activated in the PI condition (Figure 14.25a) and the HI condition (Figures 14.25b and 14.25c). Notice that there is substantial similarity between the PI and HI patterns, with overlap in the thalamus, anterior cingulate cortex, insula, parietal cortex, and prefrontal cortex. Comparing the two HI patterns shows that activation was more widespread for the subject who reported more pain (Figure 14.25b) than for the subject who had reported a lower level of pain (Figure 14.25c).

The clear relation between brain activation and pain experience and the overlap between the physically induced and hypnotically induced pain conditions support the idea that pain can occur without activation of receptors in the skin. This demonstration of a connection between perception and brain activity leads to our next section, in which we look at more evidence for links between brain activity and perception.

The Brain and Pain

One of the most obvious features of the brain activation shown in Figure 14.25 is that pain activates many areas of the brain. This is an example of distributed representation in the brain, which we introduced in Chapter 2 (see page 38). A large number of other research studies support the idea that the perception of pain is accompanied by activity that is widely distributed throughout the brain. Figure 14.26 shows a number of the structures that become activated by

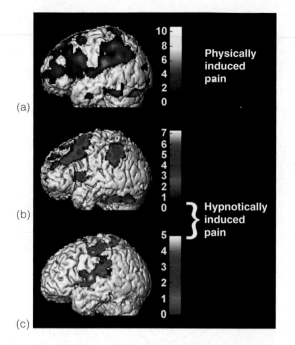

(a)

(b)

(c)

10
8
6
4
2
0
Physically induced pain

7
6
5
4
3
2
1
0

5
4
3
2
1
0
} **Hypnotically induced pain**

Figure 14.25 ▌ Brain activation for individual subjects in Derbyshire et al.'s (2004) experiment. (a) Activation by physically induced pain. (b) Activation for the subject who experienced the highest level of hypnotically induced pain. (c) Activation for the subject who experienced the lowest level of hypnotically induced pain. *(Reprinted from* Neuroimage, *23, S. W. G. Derbyshire, M. G. Whalley, V. A. Stenger, & D. A. Oakley, "Cerebral Activation During Hypnotically Induced and Imagined Pain," page 10, 2004, with permission from Elsevier.)*

pain. They include subcortical structures, such as the hypothalamus the amygdala, and the thalamus, and areas in the cortex, including the somatosensory cortex, the insula (an area deep in the cortex between the parietal and temporal regions), the anterior cingulate cortex (ACC), and the prefrontal cortex (Chapman, 1995; Derbyshire et al., 1997; Price, 2000; Rainville, 2002). All of the brain regions that are involved in pain perception, taken together, have been

called the pain matrix (Melzack, 1999; Tracey, 2005; Wager et al., 2004).

Although pain is associated with the overall pattern of firing in the pain matrix, there is also evidence that certain areas in the matrix are responsible for specific components of the pain experience.

Representation of the Sensory and Affective Components of Pain The definition of pain on page 343 states that pain is "an unpleasant sensory and emotional experience." This reference to both sensory *and* emotional experience reflects the multimodal nature of pain, which is illustrated by how people describe pain. When people describe their pain with words like *throbbing, prickly, hot,* or *dull,* they are referring to the sensory component of pain. When they use words like *torturing, annoying, frightful,* or *sickening,* they are referring to the affective (or emotional) component of pain (Melzack, 1999).

Evidence that these two components of pain are served by different areas of the brain is provided by an experiment by R. K. Hofbauer and coworkers (2001), in which participants were presented with potentially painful stimuli and were asked to rate (1) subjective pain intensity (the sensory component of pain) and (2) the unpleasantness of the pain (the affective component of pain). Hofbauer and coworkers measured brain activity using PET, as participants responded to pain induced by immersing their hands in hot water.

What makes this experiment particularly interesting is that Hofbauer and coworkers not only asked their participants to rate both the sensory and affective components of their pain, but they also used hypnotic suggestion to decrease or increase each of these components. Figure 14.27a shows that presenting suggestions to decrease or increase *subjective intensity* changed the participants' ratings of both subjective intensity (left pair of bars) and unpleasantness (right pair of bars). These changes were accompanied by changes in activity in S1, the primary somatosensory receiving area.

Figure 14.27b shows that presenting suggestions to decrease or increase the *unpleasantness* of the pain did not

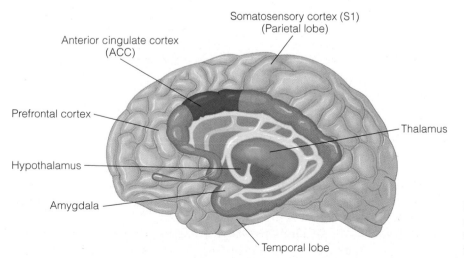

Anterior cingulate cortex (ACC)

Somatosensory cortex (S1) (Parietal lobe)

Prefrontal cortex

Hypothalamus

Amygdala

Thalamus

Temporal lobe

Figure 14.26 ▌ The perception of pain is accompanied by activation of a number of different areas of the brain. All of these areas, taken together, are called the pain matrix.

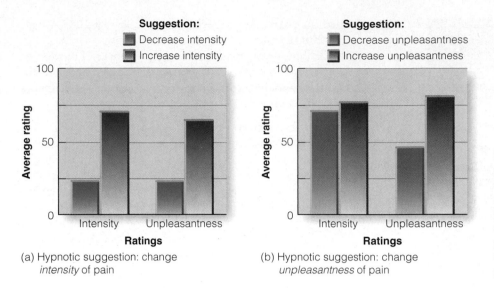

Figure 14.27 ▮ Results of Hofbauer et al.'s (2001) experiment. Participants' ratings of the intensity and the unpleasantness of pain were affected by hypnosis. (a) Results of hypnotic suggestion to decrease or increase the pain's *intensity*. (b) Results of suggestion to decrease or increase the pain's *unpleasantness*.

(a) Hypnotic suggestion: change *intensity* of pain

(b) Hypnotic suggestion: change *unpleasantness* of pain

affect ratings of subjective intensity (left bars), but did affect ratings of unpleasantness (right bars). These changes were accompanied by changes in activity in the anterior cingulate cortex (ACC), but not in S1. From these results Hofbauer concluded the ACC is important for determining unpleasantness and that unpleasantness can change even when the intensity of pain remains the same. Many other experiments have confirmed the importance of the ACC in determining the affective component of pain, and also that different structures in the brain serve different aspects of pain perception (Rainville, 2002).

Chemicals in the Brain   Another important development in our understanding of the relationship between brain activity and pain perception is the discovery of a link between chemicals called **opioids** and pain perception. This can be traced back to research that began in the 1970s on opiate drugs, such as opium and heroin, which have been used since the dawn of recorded history to reduce pain and induce feelings of euphoria.

By the 1970s, researchers had discovered that the opiate drugs act on receptors in the brain that respond to stimulation by molecules with specific structures. The importance of the molecule's structure for exciting these "opiate receptors" explains why injecting a drug called **naloxone** into a person who has overdosed on heroin can almost immediately revive the victim. Because naloxone's structure is similar to heroin's, it blocks the action of heroin by attaching itself to receptor sites usually occupied by heroin (Figure 14.28a).

Why are there opiate receptor sites in the brain? After all, they certainly have been present since long before people started taking heroin. Researchers concluded that there must be naturally occurring substances in the body that act on these sites, and in 1975 neurotransmitters were discovered that act on the same receptors that are activated by opium and heroin. One group of these transmitters are the pain-reducing **endorphins**.

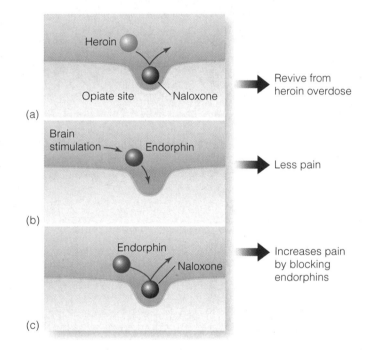

Figure 14.28 ▮ (a) Naloxone reduces the effect of heroin by occupying a receptor site normally stimulated by heroin. (b) Stimulating sites in the brain that cause the release of endorphins can reduce pain by stimulating opiate receptor sites. (c) Naloxone decreases the pain reduction caused by endorphins by keeping the endorphins from reaching the receptor sites.

Since the discovery of endorphins, researchers have accumulated a large amount of evidence linking endorphins to pain reduction. For example, pain can be decreased by stimulating sites in the brain that release endorphins (Figure 14.28b), and pain can be increased by injecting naloxone, which blocks endorphins from reaching their receptor sites (Figure 14.28c).

In addition to decreasing the analgesic effect of endorphins, naloxone also decreases the analgesic effect of placebos (see page 345). This finding, along with other evidence, suggests that the pain-reduction effect of placebos occurs because placebos cause the release of endorphins. Because placebos contain no active chemicals, their effects have always been thought to be "psychological." However, the idea that placebos cause the release of endorphins provides a physiological basis for what had previously been described in strictly psychological terms. (Also see "If You Want to Know More" item 9, "The Physiology of Placebos," on page 351.)

Finally, a recent study has identified genetic differences in people that cause their brain to release different amounts of opioids in response to painful stimuli (Zubieta et al., 2003). This study found that people whose brains released more opioids were able to withstand higher levels of pain stimulation.

Something to Consider: Pain in Social Situations

The song lyrics "It only hurts for a little while" refers not to the pain of falling down on the sidewalk but to the pain of ending a romantic relationship. In our society, "pain" goes beyond the physical pain we have been focusing on in this chapter to include, for example, the distress one feels when a relationship ends or the anguish one feels when excluded from a group. Although this may seem more like "social psychology" than "perception," there is new evidence that the pain of social loss may activate some of the brain areas that are activated by physical pain.

Naomi Eisenberger and coworkers (2003) determined how the brain responds to social loss. Participants' brain activity was measured in an fMRI scanner as they either watched or played a computer game called CyberBall. Participants were led to believe that they were playing the game with two other players who were also in fMRI scanners, although in reality there were no other players. After watching the other "players" play the game, the participant was then included in the game. After receiving seven throws from the other players (actually preprogrammed by the experimenter), it became apparent to the participant that he or she was being excluded, because the other players stopped throwing the ball to the participant.

During the exclusion part of the experiment, participants reported feeling ignored and excluded, and reported some distress. When this happened, their brain scan showed increased activation of the anterior cingulate cortex (ACC)—the same area of the brain that is activated by the emotional suffering associated with physical pain (Figure 14.26). This activation of the ACC was greater in participants who reported feeling greater social distress in response to being excluded.

If being hurt by feeling rejected activates pain-related areas in the brain, what about watching someone else experiencing pain? The answer is that watching another person experience pain also activates the ACC, especially when

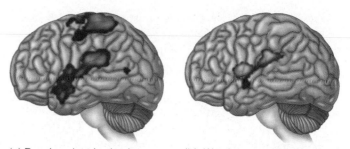

(a) Receive electric shocks   (b) Watch partner receive shocks

Figure 14.29 ▌ Singer and coworkers (2004) used fMRI to determine the areas of the brain activated by (a) receiving electric shocks and (b) watching another person receive the shocks. Singer proposes that the activation in (b) is related to empathy for the other person. Empathy did not activate the somatosensory cortex, but did activate other areas that are activated by pain, such as the insula (tucked between the parietal and temporal lobes) and anterior cingulate cortex (Figure 14.26). *(Adapted with permission from Holden, C., Imaging studies show how brain thinks about pain, Science, 303, 1121, 2004, AAAS.)*

the person watching feels empathy—an understanding and sharing of the other person's feelings.

Tania Singer and coworkers (2004) demonstrated this by bringing romantically involved couples into the laboratory and having the woman, whose brain activity was being measured by an fMRI scanner, either receive shocks herself or watch her male partner receive shocks. The results, shown in Figure 14.29, show that a number of brain areas were activated when the woman received the shocks (Figure 14.29a), and that some of the same areas were activated when she watched her partner receive shocks (Figure 14.29b).

To show that the brain activity caused by watching their partner was related to empathy, Singer had the women fill out "empathy scales" designed to measure their tendency to empathize with others. As she predicted, women with higher "empathy scores" showed higher activation of their ACC. Thus, although "social" pain may be caused by stimulation that is very different from physical pain, these two types of pain apparently share some physiological mechanisms. (Also see Avenanti et al., 2005; Lamm et al., 2007.)

TEST YOURSELF 14.2

1. What processes are involved in identifying objects by haptic exploration?
2. What are some of the physiological processes involved in recognizing objects by touch?
3. Describe the three types of pain.
4. What is the direct pathway model of pain? Describe evidence that led researchers to question this model of pain perception.
5. What is the gate control model? Be sure you understand the roles of the S-fibers, L-fibers, and central control.

6. Give examples for the following situations, which illustrate how pain is influenced by cognition and experience: expectation, shifting attention, content of emotional distraction, hypnosis.

7. Compare how the brain responds to physically induced pain and pain caused by hypnotic suggestion.

8. What is the pain matrix?

9. What does it mean to say that pain is multimodal? Describe the hypnosis experiments that identified areas involved in the sensory component of pain and the emotional component of pain.

10. Describe the role of chemicals in the perception of pain. Be sure you understand how endorphins and naloxone interact at receptor sites, and a possible mechanism that explains why pain is reduced by placebos.

11. What are some parallels between nociceptive pain and the pain associated with social situations?

THINK ABOUT IT

1. One of the themes in this book is that it is possible to use the results of psychophysical experiments to suggest the operation of physiological mechanisms or to link physiological mechanisms to perception. Cite an example of how psychophysics has been used in this way for each of the senses we have considered so far—vision, hearing, and the cutaneous senses. (p. 338)

2. Some people report situations in which they were injured but didn't feel any pain until they became aware of their injury. How would you explain this kind of situation in terms of top-down and bottom-up processing? How could you relate this situation to the studies we have discussed? (p. 344)

3. Even though the senses of vision and cutaneous perception are different in many ways, there are a number of parallels between them. Cite examples of parallels between vision and cutaneous sensations (touch and pain) for the following: "tuned" receptors, mechanisms of detail perception, receptive fields, plasticity (how changing the environment influences properties of the system), and top-down processing. Also, can you think of situations in which vision and touch interact with one another?

IF YOU WANT TO KNOW MORE

This is the largest "If You Want to Know More" section in the book because of the large amount of research that is being done on touch, pain, and the other cutaneous senses. If space were available, it would be easy to write separate chapters on touch and pain, with an additional chapter on proprioception and kinesthesis. In lieu of these chapters, here are a few of the interesting things that are being done in this extremely active area of research.

1. *A tactile illusion and the homunculus.* Recent research on monkeys has shown that tactile illusions on the skin, in which stimulation at one point causes a feeling at another point, activate the area of the brain that corresponds not to where the skin was stimulated, but to where the monkey *felt* the stimulation. (p. 332)

   Chen, L., M., Friedman, R. M., & Roe, A. W. (2003). Optical imaging of a tactile illusion in area 3b of the primate somatosensory cortex. *Science, 302,* 881–885.

   Eysel, U. T. (2003). Illusions and perceived images in the primate brain. *Science, 302,* 789–790.

2. *Plastic effects of losing a sense.* When input from one sense is eliminated, the brain area normally devoted to that sense can be taken over by another sense. For example, in people who became blind before the age of 7, the occipital cortex (which is usually associated with vision) is activated by reading Braille. (p. 333)

   Sadato, N., Pascual-Leone, A., Grafman, J., Ibanez, V., Deiber, M.-P., Dold, G., & Hallett, M. (1996). Activation of the primary visual cortex by Braille reading in blind subjects. *Nature, 380,* 526–528.

3. *Haptic recognition of emotion in facial expressions.* People can, with a small amount of training, learn to identify different facial expressions by exploring an actor's face with their hands. (p. 340)

   Lederman, S. J., Klatzky, R. L., Abramowicz, A., Salsman, K., Kitada, R., & Hamilton, C. (2007). Haptic recognition of static and dynamic expressions of emotion in the live face. *Psychological Science, 18,* 158–164.

4. *Why you can't tickle yourself.* It is generally not possible to tickle yourself. This has to do with differences between a self-produced tactile stimulus and the same stimulus presented externally. (p. 340)

   Blakemore, S. J., Wolpert, D. M., & Frith, C. D. (1998). Central cancellation of self-produced tickle sensation. *Nature Neuroscience, 1,* 635–640.

5. *How different types of stimulation affect the brain.* Research has shown that three types of stimuli—pressure, flutter, and vibration—cause maximum activation of different areas in somatosensory cortex. (p. 341)

   Friedman, R. N., Chen, L. M., & Roe, A. W. (2004). Modality maps within primate somatosensory cortex. *Proceedings of the National Academy of Sciences, 101,* 12724–12729.

6. *Pain in phantom limb.* Many people who have had a limb amputated continue to experience the limb. This experience, which is called a phantom limb, is often accompanied by feelings of pain in the limb, even though the limb is no longer present. (p. 344)

   Katz, J., & Gagliese, L. (1999). Phantom limb pain: A continuing puzzle. In R. J. Gatchel & D. C. Turk (Eds.), *Psychosocial factors in pain* (pp. 284–300). New York: Guilford Press.

Ramachandran, V. S., & Hirstein, W. (1998). The perception of phantom limbs. *Brain, 121,* 1603–1630.

7. *Pathological pain.* Pathological pain—pain that continues despite medical attempts to relieve it—is a serious problem that disrupts the lives of many people. (p. 343)

Scholz, J., & Woolf, C. J. (2002). Can we conquer pain? *Nature Neuroscience, 5,* 1062–1067.

Watkins, L. R., & Maier, S. F. (2003). When good pain turns bad. *Current Directions in Psychological Science, 12,* 232–236.

8. *Psychological factors in coping with chronic pain.* There is evidence that patients' attitudes and coping strategies can affect their ability to deal with chronic pain. (p. 345)

Ramirez-Maestre, C., Esteve, R., & Lopez, A. E. (2008). Cognitive appraisal and coping in chronic pain patients. *European Journal of Pain, 12,* 749–756.

Vaine, I., Crombez, G., Eccleston, C., Devulder, J., & DeCorte, W. (2004). Acceptance of the unpleasant reality of chronic pain: Effects upon attention to pain and engagement with daily activities. *Pain, 112,* 282–288.

9. *The physiology of placebos.* Research has shown that placebos activate the same brain structures that are activated by opioids. (p. 349)

Petrovic, P., Kalso, E., Petersson, K. M., & Ingvar, M. (2002). Placebo and opioid analgesia—imaging a shared neuronal network. *Science, 295,* 1737–1740.

Wager, T. D., Rilling, J. K., Smith, E. E., Sokolik, A., Casey, K. L., Davidson, R. J., et al. (2004). Placebo-induced changes in fMRI in the anticipation and experience of pain. *Science, 303,* 1162–1167.

KEY TERMS

Active touch (p. 340)
Affective (or emotional) component of pain (p. 347)
Cutaneous senses (p. 330)
Dermis (p. 331)
Direct pathway model of pain (p. 343)
Duplex theory of texture perception (p. 338)
Endorphin (p. 348)
Epidermis (p. 331)
Exploratory procedures (EPs) (p. 341)
Gate-control model (p. 345)
Grating acuity (p. 335)
Haptic perception (p. 340)
Homunculus (p. 332)
Inflammatory pain (p. 343)
Kinesthesis (p. 330)

Large-diameter fibers (L-fibers) (p. 345)
Mechanoreceptor (p. 331)
Medial lemniscal pathway (p. 331)
Meissner corpuscle (p. 331)
Merkel receptor (p. 331)
Multimodal nature of pain (p. 347)
Naloxone (p. 348)
Neuropathic pain (p. 343)
Nociceptive pain (p. 343)
Nociceptor (p. 343)
Opioid (p. 348)
Pacinian corpuscle (p. 331)
Pain matrix (p. 347)
Passive touch (p. 340)
Phantom limb (p. 344)
Placebo (p. 345)
Proprioception (p. 330)

Ruffini cylinder (p. 331)
Secondary somatosensory cortex (S2) (p. 332)
Sensory component of pain (p. 347)
Small-diameter fibers (S-fibers) (p. 345)
Somatosensory receiving area (S1) (p. 332)
Somatosensory system (p. 330)
Spatial cue (p. 338)
Spinothalamic pathway (p. 331)
Substantia gelatinosa (p. 345)
Tactile acuity (p. 335)
Temporal cue (p. 338)
Transmission cell (T-cell) (p. 345)
Two-point threshold (p. 335)
Ventrolateral nucleus (p. 332)

MEDIA RESOURCES

The *Sensation and Perception* Book Companion Website

www.cengage.com/psychology/goldstein

See the companion website for flashcards, practice quiz questions, Internet links, updates, critical thinking exercises, discussion forums, games, and more!

CengageNOW

www.cengage.com/cengagenow

Go to this site for the link to CengageNOW, your one-stop shop. Take a pre-test for this chapter, and CengageNOW will generate a personalized study plan based on your test results. The study plan will identify the topics you need to review and direct you to online resources to help you master those topics. You can then take a post-test to help you determine the concepts you have mastered and what you will still need to work on.

Virtual Lab

Your Virtual Lab is designed to help you get the most out of this course. The Virtual Lab icons direct you to specific media demonstrations and experiments designed to help you visualize what you are reading about. The number beside each icon indicates the number of the media element you can access through your CD-ROM, CengageNOW, or WebTutor resource.

The following lab exercises are related to material in this chapter:

1. *Anatomy of the Skin* The skin, with drag-and-drop terms to test your knowledge of the locations of basic skin structures.

2. *Surfing the Web With Touch* An ABC News feature that discusses how a vibrating computer mouse can enhance perception of textures pictured on the computer screen.

3. *Gate Control System* How different types of stimulation are processed by the gate control system.

4. *Children and Chronic Pain* An ABC News feature on how emotional factors can contribute to pain in young children.

Chapter Contents

CHAPTER 15

The Chemical Senses

OPPOSITE PAGE As this woman takes in the aroma of the wine, she is stimulating olfactory receptors in her nose. Drinking the wine will stimulate taste receptors on her tongue. The perception created by the combination of olfaction and taste is called flavor.
Tony Hutchings/Getty Images

VL The Virtual Lab icons direct you to specific animations and videos designed to help you visualize what you are reading about. The number beside each icon indicates the number of the clip you can access through your CD-ROM or your student website.

- Why is a dog's sense of smell so much better than a human's? (p. 357)
- Why does a cold inhibit the ability to taste? (p. 373)
- How do neurons in the cortex combine smell and taste? (p. 373)

We have five senses, but only two that go beyond the boundaries of ourselves. When you look at someone, it's just bouncing light, or when you hear them, it's just sound waves, vibrating air, or touch is just nerve endings tingling. Know what smell is? . . . It's made up of the molecules of what you're smelling. (Kushner, 1993, p. 17)

The character speaking the these lines in the play *Angels in America* probably did not take a course in sensation and perception and so leaves out the fact that vision and hearing are "just nerve endings tingling" as well. But his point—that smell involves taking molecules into your body—is one of the properties of the chemical senses that distinguishes them from the other senses. Thus, as you drink something, you smell it because molecules in gas form are entering your nose, and you taste it because molecules in liquid form are stimulating your tongue. Smell (which we will refer to as *olfaction*) and taste have been called molecule detectors because they endow these gas and liquid molecules with distinctive smells and tastes (Cain, 1988; Kauer, 1987).

Because the stimuli responsible for tasting and smelling are on the verge of being assimilated into the body, these senses are often seen as "gatekeepers" that (1) identify things that the body needs for survival and that should therefore be consumed and (2) detect things that would be bad for the body and that should therefore be rejected. The gatekeeper function of taste and smell is aided by a large affective, or emotional, component—things that are bad for us often taste or smell unpleasant, and things that are good for us generally taste or smell good. In addition to creating "good" and "bad" affect, smelling an odor associated with a past place or event can trigger memories, which in turn may create emotional reactions.

Because the receptors that serve taste and smell are constantly exposed not only to the chemicals that they are designed to sense but also to harmful materials such as bacteria and dirt, they undergo a cycle of birth, development, and death over 5–7 weeks for olfactory receptors and 1–2 weeks for taste receptors. This constant renewal of the receptors, which is called neurogenesis, is unique to these senses. In vision, hearing, and the cutaneous senses, the receptors are safely protected inside structures such as the eye, the inner ear, and under the skin; however, the receptors for taste and smell are relatively unprotected and therefore need to be constantly renewed.

We will consider olfaction first and then taste. We will describe the psychophysics and anatomy of each system and then how different taste and smell qualities are coded in the nervous system. Finally, we will consider flavor, which results from the interaction of taste and smell.

The Olfactory System

Functions of Olfaction

Olfaction is extremely important in the lives of many species because it is often their primary window to the environment (Ache, 1991). One important contrast between humans and other species is that many animals are macrosmatic (having a keen sense of smell that is important to their survival), whereas humans are microsmatic (having a less keen sense of smell that is not crucial to their survival). Many animals use olfaction to survive: it provides cues to orient them in space, to mark territory, and to guide them to specific places, other animals, and food sources (Holley, 1991). Olfaction is also extremely important in sexual reproduction because it triggers mating behavior in many species (Doty, 1976; Pfeiffer & Johnston, 1994).

Although olfaction may not be as central to our sensory experience as vision, hearing, or touch, some of its effects may be occurring without our awareness. Consider, for example, the phenomenon of menstrual synchrony—women who live or work together often have menstrual periods at about the same time. In the first systematic investigation of this phenomenon, Martha McClintock (1971) asked 135 females, aged 17 to 22, living in a college dormitory, to indicate when their periods began throughout the school year. She found that women who saw each other often (roommates or close friends) tended to have synchronous periods by the end of the school year. After eliminating other explanations such as awareness of the other person's period, McClintock concluded that "there is some interpersonal physiological process which affects the menstrual cycle" (p. 246).

What might this physiological process be? Twenty-seven years after the dormitory experiment, Kathleen Stern and McClintock (1998) did an experiment that led them to conclude that menstrual synchrony is caused by human pheromones—chemical signals released by an individual that affect the physiology and behavior of other individuals. They used cotton pads to collect secretions from the underarms of 9 donor women at various times in their ovulatory cycle. The pads from the donor women were treated with a small amount of alcohol and were wiped on the upper lips of other women (the recipients) who were instructed not to wash their face for 6 hours after the application.

Stern and McClintock found that underarm secretions taken from donor women in the initial phase of their cycle (just after menstruation) shortened the length of the recipients' cycles. In contrast, secretions from the ovulatory phase of the cycle lengthened the recipients' cycles. Women in a control group, who just had alcohol applied to their upper lip, did not show this effect. Apparently, there were two pheromones at work—one that shortens the cycle and one that lengthens it. What is especially interesting about these results is that they occurred even though the recipient women reported that they detected only the alcohol that was added to the pads. Thus the pheromones resulted in "chemical communication" that occurred even though odors were not consciously detected.

Although smell might work "behind the scenes" in determining a phenomenon like menstrual synchrony, there is nothing hidden about the vast sums of money people spend yearly on perfumes and deodorants (Rossiter, 1996). In addition, the emergence of a new billion-dollar-a-year industry called environmental fragrancing, which offers products to add pleasing scents to the air in both homes and businesses, attests to the fact that the role of smell in our daily lives is not inconsequential (Gilbert & Firestein, 2002; Owens, 1994).

But perhaps the most convincing argument for the importance of smell to humans comes from those who suffer from **anosmia**, the loss of the ability to smell as a result of injury or infection. People suffering from anosmia describe the great void created by their inability to taste many foods because of the close connection between smell and flavor. One woman who suffered from anosmia and then briefly regained her sense of smell stated, "I always thought I would sacrifice smell to taste if I had to choose between the two, but I suddenly realized how much I had missed. We take it for granted and are unaware that everything smells: people, the air, my house, my skin" (Birnberg, 1988; quoted in Ackerman, 1990, p. 42). Olfaction is more important in our lives than most of us realize, and, although it may not be essential to our survival, life is often enhanced by our ability to smell and becomes a little more dangerous if we lose the olfactory warning system that alerts us to spoiled food, leaking gas, or smoke from a fire. [VL] 1

Detecting Odors

Our sense of smell enables us to detect extremely low concentrations of some odorants. The **detection threshold** for odors is the lowest concentration at which an odorant can be detected.

Table 15.1 lists thresholds for a number of substances. It is notable that there is a very large range of thresholds. T-butyl mercepatan, the odorant that is added to natural gas, can be detected in very small concentrations of less than 1 part per billion in air. In contrast, to detect the vapors of acetone (the main component of nail polish remover), the concentration must be 15,000 parts per billion, and for the vapor of methanol, the concentration must be 141,000 parts per billion.

Although humans can detect extremely small concentrations of some odorants, they are much less sensitive to odors than many animals. For example, rats are 8 to 50 times more sensitive to odors than humans, and dogs are from 300 to 10,000 times more sensitive, depending on the odorant (Laing, Doty, & Breipohl, 1991). But even though humans are unaware of odors that other animals can detect, humans' individual olfactory receptors are as sensitive as any animal's. H. deVries and M. Stuiver (1961) demonstrated this by showing that human olfactory receptors can be excited by the action of just 1 molecule of odorant. This is similar to the situation in vision, in which a rod receptor can be activated by the action of just 1 quantum of light (see page 50).

Nothing can be more sensitive than 1 molecule per receptor, so how come humans are less sensitive to odors than dogs? The answer is that humans have far fewer receptors than dogs—only about 10 million receptors, compared to

TABLE 15.1 | Human Odor Detection Thresholds

COMPOUND	ODOR THRESHOLD IN AIR (PARTS PER BILLION)
Methanol	141,000
Acetone	15,000
Formaldehyde	870
Menthol	40
T-butyl mercaptan	0.3

Source: Devos et al., 1990.

about 1 billion for dogs (Dodd & Squirrell, 1980; Moulton, 1977).

Another aspect of odor detection is the *difference threshold*—the smallest *difference* in the concentration of two odors that can be detected. Measurements of the difference threshold highlight one of the most important problems in olfactory research—the control of concentrations in stimulus presentations. For example, when William Cain (1977) carefully measured the difference threshold by placing two odorants of different concentrations on absorbent cotton balls and asked participants to judge which was more intense, he found that the difference threshold averaged 19 percent. However, when Cain analyzed the stimuli he had presented on the cotton balls, he found that stimuli that were supposed to have the same concentration actually varied considerably. This variation was apparently caused by differences in the airflow pattern through the cotton in different samples.

To deal with this problem, Cain remeasured the difference threshold using a device called an **olfactometer**, which presents olfactory stimuli with much greater precision than cotton balls (Figure 15.1). Using this more precise method of presenting of stimulus, Cain found that the threshold dropped to 11 percent.

Identifying Odors

When odorant concentrations are near threshold, so a person can just detect the *presence* of an odor, the person usually cannot sense the *quality* of the odor—whether it is "floral" or "pepperminty" or "rancid." The concentration of an odorant has to be increased by as much as a factor of 3 above the threshold concentration before the person can recognize an odor's quality. The concentration at which quality can be recognized is called the **recognition threshold** (Dalton, 2002).

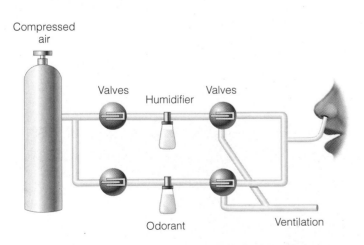

Compressed air

Valves
Humidifier
Valves

Odorant
Ventilation

Figure 15.1 ▌ This diagram shows the different components of an olfactometer. By adjusting the valves in this system, the experimenter can vary both the humidity and the concentration of olfactory stimuli reaching the subject's nose.

One of the more intriguing facts about odors is that even though humans can discriminate between as many as 100,000 different odors (Firestein, 2001), they often find it difficult to accurately identify specific odors. For example, when people are presented with the odors of familiar substances such as mint, bananas, and motor oil, they can easily tell the difference between them. However, when they are asked to *identify* the substance associated with the odor, they are successful only about half the time (Engen & Pfaffmann, 1960). J. A. Desor and Gary Beauchamp (1974) found, however, that when they presented participants with the names of the substances at the beginning of the experiment and then reminded them of the correct names when they failed to respond correctly on subsequent trials, they could, after some practice, correctly identify 98 percent of the substances.

One of the amazing things about odor identification is that knowing the correct label for the odor actually seems to transform our perception into that odor. Cain (1980) gives the example of an object initially identified as "fishy-goaty-oily." When the experimenter told the person that the fishy-goaty-oily smell actually came from leather, the smell was then transformed into that of leather.

I had a similar experience when a friend gave me a bottle of Aquavit, a Danish drink with a very interesting smell. As I was sampling this drink with some friends, we tried to identify its smell. Many odors were proposed ("anise," "orange," "lemon"), but it wasn't until someone turned the bottle around and read the label on the back that the truth became known: "Aquavit (Water of Life) is the Danish national drink—a delicious, crystal-clear spirit distilled from grain, with a slight taste of caraway." When we heard the word *caraway*, the previous hypotheses of anise, orange, and lemon were discarded, and the smell became caraway. Thus, when we have trouble identifying odors, this trouble results not from a deficiency in our olfactory system, but from an inability to retrieve the odor's name from our memory (Cain, 1979).

DEMONSTRATION

Naming and Odor Identification

To demonstrate the effect of naming substances on odor identification, have a friend collect a number of familiar objects for you and, without looking, try to identify the odors. You will find that you can identify some but not others, and when your friend tells you the correct answer for the ones you identified incorrectly, you will wonder how you could have failed to identify such a familiar smell. But don't blame your mistakes on your nose; blame them on your memory. ▌

The Puzzle of Olfactory Quality

Although we know that we can discriminate among a huge number of odors, research to determine the mechanisms be-

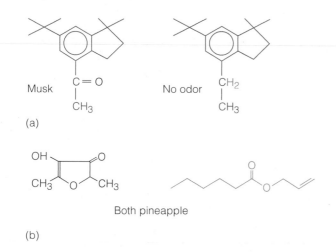

Musk   No odor

(a)

Both pineapple

(b)

Figure 15.2 ▌ (a) Two molecules that have the same structures, but one smells like musk and the other is odorless. (b) Two molecules with different structures but similar odors.

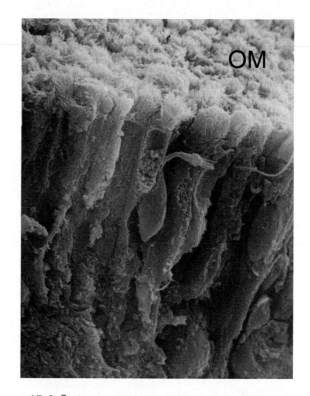

Figure 15.3 ▌ A scanning electron micrograph showing olfactory receptor neurons and supporting cells (below) and the surface of the olfactory mucosa (OM). Odorant molecules flow across the mucosa and stimulate the olfactory receptors. *(From Morrison, E. E., & Costanzo, R. M., Morphology of the human olfactory epithelium.* Journal of Comparative Neurology, 297, *1990, 1–13.)*

hind this ability is complicated by difficulties in establishing a system to bring some order to our descriptions of odor quality. Such systems exist for other senses. For example, we can describe visual stimuli in terms of their colors and can relate our perception of color to the physical property of wavelength. We can describe sound stimuli as having different pitches and relate these pitches to the physical property of frequency. However, attempts to create a way to organize odors and to relate odors to physical properties of molecules has proven to be extremely difficult.

One reason for the difficulty is that we lack a specific language for odor quality. For example, when people smell the chemical ~-ionone, they usually say that it smells like violets. This description, it turns out, is fairly accurate, but if you compare ~-ionone to real violets, they smell different. The perfume industry's solution is to use names such as "woody violet" and "sweet violet" to distinguish between different violet smells, but this hardly solves the problem we face in trying to determine how olfaction works.

Another difficulty in relating odors to molecular properties is that some molecules that have similar structures can smell different (Figure 15.2a), and molecules that have very different structures can smell similar (Figure 15.2b). We will see, however, that despite these difficulties, recent research has succeeded in demonstrating some links between (1) structural components of molecules, (2) olfactory quality, and (3) patterns of activation in the olfactory system.

The Neural Code for Olfactory Quality

How does the olfactory system know what molecules are entering the nose? The first step toward answering this question is to consider what happens when odorant molecules enter the nose and stimulate the receptors in the olfactory mucosa.

The Olfactory Mucosa

Part of the **olfactory mucosa** (OM) is shown at the top of Figure 15.3. The mucosa is a dime-sized region located high in the nasal cavity that contains the receptors for olfaction. Figure 15.4a shows the location of the mucosa, on the roof of the nasal cavity and just below the olfactory bulb. Odorant molecules are carried into the nose in an air stream (blue arrows), which brings these molecules into contact with the mucosa. Figure 15.4b shows the *olfactory receptor neurons (ORNs)* that are located in the mucosa (colored parts) and the supporting cells (tan area). $\boxed{V_L}$ **2**

Olfactory Receptor Neurons

Just as the rod and cone receptors in the retina contain molecules called visual pigments that are sensitive to light, **olfactory receptor neurons** (ORNs) in the mucosa are dotted with molecules called **olfactory receptors** that are sensitive to chemical odorants (Figure 15.4c). Other parallels between visual pigments and olfactory receptors are that they are both proteins that cross the membrane of the

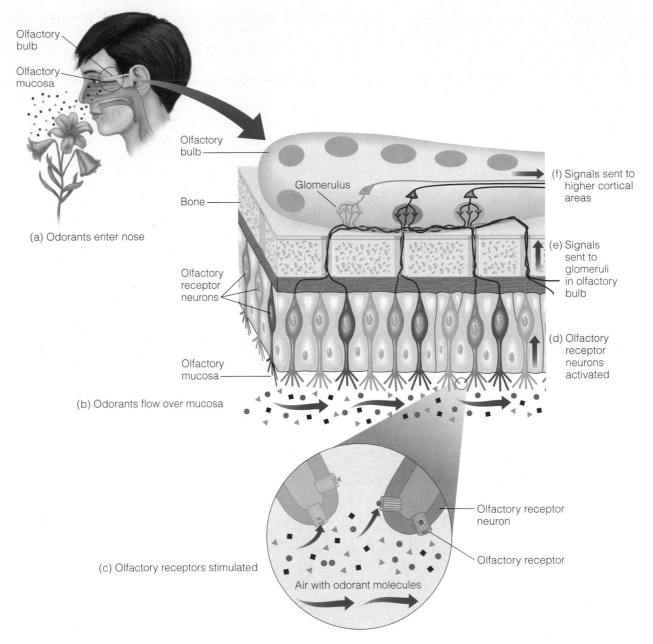

Olfactory
bulb

Olfactory
mucosa

(a) Odorants enter nose

Olfactory
bulb

Glomerulus

Bone

(f) Signals sent to
higher cortical
areas

(e) Signals
sent to
glomeruli
in olfactory
bulb

Olfactory
receptor
neurons

(d) Olfactory
receptor
neurons
activated

Olfactory
mucosa

(b) Odorants flow over mucosa

Olfactory receptor
neuron

Olfactory receptor

(c) Olfactory receptors stimulated

Air with odorant molecules

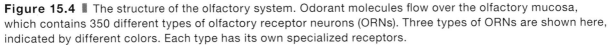

Figure 15.4 ❚ The structure of the olfactory system. Odorant molecules flow over the olfactory mucosa, which contains 350 different types of olfactory receptor neurons (ORNs). Three types of ORNs are shown here, indicated by different colors. Each type has its own specialized receptors.

receptor neurons (rods and cones for vision; ORNs for olfaction) seven times (Figure 3.6, page 48), and they are both sensitive to a specific range of stimuli. Each type of visual pigment is each sensitive to a band of wavelengths in a particular region of the visible spectrum (Figure 3.24, page 57), and each type of olfactory receptor is sensitive to a narrow range of odorants.

An important difference between the visual system and the olfactory system is that while there are only four different types of visual pigments (one rod pigment and three cone pigments), there are 350 different types of olfactory receptors, each sensitive to a particular group of odor-

ants. The discovery that there are 350 different types of olfactory receptors in the human, and 1,000 different types in the mouse, was made by Linda Buck and Richard Axel (1991), who received the 2004 Nobel Prize in Physiology and Medicine for their research on the olfactory system (also see Buck, 2004).

The large number of olfactory receptors is important because it is one reason we can identify 100,000 or more different odors, but this large number of receptor types increases the challenges in understanding how olfaction works. One thing that makes things slightly simpler is another parallel with vision: Just as a particular rod or cone receptor contains only one type of visual pigment, a particular olfactory receptor neuron (ORN) contains only one type of olfactory receptor.

Activating Olfactory Receptor Neurons

Figure 15.5a shows the surface of part of the olfactory mucosa. The circles represent ORNs, with two types of ORNs highlighted in red and blue. Remember that there are 350 different types of ORNs in the mucosa. There are about 10,000 of each type of ORN, so the mucosa contains millions of ORNs.

The first step in understanding how we perceive different odorants is to ask how the array of ORNs that blanket the olfactory mucosa respond to different odorants. One way this question has been answered is by using a technique called calcium imaging.

METHOD | Calcium Imaging

When an olfactory receptor responds, the concentration of calcium ions (Ca++) increases inside the ORN. One way of measuring this increase in calcium ions is called **calcium imaging**. This involves soaking olfactory neurons in a chemical that causes the ORN to fluoresce with a green glow when exposed to ultraviolet (380 nm) light. This green glow can be used to measure how much Ca++ had entered the neuron because *increasing* Ca++ inside the neuron *decreases* the glow. Thus, measuring the decrease in fluorescence indicates how strongly the ORN is activated.

Bettina Malnic and coworkers (1999), working in Linda Buck's laboratory, determined the response to a large number of odorants using calcium imaging. The results for a few of her odorants are shown in Figure 15.6, which indicates how 10 different ORNs are activated by each odorant. (Remember that each ORN contains only one type of olfactory receptor.) The pattern of activation is an odorant's **recognition profile**. For example, the recognition profile of octanoic acid is weak firing of ORN 79 and strong firing of ORNs 1, 18, 19, 41, 46, 51, and 83, whereas the profile for octanol is strong firing of ORNs 18, 19, 41, and 51.

From these profiles, we can see each odorant causes a different pattern of firing across ORNs. Also, odorants like octanoic acid and nonanoic acid, which have similar structures (shown on the right) often have similar profiles. We can also see, however, that this doesn't always occur (compare the patterns for bromohexanoic acid and bromooctanoic acid, which also have similar structures).

Remember that one of the puzzling facts about odor perception is that some molecules have similar structures but smell different (Figure 15.2a). When Malnic compared such molecules, she found that these molecules had differ-

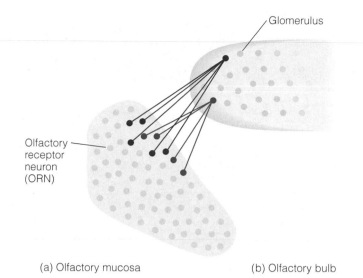

(a) Olfactory mucosa   (b) Olfactory bulb

Figure 15.5 ▌ (a) A portion of the olfactory mucosa. The mucosa contains 350 types of ORNs and about 10,000 of each type. The red circles represent 10,000 of one type of ORN, and the blue circles, 10,000 of another type. (b) All ORNs of a particular type send their signals to one or two glomeruli in the olfactory bulb.

ent recognition profiles. For example, octanoic acid and octanol differ only by one oxygen molecule, but the smell of octanol is described as "sweet," "rose," and "fresh," whereas the smell of octomonic acid is described as "rancid," "sour," and "repulsive." This difference in perception is reflected in their different profiles. Although we still can't predict which smells result from specific patterns of response, we do know that when two odorants smell different, they usually have different profiles.

The idea that an odorant's smell can be related to different response profiles is similar to the trichromatic code for color vision that we described in Chapter 9 (see page 207). Remember that each wavelength of light is coded by a different pattern of firing of the three cone receptors, and that a particular cone receptor responds to many wavelengths. The situation for odors is similar—each odorant is coded by a different pattern of firing of ORNs, and a particular ORN responds to many odorants. What's different about olfaction is that there are 350 different types of ORNs, compared to just three cone receptors for vision.

Activating the Olfactory Bulb

Activation of receptors in the mucosa causes electrical signals in the ORNs that are distributed across the mucosa. These ORNs send signals to structures called **glomeruli** in the **olfactory bulb**. Figure 15.5b illustrates a basic principle of the relationship between ORNs and glomeruli. All of the 10,000 ORNs of a paticular type send their signals to just one or two glomeruli. Each glomerulus therefore collects information about the firing of a particular type of ORN.

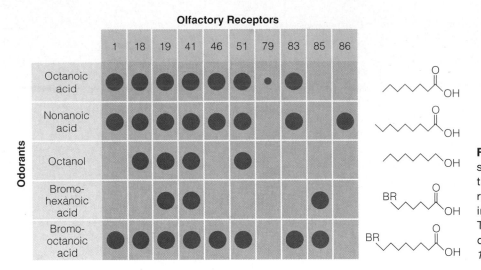

Figure 15.6 | Recognition profiles for some odorants. Large dots indicate that the odorant causes a high firing rate for the receptor listed along the top; a small dot indicates a lower firing rate for the receptor. The structures of the compounds are shown on the right. (*Adapted from Malnic et al., 1999.*)

Just as we asked how ORNs in the mucosa respond to different odorants, we can also ask how glomeruli in the olfactory bulb respond to different odorants. Naoshige Uchida and coworkers (2000) used a technique called optical imaging to answer this question.

METHOD | Optical Imaging

The technique of **optical imaging** can be used to measure the activity of large areas of the olfactory bulb by measuring how much red light is reflected from the olfactory bulb. The bulb must first be exposed by removing a patch of the skull. Red light is used because when neurons are activated, they consume oxygen from the blood. Blood that contains less oxygen reflects less red light than blood with oxygen, so areas that have been activated reflect less red light and look slightly darker than areas that have not been activated.

The optical imaging procedure involves illuminating the surface of the bulb with red light, measuring how much light is reflected, and then presenting a stimulus to determine which areas of the bulb become slightly darker. These darker areas are the areas that have been activated by the stimulus.

The results of Uchida's optical imaging experiment on the rat are shown in Figure 15.7. Each colored area represents the location of clusters of glomeruli in the olfactory bulb that are activated by the chemicals on the right. Figure 15.7a shows that each type of carboxylic acid activated a small area, and that there is some overlap between areas. Also notice that as the length of the carbon chain increases, the area of activation moves to the left. Figure 15.7b shows that a different group of chemicals—aliphatic alcohols—activates a different location on the olfactory bulb and that the same pattern occurs as before: large chain lengths activate areas farther to the left.

From these results we can conclude that the functional group associated with a particular type of compound (COOH for the acids; OH for the alcohols) determines the general area of the olfactory bulb that is activated, and the compound's chain length determines the position within each area.

Before leaving the olfactory bulb, let's return to a characteristic of odor that we considered for the olfactory receptors—molecules with similar structures can have very different odors. Christiane Linster and coworkers (2001) looked at this phenomenon in the olfactory bulb by studying pairs of molecules that have the same chemical formula, but in which a group within the molecule is rotated to a different position. Figure 15.8a shows two forms of carvone, and Figure 15.8b shows two forms of limonene. Linster studied how these molecules activated the olfactory bulb using a technique called the 2-deoxyglucose technique.

METHOD | 2-Deoxyglucose Technique

The **2-deoxyglucose technique** involves injecting a radioactive 2-deoxyglucose (2DG) molecule into an animal and exposing the animal to different chemicals. The radioactive 2DG contains the sugar glucose, which is taken up by active neurons, so by measuring the amount of radioactivity in the various parts of a structure, we can determine which neurons are most activated by the different chemicals.

The patterns of activation in the rat olfactory bulb, determined using the 2DG technique, are shown in Figure 15.8. Black arrows indicate areas that are activated by both compounds. White arrows indicate an area that is activated by one compound, but not by the other compound. The arrows indicate that the two forms of carvone have different patterns but the two forms of limonene have almost identical patterns. What's important about

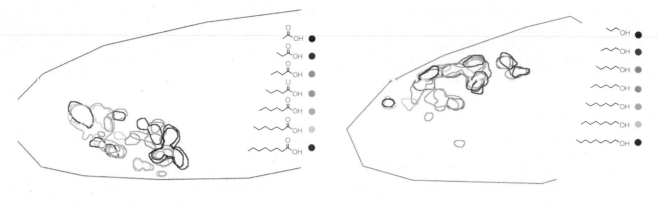

(a) Carboxylic acids

(b) Aliphatic alcohols

Figure 15.7 ❚ Areas in the olfactory bulb that are activated by various chemicals: (a) a series of carbolic acids; (b) a series of aliphatic alcohols. *(Reprinted by permission from Macmillan Publishers Ltd.: Uchida, N., Talahashi, Y. K., Tanifuji, M., & Mori, K., Odor maps in the mammalian olfactory bulb: Domain organization and odorant structural features,* Nature Neuroscience, 3, *1035–1043, Copyright 2000.)*

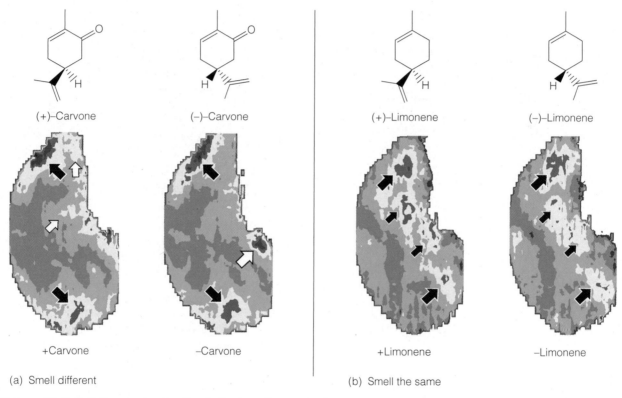

(+)–Carvone   (−)–Carvone   (+)–Limonene   (−)–Limonene

+Carvone   −Carvone   +Limonene   −Limonene

(a) Smell different

(b) Smell the same

Figure 15.8 ❚ Patterns of activation in the rat olfactory bulb. Red, orange, and yellow indicate high activation. (a) Top: Two forms of carvone. These molecules have the same chemical formula, but the molecular group at the bottom is rotated to a different position. Bottom: Activation patterns. Black arrows indicate areas in which activation was the same for the two compounds. The white arrows indicate areas activated by one compound but not the other. They show that the two forms of carvone activate different areas in the olfactory bulb. (b) Top: Two forms of limonene. These molecules also have the same chemical formula, with the molecular group at the bottom rotated to a different position. Bottom: Activation patterns. The black arrows indicate that the two forms of limonene activate similar areas in the olfactory bulb. *(From Linster, C., Johnson, B. A., Yue, E., Morse, A., Xu, Z., Hingco, E. E., Choi, Y., Choi, M., Messiha, A., & Leon, M. Perceptual correlations of neural representations evoked by odorant enantiomers.* Journal of Neuroscience, 21, *2001, 9837–9843. All rights reserved. Reproduced by permission.)*

this result is that behavioral testing of the rats showed that they could tell the difference between the two forms of carvone but could not distinguish between the two forms of limonene. Therefore, the pattern of activation on the OB is related not only to functional groups and structure, but also to the odor that is perceived. This is similar to Malnic's finding in the olfactory mucosa that molecules that smell different have different recognition profiles.

The results of experiments we have described on how ORNs and the glomeruli in the olfactory bulb respond to different chemicals have led some researchers to propose that the olfactory system codes different odorants based on the response of ORNs and the olfactory bulb to specific features of molecules, such as groups in the molecules (for example, acids have an OH group) and structural features such as chain length (see Leon & Johnson, 2003).

The idea of a direct link between odor perception and the features of molecules is illustrated by the fear response triggered in rats when they are exposed to a "cat" odor. This response occurs even for rats that have been raised in laboratories for generations and have never seen a cat (Kahn & Sobel, 2007). Another example of how molecules trigger behaviors is provided by pheromones—chemicals that trigger specific behavioral responses. An example of the action of a pheromone is the chemical released by female rabbits that triggers nursing behavior in newborn rabbits (Brennan & Zufall, 2006; Schaal et al., 2003). In these cases, a chemical with a particular molecular structure reliably leads to a specific behavioral response. One way to describe this effect is that the link between stimuli and behavior is "hardwired."

In addition to this hardwired behavior there is, however, another mode of olfactory perception that relies on processes beyond the pattern of firing in olfactory receptors. We now consider processes we will call "higher-order," both because they involve the cortex and because they involve responses to odorants that are more complicated than hardwired responses, which are always the same for a given chemical.

Higher-Order Olfactory Processing

To begin our discussion of higher-order olfactory processing, let's look at where signals are transmitted from the olfactory bulb. Figures 15.9 and 15.10 show that signals are transmitted from the olfactory bulb to the **piriform cortex** (PC) (also called the **primary olfactory cortex**) and the amygdala, and then to the **orbitofrontal cortex** (OFC) (also called the **secondary olfactory cortex**). The **amygdala** is associated with emotions and so plays a role in the emotional reactions that odors can elicit. We will focus on research involving the piriform cortex and the orbitofrontal cortex. We begin by considering some situations that occur in the environment that involve higher-order processing.

Olfaction in the Environment

When we smell something, we rarely smell one chemical in isolation. Instead, we are confronted with complex arrays of molecules, some of which combine to create familiar smells. Consider, for example, that when you walk into the kitchen and smell freshly brewed coffee, the coffee aroma is created by more than 100 different molecules. Each individual molecule activates a different pattern of ORNs in the mucosa. But we do not perceive the odors associated with the activation patterns of these individual molecules. Instead, we perceive "coffee." Thus, just understanding how individual chemicals stimulate the ORNs does not explain how a large number of chemicals can combine to result in a specific odor like coffee.

The feat of perceiving "coffee" becomes even more amazing when we consider that odors rarely occur in isolation. Thus, the coffee odor from the kitchen might be accompanied by the smells of bacon and freshly squeezed orange juice. Each of these has its own tens or hundreds of molecules, yet somehow the hundreds of different molecules that are floating around in the kitchen become three separate smells—"coffee," "bacon," and "orange juice"—when they enter your nose (Figure 15.11). This is an impressive

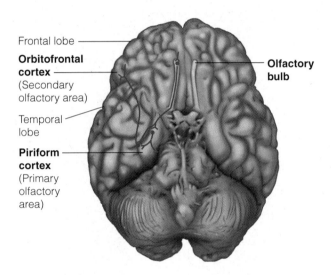

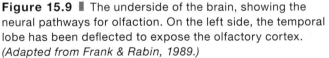

Figure 15.9 ▌ The underside of the brain, showing the neural pathways for olfaction. On the left side, the temporal lobe has been deflected to expose the olfactory cortex. *(Adapted from Frank & Rabin, 1989.)*

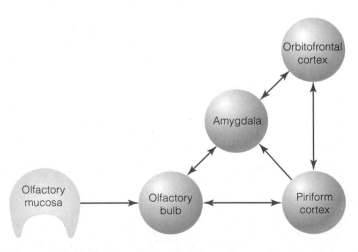

Figure 15.10 ▌ Flow diagram of the pathways for olfaction. *(Adapted from Wilson & Stevenson, 2006.)*

Figure 15.11 ▮ Hundreds of molecules from the coffee, orange juice, and bacon are mixed together in the air, but the person just perceives "coffee," "orange juice," and "bacon." This perception of three odors from hundreds of intermixed molecules is a feat of perceptual organization.

feat of perceptual organization that rivals the organization that occurs in vision, when we perceive that different overlapping objects are separate, and hearing, when we perceive individual instruments in the sound of an orchestra.

Higher-order processes in odor perception are also illustrated by situations in which people's past experiences or expectations can influence their perception. When an onion smell is labeled "pizza," people perceive it more positively than if it is labeled "body odor" (Herz, 2003), and adding red coloring to white wine causes wine tasters to describe the aroma of the white wine in terms usually associated with red wine (Morrot et al., 2001). Learning can also influence odor perception. Thus, odors that have been paired with sucrose are judged to smell sweeter when they are later presented alone (Stevenson, 2001).

All these examples—(1) many molecules creating a single perception like "coffee" or "bacon," (2) the ability to separate odors from one another in the environment, and (3) the effect of past experience and learning on odor perception—indicate that odor perception must involve more than just a hardwired "readout" of the pattern of ORN firing. Research on the physiology of higher-order processes has focused on the piriform cortex and the orbitofrontal cortex.

The Physiology of Higher-Order Processing

Research on higher-order processing in olfaction is still in its infancy. However, some research has begun looking at how odorants activate areas beyond the olfactory bulb. The picture that is emerging from this research is that individual compounds cause widespread activity across the piriform cortex. For example, Robert Rennaker and coworkers (2007) used multiple electrodes to measure neural responding in the piriform cortex. Figure 15.12 shows that isoamyl acetate causes activation across the cortex. Other compounds also cause widespread activity, and there is substantial overlap between the patterns of activity for different compounds.

The widespread activity and overlap are different from the situation in the mucosa and olfactory bulb, in which activity is more localized and doesn't overlap as much for different compounds. This overlapping activity may mean that the piriform cortex is involved in the process of perceiving complex odors such as "coffee" or "bacon" that are created from the overlapping activity of many different odorant molecules (Wilson & Stevenson, 2006).

The idea that the piriform cortex is involved in discriminating between different odors was investigated by Donald Wilson (2003), who measured the response of neurons in the rat's piriform cortex to two odorants: (1) a *mixture*—isoamyl acetate, which has a banana-like odor, plus peppermint, and (2) a *component*—the isoamyl acetate alone. Wilson was interested in how well the rat's neurons could tell the difference between the mixture and the component after the rat had been exposed to the mixture.

Wilson presented the mixture to the rat for either a brief exposure (10 seconds or about 20 sniffs) or a longer exposure (50 seconds or about 100 sniffs) and, after a short pause, measured the response to the *mixture* and to the *component*. Following 10 seconds of sniffing, the piriform neurons responded similarly to the mixture and to the component. However, following 50 seconds of sniffing, the neurons fired more rapidly to the component. Thus, after a long enough exposure to the mixture, the neurons were able to tell the difference between the mixture and the component. Similar experiments measuring responses of neurons in the olfactory bulb did not show this effect.

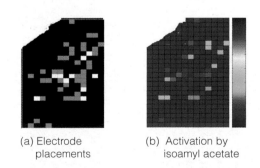

(a) Electrode placements   (b) Activation by isoamyl acetate

Figure 15.12 ▮ (a) Recording sites used by Rennaker and coworkers (2007) to determine activity of neurons in the piriform cortex of the rat. (b) The pattern of activation caused by isoamyl acetate. *(Adapted from Rennaker et al., 2007.)*

Wilson concluded from these results that, given enough time, neurons in the piriform cortex can learn to discriminate between different odors, and that this learning may be involved in our ability to tell the difference between different odors in the environment. Neurons in the piriform cortex do not, therefore, always respond in exactly the same way to a particular odorant, but can change their response, depending on conditions.

Evidence that neurons in the orbitofrontal cortex can also change their response to an odorant under different conditions is illustrated by an experiment on humans by Ivan de Araujo and coworkers (2005), who presented a test odor that was a mixture of isovaleric acid (which smells like sweat) and cheddar cheese flavoring. As participants smelled the test odor they saw the words "cheddar cheese" on some trials and "body odor" on other trials. When asked to rate the pleasantness of the odors, participants rated the test odor as more pleasant when it was labeled "cheddar cheese" than when it was labeled "body odor."

These differences in pleasantness ratings were associated with differences in activity in the orbitofrontal cortex, as measured by fMRI, with higher pleasantness ratings being associated with more activity in the orbitofrontal cortex (Figure 15.13). Thus, different labels caused the same chemical (the test odor) to result in different perceptions of pleasantness, and these different perceptions were reflected in the activity in the orbitofrontal cortex. Since the pattern of ORNs activated by the test odor is the same no matter what the label, the differences caused by the label must be a higher-order "cognitive" effect. The results of experiments on both the piriform and orbitofrontal cortex, therefore, show that to fully understand olfaction, we need to look beyond the pattern of activation of olfactory receptor neurons.

TEST YOURSELF 15.1

1. What are some of the functions of odor perception?
2. What is the difference between the detection threshold and the recognition threshold? What are some of the factors that need to be taken into account when measuring the detection threshold and the difference threshold?
3. How well can people identify odors? What is the role of memory in odor recognition?
4. Describe the following components of the olfactory system: the olfactory receptors, the olfactory receptor neurons, the olfactory bulb, the glomeruli. Be sure you understand the relation between olfactory receptors and olfactory receptor neurons, and between olfactory receptor neurons and glomeruli.
5. What is the code for olfactory quality at the level of (a) the olfactory mucosa and (b) the olfactory bulb. Be sure you understand the experiments that used calcium imaging, optical imaging, and the 2-deoxyglucose technique.
6. What are the main structures in the olfactory system past the olfactory bulb?
7. What are some characteristics of olfaction in the environment that pose challenges to the idea that odor perception is a hardwired readout of the pattern of ORN firing?
8. Describe experiments that are designed to determine the role of the piriform cortex and the oribitofrontal cortex in the higher-order processing of odor.

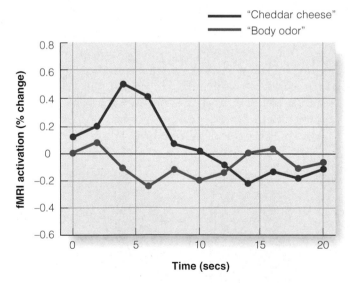

"Cheddar cheese"
"Body odor"

Figure 15.13 ▌ Activation in the orbitofrontal cortex produced by a test odor when labeled "cheddar cheese" and when labeled "body odor." *(Reprinted from De Araujo, I. E., Rolls, E. T., Velazco, M. I., Margot, C., & Cayeux, I., Cognitive modulation of olfactory processing, Neuron, 46, 671–679. Copyright 2005, with permission from Elsevier.)*

The Taste System

We will now move from olfaction, which detects molecules that enter the nose in gaseous form, to taste, which detects molecules that enter the mouth in solid or liquid form, usually as components of the foods we eat.

Functions of Taste

At the beginning of this chapter we noted that taste and smell can be thought of as "gatekeepers" that help us determine which substances we should consume and which we should avoid. This is especially true for taste because we often use taste to choose which foods to eat and which to avoid (Breslin, 2001).

Taste accomplishes its gatekeeper function by the connection between taste quality and a substance's effect. Thus, sweetness is often associated with compounds that have nutritive or caloric value and that are, therefore, important for sustaining life. Sweet compounds cause an automatic acceptance response and also trigger anticipatory metabolic responses that prepares the gastrointestinal system for processing these substances.

Bitter compounds have the opposite effect—they trigger automatic rejection responses to help the organism avoid harmful substances. Examples of harmful substances that taste bitter are the poisons strychnine, arsenic, and cyanide.

Salty tastes often indicate the presence of sodium. When people are deprived of sodium or lose a great deal of sodium through sweating, they will often seek out foods that taste salty in order to replenish the salt their body needs.

Although there are many examples of connections between a substance's taste and its function in the body, this connection is not perfect. People have often made the mistake of eating good-tasting poisonous mushrooms, and there are artificial sweeteners, such as saccharine and sucralose, that have no metabolic value. There are also bitter foods that are not dangerous and do have metabolic value. People can, however, learn to modify their responses to certain tastes, as when they develop a taste for foods they may have initially found unappealing.

Basic Taste Qualities

When dealing with the problem of describing taste quality, we are in a much better position than we were for olfaction. Although we have not been able to fit the many olfactory sensations into a small number of categories or qualities, most taste researchers generally describe taste quality in terms of five basic taste sensations: salty, sour, sweet, bitter, and umami (which has been described as meaty, brothy, or savory, and is often associated with the flavor-enhancing properties of MSG, monosodium glutamate).

Early research that supported the idea of basic tastes showed that people can describe most of their taste experiences on the basis of the four basic taste qualities (this research was done before umami became the fifth basic taste). In one study, Donald McBurney (1969) presented taste solutions to participants and asked them to make magnitude estimates of the intensity of each of the four taste qualities for each solution (see page 16 to review the magnitude estimation procedure). He found that some substances have a predominant taste and that other substances result in combinations of the four tastes. For example, sodium chloride (salty), hydrochloric acid (sour), sucrose (sweet), and quinine (bitter) are compounds that come the closest to having only one of the four basic tastes, but the compound potassium chloride (KCl) has substantial salty and bitter components (Figure 15.14). Similarly, sodium nitrate (NaNO$_3$) results in a taste consisting of a combination of salty, sour, and bitter.

Results such of these have led most researchers to accept the idea of basic tastes. As you will see in our discussion of the code for taste quality, most of the research on this problem takes the idea of basic tastes as the starting point. (See Erickson, 2000, however, for some arguments against the idea of basic tastes.)

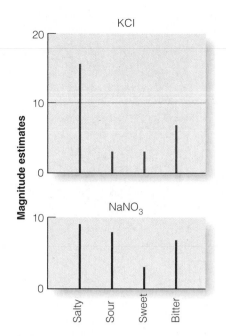

Figure 15.14 ▌ The contribution of each of the four basic tastes to the tastes of KCl and NaNO$_3$, determined by the method of magnitude estimation. The height of the line indicates the size of the magnitude estimate for each basic taste. *(From McBurney, 1969.)*

The Neural Code for Taste Quality

One of the central questions in taste research has been identification of the physiological code for taste quality. We will first describe the structure of the taste system and then describe two proposals regarding how taste quality is coded in this system.

Structure of the Taste System

The process of tasting begins with the tongue (Figure 15.15a and Table 15.2), when receptors are stimulated by taste stimuli. The surface of the tongue contains many ridges and valleys caused by the presence of structures called **papillae**, which fall into four categories: (1) filiform papillae, which are shaped like cones and are found over the entire surface of the tongue, giving it its rough appearance; (2) fungiform papillae, which are shaped like mushrooms and are found at the tip and sides of the tongue; (3) foliate papillae, which are a series of folds along the back of the tongue on the sides; and (4) circumvilliate papillae, which are shaped like flat mounds surrounded by a trench and are found at the back of the tongue (see also Figure 15.16). ▐VL▌3

All of the papillae except the filiform papillae contain **taste buds** (Figures 15.15b and 15.15c), and the whole tongue contains about 10,000 taste buds (Bartoshuk, 1971). Because the filiform papillae contain no taste buds, stimulation of the central part of the tongue, which contains only

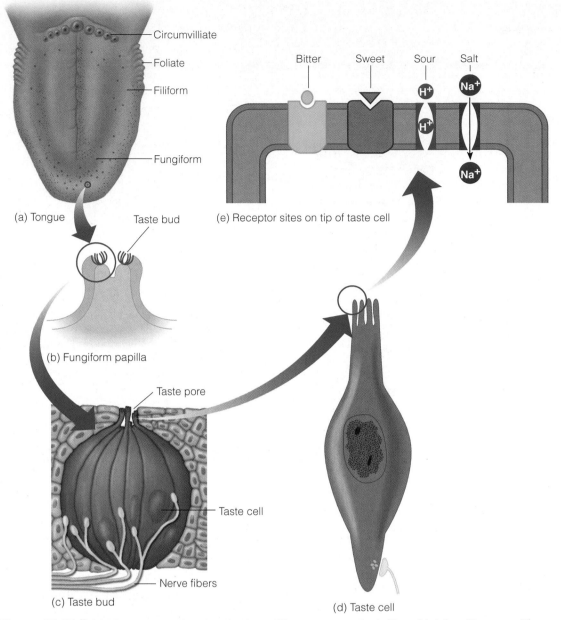

(a) Tongue

— Circumvilliate

— Foliate

— Filiform

— Fungiform

Taste bud

(b) Fungiform papilla

Taste pore

Taste cell

Nerve fibers

(c) Taste bud

(d) Taste cell

(e) Receptor sites on tip of taste cell

Bitter   Sweet   Sour   Salt

Figure 15.15 ▌ (a) The tongue, showing the four different types of papillae. (b) A fungiform papilla on the tongue; each papilla contains a number of taste buds. (c) Cross section of a taste bud showing the taste pore where the taste stimulus enters. (d) The taste cell; the tip of the taste cell is positioned just under the pore. (e) Close-up of the membrane at the tip of the taste cell, showing the receptor sites for bitter, sour, salty, and sweet substances. Stimulation of these receptor sites, as described in the text, triggers a number of different reactions within the cell (not shown) that lead to movement of charged molecules across the membrane, which creates an electrical signal in the receptor.

these papillae, causes no taste sensations. However, stimulation of the back or perimeter of the tongue results in a broad range of taste sensations.

Each taste bud (Figure 15.15c) contains 50–100 **taste cells**, which have tips that protrude into the **taste pore** (Figure 15.15d). Transduction occurs when chemicals contact receptor sites located on the tips of these taste cells (Figure 15.16e). Electrical signals generated in the taste cells are transmitted from the tongue in a number of different nerves: (1) the chorda tympani nerve (from taste cells on the front and sides of the tongue); (2) the glossopharyngeal nerve (from the back of the tongue); (3) the vagus nerve (from the mouth and throat); and (4) the superficial petronasal nerve (from the soft palette—the top of the mouth).

The fibers from the tongue, mouth, and throat make connections in the brain stem in the **nucleus of the solitary tract**, and from there, signals travel to the thalamus and then to two areas in the frontal lobe—the **insula**

TABLE 15.2 ▌ Structures in the Taste System

STRUCTURES	DESCRIPTION
Tongue	The receptor sheet for taste. Contains papillae and all of the other structures described below.
Papillae	The structures that give the tongue its rough appearance. There are four kinds, each with a different shape.
Taste buds	Contained on the papillae. There are about 10,000 taste buds.
Taste cells	Cells that make up a taste bud. There are a number of cells for each bud, and the tip of each one sticks out into a taste pore. One or more nerve fibers are associated with each cell.
Receptor sites	Sites located on the tips of the taste cells. There are different types of sites for different chemicals. Chemicals contacting the sites cause transduction by affecting ion flow across the membrane of the taste cell.

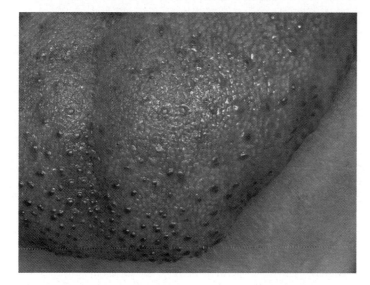

Figure 15.16 ▌ The surface of the tongue. The red dots are fungiform papillae. *(From Shahbake, M., Anatomical and psychophysical aspects of the development of the sense of taste in humans, PhD thesis, 2008, University of Western Sydney, pp. 148–153.)*

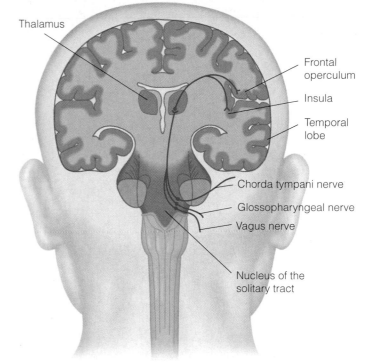

Figure 15.17 ▌ The central pathway for taste signals, showing the nucleus of the solitary tract (NST), where nerve fibers from the tongue and the mouth synapse in the medulla at the base of the brain. From the NST, these fibers synapse in the thalamus and the frontal lobe of the brain. *(From Frank & Rabin, 1989.)*

and the **frontal operculum cortex**—that are partially hidden behind the temporal lobe (Figure 15.17; Finger, 1987; Frank & Rabin, 1989). In addition, fibers serving the taste system also reach the orbitofrontal cortex (OFC), which also receives olfactory signals (Rolls, 2000; Figure 15.9).

Distributed Coding

In Chapter 2 we distinguished between two types of coding: *specificity coding*, the idea that quality is signaled by the activity in neurons that are tuned to respond to specific qualities; and *distributed coding*, the idea that quality is signaled by the pattern of activity distributed across many neurons. In that discussion, and in others throughout the book, we have generally favored distributed coding. The situation for taste, however, is not clear-cut, and there are arguments in favor of both types of coding.

Let's consider some evidence for distributed coding. Robert Erickson (1963) conducted one of the first experiments that demonstrated this type of coding by presenting a number of different taste stimuli to a rat's tongue

and recording the response of the chorda tympani nerve. Figure 15.18 shows how 13 nerve fibers responded to ammonium chloride (NH_4Cl), potassium chloride (KCl), and sodium chloride (NaCl). Erickson called these patterns the **across-fiber patterns**, which is another name for distributed coding. The red and green lines show that the across-fiber patterns for ammonium chloride and potassium chloride are similar to each other but are different from the pattern for sodium chloride, indicated by the open circles.

Erickson reasoned that if the rat's perception of taste quality depends on the across-fiber pattern, then two substances with similar patterns should taste similar. Thus, the electrophysiological results would predict that ammonium chloride and potassium chloride should taste similar and that both should taste different from sodium chloride. To test this hypothesis, Erickson shocked rats while they were drinking potassium chloride and then gave them a choice between ammonium chloride and sodium chloride. If potassium chloride and ammonium chloride taste similar, the rats should avoid the ammonium chloride when given a choice. This is exactly what they did. And when the rats were shocked for drinking ammonium chloride, they subsequently avoided the potassium chloride, as predicted by the electrophysiological results.

But what about the perception of taste in humans? When Susan Schiffman and Robert Erickson (1971) asked humans to make similarity judgments between a number of different solutions, they found that substances that were perceived to be similar were related to patterns of firing for these same substances in the rat. Solutions judged more similar psychophysically had similar patterns of firing, as distributed coding would predict.

Specificity Coding

Most of the evidence for specificity coding has been obtained from research that has focused on the taste receptors and recording neural activity early in the taste system. We begin at the receptors by describing experiments that have revealed receptors for sweet, bitter, and umami that are protein strings that cross the taste receptor membrane seven times, just like olfactory and visual receptor molecules.

The evidence supporting the existence of receptors that respond specifically to a particular taste has been obtained

by using genetic cloning, which makes it possible to add or eliminate specific receptors in mice. Ken Mueller and co-workers (2005) did a series of experiments using a chemical compound called PTC that tastes bitter to humans but is not bitter to mice. The lack of bitter PTC taste in mice is inferred by the fact that mice do not avoid even high concentrations of PTC in behavioral tests (blue curve in Figure 15.19). Because a specific receptor in the family of bitter receptors had been identified as being responsible for the bitter taste of PTC in humans, Mueller decided to see what would happen if he used genetic cloning techniques to create a strain of mice that had this human bitter-PTC receptor. When he did this, the mice with this receptor avoided high concentrations of PTC (red curve in Figure 15.19; $\boxed{V_L}$4 see Table 15.3a).

In another experiment, Mueller created a strain of mice that *lacked* a bitter receptor that responds to a compound called cyclohexamide (Cyx). Mice normally have this receptor, so they avoid Cyx. But the mice lacking this receptor did not avoid Cyx (Table 15.3b). In addition, Cyx no longer caused any firing in nerves receiving signals from the tongue. Therefore, when the taste receptor for a substance is eliminated, this is reflected in both nerve firing and the animal's behavior.

It is important to note that in all these experiments, adding or eliminating bitter receptors had no effect on neu-

TABLE 15.3 ▊ **Results of Mueller's Experiments**

CHEMICAL	NORMAL MOUSE	CLONED MOUSE
(a) PTC	No PTC receptor	Has PTC receptor
	Doesn't avoid PTC	Avoids PTC
(b) Cyx	Has Cyx receptor	No Cyx receptor
	Avoids Cyx	Doesn't avoid Cyx

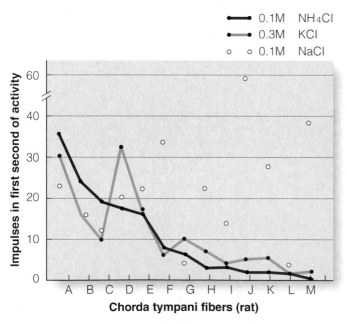

Figure 15.18 ▊ Across-fiber patterns of the response of fibers in the rat's chorda tympani nerve to three salts. Each letter on the horizontal axis indicates a different single fiber. *(Reprinted from Erickson, R. P., Sensory neural patterns and gustation. In Y. Zotterman (Ed.), Olfaction and taste, Vol. 1, pp. 205–213, figure 4. Copyright 1963, with permission from Elsevier.)*

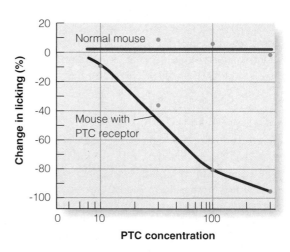

Figure 15.19 ▊ Mouse behavioral response to PTC. The blue curve indicates that a normal mouse will drink PTC even in high concentrations. The red curve indicates that a mouse that has a human bitter-PTC receptor avoids PTC, especially at high concentrations. *(Adapted from Mueller et al., 2005.)*

ral firing or behavior to sweet, sour, salty, or umami stimuli. Other research using similar techniques have identified receptors for sugar and umami (Zhao et al., 2003).

The results of these experiments in which adding a receptor makes an animal sensitive to a specific quality and eliminating a receptor makes an animal insensitive to a specific quality have been cited as support for specificity coding—that there are receptors that are specifically tuned to sweet, bitter, and umami tastes. However, not all researchers agree that the picture is so clear-cut. For example, Eugene Delay and coworkers (2006) showed that with different behavioral tests, mice that appeared to have been made insensitive to sugar by eliminating a "sweet" receptor can actually still show a preference for sugar. Based on this result, Delay suggests that perhaps there are a number of different receptors that respond to specific substances like sugar.

Another line of evidence for specificity coding in taste has come from research on how single neurons respond to taste stimuli. For example, Figure 15.20 shows how 66 fibers in the monkey's chorda tympani responded to four substances, each representing one of the basic tastes: sucrose (sweet); salt (NaCl, salty); hydrogen chloride (HCl, sour); and quinine (bitter; Sato et al., 1994). We can see that some fibers responded well to sucrose but poorly to almost all other compounds. For example, look at fiber 5's responses to each substance by following the dashed line down the record for each substance.

Fibers 1 to 16 are called sucrose-best because they respond best to sucrose. A similar situation exists for the quinine-best fibers (numbers 56–66), most of which respond only to quinine. The NaCl- and HCl-best fibers fire predominantly to one solution, but some fire to both NaCl and HCl (also see Frank et al., 1988, for similar results in the hamster).

Another finding in line with specificity theory is the effect of presenting a substance called amiloride, which blocks the flow of sodium into taste receptors. Applying amiloride to the tongue causes a decrease in the responding of neurons in the rat's brainstem (nucleus of the solitary tract) that respond best to salt (Figure 15.21a) but has little effect on neurons that respond best to a combination of salty and bitter tastes (Figure 15.21b; Scott & Giza, 1990). Thus, eliminating the flow of sodium across the membrane selectively eliminates responding of salt-best neurons, but does not affect the response of neurons that respond best to other tastes. As it turns out, the sodium channel that is blocked by amiloride is important for determining saltiness in rats and other animals, but not in humans. Recent research has identified another channel that serves the salty taste in humans (Lyall et al., 2004, 2005).

What does all of this mean? With the discovery of specific receptor mechanisms for bitter, sour, and umami, the balance in the distributed versus specificity argument appears to be shifting toward specificity (Chandrashekar et al., 2006). However, the issue is still not settled, especially because the research on specific taste receptors is so recent (Scott & Giza, 2000). More research needs to be done on

salty and sour tastes to determine whether these are also governed by specific mechanisms.

David Smith and Thomas Scott (2003) argue for distributed coding based on the finding that at more central locations in the taste system, neurons are tuned broadly, with many neurons responding to more than one taste quality. Smith and coworkers (2000) point out that just because there are neurons that might respond best to one compound like salty or sour, this doesn't mean that these tastes are signaled by just one type of neuron. They illustrate this by drawing an analogy between taste perception and the mech-

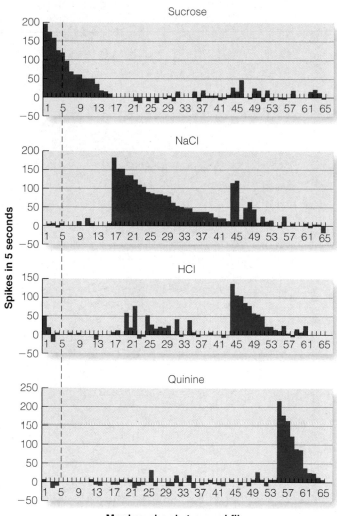

Figure 15.20 ▮ Responses of 66 different fibers in the monkey's chorda tympani nerve to four types of stimuli: sucrose (sweet); sodium chloride (salty); hydrogen chloride (sour); and quinine (bitter). To determine the response of a particular fiber, pick its number and note the height of the bars for each compound. For example, fiber 5 (dashed line) fired well to sucrose but fired poorly or not at all to any of the other compounds. Fiber 5 is therefore called a *sucrose-best fiber*. (Adapted from Sato, M., & Ogawa, H., Neural coding of taste in macaque monkeys. In K. Kurihara, N. Suzuki, & H. Ogawa (Eds.), Olfaction and taste XI, p. 398. Copyright © 1993 by Springer-Verlag. Adapted by permission.)

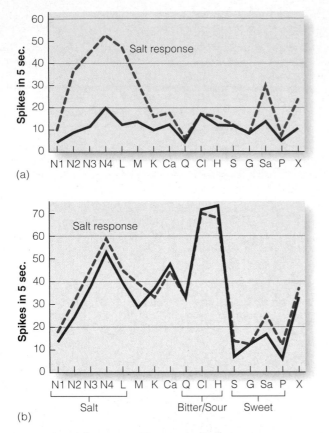

(a)

(b)

Figure 15.21 ▊ The blue lines show how two neurons in the rat NST respond to a number of different taste stimuli (along the horizontal axis). The neuron in (a) responds strongly to compounds associated with salty tastes. The neuron in (b) responds to a wide range of compounds. The red lines show how these two neurons fire after the sodium blocker amiloride is applied to the tongue. This compound inhibits the responses to salt of neuron in (a) but has little effect on neuron in (b). *(Adapted from Scott, T. R., & Giza, B. K., Coding channels in the taste system of the rat,* Science, 249, 1585–1587, figure 1. Copyright © 1990 by the American Association for the Advancement of Science. Adapted by permission.)

anism for color vision. Even though presenting a long-wavelength light that appears red may cause the highest activation in the long-wavelength cone pigment (Figure 9.10), our perception of red still depends on the combined response of both the long- and medium-wavelength pigments. Similarly, salt stimuli may cause high firing in neurons that respond best to salt, but other neurons are probably also involved in creating saltiness.

Because of arguments such as this, some researchers believe that even though there is good evidence for specific taste receptors, distributed coding is involved in determining taste as well, especially at higher levels of the system. One suggestion is that basic taste qualities could be determined by a specific code, but distributed coding could determine subtle differences between tastes within a category (Pfaffmann, 1974; Scott & Plata-Salaman, 1991). This would help explain why not all substances in a particular category have the same taste. For example, the taste of all sweet substances is not identical (Lawless, 2001).

The Perception of Flavor

Our society is obsessed with the taste of food, as evidenced by the numerous cooking shows on TV, shelves of cookbooks at the bookstore, and restaurants whose reputations are made or broken based on the taste of the food they serve. Most people look forward to eating not because it is necessary for survival but because of the pleasure it brings. Consider, for example, how Ruth Reichl (1994), then the *New York Times* food critic and currently editor of *Gourmet* magazine, describes her experience at a four-star restaurant:

> It is a surprise to dip your spoon into this mild-mannered soup and experience an explosion of flavor. Mushroom is at the base of the taste sensation, but it is haunted by citric tones—lemongrass, lime perhaps—and high at the top, a resonant note of sweetness. What is it? No single flavor ever dominates a dish. At first you find yourself searching for flavors in this complex tapestry, fascinated by the way they are woven together. In the end, you just give in and allow yourself to be seduced. Each meal is a roller coaster of sensations.

Reichl's description captures not only her enjoyment but also the complexity of some of the aspects of perceiving the flavors of food. Notice that she opens the review by commenting on the food's "flavor." What most people refer to as "taste" when describing their experience of food ("That tastes good, Mom") is usually a combination of taste, from stimulation of the receptors in the tongue, and smell, from stimulation of the receptors in the olfactory mucosa. This combination of taste and smell, as well as other sensations—such as those caused by the burning of hot peppers—is called **flavor**. Another thing Reichl captures in her review is the complexity of the perceptions created by foods. We are usually dealing with not just one or two different flavors, but many, and, as Reichl points out, the flavors often are contained within a "complex tapestry."

The fact that we are able to pick a particular flavor out of a complex tapestry of flavors becomes even more amazing when we return to the person in the kitchen in Figure 15.11, who is able to perceptually organize the effect of the hundreds of molecules entering his nose into the three classifications of coffee, orange juice, and bacon. This amazing feat of perceptual organization for olfaction also occurs for flavor. It rivals the processes that occur when we separate a complex visual scene into individual objects or the sounds of a symphony orchestra into individual instruments. We are, however, far from being able to understand how we accomplish this feat for flavor. Most of the basic research on flavor has focused on showing how taste and smell interact and on factors that influence our perception of flavor. Let's first consider evidence that flavor is the combination of taste and smell.

Flavor = Taste + Olfaction

Flavor is the overall impression that we experience from the combination of nasal and oral stimulation (Lawless, 2001). You can demonstrate how smell affects flavor with the following demonstration.

DEMONSTRATION

"Tasting" With and Without the Nose

While pinching your nostrils shut, drink a beverage with a distinctive taste, such as grape juice, cranberry juice, or coffee. Notice both the quality and the intensity of the taste as you are drinking it. (Take just one or two swallows because swallowing with your nostrils closed can cause a buildup of pressure in your ears.) After one of the swallows, open your nostrils, and notice whether you perceive a flavor. Finally, drink the beverage normally with nostrils open, and notice the flavor. You can also do this demonstration with fruits or cooked foods. ▮

During this demonstration you probably noticed that when your nostrils were closed, it was difficult to identify the substance you were drinking or eating, but as soon as you opened your nostrils, the flavor became obvious. This occurred because odor stimuli from the food reached the olfactory mucosa by following the retronasal route, from the mouth through the nasal pharynx, the passage that con-

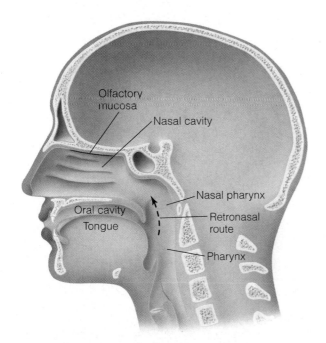

Figure 15.22 ▮ Odorant molecules released by food in the oral cavity and pharynx can travel through the nasal pharynx (dashed arrow) to the olfactory mucosa in the nasal cavity. This is the retronasal route to the olfactory receptors.

nects the oral and nasal cavities (Figure 15.22). Although pinching the nostrils shut does not close the nasal pharynx, it prevents vapors from reaching the olfactory receptors by eliminating the circulation of air through this channel (Murphy & Cain, 1980).

The importance of olfaction in the sensing of flavor has been demonstrated experimentally by using both chemical solutions and typical foods. In general, solutions are more difficult to identify when the nostrils are pinched shut (Mozell et al., 1969) and are often judged to be tasteless. For example, Figure 15.23a shows that the chemical sodium oleate has a strong soapy flavor when the nostrils are open but is judged tasteless when they are closed. Similarly, ferrous sulfate (Figure 15.23b) normally has a metallic flavor but is judged predominantly tasteless when the nostrils are closed (Hettinger et al., 1990). However, some compounds are not influenced by olfaction. For example, monosodium glutamate (MSG) has about the same flavor whether or not the nose is clamped (Figure 15.23c). Thus, in this case, the sense of taste predominates.

The results of these experiments indicate that many of the sensations that we call taste, and that we assume are caused only by stimulation of the tongue, are greatly influenced by stimulation of the olfactory receptors. Apparently, we often mislocate the source of our sensations as being in the mouth, partially because the stimuli physically enter the mouth and partially because we experience the tactile sensations associated with chewing and swallowing (Murphy & Cain, 1980; Rozin, 1982).

The Physiology of Flavor Perception

A number of cortical areas that serve both taste and olfaction are probably involved in the perception of the flavor of food. Presently, however, most of the work on the cortical response to food has focused not on the primary olfactory cortex but on the orbitofrontal cortex (OFC), because it is here that responses from taste and smell are first combined.

The OFC receives inputs from the primary cortical areas for taste and olfaction, as well as from the primary somatosensory cortex and from the inferotemporal cortex in the visual *what* pathway (Rolls, 2000; Figure 15.24). Because of this convergence of neurons from different senses, the OFC contains many bimodal neurons, those that respond to more than one sense. For example, some bimodal neurons respond to both taste and smell, and other neurons respond to taste and vision. An important property of these bimodal neurons is that they often respond to similar qualities. Thus, a cell that responds to the taste of sweet fruits would also respond to the smell of these fruits. This means that neurons are tuned to respond to qualities that occur together in the environment.

Because of these properties, and the fact that the OFC is the first place where taste and smell information is combined, it has been suggested that the OFC is a cortical center for detecting flavor and for the perceptual representation of foods (Rolls & Baylis, 1994).

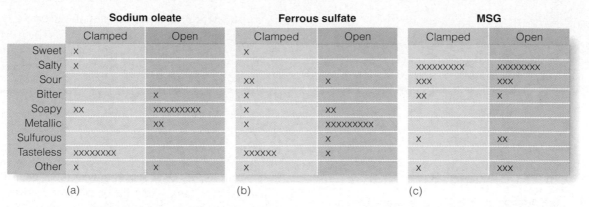

	Sodium oleate		Ferrous sulfate		MSG	
	Clamped	Open	Clamped	Open	Clamped	Open
Sweet	x		x			
Salty	x				xxxxxxxxx	xxxxxxxx
Sour			xx	x	xxx	xxx
Bitter		x	x		xx	x
Soapy	xx	xxxxxxxxx	x	xx		
Metallic		xx	x	xxxxxxxxx		
Sulfurous				x	x	xx
Tasteless	xxxxxxxx		xxxxxx	x		
Other	x	x	x		x	xxx
	(a)		(b)		(c)	

Figure 15.23 ▮ How people described the flavors of three different compounds when they tasted them with nostrils clamped shut and with nostrils open. Each X represents the judgment of one person. *(From Hettinger, T. P., Myers, W. E., & Frank, M. E., Role of olfaction in perception of non-traditional "taste" stimuli,* Chemical Senses, 15, *1990, 755–760, fig. 2, by permission of Oxford University Press.)*

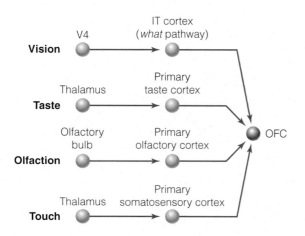

Figure 15.24 ▮ The orbitofrontal cortex (OFC) receives inputs from vision, taste, olfaction, and touch, as shown. It is the first area where signals from the taste and smell systems meet. *(From Rolls, E. T., The orbitofrontal cortex and reward,* Cerebral Cortex, 10, *2000, 284–294, fig. 2, by permission of Oxford University Press.)*

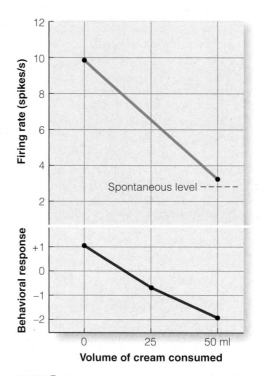

Figure 15.25 ▮ How consuming dairy cream affects the firing rate of neurons in the monkey's OFC (top panel) and the monkey's response to the cream (bottom panel). Consuming the cream causes a decrease in the neuron's response to the cream, but not to other substances (not shown). It also causes the monkey to become less interested in drinking the cream, and eventually to actively reject it. *(Adapted from Critchley & Rolls, 1996.)*

But there is also another reason to think that the OFC is important for flavor perception: Unlike neurons in the primary taste area, which are not affected by hunger, the firing of neurons in the OFC reflects the extent to which an animal will consume a particular food. Figure 15.25 shows how neurons in the monkey's OFC respond before and after ingesting dairy cream. The top graph shows that this neuron fires at about 10 spikes per second to the odor of dairy cream, and that the response decreases to 3 spikes per second (the level of spontaneous activity) after 50 ml of the cream has been presented. The bottom graph shows the monkey's behavioral reaction to presentation of the cream. At the beginning of the experiment, the monkey enthusiastically licks the feeding tube to receive the solution, but at the end it rejects the solution and tries to push it away. Thus, as the monkey's hunger for the cream decreases, the firing of the cell to the cream's odor decreases as well. What this means, according to Edmund Rolls (2004), is that the responses of neurons in the OFC are essentially reflecting the pleasantness of flavors, and in doing so, help control food intake.

Something to Consider: Individual Differences in Tasting

Although most people describe their taste preferences in terms of four basic qualities, there are genetic differences that affect people's ability to sense the taste of certain substances. One of the best-documented effects involves people's ability to taste the bitter substance phenylthiocarbamide (PTC), which we discussed earlier. Linda Bartoshuk (1980) describes the discovery of this PTC effect:

> The different reactions to PTC were discovered accidentally in 1932 by Arthur L. Fox, a chemist working at the E. I. DuPont deNemours Company in Wilmington, Delaware. Fox had prepared some PTC, and when he poured the compound into a bottle, some of the dust escaped into the air. One of his colleagues complained about the bitter taste of the dust, but Fox, much closer to the material, noticed nothing. Albert F. Blakeslee, an eminent geneticist of the era, was quick to pursue this observation. At a meeting of the American Association for the Advancement of Science (AAAS) in 1934, Blakeslee prepared an exhibit that dispensed PTC crystals to 2,500 of the conferees. The results: 28 percent of them described it as tasteless, 66 percent as bitter, and 6 percent as having some other taste. (p. 55)

People who can taste PTC are described as **tasters**, and those who cannot are called **nontasters**. Recently, additional experiments have been done with a substance called 6-*n*-propylthiouracil, or PROP, which has properties similar to those of PTC (Lawless, 1980, 2001). Researchers have found that about one-third of Americans report that PROP is tasteless and two-thirds can taste it.

What causes these differences in people's ability to taste PROP? One reason is that people have different numbers of taste buds on the tongue. Linda Bartoshuk used a technique called **video microscopy** to count the taste buds on people's tongues that contain the receptors for tasting (Bartoshuk & Beauchamp, 1994). The key result of this study was that people who could taste PROP had higher densities of taste buds than those who couldn't taste it (Figure 15.26).

But the results of an experiment by Jeannine Delwiche and coworkers (2001b) show that the density of taste buds alone cannot explain high sensitivity to PROP. After confirming that PROP tasters do have a higher density of papillae than nontasters, they devised a system for stimulating the same number of papillae in tasters and nontasters. They accomplished this by presenting stimuli to smaller areas of the tongue for the tasters. When participants rated the bitterness of PROP, the tasters' ratings were much higher than nontasters' ratings, even when the same number of papillae were stimulated.

Apparently, another factor in addition to receptor density is involved in determining individual differences in taste. Genetic studies have shown that PROP and PTC tasters have specialized receptors that are absent in nontasters (Bufe et al., 2005; Kim et al., 2003).

What does this mean for everyday taste experience? If PROP tasters also perceived other compounds as being more bitter than nontasters, this would indicate that certain foods might taste more bitter to the tasters. The evidence on this question, however, has been mixed. Some studies have reported differences between how tasters and nontasters rate the bitterness of other compounds (Bartoshuk, 1979; Hall et al., 1975), and others have not observed this difference (Delwiche et al., 2001b). However, it does appear that people who are especially sensitive to PROP, called **supertasters**, may actually be more sensitive to most bitter substances, as if the amplification in the bitter taste system is turned up for all bitter compounds (Delwiche et al., 2001a).

Although we don't completely understand the mechanisms responsible for individual differences in tasting, especially when considering everyday foods, there is no question that there is a great deal of variability in taste experience across different people. Thus, the next time you disagree with someone about the taste of a particular food, don't automatically assume that your disagreement is simply a reflection of your different preferences. It may reflect not a difference in *preference* (you like sweet things more than John does) but a difference in *taste experience* (you experience more intense sweet tastes than John does) that could be caused by differences in the types and numbers of taste receptors on your tongues.

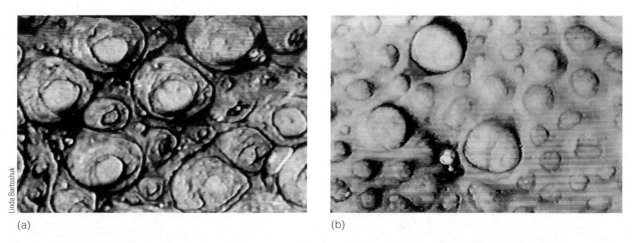

(a)   (b)

Figure 15.26 ▌ (a) Video micrograph of the tongue showing the fungiform papillae of a "supertaster"—a person who is very sensitive to the taste of PROP. (b) Papillae of a "nontaster"—someone who cannot taste PROP. The supertaster has both more papillae and more taste buds than the nontaster.

THINK ABOUT IT

1. Can you think of situations in which you have encountered a smell that triggered memories about an event or place that you hadn't thought about in years? What do you think might be the mechanism for this type of experience? (p. 365)

2. Consider the kinds of food that you avoid because you don't like the taste. Do these foods have anything in common that might enable you to explain these taste preferences in terms of the activity of specific types of taste receptors? (p. 370)

IF YOU WANT TO KNOW MORE

1. *Chemistheses.* In addition to creating experiences associated with tasting and smelling, molecules entering the nose and mouth can cause other experiences, such as the irritation of breathing ammonia or the burning sensation from eating chili peppers. This component of chemical sensitivity, which is called chemisthesis, is related to the cutaneous senses we discussed in Chapter 14.

Doty, R. L. (1995). Intranasal trigeminal chemoreception. In R. L. Doty (Ed.), *Handbook of olfaction and gustation* (pp. 821–833). New York: Marcel Dekker.

Silver, W. L., & Finger, T. E. (1991). The trigeminal system. In T. V. Getchell, R. L. Doty, L. M. Bartoshuk, & J. B. Snow (Eds.), *Smell and taste in health and disease* (pp. 97–108). New York: Raven Press.

2. *Using smell to identify people.* Humans generally do not make it a practice to smell other people at close range. However, experiments indicate that we have the capacity to recognize the smell of others and ourselves. (p. 356)

McBurney, D. H., Levine, J. M., & Cavanaugh, P. H. (1977). Psychophysical and social ratings of human body odor. *Personality and Social Psychology Bulletin, 3,* 135–138.

Russell, M. J. (1976). Human olfactory communication. *Nature, 260,* 520–522.

3. *Temporal coding in the olfactory bulb.* The code for odors may involve the way the pattern of nerve firing changes over time. (p. 361)

Spors, H., & Grinvald, A. (2002). Spatio-temporal dynamics of odor representations in the mammalian olfactory bulb. *Neuron, 34,* 301–315.

4. *Electronic nose.* Although we are far from developing a computer that can match human or animal abilities to discriminate and recognize odors, "electronic noses" have been developed that are capable of identifying some odors. (p. 365)

Nagle, H. T., Schiffman, S. S., & Gutierrez-Osuna, R. (1998). The how and why of electronic noses. *IEEE Spectrum, 35,* 22–34.

Guiterrez-Osuna, R. (in press). Electronic nose. In E. B. Goldstein (Ed.), *Sage encyclopedia of perception.* Thousand Oaks, CA: Sage.

Rock, F., Barsan, N., & Weimar, U. (2008). Electronic nose: Current status and future trends. *Chemical Reviews, 108,* 705–725.

5. *Odors can help retrieve memories.* Exposure to odors can bring back long-forgotten memories of places or events. This phenomenon has been confirmed in experiments that show that odors can help retrieve memories. (p. 365)

Aggelton, J. P., & Waskett, L. (1999). The ability of odours to serve as state-dependent cues for real-world memories: Can Viking smells aid the recall of Viking experiences? *British Journal of Psychology, 90,* 1–7.

Lyman, B. J., & McDaniel, M. A. (1990). Memory for odors and odor names: Modalities of elaboration and imagery. *Journal of Experimental Psychology: Learning, Memory, and Cognition, 16,* 656–664.

6. *Loss of memory can affect the ability to perceive odors.* Not only do odors help us retrieve memories, but memory may be necessary for the perception of odors. People who have lost their memory, through diseases such as Alzheimer's or from brain damage, can tell that odors are present, but can't tell one odor from another. (p. 364)

Eichenbaum, H., Morton, T. H., Potter, H., & Corkin, S. (1983). Selective olfactory deficits in case H.M. *Brain, 106,* 459–472.

Wilson, D. A., & Stevenson, R. J. (2003). The fundamental role of memory in olfactory perception. *Trends in Neurosciences,* 243–247.

7. *A dynamic code for taste.* As for olfaction, there is evidence that the way neurons firing changes over time provides information about taste. This information may also help determine whether an animal will decide to ingest a substance. (p. 367)

> **DiLorenzo, P. M., & Victor, J. D. (2003).** Taste response variability and temporal coding in the nucleus of the solitary tract of the rat. *Journal of Neurophysiology, 90,* 1418–1431.

> **Katz, D. B., Nicolelis, M. A. L., & Simon, S. A. (2002).** Gustatory processing is dynamic and distributed. *Current Opinion in Neurobiology, 12,* 449–454.

8. *The human brain's response to taste.* Brain imaging research has located areas that are activated by taste stimuli. (p. 367)

> **de Araujo, I. E. T., Kringelbach, M. L., Rolls, E. T., & Hobden, P. (2003).** The representation of umami taste in the human brain. *Journal of Neurophysiology, 90,* 313–319.

> **Rolls, E. T. (2004).** Smell, taste, texture, and temperature multimodal representations in the brain, and their relevance to the control of appetite. *Nutrition Reviews, 62,* S193–S204.

KEY TERMS

Across-fiber patterns (p. 369)
Amiloride (p. 371)
Amygdala (p. 364)
Anosmia (p. 357)
Bimodal neuron (p.373)
Calcium imaging (p. 361)
Detection threshold (p. 357)
Flavor (p. 372)
Frontal operculum cortex (p. 369)
Glomeruli (p. 361)
Insula (p. 368)
Macrosmatic (p. 356)
Menstrual synchrony (p. 356)
Microsmatic (p. 356)

Nasal pharynx (p. 373)
Neurogenesis (p. 356)
Nontaster (p. 375)
Nucleus of the solitary tract (p. 368)
Olfactometer (p. 358)
Olfactory bulb (p. 361)
Olfactory mucosa (p. 359)
Olfactory receptor neurons (ORNs) (p. 359)
Olfactory receptors (p. 359)
Optical imaging (p. 362)
Orbitofrontal cortex (OFC) (p. 364)
Papillae (p. 367)
Pheromone (p. 356)

Piriform cortex (PC) (p. 364)
Primary olfactory cortex (p. 364)
Recognition profile (p. 361)
Recognition threshold (p. 358)
Retronasal route (p. 373)
Secondary olfactory cortex (p. 364)
Supertaster (p. 375)
Taste bud (p. 367)
Taste cell (p. 368)
Taste pore (p. 368)
Taster (p. 375)
2-deoxyglucose technique (p. 362)
Video microscopy (p. 375)

MEDIA RESOURCES

The *Sensation and Perception* Book Companion Website

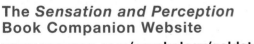

www.cengage.com/psychology/goldstein

See the companion website for flashcards, practice quiz questions, Internet links, updates, critical thinking exercises, discussion forums, games, and more!

CengageNOW

www.cengage.com/cengagenow

Go to this site for the link to CengageNOW, your one-stop shop. Take a pre-test for this chapter, and CengageNOW will generate a personalized study plan based on your test results. The study plan will identify the topics you need to review and direct you to online resources to help you master those topics. You can then take a post-test to help you determine the concepts you have mastered and what you will still need to work on.

Virtual Lab

Your Virtual Lab is designed to help you get the most out of this course. The Virtual Lab icons direct you to specific media demonstrations and experiments designed to help you visualize what you are reading about. The number beside each icon indicates the number of the media element you can access through your CD-ROM, CengageNOW, or WebTutor resource.

The following lab exercises are related to material in this chapter:

1. *The Sense of Smell* An ABC video that discusses how smell influences behavior, and possible links between the ability to smell and disease.

2. *Olfactory System* A drag-and-drop diagram to test your knowledge of structures in the olfactory system.

3. *Taste System* A drag-and-drop diagram to test your knowledge of structures in the taste system.

4. *Anti–Sweet Tooth Gum* An ABC video that describes a type of gum that eliminates sweetness by blocking receptors on the tongue that respond to sweetness.

Chapter Contents

CHAPTER 16

Perceptual Development

OPPOSITE PAGE Two views of the New York skyline. The top picture represents an adult's perception of the scene. The bottom picture simulates how a 1- to 2-month-old infant would perceive this scene.
Photographs and image processing courtesy of Anthony Movshon.

VL The Virtual Lab icons direct you to specific animations and videos designed to help you visualize what you are reading about. The number beside each icon indicates the number of the clip you can access through your CD-ROM or your student website.

- What can newborns perceive? (p. 380)
- When can an infant perceive colors? (p. 384)
- Can a newborn recognize his or her mother? (p. 387)

Our senses endow us with truly amazing capacities. We can see fine details and keep them in focus when an object moves from close to far away. We see something move and can follow the moving object with our eyes, keeping its image on our foveas so we can see the object clearly. We can perceive the location of a sound, transform pressure changes in the air into meaningful sentences, and create myriad tastes and smells from our molecular environment.

As adults, we can do all these things and more. But were we born with these abilities? Most 19th-century psychologists would have answered this question by saying that newborns and young infants experience a totally confusing perceptual world, in which they either perceive nothing or can make little sense of the stimulation to which they are exposed.

One of the things we will do in this chapter is to deal directly with this idea by asking what perceptual capacities are present in the newborn and very young infant. We will see that although newborns have great perceptual deficiencies compared to older children or adults, they can perceive quite a bit more than the 19th-century psychologists believed. But our goal in this chapter goes beyond simply establishing what newborns and young infants can perceive. We will also be considering how their perception develops as they get older and what mechanisms are responsible for early perception and this development.

Basic Visual Capacities

Why did the early psychologists think the newborn's perceptual world was either nonexistent or very confusing, whereas present-day psychologists think that newborns have some perceptual abilities? Did infants learn to see and hear better between the 19th century and now? Obviously not. What actually happened is that psychologists learned how to measure infants' perceptual abilities that were there all along. As we describe some of the techniques used to measure infant perceptual abilities, we should not lose sight of the difficulties involved in doing research on human newborns and young infants. The following statement, by a well-known researcher who studies perceptual development in 3- to 5-month-old infants, captures some of these difficulties.

> I admit I've never had the courage to run a full-blown experiment with human newborns. For those who may not be aware of the difficulties involved, running such an experiment can be a formidable task: convincing hospital administrators and personnel in the neonatal nursery that

the research is worthwhile; setting up elaborate equipment often in cramped, temporary quarters; obtaining permission from mothers who are still recovering from their deliveries; waiting, sometimes for hours, until the infant to be tested is in a quiet, alert state; coping with the infant's inevitable changes in state after testing has begun; and interpreting the infant's responses that at one moment may seem to be nothing more than a blank stare and at another moment active involvement with the stimulus. (Cohen, 1991, p. 1)

Not only do newborns and young infants exhibit behaviors such as crying, sleeping, and not paying attention while the observer is trying to test them, but the fact that they can't understand or respond to verbal instructions presents a special challenge. Even when the infant is cooperating by being quiet and paying attention, researchers are still faced with the problem of devising methods that will make it possible to determine what the infant is perceiving. As we will see, in the Methods sections in this chapter, they have come up with some ingenious solutions to this problem.

Visual Acuity

One of the most basic questions we can ask about infant perception is how well infants can perceive details. Here we encounter our first measurement challenge: how to determine visual acuity—the ability to see details—in newborns and young infants. Two of the most common methods involve using behavior (preferential looking) and electrical signals recorded from the scalp (visual evoked potential).

METHOD | Preferential Looking and Visual Evoked Potential

The key to measuring infant perception is to pose the correct question. To understand what we mean by this, let's consider two questions we can ask to determine visual acuity. One question, "What do you see?" is what you're answering when you read the letters on an eye chart in the doctor's office. Acuity is determined by noting the smallest letters a person can accurately identify. This technique is obviously not suitable for infants. To test infant acuity, we have to ask another question and use another procedure.

A question that works for infants is "Can you tell the difference between the stimulus on the left and the one on the right?" The way infants look at stimuli in their environment provides a way to determine whether they can tell the difference between two stimuli. In the **preferential looking (PL) technique**, two stimuli like the ones the infant is observing in Figure 16.1 are presented, and the experimenter watches the infant's eyes to determine where the infant is looking. In order to guard against bias, the observer does not know which stimulus is being presented on each side. If the infant looks at one stimulus more than the other, the experimenter concludes that he or she can tell the difference between them. 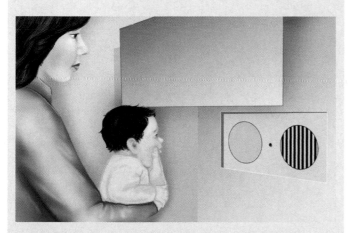 VL 1

The reason preferential looking works is that infants have *spontaneous looking preferences*; that is, they prefer to look at certain types of stimuli. For example, to measure visual acuity, we can use the fact that infants choose to look at objects with contours over ones that are homogeneous (Fantz et al., 1962). Thus, when we present a grating with large bars and a gray field that reflects the same amount of light that the grating would reflect if the bars were spread evenly over the whole area, the infant can easily see the bars and therefore looks at the side with the bars more than the side with the gray field when the grating and gray field are switched randomly from side to side on different trials. By preferentially looking at the side with the bars the infant is telling us, "I see the grating."

As we decrease the size of the bars, it becomes more difficult for the infant to tell the difference between the grating and gray stimulus, until, when they become indiscriminable, the infant looks equally at each display. We measure the infant's acuity by determining the narrowest stripe width that results in looking more to one side.

Another method for measuring acuity involves measuring an electrical response called the visual evoked potential (VEP). The VEP, which is recorded by disk electrodes placed on the back of the infant's head, over the visual cortex, is the pooled response of thousands of

neurons that are near the electrode. When a researcher is using the VEP to measure acuity, the infant looks at a gray field, which is briefly replaced by either a grating or a checkerboard pattern. If the stripes or checks are large enough to be detected by the visual system, the visual cortex generates an electrical response called the visual evoked potential. If, however, the stripes are too fine to be detected by the visual system, no response is generated. Thus, the VEP provides an objective measure of the visual system's ability to detect details.

Figure 16.2 shows acuity measuring using the preferential looking technique and the visual evoked potential technique. The VEP usually results in higher measurements of acuity, but both techniques indicate that visual acuity is poorly developed at birth (about 20/400 to 20/600 at 1 month). (The expression 20/400 means that the infant must view a stimulus from 20 feet to see the same thing that a normal adult can see from 400 feet.) Acuity increases

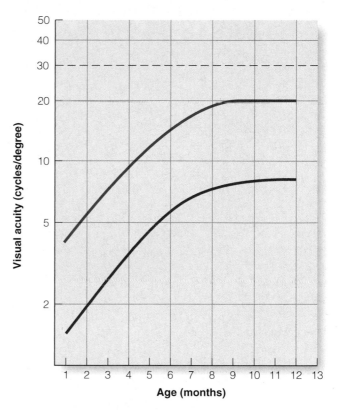

Figure 16.2 ▌ The improvement of acuity over the first year of life, as measured by the visual evoked potential technique (top curve) and the preferential looking technique (bottom curve). The numbers on the vertical axis indicate the fineness of a grating stimulus that can be detected, in cycles per degree of visual angle. Gratings with finer bars have more cycles per degree. (See page 383 and Figure 16.5 for further details about the cycles-per-degree measure.) The horizontal dashed curve represents adult acuity (20/20 vision). *(VEP curve adapted from Norcia & Tyler, 1985; PL curve adapted from Gwiazda et al., 1980, and Mayer et al., 1995.)*

Figure 16.1 ▌ An infant being tested using the preferential looking procedure. The mother holds the infant in front of the display, which consists of a grating on the right and a homogeneous gray field on the left. The grating and the gray field have the same average light intensity. An experimenter, who does not know which side the grating is on in any given trial, looks through the peephole between the grating and the gray field and judges whether the infant is looking to the left or to the right.

rapidly over the first 6 to 9 months (Banks & Salapatek, 1978; Dobson & Teller, 1978; Harris et al., 1976; Salapatek et al., 1976). This rapid improvement of acuity is followed by a leveling-off period, and full adult acuity is not reached until sometime after 1 year of age.

The reason for low acuity at birth becomes obvious when we look at the state of the cortex and the retina at birth. The infant's visual cortex is not fully developed. Figure 16.3 shows the state of cortical development at birth, at 3 months, and at 6 months (Conel, 1939, 1947, 1951). These drawings indicate that the visual cortex is only partially developed at birth and becomes more developed at 3 and 6 months, the time when significant improvements in visual acuity are occurring. However, the state of the cortex is not the whole explanation for the newborn's low visual acuity. If we look at the newborn's retina, we find that although the rod-dominated peripheral retina appears adultlike in the newborn, the all-cone fovea contains widely spaced and very poorly developed cone receptors (Abramov et al., 1982).

Figure 16.4a compares the shapes of newborn and adult foveal cones (see page 50). The newborn's cones have fat inner segments and very small outer segments, whereas the adult's inner and outer segments are larger and are about the same diameter (Banks & Bennett, 1988; Yuodelis & Hendrickson, 1986). These differences in shape and size have a number of consequences. The small size of the outer segment means that the newborn's cones contain less visual pigment and therefore do not absorb light as effectively as adult cones. In addition, the fat inner segment creates the coarse receptor lattice shown in Figure 16.4b, with large spaces between the outer segments. In contrast, when the adult cones become thin, they become packed closely together to create a fine lattice that is well suited to detecting fine details. Martin Banks and Patrick Bennett (1988) calculated that the cone receptors' outer segments effectively cover 68 percent of the adult fovea but only 2 percent of the newborn fovea. This means that most of the light entering

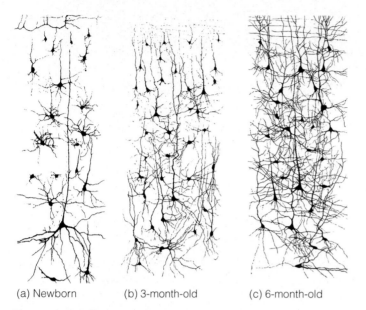

(a) Newborn   (b) 3-month-old   (c) 6-month-old

Figure 16.3 ▍ Drawings of neurons in the visual cortex of the newborn, the 3-month-old, and the 6-month-old human infant. *(Reprinted by permission of the publisher from Conel, J. L., The postnatal development of the cerebral cortex, Vol. I, III, and IV, Plates LVIII, LXIV, and LXIV, Cambridge, Mass.: Harvard University Press, Copyright © 1939, 1947, 1951, 1975 by the President and Fellows of Harvard College.)*

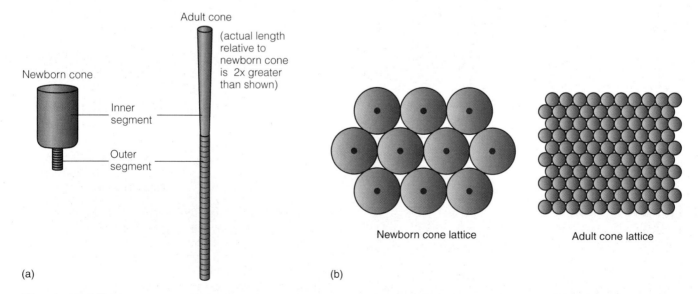

Figure 16.4 ▍ (a) Idealized shapes of newborn and adult foveal cones. (Real cones are not so perfectly straight and cylindrical.) Foveal cones are much narrower and longer than the cones elsewhere in the retina, so these look different from the one shown in Figure 3.25. (b) Receptor lattices for newborn and adult foveal cones. The newborn cone outer segments, indicated by the red circles, are widely spaced because of the fat inner segments. In contrast, the adult cones, with their slender inner segments, are packed closely together. *(Adapted from Banks & Bennett, 1988.)*

the newborn's fovea is lost in the spaces between the cones and is therefore not useful for vision.

Visual acuity provides a measure of the ability to see fine details, so an infant's acuity reflects the finest bars that he or she can resolve in a grating. However, objects in the environment come in all sizes, ranging from extremely small to very large. To determine how an infant perceives this environment, we need to determine his or her contrast sensitivity.

Contrast Sensitivity

Contrast sensitivity is measured by determining the smallest difference between the dark and light bars of a grating at which an observer can still detect the bars. We can determine how an infant perceives objects of different sizes by measuring contrast sensitivity with gratings of different bar sizes. However, rather than describing the grating in terms of fine or wide bars, researchers use a measure called spatial frequency.

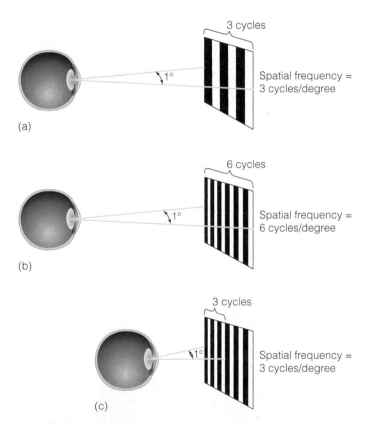

Figure 16.5 ▌ An observer's eye looking at a grating stimulus. (a) A grating in which three cycles of bars fall within a visual angle of one degree. (Each cycle includes a black bar and a white bar.) The spatial frequency of this grating is therefore 3 cycles per degree. (b) A grating with spatial frequency of 6 cycles per degree. (c) When the grating from b is moved closer, now just 3 cycles fit within the one-degree viewing angle, so the spatial frequency of this grating is now 3 cycles per degree. These examples illustrate that spatial frequency depends on both the fineness of the grating and the distance from which it is viewed.

The **spatial frequency** of a grating is the number of cycles of the grating (in which one cycle is one light bar and one dark bar) per degree of visual angle. The spatial frequency of the grating in Figure 16.5a is 3 cycles per degree, and the spatial frequency of the grating in Figure 16.5b is 6 cycles per degree. Thus, finer bars are generally associated with higher spatial frequencies. However, spatial frequency also depends on the grating's distance from the observer. Moving closer to the grating (Figure 16.5c), decreases the spatial frequency. Spatial frequency therefore is a measure of how fine the bar pattern is *on the retina*. To get a feel for a few spatial frequencies, look at Figure 16.6a from a distance of 2 feet. When viewed from this distance, the bars have spatial frequencies of about 1, 3, and 6 cycles per degree.

Determining the contrast sensitivity of gratings with different spatial frequencies results in a plot of contrast sensitivity versus spatial frequency, which is called the **contrast sensitivity function** (CSF; Figure 16.7). The top curve in this figure is the adult contrast sensitivity function. This function indicates that adults are most sensitive to gratings with spatial frequencies of about 3 cycles per degree. The adult function also indicates that adults can see low spatial frequencies (very wide bars in relation to the eye), but that their ability to see high spatial frequencies (very narrow bars) drops off rapidly above 10 cycles per degree.

Returning to the gratings in Figure 16.6a, you might notice that you have no trouble seeing all three frequencies. The reason for this is that these are high-contrast gratings—the dark bars are black and the light bars are white. But the gratings used to measure contrast sensitivity functions are low-contrast gratings, like the ones in Figure 16.6b, that are more difficult to see. Even though these are low-contrast gratings, you can probably still see the individual bars in the gratings, because you are an adult and have good contrast sensitivity. However, the situation is different for infants.

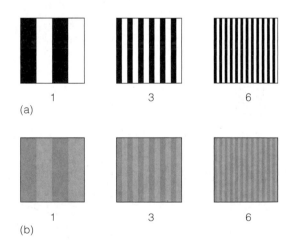

Figure 16.6 ▌ (a) When viewed from a distance of 2 feet, these gratings have spatial frequencies of 1, 3, and 6 cycles per degree, as indicated beneath each grating. (b) The same gratings with lower contrast. Low-contrast gratings such as these are used to measure contrast sensitivity, since the goal is to determine the lowest contrast that can just be seen.

The lower curves in Figure 16.7 are the contrast sensitivity functions for 1- to 3-month-old infants. These curves indicate that (1) the infants' ability to perceive contrast is restricted to low frequencies; (2) even at these low frequencies, the infants' contrast sensitivity is much lower than the adult's; and (3) infants can see little or nothing at frequencies above about 2 to 3 cycles/degree, the frequencies to which adults are most sensitive (Banks, 1982; Banks & Salapatek, 1978, 1981; Salapatek & Banks, 1978).

What does the young infants' depressed CSF tell us about their visual world? Clearly, infants are sensitive to only a small fraction of the pattern information available to the adult. At 1 month, infants can see no fine details and can see only relatively large objects with high contrast. Their vision at this age is slightly worse than adult night vision (Fiorentini & Maffei, 1973; Pirchio et al., 1978), a finding consistent with the fact that the undeveloped state of the infant's fovea forces it to see primarily with the rod-dominated peripheral retina. Thus, infants' "window on the world" is very different from adults'; infants see the world as if they are looking through a frosted glass that filters out the high frequencies that would enable them to see fine details but leaves some ability to detect larger, low-frequency forms.

We should not conclude from young infants' poor vision, however, that they can see nothing at all. At very close distances, a young infant can detect some gross features, as indicated in Figure 16.8, which simulates how infants perceive an object from a distance of about 2 feet. At birth, the contrast is so low that it is difficult to determine it is a cat, but it is possible to see very high-contrast areas. By 2 months, however, the infant's contrast perception has improved so that the image looks clearly catlike. This improvement in contrast sensitivity over the first few months is reflected in the fact that by 3 to 4 months, infants can

tell the difference between faces that look happy and those that show surprise, anger, or are neutral (LaBarbera et al., 1976; Young-Browne et al., 1977) and can tell the difference between a cat and a dog (Eimas & Quinn, 1994).

Perceiving Color

We know that our perception of color is determined by the action of three different types of cone receptors (Figure 9.9). Because the cones are poorly developed at birth, we can guess that the newborn would not have good color vision. However, research has shown that color vision develops early and that appreciable color vision is present within the first 3 to 4 months of life.

One of the challenges in determining whether infants have color vision is that perception of a light stimulus can vary on at least two dimensions: (1) its chromatic color and (2) its brightness. Thus, if we present the red and yellow patches in Figure 16.9a to a color-deficient person and ask him whether he can tell the difference between them, he might say yes, because the yellow patch looks brighter than the red one.

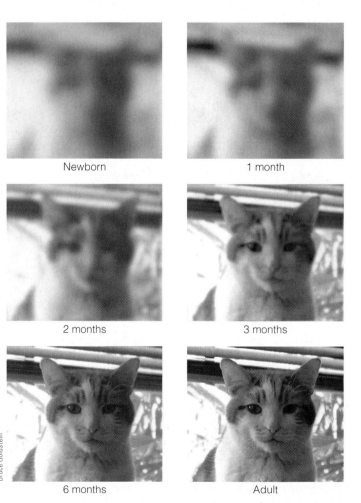

Newborn 1 month

2 months 3 months

6 months Adult

Bruce Goldstein

Figure 16.8 ▌ Simulation of perceptions of a cat located 24 inches from an observer, as seen by newborns, 1-, 2,-, 3-, and 6-month-old infants, and adults. *(Simulations courtesy of Alex Wade and Bob Dougherty.)*

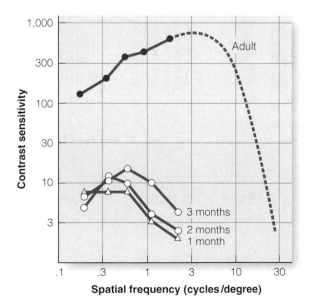

Figure 16.7 ▌ Contrast sensitivity functions for an adult and for infants tested at 1, 2, and 3 months of age.

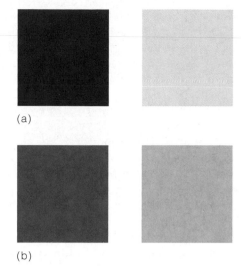

(a)

(b)

Figure 16.9 ▌ (a) Two color patches. (b) The same two patches as "seen" by a photocopy machine.

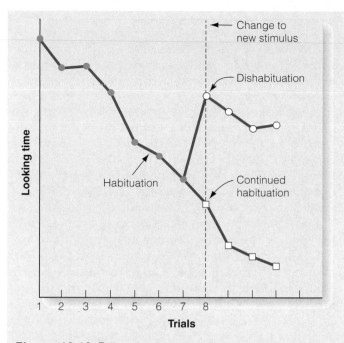

Figure 16.10 ▌ Possible results of a habituation experiment. Increased looking when the stimulus changes (trial 8) is called dishabituation. If this occurs, it means that the infant perceives the new stimulus as different from the original stimulus.

You can make this observation, if you don't have access to a color-deficient person, by using a "color-blind" black-and-white photocopier as your "observer." Photocopies of the red and yellow patches (Figure 16.9b) show that the color-blind photocopier can distinguish between the two patches because the red patch is darker than the yellow one. This means that when stimuli with different wavelengths are used to test color vision, their intensity should be adjusted so that they have the same brightness. For example, for the stimuli in Figure 16.9, it would be necessary to make the red patch lighter and the yellow patch darker. The experiment we will now describe has done this.

Marc Bornstein, William Kessen, and Sally Weiskopf (1976) assessed the color vision of 4-month-old infants by determining whether they perceive the same color categories in the spectrum as adults. People with normal trichromatic vision see the spectrum as a sequence of color categories, starting with blue at the short-wavelength end, followed by green, yellow, orange, and red, with fairly abrupt transitions between one color and the next (see the spectrum in Figure 9.4). Bornstein and coworkers used a method called *habituation* to determine whether infants can perceive the difference between these categories.

METHOD ▌ Habituation

We have seen that the preferential looking technique is based on the existence of spontaneous looking preferences. But in some cases we want to determine whether an infant perceives a difference between two stimuli that he or she normally looks at equally. Researchers have achieved this by using the following fact about infant looking behavior: When given a choice between a famil-

iar stimulus and a novel one, an infant is more likely to look at the novel one (Fagan, 1976; Slater et al., 1984).

Because infants are more likely to look at a novel stimulus, we can create a preference for one stimulus over another by familiarizing the infant with one stimulus but not with the other. In this technique, called habituation, one stimulus is presented to the infant repeatedly, and the infant's looking time is measured on each presentation (Figure 16.10). As the infant becomes more familiar with the stimulus, he or she habituates to it, looking less and less on each trial, as indicated by the green circles in Figure 16.10.

Once the infant has habituated to this stimulus, we determine whether the infant can tell the difference between it and another stimulus by presenting a new stimulus. In Figure 16.10, the new stimulus is presented on the eighth trial. If the infant can tell the difference between the habituation stimulus and the new stimulus, he or she will exhibit dishabituation, an increase in looking time when the stimulus is changed, as shown by the open red circles in Figure 16.10. If, however, the infant cannot tell the difference between the two stimuli, he or she will continue to habituate to the new stimulus (because it will not be perceived as novel), as indicated by the open blue squares in Figure 16.10. Remember that the occurrence of dishabituation means that the second stimulus appears different to the infant from the habituation stimulus.

Bornstein and his coworkers habituated infants to a 510-nm light—a wavelength that appears green to an adult with normal color vision (a trichromat)—and then presented either a 480-nm light, which looks blue to a trichromat, or a 540-nm light, which is on the other side of the blue–green border and therefore appears green to a trichromat (Figure 16.11). Because dishabituation occurred to the 480-nm light but did not occur to the 540-nm light, Bornstein concluded (a) that the 480-nm light looked different from the 510-nm light and (b) that the 540-nm light looked similar to the 510-nm light. From this result and the results of other experiments, Bornstein concluded that 4-month-old infants categorize colors the same way adult trichromats do.

Bornstein and coworkers dealt with the problem of equating brightness by setting the intensity at each wavelength so each stimulus looked equally bright to adults. This is not an ideal procedure because infants may perceive brightness differently from adults. However, as it turns out, Bornstein's result appears to be correct, because later research has confirmed Bornstein's conclusion that young infants have color vision (see Franklin & Davies, 2004; Hamer et al., 1982; Varner et al., 1985).

Perceiving Depth

At what age are infants able to use different kinds of depth information? The answer to this question is that different types of information become operative at different times. Binocular disparity becomes functional early, and pictorial depth cues become functional later.

Using Binocular Disparity One requirement for the operation of binocular disparity is that the eyes must be able to binocularly fixate so that the two eyes are both looking directly at the object, and the two foveas are therefore directed to exactly the same place. Newborns have only a rudimentary, imprecise ability to fixate binocularly, especially on objects that are changing in depth (Slater & Findlay, 1975).

Richard Aslin (1977) determined when binocular fixation develops by making some simple observations. He filmed infants' eyes while moving a target back and forth

between 12 cm and 57 cm from the infant. When the infant is directing both eyes at a target, the eyes should diverge (rotate outward) as the target moves away and should converge (rotate inward) as the target moves closer (Figure 10.2). Aslin's films indicate that although some divergence and convergence do occur in 1- and 2-month-old infants, these eye movements do not reliably direct both eyes toward the target until about 3 months of age.

Although binocular fixation may be present by 3 months of age, this does not guarantee that the infant can use the resulting disparity information to perceive depth. To determine when infants can use this information to perceive depth, Robert Fox and coworkers (1980) presented random-dot stereograms to infants ranging in age from 2 to 6 months (see page 239 to review random-dot stereograms).

The beauty of random-dot stereograms is that the binocular disparity information in the stereograms results in stereopsis (the perception of depth due to binocular disparity; see page 238). This occurs only (1) if the stereogram is observed with a device that presents one picture to the left eye and the other picture to the right eye and (2) if the observer's visual system can convert this disparity information into the perception of depth. Thus, if we present a random-dot stereogram to an infant whose visual system cannot yet use disparity information, all he or she sees is a random collection of dots.

In Fox's experiment, an infant wearing special viewing glasses was seated in his or her mother's lap in front of a television screen (Figure 16.12). The child viewed a random-dot stereogram that appeared, to an observer sensitive to disparity information, as a rectangle-in-depth, moving either

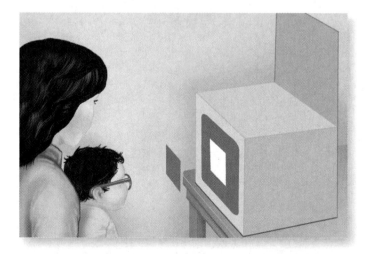

Figure 16.12 ❚ The setup used by Fox et al. (1980) to test infants' ability to use binocular disparity information. If the infant can use disparity information to see depth, he or she sees a rectangle moving back and forth in front of the screen. *(From Shea, S. L., Fox, R., Aslin, R., & Dumais, S. T., Assessment of stereopsis in human infants, Investigative Ophthalmology and Visual Science, 19, 1400–1404, figure 1. Copyright © 1980 C. V. Mosby Company, St. Louis, MO. Reprinted by permission of Elsevier.)*

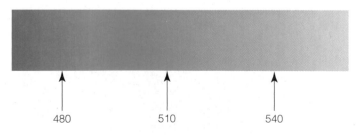

Figure 16.11 ❚ Three wavelengths (indicated by arrows) used in Bornstein, Kessen, and Weiskopf's (1976) experiment. The 510- and 480-nm lights are in different perceptual categories (one appears green, the other blue to adults), but the 510- and 540-nm lights are in the same perceptual category (both appear green to adults).

to the left or to the right. Fox's premise was that an infant sensitive to disparity will move his or her eyes to follow the moving rectangle. He found that infants younger than about 3 months of age would not follow the rectangle, but that infants between 3 and 6 months of age would follow it. He therefore concluded that the ability to use disparity information to perceive depth emerges sometime between 3½ and 6 months of age. This time for the emergence of binocular depth perception has been confirmed by other research using a variety of different methods (Shimojo et al., 1986; Teller, 1997).

Another type of depth information is provided by pictorial cues (see Chapter 10, page 231). These cues develop later than disparity, presumably because they depend on experience with the environment and the development of cognitive capabilities. In general, infants begin to use pictorial cues such as overlap, familiar size, relative size, shading, linear perspective, and texture gradients sometime between about 5 and 7 months of age (Granrud, Haake, & Yonas, 1985; Granrud & Yonas, 1984; Granrud, Yonas, & Opland, 1985; Yonas et al., 1986; Yonas, Pettersen, & Granrud, 1982). We will describe research on two of these cues—overlap and familiar size.

Depth From Familiar Size Granrud, Haake, and Yonas (1985) conducted a two-part experiment to see whether infants can use their knowledge of the sizes of objects to help them perceive depth. In the familiarization period, 5- and 7-month-old infants played with a pair of wooden objects for 10 minutes. One of these objects was large (Figure 16.13a), and one was small (Figure 16.13b). In the test period, which occurred about a minute after the familiarization period, objects (c) and (d) were presented at the same distance from the infant. The prediction was that infants sensitive to familiar size would perceive object

(c) to be closer if they remembered, from the familiarization period, that this shape was smaller than the other one. In other words, if the infant remembered the green object as being small, then seeing it as big in their field of view could lead the infant to think it was the same small object, but located much closer.

When tested monocularly, the 7-month-olds did reach for object (c), as would be predicted if they perceived it as being closer than object (d). The 5-month-olds, however, did not reach for object (c), which indicated that these infants did not use familiar size as information for depth. Thus, the ability to use familiar size to perceive depth appears to develop sometime between 5 and 7 months.

This experiment is interesting not only because it indicates when the ability to use familiar size develops, but also because the infant's response in the test phase depends on a cognitive ability—the ability to remember the sizes of the objects that he or she played with in the familiarization phase. The 7-month-old infant's depth response in this situation is therefore based on both what is perceived and what is remembered.

Perceiving Faces

Human faces are among the most important stimuli in an infant's environment. As a newborn or young infant stares up from the crib, numerous faces of interested adults appear in the infant's field of view. The face that the infant sees most frequently is usually the mother's, and there is evidence that young infants can recognize their mother's face shortly after they are born.

Recognizing Their Mother's Face

Research on the infant's ability to recognize faces provides an example of how research in perceptual development often progresses. First, an infant's ability to perceive a particular stimulus is demonstrated. Then, the result is confirmed by replicating it, perhaps also using improved procedures to rule out possible sources of bias. Finally, experiments are done to determine the information the infant is using to achieve its perception.

Using preferential looking in which 2-day-old infants were given a choice between their mother's face and a stranger's, Ian Bushnell and coworkers (1989) found that newborns looked at the mother about 63 percent of the time. This result is above the 50 percent chance level, so Bushnell concluded that the 2-day-olds could recognize their mother's face.

You may recall from our earlier discussion (page 385) that infants usually prefer novel stimuli. If that were occurring here, we would expect the infant to look at the stranger more than the mother. Why, then, does the infant prefer to look at the mother? Apparently the infant's preference for the mother is so strong that it overrides the usual tendency to prefer novel stimuli.

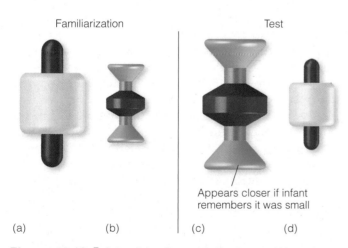

Familiarization   Test

Appears closer if infant remembers it was small

(a)   (b)   (c)   (d)

Figure 16.13 ▌ Stimuli for Granrud, Haake, and Yonas's (1985) familiar-size experiment. See text for details. *(From "Infants' Sensitivity to Familiar Size: The Effect of Memory on Spatial Perception," by C. E. Granrud, R. J. Haake, & A. Yonas, 1985, Perception and Psychophysics, 37, 459–466. Copyright © 1985 by Psychonomic Society Publications. Reprinted by permission.)*

Bushnell did control experiments to rule out the possibility that perhaps the mother was doing something to attract the infant's attention or that the infant could detect the mother's familiar smell. But to be sure that distraction and smell were not contributing factors, Gail Walton and coworkers (1992) showed that newborns still responded to the mother more than to a stranger when the faces were presented on videotape.

To determine what information the infants might be using to recognize the mother's face, Olivier Pascalis and coworkers (1995) showed that when the mother and the stranger wore pink scarves that covered their hairline, the preference for the mother disappeared. The high-contrast border between the mother's dark hairline and light forehead apparently provided important information about the mother's physical characteristics that the infant used to recognize its mother (see Bartrip et al., 2001, for another experiment that shows this).

The fact that newborns are able to perceive the difference between their mother's face and the face of a stranger raises another question: Is this ability due to a special face-sensitive mechanism that is built in at birth, or is it the result of a general perceptual mechanism?

Is There a Special Mechanism for Perceiving Faces?

The idea of an inborn face-sensitive mechanism has been proposed by John Morton and Mark Johnson (1991). They presented stimuli (see bottom of Figure 16.14) to newborns within an hour after birth and then moved the stimuli to the left and right. As they did this, they videotaped the infant's face. Later, scorers who were unaware of which stimulus had been presented viewed the tapes and noted whether the infant turned its head or eyes to follow the moving stimulus. The results in Figure 16.14 show that the newborns

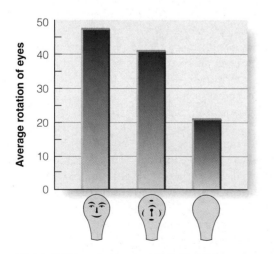

Figure 16.14 ❚ The magnitude of infants' eye movements in response to movement of each stimulus. The average rotation of the infants' eyes was greater for the facelike stimulus than for the scrambled-face stimulus or the blank stimulus. *(Adapted from Morton & Johnson, 1991.)*

looked at the moving face more than at the other moving stimuli.

Support for a special mechanism for face recognition has been provided by Martha Farah and coworkers' (2000) case study of Adam, a 16-year-old boy who contracted meningitis when he was 1 day old. This disease damaged areas in the occipital and temporal lobe usually associated with perceiving faces and left him with a condition called prosopagnosia, an inability to recognize faces, which we discussed in Chapter 4 (page 93). He could, however, still recognize other kinds of objects.

Although Adam scored below normal when tested on pictures of common household objects, vehicles, and toys (87 percent correct; normal performance is close to 100 percent), he was able to identify environmental objects well enough for everyday functioning. Faces, however, were another story. He was unable to identify any of the pictures of faces he was shown, even though many were pictures of people he watched daily on television, and he could identify friends only after hearing them talk.

Because Adam had a dissociation between object perception and face perception (see Method: Dissociations in Neuropsychology on page 89), Farah concluded that the mechanism for face perception is different from the mechanism for object perception. What makes Adam's case especially significant is that even after 16 years of observing faces, he was never able to learn to identify them. Thus, the area responsible for object perception was not able to take over the task of identifying faces.

But other evidence leads some researchers to question the idea of a separate face-recognition mechanism. For example, Ian Bushnell (2001) observed newborns over the first 3 days of life to determine whether there was a relationship between their looking behavior and the amount of time they were with their mother. He found that at 3 days of age, when the infants were given a choice between looking at a stranger's face or their mother's face, the infants who had been exposed to their mother longer were more likely to prefer her over the stranger. The two infants with the lowest exposure to the mother (an average of 1.5 hours) divided their looking evenly between the mother and stranger, but the two infants with the longest exposure (an average of 7.5 hours) looked at the mother 68 percent of the time. Analyzing the results from all of the infants led Bushnell to conclude that face perception emerges very rapidly after birth, but that experience in looking at faces does have an effect.

Chiara Turati and coworkers (2002) presented additional evidence to support the idea that early face recognition is not based on a special mechanism. They found that 1- to 4-day-old infants look longer at displays with more elements in the top half (Figure 16.15). Notice that infants looked longer at the top-heavy stimuli in pairs (a) and (b) even though in pair (b), the arrangement of the elements in the bottom-heavy stimulus looked more like a face. When two stimuli with the same number of elements on the top were compared, as in (c), the infants showed no preference, even though the display on the right looks more like a face.

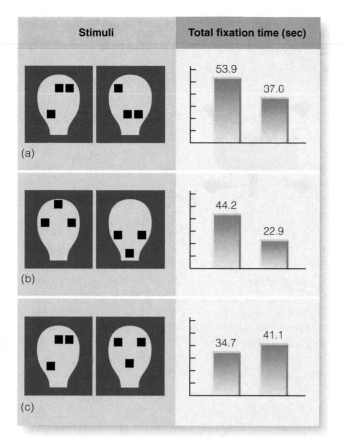

Stimuli	Total fixation time (sec)
(a)	53.9 / 37.6
(b)	44.2 / 22.9
(c)	34.7 / 41.1

Figure 16.15 ▌ Results of Turati et al.'s (2002) measurements of how long infants looked at each stimulus in the pair when they were presented simultaneously. (a) Infants looked longer at the top-heavy stimulus. (b) Infants looked longer at the top-heavy stimulus. (c) There was no significant difference in looking between these two stimuli, which are equally top-heavy.

This result could mean that infants attend to faces because faces have more elements in their top half. The infants therefore gain more experience in looking at faces, and this experience could help create an area such as the fusiform face area (FFA) that is specialized for faces (see page 93). According to this idea, infants' early preference for faces can be explained by a general mechanism of object perception. No special mechanism for face perception is needed (see Nelson, 2001).

We can summarize our description of infant face perception by noting that there is ample evidence that newborns and young infants can distinguish between different faces, and that very young infants prefer to look at facelike stimuli. There is disagreement, however, about whether this preference for faces is caused by a special mechanism dedicated to perceiving faces or by the same mechanism that serves the perception of objects in general. If this sounds familiar, it is because the same disagreement among researchers exists about the mechanism that is responsible for adults' perception of faces (see page 95). Further research on both infants and adults is needed to resolve this question. (See Quinn et al., in press.)

TEST YOURSELF 16.1

1. Why is measuring infant perception more difficult than measuring adult perception?
2. Describe two techniques that have been used to measure infant visual acuity, and the results obtained using these methods.
3. What is the connection between the development of infant visual acuity and the physiology of the cortex and the cone receptors?
4. What information about perception does measuring contrast sensitivity provide that is not provided by measuring visual acuity? What do infant contrast sensitivity functions tell us about the infant's visual world?
5. What do researchers have to take into account when determining whether infants can perceive color? How did Bornstein use the method of habituation to determine that infants can perceive color categories?
6. Describe the experiments that determined the age at which infants can (a) binocularly fixate and (b) use disparity to perceive depth.
7. How did researchers determine infants' ability to use pictorial depth information? Why do pictorial depth cues become operational at a later age than disparity?
8. Describe research on the infant's ability to recognize faces. What two explanations have been proposed for the finding that infants can recognize faces at a young age?

Perceiving Object Unity

So far, in considering how infants perceive objects, we have focused on faces. Although faces are extremely important to infants, they also see many other things and have to develop the capacity to perceptually organize all of the objects they encounter in the environment. This process of organization includes grouping some things together (see "The Gestalt Laws of Perceptual Organization," page 105) and also being able to perceive different objects as separate from one another (see "Perceptual Segregation," page 108). Because the research on the development of object perception is far too vast to cover here, we will focus on one very important aspect of object perception—the perception of object unity.

When adults look at the three men in Figure 16.16, they perceive their bodies as continuing behind the boards on which they are leaning. But would a young infant perceive the upper, middle, and lower parts of their bodies as separate units or as parts of a single object that continues behind the boards? Experiments on the perception of object unity have focused on the conditions under which an infant can perceive an object as a whole even when part of it is obscured by an occluding stimulus.

Figure 16.16 ▎ Three men whose bodies are occluded by the two boards. The perception of object unity has occurred if each man is perceived as a single object that continues behind the boards.

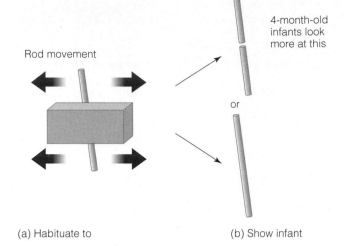

Figure 16.17 ▎ (a) Stimuli used in the habituation phase of the Kellman and Spelke (1983) experiment. A rod moves back and forth behind a rectangular occlude. (b) Two stimuli presented separately in the dishabituation phase of the experiment. *(Reprinted from Kellman, P. J., & Spelke, E. S., Perception of partly occluded objects in infancy,* Cognitive Psychology, 15, *483–524, figure 3. Copyright © 1983, with permission from Elsevier.)*

Philip Kellman and Elizabeth Spelke (1983) showed that movement helps infants perceive objects as continuing behind an occluding object. First they habituated 4-month-old infants to a rod moving back and forth behind a block (Figure 16.17a), so the infants looked less and less at this stimulus. They then presented either two separated moving rods (top stimulus in Figure 16.17b) or a single longer moving rod (bottom stimulus in Figure 16.17b). ▮VL▮ 2

The infants increased their looking when the two separated rods were presented, but did not increase their looking when the single long rod stimulus was presented. Based on this result, Kellman and Spelke concluded that the 4-month-old infants perceived the separated rods in Figure 16.17b as different from the moving rod in Figure 16.17a (remember that infants look more at the "novel" object), and that they therefore had seen the partly occluded moving rod as a whole object that continued behind the block.

This result did not occur, however, when the infant was habituated to a stationary rod and block display. Thus, movement helped the 4-month-old infants infer that the bar extended behind the block. The 4-month-olds appear to be making the following inference: if the top and bottom units are moving together, then they must be part of the same object.

If 4-month-olds perceive a moving object as continuing behind an occluding stimulus, can younger infants do this as well? When Alan Slater and coworkers (1990) repeated Kellman and Spelke's experiment with newborns, they found that when the newborns saw the moving rod during habituation, they looked more at the single rod during dishabituation. This suggests that they saw the moving rods as two separate units and not as a single rod extending behind

the occluder. Apparently newborns do *not* make the inference that 4-month-olds make about the moving display.

Thus, the capacity demonstrated at 4 months does not exist (or can't be measured using this particular procedure) at birth. But when does it appear? Scott Johnson and Richard Aslin (1995) helped determine the answer when they tested 2-month-olds and obtained results similar to those for the 4-month-olds. Apparently, the ability to use movement as a way to organize the perceptual world develops rapidly over the first few months of life.

A number of experiments like these show that at 2 months of age infants are able to perceive partially hidden objects as a single object, and that this ability becomes stronger by 4 to 6 months. But simply determining the age at which a perceptual capacity emerges is only the first step in understanding the mechanism behind this capacity. Scott Johnson and coworkers (2004) investigated the link between infants' perception of object unity and how they looked at a rod as it moved behind an occluder. They accomplished this by measuring both habituation behavior and eye movements in 3-month-old infants as the infants observed a moving rod display.

The habituation results indicated that some of the infants perceived the moving rod as continuing behind the occluder. They called these infants *perceivers*. The results also indicated that other infants did not perceive the moving rod as continuing behind the occluder. Johnson and coworkers called these infants *nonperceivers*.

Figure 16.18 shows eye fixation records measured during habituation for a perceiver (Figure 16.18a) and a nonperceiver (Figure 16.18b). The two rods in each figure indicate the left- and right-most positions of the moving rod. Notice

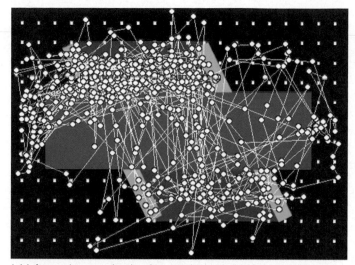

(a) Infants who perceived rod as continuing behind the occluder

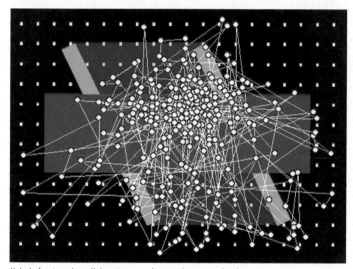

(b) Infants who did not perceive rod as continuing

Figure 16.18 ▌ How infants looked at a display during habituation, in which a rod moved back and forth behind a rectangular occluder. (a) Fixations for an infant who perceived the moving rod as a single object (a "perceiver"). (b) Fixations for an infant who did not perceive the moving rod as a single object (a "nonperceiver"). *(From S. P. Johnson, J. A. Slemmer, & D. Amso, 2004, "Where Infants Look Determines How They See: Eye Movements and Object Perception Performance in 3-Month Olds," Infancy, Vol. 6, Issue 2, pp. 185–201, Taylor & Francis. Records courtesy of Scott Johnson.)*

that in these examples, the perceiver fixated mainly on the rod, whereas the nonperceiver fixated on the rectangular occluder. Eye movement records also showed that, as a group, perceivers made more horizontal eye movements than the nonperceivers. The perceivers, therefore, tended to look at the rod and follow its movement, whereas the nonperceivers looked more at the stationary occluder and other parts of the display that were not related to perceiving the rods as extending behind the occluder. These differences between perceivers and nonperceivers mean that the infants' percep-

tion of object unity depends on the development of looking behavior that enables them to pick up information about the rod's movement. ▐VL▌3

Hearing

What do newborn infants hear, and how does hearing develop as infants get older? Although some early psychologists believed that newborns were functionally deaf, recent research has shown that newborns do have some auditory capacities and that this capacity improves as the child gets older (Werner & Bargones, 1992).

Threshold for Hearing a Tone

A simple way to find out whether infants can hear is to determine whether they will orient toward the source of a sound. Darwin Muir and Jeffry Field (1979) presented newborn infants with a loud (80-dB) rattle sound 20 cm from either their right or their left ear and found that the infants usually turned toward the sound. Newborns can therefore hear and are capable of at least crude sound localization.

More precise measurements of infants' capacities have been achieved with older infants, who have a wider repertoire of responses to sound. Lynne Werner Olsho and coworkers (1988) used the following procedure to determine infants' audibility curves. An infant is fitted with earphones and sits on the parent's lap. An observer, sitting out of view of the infant, watches the infant through a window. A light blinks on, indicating that a trial has begun, and the infant is either presented with a tone or is not. The observer's task is to decide whether or not the infant heard the tone (Olsho et al., 1987).

How can observers tell whether the infant has heard a tone? They decide by looking for responses such as eye movements, changes in facial expression, a wide-eyed look, a turn of the head, or changes in activity level. These judgments resulted in the curve in Figure 16.19a for a 2,000-Hz tone (Olsho et al., 1988). Observers only occasionally indicated that the 3-month-old infants heard the tone that was presented at low intensities or not at all. But observers were more likely to say that the infant had heard the tone when the tone was presented at high intensity. The infant's threshold was determined from this curve, and the results from a number of other frequencies were combined to create audibility functions, such as those in Figure 16.19b. The curves for 3- and 6-month-olds and adults indicate that infant and adult audibility functions look similar and that, by 6 months of age, the infant's threshold is within about 10 to 15 dB of the adult threshold.

Recognizing Their Mother's Voice

Another approach to studying hearing in infants has been to show that newborns can identify sounds they have heard before. Anthony DeCasper and William Fifer (1980)

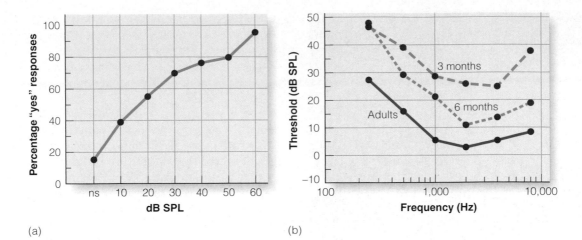

(a)   (b)

Figure 16.19 ▌ (a) Data obtained from Olsho et al.'s observer-based psychoacoustic procedure that shows the percentage of trials on which the observer indicated that a 3-month-old infant heard tones presented at different intensities. NS indicates no sound. (b) Audibility curves for 3- and 6-month-old infants determined from functions like the one in (a). The curve for 12-month-olds, not shown here, is similar to the curve for 6-month-olds. The adult curve is shown for comparison. *(Adapted from "Pure-Tone Sensitivity of Human Infants," by L. W. Olsho, E. G. Koch, E. A. Carter, C. F. Halpin, & N. B. Spetner, 1988,* Journal of the Acoustical Society of America, 84*, 1316–1324. American Institute of Physics.)*

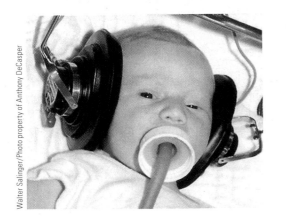

Figure 16.20 ▌ This baby, from DeCasper and Fifer's (1980) study, could control whether she heard a recording of her mother's voice or a stranger's voice by the way she sucked on the nipple. *(From DeCasper, A. J., & Fifer, W. P. (1980). Of human bonding: Newborns prefer their mothers' voices.* Science, 208*, 1174–1176.)*

demonstrated this capacity in newborns by showing that 2-day-old infants will modify their sucking on a nipple in order to hear the sound of their mother's voice. They first observed that infants usually suck on a nipple in bursts separated by pauses. They fitted infants with earphones and let the length of the pause in the infant's sucking determine whether the infant heard a recording of the mother's voice or a recording of a stranger's voice (Figure 16.20). For half of the infants, long pauses activated the tape of the mother's voice, and short pauses activated the tape of the stranger's voice. For the other half, these conditions were reversed.

DeCasper and Fifer found that the babies regulated the pauses in their sucking so that they heard their mother's voice more than the stranger's voice. This is a remarkable accomplishment for a 2-day-old, especially because most had been with their mothers for only a few hours between birth and the time they were tested.

Why did the newborns prefer their mother's voice? DeCasper and Fifer suggested that newborns recognize their mother's voice because they heard the mother talking during development in the womb. This suggestion is supported by the results of another experiment, in which DeCasper and M. J. Spence (1986) had one group of pregnant women read from Dr. Seuss's book *The Cat in the Hat* and another group read the same story with the words *cat* and *hat* replaced with *dog* and *fog*. When the children were born, they regulated the pauses in their sucking that caused them to hear the version of the story their mother had read when they were in the womb.

In another experiment, 2-day-old infants regulated their sucking to hear a recording of their native language rather than of a foreign language (Moon et al., 1993). Apparently, even when in the womb, the fetus becomes familiar with the sound cues it hears, possibly the intonation and rhythm of the mother's voice and also the sounds of specific words. (See also DeCasper et al., 1994.)

Perceiving Speech

Perceiving individual tones and being able to recognize familiar sounds are important basic skills that infants posses at an early age. As the infant develops, another skill becomes important—the ability to discern meaning through words and sentences. This ability emerges long before the infant can produce speech. The starting point for understanding speech perception in infants has been to determine how infants respond to phonemes.

The Categorical Perception of Phonemes

Remember from Chapter 13 that each language is constructed from units called phonemes—the smallest unit that when changed, changes the meaning of a word. Because of the importance of phonemes and their role as elementary units of language, some of the first research on infant speech perception focused on their perception of phonemes. This research took as its starting point the research on categorical perception of phonemes that we described in Chapter 13 (see page 314).

The main result of categorical perception experiments in adults is that even when a characteristic of the speech stimulus called voice onset time (VOT) changes over a wide range, listeners tend to hear only two categories of sound (see page 317). In the example described in Chapter 13, adults heard one sound ("da") at short VOTs and another sound ("ta") at long voice onset times. There is a place between these two extremes where changing the VOT just a little causes people's categorization of the sound to suddenly change from one sound to the other. This place is called the *phonetic boundary*.

Categorical perception was first reported for adults in 1967 (Liberman et al., 1967). In 1971, Peter Eimas and coworkers began the modern era of research on infant speech

perception by using the habituation procedure to show that infants as young as 1 month old perform similarly to adults in categorical perception experiments. The basis of these experiments was the observation that an infant will suck on a nipple in order to hear a series of brief speech sounds, but as the same speech sounds are repeated, the infant's sucking eventually habituates to a low level. By presenting a new stimulus after the rate of sucking had decreased, Eimas determined whether the infant perceived the new stimulus as sounding the same as or different from the old one.

The results of Eimas and coworkers' experiment are shown in Figure 16.21. The number of sucking responses when no sound was presented is indicated by the point at B. When a sound with voice onset time (VOT) of 20 ms (sounds like "ba" to an adult) is presented as the infant sucks, the sucking increases to a high level and then begins to decrease. When the VOT is changed to 40 ms (dashed line; sounds like "pa" to an adult), sucking increases, as indicated by the points to the right of the dashed line. This means that the infant perceives a difference between sounds with VOTs of 20 and 40 ms. The center graph, however, shows that changing the VOT from 60 to 80 ms (both sound like "pa" to an adult) has only a small effect on sucking, indicating that the infants perceive little, if any, difference between the two sounds. Finally, the results for a control group (the right graph) show that when the sound is not changed, the number of sucking responses decreases throughout the experiment.

These results show that when the VOT is shifted across the average adult phonetic boundary (left graph), the infants perceive a change in the sound, and when the VOT is shifted on the same side of the phonetic boundary (center

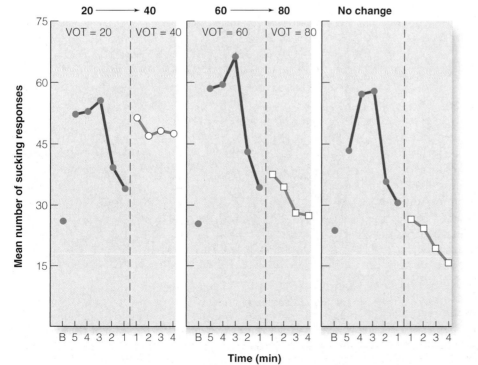

Figure 16.21 ▌ Results of a categorical perception experiment on infants using the habituation procedure. In the left panel, VOT is changed from 20 to 40 ms (across the phonetic boundary). In the center panel, VOT is changed from 60 to 80 ms (not across the phonetic boundary). In the right panel, the VOT was not changed. See text for details. *(From "Speech Perception in Infants," by P. Eimas, E. P. Siqueland, P. Jusczyk, J. Vigorito, 1971,* Science, 171, *303–306, figure 2. Copyright © 1971 by the American Association for the Advancement of Science. Reprinted by permission.)*

graph), the infants perceive little or no change in the sound. That infants as young as 1 month old are capable of categorical perception is particularly impressive, because these infants have had virtually no experience in producing speech sounds and only limited experience in hearing them.

Another impressive speech perception ability in infants is their ability to determine where in a string of sounds one word ends and another begins, a process called *speech segmentation*. This research is described on page 321 of Chapter 13.

Experience and Speech Perception

When infants are a few months old, they can distinguish between phonemes that make up their native language and also between phonemes from other languages. (Remember that although there are many possible phonemes, each language is created from one particular set of phonemes. For example, there are 11 phonemes in Hawaiian, about 49 in English, and as many as 60 in some African languages.) However, by the time infants are 1 year old, their ability to distinguish between phonemes has become "tuned" to the phonemes of the language to which they have been exposed.

This tuning is illustrated by the fact that a 4-month-old Japanese infant can distinguish between the sounds /r/ and /l/, but by the time they are 1 year old they can no longer make this distinction. This occurs because infants become sensitive only to distinctions between sounds that are important in their language, and the Japanese language does not distinguish between these two sounds (Kuhl, 2000, 2004; Kuhl et al., 1992, 1997; Werker, 1991; Werker & Tees, 1984).

Thus, infants possess mechanisms for perceiving all speech sounds fairly early in their development, and during the first year of life these mechanisms become tuned to the language that the child hears. We will return to this result at the end of the chapter when we describe research that suggests a similar "tuning" effect for perceiving faces.

Intermodal Perception

So far we have considered perceptual capacities such as seeing details, hearing sound frequencies, perceiving faces, and recognizing the mother's voice. But in the real world these things often occur together. We observe people's faces as we hear them speak; we hear an ambulance's siren as we see it racing down the street. These combinations of hearing and vision are examples of intermodal perception—coordination of information from different senses into a perceptual whole. This ability to coordinate information from different senses is something that adults routinely accomplish every day, and there is evidence that very young infants are capable of intermodal perception as well.

For example, Kelly Kaye and T. G. R. Bower (1994) showed that 1-day-old infants are capable of matching a shape they feel to a shape they can see. They placed one of two pacifiers in the infant's mouth. When the infant began

sucking, a large image of the end of one of the pacifiers appeared on a computer monitor located directly in front of the newborn (Figure 16.22). As long as the infant continued sucking, the image remained on the screen. But pausing for longer than 1 second caused the image of the other, differently shaped, pacifier to appear on the screen. Thus, the infant could determine which image appeared on the screen by the way he or she sucked on the pacifier.

The results of this experiment show that infants controlled their sucking so that in their initial exposures to the images of the pacifiers, 11 of the 12 infants caused the image of the pacifier on which they were sucking to appear on the screen longer than the image of the other pacifier. This means that newborns are capable of sensing the shape of a pacifier in their mouths and can generalize this perception from the tactual to the visual mode.

An example of intermodal perception involving vision and hearing is Patricia Kuhl and Anthony Meltzoff's (1982) experiment in which 4½-month-old infants observed films of two women's faces (Figure 16.23). One woman was repeating the vowel /i/ as in heed and the other was repeating /a/ as in hat. As the infant observed both faces, he or she heard just one of these sounds (either the /i/ or the /a/) from a loudspeaker placed between the two faces, and researchers videotaped the infants to determine where they were looking. $\boxed{V_L}$4

The result of this experiment demonstrated intermodal perception: infants looked at the face of the woman whose lip movements matched the sound they were hearing 74 percent of the time. These infants were therefore able to determine the correspondence between seeing lip movements and hearing speech sounds. (See Patterson & Werker, 1999, for another experiment that reached the same conclusion.)

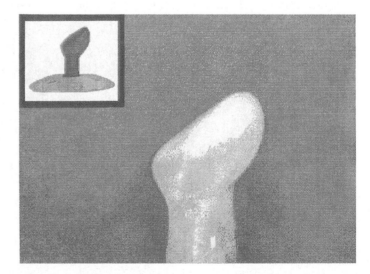

Figure 16.22 ▌ Large image: picture of the end of the pacifier as seen by infants who were looking at a TV monitor. Insert: actual pacifier on which the infant was sucking. See text for details. *(From "Learning and Intermodal Transfer of Information in Newborns," by K. L. Kaye and T. G. R. Bower, 1994, Psychological Science, 5, 286–288.)*

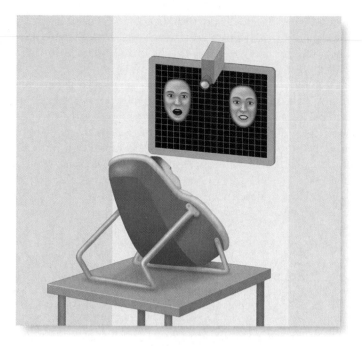

Figure 16.23 ▌ An infant viewing two faces in Kuhl and Meltzoff's (1982) experiment. Infants viewed a film showing the faces of two women, each repeating a different vowel sound. One of the vowel sounds was presented by the loudspeaker, between the faces. The infants' eye movements were videotaped as he or she observed the women's faces. *(Adapted from Kuhl & Meltzoff, 1982.)*

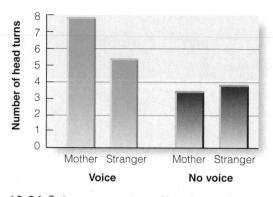

Figure 16.24 ▌ Average number of head turns in the direction of the mother's face or a stranger's face. Left pair of bars: head turns for infants whose mothers talked to them before the experiment. Right pair of bars: head turns for infants whose mothers did not talk to them. *(Adapted from Sai, 2005.)*

Infants first begin to look at faces of people who are speaking shortly after birth, when they first see their mother's face and hear her voice. According to a recent study, this pairing of face and voice may be important for determining the infant's preference for the mother's face that we described earlier in this chapter. F. Z. Sai (2005) showed two 12-hour-old newborns two faces—the mother's and a stranger's. The left pair of bars in Figure 16.24 shows that the newborns turned their heads more toward the mother's face, a finding that replicates previous results showing that newborns look more at their mother than at a stranger.

However, Sai also tested a group of newborns whose mothers did not talk to them or make any other sounds until after the infants were tested. Even though the mothers in the "no talking" group had held their infants and played with them in the same way as had the mothers in the "talking" group, the infants who had not heard their mothers talk showed no preference for the mother's face when given a choice between the mother's face and the stranger's face (right pair of bars in Figure 16.24).

Why would seeing the mother's face paired with hearing her talk facilitate recognition of the mother's face? Sai suggests that because infants are familiar with the mother's voice even before they are born, from listening to it while in the womb (see page 392), when they hear this familiar voice paired with the mother's face, this creates a link between the two and helps the infant recognize the mother's face. Thus, intermodal perception is not only present in newborns, but

it serves an important function of transferring the infant's familiarity with the mother's voice to the mother's face. (It is important to note, however, that although this result shows that hearing the mother's voice helps the newborn recognize her face, this doesn't mean that recognition cannot be achieved by other means. For example, nonhearing infants' recognition of the mother's face would presumably occur from extended visual experiences and perhaps associating seeing the mother with smelling her odor or with other cues.)

Olfaction and Taste

Do newborn infants perceive odors and tastes? Early researchers, noting that a number of olfactory stimuli elicited responses such as body movements and facial expressions from newborns, concluded that newborns can smell (Kroner, 1881, cited in Peterson & Rainey, 1911). However, some of the stimuli used by these early researchers may have irritated the membranes of the infant's nose, so the infants may have been responding to irritation rather than to smell (Beauchamp, Cowart, & Schmidt, 1991; Doty, 1991).

Modern studies using nonirritating stimuli have, however, provided evidence that newborns can smell and can discriminate between different olfactory stimuli. J. E. Steiner (1974, 1979) used nonirritating stimuli to show that infants respond to banana extract or vanilla extract with sucking and facial expressions that are similar to smiles, and that they respond to concentrated shrimp odor and an odor resembling rotten eggs with rejection or disgust (Figure 16.25).

Research investigating infants' reactions to taste has included numerous studies showing that newborns can discriminate sweet, sour, and bitter stimuli (Beauchamp, Cowart, & Schmidt, 1991). For example, newborns react with different facial expressions to sweet, sour, and bitter stimuli but show little or no response to salty stimuli (Figure 16.26; Ganchrow, 1995; Ganchrow et al., 1983; Rosenstein & Oster, 1988).

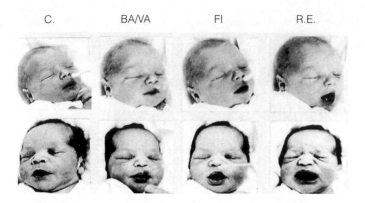

C.   BA/VA   FI   R.E.

Figure 16.25 ▌ The facial expressions of 3- to 8-hour-old infants in response to some food-related odors. In each of the horizontal rows, the reactions of the same infant can be seen to the following stimulation: C = control, odorless cotton swab; BA/VA = artificial solution of banana or vanilla; FI = artificial fish or shrimp odor; R.E. = artificial rotten egg odor. The infants were tested prior to the first breast- or bottle-feeding. *(Photographs courtesy of J. E. Steiner, The Hebrew University, Jerusalem.)*

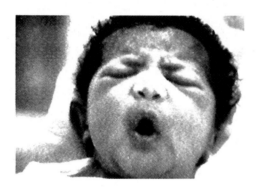

Figure 16.26 ▌ The facial expression of an infant who is less than 10 hours old to a sour taste. Specific facial expressions are also associated with bitter and sweet tastes. *(From Rosenstein, D., & Oster, H. (1988). Differential facial responses to four basic tastes in newborns.* Child Development, 59, *1555–1568.)*

Although responses to taste and olfaction do show some changes as the infant grows into childhood (for example, young infants are indifferent to the taste of salt but develop a response to salty stimuli as they get older; Beauchamp, Bertino, & Engelman, 1991; Beauchamp, Cowart, & Moran, 1986), we could argue that taste and olfaction are the most highly developed of all of the senses at birth.

Something to Consider: The Unity of Perception

It is clear that although newborn perception is not as developed as adult perception, the newborn's perceptual abilities far surpass anything imagined by the early

psychologists. Not only are infants able to perceive at birth, but they also learn quickly as they experience the environment. This learning often takes the form of perceptual systems' becoming tuned to properties of the environment.

We have already described how young infants who can distinguish between a large number of phonemes eventually lose this ability as their hearing becomes tuned to the phonemes of their own language (page 394). Interestingly enough, the same process appears to occur for distinguishing between faces. Olivier Pascalis and coworkers (2002) demonstrated this by using a procedure called paired comparison to determine the ability of infants and adults to recognize human faces and monkey faces.

METHOD ▌ Paired Comparison

One stimulus, such as the face on the left in Figure 16.27a, is presented during a familiarization period. Then during the recognition period, this "familiar" stimulus is presented with a new stimulus that the infant has never seen (so both faces in Figure 16.27a are presented together), and the amount of time the infants look at each stimulus is measured. Because infants tend to look more at novel stimuli, if they do look longer at the new face, this means that they can tell the difference between the two faces. Notice that this procedure combines components of the habituation procedure (showing a stimulus until it becomes familiar) and preferential looking (measuring looking time with two side-by-side stimuli).

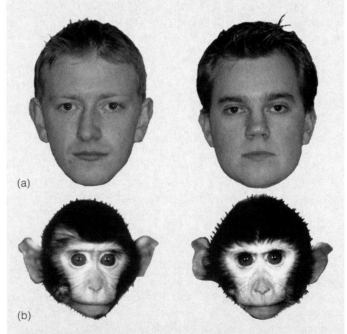

(a)

(b)

Figure 16.27 ▌ Face stimuli presented in the Pascalis et al. (2002) experiment. See text for details. *(From Pascalis, O., de Haan, M., & Nelson, C.A. (2002). Is face processing species-specific during the first year of life?* Science, 296, *1321–1323.)*

Pascalis and coworkers first tested adults using the paired-comparison procedure and measured looking time during a 5-second recognition period. The results, shown in Figure 16.28a, reveal that the adults looked more at the novel stimulus when they were familiarized with a human face and then tested with a pair of human faces (left pair of bars), but they looked equally when they were familiarized with a monkey face and then tested with a pair of monkey faces like the ones in Figure 16.27b (right pair of bars).

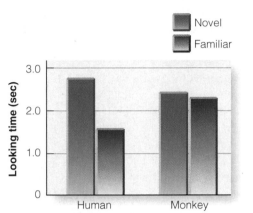

(a) Adults: distinguish between human, but not monkey

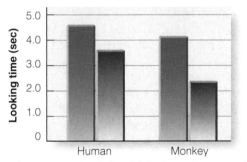

(b) 6-month-olds: distinguish between human and between monkey

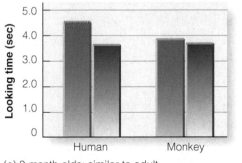

(c) 9-month-olds: similar to adult

Figure 16.28 ▌ Results of the Pascalis et al. (2002) experiment. (a) Amount of time adults looked at the face stimuli when a human face they had seen was presented with one they hadn't seen (left pair of bars), and when a monkey face they had seen was presented with one they hadn't seen (right pair of bars). (b) Amount of time 6-month-old infants looked at the human (left) and monkey (right) faces. (c) Amount of time 9-month-old infants looked at the human (left) and monkey (right) faces.

Thus, adults can distinguish between similar human faces, but not between similar monkey faces.

Figures 16.28b and 16.28c shows the results for 6- and 9-month-old infants who were tested in the same way, using a 10-second recognition period. What is striking about these results is that the 6-month-olds discriminated between both human and monkey faces, but the 9-month-olds discriminated only between the human faces. Because the older infants behaved like the adults, Pascalis concluded that, just as for speech, there is an early period during which infants learn, through experience, to discriminate between stimuli that are important in their environment.

As we saw from our discussion of intermodal perception, it may be possible that speech perception and face perception could become tuned in parallel, as infants watch faces that are producing speech. More research is needed, however, to determine whether this does, in fact, occur.

TEST YOURSELF 16.2

1. How have researchers shown that infants can perceive object unity? What type of information is important for the perception of object unity by young infants?
2. How can an infant's threshold for hearing a tone be determined? How do infants' audibility curves compare to adults'?
3. Describe the experiments that showed that newborns can recognize their mother's voice.
4. How did researchers determine that infants are capable of categorical perception of phonemes?
5. What is the evidence that experience in hearing speech tunes the speech recognition system to become selective to sounds that are used in an infant's native language?
6. What is the evidence for intermodal perception in infants? How might intermodal perception help infants recognize their mother's face?
7. What is the evidence that newborns can perceive odors and tastes?
8. Describe the idea that perception becomes tuned to stimuli in the environment, using examples from perceiving speech and perceiving faces.

THINK ABOUT IT

1. One of the basic principles of perceptual development is that some processes are "built in" or develop with typical experience (for example, visual acuity, stereopsis) and others depend more on learning and specific experiences ("tuning" for language and face perception). What are some examples of both of these kinds of processes in object perception (discussed in Chapter 5), attention (Chapter 6), movement perception (Chapter 8), and perceiving events (Chapter 10)?

2. The "other race effect" refers to the difficulty people have in distinguishing between members of a race different from their own. Social psychologists have done much of the research on this phenomenon because it plays a role in stereotyping—assigning the same characteristics to all members of a group. Describe how the other race effect relates to (a) your own experience and (b) developmental processes we have discussed in this chapter. (p. 396)

3. What types of perceptual experiences are possible before birth? Consider smell, taste, touch, hearing, and vision. (p. 387)

4. Although measurements of visual acuity indicate that newborns and very young infants see details poorly (page xxx), other research shows that young infants can recognize faces. What are some possible explanations for this apparent contradiction? (p. 387)

IF YOU WANT TO KNOW MORE

1. *Perceptual segregation.* When you see a coffee cup on a table, you perceive two different objects—the coffee cup and the table. A number of experiments have been done to determine when and under what conditions this ability appears in infants.

   Needham, A., & Ormsbee, S. M. (2003). The development of object segregation during the first year of life. In R. Kimchi, M. Behrmann, & C. Olson (Eds.), *Perceptual organization in vision: Behavioral and neural perspectives* (pp. 205–232). Mahwah, NJ: Erlbaum.

   Spelke, E. S., Gutheil, G., & Van de Walle, G. (1995). The development of object perception. In S. M. Kosslyn & D. N. Osherson (Eds.), *Visual cognition* (pp. 297–330). Cambridge, MA: MIT Press.

   Wilcox, T., Schweinle, A., & Chapa, C. (2003). Object individuation in infancy. In F. Fagan & H. Hayne (Eds.), *Progress in infancy research* (Vol. 3, pp. 193–243). Mahwah, NJ: Erlbaum.

2. *Perceptual organization.* Infants can separate figure from ground and group elements into wholes.

   Craton, L. G., & Yonas, A. (1990). The role of motion in infants' perception of occlusion. In J. T. Enns (Ed.), *The development of attention: Research and theory* (pp. 21–46). London: Elsevier.

   Quinn, P. C., Burke, S., & Rush, A. (1993). Part-whole perception in early infancy: Evidence for perceptual grouping produced by lightness similarity. *Infant Behavior and Development, 16,* 19–42.

3. *Preference for attractive faces.* Infants' preference for attractive faces suggests that we can't explain "attractiveness" just as something we learn from exposure to the media. (p. 387)

   Ramsey, J. L., Langlois, J. H., Hoss, R. A., Rubenstein, A. J., & Griffin, A. M. (2004). Origins of a stereotype: Categorization of facial attributes by 6-month-old infants. *Developmental Science, 7,* 201–211.

   Quinn, P. C., Kelly, D. J., Lee, K., Pascalis, O., & Slater, A. M. (2008). Preference for attractive faces in human infants extends beyond conspecifics. *Developmental Science, 11,* 76–83.

4. *Perceiving movement.* Infants can perceive movement at birth and develop the ability to perceive biological movement later. (p. 178)

   Bertenthal, B. I., Proffitt, D. R., Spetner, N. B., & Thomas, M. A. (1985). The development of infant sensitivity to biomechanical motions. *Child Development, 56,* 531–543.

   Fox, R., & McDaniel, C. (1982). The perception of biological motion by human infants. *Science, 218,* 486–487.

   Nelson, C. A., & Horowitz, F. D. (1987). Visual motion perception in infancy: A review and synthesis. In P. Salapatek & L. Cohen (Eds.), *Handbook of infant perception* (Vol. 2, pp. 123–153). New York: Academic Press.

5. *Development of myopia.* Myopia, or nearsightedness, affects 25 percent of adults in the United States. There is evidence linking this condition both to genetic factors (it "runs in families") and to a person's experiences. (p. 46)

   Gwiazda, J., Thorn, F., Bauer, J., & Held, R. (1993). Emmetropization and the progression of manifest refraction in children followed from infancy to puberty. *Clinical Visual Science, 8,* 337–344.

   Mutti, D. O., Zadnik, K., & Adams, A. J. (1996). Myopia: The nature versus nurture debate goes on. *Investigative Ophthalmology and Visual Science, 37,* 952–957.

   Zylbermann, R., Landau, D., & Berson, D. (1993). The influence of study habits on myopia in Jewish teenagers. *Journal of Pediatric Ophthalmology and Strabismus, 30,* 319–322.

6. *Perceiving words in speech.* Young infants can tell the difference between sentences in their native language and sentences in a foreign language. However, they can't do this when cues for separating individual words are eliminated by playing the sentences backward. (p. 54)

   Dehaene-Lambertz, G., Dehanene, S., & Hertz-Pannier, L. (2002). Functional neuroimaging of speech perception in primates. *Science, 298,* 2013–2015.

   Ramus, F., Hauser, M. D., Miller, C., Morris, D., & Mehler, J. (2000). Language discrimination by human newborns and cotton-top tamarin monkeys. *Science, 288,* 349–351.

7. *Recognizing the odor of the mother's breast.* Just as infants can recognize their mother visually, they can also recognize her by smell.

Balogh, R. D., & Porter, R. H. (1986). Olfactory preferences resulting from mere exposure in human neonates. *Infant Behavior and Development, 9,* 395–401.

Macfarlane, A. (1975). Olfaction in the development of social preferences in the human neonate. In A. Macfarlane (Ed.), *Ciba Foundation Symposium, 33,* 103–117.

Porter, R. H., & Schaal, B. (1995). Olfaction and development of social preferences in neonatal organisms. In R. L. Doty (Ed.), *Handbook of olfaction and gustation* (pp. 299–321). New York: Marcel Dekker.

8. *Perception and reasoning about the physical world.* Infants show "surprise" reactions when an environmentally unlikely event happens, such as when a figure moves behind one object and then emerges from behind another at a different location. This research looks at the links between perception, reasoning, and the knowledge infants have gained by their interactions with the environment. (p. 115)

Baillargeon, R. (2004). Infants' physical world. *Current Directions in Psychological Science, 13,* 89–94.

Wilcox, T., & Schweinle, A. (2002). Object individuation and event mapping: Developmental changes in infants' use of featural information. *Developmental Science, 5,* 132–150.

KEY TERMS

Binocularly fixate (p. 386)
Contrast sensitivity (p. 383)
Contrast sensitivity function (CSF) (p. 383)
Dishabituation (p. 385)

Habituation (p. 385)
Intermodal perception (p. 394)
Paired comparison (p. 396)
Preferential looking (PL) technique (p. 380)

Spatial frequency (p. 383)
Visual evoked potential (VEP) (p. 381)

MEDIA RESOURCES

The *Sensation and Perception* Book Companion Website

www.cengage.com/psychology/goldstein

See the companion website for flashcards, practice quiz questions, Internet links, updates, critical thinking exercises, discussion forums, games, and more!

CengageNow

www.cengage.com/cengagenow

Go to this site for the link to CengageNOW, your one-stop shop. Take a pre-test for this chapter, and CengageNOW will generate a personalized study plan based on your test results. The study plan will identify the topics you need to review and direct you to online resources to help you master those topics. You can then take a post-test to help you determine the concepts you have mastered and what you will still need to work on.

Virtual Lab

Your Virtual Lab is designed to help you get the most out of this course. The Virtual Lab icons direct you to specific media demonstrations and experiments designed to help you visualize what you are reading about. The number beside each icon indicates the number of the media element you can access through your CD-ROM, CengageNOW, or WebTutor resource.

The following lab exercises are related to the material in this chapter.

1. *Preferential Looking Procedure* A child moving his eyes between two stimuli. (Courtesy of George Hollich.)

2. *Rod Moving Behind Occluder* The stimulus used to habituate infants to a rod moving back and forth behind a block. (Courtesy of Scott Johnson.)

3. *Eye Movements Following Moving Ball* How 4- and 6-month-old infants follow a moving object that disappears behind an occluder and then reappears. (Courtesy of Scott Johnson.)

4. *Testing Intermodal Perception in Infants* Stimulus and testing procedure similar to that used in the Kuhl and Meltzoff experiment. (Courtesy of George Hollich.)

Signal Detection Theory

At the end of Chapter 1, we described a hypothetical experiment in which two subjects, Regina and Julie, were tested to determine their threshold for detecting a light (Figure 1.17). We saw that the threshold, determined by methods like constant stimuli, can depend on whether the subject is a conservative responder like Regina, who says "yes, I see the light" only if she is very sure she sees the light, or a liberal responder like Julie, who says "yes" any time she thinks the light might possibly have been presented. The difference between these two ways of responding, called a difference in *response criterion*, would cause Julie's threshold to appear to be lower than Regina's, even though the difference could actually be caused by the difference in their response criteria. A technique based on a theory called *signal detection theory* has been used to deal with this problem.

In the next section, we will describe the basic procedure of a signal detection experiment that involves detecting tones and will show how we can tell whether Regina and Julie are, in fact, equally sensitive to the tones even though their response criteria are very different. After describing the signal detection experiment, we will look at the theory on which the experiment is based.

A Signal Detection Experiment

Remember that in a psychophysical procedure such as the method of constant stimuli, at least five different stimulus intensities are presented and a stimulus is presented on every trial. In a signal detection experiment studying the detection of tones, we use only a single low-intensity tone that is difficult to hear, and we present this tone on some of the trials and present no tone at all on the rest of the trials. Thus, a signal detection experiment differs from a classical psychophysical experiment in two ways: in a signal detection experiment, (1) only one stimulus intensity is presented, and (2) on some of the trials, no stimulus is presented. Let's

consider the results of such an experiment, using Julie as our participant. We present the tone for 100 trials and no tone for 100 trials, mixing the tone and no-tone trials at random. Julie's results are as follows:

When the tone is presented, Julie

- Says "yes" on 90 trials. This correct response—saying "yes" when a stimulus is present—is called a **hit** in signal detection terminology.

- Says "no" on 10 trials. This incorrect response—saying "no" when a stimulus is present—is called a **miss**.

When no tone is presented, Julie

- Says "yes" on 40 trials. This incorrect response—saying "yes" when there is no stimulus—is called a **false alarm**.

- Says "no" on 60 trials. This correct response—saying "no" when there is no stimulus—is called a **correct rejection**.

These results are not very surprising, given that we know Julie has a low criterion and likes to say "yes" a lot. This gives her a high hit rate of 90 percent but also causes her to say "yes" on many trials when no tone is present at all, so her 90 percent hit rate is accompanied by a 40 percent false-alarm rate. If we do a similar experiment on Regina, who has a higher criterion and therefore says "yes" much less often, we find that she has a lower hit rate (say, 60 percent) but also a lower false-alarm rate (say, 10 percent). Note that although Julie and Regina say "yes" on numerous trials on which no stimulus is presented, that result would not be predicted by classical threshold theory. Classical theory would say "no stimulus, no response," but that is clearly not the case here. By adding a new wrinkle to our signal detection experiment, we can obtain another result that would not be predicted by classical threshold theory.

Without changing the tone's intensity at all, we can cause Julie and Regina to change their percentages of hits and false alarms. We do this by manipulating each person's motivation by means of **payoffs**. Let's look at how payoffs might influence Regina's responding. Remember that Regina is a conservative responder who is hesitant to say "yes." But being clever experimenters, we can make Regina say "yes'" more frequently by adding some financial inducements to the experiment. We tell Regina that we are going to reward her for making correct responses and are going to penalize her for making incorrect responses by using the following payoffs:

Hit:	Win $100
Correct rejection:	Win $10
False alarm:	Lose $10
Miss:	Lose $10

What would you do if you were in Regina's position? Being smart, you analyze the payoffs and realize that the way to make money is to say "yes" more. You can lose $10 if a "yes" response results in a false alarm, but this small loss is more than counterbalanced by the $100 you can win for a hit. Although you decide not to say "yes" on every trial—after all, you want to be honest with the experimenter about whether or not you heard the tone—you do decide to stop being so conservative. You decide to change your criterion for saying "yes." The results of this experiment are interesting. Regina becomes a more liberal responder and says "yes" a lot more, responding with 98 percent hits and 90 percent false alarms.

This result is plotted as data point L (for "liberal" response) in Figure A.1, a plot of the percentage of hits versus the percentage of false alarms. The solid curve going through point L is called a **receiver operating characteristic (ROC) curve**. We will see why the ROC curve is important in a moment, but first let's see how we determine the other points on the curve. Doing this is simple: all we have to do is to change the payoffs. We can make Regina raise her criterion and therefore respond more conservatively by means of the following payoffs:

Hit:	Win $10
Correct rejection:	Win $100
False alarm:	Lose $10
Miss:	Lose $10

This schedule of payoffs offers a great inducement to respond conservatively because there is a big reward for saying "no" when no tone is presented. Regina's criterion is therefore shifted to a much higher level, so Regina now returns to her conservative ways and says "yes" only when she is quite certain that a tone is presented; otherwise she says "no." The result of this newfound conservatism is a hit rate of only 10 percent and a minuscule false-alarm rate of 1 percent, indicated by point C (for "conservative" response) on the

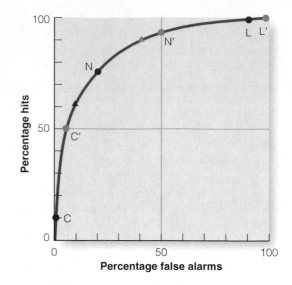

Figure A.1 ▌ A receiver operating characteristic (ROC) curve determined by testing Julie (green data points) and Regina (red data points) under three different criteria: Liberal (L and L′), neutral (N and N′) and conservative (C and C′). The fact that Regina's and Julie's data points all fall on this curve means that they have the same sensitivity to the tone. The triangles indicate the results for Julie and Regina for an experiment that did not use payoffs.

ROC curve. We should note that although Regina hits on only 10 percent of the trials in which a tone is presented, she scores a phenomenal 99 percent correct rejections on trials in which a tone is not presented. (This result follows from the fact that, if there are 100 trials in which no tone is presented, then correct rejections + false alarms = 100. Because there was one false alarm, there must be 99 correct rejections.)

Regina, by this time, is rich and decides to put a down payment on the Miata she's been dreaming about. (So far she's won $8,980 in the first experiment and $9,090 in the second experiment, for a total of $18,070! To be sure you understand how the payoff system works, check this calculation yourself. Remember that the signal was presented on 100 trials and was not presented on 100 trials.) However, we point out that she may need a little extra cash to have a satellite audio system installed in her car, so she agrees to stick around for one more experiment. We now use the following neutral schedule of payoffs:

Hit:	Win $10
Correct rejection:	Win $10
False alarm:	Lose $10
Miss:	Lose $10

With this schedule, we obtain point N (for "neutral") on the ROC curve: 75 percent hits and 20 percent false alarms. Regina wins $1,100 more and becomes the proud owner of a Miata with a satellite radio system, and we are the proud owners of the world's most expensive ROC curve.

(Do not, at this point, go to the psychology department in search of the nearest signal detection experiment. In real life, the payoffs are quite a bit less than in our hypothetical example.)

Regina's ROC curve shows that factors other than sensitivity to the stimulus determine a person's response. Remember that in all of our experiments the intensity of the tone has remained constant. Even though we changed only the person's criterion, we succeeded in drastically changing the person's responses.

Other than demonstrating that people will change how they respond to an unchanging stimulus, what does the ROC curve tell us? Remember, at the beginning of this discussion, we said that a signal detection experiment can tell us whether or not Regina and Julie are equally sensitive to the tone. The beauty of signal detection theory is that the person's sensitivity is indicated by the shape of the ROC curve, so if experiments on two people result in identical ROC curves, their sensitivities must be equal. (This conclusion is not obvious from our discussion so far. We will explain below why the shape of the ROC curve is related to the person's sensitivity.) If we repeat the above experiments on Julie, we get the following results (data points L', N', and C' in Figure A.1):

Liberal payoff:
Hits = 99 percent
False alarms = 95 percent

Neutral payoff:
Hits = 92 percent
False alarms = 50 percent

Conservative payoff:
Hits = 50 percent
False alarms = 6 percent

The data points for Julie's results are shown by the green circles in Figure A.1. Note that although these points are different from Regina's, they fall on the same ROC curve as do Regina's. We have also plotted the data points for the first experiments we did on Julie (open triangle) and Regina (filled triangle) before we introduced payoffs. These points also fall on the ROC curve.

That Regina's and Julie's data both fall on the same ROC curve indicates their equal sensitivity to the tones. This confirms our suspicion that the method of constant stimuli misled us into thinking that Julie is more sensitive, when the real reason for her apparently greater sensitivity is her lower criterion for saying "yes."

Before we leave our signal detection experiment, it is important to note that signal detection procedures can be used without the elaborate payoffs that we described for Regina and Julie. Much briefer procedures, which we will describe shortly, can be used to determine whether differences in the responses of different persons are due to differences in threshold or to differences in response criteria.

What does signal detection theory tell us about functions such as the spectral sensitivity curve (Figure 3.21) and the audibility function (Figure 11.9), which are usually determined using one of the classical psychophysical methods? When the classical methods are used to determine these functions, it is usually assumed that the person's criterion remains constant throughout the experiment, so that the function measured is due not to changes in response criterion but to changes in the wavelength or some other physical property of the stimulus. This is a good assumption because changing the wavelength of the stimulus probably has little or no effect on factors such as motivation, which would shift the person's criterion. Furthermore, experiments such as the one for determining the spectral sensitivity curve usually use highly experienced people who are trained to give stable results. Thus, even though the idea of an "absolute threshold" may not be strictly correct, classical psychophysical experiments run under well-controlled conditions have remained an important tool for measuring the relationship between stimuli and perception.

Signal Detection Theory

We will now discuss the theoretical basis for the signal detection experiments we have just described. Our purpose is to explain the theoretical bases underlying two ideas: (1) the percentage of hits and false alarms depends on a person's criterion, and (2) a person's sensitivity to a stimulus is indicated by the shape of the person's ROC curve. We will begin by describing two of the key concepts of signal detection theory (SDT): signal and noise. (See Swets, 1964.)

Signal and Noise

The signal is the stimulus presented to the person. Thus, in the signal detection experiment we just described, the signal is the tone. The noise is all the other stimuli in the environment, and because the signal is usually very faint, noise can sometimes be mistaken for the signal. Seeing what appears to be a flicker of light in a completely dark room is an example of visual noise. Seeing light where there is none is what we have been calling a false alarm, according to signal detection theory. False alarms are caused by the noise. In the experiment we just described, hearing a tone on a trial in which no tone was presented is an example of auditory noise.

Let's now consider a typical signal detection experiment, in which a signal is presented on some trials and no signal is presented on the other trials. Signal detection theory describes this procedure not in terms of presenting a signal or no signal, but in terms of presenting signal plus noise (S + N) or noise (N). That is, the noise is always present, and on some trials, we add a signal. Either condition can result in the perceptual effect of hearing a tone. A false alarm occurs when the person says "yes" on a noise trial, and a hit occurs when the person says "yes" on a signal-plus-noise trial. Now that we have defined signal and noise, we introduce the idea of probability distributions for noise and signal plus noise.

Probability Distributions

Figure A.2 shows two probability distributions. The one on the left represents the probability that a given perceptual effect will be caused by noise (N), and the one on the right represents the probability that a given perceptual effect will be caused by signal plus noise (S + N). The key to understanding these distributions is to realize that the value labeled "Perceptual effect (loudness)" on the horizontal axis is what the person experiences on each trial. Thus, in an experiment in which the person is asked to indicate whether or not a tone is present, the perceptual effect is the perceived loudness of the tone. Remember that in an SDT experiment the tone always has the same *intensity*. The *loudness* of the tone, however, can vary from trial to trial. The person perceives different loudnesses on different trials, because of either trial-to-trial changes in attention or changes in the state of the person's auditory system.

The probability distributions tell us what the chances are that a given loudness of tone is due to (N) or to (S + N). For example, let's assume that a person hears a tone with a loudness of 10 on one of the trials of a signal detection experiment. By extending a vertical dashed line up from 10 on the "Perceptual effect" axis in Figure A.2, we see that the probability that a loudness of 10 is due to (S + N) is extremely low, because the distribution for (S + N) is essentially zero at this loudness. There is, however, a fairly high probability that a loudness of 10 is due to (N), because the (N) distribution is fairly high at this point.

Let's now assume that, on another trial, the person perceives a loudness of 20. The probability distributions indicate that when the tone's loudness is 20, it is equally probable that this loudness is due to (N) or to (S + N). We can also see from Figure A.2 that a tone with a perceived loudness of 30 would have a high probability of being caused by (S + N) and only a small probability of being caused by (N).

Now that we understand the curves of Figure A.2, we can appreciate the problem confronting the person. On each trial, she has to decide whether no tone (N) was present or whether a tone (S + N) was present. However, the overlap in the probability distributions for (N) and (S + N) means that for some perceptual effects this judgment will be difficult. As we saw before, it is equally probable that a tone with a loudness of 20 is due to (N) or to (S + N). So, on a trial in which the person hears a tone with a loudness of 20, how does she decide whether or not the signal was presented? According to signal detection theory, the person's decision depends on the location of her criterion.

The Criterion

We can see how the criterion affects the person's response by looking at Figure A.3. In this figure, we have labeled three different criteria: liberal (L), neutral (N), and conservative (C). Remember that we can cause people to adopt these different criteria by means of different payoffs. According to signal detection theory, once the person adopts a criterion, he or she uses the following rule to decide how to respond on a given trial: If the perceptual effect is greater than (to the right of) the criterion, say, "Yes, the tone was present"; if the perceptual effect is less than (to the left of) the criterion, say, "No, the tone was not present." Let's consider how different criteria influence the person's hits and false alarms.

To determine how the criterion affects the person's hits and false alarms, we will consider what happens when we present (N) and when we present (S + N) under three different criteria.

Liberal Criterion

1. Present (N): Because most of the probability distribution for (N) falls to the right of the criterion, the chances are good that presenting (N) will result in a loudness to the right of the criterion. This means that the probability of saying "yes" when (N) is presented is high; therefore, the probability of a false alarm is high.

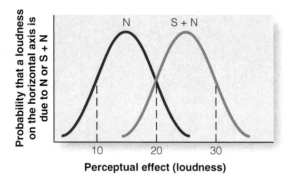

Figure A.2 ▌ Probability distributions for noise alone (N, red curve), and for signal plus noise (S + N, green curve). The probability that any given perceptual effect is caused by the noise (no signal is presented) or by the signal plus noise (signal is presented) can be determined by finding the value of the perceptual effect on the horizontal axis and extending a vertical line up from that value. The place where that line intersects the (N) and (S + N) distributions indicates the probability that the perceptual effect was caused by (N) or by (S + N).

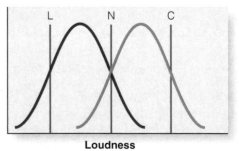

Figure A.3 ▌ The same probability distributions from Figure A.2, showing three criteria: liberal (L), neutral (N), and conservative (C). When a person adopts a criterion, he or she uses the following decision rule: Respond "yes" ("I detect the stimulus") when the perceptual effect is greater than the criterion, and respond "no" ("I do not detect the stimulus") when the perceptual effect is less than the criterion.

2. Present (S + N): Because the entire probability distribution for (S + N) falls to the right of the criterion, the chances are excellent that presenting (S + N) will result in a loudness to the right of the criterion. Thus, the probability of saying "yes" when the signal is presented is high; therefore, the probability of a hit is high. Because criterion L results in high false alarms and high hits, adopting that criterion will result in point L on the ROC curve in Figure A.4.

Neutral Criterion
1. Present (N): The person will answer "yes" only rarely when (N) is presented because only a small portion of the (N) distribution falls to the right of the criterion. The false-alarm rate, therefore, will be fairly low.

2. Present (S + N): The person will answer "yes" frequently when (S + N) is presented because most of the (S + N) distribution falls to the right of the criterion. The hit rate, therefore, will be fairly high (but not as high as for the L criterion). Criterion N results in point N on the ROC curve in Figure A.4.

Conservative Criterion
1. Present (N): False alarms will be very low because none of the (N) curve falls to the right of the criterion.

2. Present (S + N): Hits will also be low because only a small portion of the (S + N) curve falls to the right of the criterion. Criterion C results in point C on the ROC curve in Figure A.4.

You can see that applying different criteria to the probability distributions generates the solid ROC curve in Figure A.4. But why are these probability distributions necessary? After all, when we described the experiment with Regina and Julie, we determined the ROC curve simply by plotting the results of the experiment. The reason the (N) and (S + N) distributions are important is that, according to signal detection theory, the person's sensitivity to a stimulus is indicated by the distance (d′) between the peaks of the (N) and (S + N) distributions, and this distance affects the shape of the ROC curve. We will now consider how the person's sensitivity to a stimulus affects the shape of the ROC curve.

The Effect of Sensitivity on the ROC Curve

We can understand how the person's sensitivity to a stimulus affects the shape of the ROC curve by considering what the probability distributions would look like for Jamie Lynn, a person with supersensitive hearing. Jamie Lynn's hearing is so good that a tone barely audible to Regina sounds very loud to Jamie Lynn. If presenting (S + N) causes Jamie Lynn to hear a loud tone, this means that her (S + N) distribution should be far to the right, as shown in Figure A.5. In signal detection terms, we would say that Jamie Lynn's high sensitivity is indicated by the large separation (d′) between the (N) and the (S + N) probability distributions. To see how this greater separation between the probability distributions will affect her ROC curve, let's see how she would respond when adopting liberal, neutral, and conservative criteria.

Liberal Criterion
1. Present (N): high false alarms.

2. Present (S + N): high hits.

The liberal criterion, therefore, results in point L′ on the ROC curve of Figure A.4.

Neutral Criterion
1. Present (N): low false alarms. It is important to note that Jamie Lynn's false alarms for the neutral criterion will be lower than Regina's false alarms for the neutral criterion because only a very small

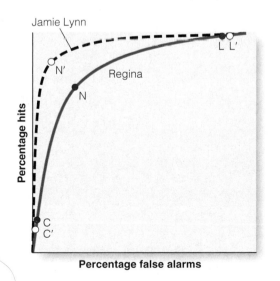

Figure A.4 ❚ ROC curves for Regina (solid curve) and Jamie Lynn (dashed curve) determined using liberal (L, L′), neutral (N, N′) and conservative (C, C′) criteria.

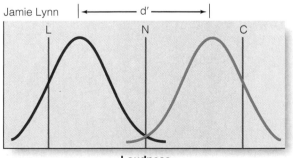

Figure A.5 ❚ Probability distributions for Jamie Lynn, a person who is extremely sensitive to the signal. The noise distribution (red) remains the same, but the (S + N) distribution (green) is shifted to the right compared to the curves in Figure A.4. Liberal (L), neutral (N) and conservative (C) criteria are shown.

portion of Jamie Lynn's (N) distribution falls to the right of the criterion, whereas more of Regina's (N) distribution falls to the right of the neutral criterion (Figure A.3).

2. Present (S + N): high hits. In this case, Jamie Lynn's hits will be higher than Regina's because almost all of Jamie Lynn's (S + N) distribution falls to the right of the neutral criterion, whereas less of Regina's does (Figure A.3). The neutral criterion, therefore, results in point N′ on the ROC curve in Figure A.4.

Conservative Criterion

1. Present (N): low false alarms.

2. Present (S + N): low hits. The conservative criterion, therefore, results in point C′ on the ROC curve.

The difference between the two ROC curves in Figure A.4 is obvious because Jamie Lynn's curve is more "bowed." But before you conclude that the difference between these two ROC curves has anything to do with where we positioned Jamie Lynn's L, N, and C criteria, see whether you can get an ROC curve like Jamie Lynn's from the two probability distributions of Figure A.3. You will find that, no matter where you position the criteria, there is no way that you can get a point like point N′ (with very high hits and very low false alarms) from the curves of Figure A.3. In order to achieve very high hits and very low false alarms, the two probability distributions must be spaced far apart, as in Figure A.5.

Thus, increasing the distance (d′) between the (N) and the (S + N) probability distributions changes the shape of the ROC curve. When the person's sensitivity (d′) is high, the ROC curve is more bowed. In practice, d′ can be determined by comparing the experimentally determined ROC curve to standard ROC curves (see Gescheider, 1976), or d′ can be calculated from the proportions of hits and false alarms that occur in an experiment by means of a mathematical procedure we will not discuss here. This mathematical procedure for calculating d′ enables us to determine a person's sensitivity by determining only one data point on an ROC curve, thus using the signal detection procedure without running a large number of trials.

Glossary

The number in parentheses at the end of each entry indicates the chapter in which the term is first used.

Ablation Removal of an area of the brain. This is usually done in experiments on animals, to determine the function of a particular area. Also called lesioning. (4)

Absolute disparity See **Angle of disparity**. (10)

Absolute threshold See **Threshold, absolute**. (1)

Absorption spectrum A plot of the amount of light absorbed by a visual pigment versus the wavelength of light. (3)

Accidental viewpoint A viewpoint relative to an object that results in perception of an accidental (or rarely encountered) property of the object. For example, although three sides of a solid cube are visible from most viewpoints, an accidental property—seeing only one side of the cube—occurs when the cube is seen from the accidental viewpoint of an end-on view. This concept is associated with the recognition-by-components theory of object perception. (5)

Accommodation (focus) In vision, bringing objects located at different distances into focus by changing the shape of the lens. (3)

Accretion A cue that provides information about the relative depth of two surfaces. Occurs when the farther object is uncovered by the nearer object due to sideways movement of an observer relative to the objects. See also **Deletion**. (10)

Achromatic color Color without hue. White, black, and all the grays between these two extremes are achromatic colors. (9)

Acoustic shadow The shadow created by the head that decreases the level of high-frequency sounds on the opposite side of the head. The acoustic shadow is the basis of the localization cue of interaural level difference. (12)

Acoustic signal The pattern of frequencies and intensities of the sound stimulus. (13)

Acoustic stimulus See **Acoustic signal**. (13)

Across-fiber patterns The pattern of firing that a stimulus causes across a number of neurons. This is the same thing as distributed coding. (15)

Action Motor activities such as moving the head or eyes and locomoting through the environment. Action is one of the major outcomes of the perceptual process. (1)

Action pathway See **Dorsal pathway**. (4)

Action potential Rapid increase in positive charge in a nerve fiber that travels down the fiber. Also called the nerve impulse. (2)

Active touch Touch in which the observer plays an active role in touching and exploring an object, usually with his or her hands. (14)

Additive color mixture See **Color mixture, additive**. (9)

Additive synthesis In hearing, the process of building a complex tone by starting with the fundamental frequency and adding pure tone harmonics. (11)

Adjustment, method of A psychophysical method in which the experimenter or the observer adjusts the stimulus intensity in a continuous manner until the observer detects the stimulus. (1)

Affective (emotional) component of pain The emotional experience associated with pain—for example, pain described as *torturing, annoying, frightful,* or *sickening.* See also **Sensory component of pain**. (14)

Affordance The information specified by a stimulus pattern that indicates how the stimulus can be used. An example of an affordance would be seeing a chair as something to sit on or a flight of stairs as something to climb. (7)

Agnosia See **Visual form agnosia**. (1)

Algorithm A procedure that is guaranteed to result in the solution to a problem. For example, the procedures we learn for addition, subtraction, and long division are algorithms. (5)

Amacrine cell A neuron that transmits signals laterally in the retina. Amacrine cells synapse with bipolar cells and ganglion cells. (3)

Ames room A distorted room, first built by Adelbert Ames, that creates an erroneous perception of the sizes of people in the room. The room is constructed so that two people at the far wall of the room appear to stand at the same distance from an observer. In actuality, one of the people is much farther away than the other. (10)

Amiloride A substance that blocks the flow of sodium into taste receptors. (15)

Amplitude In the case of a repeating sound wave, such as the sine wave of a pure tone, amplitude represents the pressure difference between atmospheric pressure and the maximum pressure of the wave. (11)

Amygdala A subcortical structure that is involved in emotional responding and in processing olfactory signals. (15)

Angle of disparity The visual angle between the images of an object on the two retinas. When images of an object fall on corresponding points, the angle of disparity is zero. When images fall on noncorresponding points, the angle of disparity indicates the degree of noncorrespondence. (10)

Angular size contrast theory An explanation of the moon illusion that states that the perceived size of the moon is determined by the sizes of the objects that surround it. According to this idea, the moon appears small when it is surrounded by large objects, such as the expanse of the sky when the moon is overhead. (10)

Anomalous trichromat A person who needs to mix a minimum of three wavelengths to match any other wavelength in the spectrum but mixes these wavelengths in different proportions from a trichromat. (9)

Anosmia Loss of the ability to smell due to injury or infection. (15)

Aperture problem A situation in which only a portion of a moving stimulus can be seen, as when the stimulus is viewed through a narrow aperture. This results in misleading information about the direction in which the stimulus is moving. (8)

Apex of the cochlea The end of the basilar membrane farthest from the middle ear. (11)

Aphasia Difficulties in speaking or understanding speech due to brain damage. (13)

Apparent distance theory An explanation of the moon illusion that is based on the idea that the horizon moon, which is viewed across the filled space of the terrain, should appear farther away than the zenith moon, which is viewed through the empty space of the sky. This theory states that because the horizon and zenith moons have the same visual angle, the farther appearing horizon moon should appear larger. (10)

Apparent motion See **Apparent movement**. (8)

Apparent movement An illusion of movement that occurs between two objects separated in space when the objects are flashed rapidly on and off, one after another, separated by a brief time interval. (5)

Architectural acoustics The study of how sounds are reflected in rooms. An important concern of architectural acoustics is how these reflected sounds change the quality of the sounds we hear. (12)

Articulator Structure involved in speech production, such as the tongue, lips, teeth, jaw, and soft palate. (13)

Atmospheric perspective. A depth cue. Objects that are farther away look more blurred and bluer than objects that are closer because we must look through more air and particles to see them. (10)

Attack The buildup of sound at the beginning of a tone. (11)

Attended stimulus The stimulus that a person is attending to at a given point in time. (1)

Attention The process of seeking out and focusing on stimuli that are of interest in a way that causes these stimuli to become more deeply processed than those that are not receiving our attention. (6)

Attentional capture The ability of motion to attract attention. (8)

Audibility curve A curve that indicates the sound pressure level (SPL) at threshold for frequencies across the audible spectrum. (11)

Audiovisual mirror neuron Neuron that responds to actions that produce sounds. These neurons respond when a monkey performs a hand action *and* when it hears the sound associated with this action. See also **Mirror neuron**. (7)

Audiovisual speech perception A perception of speech that is affected by both auditory and visual stimulation, as when a person sees a tape of someone saying /ga/ with the sound /ba/ substituted and perceives /da/. Also called the McGurk effect. (13)

Auditory canal The canal through which air vibrations travel from the environment to the tympanic membrane. (11)

Auditory grouping, principles of Principles such as similarity and good continuation that operate to group sounds into perceptual streams. See also **Auditory stream segregation**; **Auditory scene analysis**. (12)

Auditory localization The perception of the location of a sound source. (12)

Auditory masking See **Masking, auditory**. (11)

Auditory receiving area (A1) The area of the cortex, located in the temporal lobe, that is the primary receiving area for hearing. (11)

Auditory response area The psychophysically measured area that defines the frequencies and sound pressure levels over which hearing functions. This area extends between the audibility curve and the curve for the threshold of feeling. (11)

Auditory scene The sound environment, which includes the locations and qualities of individual sound sources. (12)

Auditory scene analysis The process by which listeners sort superimposed vibrations into separate sounds. See also **Auditory grouping, principles of**. (12)

Auditory space Perception of where sounds are located in space. Auditory space extends around a listener's head in all directions, existing wherever there is a sound. (12)

Auditory stream segregation The effect that occurs when a series of tones that differ in pitch or timbre are played so that the tones become perceptually separated into simultaneously occurring independent streams of sound. (12)

Autism A serious developmental disorder in which one of the major symptoms is the withdrawal of contact from other people. People with autism typically do not make eye contact with others and have difficulty telling what emotions others are experiencing in social situations. (6)

Axial myopia Myopia (nearsightedness) in which the eyeball is too long. See also **Refractive myopia**. (3)

Axon The part of the neuron that conducts nerve impulses over distances. Also called the nerve fiber. (2)

Azimuth coordinate In hearing, specifies locations that vary from left to right relative to the listener. (12)

Balint's syndrome A condition resulting from damage to a person's parietal lobe. One characteristic of this syndrome is an inability to focus attention on individual objects. (6)

Base of the cochlea The part of the basilar membrane nearest the middle ear. (11)

Basilar membrane A membrane that stretches the length of the cochlea and controls the vibration of the cochlear partition. (11)

Belongingness The hypothesis that an area's appearance is influenced by the part of the surroundings that the area appears to belong to. This principle has been used to explain the perception of lightness in the Benary cross and White's illusion. (3)

Belt area Auditory area in the temporal lobe that receives signals from the core area and sends signals to the parabelt area. (11)

Bimodal neuron A neuron that responds to stimuli associated with more than one sense. (15)

Binaural cue Sound localization cue that involves both ears. (12)

Binding The process by which features such as color, form, motion, and location are combined to create our perception of a coherent object. (6)

Binding problem The problem of how neural activity in many separated areas in the brain is combined to create a perception of a coherent object. (6)

Binocular depth cell A neuron in the visual cortex that responds best to stimuli that fall on points separated by a specific degree of disparity on the two retinas. Also called a disparity-selective cell. (10)

Binocular disparity Occurs when the retinal images of an object fall on disparate points on the two retinas. (10)

Binocular rivalry A situation in which two different images are presented simultaneously to the left and right eyes and perception alternates back and forth between the two images. (4)

Binocularly fixate Directing the two foveas to exactly the same spot. (16)

Biological motion Motion produced by biological organisms. Most of the experiments on biological motion have used walking humans with lights attached to their joints and limbs as stimuli. See also **Point-light walker**. (8)

Bipolar cell A retinal neuron that receives inputs from the visual receptors and sends signals to the retinal ganglion cells. (3)

Blind spot The small area where the optic nerve leaves the back of the eye. There are no visual receptors in this area, so small images falling directly on the blind spot cannot be seen. (3)

Border ownership When two areas share a border, as occurs in figure–ground displays, the border is usually perceived as belonging to the figure. (5)

Bottom-up processing Processing in which a person constructs a perception by analyzing the information falling on the receptors. Also called data-based processing. (1)

Brain imaging Procedures that make it possible to visualize areas of the human brain that are activated by different types of stimuli, tasks, or behaviors. The two most common techniques used in perception research are positron emission tomography (PET) and functional magnetic resonance imaging (fMRI). (4)

Broca's aphasia Language problems, caused by damage to Broca's area in the frontal lobe, characterized by labored and stilted speech and short sentences. (13)

Broca's area An area in the frontal lobe that is important for language perception and production. One effect of damage is difficulty in speaking. (13)

Calcium imaging A method of measuring receptor activity by using fluorescence to measure the concentration of calcium inside the receptor. This technique has been used to measure the activation of olfactory receptor neurons. (15)

Categorical perception In speech perception, perceiving one sound at short voice onset times and another sound at longer voice onset times. The listener perceives only two categories across the whole range of voice onset times. (13)

Cell body The part of a neuron that contains the neuron's metabolic machinery and that receives stimulation from other neurons. (2)

Center-surround antagonism The competition between the center and surround regions of a center-surround receptive field, caused by the fact that one is excitatory and the other is inhibitory. Stimulating center and surround areas simultaneously decreases responding of the neuron, compared to stimulating the excitatory area alone. (2)

Center-surround receptive field A receptive field that consists of a roughly circular excitatory area surrounded by an inhibitory area, or a circular inhibitory center surrounded by an excitatory area. (2)

Cerebral achromatopsia A loss of color vision caused by damage to the cortex. (9)

Cerebral cortex The 2-mm-thick layer that covers the surface of the brain and contains the machinery for creating perception,

as well as for other functions, such as language, memory, and thinking. (2)

Change blindness Difficulty in detecting differences between two visual stimuli that are presented with another stimulus interposed between them. Also occurs when part of a stimulus is changed very slowly. (6)

Characteristic frequency The frequency at which a neuron in the auditory system has its lowest threshold. (11)

Chromatic adaptation Prolonged exposure to light in a specific part of the visible spectrum, which adapts receptors that fire to these wavelengths by selectively bleaching a specific visual pigment. For example, adaptation to a long-wavelength light selectively bleaches the long-wavelength pigment. The perceptual effect of adapting to long-wavelength light is a decrease in sensitivity to these wavelengths. Chromatic adaptation has been proposed as one of the mechanisms responsible for color constancy. (9)

Chromatic color Color with hue, such as blue, yellow, red, or green. (9)

Cilia Fine hairs that protrude from the inner and outer hair cells of the auditory system. Bending the cilia of the inner hair cells leads to transduction. (11)

Classical psychophysical methods The methods of limits, adjustment, and constant stimuli, described by Fechner, that are used for measuring thresholds. (1)

Coarticulation The overlapping articulation that occurs when different phonemes follow one another in speech. Because of these effects, the same phoneme can be articulated differently depending on the context in which it appears. For example, articulation of the /b/ in *boot* is different from articulation of the /b/ in *boat*. (13)

Cochlea The snail-shaped, liquid-filled structure that contains the structures of the inner ear, the most important of which are the basilar membrane, the tectorial membrane, and the hair cells. (11)

Cochlear amplifier How movement of the outer hair cells in response to sound increases basilar membrane vibration and therefore amplifies the response of the inner hair cells. (11)

Cochlear implant A device in which electrodes are inserted into the cochlea to create hearing by electrically stimulating the auditory nerve fibers. This device is used to restore hearing in people who have lost their hearing because of damaged hair cells. (11)

Cochlear nucleus The nucleus where nerve fibers from the cochlea first synapse. (11)

Cochlear partition A partition in the cochlea, extending almost its full length, that separates the scala tympani and the scala vestibuli. The organ of Corti, which contains the hair cells, is part of the cochlear partition. (11)

Cognitive influences on perception How the knowledge, memories, and expectations that a person brings to a situation influence his or her perception. (1)

Coherence A term used to describe the degree of correlation between the direction of moving objects. In displays containing many moving dots, zero percent coherence means all of the dots are moving independently; 100 percent coherence means all of the dots are moving in the same direction. (8)

Color, achromatic See **Achromatic color**. (9)

Color, chromatic See **Chromatic color**. (9)

Color blindness A condition in which a person perceives no chromatic color. This can be caused by absent or malfunctioning cone receptors or by cortical damage. (9)

Color constancy The effect in which the perception of an object's hue remains constant even when the wavelength distribution of the illumination is changed. Approximate color constancy means that our perception of hue usually changes a little when the illumination changes, though not as much as we might expect from the change in the wavelengths of light reaching the eye. (9)

Color deficiency People with this condition (sometimes incorrectly called color blindness) see fewer colors than people with normal color vision and need to mix fewer wavelengths to match any other wavelength in the spectrum. (9)

Color mixture, additive The creation of colors that occurs when lights of different colors are superimposed. (9)

Color mixture, subtractive The creation of colors that occurs when paints of different colors are mixed together. (9)

Color-matching experiment A procedure in which observers are asked to match the color in one field by mixing two or more lights in another field. (9)

Common fate, law of A Gestalt law of perceptual organization that states that things that are moving in the same direction appear to be grouped together. (5)

Common region, principle of A modern Gestalt principle that states that elements that are within the same region of space appear to be grouped together. (5)

Comparator A structure hypothesized by the corollary discharge theory of movement perception. The corollary discharge signal and the sensory movement signal meet at the comparator to determine whether movement will be perceived. (8)

Complex cell A neuron in the visual cortex that responds best to moving bars with a particular orientation. (4)

Componential recovery, principle of A principle of the recognition-by-components model that states that we can rapidly and correctly identify an object if we can perceive its individual geons. (5)

Conductive hearing loss Hearing loss that occurs when the vibrations of a sound stimulus are not conducted normally from the outer ear into the cochlea. (11)

Cone of confusion A surface in the shape of a cone that extends out from the ear. Sounds originating from different locations on this surface all have the same interaural level difference and interaural time difference, so information provided by these cues is ambiguous. (12)

Cones Cone-shaped receptors in the retina that are primarily responsible for vision in high levels of illumination and for color vision and detail vision. (3)

Conflicting cues theory A theory of visual illusions proposed by R. H. Day, which states that our perception of line length depends on an integration of the actual line length and the overall figure length. (10)

Conjunction search A visual search task in which it is necessary to search for a combination (or conjunction) of two or more features on the same stimulus to find the target. An example of a conjunction search would be looking for a horizontal green line among vertical green lines and horizontal red lines. (6)

Constant stimuli, method of A psychophysical method in which a number of stimuli with different intensities are presented repeatedly in a random order. (1)

Contextual modulation When the neural response to a stimulus is influenced by the context within which the stimulus occurs. This term has been used to refer to the situation in which a neuron's response is influenced by stimulation of an area outside its receptive field. (5)

Contralateral eye The eye on the opposite side of the head from a particular structure. (4)

Contrast sensitivity Sensitivity to the difference in the light intensities in two adjacent areas. Contrast sensitivity is usually measured by taking the reciprocal of the minimum intensity difference between two bars of a grating necessary to see the bars. (3)

Contrast sensitivity function (CSF) A plot of contrast sensitivity versus the spatial frequency of a grating stimulus. (16)

Contrast threshold The intensity difference that can just barely be seen between two areas. This is often measured using gratings with alternating light and dark bars. (4)

Convergence (depth cue) See **Perspective convergence**. (10)

Convergence (neural) When many neurons synapse onto a single neuron. (2)

Core area The area in the temporal lobe that includes the primary auditory cortex (A1) and some nearby areas. Signals from the core area are transmitted to the belt area of the auditory cortex. (11)

Cornea The transparent focusing element of the eye that is the first structure through which light passes as it enters the eye. The cornea is the eye's major focusing element. (3)

Corollary discharge signal (CDS) A copy of the signal sent from the motor area of the brain to the eye muscles. The corollary discharge signal is sent to the hypothetical comparator of corollary discharge theory. (8)

Correct rejection In a signal detection experiment, saying "No, I don't detect a stimulus" on a trial in which the stimulus is not presented (a correct response). (Appendix)

Correspondence problem The visual system's matching of points on one image with similar points on the other image in order to determine binocular disparity. (10)

Corresponding retinal points The points on each retina that would overlap if one retina were slid on top of the other. Receptors at corresponding points send their signals to the same location in the brain. (10)

Cue approach to depth perception The approach to explaining depth perception that identifies information in the retinal image, and also information provided by aiming and focusing the eyes on an object that is correlated with depth in the scene. Some of the depth cues that have been identified are overlap, relative height, relative size, atmospheric perspective, convergence, and accommodation. (10)

Cutaneous senses The ability to perceive sensations, such as touch and pain, that are based on the stimulation of receptors in the skin. (14)

Dark adaptation Visual adaptation that occurs in the dark, during which the sensitivity to light increases. This increase in sensitivity is associated with regeneration of the rod and cone visual pigments. (3)

Dark adaptation curve The function that traces the time course of the increase in visual sensitivity that occurs during dark adaptation. (3)

Dark-adapted sensitivity The sensitivity of the eye after it has completely adapted to the dark. (3)

Data-based processing Another name for bottom-up processing. Refers to processing that is based on incoming data, as opposed to top-down, or knowledge-based, processing, which is based on prior knowledge. (1)

Decay The decrease in the sound signal that occurs at the end of a tone. (11)

Decibel (dB) A unit that indicates the presence of a tone relative to a reference pressure. dB = 20 log (p/p_o) where p is the pressure of the tone and p_o is the reference pressure. (11)

Deletion A cue that provides information about the relative depth of two surfaces. Deletion occurs when a farther object is covered by a nearer object due to sideways movement of an observer relative to the objects. See also **Accretion**. (10)

Dendrites Nerve processes on the cell body that receive stimulation from other neurons. (2)

Depolarization When the inside of a neuron becomes more positive, as occurs during the initial phases of the action potential. Depolarization is often associated with the action of excitatory neurotransmitters. (2)

Dermis The inner layer of skin that contains nerve endings and receptors. (14)

Desaturated Low saturation in chromatic colors as would occur when white is added to a color. For example, pink is not as saturated as red. (9)

Detached retina A condition in which the retina is detached from the back of the eye. (3)

Detection threshold See **Threshold, detection**. (15)

Deuteranopia A form of red–green color dichromatism caused by lack of the middle-wavelength cone pigment. (9)

Dichromat A person who has a form of color deficiency. Dichromats can match any wavelength in the spectrum by mixing two other wavelengths. Deuteranopes, protanopes, and tritanopes are all dichromats. (9)

Difference threshold See **Threshold, difference**. (1)

Direct pathway model of pain The idea that pain occurs when nociceptor receptors in the skin are stimulated and send their signals to the brain. This model does not account for the fact that pain can be affected by factors in addition to stimulation of the skin. (14)

Direct sound Sound that is transmitted directly from a sound source to the ears. (12)

Discriminability Generally, the ability to distinguish between one stimulus and another. In the recognition-by-components theory of object perception, discriminability is a property of geons, which indicates that each geon can be distinguished from other geons from almost all viewpoints. (5)

Dishabituation An increase in looking time that occurs when a stimulus is changed. This response is used in testing infants to see whether they can differentiate two stimuli. (16)

Disparate points See **Noncorresponding points**. (10)

Disparity-selective cell See **Binocular depth cell**. (10)

Dissociation A situation that occurs as a result of brain damage in which one function is present and another is absent. See also **Double dissociation**; **Single dissociation**. (4)

Distance coordinate In hearing, this coordinate specifies how far the sound source is from the listener. (12)

Distributed coding Type of neural code in which different perceptions are signaled by the pattern of activity that is distributed across many neurons. See also **Specificity coding**. (2)

Divided attention Directing attention to a number of things at once. (6)

Doctrine of specific nerve energies A principle proposed by Mueller, which states that our perceptions depend on "nerve energies" reaching the brain and that the specific quality we experience depends on which nerves are stimulated. For example, activating the optic nerve results in seeing, and activating the auditory nerve results in hearing. (2)

Dorsal pathway Pathway that conducts signals from the striate cortex to the parietal lobe. This is also called the *where*, the *how*, or the *action* pathway to indicate its function. (4)

Double dissociation In brain damage, when function A is present and function B is absent in one person, and function A is absent and function B is present in another. Presence of a double dissociation means that the two functions involve different mechanisms and operate independently of one another. (4)

Dual-stream model of speech perception Model that proposes a ventral stream starting in the temporal lobe that is responsible for recognizing speech, and a dorsal stream starting in the parietal lobe that is responsible for linking the acoustic signal to the movements used to produce speech. (13)

Duplex theory of texture perception The idea that texture perception is determined by both spatial and temporal cues that are detected by two types of receptors. Originally proposed by David Katz and named the "duplex theory" by Hollins. (14)

Eardrum Another term for the tympanic membrane, the membrane located at the end of the auditory canal that vibrates in response to sound. (11)

Easy problem of consciousness The problem of determining the relationship between physiological processes like nerve firing and perceptual experience. Note that this involves determining a *relationship*, not a *cause*. See also **Hard problem of consciousness**. (2)

Echolocation Locating objects by sending out high-frequency pulses and sensing the echo created when these pulses are reflected from objects in the environment. Echolocation is used by bats and dolphins. (10)

Ecological approach to perception This approach focuses on studying perception as it occurs in natural settings, particularly emphasizing the role of observer movement. (7)

Effect of the missing fundamental Removing the fundamental frequency and other lower harmonies from a musical tone does not change the tone's pitch. See also **Periodicity pitch**. (11)

Electromagnetic spectrum Continuum of electromagnetic energy that extends from very-short-wavelength gamma rays to long-wavelength radio waves. Visible light is a narrow band within this spectrum. (3)

Elevation coordinate In hearing, sound locations that are up and down relative to the listener. (12)

Emmert's law A law stating that the size of an afterimage depends on the distance of the surface against which the afterimage is viewed. The farther away the surface, the larger the afterimage appears. (10)

Endorphin Chemical that is naturally produced in the brain and that causes analgesia. (14)

End-stopped cell A cortical neuron that responds best to lines of a specific length that are moving in a particular direction. (4)

Envelope of the traveling wave A curve that indicates the maximum displacement at each point along the basilar membrane caused by a traveling wave. (11)

Environmental stimulus All of the things in our environment that we can potentially perceive at a given point in time. (1)

Enzyme cascade Sequence of reactions triggered by an activated visual pigment molecule that results in transduction. (3)

Epidermis The outer layers of the skin, including a layer of dead skin cells. (14)

Equal loudness curve A curve that indicates the sound pressure levels that result in a perception of the same loudness at frequencies across the audible spectrum. (11)

Excitatory area Area of a receptive field that is associated with excitation. Stimulation of this area causes an increase in the rate of nerve firing. (2)

Excitatory response The response of a nerve fiber in which the firing rate increases. (2)

Excitatory transmitters Neurotransmitters that cause the inside of a neuron to become more positively charged. Excitatory neurotransmitters increase the probability that an action potential will be generated and are also associated with increases in the rate of nerve firing. (2)

Excitatory-center-inhibitory-surround receptive field A center-surround receptive field in which stimulation of the center area causes an excitatory response, and stimulation of the surround causes an inhibitory response. (2)

Experience-dependent plasticity A process by which neurons adapt to the specific environment within which a person or animal lives. This is achieved when neurons change their response properties so they become tuned to respond best to stimuli that have been repeatedly experienced in the environment. See also **Neural plasticity**; **Selective rearing**. (4)

Exploratory procedures (EPs) People's movements of their hands and fingers while they are identifying three-dimensional objects by touch. (14)

Extinction A condition in which the person can identify a stimulus in the right or left visual field if just one stimulus is presented, but if two stimuli are presented, one on the left and one on the right, the person has trouble detecting the object on the left. (7)

Extrastriate body area (EBA) An area of the temporal lobe that is activated by pictures of bodies and parts of bodies. (4)

Eye The eyeball and its contents, which include focusing elements, the retina, and supporting structures. (3)

False alarm In a signal detection experiment, saying "Yes, I detect the stimulus" on a trial in which the stimulus is not presented (an incorrect response). (Appendix)

Familiar size A depth cue. Our knowledge of an object's actual size sometimes influences our perception of an object's distance. (10)

Familiarity, law of A Gestalt law of perceptual organization that states that things are more likely to form groups when the groups appear familiar or meaningful. (5)

Far point The distance at which the spot of light becomes focused on the retina. (3)

Farsightedness See **Hyperopia**. (3)

Feature detector A neuron that responds selectively to a specific feature of the stimulus. (4)

Feature integration theory A sequence of steps proposed by Treisman to explain how an object is broken down into features and how these features are recombined to result in a perception of the object. (6)

Feature search A visual search task in which a person can find a target by searching for only one feature. An example would be looking for a horizontal green line among vertical green lines. (6)

Figure When an object is seen as separate from the background (the "ground"), it is called a figure. See also **Figure–ground segregation**. (5)

Figure–ground segregation The perceptual separation of an object from its background. (5)

First harmonic See **Fundamental frequency**. (11)

Fixation The pause of the eye that occurs between eye movements as a person scans a scene. (6)

Flavor The perception that occurs from the combination of taste and olfaction. (15)

Flow See **Gradient of flow**; **Optic flow**. (7)

Focus of expansion (FOE) The point in the flow pattern caused by observer movement in which there is no expansion. According to J. J. Gibson, the focus of expansion always remains centered on the observer's destination. (7)

Focused attention stage (of perceptual processing) The stage of processing in feature integration theory in which the features are combined. This stage requires focused attention. (6)

Formant Horizontal band of energy in the speech spectrogram associated with vowels. (13)

Formant transition In the speech stimulus, the rapid shift in frequency that precedes a formant. (13)

Fovea A small area in the human retina that contains only cone receptors. The fovea is located on the line of sight, so that when a person looks at an object, the center of its image falls on the fovea. (3)

Frequency In the case of a sound wave that repeats itself, such as the sine wave of a pure tone, frequency is the number of times per second that the wave repeats itself. (11)

Frequency spectrum A plot that indicates the amplitudes of the various harmonics that make up a complex tone. Each harmonic is indicated by a line that is positioned along the frequency axis, with the height of the line indicating the amplitude of the harmonic. (11)

Frequency tuning curve Curve relating frequency and the threshold intensity for activating an auditory neuron. (11)

Frontal eyes Eyes located in front of the head, so the views of the two eyes overlap. (10)

Frontal lobe Receiving signals from all of the senses, the frontal lobe plays an important role in perceptions that involve the coordination of information received through two or more senses. It also serves functions such as language, thought, memory, and motor functioning. (2)

Frontal operculum cortex An area in the frontal lobe of the cortex that receives signals from the taste system. (15)

Functional magnetic resonance imaging (fMRI) A brain imaging technique that indicates brain activity in awake, behaving humans in response to perceptual stimuli. (4)

Fundamental frequency The first harmonic of a complex tone; usually the lowest frequency in the frequency spectrum of a complex tone. The tone's other components, called higher harmonics, have frequencies that are multiples of the fundamental frequency. (11)

Fusiform face area (FFA) An area in the human inferotemporal (IT) cortex that contains neurons that are specialized to respond to faces. (4)

Ganglion cell A neuron in the retina that receives inputs from bipolar and amacrine cells. The axons of the ganglion cells travel out of the eye in the optic nerve. (3)

Gate control model Melzack and Wall's idea that our perception of pain is controlled by a neural circuit that takes into account the relative amount of activity in large (L) fibers and small (S) fibers. This model has been used to explain how pain can be influenced by factors in addition to stimulation of receptors in the skin. (14)

Geon The volumetric features of Biederman's recognition-by-components theory of object perception. (5)

Gestalt psychology An approach to psychology that focuses on developing principles of perceptual organization, proposing that "the whole differs from the sum of its parts." (5)

Gist of a scene General description of a scene. People can identify most scenes after viewing them for only a fraction of a second, as when they flip rapidly from one TV channel to another. (5)

Global image features Information that may enable observers to rapidly perceive the gist of a scene. Features associated with specific types of scenes include degree of naturalness, degree of openness, degree of roughness, degree of expansion, and color. (5)

Global optic flow Information for movement that occurs when all elements in a scene move. The perception of global optic flow indicates that it is the observer that is moving and not the scene. (8)

Glomeruli Small structures in the olfactory bulb that receive signals from similar olfactory receptor neurons. One function of each glomerulus is to collect information about a small group of odorants. (15)

Good continuation, law of A Gestalt law of perceptual organization that states that points that, when connected, result in straight or smoothly curving lines are seen as belonging together, and that lines tend to be seen in such a way as to follow the smoothest path. (5)

Good figure, law of See **Pragnanz, law of**. (5)

Gradient of flow In an optic flow pattern, a gradient is created by movement of an observer through the environment. The "gradient" refers to the fact that the optic flow is rapid in the foreground and becomes slower as distance from the observer increases. (7)

Grandmother cell A hypothesized type of neuron that responds only to a very specific stimulus, such as a person's grandmother. (2)

Grating A stimulus pattern consisting of alternating bars with different lightnesses or colors. (4)

Grating acuity The narrowest spacing of a grooved surface on the skin for which orientation can be accurately judged; a measure of acuity on the skin. See also **Two-point threshold**. (14)

Ground In object perception, the background is called the ground. See also **Figure**. (5)

Habituation The result when the same stimulus is presented repeatedly. For example, infants look at a stimulus less and less on each succeeding trial. See also **Dishabituation**. (16)

Hair cell Neuron in the cochlea that contains small hairs, or cilia, that are displaced by vibration of the basilar membrane and fluids inside the inner ear. There are two kinds of hair cells: inner and outer. (11)

Hair cell, inner Auditory receptor cell in the inner ear that is primarily responsible for auditory transduction and the perception of pitch. (11)

Hair cells, outer Auditory receptor cells in the inner ear that amplify the response of the inner hair cells. (11)

Haptic perception The perception of three-dimensional objects by touch. (14)

Hard problem of consciousness The problem of determining how physiological processes, such as ion flow across nerve membranes, cause different perceptual experiences. (2)

Harmonics Fourier components of a complex tone with frequencies that are multiples of the fundamental frequency. (11)

Hearing The experience of perceiving sound. (11)

Hermann grid A geometrical display that results in the illusion of dark areas at the intersection of two white "corridors." This perception can be explained by lateral inhibition. (3)

Hertz (Hz) The unit for designating the frequency of a tone. One Hertz equals one cycle per second. (11)

Heuristic In perception, a rule of thumb that provides a "best guess" estimate of the identity of a particular stimulus. (5)

Hierarchical processing Processing signals through a sequence of areas. This occurs in the visual system as signals are transmitted from the LGN to the primary visual receiving area and then to higher areas. It occurs in the auditory system as signals are transmitted from the core to the belt to the parabelt regions of the cortex. (11)

Hit In a signal detection experiment, saying "Yes, I detect a stimulus" on a trial in which the stimulus is present (a correct response). (Appendix)

Homunculus Latin for "little man"; refers to the topographic map of the body in the somatosensory cortex. (14)

Horizontal cell A neuron that transmits signals laterally across the retina. Horizontal cells synapse with receptors and bipolar cells. (3)

Horopter An imaginary surface that passes through the point of fixation. Images caused by a visual stimulus on this surface fall on corresponding points on the two retinas. (10)

How **pathway** See **Dorsal pathway**. (4)

Hue The experience of a chromatic color such as red, green, yellow, or blue or combinations of these colors. (9)

Hypercolumn In the striate cortex, unit proposed by Hubel and Wiesel that combines location, orientation, and ocular dominance columns that serve a specific area on the retina. (4)

Hyperopia A condition causing poor vision in which people can see objects that are far away but do not see near objects clearly. Also called farsightedness. (3)

Hyperpolarization When the inside of a neuron becomes more negative. Hyperpolarization is often associated with the action of inhibitory neurotransmitters. (2)

Illumination edge The border between two areas created by different light intensities in the two areas. (9)

Illusory conjunction Illusory combination of features that are perceived when stimuli containing a number of features are presented briefly and under conditions in which focused attention is difficult. For example, presenting a red square and a blue triangle could potentially create the perception of a red triangle. (6)

Illusory contour Contour that is perceived even though it is not present in the physical stimulus. (5)

Illusory motion Perception of motion when there actually is none. (8)

Image displacement signal (IDS) In corollary discharge theory, the signal that occurs when an image stimulates the receptors by moving across them. (8)

Implied motion When a still picture depicts an action that involves motion, so that an observer could potentially extend the action depicted in the picture in his or her mind based on what will most likely happen next. (8)

Inattentional blindness A situation in which a stimulus that is not attended to is not perceived, even though the person is looking directly at it. (6)

Incus The second of the three ossicles of the middle ear. It transmits vibrations from the malleus to the stapes. (11)

Indexical characteristic Characteristic of the speech stimulus that indicates information about a speaker, such as the speaker's age, gender, or emotional state. (13)

Indirect sound Sound that reaches the ears after being reflected from a surface such as a room's walls. (12)

Induced motion The illusory movement of one object that is caused by the movement of another object that is nearby. (8)

Inferior colliculus A nucleus in the hearing system along the pathway from the cochlea to the auditory cortex. The inferior colliculus receives inputs from the superior olivary nucleus. (11)

Inflammatory pain Pain caused by damage to tissues, inflammation of joints, or tumor cells. This damage releases chemicals that create an "inflammatory soup" that activates nociceptors. (14)

Inhibitory area Area of a receptive field that is associated with inhibition. Stimulation of this area causes a decrease in the rate of nerve firing. (2)

Inhibitory response The response of a nerve fiber in which the firing rate decreases due to inhibition from another neuron. (2)

Inhibitory transmitters Neurotransmitters that cause the inside of a neuron to become negatively charged. Inhibitory transmitters decrease the probability that an action potential will be generated and are also associated with decreases in the rate of nerve firing. (2)

Inhibitory-center-excitatory-surround receptive field A center-surround receptive field in which stimulation of the center causes an inhibitory response and stimulation of the surround causes an excitatory response. (2)

Inner ear The innermost division of the ear, containing the cochlea and the receptors for hearing. (11)

Inner hair cell See **Hair cell, inner**. (11)

Insula An area in the frontal lobe of the cortex that receives signals from the taste system. (15)

Interaural level difference (ILD) The greater level of a sound at the closer ear when a sound source is positioned closer to one ear than to the other. This effect is most pronounced for high-frequency tones. The ILD provides a cue for sound localization. (12)

Interaural time difference (ITD) When a sound is positioned closer to one ear than to the other, the sound reaches the close ear slightly before reaching the far ear, so there is a difference in the time of arrival at the two ears. The ITD provides a cue for sound localization. (12)

Intermodal perception Coordination of information from different senses into a perceptual whole. (16)

Invariant information Environmental properties that do not change as the observer moves relative to an object or scene. For example, the spacing, or texture, of the elements in a texture gradient does not change as the observer moves on the gradient. The texture of the gradient therefore supplies invariant information for depth perception. (7)

Inverse projection problem The idea that a particular image on the retina could have been caused by an infinite number of different objects. Thus, the retinal image does not unambiguously specify a stimulus. (5)

Ions Charged molecules found floating in the liquid that surrounds nerve fibers. (2)

Ipsilateral eye The eye on the same side of the head as the structure to which the eye sends inputs. (4)

Ishihara plate A display of colored dots used to test for the presence of color deficiency. The dots are colored so that people with normal (trichromatic) color vision can perceive numbers in the plate, but people with color deficiency cannot perceive these numbers or perceive different numbers than someone with trichromatic vision. (9)

Isomerization Change in shape of the retinal part of the visual pigment molecule that occurs when the molecule absorbs a quantum of light. Isomerization triggers the enzyme cascade that results in transduction from light energy to electrical energy in the retinal receptors. (3)

Kinesthesis The sense that enables us to feel the motions and positions of the limbs and body. (14)

Knowledge Any information that the perceiver brings to a situation. See also **Top-down processing**. (1)

Knowledge-based processing Another name for top-down processing. Refers to processing that is based on knowledge, as opposed to bottom-up, or data-based, processing, which is based on incoming data. (1)

Landmark discrimination problem The behavioral task used in Ungerleider and Mishkin's experiment in which they provided evidence for the dorsal, or *where*, visual processing stream. Monkeys were required to respond to a previously indicated location. (4)

Large-diameter fiber (L-fiber) According to the gate control model, activity in L-fibers closes the gate control mechanism and therefore decreases the perception of pain. (14)

Laser-assisted in situ keratomileuis (LASIK) A process in which the cornea is sculpted with a laser in order to achieve clear vision by adjusting the focusing power of the cornea so it focuses light onto the retina. (3)

Lateral eyes Eyes located on opposite sides of an animal's head, so the views of the two eyes do not overlap or overlap only slightly, as in the pigeon and rabbit. (10)

Lateral geniculate nucleus (LGN) The nucleus in the thalamus that receives inputs from the optic nerve and, in turn, sends fibers to the cortical receiving area for vision. (4)

Lateral inhibition Inhibition that is transmitted laterally across a nerve circuit. In the retina, lateral inhibition is transmitted by the horizontal and amacrine cells. (3)

Laws of perceptual organization See **Perceptual organization, laws of**. (5)

Leisure noise Noise associated with leisure activities such as listening to music, hunting, and woodworking. Exposure to high levels of leisure noise for extended periods can cause hearing loss. (11)

Lens The transparent focusing element of the eye through which light passes after passing through the cornea and the aqueous humor. The lens's change in shape to focus at different distances is called accommodation. (3)

Level Short for sound level. Indicates the decibels or sound pressure of a sound stimulus. (11)

Light-adapted sensitivity The sensitivity of the eye when in the light-adapted state. Usually taken as the starting point for the dark adaptation curve because it is the sensitivity of the eye just before the lights are turned off. (3)

Light-from-above heuristic The assumption that light usually comes from above, which influences our perception of form in some situations. (5)

Lightness Perception of reflectance. Usually objects with high reflectance are perceived as white and objects with low reflectance are perceived as gray or black. (3)

Lightness constancy The constancy of our perception of an object's lightness under different intensities of illumination. (9)

Likelihood principle The idea proposed by Helmholtz that we perceive the object that is *most likely* to have caused the pattern of stimuli we have received. (5)

Limits, method of A psychophysical method for measuring threshold in which the experimenter presents stimuli in alternating ascending and descending order. (1)

Limulus A primitive animal more familiarly known as the horseshoe crab, which has been used in experiments studying lateral inhibition. (3)

Local disturbance in the optic array Occurs when one object moves relative to the environment, so that the stationary background is covered and uncovered by the moving object. This local disturbance indicates that the object is moving relative to the environment. (8)

Location column A column in the visual cortex that contains neurons with the same receptive field locations on the retina. (4)

Location cue In hearing, characteristics of the sound reaching the listener that provide information regarding the location of a sound source. (12)

Loudness The quality of sound that ranges from soft to loud. For a tone of a particular frequency, loudness usually increases with increasing decibels. (11)

Mach band Perception of a thin dark band on the dark side of a light–dark border and a thin light band on the light side of the border. These bands are an illusion because they occur even though corresponding intensity changes do not exist. (3)

Macrosmatic Having a keen sense of smell that is important to an animal's survival. (15)

Macular degeneration A clinical condition that causes degeneration of the macula, an area of the retina that includes the fovea and a small surrounding area. (3)

Magnitude estimation A psychophysical method in which the subject assigns numbers to a stimulus that are proportional to the subjective magnitude of the stimulus. (1)

Malleus The first of the ossicles of the middle ear. Receives vibrations from the tympanic membrane and transmits these vibrations to the incus. (11)

Masking, auditory Occurs when presentation of one sound decreases a listener's ability to hear another sound. (11)

Masking stimulus A visual pattern that, when presented immediately after a visual stimulus, decreases a person's ability to perceive the stimulus. This stops the persistence of vision and therefore limits the effective duration of the stimulus. (5)

McGurk effect See **Audiovisual speech perception**. (13)

Mechanoreceptor Receptor that responds to mechanical stimulation of the skin, such as pressure, stretching, or vibration. (14)

Medial geniculate nucleus An auditory nucleus in the thalamus that is part of the pathway from the cochlea to the auditory cortex. The medial geniculate nucleus receives inputs from the inferior colliculus and transmits signals to the auditory cortex. (11)

Medial lemniscal pathway A pathway in the spinal cord that transmits signals from the skin toward the thalamus. (14)

Meissner corpuscle A receptor in the skin, associated with RA1 mechanoreceptors. It has been proposed that the Meissner corpuscle is important for perceiving tactile slip and for controlling the force needed to grip objects. (14)

Melodic channeling See **Scale illusion**. (12)

Melody schema A representation of a familiar melody that is stored in a person's memory. Existence of a melody schema makes it more likely that the tones associated with a melody will be perceptually grouped. (12)

Memory color The idea that an object's characteristic color influences our perception of that object's color. (9)

Menstrual synchrony Women who live together experience menstrual periods that begin at approximately the same time. There is evidence that the sense of smell is involved in determining this effect. (15)

Merkel receptor A disk-shaped receptor in the skin associated with slowly adapting fibers and the perception of fine details. (14)

Metamerism The situation in which two physically different stimuli are perceptually identical. In vision, this refers to two lights with different wavelength distributions that are perceived as having the same color. (9)

Metamers Two lights that have different wavelength distributions but are perceptually identical. (9)

Method of adjustment See **Adjustment, method of**. (1)

Method of constant stimuli See **Constant stimuli, method of**. (1)

Method of limits See **Limits, method of**. (1)

Microelectrode A thin piece of wire that is small enough to record electrical signals from a single neuron. (2)

Microsmatic Having a weak sense of smell. This usually occurs in animals like humans, in which the sense of smell is not crucial for survival. (15)

Microstimulation A procedure in which a small electrode is inserted into the cortex and an electrical current is passed through the electrode that activates the neurons near the electrode. This procedure has been used to determine how activating specific groups of neurons affects perception. (8)

Middle ear The small air-filled space between the auditory canal and the cochlea that contains the ossicles. (11)

Middle-ear muscles Muscles attached to the ossicles in the middle ear. The smallest skeletal muscles in the body, they contract in response to very intense sounds and dampen the vibration of the ossicles. (11)

Mind–body problem One of the most famous problems in science: How do physical processes such as nerve impulses or sodium and potassium molecules flowing across membranes (the body part of the problem) become transformed into the richness of perceptual experience (the mind part of the problem)? (2)

Mirror neuron Neuron in the premotor area of the monkey's cortex that responds when the monkey grasps an object and also when the monkey observes someone else (another monkey or the experimenter) grasping the object. See also **Audiovisual mirror neuron**. (7)

Misapplied size constancy scaling A principle, proposed by Richard Gregory, that when mechanisms that help maintain size constancy in the three-dimensional world are applied to two-dimensional pictures, an illusion of size sometimes results. (10)

Miss In a signal detection experiment, saying "No, I don't detect a stimulus" on a trial in which the stimulus is present (an incorrect response). (Appendix)

Modular organization The organization of specific functions into specific brain structures. (2)

Module A structure that processes information about a specific behavior or perceptual quality. Often identified as a structure that contains a large proportion of neurons that respond selectively to a particular quality. (4)

Monaural cue Sound localization cue that involves one ear. (12)

Monochromat A person who is completely color-blind and therefore sees everything as black, white, or shades of gray. A monochromat can match any wavelength in the spectrum by adjusting the intensity of any other wavelength. Monochromats generally have only one type of functioning receptors, usually rods. (9)

Monochromatic light Light that contains only a single wavelength. (3)

Monocular cue Depth cue, such as overlap, relative size, relative height, familiar size, linear perspective, movement parallax, and accommodation, that works when we use only one eye. (10)

Moon illusion An illusion in which the moon appears to be larger when it is on or near the horizon than when it is high in the sky. (10)

Motion aftereffect An illusion that occurs after a person views a moving stimulus and then sees movement in the opposite direction when viewing a stationary stimulus. See also **Waterfall illusion**. (8)

Motion agnosia An effect of brain damage in which the ability to perceive motion is disrupted. (8)

Motion parallax A depth cue. As an observer moves, nearby objects appear to move rapidly whereas far objects appear to move slowly. (10)

Motor signal (MS) In corollary discharge theory, the signal that is sent to the eye muscles when the observer moves or tries to move his or her eyes. (8)

Motor theory of speech perception A theory that proposes a close link between how speech is perceived and how it is produced. The idea behind this theory is that when we *hear* a particular speech sound, this activates the motor mechanisms that are responsible for *producing* that sound, and it is the activation of these motor mechanisms that enable us to perceive the sound. (13)

Müller-Lyer illusion An illusion in which two lines of equal length appear to be of different lengths because of the addition of "fins" to the ends of the lines. (10)

Multimodal The involvement of a number of different senses in determining perception. For example, speech perception can be influenced by information from a number of different senses, including audition, vision, and touch. (13)

Multimodal nature of pain The fact that the experience of pain has both sensory and emotional components. (14)

Myopia An inability to see distant objects clearly. Also called nearsightedness. (3)

Naloxone A substance that inhibits the activity of opiates. It is hypothesized that naloxone also inhibits the activity of endorphins and therefore can have an effect on pain perception. (14)

Nasal pharynx A passageway that connects the mouth cavity and the nasal cavity. (15)

Near point The distance at which the lens can no longer accommodate enough to bring close objects into focus. Objects nearer than the near point can be brought into focus only by corrective lenses. (3)

Nearness, law of See Proximity, law of. (5)

Nearsightedness See **Myopia**. (3)

Nerve A group of nerve fibers traveling together. (2)

Nerve fiber In most sensory neurons, the long part of the neuron that transmits electrical impulses from one point to another. Also called the axon. (2)

Neural circuit A number of neurons that are connected by synapses. (2)

Neural convergence Synapsing of a number of neurons onto one neuron. (3)

Neural correlate of consciousness Connections between the firing of neurons and perceptual experience. (2)

Neural plasticity The capacity of the nervous system to change in response to experience. Examples are how early visual experience can change the orientation selectivity of neurons in the visual cortex and how tactile experience can change the sizes of areas in the cortex that represent different parts of the body. See also **Experience-dependent plasticity**; **Selective rearing**. (4)

Neural processing Operations that transform electrical signals within a network of neurons or that transform the response of individual neurons. (1)

Neural prosthesis Device that records neural signals from the brain of a paralyzed person and uses these signals to control other devices that normally (if the person weren't paralyzed) would be controlled by the person's limb or hand movements. Signals recorded from the motor cortex and parietal reach region of the cortex have been used in experimental tests of these devices. (7)

Neurogenesis The cycle of birth, development, and death of a neuron. This process occurs for the receptors for olfaction and taste. (15)

Neuron theory The idea that the nervous system consists of distinct elements or cells. (2)

Neuropathic pain Pain caused by lesions or other damage to the nervous system. (14)

Neuropsychology The study of the behavioral effects of brain damage in humans. (4)

Neurotransmitter A chemical stored in synaptic vesicles that is released in response to a nerve impulse and has an excitatory or inhibitory effect on another neuron. (2)

Neutral point The wavelength at which a dichromat perceives gray. (9)

Nociceptive pain This type of pain, which serves as a warning of impending damage to the skin, is caused by activation of receptors in the skin called nociceptors. (14)

Nociceptor A fiber that responds to stimuli that are damaging to the skin. (14)

Noise-induced hearing loss A form of sensorineural hearing loss that occurs when loud noises cause degeneration of the hair cells. (11)

Non-accidental properties (NAPs) Properties of edges in the retinal image that correspond to the properties of edges in the three-dimensional environment. For example, a non-accidental property of a rectangular solid is three parallel edges. Non-accidental properties are visible from most viewpoints. (5)

Noncorresponding points Two points, one on each retina, that would not overlap if the retinas were slid onto each other. Also called disparate points. (10)

Nontaster A person who cannot taste the compound phenylthiocarbamide (PTC). (15)

Nucleus of the solitary tract (NST) The nucleus in the brain stem that receives signals from the tongue, the mouth, and the larynx transmitted by the chorda tympani, glossopharyngeal, and vagus nerves. (15)

Object discrimination problem The behavioral task used in Ungerleider and Mishkin's experiment in which they provided evidence for the ventral, or *what*, visual processing stream. Monkeys were required to respond to an object with a particular shape. (4)

Oblique effect Enhanced sensitivity to vertically and horizontally oriented visual stimuli. This effect has been demonstrated by measuring both perception and neural responding. (5)

Occipital lobe A lobe at the back of the cortex that is the site of the cortical receiving area for vision. (2)

Occlusion Depth cue in which one object hides or partially hides another object from view, causing the hidden object to be perceived as being farther away. (10)

Octave Tones that have frequencies that are binary multiples of each other (2, 4, etc.). For example, an 800-Hz tone is one octave above a 400-Hz tone. (11)

Ocular dominance The degree to which a neuron is influenced by stimulation of each eye. A neuron has a large amount of ocular dominance if it responds only to stimulation of one eye. There is no ocular dominance if the neuron responds equally to stimulation of both eyes. (4)

Ocular dominance column A column in the visual cortex that contains neurons that respond best to stimulation of the same eye. (4)

Oculomotor cue Depth cue that depends on our ability to sense the position of our eyes and the tension in our eye muscles. Accommodation and convergence are oculomotor cues. (10)

Olfactometer A device that presents olfactory stimuli with great precision. (15)

Olfactory bulb The structure that receives signals directly from the olfactory receptors. The olfactory bulb contains glomeruli, which receive these signals from the receptors. (15)

Olfactory mucosa The region inside the nose that contains the receptors for the sense of smell. (15)

Olfactory receptor A protein string that responds to odor stimuli. (15)

Olfactory receptor neurons (ORNs) Sensory neurons located in the olfactory mucosa that contain the olfactory receptors. (15)

Ommatidium A structure in the eye of the *Limulus* that contains a small lens, located directly over a visual receptor. The *Limulus* eye is made up of hundreds of these ommatidia. The *Limulus* eye has been used for research on lateral inhibition because its receptors are large enough so that stimulation can be applied to individual receptors. (3)

Onset time The time at which a specific tone starts. When two tones start at different times, this provides information that they are coming from different sources. (12)

Opioid A chemical such as opium, heroin, and other molecules with related structures that reduce pain and induce feelings of euphoria. (14)

Opponent neuron A neuron that has an excitatory response to wavelengths in one part of the spectrum and an inhibitory response to wavelengths in the other part of the spectrum. (9)

Opponent-process theory of color vision A theory originally proposed by Hering, which claimed that our perception of color is determined by the activity of two opponent mechanisms: a blue–yellow mechanism and a red–green mechanism. The responses to the two colors in each mechanism oppose each other, one being an excitatory response and the other an inhibitory response. In addition, this theory also includes a black–white mechanism, which is concerned with the perception of brightness. See also **Opponent neuron**. (9)

Opsin The protein part of the visual pigment molecule, to which the light-sensitive retinal molecule is attached. (3)

Optic array The structured pattern of light created by the presence of objects, surfaces, and textures in the environment. (7)

Optic flow The flow of stimuli in the environment that occurs when an observer moves relative to the environment. Forward movement causes an expanding optic flow, whereas backward movement causes a contracting optic flow. Some researchers use the term *optic flow field* to refer to this flow. (7)

Optic nerve Bundle of nerve fibers that carry impulses from the retina to the lateral geniculate nucleus and other structures. Each optic nerve contains about 1 million ganglion cell fibers. (3)

Optical imaging A technique to measure the activity of large areas of the cortex by measuring the intensity of red light reflected from the cortex. (15)

Orbitofrontal cortex (OFC) An area in the frontal lobe, near the eyes, that receives signals originating in the olfactory receptors. Also known as the secondary olfactory cortex. (15)

Organ of Corti The major structure of the cochlear partition, containing the basilar membrane, the tectorial membrane, and the receptors for hearing. (11)

Orientation column A column in the visual cortex that contains neurons with the same orientation preference. (4)

Orientation tuning curve A function relating the firing rate of a neuron to the orientation of the stimulus. (4)

Ossicles Three small bones in the middle ear that transmit vibrations from the outer to the inner ear. (11)

Outer ear The pinna and the external auditory meatus. (11)

Outer hair cells See **Hair cells, outer**. (11)

Outer segments Part of the rod and cone visual receptors that contain the light-sensitive visual pigment molecules. (3)

Oval window A small, membrane-covered hole in the cochlea that receives vibrations from the stapes. (11)

Pacinian corpuscle A receptor with a distinctive elliptical shape associated with RA2 mechanoreceptors. It transmits pressure to the nerve fiber inside it only at the beginning or end of a pressure stimulus, and is responsible for our perception of vibration and fine textures that are perceived when moving the fingers over a surface. (14)

Pain matrix The network of structures in the brain that are responsible for pain perception. (14)

Paired comparison A procedure in which a participant is first familiarized with one stimulus, and then is given a choice between that stimulus and a new stimulus. Measurement of looking time indicates whether participants can tell the difference between the two stimuli. (16)

Papillae Ridges and valleys on the tongue, some of which contain taste buds. There are four types of papillae: filiform, fungiform, foliate, and circumvallate. (15)

Parabelt area Auditory area in the temporal lobe that receives signals from the belt area. (11)

Parahippocampal place area (PPA) An area in the temporal lobe that is activated by pictures of indoor and outdoor scenes. (4)

Parietal lobe. A lobe at the top of the cortex that is the site of the cortical receiving area for touch and is the termination point of the dorsal (*where* or *how*) stream for visual processing. (2)

Parietal reach region (PRR) A network of areas in the parietal cortex that contains neurons that are involved in reaching behavior. (7)

Partial color constancy A type of color constancy that occurs when changing an object's illumination causes a change in perception of the object's hue, but less change than would be expected based on the change in the wavelengths of light reaching the eye. Note that in complete color constancy, changing an object's illumination causes no change in the object's hue. (9)

Passive touch A situation in which a person passively receives tactile stimulation that is presented by someone else. (14)

Payoffs A system of rewards and punishments used to influence a participant's motivation in a signal detection experiment. (Appendix)

Penumbra The fuzzy border at the edge of a shadow. (9)

Perception Conscious sensory experience. (1)

Perceptual organization The process by which small elements become perceptually grouped into larger objects. (5)

Perceptual organization, laws of Series of rules proposed by the Gestalt psychologists that specify how we organize small parts into wholes. Some of these laws are common fate, familiarity, good continuation, good figure, nearness, and similarity. Most of these laws were originally proposed by the Gestalt psychologists, but modern researchers have proposed some additional laws. (5)

Perceptual process A sequence of steps leading from the environment to perception of a stimulus, recognition of the stimulus, and action with regard to the stimulus. (1)

Perceptual segregation Perceptual organization in which one object is seen as separate from other objects. (5)

Periodicity pitch The constancy of a complex tone's pitch when the fundamental frequency and other lower harmonics are eliminated. See also **Effect of the missing fundamental**. (11)

Peripheral retina All of the retina except the fovea and a small area surrounding the fovea. (3)

Permeability A property of a membrane that refers to the ability of molecules to pass through it. If the permeability to a molecule is high, the molecule can easily pass through the membrane. (2)

Persistence of vision A phenomenon in which perception of any stimulus persists for about 250 ms after the stimulus is physically terminated. (5)

Perspective convergence The perception that parallel lines in the distance converge as distance increases. (10)

PET See **Positron emission tomography (PET)**. (4)

Phantom limb A person's continued perception of a limb, such as an arm or a leg, even though that limb has been amputated. (14)

Phase locking Firing of auditory neurons in synchrony with the phase of an auditory stimulus. (11)

Phenomenological method Method of determining the relationship between stimuli and perception in which the observer describes what he or she perceives. (1)

Pheromone Chemical signal released by an individual that affects the physiology and behavior of other individuals. (15)

Phoneme The shortest segment of speech that, if changed, would change the meaning of a word. (13)

Phonemic restoration effect An effect that occurs in speech perception when listeners perceive a phoneme in a word even though the acoustic signal of that phoneme is obscured by another sound, such as white noise or a cough. (13)

Phonetic boundary The voice onset time when perception changes from one speech category to another in a categorical perception experiment. (13)

Physical regularities Regularly occurring physical properties of the environment. For example, there are more vertical and horizontal orientations in the environment than oblique (angled) orientations. (5)

Physiological approach to perception Analyzing perception by determining how a person's perception is related to physiological processes that are occurring within the person. This approach focuses on determining the relationship between stimuli and physiological responding and between physiological responding and perception. (1)

Pictorial cue Depth cue, such as overlap, relative height, and relative size, that can be depicted in pictures. (10)

Pineal gland Gland at the base of the brain that René Descartes identified as being the seat of the soul. (2)

Pinna The part of the ear that is visible on the outside of the head. (11)

Piriform cortex. An area under the temporal lobe that receives signals from glomeruli in the olfactory bulb. Also called the primary olfactory cortex. (15)

Pitch The quality of sound, ranging from low to high, that is most closely associated with the frequency of a tone. (11)

Pitch neurons Neurons that respond to stimuli associated with a specific pitch. These neurons fire to the pitch of a complex tone even if the first harmonic or other harmonics of the tone are not present. (11)

Place theory of hearing The proposal that the frequency of a sound is indicated by the place along the organ of Corti at which nerve firing is highest. Modern place theory is based on Békésy's traveling wave theory of hearing. (11)

Placebo A substance that a person believes will relieve symptoms such as pain but that contains no chemicals that actually act on these symptoms. (14)

Point-light walker A biological motion stimulus created by placing lights at a number of places on a person's body and having an observer view the moving-light stimulus that results as the person moves in the dark. (8)

Ponzo illusion An illusion of size in which two objects of equal size that are positioned between two converging lines appear to be different in size. Also called the railroad track illusion. (10)

Positron emission tomography (PET) A brain mapping technique that is used in awake human subjects to determine which brain areas are activated by various tasks. (4)

Power function A mathematical function of the form $P = KS^n$, where P is perceived magnitude, K is a constant, S is the stimulus intensity, and n is an exponent. (1)

Pragnanz, law of A Gestalt law of perceptual organization that states that every stimulus pattern is seen in such a way that the resulting structure is as simple as possible. Also called the law of good figure or the law of simplicity. (5)

Preattentive stage (of perceptual processing) An automatic and rapid stage of processing, proposed by feature integration theory, during which a stimulus is decomposed into individual features. (6)

Precedence effect The effect that occurs when two identical or very similar sounds reach a listener's ears separated by a time interval of less than about 50 to 100 ms, and the listener hears the sound that reaches his or her ears first. (12)

Precueing A procedure in which a cue stimulus is presented to direct an observer's attention to a specific location where a test stimulus is likely to be presented. This procedure was used by Posner to show that attention enhances the processing of a stimulus presented at the cued location. (6)

Preferential looking (PL) technique A technique used to measure perception in infants. Two stimuli are presented, and the infant's looking behavior is monitored for the amount of time the infant spends viewing each stimulus. (16)

Presbycusis A form of sensorineural hearing loss that occurs as a function of age and is usually associated with a decrease in the ability to hear high frequencies. Since this loss also appears to be related to exposure to environmental sounds, it is also called sociocusis. (11)

Presbyopia The inability of the eye to accommodate due to a hardening of the lens and a weakening of the ciliary muscles. It occurs as people get older. (3)

Primary olfactory cortex A small area under the temporal lobe that receives signals from glomeruli in the olfactory bulb. Also called the piriform cortex. (15)

Primary receiving areas Areas of the cerebral cortex that first receive most of the signals initiated by a sense's receptors. For example, the occipital cortex is the site of the primary receiving area for vision, and the temporal lobe is the site of the primary receiving area for hearing. (2)

Primary visual receiving area The occipital cortex, where visual signals that originate in the eye first reach the cortex. (4)

Principle of common region See **Common region, principle of**. (5)

Principle of componential recovery See **Componential recovery, principle of**. (5)

Principle of synchrony See **Synchrony, principle of**. (5)

Principle of uniform connectedness See **Uniform connectedness, principle of**. (5)

Principles of auditory grouping See **Auditory grouping, principles of**. (12)

Propagated response A response, such as a nerve impulse, that travels all the way down the nerve fiber without decreasing in amplitude. (2)

Proprioception The sensing of the position of the limbs. (14)

Prosopagnosia A form of visual agnosia in which the person can't recognize faces. (4)

Protanopia A form of red–green dichromatism caused by a lack of the long-wavelength cone pigment. (9)

Proximity, law of A Gestalt law of perceptual organization that states that things that are near to each other appear to be grouped together. Also called the law of nearness. (5)

Psychophysical approach to perception Analyzing perception by determining how a person's perception is related to stimuli in the environment. This approach focuses on determining the relationship between stimuli in the environment and perceptual responding. (1)

Psychophysics Traditionally, the term *psychophysics* refers to quantitative methods for measuring the relationship between properties of the stimulus and the subject's experience. In this book, all methods that are used to determine the relationship between stimuli and perception will be broadly referred to as pychophysical methods. (1)

Pupil The opening through which light reflected from objects in the environment enters the eye. (3)

Pure tone A tone with pressure changes that can be described by a single sine wave. (11)

Purkinje shift The shift from cone spectral sensitivity to rod spectral sensitivity that takes place during dark adaptation. See also **Spectral sensitivity**. (3)

Random-dot stereogram A pair of stereoscopic images made up of random dots. When one section of this pattern is shifted slightly in one direction, the resulting disparity causes the shifted section to appear above or below the rest of the pattern when the patterns are viewed in a stereoscope. (10)

Range of hearing The specific range of frequencies within which we hear sound. (11)

Ratio principle A principle stating that two areas that reflect different amounts of light will look the same if the ratios of their intensities to the intensities of their surroundings are the same. (9)

Rat–man demonstration The demonstration in which presentation of a "ratlike" or "manlike" picture influences an observer's perception of a second picture, which can be interpreted either as a rat or as a man. This demonstration illustrates an effect of top-down processing on perception. (1)

Reaction time The time between presentation of a stimulus and an observer's or listener's response to the stimulus. Reaction time is often used in experiments as a measure of speed of processing. (1)

Real motion The physical movement of a stimulus. (8)

Real-motion neuron Neuron in the monkey's cortex that responds when movement of an image across the retina is caused by movement of a stimulus, but does not respond when movement across the retina is caused by movement of the eyes. (8)

Receiver operating characteristic (ROC) curve A graph in which the results of a signal detection experiment are plotted as the proportion of hits versus the proportion of false alarms for a number of different response criteria. (Appendix)

Receptive field A neuron's receptive field is the area on the receptor surface (the retina for vision; the skin for touch) that, when stimulated, affects the firing of that neuron. (2)

Receptor A sensory receptor is a neuron sensitive to environmental energy that changes this energy into electrical signals in the nervous system. (2)

Receptor site Small area on the postsynaptic neuron that is sensitive to specific neurotransmitters. (2)

Recognition The ability to place an object in a category that gives it meaning—for example, recognizing a particular red object as a tomato. (1)

Recognition-by-components (RBC) theory A theory of object perception proposed by Biederman, which proposes that we recognize objects by decomposing them into volumetric features called geons. (5)

Recognition profile The pattern of activation of olfactory receptors caused by a particular odorant. (15)

Recognition threshold See **Threshold, recognition**. (15)

Reflectance The percentage of light reflected from a surface. (9)

Reflectance curve A plot showing the percentage of light reflected from an object versus wavelength. (9)

Reflectance edge An edge between two areas where the reflectance of two surfaces changes. (9)

Refractive myopia Myopia (nearsightedness) in which the cornea and/or the lens bends the light too much. See also **Axial myopia**. (3)

Refractory period The time period of about 1/1,000th of a second that a nerve fiber needs to recover from conducting a nerve impulse. No new nerve impulses can be generated in the fiber until the refractory period is over. (2)

Region-of-interest (ROI) approach A procedure used in brain imaging in which subjects are pretested on the stimuli to be studied. This enables researchers to establish the precise location in the brain that they will be studying for each individual person. (5)

Regularities in the environment Characteristics of the environment that occur regularly and in many different situations. (5)

Relative disparity The difference between two objects' absolute disparities. (10)

Relative height A depth cue. Objects that have bases below the horizon appear to be farther away when they are higher in the field of view. Objects that have bases above the horizon appear to be farther away when they are lower in the field of view. (10)

Relative size A cue for depth perception. When two objects are of equal size, the one that is farther away will take up less of the field of view. (10)

Representational momentum Occurs when an observer views two pictures depicting the same motion, one after another, and is asked to indicate whether the second picture is the same as or different from the first picture. Representational momentum occurs when the second picture depicts the action *later in time* but is identified by the observer as being identical to the first picture. (8)

Resonance A mechanism that enhances the intensity of certain frequencies because of the reflection of sound waves in a closed tube. Resonance in the auditory canal enhances frequencies between about 2,000 and 5,000 Hz. (11)

Resonant frequency The frequency that is most strongly enhanced by resonance. The resonance frequency of a closed tube is determined by the length of the tube. (11)

Response compression The result when doubling the physical intensity of a stimulus less than doubles the subjective magnitude of the stimulus. (1)

Response criterion In a signal detection experiment, the subjective magnitude of a stimulus above which the participant will indicate that the stimulus is present. (1)

Response expansion The result when doubling the physical intensity of a stimulus more than doubles the subjective magnitude of the stimulus. (1)

Resting potential The difference in charge between the inside and the outside of the nerve fiber when the fiber is not conducting electrical signals. Most nerve fibers have resting potentials of about –70 mV, which means the inside of the fiber is negative relative to the outside. (2)

Reticular theory An early alternative to neuron theory that held that the nervous system consisted of a large network of fused nerve cells. See also **Neuron theory**. (2)

Retina A complex network of cells that covers the inside back of the eye. These cells include the receptors, which generate an electrical signal in response to light, as well as the horizontal, bipolar, amacrine, and ganglion cells. (3)

Retinal The light-sensitive part of the visual pigment molecule. Retinal is attached to the protein molecule opsin to form the visual pigment. (3)

Retinitis pigmentosa A retinal disease that causes a gradual loss of vision. (3)

Retinotopic map A map on a structure in the visual system, such as the lateral geniculate nucleus or the cortex, that indicates locations on the structure that correspond to locations on the retina. In retinotopic maps, locations adjacent to each other on the retina are usually represented by locations that are adjacent to each other on the structure. (4)

Retronasal route The opening from the oral cavity, through the nasal pharnyx, into the nasal cavity. This route is the basis for the way smell combines with taste to create flavor. (15)

Reverberation time The time it takes for a sound produced in an enclosed space to decrease to 1/1,000th of its original pressure. (12)

Reversible figure–ground A figure-ground pattern that perceptually reverses as it is viewed, so that the figure becomes the ground and the ground becomes the figure. The best-known reversible figure–ground pattern is Rubin's vase–face pattern. (5)

Rod Rod-shaped receptor in the retina primarily responsible for vision at low levels of illumination. The rod system is extremely sensitive in the dark but cannot resolve fine details. (3)

Rod and frame illusion An illusion in which the perception of the orientation of a rod is affected by the orientation of a surrounding frame. (4)

Rod–cone break The point on the dark adaptation curve at which vision shifts from cone vision to rod vision. (3)

Rod monochromat A person who has a retina in which the only functioning receptors are rods. (3)

Ruffini cylinder A receptor structure in the skin associated with slowly adapting fibers. It has been proposed that the Ruffini cylinder is involved in perceiving "stretching." (14)

Saccade Small, rapid eye movement. (6)

Saliency map A "map" of a visual display that takes into account characteristics of the display such as color, contrast, and orientation that are associated with capturing attention. This map predicts which areas a person is most likely to attend to. (6)

Saturation (color) The relative amount of whiteness in a chromatic color. The less whiteness a color contains, the more saturated it is. (9)

Scale illusion An illusion that occurs when successive notes of a scale are presented alternately to the left and right ears. Even though each ear receives notes that jump up and down in frequency, smoothly ascending or descending scales are heard in each ear. Also called melodic channeling. (12)

Scene A view of a real-world environment that contains (1) background elements and (2) multiple objects that are organized in a meaningful way relative to each other and the background. (5)

Secondary olfactory cortex An area in the frontal lobe, near the eyes, that receives signals originating in the olfactory receptors. Also known as the orbitofrontal cortex. (15)

Secondary somatosensory receiving cortex (S2) The area in the parietal lobe next to the primary somatosensory area (S1) that processes neural signals related to touch, temperature, and pain. (14)

Selective adaptation A procedure in which a person or animal is selectively exposed to one stimulus, and then the effect of this exposure is assessed by testing with a wide range of stimuli. Exposing a person to vertical bars and then testing a person's sensitivity to bars of all orientations is an example of selective adaptation to orientation. (4)

Selective attention Focusing attention on specific objects and ignoring others. (6)

Selective permeability Occurs when a cell membrane is highly permeable to one specific type of molecule, but not to others. (2)

Selective rearing A procedure in which animals are reared in special environments. An example of selective rearing is the experiment in which kittens were reared in an environment of vertical stripes to determine the effect on orientation selectivity of cortical neurons. (4)

Selective reflection When an object reflects some wavelengths of the spectrum more than others. (9)

Selective transmission When some wavelengths pass through visually transparent objects or substances and others do not. Selective transmission is associated with the perception of chromatic color. See also **Selective reflection**. (9)

Self-produced information Generally, environmental information that is produced by actions of the observer. An example is optic flow, which occurs as a result of a person's movement and which, in turn, provides information that can be used to guide that movement. (7)

Semantic regularities Characteristics associated with the function carried out in different types of scenes. These characteristics are learned from experience. For example, most people are aware of the kinds of activities and objects that are usually associated with kitchens. (5)

Sensations Elementary elements that, according to the structuralists, combine to create perceptions. (5)

Sensoineural hearing loss Hearing loss caused by damage within the inner ear. (11)

Sensory component of pain Pain perception described with terms such as *throbbing, prickly, hot,* or *dull*. See also **Affective (emotional) component of pain**. (14)

Shadowing Listeners' repetition aloud of what they hear as they are hearing it. (13)

Signal The stimulus presented to a participant. A concept in signal detection theory. (Appendix)

Signal detection theory (SDT) A theory stating that the detection of a stimulus depends both on the participant's sensitivity to the stimulus and on the participant's response criterion. (1)

Signal-to-noise (S/N) ratio The level of a sound signal in decibels minus the level of background noise in decibels. (12)

Similarity, law of A Gestalt law stating that similar things appear to be grouped together. (5)

Simple cortical cell A neuron in the visual cortex that responds best to bars of a particular orientation. (4)

Simplicity, law of See **Pragnanz, law of**. (5)

Simultaneous contrast The effect that occurs when surrounding one color with another changes the appearance of the surrounded color. (3)

Single dissociation When, as a result of brain damage, one function is present and another is absent. Existence of a single dissociation indicates that the two functions involve different mechanisms but may not be totally independent of one another. (4)

Size constancy Occurs when the size of an object is perceived to remain the same even when it is viewed from different distances. (10)

Size–distance scaling A hypothesized mechanism that helps maintain size constancy by taking an object's perceived distance into account. According to this mechanism, an object's perceived size, S, is determined by multiplying the size of the retinal image, R, times the object's perceived distance, D. (10)

Small-diameter fiber (S-fiber) According to gate control theory, activity in S-fibers opens the gate control mechanism and therefore increases the perception of pain. (14)

Somatosensory receiving area (S1) An area in the parietal lobe of the cortex that receives inputs from the skin and the viscera that are associated with somatic senses such as touch, temperature, and pain. See also **Secondary somatosensory receiving area (S2)**. (14)

Somatosensory system The system that includes the cutaneous senses (senses involving the skin), proprioception (the sense of position of the limbs), and kinesthesis (sense of movement of the limbs). (14)

Sound (perceptual) The perceptual experience of hearing. The statement "I hear a sound" is using *sound* in that sense. (11)

Sound (physical) The physical stimulus for hearing. The statement "The sound's level was 10 dB" is using *sound* in that sense. (11)

Sound level The pressure of a sound stimulus, expressed in decibels. See also **Sound pressure level (SPL)**. (11)

Sound pressure level (SPL) A designation used to indicate that the reference pressure used for calculating a tone's decibel rating is set at 20 micropascals, near the threshold in the most sensitive frequency range for hearing. (11)

Sound spectrogram A plot showing the pattern of intensities and frequencies of a speech stimulus. (13)

Sound wave Pattern of pressure changes in a medium. Most of the sounds we hear are due to pressure changes in the air, although sound can be transmitted through water and solids as well. (11)

Sparse coding The idea that a particular object is represented by the firing of a relatively small number of neurons. (2)

Spatial cue In tactile perception, information about the texture of a surface that is determined by the size, shape, and distribution of surface elements such as bumps and grooves. (14)

Spatial frequency For a grating stimulus, the frequency with which the grating repeats itself per degree of visual angle. (One cycle of a grating includes one light bar and one dark bar.) For more natural stimuli, high spatial frequencies are associated with fine details, and low spatial frequencies are associated with grosser features. (16)

Specificity coding Type of neural code in which different perceptions are signaled by activity in specific neurons. See also **Distributed coding**. (2)

Spectral cue In hearing, the distribution of frequencies reaching the ear that are associated with specific locations of a sound. The differences in frequencies are caused by interaction of sound with the listener's head and pinnae. (12)

Spectral sensitivity The sensitivity of visual receptors to different parts of the visible spectrum. See also **Spectral sensitivity curve**. (3)

Spectral sensitivity curve The function relating a subject's sensitivity to light to the wavelength of the light. The spectral sensitivity curves for rod and cone vision indicate that the rods and cones are maximally sensitive at 500 nm and 560 nm, respectively. See also **Purkinje shift**. (3)

Speech segmentation The process of perceiving individual words from the continuous flow of the speech signal. (13)

Spinothalamic pathway One of the nerve pathways in the spinal cord that conducts nerve impulses from the skin to the somatosensory area of the thalamus. (14)

Spontaneous activity Nerve firing that occurs in the absence of environmental stimulation. (2)

Staining A technique in which neurons take up a dye that makes their structure visible. (2)

Stapes The last of the three ossicles in the middle ear. It receives vibrations from the incus and transmits these vibrations to the oval window of the inner ear. (11)

Statistical learning The process of learning about transitional probabilities and other characteristics of the environment. Statistical learning for properties of language has been demonstrated in young infants. (13)

Stereopsis The impression of depth that results from binocular disparity—the difference in the position of images of the same object on the retinas of the two eyes. (10)

Stereoscope A device that presents pictures to the left and the right eyes so that the binocular disparity a person would experience when viewing an actual scene is duplicated. The result is a convincing illusion of depth. (10)

Stevens's power law. A law concerning the relationship between the physical intensity of a stimulus and the perception of the subjective magnitude of the stimulus. The law states that $P = KS^n$, where P is perceived magnitude, K is a constant, S is the stimulus intensity, and n is an exponent. (1)

Stimulus salience Characteristics such as bright colors, high contrast, and highly visible orientations that cause stimuli to stand out and therefore attract attention. (6)

Striate cortex The visual receiving area of the cortex, located in the occipital lobe. (4)

Structuralism The approach to psychology, prominent in the late 19th and early 20th centuries, that postulated that perceptions result from the summation of many elementary sensations. The Gestalt approach to perception was, in part, a reaction to structuralism. (5)

Subcortical structure Structure below the cerebral cortex. For example, the superior colliculus is a subcortical structure in the visual system. The cochlear nucleus and superior olivary nucleus are among the subcortical structures in the auditory system. (11)

Substantia gelatinosa A nucleus in the spinal cord that, according to the gate control model, receives inputs from S-fibers and L-fibers and sends inhibition to the T-cell. (14)

Subtraction technique A technique used to analyze the results of brain imaging experiments, in which brain activity elicited by a control condition is subtracted from the activity elicited by an experimental condition to determine the activity that can be attributed to the experimental condition alone. (4)

Subtractive color mixture. See **Color mixture, subtractive**. (9)

Superior colliculus An area in the brain that is involved in controlling eye movements and other visual behaviors. This area receives about 10 percent of the ganglion cell fibers that leave the eye in the optic nerve. (4)

Superior olivary nucleus A nucleus along the auditory pathway from the cochlea to the auditory cortex. The superior olivary nucleus receives inputs from the cochlear nucleus. (11)

Supertaster A person who is especially sensitive to 6-n-propylthiouracil (PROP), a bitter substance. (15)

Synapse A small space between the end of one neuron (the presynaptic neuron) and the cell body of another neuron (the postsynaptic neuron). (2)

Synchrony As described in the synchrony hypothesis, two neurons or groups of neurons are firing in synchrony when they have the same pattern of firing. (6)

Synchrony, principle of A modern principle of perceptual organization that states that visual events that occur at the same time will be perceived as belonging together. (5)

Synchrony hypothesis The idea that when an object causes neurons in different parts of the cortex to fire, the timing of the firing of these neurons will be synchronized. This synchrony indicates that all of these neurons are responding to the same object. This idea has been proposed as a solution to the binding problem. (6)

Tactile acuity The smallest details that can be detected on the skin. (14)

Taste bud A structure located within papillae on the tongue that contains the taste cells. (15)

Taste cell Cell located in taste buds that causes the transduction of chemical to electrical energy when chemicals contact receptor sites or channels located at the tip of this cell. (15)

Taste pore An opening in the taste bud through which the tips of taste cells protrude. When chemicals enter a taste pore, they stimulate the taste cells and result in transduction. (15)

Taster A person who can taste the compound phenylthiocarbamide (PTC). (15)

Tectorial membrane A membrane that stretches the length of the cochlea and is located directly over the hair cells. Vibrations of the cochlear partition cause the tectorial membrane to bend the hair cells by rubbing against them. (11)

Temporal coding The connection between the frequency of a sound stimulus and the timing of the auditory nerve fiber firing.

Temporal cue In tactile perception, information about the texture of a surface that is determined by the rate of vibrations that occur as we move our fingers across the surface. (14)

Temporal lobe A lobe on the side of the cortex that is the site of the cortical receiving area for hearing and the termination point for the ventral, or *what*, stream for visual processing. A number of areas in the temporal lobe, such as the fusiform face area and the extrastriate body area, serve functions related to perceiving and recognizing objects. (2)

Texture gradient The visual pattern formed by a regularly textured surface that extends away from the observer. This pattern provides information for distance because the elements in a texture gradient appear smaller as distance from the observer increases. (10)

Theory of natural selection The idea that genetically based characteristics that enhance an animal's ability to survive, and therefore reproduce, will be passed on to future generations. (4)

Theory of unconscious inference The idea proposed by Helmholtz that some of our perceptions are the result of unconscious assumptions that we make about the environment. See also **Likelihood principle**. (5)

Threshold, absolute The minimum stimulus energy necessary for an observer to detect a stimulus. (1)

Threshold, detection The minimum amount of energy that can be detected. The detection threshold for smell is the lowest concentration at which an odorant can be detected. This threshold is distinguished from the recognition threshold, which requires a higher concentration of odorant. (15)

Threshold, difference The minimal detectable difference between two stimuli. (1)

Threshold, recognition For smell, the concentration at which the quality of an odor can be recognized. (15)

Timbre The quality that distinguishes between two tones that sound different even though they have the same loudness, pitch, and duration. Differences in timbre are illustrated by the sounds made by different musical instruments. (11)

Tone chroma The perceptual similarity of notes separated by one or more octaves. (11)

Tone height The increase in pitch that occurs as frequency is increased. (11)

Tonotopic map An ordered map of frequencies created by the responding of neurons within structures in the auditory system. There is a tonotopic map of neurons along the length of the cochlea, with neurons at the apex responding best to low frequencies and neurons at the base responding best to high frequencies. (11)

Top-down processing Processing that starts with the analysis of high-level information, such as the knowledge a person brings to a situation. Also called knowledge-based processing. Distinguished from bottom-up, or data-based processing, which is based on incoming data. (1)

Transduction In the senses, the transformation of environmental energy into electrical energy. For example, the retinal receptors transduce light energy into electrical energy. (1)

Transitional probabilities In language, the chances that one sound will follow another sound. Every language has transitional probabilities for different sounds. Part of learning a language involves learning about the transitional probabilities in that language. (13)

Transmission cell (T-cell) According to gate control theory, the cell that receives input from the L- and S-fibers. Activity in the T-cell determines the perception of pain. (14)

Traveling wave In the auditory system, vibration of the basilar membrane in which the peak of the vibration travels from the base of the membrane to its apex. (11)

Trichromat A person with normal color vision. Trichromats can match any wavelength in the spectrum by mixing three other wavelengths in various proportions. (9)

Trichromatic theory of color vision. A theory proposing that our perception of color is determined by the ratio of activity in three receptor mechanisms with different spectral sensitivities. (9)

Tritanopia A form of dichromatism thought to be caused by a lack of the short-wavelength cone pigment. (9)

Tuning curve, frequency See **Frequency tuning curve**. (11)

Tuning curve, orientation See **Orientation tuning curve**. (4)

2-deoxyglucose technique A procedure that involves injecting a radioactive 2-deoxyglucose (2DG) molecule into an animal and exposing the animal to oriented stimuli. The 2DG is taken up by neurons that respond to the orientation. This procedure is used to visualize orientation columns in the cortex. (15)

Two-point threshold. The smallest separation between two points on the skin that is perceived as two points; a measure of acuity on the skin. See also **Grating acuity**. (14)

Tympanic membrane A membrane at the end of the auditory canal that vibrates in response to vibrations of the air and transmits these vibrations to the ossicles in the middle ear. (11)

Uniform connectedness, principle of A modern Gestalt principle that states that connected regions of a visual stimulus are perceived as a single unit. (5)

Unilateral dichromat A person who has dichromatic vision in one eye and trichromatic vision in the other eye. People with this condition (which is extremely rare) have been tested to determine what colors a dichromats perceive by asking them to compare the perceptions they experience with their dichromatic eye and their trichromatic eye. (9)

Ventral pathway Pathway that conducts signals from the striate cortex to the temporal lobe. Also called the *what* pathway because it is involved in recognizing objects. (4)

Ventricles Cavities located at the center of the brain that were identified by Galen as the source of "spirits" that determined human health, thoughts, and emotions. (2)

Ventriloquism effect See **Visual capture**. (12)

Ventrolateral nucleus Nucleus in the thalamus that receives signals from the cutaneous system. (14)

Video microscopy A technique that has been used to take pictures of papillae and taste buds on the tongue. (15)

Viewpoint invariance Objects that have properties that don't change when viewed from different angles. The geons in the recognition-by-components theory of object perception are view invariant. (5)

Visible light The band of electromagnetic energy that activates the visual system and that, therefore, can be perceived. For humans, visible light has wavelengths between 400 and 700 nanometers. (3)

Visual acuity The ability to resolve small details. (3)

Visual angle The angle of an object relative to an observer's eyes. This angle can be determined by extending two lines from the eye—one to one end of an object and the other to the other end of the object. Because an object's visual angle is always determined relative to an observer, its visual angle changes as the distance between the object and the observer changes. (10)

Visual capture When sound is heard coming from its seen location, even though it is actually originating somewhere else. Also called the ventriloquism effect. (12)

Visual direction strategy A strategy used by moving observers to reach a destination by keeping their body oriented toward the target. (7)

Visual evoked potential (VEP) An electrical response to visual stimulation recorded by the placement of disk electrodes on the back of the head. This potential reflects the activity of a large population of neurons in the visual cortex. (16)

Visual form agnosia The inability to recognize objects. (1)

Visual pigment A light-sensitive molecule contained in the rod and cone outer segments. The reaction of this molecule to light results in the generation of an electrical response in the receptors. (3)

Visual pigment bleaching The change in the color of a visual pigment that occurs when visual pigment molecules are isomerized by exposure to light. (3)

Visual pigment molecules Light-sensitive molecules in the outer segments of the rod and cone visual receptors that are responsible for the transformation of light energy into electrical energy. The molecule consists of a large protein component called opsin and a small light-sensitive component called retinal. (3)

Visual pigment regeneration Occurs after the visual pigment's two components—opsin and retinal—have become separated due to the action of light. Regeneration, which occurs in the dark, involves a rejoining of these two components to reform the visual pigment molecule. This process depends on enzymes located in the pigment epithelium. (3)

Visual search A procedure in which a person's task is to find a particular element in a display that contains a number of elements. (1)

Voice onset time (VOT) In speech production, the time delay between the beginning of a sound and the beginning of the vibration of the vocal chords. (13)

Waterfall illusion An aftereffect of movement that occurs after viewing a stimulus moving in one direction, such as a waterfall. Viewing the waterfall makes other objects appear to move in the opposite direction. (8)

Wavelength For light energy, the distance between one peak of a light wave and the next peak. (3)

Weber fraction The ratio of the difference threshold to the value of the standard stimulus in Weber's law. (1)

Weber's law A law stating that the ratio of the difference threshold (DL) to the value of the stimulus (S) is constant. According to this relationship, doubling the value of a stimulus will cause a doubling of the difference threshold. The ratio DL/S is called the Weber fraction. (1)

Wernicke's aphasia An inability to comprehend words or arrange sounds into coherent speech, caused by damage to Wernicke's area. (13)

Wernicke's area An area in the temporal lobe involved in speech perception. Damage to this area causes Wernicke's aphasia, which is characterized by difficulty in understanding speech. (13)

***What* pathway** See **Ventral pathway**. (4)

***Where* pathway** See **Dorsal pathway**. (4)

White's illusion A display in which two rectangles are perceived as differing in lightness even though they both reflect the same amount of light and even though the rectangle that is perceived as lighter receives more lateral inhibition than the one perceived as darker. (3)

Word deafness Occurs in the most extreme form of Wernicke's aphasia, when a person cannot recognize words, even though the ability to hear pure tones remains intact. (13)

Young-Helmholtz theory of color vision. See **Trichromatic theory of color vision**. (9)

References

Abramov, I., & Gordon, J. (1994). Color appearance: On seeing red, or yellow, or green, or blue. *Annual Review of Psychology, 45,* 451–485.

Abramov, I., Gordon, J., Hendrickson, A., Hainline, L., Dobson, V., & LaBossiere, E. (1982). The retina of the newborn human infant. *Science, 217,* 265–267.

Ache, B. W. (1991). Phylogeny of smell and taste. In T. V. Getchell, R. L. Doty, L. M. Bartoshuk, & J. B. Snow (Eds.), *Smell and taste in health and disease* (pp. 3–18). New York: Raven Press.

Ackerman, D. (1990). *A natural history of the senses.* New York: Vintage Books.

Acoustical Society of America. (2000). *Classroom acoustics.* Melville, NY: Author.

Adelson, E. H. (1993). Perceptual organization and the judgment of brightness. *Science, 262,* 2042–2044.

Adelson, E. H. (1999). Light perception and lightness illusions. In M. Gazzaniga (Ed.), *The new cognitive neurosciences* (pp. 339–351). Cambridge, MA: MIT Press.

Adrian, E. D. (1928). *The basis of sensation.* New York: Norton.

Adrian, E. D. (1932). The mechanism of nervous action. Philadelphia: University of Pennsylvania Press.

Aguirre, G. K., Zarahn, E., & D'Esposito, M. (1998). An area within human ventral cortex sensitive to "building" stimuli: Evidence and implications. *Neuron, 21,* 373–383.

Alain, C., Arnott, S. R., Hevenor, S., Graham, S., & Grady, C. L. (2001). "What" and "where" in the human auditory system. *Proceedings of the National Academy of Sciences, 98,* 12301–12306.

Alpern, M., Kitahara, K., & Krantz, D. H. (1983). Perception of color in unilateral tritanopia. *Journal of Physiology, 335,* 683–697.

Andersen, R. A., Musallam, S., & Pesaran, B. (2004). *Current Opinion in Neurobiology, 14,* 1–7.

Anderson, B. L., & Winawer, J. (2005). Image segmentation and lightness perception. *Nature, 434,* 79–83.

Appelle, S. (1972). Perception and discrimination as a function of stimulus orientation: The "oblique effect" in man and animals. *Psychological Bulletin, 78,* 266–278.

Arbib, M. A. (2001). The mirror system hypothesis for the language-ready brain. In A. Cangelosi & D. Parisi (Eds.), *Computational approaches to the evolution of language and communication.* Berlin: Springer-Verlag.

Ashbridge, E., Cowey, A., & Wade, D. (1999). Does parietal cortex contribute to feature binding? *Neuropsychologia, 37,* 999–1004.

Aslin, R. N. (1977). Development of binocular fixation in human infants. *Journal of Experimental Child Psychology, 23,* 133–150.

Avenanti, A., Bueti, D., Galati, G., & Aglioti, S. M. (2005). Transcranial magnetic stimulation highlights the sensorimotor side of empathy for pain. *Nature Neuroscience, 8,* 955–960.

Azzopardi, P., & Cowey, A. (1993). Preferential representation of the fovea in the primary visual cortex. *Nature, 361,* 719–721.

Baars, B. J. (2001). The conscious access hypothesis: Origins and recent evidence. *Trends in Cognitive Sciences, 6,* 47–52.

Bach, M., & Poloschek, C. M. (2006). Optical illusions. *Advances in Clinical Neuroscience and Rehabilitation, 6,* 20–21.

Backhaus, W. G. K. (1998). Physiological and psychophysical simulations of color vision in humans and animals. In W. G. K. Backhaus, R. Kliegl, & J. S. Werner (Eds.), *Color vision: Perspectives from different disciplines* (pp. 45–77). New York: Walter de Gruyter.

Backus, B. T., Fleet, D. J., Parker, A. J., & Heeger, D. J. (2001). Human cortical activity correlates with stereoscopic depth perception. *Journal of Neurophysiology, 86,* 2054–2068.

Baird, J. C., Wagner, M., & Fuld, K. (1990). A simple but powerful theory of the moon illusion. *Journal of Experimental Psychology: Human Perception and Performance, 16,* 675–677.

Banks, M. S. (1982). The development of spatial and temporal contrast sensitivity. *Current Eye Research, 2,* 191–198.

Banks, M. S., & Bennett, P. J. (1988). Optical and photoreceptor immaturities limit the spatial and chromatic vision of human neonates. *Journal of the Optical Society of America, A5,* 2059–2079.

Banks, M. S., & Salapatek, P. (1978). Acuity and contrast sensitivity in 1-, 2-, and 3-month-old human infants. *Investigative Ophthalmology and Visual Science, 17,* 361–365.

Banks, M. S., & Salapatek, P. (1981). Infant pattern vision: A new approach based on the contrast sensitivity function. *Journal of Experimental Child Psychology, 31,* 1–45.

Bar, M. (2004). Visual objects in context. *Nature Reviews Neuroscience, 5,* 617–629.

Barber, T. X., & Hahn, K. W. (1964). Experimental studies in "hypnotic" behaviour: Physiologic and subjective effects of imagined pain. *Journal of Nervous and Mental Disorders, 139,* 416–425.

Bardy, B. G., & Laurent, M. (1998). How is body orientation controlled during somersaulting? *Journal of Experimental Psychology: Human Perception and Performance, 24,* 963–977.

Barlow, H. B. (1995). The neuron in perception. In M. S. Gazzaniga (Ed.), *The cognitive neurosciences* (pp. 415–434). Cambridge, MA: MIT Press.

Barlow, H. B., Blakemore, C., & Pettigrew, J. D. (1967). The neural mechanism of binocular depth discrimination. *Journal of Physiology, 193,* 327–342.

Barlow, H. B., & Mollon, J. D. (Eds.). (1982). *The senses.* Cambridge, UK: Cambridge University Press.

Bartley, H. (1951). The psychophysiology of vision. In S. S. Stevens (Ed.), *Handbook of Experimental Psychology.* New York: Macmillan.

Bartoshuk, L. M. (1971). The chemical senses: I. Taste. In J. W. Kling & L. A. Riggs (Eds.), *Experimental psychology* (3rd ed.). New York: Holt, Rinehart and Winston.

Bartoshuk, L. M. (1979). Bitter taste of saccharin: Related to the genetic ability to taste the bitter substance propylthioural (PROP). *Science, 205,* 934–935.

Bartoshuk, L. M. (1980, September). Separate worlds of taste. *Psychology Today, 243,* 48–56.

Bartoshuk, L. M., & Beauchamp, G. K. (1994). Chemical senses. *Annual Review of Psychology, 45,* 419–449.

Bartrip, J., Morton, J., & deSchonen, S. (2001). Responses to mother's face in 3-week- to 5-month-old infants. *British Journal of Developmental Psychology, 19,* 219–232.

Battaglini, P. P., Galletti, C., & Fattori, P. (1996). Cortical mechanisms for visual perception of object motion and position in space. *Behavioural Brain Research, 76,* 143–154.

Battelli, L., Cavanagh, P., & Thornton, I. M. (2003). Perception of biological motion in parietal patients. *Neuropsychologia, 41*, 1808–1816.

Baylis, G. C., & Driver, J. (1993). Visual attention and objects: Evidence for hierarchical coding of location. *Journal of Experimental Psychology: Human Perception and Performance, 19*, 451–470.

Baylor, D. (1992). Transduction in retinal photoreceptor cells. In P. Corey & S. D. Roper (Eds.), *Sensory transduction* (pp. 151–174). New York: Rockefeller University Press.

Beauchamp, G. K., Bertino, M., & Engelman, K. (1991). Human salt appetite. In M. I. Friedman, M. G. Tordoff, & M. R. Kare (Eds.), *Chemical senses: Appetite and nutrition* (pp. 85–107). New York: Marcel Dekker.

Beauchamp, G. K., Cowart, B. J., & Moran, M. (1986). Developmental changes in salt acceptability in human infants. *Developmental Psychobiology, 19*, 17–25.

Beauchamp, G. K., Cowart, B. J., & Schmidt, H. J. (1991). Development of chemosensory sensitivity and preference. In T. V. Getchell, R. L. Doty, L. M. Bartoshuk, & J. B. Snow (Eds.), *Smell and taste in health and disease* (pp. 405–416). New York: Raven Press.

Beecher, H. K. (1959). *Measurement of subjective responses*. New York: Oxford University Press.

Behrmann, M., Geng, J. J., & Shomstein, S. (2004). Parietal cortex and attention. *Current Opinion in Neurobiology, 14*, 212–217.

Békésy, G. von (1960). *Experiments in hearing*. New York: McGraw-Hill.

Belin, P., Zatorre, R. J., Lafaille, P., Ahad, P., & Pike, B. (2000). Voice-selective areas in human auditory cortex. *Nature, 403*, 309–312.

Benary, W. (1924). Beobachtungen zu einem Experiment uber Helligkeitzkontrast . *Psychologische Forschung, 5*, 131–142.

Bendor, D., & Wang, X. (2005). The neuronal representation of pitch in primate auditory cortex. *Nature, 436*, 1161–1165.

Beranek, L. L. (1996). *Concert and opera halls: How they sound*. Woodbury, NY: Acoustical Society of America.

Berger, K. W. (1964). Some factors in the recognition of timbre. *Journal of the Acoustical Society of America, 36*, 1881–1891.

Berthenthal, B. I., Rose, J. L., & Bai, D. L. (1997). Perception–action coupling in the development of visual control of posture. *Journal of Experimental Psychology: Human Perception and Performance, 23*, 1631–1643.

Biederman, I. (1987). Recognition-by-components: A theory of human image understanding. *Psychological Review, 94*, 115–147.

Biederman, I. (1995). Visual object recognition. In S. F. Kosslyn & D. N. Osherson (Eds.), *An invitation to cognitive science: Vol. 2. Visual cognition* (2nd ed., pp. 121–165). Cambridge, MA: MIT Press.

Biederman, I., & Cooper, E. E. (1991). Priming contour-deleted images: Evidence for intermediate representations in visual object recognition. *Cognitive Psychology 23*, 393–419.

Birnberg, J. R. (1988, March 21). My turn. *Newsweek*.

Bisley, J. W., & Goldberg, M. E. (2003). Neuronal activity in the lateral intraparietal area and spatial attention. *Science, 299*, 81–86.

Blake, R., & Hirsch, H. V. B. (1975). Deficits in binocular depth perception in cats after alternating monocular deprivation. *Science, 190*, 1114–1116.

Blake, R., & Wilson, H. R. (1991). Neural models of stereoscopic vision. *Trends in Neuroscience, 14*, 445–452.

Blakemore, C., & Cooper, G. G. (1970). Development of the brain depends on the visual environment. *Nature, 228*, 477–478.

Blauert, J. (1997). *Spatial hearing: The psychophysics of human sound localization* (Rev. ed.). Cambridge, MA: MIT Press.

Block, N. (in press). Consciousness, accessibility, and the mesh between psychology and neuroscience. *Behavioral and Brain Sciences*.

Blumstein, S. E., Baker, E., & Goodglass, H. (1977). Phonological factors in auditory comprehension in aphasia. *Neuropsychologia, 15*, 19–30.

Boring, E. G. (1942). Sensation and perception in the history of experimental psychology. New York: Appleton-Century-Crofts.

Bornstein, M. H., Kessen, W., & Weiskopf, S. (1976). Color vision and hue categorization in young human infant. *Journal of Experimental Psychology: Human Perception and Performance, 2*, 115–119.

Bosking, W. H., Zhang, Y., Schofield, B., & Fitzpatrick, D. (1997). Orientation selectivity and the arrangement of horizontal connections in tree shrew striate cortex. *Journal of Neuroscience, 17*, 2112–2127.

Bowmaker, J. K., & Dartnall, H. J. A. (1980). Visual pigments of rods and cones in a human retina. *Journal of Physiology, 298*, 501–511.

Boynton, R. M. (1979). *Human color vision*. New York: Holt, Rinehart and Winston.

Bradley, D. R., & Petry, H. M. (1977). Organizational determinants of subjective contour: The subjective Necker cube. *American Journal of Psychology, 90*, 253–262.

Brainard, D. H., & Wandell, B. A. (1986). Analysis of the retinex theory of color vision. *Journal of the Optical Society of America, A3*, 1651–1661.

Bregman, A. S. (1990). *Auditory scene analysis*. Cambridge, MA: MIT Press.

Bregman, A. S. (1993). Auditory scene analysis: Hearing in complex environments. In S. McAdams & E. Bigand (Eds.), *Thinking in sound: The cognitive psychology of human audition* (pp. 10–36). Oxford, UK: Oxford University Press.

Bregman, A. S., & Campbell, J. (1971). Primary auditory stream segregation and perception of order in rapid sequence of tones. *Journal of Experimental Psychology, 89*, 244–249.

Bregman, A. S., & Rudnicky, A. I. (1975). Auditory segregation: Stream or streams? *Journal of Experimental Psychology: Human Perception and Performance, 1*, 263–267.

Brennan, P. A., & Zufall, F. (2006). Pheromonal communication in vertebrates. *Nature, 444*, 308–315.

Breslin, P. A. S. (2001). Human gustation and flavour. *Flavour and Fragrance Journal, 16*, 439–456.

Bridgeman, B., & Stark, L. (1991). Ocular proprioception and efference copy in registering visual direction. *Vision Research, 31*, 1903–1913.

Britten, K. H., & van Wezel, R. J. A. (2002). Area MST and heading perception in macaque monkeys. *Cerebral Cortex, 12*, 692–701.

Brosch, M., Bauer, R., & Eckhorn, R. (1997). Stimulus-dependent modulations of correlated high-frequency oscillations in cat visual cortex. *Cerebral Cortex, 7*, 70–76.

Brown, A. A., Dowell, R. C., & Clark, G. M. (1987). Clinical results for postlingually deaf patients implanted with multichannel cochlear prosthetics. *Annals of Otology, Rhinology, and Laryngology, 96*(Suppl. 128), 127–128.

Brown, P. K., & Wald, G. (1964). Visual pigments in single rods and cones of the human retina. *Science, 144*, 45–52.

Buchsbaum, G., & Gottschalk, A. (1983). Trichromacy, opponent colours coding and optimum colour information transmission in the retina. *Proceedings of the Royal Society of London B, 220*, 89–110.

Buck, L. B. (2004). Olfactory receptors and coding in mammals. *Nutrition Reviews, 62*, S184–S188.

Buck, L., & Axel, R. (1991). A novel multigene family may encode odorant receptors: A molecular basis for odor recognition. *Cell, 65*, 175–187.

Bufe, B., Breslin, P. A. S., Kuhn, C., Reed, D. R., Tharp, C. D., Slack, J. P., et al. (2005). The molecular basis of individual differences in phenylthiocarbamide and propylthiouracil bitterness perception. *Current Biology, 15*, 322–327.

Bugelski, B. R., & Alampay, D. A. (1961). The role of frequency in developing perceptual sets. *Canadian Journal of Psychology, 15*, 205–211.

Burns, M. & Lamb, T. D. (2004). Visual transduction by rod and cone photoreceptors. In L. M. Chalupa & J. S. Werner (Eds.), *The visual neurosciences*. Cambridge, MA: MIT Press.

Burton, A. M., Young, A. W., Bruce, V., Johnston, R. A., & Ellis, A. W. (1991). Understanding covert recognition. *Cognition, 39*, 129–166.

Bushnell, I. W. R. (2001). Mother's face recognition in newborn infants: Learning and memory. *Infant and Child Development, 10*, 67–74.

Bushnell, I. W. R., Sai, F., & Mullin, J. T. (1989). Neonatal recognition of the mother's face. *British Journal of Developmental Psychology, 7*, 3–15.

Cain, W. S. (1977). Differential sensitivity for smell: "Noise" at the nose. *Science, 195*, 796–798.

Cain, W. S. (1979). To know with the nose: Keys to odor identification. *Science, 203*, 467–470.

Cain, W. S. (1980). Sensory attributes of cigarette smoking. *Branbury Report: 3. A safe cigarette?* (pp. 239–249). Cold Spring Harbor, NY: Cold Spring Harbor Laboratory.

Cain, W. S. (1988). Olfaction. In R. A. Atkinson, R. J. Herrnstein, G. Lindzey, & R. D. Luce (Eds.), *Stevens' handbook of experimental psychology: Vol. 1. Perception and motivation* (Rev. ed., pp. 409–459). New York: Wiley.

Calder, A. J., Beaver, J. D., Winston, J. S., Dolan, R. J., Jenkins, R., Eger, E., et al. (2007). Separate coding of different gaze directions in the superior temporal sulcus and inferior parietal lobule. *Current Biology, 17*, 20–25.

Calton, J. L., Dickenson, A. R., & Snyder, L. H. (2002). Non-spatial, motor-specific activation in posterior parietal cortex. *Nature Neuroscience, 5*, 580–588.

Calvert, G. A., Bullmore, E. T., Brammer, M. J., Campbell, R., Williams, S. C. R., McGuire, P. K., et al. (1997). Activation of auditory cortex during silent lipreading. *Science, 276*, 593–595.

Calvo-Merino, B., Glaser, D. E., Grezes, J., Passingham, R. E., & Haggard, P. (2005). Action observation and acquired motor skills: An fMRI study with expert dancers. *Cerebral Cortex, 15*, 1243–1249.

Calvo-Merino, B., Grezes, J., Glaser, D. E., Passingham, R. E., & Haggard, P. (2006). Seeing or doing? Influence of visual and motor familiarity in action observation. *Current Biology, 16*, 1905–1910.

Campbell, F. W., Kulikowski, J. J., & Levinson, J. (1966). The effect of orientation on the visual resolution of gratings. *Journal of Physiology (London), 187*, 427–436.

Carello, C., & Turvey, M. T. (2004). Physics and psychology of the muscle sense. *Current Directions in Psychological Science, 13*, 25–28.

Carlile, S., Leong, P., Hyams, S. (1997). The nature and distribution of errors in sound localization by human listeners. *Hearing Research, 114*, 179–196.

Carr, R. E., & Ripps, H. (1967). Rhodopsin kinetics and rod adaptation in Oguchi's disease. *Investigative Ophthalmology, 6*, 426–436.

Carrasco, M. (in press). Attention: Effect on perception. In E. B. Goldstein (Ed.), *Sage encyclopedia of perception*. Thousand Oaks, CA: Sage.

Carrasco, M., Ling, S., & Read, S. (2004). Attention alters appearance. *Nature Neuroscience, 7*, 308–313.

Carrasco, M., Loula, F., & Ho, Y.-X. (2006). How attention enhances spatial resolution: Evidence from selective adaptation to spatial frequency. *Perception and Psychophysics, 68*, 1004–1012.

Casagrande, V. A., & Norton, T. T. (1991). Lateral geniculate nucleus: A review of its physiology and function. In J. R. Coonley-Dillon (Vol. Ed.) & A. G. Leventhal (Ed.), *Vision and visual dysfunction: The neural basis of visual function* (Vol. 4, pp. 41–84). London: Macmillan.

Catmur, C., Walsh, V., & Heyes, C. (2007). Sensorimotor learning configures the human mirror system. *Current Biology, 17*, 1527–1531.

CBS News. (2001, September 4). The cochear implant controversy. *CBS Sunday Morning.* http://www.cbsnews.com/stories/1998/06/01/sunday/main10719.shtml

Chandrashekar, J., Hoon, M. A., Ryba, N. J. P., & Zuker, C. S. (2006). The receptors and cells for mammalian taste. *Nature, 444*, 288–294.

Chapman, C. R. (1995). The affective dimension of pain: A model. In B. Bromm & J. Desmedt (Eds.), *Pain and the brain: From nociception to cognition: Advances in pain research and therapy* (Vol. 22, pp. 283–301). New York: Raven.

Chella, A., Frixione, M., & Gaglio, S. (2000). Understanding dynamic scenes. *Artificial Intelligence, 123*, 89–132.

Chino, Y., Smith, E., Hatta, S., & Cheng, H. (1997). Postnatal development of binocular disparity sensitivity in neurons of the primate visual cortex. *Journal of Neuroscience, 17*, 296–307.

Cholewaik, R. W., & Collins, A. A. (2003). Vibrotactile localization on the arm: Effects of place, space, and age. *Perception and Psychophysics, 65*, 1058–1077.

Churchland, P. S., & Ramachandran, V. S. (1996). Filling in: Why Dennett is wrong. In K. Atkins (Ed.), *Perception*. Oxford, UK: Oxford University Press.

Clarke, S., Thiran, A. B., Maeder, P., Adriani, M., Vernet, O., Regli, L., et al. (2002). What and where in human auditory: Selective deficits following focal hemispheric lesions. *Experimental Brain Research, 147*, 8–15.

Clulow, F. W. (1972). *Color: Its principles and their applications*. New York: Morgan & Morgan.

Cohen, J. D., & Tong, F. (2001). The face of controversy. *Science, 293*, 2405–2407.

Cohen, L. B. (1991). Infant attention: An information processing approach. In M. J. Weiss & P. R. Zelazo (Eds.), *Newborn attention: Biological constraints and the influence of experience* (pp. 1–21). Norwood, NJ: Ablex.

Cohen, M. R., & Newsome, W. T. (2004). What electrical microstimulation has revealed about the neural basis of cognition. *Current Opinion In Neurobiology, 14*, 169–177.

Colby, C. L., Duhamel, J.-R., & Goldberg, M. E. (1995). Oculocentric spatial representation in parietal cortex. *Cerebral Cortex, 5*, 470–481.

Cole, J. (1995). *Pride and a daily marathon*. Cambridge, MA: MIT Press.

Collett, T. S. (1978). Peering—a locust behavior pattern for obtaining motion parallax information. *Journal of Experimental Biology, 76*, 237–241.

Collett, T. S., & Harkness, L. I. K. (1982). Depth vision in animals. In D. J. Ingle, M. A. Goodale, & R. J. W. Mansfield (Eds.), *Analysis of visual behavior* (pp. 111–176). Cambridge, MA: MIT Press.

Coltheart, M. (1970). The effect of verbal size information upon visual judgments of absolute distance. *Perception and Psychophysics, 9*, 222–223.

Comel, M. (1953). Fisiologia normale e patologica della cute umana. Milan, Italy: Fratelli Treves Editori.

Conel, J. L. (1939). *The postnatal development of the cerebral cortex* (Vol. 1). Cambridge, MA: Harvard University Press.

Conel, J. L. (1947). *The postnatal development of the cerebral cortex* (Vol. 2). Cambridge, MA: Harvard University Press.

Conel, J. L. (1951). *The postnatal development of the cerebral cortex* (Vol. 3). Cambridge, MA: Harvard University Press.

Connolly, J. D., Andersen, R. A., & Goodale, M. A. (2003). fMRI evidence for a "parietal reach region" in the human brain. *Experimental Brain Research, 153*, 140–145.

Coppola, D. M., White, L. E., Fitzpatrick, D., & Purves, D. (1998). Unequal distribution of cardinal and oblique contours in ferret visual cortex. *Proceedings of the National Academy of Sciences, 95*, 2621–2623.

Costanzo, R. M., & Gardner, E. B. (1980). A quantitative analysis of responses of direction-sensitive neurons in somatosensory cortex of awake monkeys. *Journal of Neurophysiology, 43*, 1319–1341.

Cowey, A., & Heywood, C. A. (1997). Cerebral achromatopsia: Colour blindness despite wavelength processing. *Trends in Cognitive Science, 1*, 133–139

Craig, J. C., & Lyle, K. B. (2001). A comparison of tactile spatial sensitivity on the palm and fingerpad. *Perception and Psychophysics, 63*, 337–347.

Craig, J. C., & Lyle, K. B. (2002). A correction and a comment on Craig and Lyle (2001). *Perception and Psychophysics, 64*, 504–506.

Crick, F. C., & Koch, C. (2003). A framework for consciousness. *Nature Neuroscience, 6*, 119–127.

Critchley, H. D., & Rolls, E. T. (1996). Hunger and satiety modify the responses of olfactory and visual neurons in the primary orbitofrontal cortex. *Journal of Neurophysiology, 75*, 1673–1686.

Culler, E. A., Coakley, J. D., Lowy, K., & Gross, N. (1943). A revised frequency-map of the guinea-pig cochlea. *American Journal of Psychology, 56*, 475–500.

Cutting, J. E., & Vishton, P. M. (1995). Perceiving layout and knowing distances: The integration, relative potency, and contextual use of different information about depth. In W. Epstein & S. Rogers (Eds.), *Handbook of perception and cognition: Perception of space and motion* (pp. 69–117). New York: Academic Press.

Dallos, P. (1996). Overview: Cochlear neurobiology. In P. Dallos, A. N. Popper, & R. R. Fay (Eds.), *The cochlea* (pp. 1–43). New York: Springer.

Dalton, D. S., Cruickshanks, K. J., Wiley, T. L., Klein, B. E. K., Klein, R., & Tweed, T. S. (2001). Association of leisure-time noise exposure and hearing loss. *Audiology, 40*, 1–9.

Dalton, J. (1948). Extraordinary facts relating to the vision of colour: With observations. In W. Dennis (Ed.), *Readings in the history of psychology* (pp. 102–111). New York: Appleton-Century-Crofts. (Original work published 1798)

Dalton, P. (2002). Olfaction. In S. Yantis (Ed.), *Stevens' handbook of experimental psychology: Sensation and perception* (3rd ed., pp. 691–756). New York: Wiley.

Damasio, H., & Damasio, A. R. (1980). The anatomical basis of conduction aphasia. *Brain, 103,* 337–350.

Dartnall, H. J. A., Bowmaker, J. K., & Mollon, J. D. (1983). Human visual pigments: Microspectrophotometric results from the eyes of seven persons. *Proceedings of the Royal Society of London B, 220,* 115–130.

Darwin, C. J. (1997). Auditory grouping. *Trends in Cognitive Sciences, 1,* 327–333.

Darwin, C. J. (in press). Auditory scene analysis. In E. B. Goldstein (Ed.), *Sage encyclopedia of perception.* Thousand Oaks, CA: Sage.

David, A. S., & Senior, C. (2000). Implicit motion and the brain. *Trends in Cognitive Sciences, 4,* 293–295.

Day, R. H. (1989). Natural and artificial cues, perceptual compromise and the basis of veridical and illusory perception. In D. Vickers & P. L. Smith (Eds.), *Human information processing: Measures and mechanisms* (pp. 107–129). North Holland, The Netherlands: Elsevier Science.

Day, R. H. (1990). The Bourdon illusion in haptic space. *Perception and Psychophysics, 47,* 400–404.

de Araujo, I. E., Rolls, E. T., Velazco, M. I., Margot, C., & Cayeux, I. (2005). Cognitive modulation of olfactory processing. *Neuron, 46,* 671–679.

DeAngelis, G. C., Cumming, B. G., & Newsome, W. T. (1998). Cortical area MT and the perception of stereoscopic depth. *Nature, 394,* 677–680.

DeAngelis, G. C., Cumming, B. G., & Newsome, W. T. (2000). A new role for cortical area MT: The perception of stereoscopic depth. In M. Gazzaniga (Ed.), *The new cognitive neurosciences* (pp. 305–314). Cambridge, MA: MIT Press.

DeCasper, A. J., & Fifer, W. P. (1980). Of human bonding: Newborns prefer their mothers' voices. *Science, 208,* 1174–1176.

DeCasper, A. J., Lecanuet, J.-P., Busnel, M.-C., Deferre-Granier, C., & Maugeais, R. (1994). Fetal reactions to recurrent maternal speech. *Infant Behavior and Development, 17,* 159–164.

DeCasper, A. J., & Spence, M. J. (1986). Prenatal maternal speech influences newborn's perception of speech sounds. *Infant Behavior and Development, 9,* 133–150.

Delahunt, P. B., & Brainard, D. H. (2004). Does human color constancy incorporate the statistical regularity of natural daylight? *Journal of Vision, 4,* 57–81.

Delay, E. R., Hernandez, N. P., Bromley, K., & Margolskee, R. F. (2006). Sucrose and monosodium glutamate taste thresholds and discrimination ability of T1R3 knockout mics. *Chemical Senses, 31,* 351–357.

DeLucia, P., & Hochberg, J. (1985). Illusions in the real world and in the mind's eye [Abstract]. *Proceedings of the Eastern Psychological Association, 56,* 38.

DeLucia, P., & Hochberg, J. (1986). Real-world geometrical illusions: Theoretical and practical implications . *Proceedings of the Eastern Psychological Association, 57,* 62.

DeLucia, P., & Hochberg, J. (1991). Geometrical illusions in solid objects under ordinary viewing conditions. *Perception and Psychophysics, 50,* 547–554.

Delwiche, J. F., Buletic, Z., & Breslin, P. A. S. (2001a). Covariation in individuals' sensitivities to bitter compounds: Evidence supporting multiple receptor/transduction mechanisms. *Perception and Psychophysics, 63,* 761–776.

Delwiche, J. F., Buletic, Z., & Breslin, P. A. S. (2001b). Relationship of papillae number to bitter intensity of quinine and PROP within and between individuals. *Physiology and Behavior, 74,* 329–337.

Denes, P. B., & Pinson, E. N. (1993). *The speech chain* (2nd ed.). New York: Freeman.

Derbyshire, S. W. G., Jones, A. K. P., Gyulia, F., Clark, S., Townsend, D., & Firestone, L. L. (1997). Pain processing during three levels of noxious stimulation produces differential patterns of central activity. *Pain, 73,* 431–445.

Derbyshire, S. W. G., Whalley, M. G., Stenger, V. A., & Oakley, D. A. (2004). Cerebral activation during hypnotically induced and imagined pain. *Neuroimage, 23,* 392–401.

Desor, J. A., & Beauchamp, G. K. (1974). The human capacity to transmit olfactory information. *Perception and Psychophysics, 13,* 271–275.

Deutsch, D. (1975). Two-channel listening to musical scales. *Journal of the Acoustical Society of America, 57,* 1156–1160.

Deutsch, D. (1996). The perception of auditory patterns. In W. Prinz & B. Bridgeman (Eds.), *Handbook of perception and action* (Vol. 1, pp. 253–296). San Diego, CA: Academic Press.

Deutsch, D. (1999). *The psychology of music* (2nd ed.). New York: Academic Press.

DeValois, R. L. (1960). Color vision mechanisms in monkey. *Journal of General Physiology, 43,* 115–128.

DeValois, R. L., Abramov, I., & Jacobs, G. H. (1966). Analysis of response of LGN cells. *Journal of the Optical Society of America, 56,* 966–977.

DeValois, R. L., & Jacobs, G. H. (1968). Primate color vision. *Science, 162,* 533–540.

DeValois, R. L., Yund, E. W., & Hepler, N. (1982). The orientation and direction selectivity of cells in macaque visual cortex. *Vision Research, 22,* 531–544.

deVries, H., & Stuiver, M. (1961). The absolute sensitivity of the human sense of smell. In W. A. Rosenblith (Ed.), *Sensory communication.* Cambridge, MA: MIT Press.

deWied, M., & Verbaten, M. N. (2001). Affective pictures processing, attention, and pain tolerance. *Pain, 90,* 163–172.

Di Pellegrino, G., Rafal, R, & Tipper, S. P. (2005). Implicitly evoked actions modulate visual selection: Evidence from parietal extinction. *Current Biology, 15,* 1469–1472.

Dobson, V., & Teller, D. (1978). Visual acuity in human infants: Review and comparison of behavioral and electrophysiological studies. *Vision Research, 18,* 1469–1483.

Dodd, G. G., & Squirrell, D. J. (1980). Structure and mechanism in the mammalian olfactory system. *Symposium of the Zoology Society of London, 45,* 35–56.

Doty, R. L. (Ed.). (1976). *Mammalian olfaction, reproductive processes and behavior.* New York: Academic Press.

Doty, R. L. (1991). Olfactory system. In T. V. Getchell, R. L. Doty, L. M. Bartoshuk, & J. B. Snow (Eds.), *Smell and taste in health and disease* (pp. 175–203). New York: Raven Press.

Dougherty, R. F., Koch, V. M., Brewer, A. A., Fischer, B., Modersitzki, J., & Wandell, B. A. (2003). Visual field representations and locations of visual areas V1/2/3 in human visual cortex. *Journal of Vision, 3,* 586–598.

Dowling, J. E., & Boycott, B. B. (1966). Organization of the primate retina. *Proceedings of the Royal Society of London, 166B,* 80–111.

Dowling, W. J., & Harwood, D. L. (1986). *Music cognition.* New York: Academic Press.

Downar, J., Crawley, A. P., Mikulis, D. J., & Davis, K. D. (2001). The effect of task relevance on the cortical response to changes in visual and auditory stimuli: An event-related fMRI study. *Neuroimage, 14,* 1256–1267.

Downing, P. E., Jiang, Y., Shuman, M., & Kanwisher, N. (2001). Cortical area selective for visual processing of the human body. *Science, 293,* 2470–2473.

Driver, J., & Baylis, G. C. (1989). Movement and visual attention: The spotlight metaphor breaks down. *Journal of Experimental Psychology: Human Perception and Performance, 15,* 448–456.

Driver, J., & Baylis, G. C. (1998). Attention and visual object segmentation. In R. Parasuraman (Ed.), *The attentive brain* (pp. 299–325). Cambridge, MA: MIT Press.

Dubno, J. (in press). Ageing and hearing. In E. B. Goldstein (Ed.), *Sage encyclopedia of perception.* Thousand Oaks, CA: Sage.

Dudley, D. L., Holmes, T. H., Martin, C. J., & Ripley, H. S. (1966). Hypnotically induced facsimile of pain. *Archives of General Psychiatry, 15,* 258–265.

Duffy, C. J., & Wurtz, R. H. (1991). Sensitivity of MST neurons to optic flow stimuli: 2. Mechanisms of response selectivity revealed by small-field stimuli. *Journal of Neurophysiology, 65,* 1346–1359.

Duncan, R. O., & Boynton, G. M. (2003). Cortical magnification within human primary visual cortex correlates with acuity thresholds. *Neuron, 36,* 659–671.

Duncan, R. O., & Boynton, G. M. (2007). Tactile hyperacuity thresholds correlate with finger maps in primary somatosensory cortex (S1). *Cerebral Cortex, 17,* 2878–2891.

Durrant, J., & Lovrinic, J. (1977). *Bases of hearing science*. Baltimore: Williams & Wilkins.

Dyde, R. T., & Milner, A. D. (2002). Two illusions of perceived orientation: One fools all of the people some of the time, but the other fools all of the people all of the time. *Experimental Brain Research, 144*, 518–527.

Ecker, A. J., & Heller, L. M. (2005). Auditory-visual interactions in the perception of a ball's path. *Perception, 34*, 59–75.

Edwards, R. (in press). Cochlear implants: Controversy. In E. B. Goldstein (Ed.), *Sage encyclopedia of perception*. Thousand Oaks, CA: Sage.

Egan, J. P., & Hake, H. W. (1950). On the masking pattern of a simple auditory stimulus. *Journal of the Acoustical Society of America, 22*, 622–630.

Egly, R., Driver, J., & Rafal, R. D. (1994). Shifting visual attention between objects and locations: Evidence from normal and parietal lesion subjects. *Journal of Experimental Psychology: General, 123*, 161–177.

Eimas, P. D., & Corbit, J. D. (1973). Selective adaptation of linguistic feature detectors. *Cognitive Psychology, 4*, 99–109.

Eimas, P. D., & Quinn, P. C. (1994). Studies on the formation of perceptually based basic-level categories in young infants. *Child Development, 65*, 903–917.

Eimas, P. D., Siqueland, E. R., Jusczyk, P., & Vigorito, J. (1971). Speech perception in infants. *Science, 171*, 303–306.

Eisenberger, N. I., Lieberman, M. D., & Williams, K. D. (2003). Does rejection hurt? An fMRI study of social exclusion. *Science, 302*, 290–292.

Elbert, T., Pantev, C., Wienbruch, C., Rockstroh, B., & Taub, E. (1995). Increased cortical representation of the fingers of the left hand in string players. *Science, 270*, 305–307.

Emmert, E. (1881). Grossenverhaltnisse der Nachbilder. *Klinische Monatsblätter für Augenheilkunde, 19*, 443–450.

Engel, A. K., Fries, P., Konig, P., Brecht, M., & Singer, W. (1999). Temporal binding, binocular rivalry, and consciousness. *Consciousness and Cognition, 8*, 128–151.

Engel, S., Zhang, X., & Wandell, B. (1997). Colour tuning in human visual cortex measured with functional magnetic resonance imaging. *Nature, 388*, 68–71.

Engen, T. (1972). Psychophysics. In J. W. Kling & L. A. Riggs (Eds.), *Experimental psychology* (3rd ed., pp. 1–46). New York: Holt, Rinehart and Winston.

Engen, T., & Pfaffmann, C. (1960). Absolute judgments of odor quality. *Journal of Experimental Psychology, 59*, 214–219.

Epstein, R. A. (2005). The cortical basis of visual scene processing. *Visual Cognition, 12*, 954–978.

Epstein, R., Harris, A., Stanley, D., & Kanwisher, N. (1999). The parahippocampal place area: Recognition, navigation, or encoding? *Neuron, 23*, 115–125.

Epstein, R., & Kanwisher, N. (1998). A cortical representation of the local visual environment. *Nature, 392*, 598–601.

Epstein, W. (1965). Nonrelational judgments of size and distance. *American Journal of Psychology, 78*, 120–123.

Erickson, R. (1975). *Sound structure in music*. Berkeley: University of California Press.

Erickson, R. P. (1963). Sensory neural patterns and gustation. In Y. Zotterman (Ed.), *Olfaction and taste* (Vol. 1, pp. 205–213). Oxford, UK: Pergamon Press.

Erickson, R. P. (2000). The evolution of neural coding ideas in the chemical senses. *Physiology and Behavior, 69*, 3–13.

Evarts, E. V. (1966). Methods for recording activity of individual neurons in moving animals. In R. F. Rushmer (Ed.), *Methods in medical research* (Vol. 11, pp. 241–250). Chicago: Yearbook.

Fagan, J. F. (1976). Infant's recognition of invariant features of faces. *Child Development, 47*, 627–638.

Fajen, B. R., & Warren, W. H. (2003). Behavioral dynamics of steering, obstacle avoidance and route selection. *Journal of Experimental Psychology: Human Perception and Performance, 29*, 343–362.

Fantz, R. L., Ordy, J. M., & Udelf, M. S. (1962). Maturation of pattern vision in infants during the first six months. *Journal of Comparative and Physiological Psychology, 55*, 907–917.

Farah, M. J., Rabinowitz, C., Quinn, G. E., & Liu, G. T. (2000). Early commitment of neural substrates for face recognition. *Cognitive Neuropsychology, 17*, 117–123.

Fechner, G. T. (1966). *Elements of Psychophysics*. New York: Holt, Rinehart and Winston. (Original work published 1860)

Fei Fei, L., Iyer, A., Koch, C., & Perona, P. (2007). What do we perceive in a glance of a real-world scene? *Journal of Vision, 7*, 1–29.

Felleman, D. J., & Van Essen, D. C. (1991). Distributed hierarchical processing in the primate cerebral cortex. *Cerebral Cortex, 1*, 1–47.

Fettiplace, R., & Hackney, C. M. (2006). The sensory and motor roles of auditory hair cells. *Nature Reviews Neuroscience, 17*, 19–28.

Fields, H. L., & Basbaum, A. I. (1999). Central nervous system mechanisms of pain modulation. In P. D. Wall & R. Melzack (Eds.), *Textbook of pain* (pp. 309–328). New York: Churchill Livingstone.

Finger, T. E. (1987). Gustatory nuclei and pathways in the central nervous system. In T. E. Finger & W. L. Silver (Eds.), *Neurobiology of taste and smell* (pp. 331–353). New York: Wiley.

Finniss, D. G., & Benedetti, F. (2005). Mechanisms of the placebo response and their impact on clinical trials and clinical practice. *Pain, 114*, 3–6.

Fiorentini, A., & Maffei, L. (1973). Contrast in night vision. *Vision Research, 13*, 73–80.

Firestein, S. (2001). How the olfactory system makes sense of scents. *Nature, 413*, 211–218.

Fletcher, H., & Munson, W. A. (1933). Loudness: Its definition, measurement, and calculation. *Journal of the Acoustical Society of America, 5*, 82–108.

Fortenbaugh, F. C., Hicks, J. C., Hao, L., & Turano, K. A. (2006). High-speed navigators: Using more than what meets the eye. *Journal of Vision, 6*, 565–579.

Fox, C. R. (1990). Some visual influences on human postural equilibrium: Binocular versus monocular fixation. *Perception and Psychophysics, 47*, 409–422.

Fox, R., Aslin, R. N., Shea, S. L., & Dumais, S. T. (1980). Stereopsis in human infants. *Science, 207*, 323–324.

Frank, M. E., Bieber, S. L., & Smith, D. V. (1988). The organization of taste sensibilities in hamster chorda tympani nerve fibers. *Journal of General Physiology, 91*, 861–896.

Frank, M. E., & Rabin, M. D. (1989). Chemosensory neuroanatomy and physiology. *Ear, Nose and Throat Journal, 68*, 291–292, 295–296.

Franklin, A., & Davies, R. L. (2004). New evidence for infant colour categories. *British Journal of Developmental Psychology, 22*, 349–377.

Freyd, J. (1983). The mental representation of movement when static stimuli are viewed. *Perception and Psychophysics, 33*, 575–581.

Friedman-Hill, S. R., Robertson, L. C., & Treisman, A. (1995). Parietal contributions to visual feature binding: Evidence from a patient with bilateral lesions. *Science, 269*, 853–855.

Frisina, R. D. (2001). Subcortical neural coding mechanisms for auditory temporal processing. *Hearing Research, 158*, 1–27.

Fritz, J., Shamma, S., Elhilali, M., & Klein, D. (2003). Rapid task-related plasticity of spectrotemporal receptive fields in primary auditory cortex. *Nature Neuroscience, 6*, 1216–1223.

Fuld, K., Wooten, B. R., & Whalen, J. J. (1981). Elemental hues of short-wave and spectral lights. *Perception and Psychophysics, 29*, 317–322.

Furmanski, C. S., & Engel, S. A. (2000). An oblique effect in human primary visual cortex. *Nature Neuroscience, 3*, 535–536.

Gallese, V., Fadiga, L., Fogassi, L., & Rizzolatti, G. (1996). Action recognition in the premotor cortex. *Brain, 119*, 593–609.

Galletti, C., & Fattori, P. (2003). Neuronal mechanisms for detection of motion in the field of view. *Neuropsychologia, 41*, 1717–1727.

Ganchrow, J. R. (1995). Ontogeny of human taste perception. In R. L. Doty (Ed.), *Handbook of olfaction and gustation* (pp. 715–729). New York: Marcel Dekker.

Ganchrow, J. R., Steiner, J. E., & Daher, M. (1983). Neonatal facial expressions in response to different qualities and intensities of gustatory stimuli. *Infant Behavior and Development, 6*, 473–484.

Gardner, M. B., & Gardner, R. S. (1973). Problem of localization in the median plane: Effect of pinnae cavity occlusion. *Journal of the Acoustical Society of America, 53*, 400–408.

Gauthier, I., Skudlarski, P., Gore, J. C., & Anderson, A. W. (2000). Expertise for cars and birds recruits brain areas involved in face recognition. *Nature Neuroscience, 3*, 191–197.

Gauthier, I., Tarr, M. J., Anderson, A. W., Skudlarski, P., & Gore, J. C. (1999). Activation of the middle fusiform face area increases with expertise in recognizing novel objects. *Nature Neuroscience, 2*, 568–573.

Gegenfurtner, K. R. (2001). Color in the cortex revisited. *Nature Neuroscience, 4*, 339–340.

Gegenfurtner, K. R. (2003). Cortical mechanisms of colour vision. *Nature Reviews Neuroscience, 4*, 563–572.

Gescheider, G. A. (1976). Psychophysics: Method and theory. Hillsdale, NJ: Erlbaum.

Gibson, J. J. (1950). *The perception of the visual world*. Boston: Houghton Mifflin.

Gibson, J. J. (1962). Observations on active touch. *Psychological Review, 69*, 477–491.

Gibson, J. J. (1979). *The ecological approach to visual perception*. Boston: Houghton Mifflin.

Gilbert, A. N., & Firestein, S. (2002). Dollars and scents: Commercial opportunities in olfaction and taste. *Nature Neuroscience, 5*, 1043–1045.

Gilbert, C. D., & Wiesel, T. N. (1989). Columnar specificity of intrinsic horizontal and corticocortical connections in cat visual cortex. *Journal of Neuroscience, 9*, 2432–2442.

Gilchrist, A., Kossyfidis, C., Agostino, T., Li, X., Bonato, F., Cataliotti, J., et al. (1999). An anchoring theory of lightness perception. *Psychological Review, 106*, 795–834.

Gilchrist, A. L. (Ed.) (1994). *Lightness, brightness, and transparency*. Hillsdale, NJ: Erlbaum.

Gilinsky, A. S. (1951). Perceived size and distance in visual space. *Psychological Review, 58*, 460–482.

Girard, P., Lomber, S. G., & Bullier, J. (2002). Shape discrimination deficits during reversible deactivation of area V4 in the macaque monkey. *Cerebral Cortex, 12*, 1146–1156.

Glanz, J. (2000, April 18). Art + physics = beautiful music. *New York Times*, pp. D1–D4.

Glickstein, M. (1988, September). The discovery of the visual cortex. *Scientific American, 259*, 118–127.

Gobbini, M. I., & Haxby, J. V. (2007). Neural systems for recognition of familiar faces. *Neuropsychologia, 45*, 32–41.

Goffaux, V., Jacques, C., Mauraux, A., Oliva, A., Schynsand, P. G., & Rossion, B. (2005). Diagnostic colours contribute to the early stages of scene categorization: Behavioural and neurophysiological evidence. *Visual Cognition, 12*, 878–892.

Goffaux, V., & Rossion, B. (2006). Faces are "spatial": Holistic face perception is supported by low spatial frequencies. *Journal of Experimental Psychology: Human Perception and Performance, 32*, 1023–1039.

Goldstein, E. B. (2001). Pictorial perception and art. In E. B. Goldstein (Ed.), *Blackwell handbook of perception* (pp. 344–378). Oxford, UK: Blackwell.

Goldstein, E. B. (2002). *Sensation and perception* (6th ed.). Belmont, CA: Wadsworth.

Goldstein, E. B. (in press). Pictorial depiction and perception. In E. B. Goldstein (Ed.), *Sage encyclopedia of perception*. Thousand Oaks, CA: Sage.

Goldstein, E. B., & Fink, S. I. (1981). Selective attention in vision: Recognition memory for superimposed line drawings. *Journal of Experimental Psychology: Human Perception and Performance, 7*, 954–967.

Goodale, M. A., & Humphrey, G. K. (1998). The objects of action and perception. *Cognition, 67*, 181–207.

Goodale, M. A., & Humphrey, G. K. (2001). Separate visual systems for action and perception. In E. B. Goldstein (Ed.), *Blackwell handbook of perception* (pp. 311–343). Oxford, UK: Blackwell.

Goodwin, A. W. (1998). Extracting the shape of an object from the responses of peripheral nerve fibers. In J. W. Morley (Ed.), *Neural aspects of tactile sensation* (pp. 55–87). New York: Elsevier Science.

Gordon, J., & Abramov, I. (2001). Color vision. In E. B. Goldstein (Ed.), *Blackwell handbook of perception* (pp. 92–127). Oxford, UK: Blackwell.

Gottlieb, J. P., Kununoki, M., & Goldberg, M. (2002). The representation of visual salience in monkey parietal cortex. *Nature, 391*, 481–483.

Gouras, P. (1991). Color vision. In E. R. Kandel, J. H. Schwartz, & T. M. Jessell (Eds.), *Principles of neural science* (3rd ed., pp. 467–480). New York: Elsevier.

Graham, C. H., Sperling, H. G., Hsia, Y., & Coulson, A. H. (1961). The determination of some visual functions of a unilaterally color-blind subject: Methods and results. *Journal of Psychology, 51*, 3–32.

Granrud, C. E., Haake, R. J., & Yonas, A. (1985). Infants' sensitivity to familiar size: The effect of memory on spatial perception. *Perception and Psychophysics, 37*, 459–466.

Granrud, C. E., & Yonas, A. (1984). Infants' perception of pictorially specified interposition. *Journal of Experimental Child Psychology, 37*, 500–511.

Granrud, C. E., Yonas, A., & Opland, E. A. (1985). Infants' sensitivity to the depth cue of shading. *Perception and Psychophysics, 37*, 415–419.

Graziano, M. S. A., Andersen, R. A., & Snowden, R. J. (1994). Tuning of MST neurons to spiral motions. *Journal of Neuroscience, 14*, 54–67.

Gregory, R. L. (1966). *Eye and brain*. New York: McGraw-Hill.

Grelotti, D. J., Gauthier, I., & Schultz, R. T. (2002). Social interest and the development of cortical face specialization: What autism teaches us about face processing. *Developmental Psychobiology, 40*, 213–225.

Grelotti, D. J., Klin, A. J., Gauthier, I., Skudlarski, P., Cohen, D. J., Gore, J. C., et al. (2005). fMRI activation of the fusiform gyrus and amygdala to cartoon characters but not to faces in a boy with autism. *Neuropsychologia, 43*, 373–385.

Griffin, D. R. (1944). Echolocation by blind men and bats. *Science, 100*, 589–590.

Grill-Spector, K., Knouf, N., & Kanwisher, N. (2004). The fusiform face area subserves face perception, not generic within-category identification. *Nature Neuroscience, 7*, 555–562.

Gross, C. G. (2002). The genealogy of the "grandmother cell." *Neuroscientist, 8*, 512–518.

Gross, C. G., Bender, D. B., & Roche-Miranda, C. E. (1969). Visual receptive fields of neurons in inferotemporal cortex of the monkey. *Science, 166*, 1303–1306.

Grossman, E. D., Batelli, L., & Pascual-Leone, A. (2005). Repetitive TMS over posterior STS disrupts perception of biological motion. *Vision Research, 45*, 2847–2853.

Grossman, E. D., & Blake, R. (2001). Brain activity evoked by inverted and imagined biological motion. *Vision Research, 41*, 1475–1482.

Grossman, E. D., & Blake, R. (2002). Brain areas active during visual perception of biological motion. *Neuron, 56*, 1167–1175.

Growing up different. (2001, November 13). *Scientific American Frontiers*. Public Broadcasting System.

Gulick, W. L., Gescheider, G. A., & Frisina, R. D. (1989). *Hearing*. New York: Oxford University Press.

Gullberg, M., & Holmqvist, K. (2006). What speakers do and what addressees look at. *Pragmatics & Cognition, 14*, 53–82.

Gwiazda, J., Brill, S., Mohindra, I., & Held, R. (1980). Preferential looking acuity in infants from two to fifty-eight weeks of age. *American Journal of Optometry and Physiological Optics, 57*, 428–432.

Haarmeier T., Their, P., Repnow, M., & Petersen, D. (1997). False perception of motion in a patient who cannot compensate for eye movements. *Nature, 389*, 849–852.

Hall, D. A., Fussell, C., & Summerfield, A. Q. (2005). Reading fluent speech from talking faces: Typical brain networks and individual differences. *Journal of Cognitive Neuroscience, 17*, 939–953.

Hall, M. J., Bartoshuk, L. M., Cain, W. S., & Stevens, J. C. (1975). PTC taste blindness and the taste of caffeine. *Nature, 253*, 442–443.

Hamer, R. D., Alexander, K. R., & Teller, D. Y. (1982). Rayleigh discriminations in young human infants. *Vision Research, 22*, 575–587.

Handford, M. (1997). *Where's Waldo?* Cambridge, MA: Candlewick Press.

Hansen, T., Olkkonen, M., Walter, S., & Gegenfurtner, K. R. (2006). Memory modulates color appearance. *Nature Neuroscience, 9*, 1367–1368.

Harris, J. M., & Rogers, B. J. (1999). Going against the flow. *Trends in Cognitive Sciences, 3*, 449–450.

Harris, L., Atkinson, J., & Braddick, O. (1976). Visual contrast sensitivity of a 6-month-old infant measured by the evoked potential. *Nature, 246,* 570–571.

Hartline, H. K., Wagner, H. G., & Ratliff, F. (1956). Inhibition in the eye of *Limulus. Journal of General Physiology, 39,* 651–673.

Hartmann, M. (1999). How we localize sound. *Physics Today on the Web* http://www.aip.org/pt/nov99/locsound.html

Haxby, J. V., Hoffman, E. A., & Gobbini, M. I. (2000). The distributed human neural system for face perception. *Trends in Cognitive Science, 46,* 223–233.

Hayhoe, M., & Ballard, C. (2005). Eye movements in natural behavior. *Trends in Cognitive Sciences, 9,* 188–194.

Hecaen, H., & Angelerques, R. (1962). Agnosia for faces (prosopagnosia). *Archives of Neurology, 7,* 92–100.

Hecht, S., Shlaer, S., & Pirenne, M. H. (1942). Energy, quanta, and vision. *Journal of General Physiology, 25,* 819–840.

Heise, G. A., & Miller, G. A. (1951). An experimental study of auditory patterns. *American Journal of Psychology, 57,* 243–249.

Helmholtz, H. von. (1852). On the theory of compound colors. *Philosophical Magazine, 4,* 519–534.

Helmholtz, H. von. (1911). *Treatise on physiological optics* (J. P. Southall, Ed. & Trans.; 3rd ed., Vols. 2 & 3). Rochester, NY: Optical Society of America. (Original work published 1866)

Helson, H. (1933). The fundamental propositions of Gestalt psychology. *Psychological Review, 40,* 13–32.

Henderson, J. M. (2003). Human gaze control during real-world scene perception. *Trends in Cognitive Sciences, 7,* 498–503.

Henderson, J. M., & Hollingworth, A. (1999). High-level scene perception. *Annual Review of Psychology, 50,* 243–271.

Henderson, J. M., & Hollingworth, A. (2003). Eye movements, visual memory, and scene representation. In M. Peterson & G. Rhodes (Eds.), *Perception of faces, objects, and scenes: Analytic and holistic processes* (pp. 356–383). New York: Oxford University Press.

Hering, E. (1878). *Zur Lehre vom Lichtsinn.* Vienna: Gerold.

Hering, E. (1905). Grundzuge der Lehre vom Lichtsinn. In *Handbuch der gesamter Augenheilkunde* (Vol. 3, Chap. 13). Berlin.

Hering, E. (1964). *Outlines of a theory of the light sense* (L. M. Hurvich & D. Jameson, Trans.). Cambridge, MA: Harvard University Press.

Hershenson, M. (Ed.). (1989). *The moon illusion.* Hillsdale, NJ: Erlbaum.

Herz, R. (2003). The effect of verbal context on olfactory perception. *Journal of Experimental Psychology: General, 132,* 595–606.

Hess, E. H. (1965). Attitude and pupil size. *Scientific American, 212,* 46–54.

Hettinger, T. P., Myers, W. E., & Frank, M. E. (1990). Role of olfaction in perception of nontraditional "taste" stimuli. *Chemical Senses, 15,* 755–760.

Heywood, C. A., & Cowey, A. (1998). With color in mind. *Nature Neuroscience, 1,* 171–173.

Heywood, C. A., Cowey, A., & Newcombe, F. (1991). Chromatic discrimination in a cortically colour blind observer. *European Journal of Neuroscience, 3,* 802–812.

Hickock, G., & Poeppel, D. (2007). The cortical organization of speech processing. *Nature Reviews Neuroscience, 8,* 393–401.

Hinkle, D. A., & Connor, C. E. (2002). Three-dimensional orientation tuning in macaque area V4. *Nature Neuroscience, 5,* 665–670.

Hochberg, J. E. (1971). Perception. In J. W. Kling & L. A. Riggs (Eds.), *Experimental psychology* (3rd ed., pp. 396–550). New York: Holt, Rinehart and Winston.

Hochberg, J. E. (1987). Machines should not see as people do, but must know how people see. *Computer Vision, Graphics and Image Processing, 39,* 221–237.

Hochberg, L. R., Serruya, M. D., Friehs, G. M., Mukand, J. A., Saleh, M., Caplan, A. H., et al. (2006). Neuronal ensemble control of prosthetic devices by a human with tetraplegia. *Nature, 442,* 164–171.

Hodgetts, W. E., & Liu, R. (2006). Can hockey playoffs harm your hearing? *CMAJ, 175,* 1541–1542.

Hofbauer, R. K., Rainville, P., Duncan, G. H., & Bushnell, M. C. (2001). Cortical representation of the sensory dimension of pain. *Journal of Neurophysiology, 86,* 402–411.

Hoffman, E. J., Phelps, M. E., Mullani, N. A., Higgins, C. S., & Ter-Pogossian, M. M. (1976). Design and performance characteristics of a whole-body positron transaxial tomography. *Journal of Nuclear Medicine, 17,* 493–502.

Hoffman, H. G., Doctor, J. N., Patterson, D. R., Carrougher, G. J., & Furness, T. A., III. (2000). Virtual reality as an adjunctive pain control during burn wound care in adolescent patients. *Pain, 85,* 305–309.

Hofman, F. M., Van Riswick, J. G. A., & Van Opstal, A. J. (1998). Relearning sound localization with new ears. *Nature Neuroscience, 1,* 417–421.

Holden, C. (2004). Imaging studies show how brain thinks about pain. *Science, 303,* 1131.

Holley, A. (1991). Neural coding of olfactory information. In T. V. Getchell, R. L. Doty, L. M. Bartoshuk, & J. B. Snow (Eds.), *Smell and taste in health and disease* (pp. 329–343). New York: Raven Press.

Hollingsworth, A. (2005). Memory for object position in natural scenes. *Visual Cognition, 12,* 1003–1016.

Hollins, M., Bensmaia, S. J., & Roy, E. A. (2002). Vibrotaction and texture perception. *Behavioural Brain Research, 135,* 51–56.

Hollins, M., Bensmaia, S. J., & Washburn, S. (2001). Vibrotactile adaptation impairs discrimination of fine, but not coarse, textures. *Somatosensory and Motor Research, 18,* 253–262.

Hollins, M., & Risner, S. R. (2000). Evidence for the duplex theory of texture perception. *Perception and Psychophysics, 62,* 695–705.

Holway, A. H., & Boring, E. G. (1941). Determinants of apparent visual size with distance variant. *American Journal of Psychology, 54,* 21–37.

Hsiao, S. S., Johnson, K. O., Twombly, A., & DiCarlo, J. (1996). Form processing and attention effects in the somatosensory system. In O. Franzen, R. Johannson, & L. Terenius (Eds.), *Somesthesis and the neurobiology of the somatosensory cortex* (pp. 229–247). Basel: Biorkhauser Verlag.

Hsiao, S. S., O'Shaughnessy, D. M., & Johnson, K. O. (1993). Effects of selective attention on spatial form processing in monkey primary and secondary somatosensory cortex. *Journal of Neurophysiology, 70,* 444–447.

Hubel, D. H. (1959). Single unit activity in striate cortex of unrestrained cats. *Journal of Physiology, 147,* 226–238.

Hubel, D. H. (1982). Exploration of the primary visual cortex, 1955–1978. *Nature, 299,* 515–524.

Hubel, D. H., & Wiesel, T. N. (1959). Receptive fields of single neurons in the cat's striate cortex. *Journal of Physiology, 148,* 574–591.

Hubel, D. H., & Wiesel, T. N. (1961). Integrative action in the cat's lateral geniculate body. *Journal of Physiology, 155,* 385–398.

Hubel, D. H., & Wiesel, T. N. (1965). Receptive fields and functional architecture in two non-striate visual areas (18 and 19) of the cat. *Journal of Neurophysiology, 28,* 229–289.

Hubel, D. H., & Wiesel, T. N. (1970). Stereoscopic vision in macaque monkey: Cells sensitive to binocular depth in area 18 of the macaque monkey cortex. *Nature, 225,* 41–42.

Hudspeth, A. J. (1983). The hair cells of the inner ear. *Scientific American, 248,* 54–64.

Hudspeth, A. J. (1989). How the ear's works work. *Nature, 341,* 397–404.

Hübener, M., Shoham, D., Grinvald, A., & Bonhoeffer, T. (1997). Spatial relationships among three columnar systems in cat area 17. *Journal of Neuroscience, 17,* 9270–9284.

Humphrey, A. L., & Saul, A. B. (1994). The temporal transformation of retinal signals in the lateral geniculate nucleus of the cat: Implications for cortical function. In D. Minciacchi, M. Molinari, G. Macchi, & E. G. Jones (Eds.), *Thalamic networks for relay and modulation* (pp. 81–89). New York: Pergamon Press.

Humphreys, G. W., & Riddoch, M. J. (2001). Detection by action: Neuropsychological evidence for action-defined templates in search. *Nature Neuroscience, 4,* 84–88.

Hurvich, L. (1981). *Color vision.* Sunderland, MA: Sinauer Associates.

Hyvärinen, J., & Poranen, A. (1974). Function of the parietal associative area 7 as revealed from cellular discharges in alert monkeys. *Brain, 97,* 673–692.

Hyvärinen, J., & Poranen, A. (1978). Movement-sensitive and direction and orientation-selective cutaneous receptive fields in the hand area of the postcentral gyrus in monkeys. *Journal of Physiology, 283,* 523–537.

Ilg, U. J., Bridgeman, B., & Hoffmann, K. P. (1989). Influence of mechanical disturbance on oculomotor behavior. *Vision Research, 29,* 545–551.

Ishai, A. (2008). Let's face it: It's a cortical network. *Neuroimage, 40,* 415–419.

Ishai, A., Pessoa, L., Bikle, P. C., & Ungerleider, L. G. (2004). Repetition suppression of faces is modulated by emotion. *Proceedings of the National Academy of Sciences USA, 101,* 9827–9832.

Ishai, A., Ungerleider, L. G., Martin, A., & Haxby, J. V. (2000). The representation of objects in the human occipital and temporal cortex. *Journal of Cognitive Neuroscience, 12,* 35–51.

Ishai, A., Ungerleider, L. G., Martin, A., Schouten, J. L., & Haxby, J. V. (1999). Distributed representation of objects in the human ventral visual pathway. *Proceedings of the National Academy of Sciences USA, 96,* 9379–9384.

Ito, M., Tamura, H., Fujita, I., & Tanaka, K. (1995). Size and position invariance of neuronal responses in monkey inferotemporal cortex. *Journal of Neurophysiology, 73,* 218–226.

Iwamura, Y. (1998). Representation of tactile functions in the somatosensory cortex. In J. W. Morley (Ed.), *Neural aspects of tactile sensation* (pp. 195–238). New York: Elsevier Science.

Jacobson, A., & Gilchrist, A. (1988). The ratio principle holds over a million-to-one range of illumination. *Perception and Psychophysics, 43,* 1–6.

James, W. (1981). *The principles of psychology* (Rev. ed.). Cambridge, MA: Harvard University Press. (Original work published 1890)

Jameson, D. (1985). Opponent-colors theory in light of physiological findings. In D. Ottoson & S. Zeki (Eds.), *Central and peripheral mechanisms of color vision* (pp. 8–102). New York: Macmillan.

Janzen, G., & van Turennout, M. (2004). Selective neural representation of objects relevant for navigation. *Nature Neuroscience, 7,* 673–677.

Jasper, H. H., Ricci, G. F., & Doane, B. (1958). Patterns of cortical neuronal discharge during conditioned responses in monkeys. In G. E. W. Wolstenholme & C. M. O'Connor (Eds.), *Neurological basis of behavior* (pp. 277–294). London: Churchill.

Jeffress, L. A. (1948). A place theory of sound localization. *Journal of Comparative and Physiological Psychology, 41,* 35–39.

Jenkins, W. M., & Merzenich, M. M. (1987). Reorganization of neocortical representations after brain injury: A neurophysiological model of the bases of recovery from stroke. *Progress in Brain Research, 71,* 249–266.

Jensen, T. S., & Nikolajsen, L. (1999). Phantom pain and other phenomena after amputation. In P. D. Wall & R. Melzack (Eds.), *Textbook of pain* (pp. 799–814). New York: Churchill Livingstone.

Jin, E. W., & Shevell, S. K. (1996). Color memory and color constancy. *Journal of the Optical Society of America, A, 13,* 1981–1991.

Johansson, G. (1973). Visual perception of biological motion and a model for its analysis. *Perception and Psychophysics, 14,* 201–211.

Johansson, G. (1975). Visual motion perception. *Scientific American, 232,* 76–88.

Johnson, K. O. (2002). Neural basis of haptic perception. In H. Pashler & S. Yantis (Eds.), *Steven's handbook of experimental psychology: Vol. 1. Sensation and perception* (3rd ed., pp. 537–583). New York: Wiley.

Johnson, M. H., Dziurawiec, S., Ellis, H., & Morton, J. (1991). Newborns' preferential tracking of face-like stimuli and its subsequent decline. *Cognition, 90,* 1–19.

Johnson, S. P., & Aslin, R. N. (1995). Perception of object unity in 2-month-old infants. *Developmental Psychology, 31,* 739–745.

Johnson, S. P., Slemmer, J. A., & Amso, D. (2004). Where infants look determines how they see: Eye movement and object perception performance in 3-month-olds. *Infancy, 6,* 185–201.

Johnstone, B. M., & Boyle, A. J. F. (1967) Basilar membrane vibrations examined with the Mossbauer technique. *Science, 158,* 390–391.

Jones, M. R., & Yee, W. (1993). Attending to auditory events: The role of temporal organization. In S. McAdams & E. Bigand (Eds.), *Thinking in sound: The cognitive psychology of human audition* (pp. 69–112). Oxford, UK: Oxford University Press.

Judd, D. B., MacAdam, D. L., & Wyszecki, G. (1964). Spectral distribution of typical daylight as a function of correlated color temperature. *Journal of the Optical Society of America, 54,* 1031–1040.

Julesz, B. (1971). *Foundations of cyclopean perception.* Chicago: University of Chicago Press.

Kaas, J. H., & Hackett, T. A. (1999). "What" and "where" processing in auditory cortex. *Nature Neuroscience, 2,* 1045–1047.

Kaas, J. H., Hackett, T. A., & Tramo, M. J. (1999). Auditory processing in primate cerebral cortex. *Current Opinion in Neurobiology, 9,* 164–170.

Kahn, R. M., & Sobel, N. (2007). How the nose knows what it knows. *Nature Neuroscience, 10,* 7.

Kamitani, Y., & Tong, F. (2005). Decoding the visual and subjective contents of the human brain. *Nature Neuroscience, 8,* 679–685.

Kandel, E. R., & Jessell, T. M. (1991). Touch. In E. R. Kandel, J. H. Schwartz, & T. M. Jessell (Eds.), *Principles of neural science* (3rd ed., pp. 367–384). New York: Elsevier.

Kanwisher, N. (2003). The ventral visual object pathway in humans: Evidence from fMRI. In L. M. Chalupa & J. S. Werner (Eds.), *The visual neurosciences* (pp. 1179–1190). Cambridge, MA: MIT Press.

Kanwisher, N., McDermott, J., & Chun, M. M. (1997). The fusiform face area: A module in human extrastriate cortex specialized for face perception. *Journal of Neuroscience, 17,* 4302–4311.

Kaplan, E., Mukherjee, P., & Shapley, R. (1993). Information filtering in the lateral geniculate nucleus. In R. Shapley & D. Man-Kit Lam (Eds.), *Contrast sensitivity* (Vol. 5). Cambridge, MA: MIT Press.

Kaplan, G. (1969). Kinetic disruption of optical texture: The perception of depth at an edge. *Perception and Psychophysics, 6,* 193–198.

Kastner, S., Pinsk, M. A., DeWeerd, P., Desimone, R., & Ungerleider, L. G. (1999). Increased activity in human visual cortex during directed attention in the absence of visual stimulation. *Neuron, 22,* 751–761.

Katz, J., & Gagliese, L. (1999). Phantom limb pain: A continuing puzzle. In R. J. Gatchel & D. C. Turk (Eds.), *Psychosocial factors in pain* (pp. 284–300). New York: Guilford.

Kauer, J. S. (1987). Coding in the olfactory system. In T. E. Finger & W. C. Silver (Eds.), *Neurobiology of taste and smell* (pp. 205–231). New York: Wiley.

Kaufman, L., & Rock, I. (1962a). The moon illusion. *Science, 136,* 953–961.

Kaufman, L., & Rock, I. (1962b). The moon illusion. *Scientific American, 207,* 120–132.

Kay, K. N., Naselaris, T., Prenger, R. J., & Gallant, J. L. (2008). Identifying natural images from human brain activity. *Nature, 452,* 352–355.

Kaye, K. L., & Bower, T. G. R. (1994). Learning and intermodal transfer of information in newborns. *Psychological Science, 5,* 286–288.

Kellman, P., & Spelke, E. (1983). Perception of partly occluded objects in infancy. *Cognitive Psychology, 15,* 483–524.

Kersten, D., Mamassian, P., & Yuille, A. (2004). Object perception as Bayesian inference. *Annual Review of Psychology, 55,* 271–304.

Khanna, S. M., & Leonard, D. G. B. (1982). Basilar membrane tuning in the cat cochlea. *Science, 215,* 305–306.

Kiefer, J., von Ilberg, C., Reimer, B., Knecht, R., Gall, V., Diller, G., et al. (1996). Results of cochlear implantation in patients with severe to profound hearing loss: Implications for the indications. *Audiology, 37,* 382–395.

Kim, U. K., Jorgenson, E., Coon, H., Leppert, M., Risch, N., & Drayna, D. (2003). Positional cloning of the human quantitative trait locus underlying taste sensitivity to phenylthiocarbamide. *Science, 299,* 1221–1225.

King, A. J., Schnupp, J. W. H., & Doubell, T. P. (2001). The shape of ears to come: Dynamic coding of auditory space. *Trends in Cognitive Sciences, 5,* 261–270.

King, W. L., & Gruber, H. E. (1962). Moon illusion and Emmert's law. *Science, 135,* 1125–1126.

Klatzky, R. L., Lederman, S. J., Hamilton, C., Grindley, M., & Swendsen, R. H. (2003). Feeling textures through a probe: Effects of probe and surface geometry and exploratory factors. *Perception and Psychophysics, 65,* 613–631.

Klatzky, R. L., Lederman, S. J., & Metzger, V. A. (1985). Identifying objects by touch: An "expert system." *Perception and Psychophysics, 37,* 299–302.

Kleffner, D. A., & Ramachandran, V. S. (1992). On the perception of shape from shading. *Perception and Psychophysics, 52,* 18–36.

Klin, A., Jones, W., Schultz, R., & Volkmar, F. (2003). The enactive mind, or from actions to cognition: Lessons from autism. *Philosophical Transactions of the Royal Society of London B, 345*–360.

Knill, D. C., & Kersten, D. (1991). Apparent surface curvature affects lightness perception. *Nature, 351*, 228–230.

Kobatake, E., & Tanaka, K. (1994). Neuronal selectivities to complex object features in the ventral visual pathway of the macaque cerebral cortex. *Journal of Neurophysiology, 71*, 856–867.

Kohler, E., Keysers, C., Umilta, M. A., Fogassi, L., Gallese, V., & Rizzolatti, G. (2002). Hearing sounds, understanding actions: Action representation in mirror neurons. *Science, 297*, 846–848.

Kolb, N., & Whishaw, I. Q. (2003). *Fundamentals of neuropsychology* (5th ed.). New York: Worth.

Konorski, J. (1967). *Integrative activity of the brain: An interdisciplinary approach.* Chicago: University of Chicago Press.

Kosaki, H., Hashikawa, T., He, J., & Jones, E. G. (1997). Tonotopic organization of auditory cortical fields delineated by parvalbumin immunoreactivity in macaque monkeys. *Journal of Comparative Neurology, 386*, 304–316.

Kosslyn, S. M. (1994). *Image and brain: The resolution of the imagery debate.* Cambridge, MA: MIT Press.

Kourtzi, Z., & Kanwisher, N. (2000). Activation of human MT/MST by static images with implied motion. *Journal of Cognitive Neuroscience, 12*, 48–55.

Kroner, T. (1881). Über die Sinnesempfindungen der Neugeborenen. *Breslauer aerzliche Zeitschrift.* (Cited in Peterson & Rainey, 1911)

Kruger, L. E. (1970). David Katz: Der Aufbau der Tastwelt [The world of touch: A synopsis]. *Perception and Psychophysics, 7*, 337–341.

Kuhl, P. K. (2000). Language, mind and brain: Experience alters perception. In M. Gazzaniga (Ed.), *The new cognitive neurosciences* (pp. 99–115). Cambridge, MA: MIT Press.

Kuhl, P. K. (2004). Early language acquisition: Cracking the speech code. *Nature Reviews: Neuroscience, 5*, 831–843.

Kuhl, P. K., Kirtani, S., Deguchi, T., Hayashi, A., Stevens, E. B., Dugger, C. D., & Iverson, P. (1997). Effects of language experience on speech perception: American and Japanese infants' perception of /ra/ and /la/. *Journal of the Acoustical Society of America, 102*, 3125.

Kuhl, P. K., & Meltzoff, A. N. (1982). The bimodal perception of speech in infancy. *Science, 218*, 1138–1141.

Kuhl, P. K., Williams, K. A., Lacerda, F., Stevens, K. N., & Lindblom, B. (1992). Linguistic experience alters phonetic perception in infants by 6 months of age. *Science, 255*, 606–608.

Kuhn, G., & Land, M. F. (2006). There's more to magic than meets the eye. *Current Biology, 16*, R950–R951.

Kushner, T. (1993). *Angels in America.* New York: Theatre Communications Group.

Kwee, I., Fujii, Y., Matsuzawa, H., & Nakada, T. (1999). Perceptual processing of stereopsis in humans: GH high-field (3.0 tesla) functional MRI study. *Neurology, 53*, 1599–1601.

LaBarbera, J. D., Izard, C. E., Vietze, P., & Parisi, S. A. (1976). Four- and six-month-old infants' visual responses to joy, anger, and neutral expressions. *Child Development, 47*, 535–538.

Laing, D. D., Doty, R. L., & Breipohl, W. (Eds.). (1991). *The human sense of smell.* New York: Springer.

Lamm, C., Batson, C. D., & Decdety, J. (2007). The neural substrate of human empathy: Effects of perspective-taking and cognitive appraisal. *Journal of Cognitive Neuroscience, 19*, 42–58.

Lamme, V. A. F. (1995). The neurophysiology of figure–ground segregation in primary visual cortex. *Journal of Neuroscience, 15*, 1605–1615.

Lamme, V. A. F., & Roelfsema, P. R. (2000). The distinct modes of vision offered by feedforward and recurrent processing. *Trends in Neurosciences, 23*, 571–579.

Land, E. H. (1983). Recent advances in retinex theory and some implications for cortical computations: Color vision and the natural image. *Proceedings of the National Academy of Sciences USA, 80*, 5163–5169.

Land, E. H. (1986). Recent advances in retinex theory. *Vision Research, 26*, 7–21.

Land, E. H., & McCann, J. J. (1971). Lightness and retinex theory. *Journal of the Optical Society of America, 61*, 1–11.

Land, M. F., & Hayhoe, M. (2001). In what ways do eye movements contribute to everyday activities? *Vision Research, 41*, 3559–3565.

Land, M. F., & Horwood, J. (1995). Which parts of the road guide steering? *Nature, 377*, 339–340.

Land, M. F., & Lee, D. N. (1994). Where we look when we steer. *Nature, 369*, 742–744.

Land, M. F., Mennie, N., & Rusted, J. (1999). The roles of vision and eye movements in the control of activities of daily living. *Perception, 28*, 1311–1328.

Larsen, A., Madsen, K. H., Lund, T. E., & Bundesen, C. (2006). Images of illusory motion in primary visual cortex. *Journal of Cognitive Neuroscience, 18*, 1174–1180.

Lavie, N., & Driver, J. (1996). On the spatial extent of attention in object-based visual selection. *Perception and Psychophysics, 58*, 1238–1251.

Lawless, H. (1980). A comparison of different methods for assessing sensitivity to the taste of phenylthiocarbamide PTC. *Chemical Senses, 5*, 247–256.

Lawless, H. (2001). Taste. In E. B. Goldstein (Ed.), *Blackwell handbook of perception* (pp. 601–635). Oxford, UK: Blackwell.

Lederman, S. J., & Klatzky, R. L. (1987). Hand movements: A window into haptic object recognition. *Cognitive Psychology, 19*, 342–368.

Lederman, S. J., & Klatzky, R. L. (1990). Haptic classification of common objects: Knowledge-driven exploration. *Cognitive Psychology, 22*, 421–459.

Lee, D. N. (1980). The optic flow field: The foundation of vision. *Transactions of the Royal Society, 290B*, 169–179.

Lee, D. N., & Aronson, E. (1974). Visual proprioceptive control of standing in human infants. *Perception and Psychophysics, 15*, 529–532.

LeGrand, Y. (1957). *Light, color and vision.* London: Chapman & Hall.

Lennie, P., Krauskopf, J., & Sclar, G. (1990). Chromatic mechanisms in striate cortex of macaque. *Journal of Neuroscience, 10*, 649–669.

Leon, M., & Johnson, B. A. (2003). Olfactory coding in the mammalian olfactory bulb. *Brain Research Reviews, 42*, 23–32.

Leventhal, A. G., Thompson, K. G., Liu, D., Zhou, Y., & Ault, S. J. (1995). Concomitant sensitivity to orientation, direction, and color of cells in layers 2, 3, and 4 of monkey striate cortex. *Journal of Neuroscience, 15*, 1808–1818.

Levin, D., Momen, N., Drivdahl, S. B., & Simons, D. (2000). Change blindness blindness: The metacognitive error of overestimating change-detection ability. *Visual Cognition, 7*, 397–412.

Levin, D., & Simons, D. (1997). Failure to detect changes to attended objects in motion pictures. *Psychonomic Bulletin and Review, 4*, 501–506.

Li, L., Sweet, B. T., & Stone, L. S. (2006). Humans can perceive heading without visual path information. *Journal of Vision, 6*, 874–881.

Liberman, A. M., Cooper, F. S., Harris, K. S., & MacNeilage, P. F. (1963). A motor theory of speech perception. *Proceedings of the Symposium on Speech Communication Seminar* (Vol. 2, Paper D3). Stockholm: Royal Institute of Technology.

Liberman, A. M., Cooper, F. S., Shankweiler, D. P., & Studdert-Kennedy, M. (1967). Perception of the speech code. *Psychological Review, 74*, 431–461.

Liberman, A. M., & Mattingly, I. G. (1989). A specialization for speech perception. *Science, 243*, 489–494.

Liberman, M. C., & Dodds, L. W. (1984). Single-neuron labeling and chronic cochlear pathology: III. Stereocilia damage and alterations of threshold tuning curves. *Hearing Research, 16*, 55–74.

Lindsay, P. H., & Norman, D. A. (1977). *Human information processing* (2nd ed.). New York: Academic Press.

Linster, C., Johnson, B. A., Yue, E., Morse, A., Xu, Z., Hingco, E. E., et al. (2001). Perceptual correlates of neural representations evoked by odorant enantiomers. *Journal of Neuroscience, 21*, 9837–9843.

Litovsky, R. Y., Colburn, H. S., Yost, W. A., & Guzman, S. J. (1999). The precedence effect. *Journal of the Acoustical Society of America, 106*, 1633–1654.

Litovsky, R. Y., Fligor, B. J., & Tramo, M. J. (2002). Functional role of the human inferior colliculus in binaural hearing. *Hearing Research, 165*, 177–188.

Litovsky, R. Y., Rakerd, B., Yin, T. C. T., & Hartmann, W. M. (1997). Psychophysical and physiological evidence for a precedence effect in the median saggital plane. *Journal of Neurophysiology, 77,* 2223–2226.

Livingstone, M. S., & Hubel, D. H. (1988). Segregation of form, color, movement, and depth: Anatomy, physiology, and perception. *Science, 240,* 740–749.

Lomber, S. G., & Malhotra, S. (2008). Double dissociation of "what" and "where" processing in auditory cortex. *Nature Neuroscience, 11,* 609–616.

Loomis, J. M., DaSilva, J. A., Fujita, N., & Fulusima, S. S. (1992). Visual space perception and visually directed action. *Journal of Experimental Psychology: Human Perception and Performance, 18,* 906–921.

Lorteije, J. A. M., Kenemans, J. L., Jellema, T., van der Lubbe, R. H. J., de Heer, F., & van Wezel, R. J. A. (2006). Delayed response to animate implied motion in human motion processing areas. *Journal of Cognitive Neuroscience, 18,* 158–168.

Lowenstein, W. R. (1960). Biological transducers. *Scientific American, 203,* 98–108.

Luck, S. J. (2004). Understanding awareness: One step closer. *Nature Neuroscience, 7,* 208–209.

Lyall, V., Heck, G. L., Phan, T. H., Mummalaneni, S., Malik, S. A., Vinnikova, A. K., et al. (2005). Ethanol modulates the VR-1 variant amiloride-insensitive salt taste receptor: I. Effect on TRC volume and Na + flux. *Journal of General Physiology, 125,* 569–585.

Lyall, V., Heck, G. L., Vinnikova, A. K., Ghosh, S., Phan, T.-H. T., Alam, R. I., et al. (2004). The mammalian amiloride-insensitive non-specific salt taste receptor is a vanilloid receptor-1 variant. *Journal of Physiology, 558,* 147–159.

Mack, A., & Rock, I. (1998). Inattentional blindness. Cambridge, MA: MIT Press.

Maguire, E. A., Frith, C. D., Burgess, N., Donnett, J. G., & O'Keefe, J. (1998). Knowing where things are: Parahippocampal involvement in encoding object locations in virtual large-scale space. *Journal of Cognitive Neuroscience, 10,* 61–76.

Malnic, B., Hirono, J., Sata, T., & Buck, L. B. (1999). Combinatorial receptor codes for odors. *Cell, 96,* 713–723.

Mamassian, P., Knill, D., & Kersten, D. (1998). The perception of cast shadows. *Trends in Cognitive Sciences, 2,* 288–295.

Maunsell, J. H. R. (2004). The role of attention in visual cerebral cortex. In L. M. Chalupa & J. S. Werner (Eds.), *The visual neurosciences* (pp. 1538–1545). Cambridge, MA: MIT Press.

Mayer, D. L., Beiser, A. S., Warner, A. F., Pratt, E. M., Raye, K. N., & Lang, J. M. (1995). Monocular acuity norms for the Teller Acuity Cards between ages one month and four years. *Investigative Ophthalmology and Visual Science, 36,* 671–685.

McAlpine, D. (2005). Creating a sense of auditory space. *Journal of Physiology, 566,* 21–28.

McBurney, D. H. (1969). Effects of adaptation on human taste function. In C. Pfaffmann (Ed.), *Olfaction and taste* (pp. 407–419). New York: Rockefeller University Press.

McClintock, M. K. (1971). Menstrual synchrony and suppression. *Nature, 229,* 244–245.

McFadden, S. A. (1987). The binocular depth stereoacuity of the pigeon and its relation to the anatomical resolving power of the eye. *Vision Research, 27,* 1967–1980.

McFadden, S. A., & Wild, J. M. (1986). Binocular depth perception in the pigeon. *Journal of Experimental Analysis of Behavior, 45,* 149–160.

McGurk, H., & MacDonald, T. (1976). Hearing lips and seeing voices. *Nature, 264,* 746–748.

Meader, P. P., Meuli, R. A., Adriani, M., Bellmann, A., Fornari, E., Thiran, J. P., et al. (2001). Pathways involved in sound recognition and localization: A human fMRI study. *Neuroimage, 14,* 802–816.

Mehler, J. (1981). The role of syllables in speech processing: Infant and adult data. *Transactions of the Royal Society of London, B295,* 333–352.

Melzack, R. (1992). Phantom limbs. *Scientific American, 266,* 121–126.

Melzack, R. (1999). From the gate to the neuromatrix. *Pain, Suppl. 6,* S121–S126.

Melzack, R., & Wall, P. D. (1965). Pain mechanisms: A new theory. *Science, 150,* 971–979.

Melzack, R., & Wall, P. D. (1988). *The challenge of pain* (Rev. ed.). New York: Penguin Books.

Menz, M. D., & Freeman, R. D. (2003). Stereoscopic depth processing in the visual cortex: A coarse-to-fine mechanism. *Nature Neuroscience, 6,* 59–65.

Menzel, R., & Backhaus, W. (1989). Color vision in honey bees: Phenomena and physiological mechanisms. In D. G. Stavenga & R. C. Hardie (Eds.), *Facets of vision* (pp. 281–297). Berlin: Springer-Verlag.

Menzel, R., Ventura, D. F., Hertel, H., deSouza, J., & Greggers, U. (1986). Spectral sensitivity of photoreceptors in insect compound eyes: Comparison of species and methods. *Journal of Comparative Physiology, 158A,* 165–177.

Merigan, W. H., & Maunsell, J. H. R. (1993). How parallel are the primate visual pathways? *Annual Review of Neuroscience, 16,* 369–402.

Merskey, H. (1991). The definition of pain. *European Journal of Psychiatry, 6,* 153–159.

Merzenich, M. M., Recanzone, G., Jenkins, W. M., Allard, T. T., & Nudo, R. J. (1988). Cortical representational placticity. In P. Rakic & W. Singer (Eds.), *Neurobiology of neocortex* (pp. 42–67). New York: Wiley.

Micelli, G., Silveri, M., Villa, G., & Caramazza, A. (1984). On the basis of the agrammatics' difficulty in producing main verbs. *Cortex 20,* 207–220.

Middlebrooks, J. C., & Green, D. M. (1991). Sound localization by human listeners. *Annual Review of Psychology, 42,* 135–159.

Miller, G. A., & Heise, G. A. (1950). The trill threshold. *Journal of the Acoustical Society of America, 22,* 637–683.

Miller, G. A., & Isard, S. (1963). Some perceptual consequences of linguistic rules. *Journal of Verbal Learning and Verbal Behavior, 2,* 212–228.

Miller, I. J. (1995). *Anatomy of the peripheral taste system*. In R. L. Doty (Ed.), Handbook of olfaction and gustation (pp. 521–548). New York: Marcel Dekker.

Miller, J. D. (1974). Effects of noise on people. *Journal of the Acoustical Society of America, 56,* 729–764.

Milner, A. D., & Goodale, M. A. (1995). The visual brain in action. New York: Oxford University Press.

Milner, A. D., & Goodale, M. A. (2006). The visual brain in action (2nd ed.). New York: Oxford University Press.

Mishkin, M., Ungerleider, L. G., & Macko, K. A. (1983). Object vision and spatial vision: Two central pathways. *Trends in Neuroscience, 6,* 414–417.

Møller, A. R. (2000). *Hearing: Its physiology and pathophysiology*. New York: Academic Press.

Mollon, J. D. (1989). "Tho' she kneel'd in that place where they grew . . ." *Journal of Experimental Biology, 146,* 21–38.

Mollon, J. D. (1997). "Tho she kneel'd in that place where they grew . . ." The uses and origins of primate colour visual information. In A. Byrne & D. R. Hilbert (Eds.), *Readings on color: Vol. 2. The science of color* (pp. 379–396). Cambridge, MA: MIT Press.

Montagna, W., & Parakkal, P. F. (1974). *The structure and function of skin* (3rd ed.). New York: Academic Press.

Mon-Williams, M., & Tresilian, J. R. (1999). Some recent studies on the extraretinal contribution to distance perception. *Perception, 28,* 167–181.

Monzée, J., Lamarre, Y., & Smith, A. M. (2003). The effects of digital anesthesia on force control using a precision grip. *Journal of Neurophysiology, 89,* 672–683.

Moon, C., Cooper, R. P., & Fifer, W. P. (1993). Two-day-olds prefer their native language. *Infant Behavior and Development, 16,* 495–500.

Moore, C. M., Yantis, S., & Vaughan, B. (1998). Object-based visual selection: Evidence from perceptual completion. *Psychological Science, 9,* 104–110.

Moran, J., & Desimone, R. (1985). Selective attention gates visual processing in the extrastriate cortex. *Science, 229,* 782–784.

More noise than signal [Editorial]. (2007). *Nature Neuroscience, 10,* 799.

Morimoto, C. H., & Mimica, M. R. M. (2005). Eye gaze tracking techniques for interactive applications. *Computer Vision and Image Understanding, 98,* 4–24.

Morrison, E. E., & Moran, D. T. (1995). Anatomy and ultrastructure of the human olfactory neuroepithelium. In R. L. Doty (Ed.), *Handbook of olfaction and gustation* (pp. 75–101). New York: Marcel Dekker.

Morrot, G., Brochet, F., & Dubourdieu, D. (2001). The color of odors. *Brain and Language, 79*, 309–320.

Morton, J., & Johnson, M. H. (1991). CONSPEC and CONLEARN: A two-process theory of infant face recognition. *Psychological Review, 98*, 164–181.

Moulton, D. G. (1977). Minimum odorant concentrations detectable by the dog and their implications for olfactory receptor sensitivity. In D. Miller-Schwarze & M. M. Mozell (Eds.), *Chemical signals in vertebrates* (pp. 455–464). New York: Plenum Press.

Mountcastle, V. B., Lynch, J. C., Georgopoulos, A., Sakata, H., & Acuña, C. (1975). Posterior parietal association cortex of the monkey: Command functions for operations within extrapersonal space. *Journal of Neurophysiology, 38*, 871–908.

Mountcastle, V. B., & Powell, T. P. S. (1959). Neural mechanisms subserving cutaneous sensibility, with special reference to the role of afferent inhibition in sensory perception and discrimination. *Bulletin of the Johns Hopkins Hospital, 105*, 201–232.

Movshon, J. A., & Newsome, W. T. (1992). Neural foundations of visual motion perception. *Current Directions in Psychological Science, 1*, 35–39.

Mozell, M. M., Smith, B. P., Smith, P. E., Sullivan, R. L., & Swender, P. (1969). Nasal chemoreception in flavor identification. *Archives of Otolaryngology, 90*, 131–137.

Mueller, K. L., Hoon, M. A., Erlenbach, I., Chandrashekar, J., Zuker, C. S., & Ryba, N. J. P. (2005). The receptors and coding logic for bitter taste. *Nature, 434*, 225–229.

Muir, D., & Field, J. (1979). Newborn infants orient to sounds. *Child Development, 50*, 431–436.

Murphy, C., & Cain, W. S. (1980). Taste and olfaction: Independence vs. interaction. *Physiology and Behavior, 24*, 601–606.

Murphy, K. J., Racicot, C. I., & Goodale, M. A. (1996). The use of visuomotor cues as a strategy for making perceptual judgements in a patient with visual form agnosia. *Neuropsychology, 10*, 396–401.

Musallam, S., Corneil, B. D., Greger, B., Scherberger, H., & Andersen, R. A. (2004). Cognitive control signals for neural prosthetics. *Science, 305*, 258–262.

Mythbusters. (2007). Episode 71: Pirate special. Program first aired on the Discovery Channel, January 17, 2007.

Narayan, S. S., Temchin, A. N., Recio, A., & Ruggero, M. A. (1998). Frequency tuning of basilar membrane and auditory nerve fibers in the same cochleae. *Science, 282*, 1882–1884.

Nathans, J., Thomas, D., & Hogness, D. S. (1986). Molecular genetics of human color vision: The genes encoding blue, green, and red pigments. *Science, 232*, 193–202.

Neisser, U., & Becklen, R. (1975). Selective looking: Attending to visually specified events. *Cognitive Psychology, 7*, 480–494.

Neitz, M., Neitz, J., & Jacobs, G. H. (1991). Spectral tuning of pigments underlying red–green color vision. *Science, 252*, 971–974.

Nelken, I. (2004). Processing of complex stimuli and natural scenes in the auditory cortex. *Current Opinion in Neurobiology, 14*, 474–480.

Nelson, C. A. (2001). The development and neural basis of face recognition. *Infant and Child Development, 10*, 3–18.

Neuenschwander, S., & Singer, W. (1996). Long-range synchronization of oscillatory light responses in the cat retina and lateral geniculate nucleus. *Nature, 379*, 728–733.

Newsome, W. T., Britten, K. H., & Movshon, J. A. (1989). Neuronal correlates of a perceptual decision. *Nature, 341*, 52–54.

Newsome, W. T., & Paré, E. B. (1988). A selective impairment of motion perception following lesions of the middle temporal visual area (MT). *Journal of Neuroscience, 8*, 2201–2211.

Newsome, W. T., Shadlen, M. N., Zohary, E., Britten, K. H., & Movshon, J. A. (1995). Visual motion: Linking neuronal activity to psychophysical performance. In M. S. Gazzaniga (Ed.), *The cognitive neurosciences* (pp. 401–414). Cambridge, MA: MIT Press.

Newton, I. (1704). *Optiks.* London: Smith and Walford.

Nobre, A., Allison, T., & McCarthy, G. (1994). Word recognition in the human inferior temporal lobe. *Nature, 372*, 260–263.

Norcia, A. M., & Tyler, C. W. (1985). Spatial frequency sweep VEP: Visual acuity during the first year of life. *Vision Research, 25*, 1399–1408.

Nordby, K. (1990). Vision in a complete achromat: A personal account. In R. F. Hess, L. T. Sharpe, & K. Nordby (Eds.), *Night vision* (pp. 290–315). Cambridge, UK: Cambridge University Press.

Ohzawa, I. (1998). Mechanisms of stereoscopic vision: The disparity energy model. *Current Opinion in Neurobiology, 8*, 509–515.

Oliva, A., & Torralba, A. (2001). Modeling the shape of the scene: A holistic representation of the spatial envelope. *International Journal of Computer Vision, 42*, 145–175.

Oliva, A., & Torralba, A. (2006). Building the gist of a scene: The role of global image features in recognition. *Progress in Brain Research, 155*, 23–36.

Oliva, A., & Torralba, A. (2007). The role of context in object recognition. *Trends in Cognitive Sciences, 11*, 521–527.

Olshausen, B. A., & Field, D. J. (2004). Sparse coding of sensory inputs. *Current Opinion in Neurobiology, 14*, 481–487.

Olsho, L. W., Koch, E. G., Carter, E. A., Halpin, C. F., & Spetner, N. B. (1988). Pure-tone sensitivity of human infants. *Journal of the Acoustical Society of America, 84*, 1316–1324.

Olsho, L. W., Koch, E. G., Halpin, C. F., & Carter, E. A. (1987). An observer-based psychoacoustic procedure for use with young infants. *Developmental Psychology, 23*, 627–640.

Olson, C. R., & Freeman, R. D. (1980). Profile of the sensitive period for monocular deprivation in kittens. *Experimental Brain Research, 39*, 17–21.

Olson, H. (1967). *Music, physics, and engineering* (2nd ed.). New York: Dover.

Ooi, T. L., Wu, B., & He, Z. J. (2001). Distance determined by the angular declination below the horizon. *Nature, 414*, 197–200.

Orban, G. A., Lagae, L., Verri, A., Raiguel, S., Xiao, D., Maes, H., et al. (1992). First-order analysis of optical flow in monkey brain. *Proceedings of the National Academy of Sciences, 89*, 2595–2599.

Orban, G. A., Vandenbussche, E., & Vogels, R. (1984). Human orientation discrimination tested with long stimuli. *Vision Research, 24*, 121–128.

Owens, E. (1989). Present status of adults with cochlear implants. In E. Owens & D. K. Kessler (Eds.), *Cochlear implants in young deaf children* (pp. 25–52). Boston: Little, Brown.

Owens, M. (1994, June 6). Designers discover the sweet smell of success. *New York Times.*

Pack, C. C., & Born, R. T. (2001). Temporal dynamics of a neural solution to the aperture problem in visual area MT of macaque brain. *Nature, 409*, 1040–1042.

Pack, C. C., Livingston, M. S., Duffy, K. R., & Born, R. T. (2003). End-stopping and the aperture problem: Two-dimensional motion signals in macaque V1. *Neuron, 59*, 671–680.

Palmer, A. R. (1987). Physiology of the cochlear nerve and cochlear nucleus. In M. P. Haggard & E. F. Evans (Eds.), *Hearing* (pp. 838–855). Edinburgh: Churchill Livingstone.

Palmer, S. E. (1975). The effects of contextual scenes on the identification of objects. *Memory and Cognition, 3*, 519–526.

Palmer, S. E. (1992). Common region: A new principle of perceptual grouping. *Cognitive Psychology, 24*, 436–447.

Palmer, S. E., & Rock, I. (1994). Rethinking perceptual organization: The role of uniform connectedness. *Psychonomic Bulletin and Review, 1*, 29–55.

Palmeri, T. J., Goldinger, S. D., & Pisoni, D. B. (1993). Episodic encoding of voice attributes and recognition memory for spoken words. *Journal of Experimental Psychology: Learning Memory and Cognition, 19*, 309–328.

Pantev, C., Oostenveld, R., Engelien, A., Ross, B., Roberts, L. E., & Hoke, M. (1998). Increased auditory cortical representation in musicians. *Nature, 392*, 811–814.

Parker, A. J. (2007). Binocular depth perception and the cerebral cortex. *Nature Reviews Neuroscience, 8*, 379–391.

Parkhurst, D., Law, K., & Niebur, E. (2002). Modeling the role of salience in the allocation of overt visual attention. *Vision Research, 42*, 107–123.

Parkin, A. J. (1996). *Explorations in cognitive neuropsychology*. Oxford, UK: Blackwell.

Pascalis, O., de Haan, M., & Nelson, C. A. (2002). Is face processing species-specific during the first year of life? *Science, 296*, 1321-1323.

Pascalis, O., deSchonen, S., Morton, J., Deruelle, C., & Fabre-Grenet, M. (1995). Mother's face recognition by neonates: A replication and an extension. *Infant Behavior and Development, 18*, 79-85.

Pasternak, T., & Merigan, E. H. (1994). Motion perception following lesions of the superior temporal sulcus in the monkey. *Cerebral Cortex, 4*, 247-259.

Patterson, M. L., & Werker, J. F. (1999). Matching phonetic information in lips and voice is robust in 4.5 month old infants. *Infant Behavior and Development, 22*, 237-247.

Pelphrey, K. A., Mitchell, T. V., McKeown, M. J., Goldstein, J., Allison, T., & McCarthy, G. (2003). Brain activity evoked by the perception of human walking: Controlling for meaningful coherent motion. *Journal of Neuroscience, 23*, 6819-6825.

Pelphrey, K. A., Morris, J. P., & McCarthy, G. (2005). Neural basis of eye gaze processing deficits in autism. *Brain, 128*, 1038-1048.

Pelphrey, K. A., Viola, R. J., & McCarthy, G. (2004). When strangers pass. *Psychological Science, 15*, 598-603.

Penfield, W., & Rasmussen, T. (1950). *The cerebral cortex of man*. New York: Macmillan.

Peng, J. H., Tao, Z. Z., Huang, Z. W. (2007). Risk of damage to hearing from personal listening devices in young adults. *Journal of Otolaryngology, 36*, 181-185.

Perl, E. R., & Kruger, L. (1996). In L. Kruger (Ed.), *Pain and touch* (pp. 179-221). San Diego, CA: Academic Press.

Peterson, F., & Rainey, L. H. (1911). The beginnings of mind in the newborn. *Bulletin of the Lying-In Hospital, 7*, 99-122.

Pfaffmann, C. (1974). Specificity of the sweet receptors of the squirrel monkey. *Chemical Senses, 1*, 61-67.

Pfeiffer, C. A., & Johnston, R. E. (1994). Hormonal and behavioral responses of male hamsters to females and female odors: Roles of olfaction, the vemeronasal system, and sexual experience. *Physiology and Behavior, 55*, 129-138.

Philbeck, J. W., Loomis, J. M., & Beall, A. C. (1997). Visually perceived location is an invariant in the control of action. *Perception and Psychophysics, 59*, 601-612.

Phillips, J. R., & Johnson, K. O. (1981). Tactile spatial resolution: II. Neural representation of bars, edges, and gratings in monkey primary afferent. *Journal of Neurophysiology, 46*, 1177-1191.

Pierno, A. C., Becchio, C., Wall, M. B., Smith, A. T., Turella, L., & Castiello, U. (2006). When gaze turns into grasp. *Journal of Cognitive Neuroscience, 18*, 2130-2137.

Pirchio, M., Spinelli, D., Fiorentini, A., & Maffei, L. (1978). Infant contrast sensitivity evaluated by evoked potentials. *Brain Research, 141*, 179-184.

Plack, C. J. (2005). *The sense of hearing*. New York: Erlbaum.

Plug, C., & Ross, H. E. (1994). The natural moon illusion: A multifactor account. *Perception, 23*, 321-333.

Pokorny, J., Shevell, S. K., & Smith, V. C. (1991). Color appearance and color constancy. In P. Gouras (Ed.), *The perception of color: Vol. 6. Vision and visual dysfunction* (pp. 43-61). Boca Raton, FL: CRC Press.

Poremba, A., Saunders, R. C., Crane, A. M., Cook, M., Sokoloff, L., & Mishkin, M. (2003). Functional mapping of the primate auditory system. *Science, 299*, 568-572.

Posner, M. I., Nissen, M. J., & Ogden, W. C. (1978). Attended and unattended processing modes: The role of set for spatial location. In H. L. Pick & I. J. Saltzman (Eds.), *Modes of perceiving and processing information*. Hillsdale, NJ: Erlbaum.

Potter, M. C. (1976). Short-term conceptual memory for pictures. *Journal of Experimental Psychology (Human Learning), 2*, 509-522.

Price, D. D. (2000). Psychological and neural mechanisms of the affective dimension of pain. Science, 288, 1769-1772.

Prinzmetal, W., Shimamura, A. P., & Mikolinski, M. (2001). The Ponzo illusion and the perception of orientation. *Perception and Psychophysics, 63*, 99-114.

Proffitt, D. R., Stefanucci, J., Banton, T., & Epstein, W. (2003). The role of effort in perceiving distance. *Psychological Science, 14*, 106-112.

Puce, A., Allison, T., Bentin, S., Gore, J. C., & McCarthy, G. (1998). Temporal cortex activation in humans viewing eye and mouth movements. *Journal of Neuroscience, 18*, 2188-2199.

Puce, A., & Perrett, D. (2003). Electrophysiology and brain imaging of biological motion. *Philosophical Transactions of the Royal Society of London B, 358*, 435-445.

Qui, F. T., & von der Heydt, R. (2005). Figure and ground in the visual cortex: V2 combines stereoscopic cues with Gestalt rules. *Neuron, 7*, 155-166.

Quinn, P. C., Lee, K., Pascalis, O., & Slater, A. M. (in press). Perceptual development: Face perception. In E. B. Goldstein (Ed.), *Encyclopedia of perception*. Thousand Oaks, CA: Sage.

Quinn, P. C., Rosano, J. L., & Wooten, B. R. (1988). Evidence that brown is not an elemental color. *Perception and Psychophysics, 43*, 156-164.

Quiroga, R. Q., Reddy, L., Kreiman, G., Koch, C., & Fried, I. (2005). Invariant visual representation by single neurons in the human brain. *Nature, 435*, 1102-1107.

Quiroga, R. Q., Reddy, L., Kreiman, G., Koch, C., & Fried, I. (2008). Sparse but not "grandmother-cell" coding in the medial temporal lobe. *Trends in Cognitive Sciences, 12*, 87-91.

Raffi, M., Squatrito, S., & Maioli, M. G. (2002). Responses to optic flow in the monkey parietal area. *Cerebral Cortex, 12*, 639-646.

Rainville, P. (2002). Brain mechanisms of pain affect and pain modulation. *Current Opinion in Neurobiology, 12*, 195-204.

Ramachandran, V. S. (1992, May). Blind spots. *Scientific American*, 86-91.

Ramachandran, V. S., & Anstis, S. M. (1986, May). The perception of apparent motion. *Scientific American*, 102-109.

Ramachandran, V. S., & Hirstein, W. (1998). The perception of phantom limbs. *Brain, 121*, 1603-1630.

Ratner, C., & McCarthy, J. (1990). Ecologically relevant stimuli and color memory. *Journal of General Psychology, 117*, 369-377.

Rauschecker, J. P. (1997). Processing of complex sounds in the auditory cortex of cat, monkey, and man. *Acta Otolaryngol, 532*(Suppl.), 34-38.

Rauschecker, J. P. (1998). Cortical processing of complex sounds. *Current Opinion in Neurobiology, 8*, 516-521.

Rauschecker, J. P., & Tian, B. (2000). Mechanisms and streams for processing of "what" and "where" in auditory cortex. *Proceedings of the National Academy of Sciences USA, 97*, 11800-11806.

Reale, R. A., & Imig, T. J. (1980). Tonotopic organization in auditory cortex of the cat. *Journal of Comparative Neurology, 192*, 265-291.

Recanzone, G. H., Schreiner, C. E., & Merzenich, M. M. (1993). Plasticity in the frequency representation of primary auditory cortex following discrimination training in adult owl monkeys. *Journal of Neuroscience, 13*, 87-103.

Reddy, L., Moradi, F., & Koch, C. (2007). Top-down biases win against focal attention in the fusiform face area. *Neuroimage, 38*, 730-739.

Reddy, L., Reddy, L., & Koch, C. (2006). Face identification in the near-absence of focal attention. *Vision Research, 46*, 2336-2343.

Reed, C. L., & Vinson, N. G. (1996). Conceptual effects on representational momentum. *Journal of Experimental Psychology: Human Perception and Performance, 22*, 839-850.

Regan, D. (1986). Luminance contrast: Vernier discrimination. *Spatial Vision, 1*, 305-318.

Regan, D., & Cynader, M. (1979). Neurons in area 18 of cat visual cortex selectively sensitive to changing size: Nonlinear interactions between responses to two edges. *Vision Research, 19*, 699-711.

Reichl, R. (1994, March 11). Dining in New York. *New York Times*.

Rennaker, R. L., Chen, C.-F. F., Ruyle, A. M., Sloan, A. M., & Wilson, D. A. (2007). Spatial and temporal distribution of odorant-evoked activity in the piriform cortex. *Journal of Neuroscience, 27*, 1534-1542.

Rensink, R. A. (2002). Change detection. *Annual Review of Psychology, 53*, 245-277.

Rensink, R. A., O'Regan, J. K., & Clark, J. J. (1997). To see or not to see: The need for attention to perceive changes in scenes. *Psychological Science, 8*, 368–373.

Reynolds, J. H., & Desimone, R. (2003). Interacting roles of attention and visual salience in V4. *Neuron, 37*, 853–863.

Riesenhuber, M., & Poggio, T. (2000). Models of object recognition. *Nature Neuroscience Supplement, 3*, 1199–1204.

Riesenhuber, M., & Poggio, T. (2002). Neural mechanisms of object recognition. *Current Opinion in Neurobiology, 12*, 162–168.

Ringbach, D. L. (2003). Look at the big picture (details will follow). *Nature Neuroscience, 6*, 7–8.

Risset, J. C., & Mathews, M. W. (1969). Analysis of musical instrument tones. *Physics Today, 22*, 23–30.

Rivera-Gaxiola, M., Silva-Pereyra, J., & Kuhl, P. K. (2005). Brain potentials to native and non-native speech contrasts in 7- and 11-month-old American infants. *Developmental Science, 8*, 162–172.

Rizzolatti, G., & Arbib, M. A. (1998). *Trends in Neurosciences, 21*, 188–194.

Rizzolatti, G., Fadiga, L., Gallese, V., & Fogassi, L. (1996). Premotor cortex and the recognition of motor actions. *Cognitive Brain Research, 3*, 131–141.

Rizzolatti, G., Forgassi, L., & Gallese, V. (2000). Cortical mechanisms subserving object grasping and action recognition: A new view on the cortical motor functions. In M. Gazzaniga (Ed.), *The new cognitive neurosciences* (pp. 539–552). Cambridge, MA: MIT Press.

Rizzolatti, G., Forgassi, L., & Gallese, V. (2006, November). Mirrors in the mind. *Scientific American*, pp. 54–63.

Robbins, J. (2000, July 4). Virtual reality finds a real place. *New York Times*.

Robertson, L., Treisman, A., Friedman-Hill, S., & Grabowecky, M. (1997). The interaction of spatial and object pathways: Evidence from Balint's syndrome. *Journal of Cognitive Neuroscience, 9*, 295–317.

Robinson, D. L., & Wurtz, R. (1976). Use of an extra-retinal signal by monkey superior colliculus neurons to distinguish real from self-induced stimulus movement. *Journal of Neurophysiology, 39*, 852–870.

Robles-De-La-Torre, G. (2006). The importance of the sense of touch in virtual and real environments. *IEEE Multimedia, 13*(3), 24–30.

Rock, I. (1983). *The logic of perception*. Cambridge, MA: MIT Press.

Rock, I., & Kaufman, L. (1962). The moon illusion: Part 2. *Science, 136*, 1023–1031.

Rollman, G. B. (1991). Pain responsiveness. In M. A. Heller & W. Schiff (Eds.), *The psychology of touch* (pp. 91–114). Hillsdale, NJ: Erlbaum.

Rolls, E. T. (2000). The orbitofrontal cortex and reward. *Cerebral Cortex, 10*, 284–294.

Rolls, E. T. (2004). Smell, taste, texture, and temperature multimodal representations in the brain, and their relevance to the control of appetite. *Nutrition Reviews, 62*, S193–S204.

Rolls, E. T., & Baylis, L. L. (1994). Gustatory, olfactory, and visual convergence within the primate orbitofrontal cortex. *Journal of Neuroscience, 14*, 5437–5452.

Rolls, E. T., & Tovee, M. J. (1995). Sparseness of the neuronal representation of stimuli in the primate temporal visual cortex. *Journal of Neurophysiology, 73*, 713–726.

Romanski, L. M., Tian, B., Fritz, J., Mishkin, M., Goldman-Rakic, P. S., & Rauschecker, J. P. (1999). Dual streams of auditory afferents target multiple domains in the prefrontal cortex. *Nature Neuroscience, 2*, 1131–1136.

Romo, R., Hernandez, A., Zainos, A., & Salinas, E. (1998). Somatosensory discrimination based on cortical microstimulation. *Nature, 392*, 387–390.

Rose, D. (1996). Reflections on (or by?) grandmother cells. *Perception, 25*, 881.

Rosenstein, D., & Oster, H. (1988). Differential facial responses to four basic tastes in newborns. *Child Development, 59*, 1555–1568.

Roskies, A. L. (1999). The binding problem. *Neuron, 24*, 7–9.

Rossiter, K. J. (1996). Structure-odor relationships. *Chemical Reviews, 96*, 3201–3240.

Rowe, M. J., Turman, A. A., Murray, G. M., & Zhang, H. Q. (1996). Parallel processing in somatosensory areas I and II of the cerebral cortex. In O. Franzen, R. Johansson, & L. Terenius (Eds.), *Somesthesis and the neurobiology of the somatosensory cortex* (pp. 197–212). Basel: Birkhauser Verlag.

Rozin, P. (1982). "Taste-smell confusions" and the duality of the olfactory sense. *Perception and Psychophysics, 31*, 397–401.

Rubin, P., Turvey, M. T., & Van Gelder, P. (1976). Initial phonemes are detected faster in spoken words than in spoken nonwords. *Perception and Psychophysics, 19*, 394–398.

Rushton, S. K., Harris, J. M., Lloyd, M. R., & Wann, J. P. (1998). Guidance of locomotion on foot uses perceived target location rather than optic flow. *Current Biology, 8*, 1191–1194.

Rushton, S. K., & Salvucci, D. D. (2001). An egocentric account of the visual guidance of locomotion. *Trends in Cognitive Sciences, 5*, 6–7.

Rushton, W. A. H. (1961). Rhodopsin measurement and dark adaptation in a subject deficient in cone vision. *Journal of Physiology, 156*, 193–205.

Rushton, W. A. H. (1964). Color blindness and cone pigments. *American Journal of Optometry and Archives of the American Academy of Optometry, 41*, 265–282.

Rust, N. C., Mante, V., Simoncelli, E. P., & Movshon, J. A. (2006). How MT cells analyze the motion of visual patterns. *Nature Neuroscience, 9*, 1421–1431.

Sackett, B. (1972). Counting every quantum. *Journal of Physiology, 223*, 131–150.

Sacks, O. (1985). *The man who mistook his wife for a hat*. London: Duckworth.

Saffran, J. R., Aslin, R. N., & Newport, E. L. (1996). Statistical learning by 8-month-old infants. *Science, 274*, 1926–1928.

Sai, F. Z. (2005). The role of the mother's voice in developing mother's face preference: Evidence for intermodal perception at birth. *Infant and Child Development, 14*, 29–50.

Sakata, H., & Iwamura, Y. (1978). Cortical processing of tactile information in the first somatosensory and parietal association areas in the monkey. In G. Gordon (Ed.), *Active touch* (pp. 55–72). Elmsford, NY: Pergamon Press.

Sakata, H., Taira, M., Mine, S., & Murata, A. (1992). Hand-movement-related neurons of the posterior parietal cortex of the monkey: Their role in visual guidance of hand movements. In R. Caminiti, P. B. Johnson, & Y. Burnod (Eds.), *Control of arm movement in space: Neurophysiological and computational approaches* (pp. 185–198). Berlin: Springer-Verlag.

Salapatek, P., & Banks, M. S. (1978). Infant sensory assessment: Vision. In F. D. Minifie & L. L. Lloyd (Eds.), *Communicative and cognitive abilities: Early behavioral assessment* (pp. 61–106). Baltimore: University Park Press.

Salapatek, P., Bechtold, A. G., & Bushnell, E. W. (1976). Infant visual acuity as a function of viewing distance. *Child Development, 47*, 860–863.

Salasoo, A., & Pisoni, D. B. (1985). Interaction of knowledge sources in spoken word identification. *Journal of Memory and Language, 24*, 210–231.

Samuel, A. G. (1981). Phonemic restoration: Insights from a new methodology. *Journal of Experimental Psychology: General, 110*, 474–494.

Samuel, A. G. (1990). Using perceptual-restoration effects to explore the architecture of perception. In G. T. M. Altmann (Ed.), *Cognitive models of speech processing* (pp. 295–314). Cambridge, MA: MIT Press.

Samuel, A. G. (1997). Lexical activation produces potent phonemic percepts. *Cognitive Psychology, 32*, 97–127.

Samuel, A. G. (2001). Knowing a word affects the fundamental perception of the sounds within it. *Psychological Science, 12*, 348–351.

Sato, M., & Ogawa, H. (1993). Neural coding of taste in macaque monkeys. In K. Kurihari, N. Suzuki, & H. Ogawa (Eds.), *Olfaction and taste* (Vol.1, pp. 388–392). Tokyo: Springer-Verlag.

Sato, M., Ogawa, H., & Yamashita, S. (1994). Gustatory responsiveness of chorda tympani fibers the cynomolgus monkey. *Chemical Senses, 19*, 381–400.

Schaal, B., Coureaud, G., Langlois, D., Ginies, C., Semon E., & Perrier, G. (2003). Chemical and behavioural characterization of the rabbit mammary pheromone. *Nature, 424*, 68–72.

Schiffman, H. R. (1967). Size-estimation of familiar objects under informative and reduced conditions of viewing. *American Journal of Psychology, 80*, 229–235.

Schiffman, S. S., & Erickson, R. P. (1971). A psychophysical model for gustatory quality. *Physiology and Behavior, 7*, 617–633.

Schmuziger, N., Patscheke, J., & Probst, R. (2006). Hearing in nonprofessional pop/rock musicians. *Ear and Hearing, 27*, 321–330.

Schnapf, J. L., Kraft, T. W., & Baylor, D. A. (1987). Spectral sensitivity of human cone photoreceptors. *Nature, 325*, 439–441.

Schneider, P., Scherg, M., Dosch, H. G., Specht, H. J., Gutschalk, A., & Rupp, A. (2002). Morphology of Heschl's gyrus reflects enhanced activation in the auditory cortex of musicians. *Nature Neuroscience, 3*, 688–694.

Scholz, J., & Woolf, C. J. (2002). Can we conquer pain? *Nature Neuroscience, 5*, 1062–1067.

Schreiner, C. H., & Mendelson, J. R. (1990). Functional topography of cat primary auditory cortex: Distribution of integrated excitation. *Journal of Neurophysiology, 64*, 1442–1459.

Schubert, E. D. (1980). *Hearing: Its function and dysfunction*. Wien: Springer-Verlag.

Scott, S. H. (2006). Converting thoughts into action. *Nature, 442*, 141–142.

Scott, T. R., & Giza, B. K. (1990). Coding channels in the taste system of the rat. *Science, 249*, 1585–1587.

Scott, T. R., & Giza, B. K. (2000). Issues of gustatory neural coding: Where they stand today. *Physiology and Behavior, 69*, 65–76.

Scott, T. R., & Plata-Salaman, C. R. (1991). Coding of taste quality. In T. V. Getchell, R. L. Doty, L. M. Bartoshuk, & J. B. Snow (Eds.), *Smell and taste in health and disease* (pp. 345–368). New York: Raven Press.

Sedgwick, H. (2001). Visual space perception. In E. B. Goldstein (Ed.), *Blackwell handbook of perception* (pp. 128–167). Oxford, UK: Blackwell.

Segui, J. (1984). The syllable: A basic perceptual unit in speech processing? In H. Bouma & D. G. Gouwhuis (Eds.), *Attention and performance X* (pp. 165–181). Hillsdale, NJ: Erlbaum.

Sekuler, R., Sekuler, A. B., & Lau, R. (1997). Sound alters visual motion perception. *Nature, 385*, 308.

Senior, C., Barnes, J., Giampietro, V., Simmons, A., Bullmore, E. T., Brammer, M., & David, A. S. (2000). The functional neuoroanatomy of implicit-motion perception or "representational momentum." *Current Biology, 10*, 16–22.

Sereno, M. E., Trinath, T., Augath, M., & Logothetis, N. K. (2002). Three dimensional shape representation in monkey cortex. *Neuron, 33*, 635–652.

Serruya, M. D., Hatsopoulos, N. G., Paminski, L., Fellows, M. R., & Donoghue, J. P. (2002). Instant neural control of a movement signal. *Nature, 416*, 141–142.

Shafritz, K. M., Gore, J. C., & Marois, R. (2002). The role of the parietal cortex in visual feature binding. *Proceedings of the National Academy of Sciences, 99*, 10917–10922.

Shams, L., Kamitani, Y., & Shimojo, S. (2000). What you see is what you hear. *Nature, 408*, 788.

Shein, S. J., & Desimone, R. (1990). Spectral properties of V4 neurons in the macaque. *Journal of Neuroscience, 10*, 3369–3389.

Sheinberg, D. L., & Logothetis, N. K. (1997). The role of temporal cortical areas in perceptual organization. *Proceedings of the National Academy of Sciences, 94*, 3408–3413.

Sheinberg, D. L., & Logothetis, N. K. (2001). Noticing familiar objects in real world scenes: The role of temporal cortical neurons in natural vision. *Journal of Neuroscience, 21*, 1340–1350.

Sherman, S. M., & Koch, C. (1986). The control of retinogeniculate transmission in the mammalian lateral geniculate nucleus. *Experimental Brain Research, 63*, 1–20.

Shimamura, A. P., & Prinzmetal, W. (1999). The mystery spot illusion and its relation to other visual illusions. *Psychological Science, 10*, 501–507.

Shimojo, S., Bauer, J., O'Connell, K. M., & Held, R. (1986). Pre-stereoptic binocular vision in infants. *Vision Research, 26*, 501–510.

Shinkareva, S. V., Mason, R. A., Malave, V. L., Wang, W., Mitchell, T. M., & Just, M. (2008). Using fMRI brain activation to identify cognitive states associated with perception of tools and dwellings. *PLoS ONE, 3*(1), e1394. doi:10.1371/journal.pone.0001394

Shinoda, H., Hayhoe, M. M., & Shrivastava, A. (2001). What controls attention in natural environments? *Vision Research, 41*, 3535–3545.

Simons, D. J., & Chabris, C. F. (1999). Gorillas in our midst: sustained inattentional blindness for dynamic events. *Perception, 28*, 1059–1074.

Singer, T., Seymour, B., O'Doherty, J., Kaube, H., Dolan, R. J., & Frith, C. D. (2004). Empathy for pain involves the affective but not sensory components of pain. *Science, 303*, 1157–1162.

Sinha, P. (2002). Recognizing complex patterns. *Nature Neuroscience, 5*, 1093–1097.

Sinha, P., Balas, B., Ostrovsky, Y., & Russell, R. (2006). Face recognition by humans: Nineteen results all computer vision researchers should know about. *Proceedings of the IEEE, 94*, 1948–1962.

Slater, A. M., & Findlay, J. M. (1975). Binocular fixation in the newborn baby. *Journal of Experimental Child Psychology, 20*, 248–273.

Slater, A. M., Morison, V., & Rose, D. (1984). Habituation in the newborn. *Infant Behavior and Development, 7*, 183–200.

Slater, A. M., Morison, V., Somers, M., Mattock, A., Brown, E., & Taylor, D. (1990) Newborn and older infants' perception of partly occluded objects. *Infant Behavior and Development, 13*, 33–49.

Sloan, L. L., & Wollach, L. (1948). A case of unilateral deuteranopia. *Journal of the Optical Society of America, 38*, 502–509.

Smith, D. V., & Scott, T. R. (2003). Gustatory neural coding. In R. L. Doty (Ed.), *Handbook of olfaction and gustation* (2nd ed.). New York: Marcel Dekker.

Smith, D. V., St. John, S. J., & Boughter, J. D., Jr. (2000). Neuronal cell types and taste quality coding. *Physiology and Behavior, 69*, 77–85.

Smith, M. A., Majaj, N. J., & Movshon, J. A. (2005). Dynamics of motion signaling by neurons in macaque area MT. *Nature Neuroscience, 8*, 220–228.

Snyder, L. H., Batista, A. P., & Andersen, R. A. (2000). Intention-related activity in the posterior parietal cortex: A review. *Vision Research, 40*, 1433–1441.

Sobel, E. C. (1990). The locust's use of motion parallax to measure distance. *Journal of Comparative Physiology, 167*, 579–588.

Solomon, S. G., & Lennie, P. (2007). The machinery of colour vision. *Nature Reviews Neuroscience, 8*, 276–286.

Sommer, M. A., & Crapse, T. B. (in press). Corollary discharge. In E. B. Goldstein (Ed.), *Sage encyclopedia of perception*. Thousand Oaks, CA: Sage.

Sommer, M. A., & Wurtz, R. H. (2006). Influence of the thalamus on spatial visual processing in frontal cortex. *Nature, 444*, 374–377.

Sommer, M. A., & Wurtz, R. H. (2008). Brain circuits for the internal monitoring of movements. *Annual Review of Neuroscience, 31*, 317–338.

Soto-Faraco, S., Lyons, J., Gazzaniga, M., Spence, C., & Kingstone, A. (2002). The ventriloquist in motion: Illusory capture of dynamic information across sensory modalities. *Cognitive Brain Research, 14*, 139–146.

Soto-Faraco, S., Spence, C., Lloyd, D., & Kingstone, A. (2004). Moving multisenosry research along: Motion perception across sensory modalities. *Current Directions in Psychological Science, 13*, 29–32.

Spiers, H. J., & Maguire, E. A. (2006). Thoughts, behavior, and brain dynamics during navigation in the real world. *Neuroimage, 31*, 1826–1840.

Srinivasan, M. V., & Venkatesh, S. (Eds.). (1997). *From living eyes to seeing machines*. New York: Oxford University Press.

Stark, L., & Bridgeman, B. (1983). Role of corollary discharge in space constancy. *Perception and Psychophysics, 34*, 371–380.

Steiner, J. E. (1974). Innate, discriminative human facial expressions to taste and smell stimulation. *Annals of the New York Academy of Sciences, 237*, 229–233.

Steiner, J. E. (1979). Human facial expressions in response to taste and smell stimulation. *Advances in Child Development and Behavior, 13*, 257–295.

Stern, K., & McClintock, M. K. (1998). Regulation of ovulation by human pheromones. *Nature, 392*, 177–179.

Stevens, S. S. (1957). On the psychophysical law. *Psychological Review, 64*, 153–181.

Stevens, S. S. (1961). To honor Fechner and repeal his law. *Science, 133*, 80–86.

Stevens, S. S. (1962). The surprising simplicity of sensory metrics. *American Psychologist, 17*, 29–39.

Stevenson, R. J. (2001). Associative learning and odor quality perception: How sniffing an odor mixture can alter the smell of its parts. *Learning and Motivation, 32*, 154–177.

Stiles, W. S. (1953). Further studies of visual mechanisms by the two-color threshold method. *Coloquio sobre problemas opticos de la vision* (Vol. 1, pp. 65–103). Madrid: Union Internationale de Physique Pure et Appliquée.

Stoerig, P. (1998). Wavelength information processing versus color perception: Evidence from blindsight and color-blind sight. In W. G. K. Backhaus, R. Kliegl, & J. S. Werner (Eds.), *Color vision: Perspectives from different disciplines* (pp. 131–147). New York: Walter de Gruyter.

Stoffregen, T. A., Smart, J. L., Bardy, B. G., & Pagulayan, R. J. (1999). Postural stabilization of looking. *Journal of Experimental Psychology: Human Perception and Performance, 25*, 1641–1658.

Strange, W. (Ed.). (1995). Speech perception and linguistic experience: Issues in cross-language research. Timonium, MD: York.

Sufka, K. J., & Price, D. D. (2002). Gate control theory reconsidered. *Brain and Mind, 3*, 277–290.

Suga, N. (1990, June). Biosonar and neural computation in bats. *Scientific American*, 60–68.

Sumby, W. H., & Pollack, J. (1954). Visual contributions to speech intelligibility in noise. *Journal of the Acoustical Society of America, 26*, 212–215.

Sumner, P., & Mollon, J. D. (2000). Catarrhine photopigments are optimized for detecting targets against a foliage background. *Journal of Experimental Biology, 23*, 1963–1986.

Sun, H.-J., Campos, J., Young, M., Chan, G. S. W., & Ellard, C. G. (2004). The contributions of static visual cues, nonvisual cues, and optic flow in distance estimation. *Perception, 33*, 49–65.

Svaetichin, G. (1956). Spectral response curves from single cones. *Acta Physiologica Scandinavica Supplementum, 134*, 17–46.

Swets, J. A. (1964). *Signal detection and recognition by human observers*. New York: Wiley.

Taira, M., Mine, S., Georgopoulis, A. P., Murata, A., & Sakata, H. (1990). Parietal cortex neurons of the monkey related to the visual guidance of hand movement. *Experimental Brain Research, 83*, 29–36.

Tanaka, J. W., & Presnell, L. M. (1999). Color diagnosticity in object recognition. *Perception and Psychophysics, 61*, 1140–1153.

Tanaka, J. W., Weiskopf, D., & Williams, P. (2001). The role of color in high-level vision. *Trends in Cognitive Sciences, 5*, 211–215.

Tanaka, K. (1993). Neuronal mechanisms of object recognition. *Science, 262*, 684–688.

Tanaka, K., Siato, H.-A., Fukada, Y., & Moriya, M. (1991). Coding visual images of objects in inferotemporal cortex of the Macaque monkey. *Journal of Neurophysiology, 66*, 170–189.

Tatler, B. W., & Kuhn, G. (2007). Don't look now: The magic of misdirection. In R. P. G. van Gompel, M. H. Fischer, W. S. Murray, & R. L. Hill (Eds.), *Eye movements: A window on mind and brain* (pp. 697–714). Oxford, UK: Elsevier.

Taylor, D. A., Helms, T. S. I., & Schwartz, A. B. (2002). Direct cortical control of 3D neuroprosthetic devices. *Science, 296*, 1829–1832.

Teghtsoonian, R. (1971). On the exponents in Stevens's Law and the constant in Ekman's Law. *Psychological Review, 78*, 78–80.

Teller, D. Y. (1990). The domain of visual science. In L. Spellman & J. S. Werner (Eds.), *Visual perception: The neurophysiology foundations* (pp. 11–21). San Diego, CA: Academic Press.

Teller, D. Y. (1997). First glances: The vision of infants. *Investigative Ophthalmology and Visual Science, 38*, 2183–2199.

Ter-Pogossian, M. M., Phelps, M. E., Hoffman, E. J., & Mullani, N. A. (1975). A positron-emission tomograph for nuclear imaging (PET). *Radiology, 114*, 89–98.

Terwogt, M. M., & Hoeksma, J. B. (1994). Colors and emotions: Preferences and combinations. *Journal of General Psychology, 122*, 5–17.

Tian, B., Reser, D., Durham, A., Kustov, A., & Rauschecker, J. P. (2001). Functional specialization in rhesus monkey auditory cortex. *Science, 292*, 290–293.

Tong, F., Nakayama, K., Vaughn, J. T., & Kanwisher, N. (1998) Binocular rivalry and visual awareness in human extrastriate cortex. *Neuron, 21*, 753–759.

Tonndorf, J. (1960). Shearing motion in scalia media of cochlear models. *Journal of the Acoustical Society of America, 32*, 238–244.

Tonndorf, J., & Khanna, S. M. (1968). Submicroscopic displacement amplitudes of the tympanic membrane (cat) measured by laser interferometer. *Journal of the Acoustical Society of America, 44*, 1546–1554.

Tracey, I. (2005.) Nociceptive processing in the human brain. *Current Opinion in Neurobiology, 15*, 478–487.

Tramo, M. J., Gaurav, D. S., & Braida, L. D., (2002). Functional role of auditory cortex in frequency processing and pitch perception. *Journal of Neurophysiology, 87*, 122–139.

Treisman, A. (1988). Features and objects: The fourteenth Bartlett memorial lecture. *Quarterly Journal of Experimental Psychology, 40A*, 207–237.

Treisman, A. (1993). The perception of features and objects. In A. Baddeley & L. Weiskrantz (Eds.), *Attention: Selection, awareness, and control* (pp. 5–34). Oxford, UK: Clarendon Press.

Treisman, A. (1999). Solutions to the binding problem: Progress through controversy and convergence. *Neuron, 24*, 105–110.

Treisman, A. (2005). Attention and binding. Presentation to the Cognitive Science Group, University of Arizona, February 4, 2005.

Treisman, A., & Gelade, G. (1980). A feature-integration theory of attention. *Cognitive Psychology, 12*, 97–136.

Treisman, A., & Schmidt, H. (1982). Illusory conjunctions in the perception of objects. *Cognitive Psychology, 14*, 107–141.

Tresilian, J. R., Mon-Williams, M., & Kelly, B. (1999). Increasing confidence in vergence as a cue to distance. *Proceedings of the Royal Society of London, 266B*, 39–44.

Truax, B. (1984). *Acoustic communication*. Norwood, NJ: Ablex.

Tsao, D. Y., Freiwald, W. A., Tootell, R. B., & Livingstone, M. S. (2006). A cortical region consisting entirely of face-selective cells. *Science, 311*, 670–674.

Ts'o, D. Y., Roe, A. R., & Gilbert, C. D. (2001). A hierarchy of the functional organization for color, form, and disparity in primate visual area V2. *Vision Research, 41*, 1333–1349.

Tsutsui, K. I., Sakata, H., Naganuma, T., & Taira, M. (2002). Neural correlates for perception of 3D surface orientation from texture gradient. *Science, 298*, 402–412.

Tsutsui, K. I., Tiara, M., & Sakata, H. (2005). Neural mechanisms of three-dimensional vision. *Neuroscience Research, 51*, 221–229.

Turati, C., Simion, F., Milani, I., & Umilta, C. (2002). Newborns' preference for faces: What is crucial? *Developmental Psychology, 38*, 875–882.

Turk, D. C., & Flor, H. (1999). Chronic pain: A biobehavioral perspective. In R. J. Gatchel & D. C. Turk (Eds.), *Psychosocial factors in pain* (pp. 18–34). New York: Guilford Press.

Turman, A. B., Morley, J. W., & Rowe, M. J. (1998). Functional organization of the somatosensory cortex in the primate. In J. W. Morley (Ed.), *Neural aspects of tactile sensation* (pp. 167–193). New York: Elsevier Science.

Tye-Murray, N., Spencer, L., & Woodworth, G. G. (1995). Acquisition of speech by children who have prolonged cochlear implant experience. *Journal of Speech and Hearing Research, 38*, 327–337.

Tyler, C. W. (1997a). Analysis of human receptor density. In V. Lakshminarayanan (Ed.), *Basic and clinical applications of vision science* (pp. 63–71). Norwell, MA: Kluwer Academic.

Tyler, C. W. (1997b). Human cone densities: Do you know where all your cones are? Unpublished manuscript.

Uchida, N., Takahashi, Y. K., Tanifuji, M., & Mori, K. (2000). Odor maps in the mammalian olfactory bulb: Domain organization and odorant structural features. *Nature Neuroscience, 3*, 1035–1043.

Uchikawa, K., Uchikawa, H., & Boynton, R. M. (1989). Partial color constancy of isolated surface colors examined by a color-naming method. *Perception, 18*, 83–91.

Uka, T., & DeAngelis, G. C. (2003). Contribution of middle temporal area to coarse depth discrimination: Comparison of neuronal and psychophysical sensitivity. *Journal of Neuroscience, 23*, 3515–3530.

Ungerleider, L. G., & Haxby, J. V. (1994). "What" and "where" in the human brain. *Current Opinion in Neurobiology, 4,* 157–165.

Ungerleider, L. G., & Mishkin, M. (1982). Two cortical visual systems. In D. J. Ingle, M. A. Goodale, & R. J. Mansfield (Eds.), *Analysis of visual behavior* (pp. 549–580). Cambridge, MA: MIT Press.

Ungerleider, L. G., & Pasternak, T. (2003). Ventral and dorsal cortical processing streams. In L. M. Chalupa & J. S. Werner (Eds.), *The visual neurosciences* (pp. 541–562). Cambridge, MA: MIT Press.

Valdez, P., & Mehribian, A. (1994). Effect of color on emotions. *Journal of Experimental Psychology: General, 123,* 394–409.

Vallbo, A. B., & Johansson, R. S. (1978). The tactile sensory innervation of the glabrous skin of the human hand. In G. Gordon (Ed.), *Active touch* (pp. 29–54). New York: Oxford University Press.

Van Essen, D. C., & Anderson, C. H. (1995). Information processing strategies and pathways in the primate visual system. In S. F. Zornetzer, J. L. Davis, & C. Lau (Eds.), *An introduction to neural and electronic networks* (2nd ed., pp. 45–75). San Diego: Academic Press.

Van Wanrooij, M. M., & Van Opstal, A. J. V. (2005). Relearning sound localization with a new ear. *Journal of Neuroscience, 25,* 5413–5424.

Varner, D., Cook, J. E., Schneck, M. E., McDonald, M., & Teller, D. Y. (1985). Tritan discriminations by 1- and 2-month-old human infants. *Vision Research, 25,* 821–831.

Vecera, S. P., Vogel, E. K., & Woodman, G. F. (2002). Lower region: A new cue for figure–ground assignment. *Journal of Experimental Psychology: General, 131,* 194–205.

Vermeij, G. (1997). *Privileged hands: A scientific life.* New York: Freeman.

Vinson, N. G., & Reed, C. L. (2002). Sources of object-specific effects in representational momentum. *Visual Cognition, 9,* 41–65.

von der Emde, G., Schwarz, S., Gomez, L., Budelli, R., & Grant, K. (1998). Electric fish measure distance in the dark. *Nature, 395,* 890–894.

von Holst, E. (1954). Relations between the central nervous system and the peripheral organs. *British Journal of Animal Behaviour, 2,* 89–94.

von Kriegstein, K., Kleinschmidt, A., Sterzer, P., & Giraud, A.-L. (2005). Interaction of face and voice areas in speaker recognition. *Journal of Cognitive Neuroscience, 17,* 367–376.

Wager, T. D., Rilling, J. K., Smith, E. E., Sokolik, A., Casey, K. L., Davidson, R. J., et al. (2004). Placebo-induced changes in fMRI in the anticipation and experience of pain. *Science, 303,* 1162–1167.

Wald, G. (1964). The receptors of human color vision. *Science, 145,* 1007–1017.

Wald, G., & Brown, P. K. (1958). Human rhodopsin. *Science, 127,* 222–226.

Waldrop, M. M. (1988). A landmark in speech recognition. *Science, 240,* 1615.

Wall, P. D., & Melzack, R. (Eds.). (1994). *Textbook of pain* (3rd ed.). Edinburgh, UK: Churchill Livingstone.

Wallach, H. (1963). The perception of neutral colors. *Scientific American, 208,* 107–116.

Wallach, H., Newman, E. B., & Rosenzweig, M. R. (1949). The precedence effect in sound localization. *American Journal of Psychology, 62,* 315–336.

Walls, G. L. (1942). *The vertebrate eye.* New York: Hafner. (Reprinted in 1967)

Walton, G. E., Bower, N. J. A., & Power, T. G. R. (1992). Recognition of familiar faces by newborns. *Infant Behavior and Development, 15,* 265–269.

Wandell, B. A., Dumoulin, S. O., & Brewer, A. A. (2007a). Visual field maps in human cortex. *Neuron, 56,* 366–383.

Wandell, B. A., Dumoulin, S. O., & Brewer, A. A. (2007b). Visual areas in humans. L. Squire (Ed.). *Encyclopedia of neuroscience.* New York: Academic Press.

Wang, X., Zhang, M., Cohen, I. S., & Goldberg, M. E. (2007). The proprioceptive representation of eye position in monkey primary somatosensory cortex. *Nature Neuroscience, 10,* 640–646.

Wann, J., & Land, M. (2000). Steering with or without the flow: Is the retrieval of heading necessary? *Trends in Cognitive Science, 4,* 319–324.

Warren, R. M. (1970). Perceptual restoration of missing speech sounds. *Science, 167,* 392–393.

Warren, R. M., Obuseck, C. J., & Acroff, J. M. (1972). Auditory induction of absent sounds. *Science, 176,* 1149.

Warren, S., Hamalainen, H., & Gardner, E. P. (1986). Objective classification of motion- and direction-sensitive neurons in primary somatosensory cortex of awake monkeys. *Journal of Neurophysiology, 56,* 598–622.

Warren, W. H. (1995). Self-motion: Visual perception and visual control. In W. Epstein & S. Rogers (Eds.), *Handbook of perception and cognition: Perception of space and motion* (pp. 263–323). New York: Academic Press.

Warren, W. H. (2004). Optic flow. In L. M. Chalupa & J. S. Werner (Eds.), *The visual neurosciences* (pp. 1247–1259). Cambridge, MA: MIT Press.

Warren, W. H., Kay, B. A., & Yilmaz, E. H. (1996). Visual control of posture during walking: Functional specificity. *Journal of Experimental Psychology: Human Perception and Performance, 22,* 818–838.

Wassenhove, V. van, Grant, K. W., & Poeppel, D. (2005). Visual speech speeds up the neural processing of auditory speech. *Proceedings of the National Academy of Sciences, 102,* 1181–1186.

Watkins, K. E., Strafella, A. P., & Paus, T. (2003). Seeing and hearing speech excites the motorsystem involved in speech production. *Neuropsychologia, 41,* 989–994

Watkins, L. R., & Maier, S. F. (2003). When good pain turns bad. *Current Directions in Psychological Science, 12,* 232–236.

Weinstein, S. (1968). Intensive and extensive aspects of tactile sensitivity as a function of body part, sex, and laterality. In D. R. Kenshalo (Ed.), *The skin senses* (pp. 195–218). Springfield, IL: Thomas.

Weisenberg, M. (1977). Pain and pain control. *Psychological Bulletin, 84,* 1008–1044.

Weissberg, M. (1999). Cognitive aspects of pain. In P. D. Wall & R. Melzack (Eds.), *Textbook of pain* (4th ed., pp. 345–358). New York: Churchill Livingstone.

Werker, J. F. (1991). The ontogeny of speech perception. In I. G. Mattingly & M. Studdert-Kennedy (Eds.), *Modularity and the motor theory of speech perception* (pp. 91–109). Hillsdale, NJ: Erlbaum.

Werker, J. F., & Tees, R. C. (1984). Cross-language speech perception: Evidence for perceptual reorganization during the first year of life. *Infant Behavior and Development, 7,* 49–63.

Werner, L. A., & Bargones, J. Y. (1992). Psychoacoustic development of human infants. In C. Rovee-Collier & L. Lipsett (Eds.), *Advances in infancy research* (Vol. 7, pp. 103–145). Norwood, NJ: Ablex.

Wertheimer, M. (1912). Experimentelle Studien über das Sehen von Beuegung. *Zeitchrift für Psychologie, 61,* 161–265.

Wever, E. G. (1949). *Theory of hearing.* New York: Wiley.

Wexler, M., Panerai, I. L., & Droulez, J. (2001). Self-motion and the perception of stationary objects. *Nature, 409,* 85–88.

Whalley, M. G., & Oakley, D. A. (2003). Psychogenic pain: A study using multidimensional scaling. *Contemporary Hypnosis, 20,* 16–24.

White, M. (1981). The effect of the nature of the surround on the perceived lightness of grey bars within squarewave test gratings. *Perception, 10,* 215–230.

Wiech, K., Ploner, M., & Tracey, I. (2008). Neurocognitive aspects of pain perception. *Trends in Cognitive Sciences, 12,* 306–313.

Wightman, F. L., & Kistler, D. J. (1997). Monaural sound localization revisited. *Journal of the Acoustical Society of America, 101,* 1050–1063.

Wightman, F. L., & Kistler, D. J. (1998). Of Vulcan ears, human ears and "earprints." *Nature Neuroscience, 1,* 337–339.

Wilkie, R. M., & Wann, J. P. (2003). Eye-movements aid the control of locomotion. *Journal of Vision, 3,* 677–684.

Williams, S. M., McCoy, A. N., & Purves, D. (1998). The influence of depicted illumination on brightness. *Proceedings of the National Academy of Sciences USA, 95,* 13296–13300.

Willis, T. (1965). *The anatomy of the brain and nerves* (W. Feindel, Ed.). Montreal: McGill University Press. (Original work published 1664)

Wilson, D. A. (2003). Rapid, experience-induced enhancement in odorant discrimination by anterior piriform cortex neurons. *Journal of Neurophysiology, 90,* 65–72.

Wilson, D. A., & Stevenson, R. J. (2006). *Learning to smell.* Baltimore: Johns Hopkins University Press.

Wilson, J. R., Friedlander, M. J., & Sherman, M. S. (1984). Ultrastructural morphology of identified X- and Y-cells in the cat's lateral geniculate nucleus. *Proceedings of the Royal Society, 211 B,* 411–436.

Wissinger, C. M., VanMeter, J., Tian, B., Van Lare, J., Pekar, J., & Rauschecker, J. P. (2001). Hierarchical organization of the human auditory cortex revealed by functional magnetic resonance imaging. *Journal of Cognitive Neuroscience, 13,* 1–7.

Witt, J. K., Proffitt, D. R., & Epstein, W. (2004). Perceiving distance: A role of effort and intent. *Perception, 33,* 577–590.

Wolpaw, J. R. (2007). Brain–computer interfaces as new brain output pathways. *Journal of Physiology, 597,* 613–619.

Wysecki, G., & Stiles, W. S. (1965). *Color science: Concepts and methods, quantitative data and formulae.* New York: Wiley.

Yarbus, A. (1967). *Eye movements and vision.* New York: Plenum Press.

Yonas, A., Granrud, C. E., Arterberry, M. E., & Hanson, B. L. (1986). Infant's distance from linear perspective and texture gradients. *Infant Behavior and Development, 9,* 247–256.

Yonas, A., Pettersen, L., & Granrud, C. E. (1982). Infant's sensitivity to familiar size as information for distance. *Child Development, 53,* 1285–1290.

Yost, W. A. (1997). The cocktail party problem: Forty years later. In R. H. Kilkey & T. R. Anderson (Eds.), *Binaural and spatial hearing in real and virtual environments* (pp. 329–347). Hillsdale, NJ: Erlbaum.

Yost, W. A. (2001). Auditory localization and scene perception. In E. B. Goldstein (Ed.), *Blackwell handbook of perception* (pp. 437–468). Oxford, UK: Blackwell.

Yost, W. A., & Guzman, S. J. (1996). Auditory processing of sound sources: Is there an echo in here? *Current Directions in Psychological Science, 5,* 125–131.

Yost, W. A., & Sheft, S. (1993). Auditory processing. In W. A. Yost, A. N. Popper, & R. R. Fay (Eds.), *Handbook of auditory research* (Vol. 3). New York: Springer-Verlag.

Young, R. S. L., Fishman, G. A., & Chen, F. (1980). Traumatically acquired color vision defect. *Investigative Ophthalmology and Visual Science, 19,* 545–549.

Young, T. (1802). On the theory of light and colours. *Transactions of the Royal Society of London, 92,* 12–48.

Young-Browne, G., Rosenfield, H. M., & Horowitz, F. D. (1977). Infant discrimination of facial expression. *Child Development, 48,* 555–562.

Yuille, A., & Kersten, D. (2006). Vision as Bayesian inference: Analysis by synthesis? *Trends in Cognitive Sciences, 10,* 301–308.

Yuodelis, C., & Hendrickson, A. (1986). A qualitative and quantitative analysis of the human fovea during development. *Vision Research, 26,* 847–855.

Zacks, J. M. (2004). Using movement and intentions to understand simple events. *Cognitive Science, 28,* 979–1008.

Zacks, J. M., & Swallow, K. M. (2007). Event segmentation. *Current Directions in Psychological Science, 16,* 80–84.

Zapadia, M. K., Ito, M., Gilbert, C. G., & Westheimer, G. (1995). Improvement in visual sensitivity by changes in local context: Parallel studies in human observers and in V1 of alert monkeys. *Neuron, 15,* 843–856.

Zeki, S. (1983a). Color coding in the cerebral cortex: The reaction of cells in monkey visual cortex to wavelengths and colours. *Neuroscience, 9,* 741–765.

Zeki, S. (1983b). Color coding in the cerebral cortex: The responses of wavelength-selective and color coded cells in monkey visual cortex to changes in wavelength composition. *Neuroscience, 9,* 767–781.

Zeki, S. (1990). A century of cerebral achromatopsia. *Brain, 113,* 1721–1777.

Zeki, S., & Marini, L. (1998). Three cortical stages of colour processing in the human brain. *Brain, 121,* 1669–1685.

Zhang, T., & Britten, K. H. (2006). The virtue of simplicity. *Nature Neuroscience, 9,* 1356–1357.

Zhao, G. Q., Zhang, Y., Hoon, M., Chandrashekar, J., Erienbach, I., Ryba, N. J. P., et al. (2003). The receptors for mammalian sweet and umami taste. *Cell, 115,* 255–266.

Zihl, J., von Cramon, D., & Mai, N. (1983). Selective disturbance of movement vision after bilateral brain damage. *Brain, 106,* 313–340.

Zihl, J., von Cramon, D., Mai, N., & Schmid, C. (1991). Disturbance of movement vision after bilateral posterior brain damage. *Brain, 114,* 2235–2252.

Zimmer, C. (2004). A distant mirror for the brain. *Science, 303,* 43–44.

Zubieta, J.-K., Heitzeg, M. M., Smith, Y. R., Buyeller, J. A., Xu, K., Xu, Y., et al. (2003). COMT val158met genotype affects mu-opioid neurotransmitter responses to a pain stressor. *Science, 299,* 1240–1243.

Zue, V. W., & Glass, J. R. (2000). Conversational interfaces: Advances and challenges. *Proceedings of the IEEE, 88,* 1166–1180.

Name Index

Subject Index